THE PANARION
OF
EPIPHANIUS OF SALAMIS

NAG HAMMADI
AND
MANICHAEAN STUDIES

FORMERLY

NAG HAMMADI STUDIES

EDITED BY

J.M. ROBINSON & H.J. KLIMKEIT

Editorial Board

XXXVI

THE PANARION
OF
EPIPHANIUS OF SALAMIS

Books II and III (Sects 47-80, *De Fide*)

TRANSLATED BY

FRANK WILLIAMS

E.J. BRILL
LEIDEN · NEW YORK · KÖLN
1994

The paper in this book meets the guidelines for permanence and durability of the Committee on Production Guidelines for Book Longevity of the Council on Library Resources.

Library of Congress Cataloging-in-Publication Data

(Revised for volumes 2-3)

Epiphanius, Saint, Bp. of Constantia in Cyprus.
The Panarion of Epiphanius of Salamis.

(Nag Hammadi studies, 0169-9350 ; 35) (Nag Hammadi and Manichaean studies, 0929-2470 ; 36)
    Includes bibliographical references and index.
    Contents: bk. 1. Sects 1-46 — bk. 2-3. Sects 47-80, De fide (1 v.)
    1. Heresies, Christian—History—Early church, ca. 30-600.   2. Gnosticism.   I. Title.   II. Series.
BR65.E653P36 1987   273'.4   87-6375
ISBN 90-04-07926-2 (bk. 1)
ISBN 90-04-09898-4 (bk. 2-3)

Die Deutsche Bibliothek – CIP-Einheitsaufnahme

Epiphanius <Constantiensis>:
[The Panarion]
The Panarion of Epiphanius of Salamis. - Leiden ; New York ; Köln : Brill
    Einheitssacht.: Panarium <engl.>
Books 2/3 = Sects 47-80. De fide / transl. by Frank Williams.
 -1993
 (Nag Hammadi studies ; 36)
 ISBN 90-04-09898-4
NE: Williams, Frank [Übers.]; GT

ISSN   0929-2470
ISBN   90 04 09898 4

CONTENTS

(Most sections of the work are titled as in the manuscripts. Modern titles are noted with an asterisk.)

ACKNOWLEDGEMENTS

A large portion of the work on this translation was made possible by a grant from the National Endowment for the Humanities of the United States of America, for which I am most grateful.

I am indebted to Hans-J. Klimkeit for making his valuable *Manichaean Texts from the Silk Road* available to me in advance of publication.

I owe many thanks to Professor James M. Robinson, of the Institute for Antiquity and Christianity, for the timely help of many kinds which has made this publication possible.

Finally, I am especially grateful to my wife Charlotte, without whose patience, understanding and encouragement it would have been very difficult to do this work.

INTRODUCTION

The following translation of Books II and III of the *Panarion* of Epiphanius of Salamis, together with Epiphanius' Appendix which is usually called *De Fide*, will complete our version of his *Panarion*. Our rendering of Book I, *The Panarion of Epiphanius of Salamis, Book I (Sects 1–46)*, appeared in 1987 as Volume XXXV of *Nag Hammadi Studies*. For an overview of Epiphanius' life and writings the reader is referred to the Introduction to that volume.

Our translation renders Karl Holl's text in *Die griechischen christlichen Schriftsteller der ersten drei Jahrhunderte*, working with the second editions by Jürgen Dummer of Sects 34–64, published by the Akademie Verlag, Berlin, in 1980, and of Sects 65–85 with *De Fide*, from the same press in 1985. Dummer has updated the *Textapparat* and *Sachapparat* of Holl's two original volumes, which were published by Hinrichs in 1928 and 1933 respectively. (The *Sachapparat* of the 1933 volume was, however, completed from Sect 67 on by Hanz Lietzmann following Holl's death.)

Dummer's second editions reprint Holl-Lietzmann as it stands and add two Appendices containing the new work on the content of the *Panarion* and its text. The Appendix concerned with content appears to be entirely Dummer's work; that concerned with text collects the readings suggested by himself and other scholars for various passages in the *Panarion* up until the dates of Dummer's publications. Dummer insists on few of these new readings, but we regularly render them in preference to Holl as embodying the latest work on the text, and subjoin a footnote which gives the key words of the new reading, followed by the corresponding keywords from Holl. Where we occasionally prefer Holl's to the later suggestion, the order in the footnote is reversed. Because of the limits of our publication we must refer the reader who desires fuller information about the text to Holl-Dummer and the authorities cited by Dummer.

A problem is posed by the text of the *Syntagmation* of Aetius the Anomoean, which Epiphanius reproduces *in toto* at 76,11–12, and then refutes paragraph by paragraph. The text of the *Syntagmation*, which was corrupt and in places almost unintelligible, was reedited in 1968 with a translation and commentary by L. R. Wickham, giving a much more satisfactory text, which Dummer accepts. But did Epiphanius in fact possess this good text? At 77,54,3 he faults Aetius for calling God αὐτογέννητος, "self-begotten; this stands in the text of Holl, but Aetius could not have written it, and Wickham emends it to αὐτὸ ἀγέννητος.

This, however, is the only point at which a refutation of Epiphanius depends upon a reading in Aetius which may be corrupt. There is thus no way of judging what the rest of Epiphanius' text of Aetius was like. We therefore translate Wickham's emendations noting them in the usual way, and avoid having to offer some very forced renderings of Aetius.

The question has been raised whether a translation of the *Panarion* at this time, when portions of Holl's text have been challenged by a number of scholars and a revision is in progress, is premature. We reply that a full revision of the *Panarion* is likely to be a very protracted undertaking,[1] while on the other hand experience shows that a translation is needed now. Whatever the deficiencies of Holl's edition it certainly presents a workmanlike text, many of whose readings can withstand careful scrutiny. It ought to be possible, when the revised text of the *Panarion* is published, to issue a list of alternative translations as a supplement or appendix, which will bring this version into harmony with the revision.

While ours remains the only version in a modern language of the complete *Panarion*, a volume of selections from the *Panarion*, translated by Phillip R. Amidon, S. J., appeared in 1990.[2] Amidon renders Epiphanius' descriptions of sects and his narrative material but omits most of the refutations, thus translating about half of the *Panarion*. The current translator has compared the relevant portions of Amidon's work, with profit, with his own.

Other modern translations of portions of the *Panarion* which we have utilized are Wickham, already mentioned; Strobel's versions of the calendar material at 51,26,1–8 and 70,12,4–13,6, included in his *Ursprung und Geschichte*; and Robertson's of Athanasius' *Epistula ad Epictetum*, which Epiphanius quotes in full at 77,3,1–13,6. We have consulted Riggi's *Epifanio contro Mani*, which renders Sect 66, at some points, but meager acquaintance with the Italian language precluded our making as much use of this as we could have wished. It did not seem necessary to compare our Sect 78 with the older German versions of this polished work (Wolfsgruber, 1880; Hörmann, 1919), since they were made from the Migne text.

Aside from the textual notes, the footnotes chiefly call attention

---

[1] Cf. Dummer's comment in "Zur Epiphanius-Ausgabe," p. 120, n. 8.
[2] Amidon, Philip R., S. J., Tr., *The Panarion of St. Epiphanius, Bishop of Salamis: Selected Passages*, New York, Oxford: Oxford University Press, 1990.

to material from Patristic and other ancient sources which parallels the doctrines and ideas alluded to by Epiphanius. The object of these notes is to place Epiphanius' work in its context, as well as to provide documentation for him and a check on his accuracy. (For translation notes there is unfortunately seldom room.) Our notes are a revision of Holl-Lietzmann, and are updated with references that were not available to those scholars. This updating is not as extensive as it was in our previous volume because Books II and III do not contain as much anti-Gnostic material as did Book I. However a fair amount was still needed, particularly in Sect 66, *Against Manichaeans.*

Indeed the annotation of Sect 66 presented special problems. Comparatively little Manichaean literature had been published when Holl and Lietzmann wrote, and they were forced to rely chiefly on Patristic sources, with a few rather obscure citations of Manichaean authors. Now, sixty years later, so much Manichaean writing is available that it is difficult for a book of this sort to do it justice. Full documentation of Sect 66 from published Manichaean works might well require a slim volume of its own; we have had to content ourselves with citing a selection of passages which seem representative, drawing them when possible from the publications most readily accessible.

Book I of the *Panarion* was largely a polemic against Gnostic and Jewish Christian ideas. Except for Sect 66 and the not very important Sect 56, Books II and III are concerned with non-Gnostic matters: the Trinity, the Incarnation of Christ, the divinity and personality of the Holy Spirit, Origenism, the resurrection of the body, the Christian calendar, penance, celibacy, and the rules of monastic discipline. All these were burning issues in Epiphanius' day, and Epiphanius was actively involved in controversies over them all. Living, as he did, in the troubled times between the Council of Nicaea and the First Council of Constantinople, he is a primary witness to the persons, events and thought of this creative but difficult period. It is hoped that this translation will be of service to students of Church History, Systematic Theology and the History of Doctrine, as well as to those whose interests lie in Gnosticism and Manichaeism.

The sources of Epiphanius' information in Books II and III are more varied than those of Book I. Sources which can be readily observed or conjectured are mentioned in the notes to each Sect. Interestingly, Epiphanius does not show the heavy literary dependence upon Athanasius which one might have expected.[3] He has

---

[3] Dechow suggests possible dependence on Peter of Alexandria, *Dogma and Mysticism,* p. 99.

certainly read some of Athanasius' works, and has learned much from the man, with whom he was personally acquainted and whom he intensely admired. But beyond the necessary technical terms of theology Epiphanius' phraseology is not particularly Athanasian. He shows considerable sympathy for the Melitians whom Athanasius detests, and worries through six chapters (69,21–26) over the interpretation of Proverbs 8:22, a matter which gives Athanasius little trouble.

As a theologian Epiphanius has long been underrated. While he need not now be overrated in compensation, it should be possible to arrive at a more just estimate of his worth than that which obtained in former generations.

Epiphanius cannot be placed on a level with, say, the Cappadocian Fathers. He was a "rough diamond," untrained in the Greek classics and with little or no background in philosophy. However he was very well schooled in scripture, exegesis and Christian matters, and in dealing with these his natural quickness would have made him a formidable opponent in debate. Examples of the sureness with which he could dispose of a theological problem in terms of fourth century exegesis are Sect 48, The Montanists, Sect 62, The Sabellians, and numerous others. Nor is Epiphanius without originality; Sect 78, his defense of the divinity of the Holy Spirit, shows how fertile his use of scriptural exegesis could be. On the other hand, when out of his field he can turn in a poor performance. In Sect 76, where he attempts to meet the Aristotelian Aetius on his home ground, the results are wordy, labored and often not to the point.

To Epiphanius' credit is his lively imagination. Sects 68 and the beginnings of 64 and 69 are examples of the verve with which he tells a story. Long passages of exegetical debate can suddenly be illuminated with homely illustrations, of attractive aptness.

Some of these reflect Epiphanius' experience as an islander and sea voyager. Persons with property are to be received into the church on an equal footing with persons who renounce property because *God's ship takes any passenger except a bandit. If it finds that someone is a robber and bandit it does not take him on board—or a runaway, in rebellion against his owners. Thus God's holy church does not accept fornication, adultery, the denial of God, and those who defy the authority of God's ordinance and his apostles. But it takes the man on important business, the experienced seamen—the pilot and < helmsman* >, the bow lookout, the man in the stern (the one most used to command), the one who knows even a bit about cargo and lading—and someone who just wants to cross the ocean without drowning.* (44,4,5–7)

One suspects that personal experience lies behind the following passage, in which Epiphanius pillories sectarianism in general as a collection of abortive shortcuts (39,l2,2–3): *It is < as though > one found a break in a wall beside a highway, thought of going through it, left the road and turned off < there >, in the belief that a place where he could turn and pick up the road again was right close by. But he did not know that the wall was very high and ran on for a long·way; he kept running into it and not finding a place to get out, and in fact went for more than a signpost, or mile, farther without reaching the road. And so he would turn and keep going, tiring himself out and finding no way to get back to his route; and perhaps he could never find one unless he went back through the place where he had come in.* Epiphanius often shows himself concerned with the reader, and one wonders whether he inserts such paragraphs to relieve what he is wont to call the "hard labor of reading."

Particularly because of their long quotations from other writers, Epiphanius' Books II and III contain a variety of styles and manners. These can range all the way from the dignified cadences of formal ecclesiastical correspondence, through the lyricism of enthused homiletics, to the language of disputation, and sharp invective. Probably the disputation predominates. Epiphanius' age, echoing the Platonic dialogues of centuries before and anticipating the debates of the medieval universities, believed that the truth could be uncovered through public disputation. Debates were held in churches, in village squares, surely in monasteries. The long passages of exegesis, full of abbreviated technical phrases and interspersed with condemnations and sharp name-calling, might well represent the way in which Epiphanius and his contemporaries conducted their disputations.

As far as possible we have tried to render all this in a dignified modern English. The manner of the translation will vary with the manner of the passage being translated. Scriptural citations, however, are usually given in language approximating the King James version of the Bible; this sets them off from the text of Epiphanius and reflects the extreme reverence for scripture which is so obvious in his writings.

The twin overall goals of the translation have been accuracy and readability. The translator apologizes for flaws of accuracy and style which no amount of care can entirely eliminate from a work of this length.

Frank Williams
The University of Texas at El Paso
November 11, 1992

ABBREVIATIONS

Act. Arch.	*Acta Archelai cum Manete Disputantis*
Act. Perpet.	*Acta Perpetuae*
Alex. Lycop.	Alexander of Lycopolis
Anc.	*Ancoratus*
Ant.	*Antiquitates Judaeorum*
APAW	*Abhandlungen der Königlichen Preussischen Akademie der Wissenschaften*, Berlin
Apol. Ep. Dion.	Apolinaris, *Epistula ad Dionysium*
App.	Appendix
Asc. Isa.	*Ascension of Isaiah*
Ath. Ap. De Fuga	Athanasius *Apologia de Fuga*
Ap. Sec.	*Apologia Secunda*
C. Apol.	*Contra Apolinarem*
De Sent. Dion.	*De Sententiis Dionysii*
Dial. II Trin.	*Dialogus Secundus De Trinitate*
Ep. Ad Serap.	*Epistula ad Serapionem de Morte Arii*
Nic.	*De Decretis Nicaeae Synodis*
Or. I C. Ar.	*Oratio I contra Arianos*
Or. II C. Ar.	*Oratio II contra Arianos*
Or. III C. Ar.	*Oratio III contra Arianos*
Syn.	*De Synodis*
Aug. Adeim.	Augustine *Contra Adeimantum*
C. Faust.	*Contra Faustum*
Fel.	*Contra Felicem*
Serm. Dom. Mont.	*De Sermone Domini in Monte*
Bas. Caes.	Basil of Caesarea
BSOAS	*Bulletin of the School of Oriental and African Studies*, London
CG	*Cairo Gnosticus* (Nag Hammadi)
Chrys.Comment. Ad Isa.	Chrysostom *Commentaria ad Isaiam*
De Melch.	*De Melchizedek*
Hom. 6 In Heb.	*Homilia 6 in Hebraeos*
In Gen. Sermo	*In Genesim Sermo*
Clem. Alex.	Clement of Alexandria
Theod.	*Excerpta Theodoti*
Paedag.	*Paedagogus*
Strom.	*Stromateis*
CM	Cologne Mani Codex
Const. Ap.	*Constitutiones Apostolicae*
Consularia Constantia	*Consularia Constantia*
Cyr. Cat.	Cyril of Jerusalem
	Catechetical Lectures
C. Ap.	*Contra Apionem*
Dial. Mont. Orth.	*Dialogus Montanistae cum Orthodoxo*
Didasc.	*Didascalia*
Did. Com. Act.	Didymus *Commentaria in Acta*
De Trin.	*De Trinitate*
Div. Inst.	*Divinae Institutiones*
Epiph.	Epiphanius
Ep.	*Epistula*
Ep. Ad Alex.	*Epistula ad Alexandrum*

Ep. Barn.	*Epistle of Barnabas*
Eus. Dem. Ev.	Eusebius *Demonstratio Evangelica*
H. E.	*Historia Ecclesiastica*
Praep. Ev.	*Praeparatio Evangelica*
Vit. Const.	*Vita Constantini*
Filast.	
Haer.	Filastrius *Contra Omnes Haereses*
Gel.	Gelasius
Greg. Naz.	Gregory Nazianzus
Carm. Hist. I De Suo Ipso	*Carmen Historica I de Suo Ipso*
C. Eunom.	*Contra Eunomium*
Hippol.	Hippolytus
C. Noet.	*Contra Noetum*
Haer.	*Contra Omnes Haereses*
In Dan.	*Commentaria in Danielem*
Hist. Aceph.	*Historia Acephala*
Hist. Laus.	*Historial Lausiaca*
*HR*II	F. W. K. Müller, *Handschriftliche-Reste in Estrangelo-Schrift aus Turfan*, Anhang APAW, 1904
Iren. Haer.	Irenaeus *Contra Omnes Haereses*
Jer. Adv. Jov.	Jerome *Adversus Jovinianum*
Chron.	*Chronicle*
Com. In Isa.	*Commentaria in Isaiam*
C. Rufin.	*Contra Rufinum*
In Tit.	*Commentaria in Titum*
Vir. Ill.	*De Viris Illustribus*
Jub.	*Book of Jubilees*
Jul. Af.	Julius Africanus
Keph.	*Kephalaia*
Leg.	*Legatio*
Mand.	*Mandata*
Man. Hom.	*Manichaean Homilies*
Man. Ps.	*Manichaean Psalms*
*MM*II	F. C. Andreas, W. Henning, *Mitteliranische Manichaica aus Chinesischen-Turkestan*, SPAW 1932, 1933, 1934
MSG	Migne *Scriptores Graeci*
MSL	Migne *Scriptores Latini*
NGWG	*Nachrichten von der Gesellschaft der Wissenschaften zu Göttingen*
NHL	Nag Hammadi Library
Apoc. Adam	*Apocalypse of Adam*
Apoc. Jas.	*Apocryphon of James*
Apocry. John	*Apocryphon of John*
Gosp. Tr.	*Gospel of Truth*
Gr. Pow.	*Concept of Our Great Power*
Melch.	*Melchizedek*
Nat. Arch.	*Nature of the Archons*
Orig. Wld.	*Origin of the World*
Testim. Tr.	*Testimony of Truth*
Tri. Prot.	*Triple Protennoia*
Nic. H. E.	Nicephorus *Historia Ecclesiastica*
Orig. Cels.	Origen *Contra Celsum*
Com. In Mat.	*Commentaria in Matthaeum*

Princ.	*De Principiis*
Pan.	*Panarion*
Philost.	Philostratus
PS	*Pistis Sophia*
Ps.-Ath.	Pseudo-Athanasius
C. Apolin.	*Contra Apolinarem*
Haer.	*Contra Omnes Haereses*
Ps.-Tert.	Pseudo-Tertullian
Serap. Thm.	Serapion of Thmuis
Soc.	Socrates *Historia Ecclesiastica*
Soz.	Sozomen *Historia Ecclesiastica*
SPAW	*Sitzungsberichte der Königlichen Preussischen Akademie der Wissenschaften, Berlin*
Tert. Adv. Hermog.	Tertullian *Adversus Hermogenem*
Adv. Marc.	*Adversus Marcum*
Adv. Prax.	*Adversus Praxeam*
Carn. Res.	*De Carnis Resurrectione*
Jejun.	*De Jejunia*
Monog.	*De Monogamia*
Pudic.	*De Pudicitia*
Virg. Vel.	*De Virginibus Velandis*
Theodoret	Theodoret
Haer. Fab.	*Haereticorum Fabulae*
Theophilus	Theophilus
Ad Autol.	*Ad Autolycum*
Tit. Bost. Man.	Titus of Bostra, *Adversus Manichaeos*
TPS	*Transactions of the Philosophical Society, London*
T	*Talmud Babli*
Trall.	Pseudo-Ignatius, *Epistula ad Trallianos*
Vit. Epiph.	*Vita Epiphanii*

Sigla

< >	enclose a conjectural reading placed in the text by Holl
< * >	enclose a conjectural reading left in the apparatus by Holl
[ ]	enclose words supplied by the translator for clarity
( )	enclose parenthetical material in Epiphanius
(i. e.)	enclose translator's explanatory note
†	marks a word emended by Holl

WORKS CITED

Achelis, Hans and Flemming, Johannes, *Die Syrische Didascalia übersetzt und erklärt*, Leipzig: Hinrichs, 1904

Allberry, C. R. C., *A Manichaean Psalm Book*, Stuttgart: W. Kohlhammer Verlag, 1938

Amidon, *The Panarion of St. Epiphanius, Bishop of Salamis: Selected Passages*, New York, Oxford: Oxford University Press, 1990

Asmussen, Jes P., *Manichaean Literature*, Delmar, N. Y.: Scholars' Facsimiles and Reprints, 1975

Brightman, Frank Edward, *Liturgies Eastern and Western*, Volume I, *Eastern*, Oxford: Clarendon Press, 1965

Charlesworth, James S., *The Old Testament Pseudepigrapha*, Garden City, N. Y.: Doubleday and Co., 1983

Corssen, Peter, *Monarchische Prologe zu den vier Evangelien*, Leipzig: Hinrichs, 1896

Dechow, Jon, *Dogma and Mysticism in Early Christianity: Epiphanius of Cyprus and the Legacy of Origen*, Dissertation, University of Pennsylvania, 1975, Available from Microfilms International, Ann Arbor, MI

Dummer, Jürgen, "Die Epiphanius-Ausgabe der Griechischen Christlichen Schriftsteller," *Texte und Textkritik*, ed. Jürgen Dummer with Johannes Irmscher, Franz Paschalis, Kurt Treu, pp. 119–125

Field, Frederick, *Origenis Hexapla quae Supersunt*, Holdesheim: G. Olms, 1964

Flügel, *Mani, seine Lehre und seine Schriften, ein Beitrag zur Geschichte des Manichäismus aus den Fihrist des Abu'l Farasch Muhammed ben ishak al-warrah*, repr. Osnabrück: Biblio Verlag, 1969

Hahn, August, *Bibliothek der Symbole und Glaubensregeln der alten Kirche*, Breslau: E. Morgenstern, 1897

Helm, Rudolf, *Die Chronik des Hieronymus*, Berlin: Akademie Verlag, 1956

Hennecke, Edgar, *New Testament Apocrypha*, ed. Wilhelm Schneemelcher, trans. A. J. H. Higgins and others, London: Lutterworth Press, 1963

Hinrichs, A. and Koenen, L., *Der Kölner Mani-Kodex*, Germany: Westdeutscher Verlag, 1987

Holl, Karl, *Epiphanius II: Panarion haer. 34–64*, rev. ed. Jürgen Dummer, Berlin: Akademie Verlag, 1980

Holl, Karl, *Epiphanius III: Panarion haer. 65–80, De Fide*, rev. ed. Jürgen Dummer, Berlin: Akademie Verlag, 1985

Hörmann, Josef, "Gegen die Antidikomarianiten," *Des heiligen Epiphanius von Salamis ausgewählte Schriften*, Kempten und München: Verlag der Jos. Köselschen Buchhandlung, 1919, pp. 233–263

Klimkeit, Hans-J., *Gnostic Texts from the Silk Road: Iranic and Turkic Manichaean Documents from Central Asia*, San Francisco, Harper Collins, forthcoming

Labriolle, Pierre, *Les Sources de l'Histoire du Montanisme*, repr. New York: A M S Press, 1980

Lietzmann, Hans, *Apollinaris von Laodicea und seine Schule*, Tübingen, J. C. B. Mohr, 1904

Loofs, Friedrich, *Paulus von Samosata*, Leipzig: Hinrichs, 1924

Pognon, *Inscriptions Mandaïtes des Coupes de Khouaber*, Paris: Impremerie Nationale, 1898

Polotsky, Hans Jacob and Böhlig, Alexander, *Kephalaia*, Stuttgart: W. Kohlhammer Verlag, 1934

Polotsky, Hans Jacob, *Manichäische Homilien*, Stuttgart: W. Kohlhammer Verlag, 1934

Reichardt, Walther, *Die Briefe des Sextus Julius Africanus an Aristides und Origenes*, Leipzig: Hinrichs, 1904

Riggi, C., "Nouvelle lecture du Panarion LIX (Épiphane et le divorce)," *Studia Patristica XII. Papers presented to the Sixth International Conference on Patristic Studies held in Oxford, 1971,* ed. E. A. Livingstone, Part I Berlin 1975 (TU 115) pp. 129–134

Routh, Martinus Josephus, *Reliquiae Sacrae,* Oxford: Oxford Press, 1846

Robertson, Archibald trans., "Ad Epictetum," *Nicene and Post-Nicene Fathers,* ed. Philip Schaff and Henry Wace, repr. Grand Rapids: Eerdmans, 1978, IV pp. 570–574

Schmidt, Karl, *Gespräche Jesu mit seinen Jüngern nach der Auferstehung,* Hildesheim: Olms, 1967

Schwarz, Eduard, "Christliche und Jüdische Ostertafeln," APAW 1905

Strobel, August, *Ursprung und Geschichte der frühchristlichen Osterkalendar,* Berlin: Addademie Verlag, 1971

Wickham, L. R., "The Syntagmation of Aetius the Anomoean," JTS 19, 1968, pp. 532–569

Wolfsgruber, C., *Des heiligen Epiphanius von Salamis ausgewählte Schriften,* Kempten und München: Verlag der Jos. Köselschen Buchhandlung, 1880

ANACEPHALAEOSIS IV

Here likewise are the contents of this first Section of Volume Two; counted consecutively from the beginning of the sections it is Section Four. It contains eighteen Sects:

47. Encratites, who are an outgrowth of Tatian, reject marriage and say that it is of Satan, and forbid the eating of any sort of meat.

48. Phrygians, also called Montanists and Tascodrugians. They accept the Old and the New Testaments but, by boasting of a Montanus and a Priscilla, introduce other prophets after the [canonical] prophets.

49. (1) Pepuzians, also called Quintillianists, with whom Artotyrites are associated. They derive from the Phrygians but teach different doctrines. They venerate Pepuza, a deserted city between Galatia, Cappadocia and Phrygia, and regard this as Jerusalem. (There is another Pepuza as well.) And they allow women to rule and to act as priests.

(2) Their initiation is the stabbing of a small child. And they tell the story that Christ was revealed in female form to Quintilla, or Priscilla, there in Pepuza.

(3) They too use the Old and the New Testaments, revising them to suit their own taste.

50. Quartodecimans, who celebrate the Passover on one day of the year, whichever day is the fourteenth of the month—whether it is a Sabbath or a Lord's Day—and both fast and hold a vigil on that day.

51. Alogi, or so I have named them, who reject the Gospel of John and the eternal divine Word in it, who has descended from the Father. They do not accept either John's Gospel itself, or his Revelation.

52. (1) Adamians, by some called Adamizers, whose doctrine is not true but ridiculous. (2) For they assemble stark naked, men and women alike, and conduct their readings, prayers and everything else in that condition. This is because they are pretendedly single and continent and, since they regard their church as Paradise, do not allow marriage.

53. Sampsaeans, also called Elkasaites, who live to this day in Arabia, the country lying north of the Dead Sea. They have been deceived by Elxai, a false prophet (2) whose descendants were

Marthus and Marthana, two women who are still worshipped as goddesses by the sect. All their customs are quite like the Ebionites'.

54.   Theodotians, who derive from Theodotus the shoemaker, of Byzantium. He excelled in the Greek education, but when he was arrested with others during the persecution in his time, only he fell away. Because he was reproached after the martyrdom of the others, to escape the charge of denying God he thought of the expedient of calling Christ a mere man, and taught in this vein.

55.   Melchizedekians, who honor Melchizedek and claim he is a power of some sort and not a mere man, and have dared to ascribe everything to his name and say so.

56.   Bardesians. Bardesianes came from Mesopotamia. At first he was a follower of the true faith and excelled in wisdom, but after he swerved from the truth he taught like Valentinus, except for a few small points < in > which he differs from Valentinus.

57.   (1) Noetians. Noetus was from Smyrna in Asia. From conceit he taught, among other things, that Christ is the Son-Father,[1] < and said > that the Father, the Son and the Holy Spirit are the same. (2) He also said that he was Moses; his brother, he said, was Aaron.

58.   (1) Valesians. They live, I believe, in the chief village of Philadelphia in Arabia, Bacathus; they make eunuchs of all who happen by and accept their hospitality. Most of them are castrated eunuchs themselves. (2) They teach certain other things which are full of heresy, reject < the teachings > of the Law and the Prophets, and introduce certain other obscenities.

59.   Purists (Cathari), who are connected with Navatus of Rome, entirely reject the twice-married, and do not accept repentance.

60.   Angelics. These have entirely died out. Either they boasted of angelic rank, or † they[2] were called Angelics < because they worshipped* > angels.

61.   Apostolics, also called Apotactics. These too < live > in Pisidia; they accept only persons who renounce the world, and they pray by themselves. They are quite like the Encratites, but have opinions which are different from theirs.

62.   Sabellians, whose opinions are like the Noetians' except that they deny that the Father has suffered.

63.   Origenists, the disciples of one Origen. They are obscene, have unspeakable practices, and devote their bodies to corruption.

64.   Other Origenists, the disciples of the Origen who is called

---

[1] υἱόσπατηρ
[2] Holl: προσκυνεῖν < οὕτως ἐπεκλήθησαν >; MSS: προσκεκλῆσθαι

Adamantius the Author. They reject the resurrection of the dead, represent Christ and the Holy Spirit as creatures, allegorize Paradise, the heavens and all the rest, and foolishly say that Christ's kingdom will come to an end.

These, in turn, are the eighteen Sects of Volume Two, Section One.

Against Encratites.[1] Number 47, but 67 of the series

1,1   Certain persons whom we call Encratites are Tatian's successors. They were led astray and deceived by Tatian in person, but have ideas different from his and have devoted themselves to worse foolishness in their own turn. (2) Even today their numbers are increasing in Pisidia and the land called Scorched Phrygia.[2] (Perhaps the country has come to be called this by divine dispensation, for this very reason—its inhabitants have been scorched by the perversity of such error, and so much of it. For there are many sects in the area.)

1,3   There are also Encratites in Asia, Isauria, Pamphylia, Cilicia and Galatia. And by now this sect < has > also < been planted > in Rome < to a > certain extent, and at Antioch in Syria, though not everywhere.

1,4   Encratites too say that there are certain sovereign authorities,[3] and that the < power > of the devil is ranged against God's creatures[4] because the devil is not subject to God; he has power of his own and acts as in his own right, and not as though he had fallen into perversity.[5] For they do not agree with the church, but differ from its declaration of the truth.

1,5   For scriptures they use principally the so-called Acts of Andrew, and of John, and of Thomas, and certain apocrypha,[6] and

---

[1] Epiphanius may have used Iren. Haer. 1.28.1, but clearly has contemporary knowledge of the Encratites. Other ancient discussions are found at Hippol. Haer. 8.7; Eus. H. E. 4.28–30; Clem. Alex. Paedag. 2.2.33; Strom. 1.91.5; 3.76.25; 7.108.2. The apocryphal Acts of John, Andrew and Thomas afford many instances of the sort of teachings described here.

[2] Basil of Caesarea Ep. 188; 198; 236

[3] ἀρχαί Typically Gnostic terms for such beings are found at Acts of John 94; 95; 98–99; Acts of Andrew 20; Acts of Thomas 27; 50; 121; 132; 133; 148.

[4] "Let rulers be broken, let powers fall" is said of Satan's host at Acts of John 114.

[5] The apocryphal Acts represent the devil as a powerful, dangerous being, Acts of Andrew 27; Acts of Thomas 31; 32; 34; 44; 76. At Acts of Thomas 31 the devil says, "The Son of God hath wronged me against my will, and taken them that were his own from me."

[6] The Nag Hammadi tractate, Thomas the Contender (CG II, 7) contains a sharp polemic against sex, but there is no evidence that the Encratites used it.

any sayings from the Old Testament that they care to.

1,6   They declare that marriage is plainly the work of the devil.[7]
And they regard meat as an abomination—though they do not
prohibit it for the sake of continence or as a pious practice, but
from fear and for appearance' sake, and in order not to be
condemned for eating flesh.[8]

1,7   Encratites too celebrate mysteries with water.[9] They do not
drink wine at all,[10] and claim that it is of the devil, and that those
who drink and use it are malefactors and sinners. (8) And yet they
believe in the resurrection of the dead, showing that, for people
who have gone this far wrong, everything is crazy. (9) Indeed, a
person with sense can see and puzzle over everything that heretics
say and do, and be thrown into consternation because of them;
none of their speech and behavior hangs together and admits of
any appearance of truth.

2,1   For if they use the Old and New Testaments, where are
there any different authorities? The two Testaments agree on one
< authority > and proclaim the knowledge of < one Godhead >. (2)
And if there is a resurrection of the dead, how can lawful wedlock
be of the devil? For God says, "Be fruitful and multiply;"[11] and the
Lord says, in the Gospel, "What God hath joined together, let not
man put asunder."[12] And the apostle says, "Marriage is honorable,
and the bed undefiled."[13]

2,3   But when they are confronted with such arguments they
malign Paul by calling him a drunkard.[14] And they hunt for texts
against wine-drinkers to suit their taste and support their fiction,
seize on them, and say that anything like wine is of the devil. "Noah
drank wine," they say, "and was stripped naked. (4) Lot got drunk,
and unknowingly lay with his own daughters. The calf was made
during a drinking bout. And the scripture says, 'Who hath confusion? Who hath contentions? Who hath resentments and gossip?

---

[7] Marriage is called "the work of the serpent" at Acts of Thomas 57. Condemnations of matrimony occur in the apocryphal Acts, e.g. at Acts of John
63; 113; Acts of Andrew 28;35; Acts of Thomas 12–16; 96–103; 131. Cf. Iren.
Haer. 1.28.1; Hippol. Haer. 8.20.15; Clem. Alex. Strom. 1.71.5; 2.46.3.
[8] Iren. Haer. 1.28.1; Hippol. Haer. 8.20.1; Basil of Cesarea Ep. 236,4.
[9] Acts of Thomas 121. Cyprian of Carthage Ep. 63 is a tract against the
practice, which suggests that it sometimes occurred in catholic circles.
[10] Hippol. Haer. 8.20.1; Clem. Alex. Paedag. 2.32.1–3; Basil of Caesarea Ep.
236,4.
[11] Gen. 1:28
[12] Matt. 19:6; Mark 10:9
[13] Heb. 13:4
[14] In his Prologue to the Epistle to Titus, Jerome says that "Tatian, the patriarch
of the Encratites" repudiated several of the Pauline Epistles.

Who hath afflictions without cause? Whose eyes are inflamed? Is it not they that tarry long at wine, that seek out the place where drinking is?'"[15]

2,5   And they track down other texts of this kind and make a collection of them for their credibility's sake, without realizing that all immoderation is in every way grievous, and declared to be outside of the prescribed bounds. (6) For I would say this not merely of wine, but of every form of intemperance. The Lord was teaching this lesson when he said, "Let not your hearts be overcharged with surfeiting and drunkenness and cares of this life."[16] So was the text, "If thou be given to appetite, be not desirous of a rich man's meats, for these attend on a life of deceit."[17] (7) And further, when the holy apostle was ridding the church of the intemperate and greedy he said, in anger at their gluttonous desires, "Meats for the belly, and the belly for meats; but God shall destroy both it and them."[18]

2,8   Besides, Esau lost his birthright over a wheat mash—as the scripture says, calling the same thing a "wheat mash" and a "lentil mash."[19] (I imagine it was not made of wheat—that is, not made of grain. I think the scripture was probably describing the leftover lentils—which had already been boiled, and which had been put back on the fire and heated up again—as "< boiled > on the fire," because they had been heated up after cooling off.) (9) And as Noah was stripped naked because of wine but came to no harm, so Esau came to the harm of losing his birthright, but from hunger and greed rather than wine. And no falsely applied text is of any avail in the face of the truth, nor is any invention of dramatic fiction.

3,1   They take pride in a pretended continence, but all their conduct is risky. For they are surrounded by women, deceive women in every way, travel and eat with women and are served by them. For they are outside of the truth, "having the form of godliness, but denying the power thereof."[20] (2) For if a person neglects any part of a work such as this, through the one part which he neglects he has given up the whole of it. And so it is that their mysteries are celebrated only with water, and are not mysteries but false mysteries, celebrated in imitation of the true ones. (3) Hence the

---

[15] Prov. 23:29–30
[16] Luke 21:34
[17] Prov. 23:3
[18] 1 Cor. 6:13
[19] Cf. LXX Gen. 25:30 with 25:34. Epiphanius here takes πυρός, "wheat," as the genitive of πῦρ, "fire."
[20] 2 Tim. 3:5

Encratites will be defeated on this point too, by the plain words of the Savior, "I will not drink henceforth of this *fruit of the vine*, until I drink it new with you in the kingdom of God."[21]

3,4   Disabling this sect in its turn with the mighty hand of the truth—like a stinging insect deprived of teeth—let us go on to the rest, calling on the God of all, as we always do, to be our guide and our defender against horrors, and to be the help of our judgment as he is the giver of our wisdom. May I thus learn the truth from him and be able to expose the < nonsense* > of the others and, by the speech of the truth, make the medicinal antidote for them from many fragrant herbs. May it be given ungrudgingly: for healing, to those who have already contracted [the disease]; as a treatment, to whose who are coming down with it; as a preventative, to those who are about to learn something they did not know; and to myself, for God's salvation and reward.

Against those who are called Phrygians or Montanists[1] or, also, Tascodrugians. Number 28, but 48 of the series

1,1   Another sect emerges in its turn after these, and is called the sect of the Phrygians. It originated at the same time as the Encratites, and is their successor. (2) For the Montanists had their beginning about the nineteenth year of Hadrian's successor Antoninus Pius,[2] while Marcion, Tatian, and the Encratites who succeeded him, began in Hadrian's time and after Hadrian.

1,3   These Phrygians too, as we call them, accept every scripture of the Old and the New Testaments and affirm the resurrection of the dead as well. But they boast of having Montanus for a prophet, and Priscilla and Maximilla for prophetesses, and have lost their wits by paying heed to them. (4) They agree with the holy catholic church about the Father, the Son and the Holy Spirit,[3] but have

---

[21] Matt. 26:29

[1] Epiphanius' literary source for this Sect would have been a short collection of Montanist prophecies; for the existence of Montanist books see Hippol. Haer. 8.19.1; Eus. H. E. 5.18.5; Labriolle (Dial. Mont. Orth.) p. 106; Jer. Vir. Ill. 40; Theod. Haer. Fab. 3.1. The Epiphanian style, and the absence of the marks of the adaptation of sources, make it certain that Epiphanius' refutation is his own. Other ancient sources for Montanism are Hippol. Haer. 8.6.19; 10.25–28; Eus. H. E. 5.3.16–19; Jer. Ep. 41; Filast. Haer. 49; Cyr. Cat. 16.18; Did. De Trin. 3.41; the Montanist works of Tertullian, and the sources collected in Labriolle.
[2] Clem. Alex. Strom. 3.106.4–5
[3] The Montanist Tertullian detests monarchianism (Adv. Prax. 1.1–3; 5) and attributes his essentially catholic doctrine of the the Trinity to the Paraclete (Adv. Prax. 2.1; 8.5). Montanists are, however, accused of monarchianism at Labriolle (Dial. Mont. Orth.) pp. 97–98; Jer. Ep. 41.3, cf. Orig. Cels. 8.9. Hippolytus

separated themselves by "giving heed to seducing spirits and doctrines of devils"[4] and saying, "We must receive the gifts of grace as well."

1,5   God's holy church also receives the gifts of grace—but the real gifts, which have already been tried in God's holy church through the Holy Spirit, and by prophets and apostles, and the Lord himself. (6) For the apostle John says in his Epistle, "Try the spirits, whether they be of God;"[5] and again, "Ye have heard that Antichrist cometh, and now many Antichrists have come. They went out from us, but they were not of us; for if they had been of us, they would have continued with us: but that it might be made known that they were not of us. For this cause write I unto you, little children,"[6] and so on. (7) The Phrygians are truly not "of" the saints themselves. They "went out" by their contentiousness, and "gave heed" to spirits of error and fictitious stories.

2,1   For look here, their religion itself is proof that they cannot keep their contentiously made promises. If we must receive gifts of grace, and if there must be gifts of grace in the church, why do they have no more prophets after Montanus, Priscilla and Maximilla?[7] Has grace stopped working, then? Never fear, the grace in the holy church does not stop working! (2) But if the prophets prophesied up to a certain time, and no more < after that* >, then neither Priscilla nor Maximilla prophesied; < they delivered their prophecies after > the ones which were tried by the holy apostles, in the holy church.

2,3   Their stupidity will be exposed in two ways, then. Either they should show that there are prophets after Maximilla, so that their so-called "grace" will not be inoperative. Or Maximilla will be proved a false prophet, since she dared to receive inspiration after the end of the prophetic gifts—not from the Holy Spirit but from devils' imposture—and delude her audience.

2,4   And see how they can be refuted from the very things they say! Their so-called prophetess, Maximilla, says, "After me will be no prophet more, but the consummation." (5) Look here, the Holy Spirit and the spirits of error are perfectly recognizable! Everything the prophets have said, they also said rationally and with understanding; and the things they said have come true and

---

(Haer.8.19.3; Ps.-Tert. 7.2) and Didymus (De Trin.3.41.1) distinguish between Montanists who are monarchian and those who are not.

[4] 1 Tim. 4:1. For the use of this text against Montanists cf. Tert. Jejun. 2:5; Orig. Com. in Mat. 15.30.

[5] 1 John 4:1

[6] Cf. 1 John 2:18–19.

[7] So argued at Eus. H. E. 5.17.4 (anonymous anti-Montanist)

are still coming true. (6) But Maximilla said that the consummation would come after her, and no consummation has come yet—
even after so many emperors, and such a lapse of time! (7) There
have been about † 206[8] years from Maximilla's time until ours, the
twelfth year of Valentinian and Valens and the < eighth > of Gratian's,[9]
and we have yet to see the consummation announced by this woman
who boasted of being a prophetess, but did not even know the
day of her own death.

2,8   Plainly, none who have estranged themselves from the truth
have retained any soundness of reason. Like babes bitten by the
perennial deceiver, the serpent, they have surrendered themselves
to destruction and to being caught outside the fold and dragged
off to be the wolf's meat < and > thus perish. This is because they
did not hold on to the Head but deserted the truth and hazarded
themselves in shipwreck, and in the surf of all sorts of error. (9)
If Maximilla says there will never be another prophet, she is denying
that they have the gift, and that it is still to be found among them.
If their gift persists [only] until Maximilla, then, as I said before,
she had no gifts of grace either.[10]

3,1   For she has gone astray. The Lord has set his seal on the
church, and perfected the gifts of grace < in > her. When prophets
were needed the same saints, filled with the Holy Spirit, delivered
all the prophecies for our benefit[11]—[delivered them] in the true
Spirit, with sound mind and a rational intellect, in proportion to
their < faith > in the gifts of grace the Spirit was giving to each,
and "in proportion to the faith."[12] (2) But what have these people
said that was beneficial? What have they said that was in proportion
to the faith? Indeed, how can they be any but the persons of whom
the Lord said, "Beware of false prophets, who come to you in
sheep's clothing, but inwardly they are ravening wolves?"[13]

3,3   By comparing what they have said with < the teachings >
of the Old and New Testaments—which are true, and which have
been delivered and prophesied in truth—let us determine which
is < really > prophecy, and which false prophecy. (4) A prophet
always spoke with composure and understanding, and delivered

---

[8] Holl: σϝ; MSS: διακόσια ἐνενήκοντα
[9] 376 C. E. Epiphanius has been at work on the Panarion for about a year
at this point; cf. Proem II.2.
[10] So argued at Eus. H. E. 5.17.4
[11] Cf. 1 Cor. 12:7.
[12] Cf. Rom. 12:6.
[13] Matt. 7:15

his oracles by the Holy Spirit's inspiration.[14] He said everything with a sound mind like "Moses, the servant of God and faithful in all his house, who saw the glory of God < apparently, and not in dark speeches."[15] And thus the man who *saw** > was called a prophet in the Old Testament. (5) Scripture says, "The vision which Isaiah the son of Amoz, the prophet, *saw*.[16] I *saw* < the > Lord sitting upon a throne high and lifted up. And I *saw* Seraphim and Cherubim, and I heard the Lord saying unto me, Go and tell this people, Hear indeed and ye shall not understand; and see indeed, and ye shall not perceive."[17] And after the Lord had told him this he went to the people and said, "Thus saith the Lord." (6) Can't you see that this is the speech of a sober person who is not out of his senses, and that the oracle was not delivered as the speech of a mind distraught?

3,7   Similarly, when the prophet Ezekiel heard the Lord say, "Bake thee bread on human dung,"[18] he said, "Not so, Lord; nothing common or unclean hath at any time come into my mouth."[19] (8) Because he understood the threat the Lord had addressed to him he did not go ahead and do [it] as though he were out of his senses. Since his mind was sound and rational he prayed and said, "Not so, Lord." These—both the teaching and the discussion—are marks of < the > true prophets, whose minds are sound in the Holy Spirit.

3,9   And who can deny that Daniel was filled with all wisdom and in possession of his senses? He found the answers to Nebuchadnezzar's riddles, (10) recalled Nebuchadnezzar's dreams when they had eluded even the dreamer, and with his soundness of mind and the superiority of his gift, gave the explanation at once. For he had wisdom greater than everyone's by the gift of the Holy Spirit, who truly gives wisdom—to the prophet and to those who, through the prophet, are vouchsafed the teaching of the truth.

3,11   But when the Phrygians profess to prophesy, it is plain that they are not sound of mind and rational. Their words are ambiguous and odd, with nothing right about them. (4,1) Montanus, for instance, says, "Lo, the man is as a lyre, and I fly over him

---

[14] Eus. H. E. 5.17.2–3 (anonymous anti-Montanist): "But the false prophet prophesies in ecstasy . . . They cannot show that any of the truly inspired prophets in the Old or the New Testament was of this sort . . . "
[15] Nu. 12:7–8
[16] Isa. 1:1
[17] Cf. Isa. 6:1–3;9.
[18] Ezek. 4:12
[19] Ezek. 4:4; Acts 10:14

as a pick. The man sleepeth, while I watch. Lo, it is the Lord that distracteth the hearts of men, and that giveth the heart to man."[20]

4,2 Now what rational person who receives the "profitable" message with understanding and cares for his salvation, can fail to despise a false religion like this, and the speech of someone who boasts of being a prophet but cannot talk like a prophet? (3) For the Holy Spirit never spoke in him. Such expressions as "I fly," and "strike," and "watch," and "The Lord distracteth men's hearts," are the utterances of an ecstatic. They are not the words of a rational man, but of someone of a different stamp from the Holy Spirit who spoke in the prophets.

4,4 When the Phrygians are out to combine falsehood with truth and rob those who care for accuracy of their intelligence, they collect[21] heaps of texts to make a false case for their imposture, and < to prove their lies from them* >, say that certain scriptures bear a resemblance to it. < For instance >, the holy scripture has said, "God sent an 'ecstasy' upon Adam, and he slept."[22]

But Adam's case was nothing like theirs. (5) In their case God did not mean to fashion a body—his reason for putting Adam into a trance—and, of his extreme lovingkindness, give them a similar experience. (6) God brought the unconsciousness of sleep upon Adam, not distraction of mind.

There are many different forms of ecstasy. We call stupefaction from excess of wonder an ecstasy; and madness is called *ecstasy* because it is *out* of touch with reality. (7) But Adam's "ecstasy" of sleep was so called in a different sense, one related to the activity of his body, especially because the holy Adam whom God's hand had fashioned was cast into a very deep trance.

5,1 For it is indeed plain that the sacred scripture was right to call this *ecstasy*. When someone is asleep, all his senses leave him and take a rest. Though the sense of sight is there, for example, but does not see; the eye is closed, and the mover in the man, the spirit or soul, is at rest. (2) If there is an unpleasant odor in the house or even a pleasant one, the sense of smell is there but does not perceive the odor; this sense has departed to take a rest. (3) If there are bitter, or salty or sweet fluids in the mouth, the

---

[20] Tertullian maintains that a prophet loses his senses because he is overshadowed by the power of God, and cannot know what he has said, Adv. Marc. 4.22.4–5. At Adv. Marc. 5.8.12 he equates ecstasy with *amentia*.

[21] Reading ἐπισωρεύουσι [τε] λόγους, with the omission of τε

[22] LXX Gen. 2:21. Tertullian, who regards dreams as a kind of madness, explains Adam's "ecstasy" similarly at De Anima 45.1–6; 23.

sense of taste does not perceive them; it lies in the ecstasy of rest without doing what it did in the man when he was awake.

5,4 The ear is there, but the hearing is not functioning as a sense. And if people are talking in the house it often does not hear what anyone says unless the man wakes up; for the time being, its function is suspended. (5) Creatures can be crawling on our bodies, but we do not feel their touch on our bodies unless their onslaught is severe; the whole body has abandoned its activity for the rest of sleep.

5,6 For the body is made of earth and envelops the soul, and since God made it serviceable to us in this way, it is allowed a time of withdrawal from its full sensation to a state of rest. The soul itself does not abandon its function of governance or thought. (7) It often imagines and sees itself as though it were awake, and walks around, does work, crosses the sea, addresses crowds—and sees itself in more situations, and more striking ones, in its dreams. (8) But it is not like a madman, or an ecstatic in a transport. He takes frightful things in hand while awake in body and soul,[23] and often does grievous harm to himself and his neighbors. He does not know what he is saying and doing, for he has fallen into the ecstasy of folly.

6,1 Beloved, I have had to gather all this material < about > the various kinds of ecstasy because of the text, "The Lord sent an ecstasy upon Adam, and he slept."[24] (2) And I have explained why going to sleep is called an "ecstasy from the Lord" in that passage. It is because of the compassion and lovingkindess God has granted to all, so that one may be removed from care and the business of living to the rest of sleep. (3) In Adam's case, however, God further called it ecstasy because it made him insensitive to pain for a time, because of the side God meant to take from him and make into his wife.

6,4 But Adam's senses and wits were not in abeyance. He recognized Eve as soon as he awoke, and said, "This is now bone of my bone and flesh of my flesh; she shall be called 'wife,' for she was taken out of her husband."[25] (5) And as you see, he was aware of the past and the present, and made a prophecy of the future. Look here, by saying "bone of my bone" he took notice of what had happened while he was asleep. And he was aware of the present; after his wife had been made he was aware that she had been taken

---

[23] Cf. Tertullian's description of dreams at De Anima 45; dreams, while a form of madness, are healthy and natural.
[24] Gen. 2:21
[25] Gen. 2:23

from < his > body. (6) And of the future he prophesied, "For this cause shall a man leave his father and his mother and shall cleave unto his wife, and they two shall be one flesh."[26] These are not the words of a man in an ecstasy or without understanding, but of a person of sound mind.

7,1 But if I must also speak of, "I said in my ecstasy, all men are liars,"[27] the meaning of this, again, is different. These are not the words of a madman and an ecstatic < as the Phrygians claim* >— far from it!—(2) but of someone who is very surprised, and is taking more than usual account < of > things < not > fit to be said and done. For since the prophet was astonished, he also speaks with astonishment here.[28]

7,3 The prophets fell into trances, < but* > not into distraction. Peter too was in an "ecstasy,"[29] not because he was irrational but because he saw things other than what men usually see in the everyday world. (4) "For he saw a sheet let down, bound at the four corners, and in it all manner of four-footed beasts and creeping things and birds of the air."[30] (5) Observe that St. Peter was rational, and not out of his mind. For when he heard < the words >, "Arise, kill and eat,"[31] he did not obey like a person of unsound mind, but told the Lord, "Not so, Lord; nothing common or unclean hath at any time come into my mouth."[32]

7,6 And the holy David said, "< I said >, all men are liars."[33] In saying, "I said," he was speaking for himself, and saying that people lie. Thus he was not lying—but he expressed great astonishment because he was amazed and astounded at God's lovingkindness and the things the Lord had told him. (7) And, seeing that everyone is in need of God's mercy, he ascribed truth-telling to the Lord alone, and realized that every human being is deserving of punishment—thus evidencing the true Spirit, who spoke in the prophets and revealed to them the depths of the exact knowledge of God.

7,8 Abraham too fell into ecstasy—not the abeyance of his wits but the distraction of fear. He saw the furnace and the torches

---

[26] Gen. 2:24
[27] Ps. 115:2
[28] Didymus the Blind explains the "ecstasy" can mean astonishment, Labriolle p. 161 (Did. Com. Acts 10:10).
[29] Tertullian uses Peter as an example of "ecstasy," Adv. Marc. 4.22.4–5. Cf. Didymus the Blind at Labriolle p. 161.
[30] Acts 10:11–12
[31] Acts 10:13
[32] Cf. Acts 10:14.
[33] Ps. 115:2

about sundown < and was afraid, as* > other prophets said when
they saw visions in their right minds. (9) Moses, for example, said,
"I fear exceedingly and quake."[34] But Abraham knew what the
Lord was saying, for < scripture says >, "Thou shalt *know* of a surety
that thy seed shall be a stranger 400 years in a land that is not
theirs."[35] (10) And you see how plain it is that everything was said
in truth by the prophets with sound mind and sober reason, and
not in madness.

8,1   But even though they choose to reply, "The first gifts are
not like the last ones,"[36] how can they prove it? The holy prophets
and the holy apostles prophesied alike. (2) In the first place, those
who saw the two men in white when the Savior ascended into
heaven did not see them in derangement, but with sound minds
heard [them say], "Ye men of Galilee, why stand ye gazing up onto
heaven? This same Jesus, who is taken up from you into heaven,
shall so come,"[37] and so on. (3) And then, as I said, Peter was
in his right mind when he saw, heard, and gave his answer, and
said, "Not so, Lord."[38]

8,4   Agabus spoke prophetically and hinted at his meaning with
an unusual gesture, when he took Paul's girdle, bound his own
feet, and said, "He whose girdle this is, him shall they bind and
carry to Jerusalem."[39] (5) And in turn, prophets came down to
Antioch and declared that there would be a world-wide famine,
and their prediction did not fail; to show that they were true prophets,
the scripture adds at once, "Which thing came to pass in the days
of Claudius Caesar."[40]

8,6   And the most holy apostle Paul prophesied, "Now the Spirit
saith expressly that in the last days harsh times shall come,"[41] and
so on. (7) And again, in another place, "Some shall fall away from
sound doctrine, giving heed to seducing < spirits > and doctrines
of devils, forbidding to marry and commanding to abstain from
meats, which God hath created to be partaken of by us < who
receive them > with thanksgiving.[42] (8) The material before this
< will > itself < make it plain > that < this > has clearly come true,

---

[34] Deut. 9:19; Heb. 12:21
[35] Gen. 15:13
[36] Tertullian says that the Paraclete's instructions are novelties of discipline
but not doctrine, Monog. 3.8; 9; Virg. Vel. 1.2–4.
[37] Acts 1:11
[38] Acts 10:14
[39] Acts 21:11
[40] Acts 21:11
[41] 2 Tim. 3:1
[42] 1 Tim. 4:1;3

in you and others like you. Most of these sects forbid marriage and prescribe abstinence from foods, though they do not enjoin these things for discipline's sake or for greater virtue with its rewards and crowns, but because they regard these creatures of the Lord as abominations.

9,1   Now the holy catholic church reveres virginity, the single life and purity, commends widowhood, and honors and accepts lawful wedlock; but it forbids fornication, adultery and unchastity. (2) This will show the character of the holy catholic church and the false customs of the others—[show], < likewise >, who has seen fit to avoid every imposture, crooked path and uphill track. (3) For I have said before—as has just been said by the most holy apostle and I shall now repeat—that it was to make us secure and distinguish the character of the holy catholic church from the imposture of the sects, that Paul said how arrogantly the sects which forbid matrimony and prescribe abstinence from foods prohibit God's good ordinances by law.

9,4   For it was < with > a certain fitness that the divine Word said, "Wilt thou be perfect?"[43] in the Gospel. Although he makes allowances for human clay and its frailty, he rejoices in those who can show the marks of piety and choose to practice virginity, purity and continence. Still, he honors marriage to one spouse, (5) even though he prefigures the gifts of the priesthood chiefly by means of persons who stayed continent after one marriage, and persons who remained virgin, and his holy apostles so established the canonical rule of the priesthood, with decency and holiness.[44] (6) But if, from frailty, someone needs to contract a second marriage after the death of his wife, the rule of the truth does not prohibit this—that is, provided he is not a priest.

9,7   But these people do forbid it—"forbidding to marry,"[45] as scripture says. They expel anyone who has contracted a second marriage, and make their rule against second marriage a matter of compulsion.

9,8   For our part, we lay necessity on no one. As a good counsel we urge those who can [to follow this rule], but we lay no necessity on one who cannot, and surely do not expel him from life.[46] (9)

[43] Matt. 19:21
[44] Didasc. 4, Achelis-Flemming p. 14
[45] 1 Tim. 4:3. This discipline was crucial to Montanists, cf. Tert. Pudic. 1.20; Adv. Marc. 1.29.4; Carn. Res. 8.4; De Monogamia, especially 1.2; 14.3. Cf. Eus. H. E. 5.18.2; Jer. Ep. 41.3.1.
[46] Montanists regarded second marriages as adultery (Tert. Monog. 15.1; Adv. Hermog. 1.2) and excommunicated those who contracted them (Jer. Ep. 41.3.1).

The holy word everywhere declared that we must bear with the frailty of the weak. We shall find at once that, to shame people like these < who expel persons* > who do not have the same gift as they, the holy apostle says, "Younger widows refuse; (10) for after they wax wanton against Christ they will marry, having condemnation because they have left their first faith."[47] For widows who have promised and broken their promise have condemnation, while those who made no promise, but married from frailty, will not have condemnation. If they were to have condemnation, why did Paul say, "Let them marry, guide the house."[48]

10,1 We find then that every prophet, whether in the Old Testament or in the New, prophesies with understanding, as St. John said in Revelation: "The Lord *revealed* these things to his servants through his servant John,"[49] and, "Thus saith the Lord." (2) The person who said this was sound of mind and understanding—see how < he says the same as the Old Testament prophets who say* >, "Thus saith the Lord," and "the vision which he saw."

10,3 But this Montanus, who has deceived his victims with his boast of being a prophet, describes things which are not consistent with sacred scripture. For in his so-called prophecy he says, "Why sayest thou, [Only] he that is more than man can be saved?[50] For the righteous shall shine an hundredfold brighter than the sun; and the least of you that are saved, an hundredfold brighter than the moon."

10,4 But the Lord confounds him. And it is he who has the power to grant radiance to the faces of the saints, who made Moses' face shine, and who will transform his saints, who are sown in dishonor and raised in glory, at the coming resurrection of bodies. (5) Not transform bodies other than their own but change their own bodies, raised entire, and receiving glory, after < the resurrection >, from him who gives glory unstintingly to his saints. For as Lord and God he has the power to grant and bestow glory.

10,6 But although he has < the power > to grant this, he did not make promises like Montanus'; he said, "Your faces shall shine *as* the sun."[51] Now if Jesus Christ, who has the power and is our true Master and Lord, says that the faces of the righteous will shine

---

[47] 1 Tim. 5:11–12. Tertullian takes this passage to mean that the church should not receive younger widows as converts, Monog. 13.1.
[48] 1 Tim. 5:14
[49] Cf. Rev. 1:1.
[50] A protest against the rigor of second century penitential discipline?
[51] Cf. Matt. 13:43

as the sun, how can Montanus promise a hundred times more? (7) Only if he is like the one who promised Adam, "Ye shall be as gods,"[52] and secured his expulsion from the glory he had and the enjoyment of Paradise, and his degradation to the corruption of death.

11,1   The same Montanus goes on to add, "I am the Lord God, the Almighty, dwelling in a man." (2) Happily the sacred scripture, and the course of the Holy Spirit's teaching, keeps us safe by giving us warnings so that we will know which are the counterfeits of the strange spirit and the opposites of the truth. (3) Simply by saying this, Montanus has suggested that we remember the words of the Lord. For the Lord says in the Gospel, "I came in my Father's name and ye received me not. Another shall come in his own name, and such a one will ye receive."[53] (4) Montanus is thus in total disagreement with the sacred scriptures, as any attentive reader can see. And since he is in disagreement, < he himself >, and the sect which like him boasts of having prophets and gifts, are strangers to the holy catholic church. He did not receive these gifts; he departed from them.

11,5   What rational person would dare to call these people prophets instead of < saying > that such prophets are deceivers? Christ taught us, "I send unto you the Spirit, the Paraclete,"[54] and to give the signs of the Paraclete, said, "He shall glorify me."[55] (6) And in fact it is plain that the holy apostles glorified the Lord after receiving the Paraclete Spirit, while this Montanus glorifies himself. The Lord glorified his Father; and in turn, the Lord Christ glorified the Spirit by calling him the Spirit of truth. Montanus, however, glorifies only himself, and says that he is the Father almighty, and that < the deceitful spirit* > which dwells in him < is the Paraclete* > —proof positive that he is not the Father, was not sent by the Father, and has received nothing from the Father. (7) "In the Lord was all the fullness of the Godhead pleased to dwell bodily,"[56] and "Of his fullness have all the prophets received,"[57] as St. John has told us. (8) And see how all the ancient [prophets] announced Christ, and how those who came after them glorified Christ and confessed him. But Montanus intruded himself by saying that he was somebody, proof that he is not Christ, was not sent

---

[52] Gen. 3:5
[53] John 5:43
[54] Cf. John 16:7.
[55] John 16:4
[56] Col. 2:9
[57] Cf. John 1:16.

by Christ, and has received nothing from Christ.

11,9   This pathetic little man, Montanus, says in turn, "Neither angel nor messenger, but I the Lord, God the Father, have come."[58] By saying this he will be exposed as a heretic, for he does not glorify Christ, whom every regular gift which has been given in the holy church truly glorified. (10) For we shall find that Montanus is outside the body of the church and the Head of all, and "does not hold the Head, from whom the whole body, knit together, increaseth,"[59] as scripture says. For the actual true Son, our Lord Jesus Christ, showed that he was a Son; but Montanus even says that he is the Father.

12,1   When you Phrygians say you left the church over gifts of grace,[60] how can we believe you? Even though you are disguised with the title of "Christian," you have launched another enemy attack on us. You have taken up the barbarians' quarrel and mimicked the enmity of the Trojans, who were also Phrygians! (2) Things that are different from gifts and—as your own prophets say—not the same kind that the Lord promises, cannot be gifts.

12,3   And in turn, you introduce us to—Maximilla! Even your names are different and scary, with nothing pleasant and melodious about them, but with a certain wildness and savagery. (4) At once this Maximilla, who belongs to these so-called Phrygians— listen to what she says, children of Christ! "Hearken not unto me, but hearken unto Christ!"[61]

12,5   Even where she seemed to be glorifying Christ, she was wrong. If she were Christ's she would talk like the holy apostles, as each < of them > says—Peter first, who says, "We have heard of him."[62] And the Lord himself says, "He that heareth you, heareth me."[63] And Paul says, "Be ye imitators of me, as I am of Christ."[64]

12,6   But in the act of lying she tells the truth, even against her will. She is right to say not to listen to her, but to Christ. Unclean spirits are often forced to denounce themselves < as > not of the truth and to show, willy nilly and under duress, who their Lord is.[65] (7) As the damsel with the oracular spirit said, "These

---

[58] Cf. Isa. 63:9. At Adv. Marc. 4.22.11 Tertullian applies this saying to Christ himself.

[59] Col. 2:19

[60] Tert. Adv. Prax. 1.7, "*et nos quidem postea agnitio paracleti atque defensio disjunxit a psychicis.*

[61] Cf. Luke 10:16

[62] Cf. Acts 4:20; 2 Pet. 1:18.

[63] Luke 10:16

[64] 1 Cor. 11:1

[65] Catholic exorcists exorcise Montanist prophets at Eus. H. E. 5.16.7

men are servants of the most high God;"[66] and [as the demon in the Gospel said], "Why hast thou come before the time to torment us? I know thee who thou art, the holy one of God."[67] So Maximilla, under compulsion, said not to listen to her, but to Christ. (8) Now how can those who have heard this from her and believed her care to listen to her—when they have learned from her not to listen to her, but to the Lord! In fact if they had any sense they shouldn't listen to her, since her oracles are of the earth.

12,9   And don't tell me that she was in a rational state! A rational person doesn't condemn himself in his own teaching. If she said anything like, "Don't listen to me," what sort of spirit was speaking in her? (10) For if she spoke humanly, then she was not in the Holy Spirit—for it is plain that in saying, "Do not listen to me," she was speaking humanly, and was not in the Holy Spirit. But if she was not in the Holy Spirit from on high but was thinking humanly, she knew nothing and was no prophetess. For she did not have the Holy Spirit, but spoke and delivered her oracles with human intelligence.

12,11   But if she did speak and prophesy in the Holy Spirit— what sort of Holy Spirit would say, "Don't listen to me?" The blindness of deceit is stone blind—and great is the word of God, which gives us understanding in every way, so that we may know what has been spoken by the Holy Spirit's inspiration, here in the person of the Father, there in the person of the Son, there in the person of the Holy Spirit!

12,12   And if the spirit in Maximilla were a holy < spirit >, it would not forbid his own utterances. "*One* is the Holy Spirit, that divideth to each as he will."[68] (13) And if he has the power to divide as he will, and is called the Spirit of knowledge and the Spirit of piety, and is said to be the Spirit of God and the Spirit of Christ, proceeding from the Father and receiving of the Son and not foreign to the Father and the Son—then he didn't say, "Do not listen to me!" (14) For the Spirit gave Christ's message and Christ sends the Spirit, and casts out devils by the Holy Spirit. And the Son gives the Father's message and the Father sanctified the Son and sent him into the world, that they might know him, and might glorify him as they glorify the Father. And the notion of those who separate themselves from the following of Christ is all wrong.

(Apolinarius); 18.13 (Apollonius); 19.3 (Serapion); Firmilian/Cyprian Ep. 45.10.
[66] Acts 16:16–17
[67] Matt. 8:29; Mark 1:24
[68] 1 Cor. 12:11

13,1   In turn the same Maximilla—this "rational knowledge and teaching," if I may be sarcastic—says, "The Lord hath sent me perforce, willing and not willing, to be votary, herald and interpreter of this burden and covenant and promise, to impart the knowledge of God."[69] (2) Let us look to the firm foundation of our life, beloved, and the lighted pathway, and not trip on words of the adversary and the strange spirit's prey. (3) See the prophet here, who spoke like that and denounced herself, not willingly but under compulsion. Our Lord did not come into the world unwillingly, and was not sent under compulsion by the Father. (4) He has the will in concert with the Father, and its performance in concert with the Holy Spirit. And as he himself has the will—and the giving of grace to all, not perforce but by his superabundant lovingkindness—in concert with the Father, even so, those whom he has called, he has called of their own choice, imposing no necessity and clapping no collars on them. (5) For he says, "Ye that thirst, *come* to me,"[70] and again, "If any man *will come* after me let him follow me."[71] And he said the same through Isaiah: "If ye be *willing* and hearken."[72] And later, to show who was speaking, the prophet said, "For the mouth of the Lord hath spoken these things."[73]

13,6   And are you fully aware of their disagreement with the sacred text, and the difference between their notion and opinion, and the faith and following of God? (7) For Maximilla also said that she compelled the willing and the unwilling [to know God]— so that her very words make her a liar. She neither taught the knowledge of God—which she did not know—to the willing, nor compelled the unwilling [to learn it]. (8) It goes without saying that the whole world does not know Maximilla's name, or her misstatements. And their erroneous notion is all wrong, and no part of God's truth.

14,1   Phrygians also venerate a deserted spot in Phrygia, a town once called Pepuza though it is now leveled, and say that the heavenly Jerusalem will descend there.[74] (2) And so they resort there, celebrate

---

[69] ἀπέστειλέ με κύριος ... ἠναγκασμένον, θέλοντα καὶ μὴ θέλοντα, γνωθεῖν γνῶσιν θεοῦ. Maximilla refers to herself in the masculine; Epiphanius, however, reads, "The Lord hath sent me to impart knowledge of God to the willing and the unwilling," and refutes on that basis.

[70] John 7:37

[71] Matt. 16:24

[72] Isa. 1:19

[73] Isa. 58:14

[74] Eus. H. E. 5.18.1; 13; Cyr. Cat. 16.8; Filast. Haer. 49.4. Tertullian speaks of the descent of heavenly Jerusalem without mentioning Pepuza, Adv. Marc.

certain mysteriess[75] on the site, and, as they suppose, sanctify
< themselves >. For this breed is also to be found in Cappadocia
and Galatia—and in Phrygia as I said, which is why the sect is called
the Phrygian. But they are in Cilicia too and, for the most part,
in Constantinople.

14,3   But to omit nothing that bears on the name of every sect
I have discussed, I shall also speak, in its turn, of the Tascodrugians'.
For this name is used either in this sect itself, or the one after
it, which is called the sect of the Quintillianists—for this name too
originates with these people themselves.

14,4   They are called Tascodrugians for the following reason.
Their word for "peg" is "tascus," and "drungus" is their word for
"nostril" or "snout." And since they put their licking finger, as we
call it, on their nostril when they pray, for dejection, if you please,
and would-be righteousness, some people have given them the
name of Tascodrugians, or "nose-pickers."[76]

14,5   They say that a shocking, wicked thing is done in this
sect—or in its sister sect, the one called the sect of the Quintillianists
or Priscillianists, and Pepuzians. (6) At a certain festival they pierce
a child—just a little baby—all over its body with bronze needles
and get its blood for sacrifice, if you please.[77]

15,1   But I am content with what I have said about this sect
in its turn, beloved. I promised to withhold nothing about any sect
I know, but to disclose what I have learned by word of mouth,
and from treatises, documents, and persons who truly confirmed
my notion. (2) Thus, by writing no more than I know, I will < not >
appear to be guilty of inventing my own false charges against people,
and of getting into the same position as they by not telling the
truth, but declaring things that they have neither seen, heard, nor
learned from the true teaching of the Holy Spirit.

15,3   I give all the facts, as I said, with accuracy, about each
sect, and make these shocking disclosures for the readers' correction. And I prepare a sort of medicine made of refutation from
the words of sacred scripture and right reasonings, (4) and compound < it > in the Lord for two purposes: for the recovery of the

---

3.24.3–4. Jerome says that Montanist patriarchs reside at Pepuza, Ep. 41.3.2.
   [75] Tertullian speaks of distinctively Montanist rites *in diversis provinciis*, Jejun.
13.5, cf. 13.8.
   [76] Filast. Haer. 76 appears to describe this group under the name of
"Passalorinchitae." At Haer. 75 he speaks of "Ascodrugians," who dance wildly
around an inflated wineskin.
   [77] Cyr. Cat. 16.8; Jer. Ep. 41.4.1. Theod. Haer. Fab. 3.2 and Praedestinatus
26 report this as a rumor which may not be true.

sufferers from their illness and great pain, but for (5) a prophylactic, as it were, for those who have never contracted the disease.
Thus may I too be called a disciple of the Lord's disciples for
imparting the medicine of the truth to the wise, and a disciple
of the Savior himself, the help of bodies and souls.

15,6 Now, with the power of Christ, let me set myself to go
on to the rest, since I feel that this here will be enough for this
sect. I have crushed its poison, and the venom on its hooked fangs,
with the cudgel of the truth of the cross. For it is like the viper
of hemorrhage, whose mischief is to drain the blood from its victims'
entire bodies and so cause their deaths. (7) For this sect and the
sect of Quintillianists do the same thing. They stab the body of
an innocent child and get its blood to drink, and delude their
victims by < pretending* >, if you please, that this is initiation in
the name of Christ.

15,8 But as we go on to the rest by the power of Christ, let
us call upon his truth that we may track down the meaning of each
imposture, and after detecting and refuting it, render our accustomed thanks in all things to God.

*Against Quintillianists or Pepuzians, also known as Priscillianists,[1]
with whom the Artotyrites are associated. 29, but 49 of the series*

1,1 The Quintillianists in their turn, who are also called Pepuzians
and known as Artotyrites and Priscillianists, are the same as the
Phrygians and derive from them, but in a certain way are different.
(2) For the Quintillianists or Priscillianists say that either Quintilla[2]
or Priscilla—I cannot say for certain, but one of them, as I said,
slept in Pepuza, and Christ came to her and slept beside her under
the following circumstances, as the deluded woman said: (3) "Christ
came to me dressed in a white robe," she said, "in the form of
a woman,[3] imbued me with wisdom, and revealed to me that this
place is holy, and that Jerusalem will descend from heaven here."

1,4 And so even to this day, they say, certain women—men
too—are initiated there on the site, so that those women or men

---

[1] Only Epiphanius distinguishes this group from the Montanists, though Ps.-
Tert. 7.2 suggests that there are Montanist sub-groups named for their leaders.
Epiphanius might have conjectured the existence of this sect from the distinc-
tiveness of Priscilla's vision, or from its occurrence in a document different from
his collection of Montanist prophecies.

[2] Only Epiphanius mentions Quintilla.

[3] "Tetrad" appears in female form at Iren. Haer. 1.14.1; Protennoia does the
same at NHL Tri. Prot. 42,17–18.

may await Christ and see him.[4] (5) (They have women they call prophetesses.[5] I am not sure, though, whether this custom is theirs or the Phrygians'; they are associated and have the same ideas.)

2,1   They use the Old and the New Testaments, and likewise affirm the resurrection of the dead. Their founder is Quintilla, along with Priscilla who was also a Phrygian prophetess.

2,2   They cite many texts which have no relevance, and give thanks to Eve because she was the first to eat from the tree of wisdom.[6] And as scriptural support for their ordination of women as clergy, they say that Moses' sister was a prophetess.[7] What is more, they say, Philip had four daughters who prophesied.[8]

2,3   In their church seven virgins with lamps often come in, if you please, dressed in white, to prophesy to the people. (4) They deceive the congregation with a show of some sort of inspiration and make them all weep by shedding tears and pretending to mourn for humankind, as though to encourage them to the mourning of penitence.[9] (5) They have woman bishops, presbyters and the rest;[10] they say that none of this makes any difference because "In Christ Jesus there is neither male nor female."[11] (6) This is what I have learned [about them]. However, they call them Artotyrites because they set bread and cheese on the altar in their mysteries and celebrate their mysteries with them.[12]

3,1   But every human illusion < comes of > deserting the right faith and opting for something impossible, and for various frenzies and secret rites. For if they do not cling to the anchor of the truth but entrust themselves < to their own reason* >, their minds are always maddened, and bring them [to frenzy] for any reason at all. (2) Even though it is because of Eve that they ordain women to the episcopate and presbyterate, they should listen to the Lord when he says, "Thy resort shall be to thine husband, and he shall rule over thee."[13] (3) And they have overlooked the command of

---

[4] Or, "may live long enough to see Christ."

[5] Tertullian considers woman prophets a mark of divine endorsement and cites 1 Cor. 11:5 (Adv. Marc. 5.8.11); cf. De Anima 9.4.

[6] Eve is the "instructor of life" at NHL Orig. Wld. 113,33; cf. Apoc. Adam 69,14–18.

[7] Did. Trin. 3.41.23

[8] Eus. H. E. 3.17.4; 5.17.3; Did. Trin. 3.41.3

[9] For Montanist emphasis on penitence see Eus. H. E. 5.18.9.

[10] A prophetess celebrates the Eucharist, preaches and baptizes at Firmilian/ Cyprian Ep. 75.10; Epiphanius criticizes Marcionite baptism by women at Pan. 42,4,5.

[11] Gal. 3:28

[12] Sacramental use of cheese is found at Act. Perpet. 4.9; possibly of milk at Tert. Adv. Marc. 1.14.3.

[13] Gen. 3:16

the apostle, "I suffer not a woman to speak, or to have authority over a man,"[14] and again, "The man is not of the woman, but the woman of the man,"[15] and, "Adam was not deceived, but Eve, deceived first, fell into condemnation."[16]

What prolific error there is in this world!

3,4   And now that < I have squashed* > a toothless, witless < serpent* > like a gecko, I shall pass this sect by, beloved, and go on to the rest, calling upon God as the help of my lowliness, and for the fulfillment of my promise.

Against Quartodecimans.[1] *Number 30, but 50 of the series*

1,1   After these two intermingled sects of Phrygians and Quintillianists or Priscillianists, another one, called the sect of the Quartodecimans, appeared in its turn. (2) These too hold all the doctrines that the church does; but they are foiled in everything because they do not adhere to the proper order and teaching but to Jewish fables. And yet their doctrines are not the same as the Jews', "For they know not what they say nor whereof they affirm."[2]

1,3   The Quartodecimans contentiously keep the Passover on one day, once a year,[3] even though their doctrine of the Father, the Son and the Holy Spirit is good and in agreement with < ours >, and they accept the prophets, apostles and evangelists, and likewise confess the resurrection of the flesh and the coming judgment, and everlasting life. (4) But they have fallen into an error, and one of no small importance, by following the letter, if you please, of the Law's saying, "Cursed is he who shall not keep the Passover on the fourteenth day of the month."[4] (5) Others though, who keep the same one day and fast and celebrate the mysteries on the same one day, boast that they have found the precise date in the Acts of Pilate, if you please; it says there that the Savior suffered on the eighth before the Kalends of April.[5]

---

[14] 1 Tim. 2:12
[15] 1. Cor. 11:8
[16] 1 Tim. 2:14

[1] Cf. Eus. H. E. 5.23–24; Hippol. Haer. 8.18; Ps.-Tert. 8.1. These are authors Epiphanius knows, but at 1,5–8 he shows further knowledge, independent of them, of the Quartodecimans.
[2] 1 Tim. 1:7
[3] I. e., rather than keeping a week-long fast. Cf. Eus. H.E. 5.24.12 (Irenaeus).
[4] Cf. Lev. 23:5; Nu.. 9:4–5; Deut. 27:28, and see Hippol. Haer. 8.18.1.
[5] I.e., the day of the spring equinox. Cf. Acts of Pilate, Prologue; Hippol. In Dan. 4:23; Tert. Adv. Jud. 8.

1,6   They keep the Passover on whichever day it is that the
fourteenth of the month falls;[6] but the ones in Cappadocia keep
the same one day on the eighth before the Kalends of April. (7)
And there is no little dissension in their ranks, since some say the
fourteenth day of the month, but some, the eighth before the
Kalends of April. (8) Furthermore, I have found copies of the Acts
of Pilate which say that the passion came on the fifteenth before
the Kalends of April.[7] But in fact, as I know from much minute
investigation, I have found that the Savior suffered on the thirteenth before the Kalends of April.[8] Some, however, say it was the
tenth before the Kalends of April.[9]

1,9   But the Quartodecimans too have departed from the prescribed path. (But I am afraid of making my discussion of them
extremely long too, for I have a great deal to say.) (2,1) After he
had finished the entire Law, the law-giver Moses was commanded
by God to put all the curses in the last book, Deuteronomy—not
only the curse about the Passover, but the ones about circumcision, tithing and offerings. (2) Thus if they avoided one curse they
fell foul of many. They would be accursed if they were not circumcised, accursed if they did not tithe; and they are accursed for
not presenting offerings at Jerusalem. (3) Shame on the people
who get themselves into many kinds of foolishness! Well may we
quote the wise saying of the Preacher, expressly set forth for us
by the Holy Spirit: "This the preacher doth know, that God hath
made the wise man a straight path, but they have sought for themselves many ways."[10]

2,4   In what way is their notion not wrong? In the first place,
if they keep the Passover on the fourteenth of the month, they
need to take the lamb on the tenth and keep it until the fourteenth, and there is no longer one day of fasting but five: the tenth,
eleventh, twelfth, thirteenth and fourteenth. (5) But if the paschal
lamb is killed toward evening, the opening of this fourteenth day
makes six days in the fast, and there will no longer be one fast
day—and their quest for one day has failed, since there is no one day.

2,6   For the types [of the Lord's death and resurrection] have
been combined at the cost of no little reverent study. Christ had

---

[6] So Hippol. Haer. 8.18.1.
[7] Probably a variant date of the spring equinox (Strobel p. 223)
[8] This date is given in the spurious Acta of the Council of Caesarea 1; Martin
of Bracara De Pascha 1; Niceta Remesiana (=Tractatus Athanasii) 1; Soz. Hist.
7,18. Sozomen says that it is the date celebrated by Montanists.
[9] Consularia Constant. MG. Auct. Antiq. 9.220; Chronicon Paschale 218;
Lactantius Div. Inst. 4.10.8.
[10] Eccles. 7:29

to be slain on the fourteenth of the month in accordance with the Law, so that the light that illumined them under the Law would go out for them, since the sun had risen and hidden the light of the moon. (7) For the moon is on the wane after the fourteenth. Hence even in the Law the Jewish synagogue lost its luster after Christ's incarnation and passion, and the Gospel outshone it—although, because the Law was not abolished but served to prove the truth, the Law was not destroyed but fulfilled.

2,8 So too, at the celebration of the Passover in Jericho the sacred scripture at once added, "And the children of Israel kept the Passover and ate it in Gilgal, and the manna ceased."[11] (9) This was its further testimony to them, and its prophecy that their angelic, heavenly food, which they called manna,[12] would come to an end because of the Lord's suffering for their denial of God.

3,1 But God's holy church does not miss the truth in any way in her fixing of the date for this mystery. (2) She uses not only the fourteenth day, but also the seven days which recur < in the > order of the seven days of the week, so that the resurrection and the festival will correspond with the Lord's deeds < just as > they do with the type. (3) And she uses not only the fourteenth day of the lunar month, but the course of the sun as well, to keep us from observing two Passovers in one year and not even one in another.

3,4 We observe the fourteenth day, then, but we wait until after the equinox and bring the end of our full observance [of the commandment][13] to the sacred Lord's Day. But we take the lamb on the tenth day by acknowledging the name of Jesus through its "iota,"[14] so that, < through* > their canonical and true < treatment* >, we will miss no one of the observances of this life-giving < festival* > of the Passover as the whole truth prescribes them.

3,5 However, since by Christ's power I am done with the swollenness of this gudgeon or toad, I shall pass it by and give my attention to the rest, making my usual supplication for God's help.

---

[11] Josh. 5:10–12
[12] I. e., the Law
[13] The commandment, "They shall take to them every man a lamb . . ." Exod. 12:3–6
[14] Ten

*Against the sect which does not accept the Gospel according to John,
and his Revelation.[1] 31, but 51 of the series*

1,1   Following these sects—after the Phrygians and Quintillianists
and the ones called Quartodecimans—another sect sprang up. It
is like a snake without much strength, which cannot stand the odor
of dittany—that is, storax—or of frankincense or southernwood,
or the smell of pitch, incense, lignite or hartshorn. (2) For those
who are familiar with them say that these substances have the effect
of driving poisonous snakes away; and some call dittany "tittany"
(τίκταμνον) because professional physicians use it as an aid for
women in childbirth (τικτούσων). I may thus appropriately compare it with the divine Word who descended from the heavens,
and has been begotten of the Father outside of time and without
beginning.

1,3   Solomon says of a foolish, worthless woman, "She hateth
a word of sureness."[2] These people too have hated the surenesses
of the Gospel, since they are of the earth and angry with the
heavens. (4) Therefore, for fear of the Holy Spirit's voice which
says, "The voice of the Lord restoreth the hinds,"[3] < they reject his
proclamation of the divine Word* > who told his servants and apostles, "Lo, I have given you power to tread upon serpents and scorpions,
and over all the power of the enemy."[4] (5) For this is the voice
that restores the hinds, the voice which resounded in the world
through the holy apostles and evangelists, to trample on the devil's
opposition. One of these, St. John, checked this with the utmost
effectiveness, and tried the power of the deceived, and of the snake-
like heretics.

2,1   But they will not prevail in the ark. The holy Noah is ordered
by God's direction to make the ark secure (ἐπασφαλίσασθαι), as
God says to him, "Thou shalt pitch (ἀσφαλτώσεις) it within and
without"[5]—to prefigure God's holy church, which has the power
of pitch, which drives the horrid, baneful, snake-like teachings away.
For where pitch is burned, no snake can remain. (2) The holy
storax incense stuns them, and they avoid its sweet odor. And the
power of southernwood or frankincense < drives them away* > if

---

[1] Individuals or groups who took this position are described at Iren. Haer.
3.11.9; Eus. H. E. 7.25.1–3 (Dionysius of Alexandria); Hippol. Capitula Adversus Gaium. Epiphanius may have known the works of some such school, cf.
51,29,1; 5.
[2] Prov. 11:15
[3] Ps. 28:9
[4] Luke 10:19
[5] Gen. 6:14

it grows down over the serpent itself and sprouts above its den.

2,3   For in the place—I mean Asia—where Ebion, Cerinthus and their supporters preached that Christ is a mere man and the product of sexual intercourse, the Holy Spirit caused this sacred plant or shrub to sprout, and it has driven the serpent away and destroyed the devil's tyranny. (4) For in his old age St. John was told by the Holy Spirit to preach there,[6] and bring back those who had lost their way on the journey—[bring them], not by force but of their own free choice, by revealing to the obedient the divine light in God's holy teaching. (5) But how long shall I go on? It is a fact that no snake can remain or have its den where southernwood grows; and where God's true teaching is, a den of snake-like teaching cannot prevail but will be destroyed.

3,1   Now these Alogi say—this is what I call them. They shall be so called from now on, and let us give them this name, beloved, Alogi. (2) For they believed in the heresy for which < that* > name < was a good one* >, since it rejects the books by John. As they do not accept the Word which John preaches, they shall be called Dumb ("Αλογοι). (3) As complete strangers to the truth's message they deny its purity, and accept neither John's Gospel nor his Revelation.

3,4   And if they accepted the Gospel but rejected the Revelation, I would say they might be doing it from scrupulousness, and refusing to accept an "apocryphon" because of the deep and difficult sayings in the Revelation. (5) But since they do not accept the books in which St. John actually proclaimed his Gospel, it must be plain to everyone that they and their kind are the ones of whom St. John said in his General Epistles, "It is the last hour and ye have heard that Antichrist cometh; even now, lo, there are many Antichrists."[7] (6) For they offer excuses [for their behavior]. Knowing, as they do, that St. John was an apostle and the Lord's beloved, that the Lord rightly revealed the mysteries to him, and < that he* > leaned upon his breast, they are ashamed to contradict him and try to object to these mysteries for a different reason. For they say that they are not John's composition but Cerinthus', and have no right to a place in the church.

4,1   And it can be shown at once, from this very attack, that they "understand neither what they say nor whereof they affirm."[8]

---

[6] Iren. Haer. 3.2.1, and the reconstructed monarchian prologue at Corssen, pp. 80–81
[7] 1 John 2:16
[8] 1 Tim. 1:7

How can the words which are directed against Cerinthus be by Cerinthus? (2) Cerinthus says that Christ is of recent origin and a mere man, while John has proclaimed that < he > is the eternal Word, and has come from on high and been made flesh. From the very outset, then, their worthless quibble is exposed as foolish, and unaware of its own refutation. (3) For they appear to believe what we do; but because they do not hold to the certainties of the message God has revealed to us through St. John, they will be convicted of shouting against the truth about things which they do not know. (4) They will be known to them, though, if they choose to sober up and take notice; I am not discarding the teachings of the Holy Spirit in all their importance and certainty.

4,5   For they say against themselves—I prefer not to say, "against the truth"—that John's books do not agree with the other apostles.[9] And now they think they can attack his holy, inspired teaching. (6) "And what did he say?" they argue. "'In the beginning was the Word, and the Word was with God, and the Word was God.'[10] And, 'The Word was made flesh and dwelt among us, and we knew his glory, glory as of an only Son of a Father, full of grace and truth.'[11] (7) And immediately afterwards, 'John bare witness and cried, saying, This he of whom I spake unto you,'[12] and, 'This is the Lamb of God, that taketh away the sin of the world.'[13]

"And next he says, 'They that heard him said, Rabbi, where dwellest thou?'[14] and in the same breath, (8) 'On the morrow Jesus would go forth into Galilee, and findeth Philip, and saith unto him, Follow me.'[15] (9) And shortly thereafter he says, 'And after three days there was a marriage in Cana of Galilee, and Jesus was called, and his disciples, to the marriage supper, and his mother was there.'[16] (10) But the other evangelists say that he spent forty days in the wilderness tempted by the devil, and then came back and chose his disciples."

4,11   And stupid as they are, they don't know that each evangelist was concerned to say what the others had said, in agreement with them, while at the same time revealing what they had not said, but had omitted. For the will was not theirs; both their order and their teaching came from the Holy Spirit. (12) If our oppo-

---

[9] So, apparently, the second century heretic Gaius, Labriolle p. 48
[10] John 1:1
[11] John 1:14
[12] John 1:15; 30
[13] John 1:29
[14] John 1:38
[15] John 1:43
[16] John 2:1–2

nents want to attack John, they must learn that the other three did not begin with the same sequence of events.

For Matthew was the first to become an evangelist. He was directed to issue the Gospel first. (I have spoken largely of this in another Sect;[17] however, I shall not mind dealing with the same things again, as proof of the truth and in refutation of the erring.) (5,1) As I said, Matthew was privileged to be the first < to issue > the Gospel, and this was absolutely right. Because he had repented of many sins, and had risen from the receipt of custom and followed Him who came for man's salvation and said, "I am not come to call the righteous, but sinners to repentance,"[18] it was Matthew's duty to present the message of salvation < first >, as an example for us, who would be saved like this man who was restored in the tax office and turned from his iniquity. From him men would learn the graciousness of Christ's advent.

5,2   For after the forgiveness of his sins it was granted him to raise the dead, cleanse leprosy, and work miracles of healing and cast out devils, so that he would not merely persuade his hearers by his speech, but publish[19] good tidings with actual deeds—[publish] the tidings of their salvation through repentance, to the perishing; the tidings that they would arise, to the fallen; and the tidings that they would be quickened, to the dead.

5,3   Matthew himself wrote and issued the Gospel in the Hebrew alphabet, and did not begin at the beginning, but traced Christ's pedigree from Abraham. "Abraham begat Isaac," he said, "and Isaac begat Jacob,"[20] and so on down to Joseph and Mary. (4) And he wrote at the beginning, "The book of the generation of Jesus Christ, the son of David," and then said, "the son of Abraham."[21] Then, coming to his main point, he said, "The birth of Jesus Christ was on this wise. When as his mother Mary was espoused to Joseph, before they came together she was found with child of the Holy Ghost. (5) And Joseph, being a just man, sought to put her away privily. And lo, the angel of the Lord appeared to him in a dream saying, Put not away thy wife; for that which is conceived in her is of the Holy Ghost. (6) For lo, she shall bear a son, and thou shalt call his name Jesus. He shall save his people from their sins. And this was done," he said, "to fulfill that which was spoken of

---

[17] Pan. 20,8,4; 30,3,7
[18] Matt. 9:13
[19] Klostermann: κηρύξῃ; Holl < δύνηται > κηρύξαι
[20] Matt. 1:2
[21] Matt. 1:1

the Lord by the prophet, saying, Behold the virgin shall be with child,"[22] and so on.

5,7   "And Joseph," he said, "being raised from sleep, did so and took unto him his wife, and knew her not till she brought forth her first-born son, and he called his name Jesus. (8) Now when Jesus was born in Bethlehem of Judaea in the days of Herod the king, behold, there came wise men from the east to Jerusalem, saying, Where is he that is born king of the Jews? For we have seen his star in the east, and are come to worship him."[23]

5,9   Now then, where is the story of Zacharias? Where are the subjects Luke discussed? Where is the vision of the angel? Where is John the Baptist's prophecy? Where is the rebuke of Zacharias, so that he could not speak until the angel's words had come true?

5,10   Where are the things that Gabriel told the Virgin? Where is his reassurance, when Mary answered the angel himself with wisdom and asked, "How shall this be, seeing I know not a man?"[24] And where is his accurate and clear explanation, "The Spirit of the Lord shall come upon thee, and the power of the Highest shall overshadow thee?"[25]

6,1   Well, what shall I say? Because Matthew did not report the events which Luke related, can St. Matthew be at odds with the truth? Or is St. Luke not telling the truth, because he has said < nothing > about the first things Matthew dealt with? (2) Didn't God give each evangelist his own assignment, so that each of the four evangelists whose duty was to proclaim the Gospel could find what he was to do and proclaim some things in agreement and alike to show that they were from the same source, but otherwise[26] describe what another had omitted, as each received his proportionate share from the Spirit?

6,3   Now what shall we do? Matthew declares that Mary gave birth in Bethlehem < and > < shows* > Christ's incarnation in Abraham's and David's line. St. Mark, we find, says none of this; (4) he introduces the Gospel with the affair at the Jordan and says, "The beginning of the Gospel, as it is written in Isaiah the prophet, A voice of one crying in the wilderness."[27] (5) < Is Mark lying, then? Of course not! There was no reason for him to repeat information which had already been given* >. Similarly, the things St. John

---

[22] Matt. 1:18–23
[23] Matt. 1:24–2:2
[24] Luke 1:34
[25] Luke 1:35
[26] Klostermann: ἄλλος < ἄλλως >; MSS: ἄλλος
[27] Mark 1:1–3

discussed, and confirmed in the Holy Spirit, were not just meant to repeat what had already been proclaimed, but to speak of the teachings the others had had to leave to John.

6,6   For the whole essence of the Gospel was of this nature. After Matthew had proclaimed Christ's generation, his conception through the Holy Spirit, < and > his incarnation as a descendant of David and Abraham, an error arose in those who did not understood the narrative which was intended in good faith to provide assurance of these things from the Gospel. (Not that the Gospel was responsible for their error; their own wrong notion was.) (7) And this was why Cerinthus and Ebion held that Christ was a mere man, and < misled* > Merinthus,[28] Cleobius[29] or Cleobulus,[30] Claudius, Demas[31] and Hermogenes,[32] who had loved this world and left the way of the truth. (8) For they contradicted the Lord's disciples at that time, and tried to use the genealogy from Abraham and David as proof of their nonsense—not in good faith, but seizing on it as an excuse. (9) For they were often contradicted by St. John and his friends, Leucius and many others. But shamelessness struck its forehead, and did its best to bring its own woes on itself.

6,10   Mark, who came directly after Matthew, was ordered to issue the Gospel by St. Peter at Rome, and after writing it was sent by St. Peter to Egypt. (11) He one of the seventy-two who had been dispersed because of the Lord's saying, "Unless a man eat my flesh and drink my blood, he is not worthy of me"[33]—as < can be > plainly proved to the readers of the Gospels. Still, after his restoration by Peter he was privileged to proclaim the Gospel by the Holy Spirit's inspiration.

6,12   He began his proclamation where the Spirit told him, and opened it at the fifteenth year of Tiberius Caesar, thirty years after Matthew's account. (13) Since he was a second evangelist, and gave no clear indication of the divine Word's descent from on high—he does it vividly everywhere, but not with as much precision [as Matthew]—these misguided people had their perceptions darkened a second time, and were not held worthy of the Gospel's illumination. (14) "Look," they said, "here is a second Gospel too with an account of Christ, and nowhere does it say that his generation is heavenly.

---

[28] Pan. 28,8,1. But there Epiphanius is unsure whether Merinthus is a heretic so named, or an alternate name for Cerinthus.

[29] Eus. H. E. 4.22.5 (Hegesippus); Didascalia 23, Achelis-Flemming p. 121; Const. Ap. 6.8.1

[30] Cf. Ps.-Ignatius Trall. 11.

[31] Col. 4:14; Philem. 24; 2 Tim. 4:10

[32] 2 Tim. 1:15

[33] Cf. John 6:53.

Instead," they said, "the Spirit descended upon him in the Jordan and < there was* > a voice, 'This is my beloved Son, with whom I am well pleased.'"[34]

7,1   Since this was these stupid people's state of mind, the Holy Spirit compelled and urged St. Luke to raise their misguided minds from the lowest depths, as it were, and once again take up what the other evangelists had omitted. (2) < But > lest some misguided person should think his description of Christ's generation fictitious, he carried the matter back, and for accuracy's sake went through his whole account in the fullest detail. (3) And he produced those who had been ministers of the word as his witnesses in support of the truth; and he said, "Inasmuch as many have attacked,"[35] to show that there were attackers—I mean Cerinthus, Merinthus and the others.

7,4   What does he say next? "It seemed good to me, having attended closely to them which from the beginning were eyewitnesses and ministers of the word, to write unto thee, most excellent Theophilus"—whether he said this because he was then writing to someone named Theophilus, or to every lover of God—"< that thou mayest know > the certainty of the things wherein thou hast been instructed."[36] (5) And he said that the instruction was already written, as though Theophilus had already been instructed by others, but had not learned the exact truth from them with certainty.

7,6   Next he says, "There was in the days of Herod the king a priest named Zacharias of the course of the high priest Abijah, and his wife was of the daughters of Aaron, and her name was Elizabeth."[37] (7) And he begins before Matthew. Matthew had indicated a period of thirty years from the beginning, while Mark—like Matthew and Luke—had set down what happened after < the > thirty years, the true occurrence at the Jordan. (8) But Matthew began his account thirty years before the event at the Jordan and the baptism. Luke, on the other hand, described the six month period before the Savior's conception, and again, the period of the nine months plus a few days following the conception of the Lord, so that the entire period of time [described in Luke] is thirty-one years and more.

7,9   Luke also describes the shepherds' vision, [which was shown them] by the angels who brought them the tidings. And he de-

---

[34] Cf. Mark 1:10–11.
[35] Luke 1:1
[36] Luke 1:3–4
[37] Luke 1:5

scribes how Christ was born in Bethlehem, laid in a manger in swaddling clothes, and circumcised the eighth day; and how they made an offering for him forty days later in obedience to the Law, Simeon took < him > in his arms, and Anna the daughter of Phanuel gave thanks for him; and how he went away to Nazareth and returned to Jerusalem each year with his parents, who made the offerings for him that the Law required. But neither Matthew nor Mark has dealt with any of this, and certainly not John.

8,1 And so, in the course of their refutations of the Gospel account, certain other Greek philosophers—I mean Porphyry, Celsus,[38] and that dreadful, deceitful serpent of Jewish extraction, Philosabbatius—accuse the holy apostles, though they [themselves] are natural and carnal, make war by fleshly means and cannot please God, and have not understood < the things which have been said > by the Spirit.

8,2 Tripping over the words of the truth because of the blindness of their ignorance, each < of them > lit upon this point and said, "How can the day of his birth in Bethlehem have a circumcision eight days after it, and forty days later the pilgrimage to Jerusalem and the things Simeon and Anna did for him, (3) when an angel appeared to him the night he was born, after the arrival of the magi who came to worship him, and who opened their bags and offered him gifts? As it says, 'An angel appeared to him saying, Arise, take thy wife and the young child and go unto Egypt, for Herod seeketh the young child's life.'[39] (4) Now then, if he was taken to Egypt the very night he was born and was there until Herod died, how can he stay [in Bethlehem] for eight days and be circumcised? Or how can Luke < fail to* > be caught in a lie < when he tells us that Jesus was brought to Jerusalem after* > forty < days* >?"—so they say in blasphemy against their own heads, because he says, "On the fortieth day they brought him to Jerusalem and < returned > to Nazareth from there."[40]

9,1 And in their ignorance they do not know the power of the Holy Spirit; for he granted each evangelist to describe the true events of each time and season. And Matthew reported only Christ's generation by the Holy Spirit and conception without a man's seed, but said nothing about circumcision, or the two years—any of the things that happened to him after his birth. (2) Instead,

---

[38] See Orig. C. Cels. 1.40; 48; 91.5–7. Origen also mentions the seeming discrepancy between Matthew and Luke at In Joh. 10.3.
[39] Matt. 2:13
[40] Cf. Luke 2:22; 39.

as the true word of God bears witness, he describes the coming of the magi. For Herod asked the magi for the time, and demanded the exact time of the star's appearance, and Matthew gave the magi's answer, that it was no more than two years before. Thus this period of time is not the period Luke treats of.

9,3   Luke, however, describes the events before < the > two years—whereas Matthew spoke of Christ's birth and then skipped to the time two years later and indicated what happened after < the > two years. (4) And so, when Herod deliberated after the magi's departure by another route, he assumed that < the > new-born child himself would be found among all the other children and killed along with them. (5) For he ordered the killing of all the children in the vicinity of Bethlehem who had been two years old or less on the very day the magi came to him. Who, then, can fail to realize that the child who had been born was two years old when the magi came?

9,6   Indeed, the account itself clarifies everything. For Luke says that the child was swaddled as soon as he was born, and lay in a manger and cave because there was no room in the inn. (7) For a census was then underway, and the people who had been scattered at the time of the wars in the Maccabees' time were dispersed all over the world, and very few had continued to live in Bethlehem. And thus Bethlehem is called the *city* of David in one copy of the Evangelists, while in another it calls it a village, because it had come to occupy a small area. (8) But when the emperor Augustus' order was issued, and those who had been dispersed had to go to Bethlehem for enrollment because of their family origins, the influx of the multitudes filled the place, and because of the crowding there was no room in the inn.

9,9   But then, after the census, each one went back to his own place of abode, and room was made in Bethlehem. (10) Now when < the > first year was over and the second year had passed, Christ's parents came from Nazareth to Bethlehem as though to the original gathering—coming as a sort of memorial of the events in Bethlehem. (11) Thus the magi's arrival was on this occasion, and probably not during Mary's and Joseph's visit because of the time of the census, which Luke mentions. For the magi did not find Mary in the cavern where she gave birth; as the Gospel says, the star led them to the place where the young child was. (12) And they entered *the house* and found the baby with Mary—no longer in a manger, no longer in a cave, but in a house—showing the exact truth and the two-year interval, that is, from Christ's birth until the arrival of the magi.

9,13 And the angel appeared that night, two years after the birth, and said to take the mother and child to Egypt. Thus Joseph did not go back again to Nazareth but escaped to Egypt with the child and his mother, and spent another two years there. And so, after Herod's death, the angel < appeared* > again < and* > sent them back to Judaea.

10,1 The Lord was born in the thirty-third year of Herod, the magi came in the thirty-fifth, and in the thirty-seventh year Herod died and his son Archelaus inherited the throne and reigned for nine years, as I have already said in other places.[41] (2) When Joseph heard of Archelaus he returned and went to Nazareth to make his home, and from there, in turn, went each year to Jerusalem.

10,3 Do you see the precision as to every event that is found in the sacred Gospels? But because the ignorant have blinded their own minds and do not know the intent of each saying, they simply shout and rave against the holy < evangelists >, saying nothing truthful but depriving themselves of life.

10,4 And then, after the first part of his narrative, Luke tells in turn how Christ went to Jerusalem in his twelfth year, leaving no opportunity for those who think, as Cerinthus, Ebion and the rest supposed, that Christ simply appeared in the world as a grown man and came to the Jordan to John. (5) For the serpent is a dreadful one, crawls a crooked course, and does not stand by one opinion; some suppose that Christ was engendered by sexual congress and a man's seed, but others, that he simply appeared as a grown man.

10,6 And this is why the holy evangelists write with precision, describing everything in exact detail. As though raising his mind from earth to the heavens, Luke expressly said, "And Jesus began to be about thirty years of age, being, *as was supposed*, the son of Joseph."[42] (7) Supposition is not fact; Joseph was in the position of a father to Jesus because this pleased God, but since he had no relations with Mary he was not his father. (8) He was simply called her husband because he was espoused to her as an old man of about eighty, with six sons (sic!)[43] by his actual first wife. But he was given this charge, as I have explained more precisely elsewhere. Without conjugal relations, how could he be Christ's father? This is not possible.

---

[41] E.g., at De Incarnatione 2,1–3
[42] Luke 3:23
[43] Anc. 60,1–3; Pan. 30,29,8; 11; 78,7–9. But Epiphanius regularly gives Joseph four sons and two daughters, cf. Anc. 60,1; Pan. 78,7,6.

11,1   But you will ask me, if he did not have her, why was he called her husband? Whoever doubts this does not know the Law's provision that once a woman is designated a man's wife, she is called the wife of the man so designated, even though she is a virgin and still in her father's house. And thus the holy angel said, "Fear not to take unto thee thy *wife*."[44]

11,2   And lest it be thought that < there is > some error in the Gospels—for the mystery is awesome and beyond human telling, and only to the Holy Spirit's children is the statement of it plain and clear—(3) < he says >, "He was about thirty years old, *supposedly* the son of Joseph, the son of Eli, the son of Matthan,"[45] and traces his ancestry to Abraham, where Matthew began. But he goes past Noah and comes to Adam, to indicate the first man, who was sought for by the One who came from his clay—that is, the One who came from the holy Virgin Mary. (4) (For Christ has come for that first man, and for those of his descendants who desire to inherit eternal life.)

And he goes past Adam and says, "Son of God."[46] (5) From this, at length, it was perfectly plain that he was the Son of God, but that he had come in the flesh as Adam's lineal descendant. But once more the misguided did not see the light; in their self-deceit, < and their preference of falsehood* > to truth, they disputed the statement. (6) "Here is a third Gospel, Luke's," they said—(for Luke was given this commission. He too was one of the seventy-two who had been scattered because of the Savior's saying. But he was brought back to the Lord by St. Paul and told to issue his Gospel. And he preached in Dalmatia, Gaul, Italy and Macedonia first, but originally in Gaul, as Paul says of certain of his followers in his epistles, "Crescens is in Gaul."[47] It does not say, "in Galatia," as some wrongly believe, but "in Gaul.")

12,1   But to return to the subject. Although Luke had traced Christ's pedigree from its end to its beginning and reached the point where, to turn the misguided from their error, he hinted at the divine Word's advent and simultaneous union with his human nature, they did not understand. (2) Later, therefore, though from caution and humility he had declined to be an evangelist, the Holy Spirit compelled John to issue the Gospel in his old age when he was past ninety, after his return from Patmos under Claudius Caesar, and several years of his residence in Asia.

---

[44] Matt. 1:20
[45] Luke 3:23–24
[46] Luke 3:38
[47] 2 Tim 4:19

12,3   And John did not need to speak in detail of the [Savior's] advent; that had already been confirmed. But, as though he were following behind people and saw them in front of him choosing very rough, circuitous, thorny paths, John was concerned to recall them to the straight way, and took care to call out to them for their protection, "Why are you going wrong? Which turn are you taking? Where are you wandering off to, Cerinthus, Ebion and the rest? It is not as you suppose.

12,4   "Sure, plainly Christ was conceived in the flesh; look, I confess myself that the Word was made flesh. But don't suppose that he existed only from the time when he was made flesh. He doesn't exist from Mary's time only, as each of us exists from the time of our conception, but not before. (5) The holy divine Word, the Son of God, our Lord Jesus Christ, isn't just from Mary's time, or just from Joseph's time, or Eli's, Levi's, Zorubbabel's, Shealtiel's, Nathan's, David's, Jacob's or Isaac's. And not just from the time of Abraham, Noah or Adam, or the fifth day of creation, the fourth, the third, the second, or the beginning of heaven and earth, or the beginning of the universe.

12,6   "No, '*In the beginning* was the Word, and the Word was with God, and the Word was God. All things were made by him, and without him was not anything made that was made,'[48] and so on. (7) And then, 'There was a man sent from God, whose name was John. The same came for a witness, to bear witness of the light, that all men through him might believe. He was not the light, but was sent to bear witness of the light. The true light, that lighteneth every man, was coming into the world. He was in the world, and the world was made by him, and the world knew him not. He came unto his own, and his own received him not. But as many as received him, to them gave he power to become the sons of God, who were born not of blood and flesh, but of God. (8) And the Word was made flesh,' he said, 'and dwelt among us. John bare witness of him and cried saying, This is he of who I spake unto you, and, Of his fullness we have all received.[49] And he said, I am not the Christ, but the voice of one crying in the wilderness.' "[50]

13,1   And when he describes all this he says, "These things were done in Bethabara"—"Bethany" in other copies—"beyond Jordan."[51] (2) And after this he states that John's disciples asked Jesus,

---

[48] John 1:1–2
[49] John 1:6–16
[50] John 1:20; 23
[51] John 1:28. Origen reads "Bethabara" at In Joh. 6.40.

"Rabbi, where dwellest thou? And he said, Come and see. And they went, and remained with him that day."[52] (3) And the next day "It was about the tenth hour; one of the two which had followed him was Andrew, Simon Peter's brother. He first findeth his own brother Simon and saith unto him, We have found Messiah, which is, being interpreted, Christ. He brought him to Jesus. Jesus looking on him saith, Thou art Simon the son of Jonah; thou shalt be called Cephas, which is by interpretation Peter.

13,4 "On the morrow he would go forth into Galilee and findeth Philip, and Jesus saith unto him, Follow me. Now Philip was of Bethsaida, the city of Andrew and Peter. Philip findeth Nathanael and saith unto him, We have found him of whom Moses in the Law, and the prophets did write, Jesus of Nazareth, the son of Joseph. And Nathanael said unto him, Can there any good thing come out of Nazareth? Philip said unto him, Come and see. (5) Jesus seeing Nathanael come unto him saith of him, Behold an Israelite indeed, in whom is no guile. Nathanael saith unto him, Whence knowest thou me? Jesus answered and said unto him, Before that Philip called thee, when thou wast under the fig tree, I saw thee. Nathanael answered him and said, Rabbi, thou art the Son of God, thou art the king of Israel. (6) Jesus answered and said unto him, Because I said unto thee, I saw thee under the fig tree, believest thou? Verily, verily I say unto you, Ye shall see heaven opened, and the angels of God ascending and descending upon the Son of Man. (7) And the third day there was a marriage in Cana of Galilee,"[53] and so on.

All this will show that he came back to the Jordan after the forty days of the temptation, his return from the temptation itself, and his start for Nazareth and Galilee, as the other three evangelists have said. (8) This will also be shown by the words of John [the Baptist], "Behold the Lamb of God, which taketh away the sin of the world."[54] And on another day, as he saw him on his way, he said, "This is he of whom I said unto you, He that cometh after me is preferred before me, for he was before me."[55] "And John bore witness," it says, "I saw the Spirit in the form of a dove descending and coming upon him."[56]

13,9 "*Bore* witness" and "This is he of whom I *said* unto you,"

---

[52] John 1:38–39
[53] John 1:39–2:1
[54] John 1:29
[55] John 1:30
[56] Cf. John 1:32.

suggest that John is speaking of two different times already past, to show that this is not the same as the time of the baptism, but a different one. (10) For Jesus did not go straight to John from the temptation, but went to Galilee first and then from Galilee to the Jordan, making this < his second meeting* > with John. And so John says, "This was he of whom I *said* unto you;" and the Gospel goes on to say, "And John *bore* witness, I saw"—as though the thing had already taken place some time before.

14,1   The beginning of Peter's and Andrew's call is shown after this. For Andrew went to visit Jesus—one of the two who followed him, who were John's disciples but still lived in Galilee and now and then spent time with John. (2) And just after Andrew had stayed with him that day—it was about the sixth hour—he happened to meet his brother Simon that very same day, and said the words I have already mentioned, "We have found the Messiah." And he brought him to the Lord and so on, as the sequel—that Jesus told him, "Thou shalt be called Cephas"—indicates.

14,3   "And the day following," it says, "Jesus would go forth into Galilee, and findeth Philip, and saith unto him, Follow me. Now Philip was of Bethsaida, the city of Andrew and Peter."[57] (4) And you see that this allows me to suppose—of the two disciples of John who had followed Jesus[58] he gave only the name of the one, Andrew, but did not give the name of the other. (5) This makes me think that, because they came from the same place, lived together, had the same trade and worked together, this disciple whose name he did not give was either John or James, < but > one of the sons of Zebedee. (6) For they should have been called first and then Philip, according to the order in the Gospels: Peter first, then Andrew, then James, then John, and Philip after these. But never mind this now; there is a great deal of followup to this matter.

15,1   But it is time to return to the subject < and point out* > that, obviously, just as they < continued* > to practice their trade and attend to their discipleship while they were disciples of John, so, after spending their first day with Jesus, they went back the next day and fished, as the course of the other Gospels indicates. (2) For after Jesus left on the following day, the sequel [in John] says at once, "On the third day there was a marriage in Cana of Galilee, and the mother of Jesus was there. And Jesus was called, and his disciples, to the marriage."[59] (3) But from both these precise state-

---

[57] John 1:43–44
[58] I.e., at John 1:35
[59] John 2:1–2

ments and the subject of them, we are given to understand that Jesus had also brought other disciples who [unlike Peter and the others] had remained with him—perhaps Nathanael and Philip, and some others. Andrew and the rest had left, but those who had remained with him were also invited to the wedding.

15,4   And after performing this first miracle he went down to Capernaum and made his home there. And then he began to perform other miracles there—when he healed the man's withered hand, and Peter's mother-in-law as well. (5) (Peter was from Bethsaida but had married a woman from Capernaum, for the two places are not far apart. Jesus cured Peter's mother-in-law of fever and, because she was cured, she waited on them, so that the sequence of events is < plain* >.)

15,6   And after this he returned to Nazareth where he had been brought up. He then read the roll of the prophet Isaiah, and afterwards anticipated them himself and said, "Ye will surely say unto me this parable, Physician, heal thyself. What signs we have heard have been done in Capernaum, do also here in thy country."[60] And do you see the truthfulness of what follows? "And he did nothing[61] because of their unbelief."[62]

15,7   From there he went to Capernaum and settled there once more. And going to the sea, as Matthew says, he saw Simon Peter and his brother Andrew casting their nets—and, once again, James and John the sons of Zebedee. And he called them for good, and they finally threw their nets away and followed him.

15,8   And Luke also makes it quite clear that at last they followed him for good and no longer put their call off. He says, "When he was come unto the lake Gennesareth he saw Simon Peter and Andrew mending their nets, and he entered into the ship which was Simon Peter's and Andrew's"[62a]—and this means that he already knew them, and they allowed this out of habit—and he boarded it and sat down. (9) When he told Peter, after his teaching, "Launch out into the deep and let down your nets,"[63] and they said, "Master,"[64] they were already calling him Master because of John's testimony. For they had heard, "Behold the Lamb

---

[60] Cf. Luke 4:23
[61] MSS and Delahaye: ουδέν; Holl: οὐδὲν < σημεῖον >
[62] Cf. Matt. 13:58; Mark 6:5.
[62a] Cf. Luke 5:1–3.
[63] Luke 5:4
[64] Luke 5:4–5

of God which taketh away the sin of the world"[65] said < of > him
on a previous occasion, and had spent the one day with him. (10)
And they went out for their second and later catch, when they
were amazed at the number of the fish, and Peter said, "Depart
from me; for I am a sinful man, O Lord."[66] (Perhaps, indeed, he
was sorry, because he had been called before and had gone back
to his fish and the whole business of fishing.) (11) But to hearten
him Jesus said, "Fear not;" he had not been rejected but could
still lay claim to his call. For Jesus said, "From henceforth thou
shalt catch men"[67] when they motioned their partners in the other
boat to come and help with the catch. (12) For as it says, they
were Simon's partners; I have mentioned this already because of
the two who had followed Jesus < and > heard John say, < "Behold
the Lamb of God." >[68] One of these two was Andrew, < as > I said,
and I have a very good notion that the other, in turn, might have
been one of the sons of Zebedee, because they were co-workers,
in the same business, and partners.

15,13   And then, as it says, after all this the four left their boats
and simply threw everything down and followed him, as Luke testifies.
(14) And thus it is fully demonstrated that there is no obscurity
or contradiction in the holy Gospels or between the evangelists,
but that everything is plain. (15) There are, however, differences
of time! For from this time forward, after Peter, John and the
others had finally joined and followed him, he went teaching
throughout Galilee and Judaea. And then, as the Gospel became
widespread, he performed the rest of the miracles. Thus the overall
order of events is this:

16,1   first, he was baptized on the twelfth of the Egyptian month
Athyr, the sixth before the Ides of November † in the Roman
calendar.[69] (In other words, he was baptized a full sixty days before
the Epiphany, which is the day of his birth in the flesh, (2) as
the Gospel according to Luke testifies, "Jesus *began to be* about
thirty years old, being, as was supposed, the son of Joseph."[70] Actually,
he was twenty-nine years and ten months old—thirty years old but
not quite—when he came for his baptism. This is why it says, "*began
to be* about thirty years old." Then he was sent into the wilderness.

16,3   Those forty days of the temptation appear next, and the

---

[65] John 1:29
[66] Luke 5:8
[67] Luke 5:10
[68] John 1:29
[69] Holl: ὅ ἐστιν κατὰ Ῥωμαίους; MSS: ὡς ἔφημεν
[70] Luke 3:23

slightly more than two weeks—[two weeks] and two days—which he spent after his return from the temptation to Galilee, that is, to Nazareth and its vicinity. (4) And one day when he went to John—the day John said, "Behold the Lamb of God, which taketh away the sin of the world."[71] And the next day < when > "John, again, stood, and two of his disciples, and looking upon Jesus as he walked, said, Behold the Christ, the Lamb of God."[72] Then it says, "The two disciples heard him and followed Jesus."[73]

16,5   As I said, this was the eighteenth day after the temptation, but the first after [Jesus' encounter with] John, when Andrew and the others followed Jesus and stayed with him that day—it was about the tenth hour—and when Andrew found his brother Simon and brought him to Jesus. (6) Then the Gospel says, "On the morrow the Lord would go forth into Galilee, and findeth Philip, and saith unto him, Follow me."[74] As the sequence of the Gospel indicates, this was the nineteenth day after the temptation, < and it includes* > the call of Philip and Nathanael.

16,7   And then, it says, there was a wedding in Cana of Galilee on the third day after the two days I have mentioned which followed [the encounter with] John. Now if the twenty days are added to the forty days of the temptation, this makes two months. And when these are combined with the ten months they make a year, or, in other words, a full thirty years from the birth of the Lord. (8) And we find that Christ performed his first miracle, the changing of the water into wine, at the end of his thirtieth year, as you must realize if you follow the orders of the events in the Gospels closely. (9) And then, after this first miracle, he performed the other miracles and presented his teaching, showing his wondrous, inexpressible lovingkindness to all, and the wonderworking in the Gospels—so I have often been obliged to say because of the ignorance of the misguided people who venture to contradict the Gospels' accurate account, as it is set forth in order by the Holy Spirit.

17,1   This amount of accurate demonstration will leave no room for those who are their own opponents—I won't say, the truth's, because they can't be. (2) For it is plain that the beginnning of the rest of the affair follows the baptism. Thus it is shown that the Lord underwent the forty day temptation in the wilderness after the day of the baptism, even though the Holy Spirit saw no need to make this known through John; it had already been indicated

---

[71] John 1:29
[72] Cf. John 1:35–36.
[73] John 1:37
[74] John 1:43

by the three evangelists. (3) And again, the other evangelists were not concerned with the other matters, since each is assisted by each. For when the truth is gathered from all the evangelists it is shown to be one, and not in conflict with itself.

17,4   For directly after the temptation, as I said, he went from the wilderness to Nazareth and stayed there, and no disciples were with him as yet. And from there he went down to John, and at once Peter was called through Andrew, and Nathanael through Philip. (5) But even though he sees that Andrew met Jesus first and then Peter was called, and through Andrew at that, no one need waste his time on doubts about this as well, and begin to be distressed about it. (6) Andrew met Jesus first because Andrew was younger in years than Peter. But later, in turn, when they renounced the world for good, it was at Peter's instance. For he was his brother's mentor; and the Lord knew this, for he is God, understands the inclinations of hearts, knows who is worthy to be ranked first, and chose Peter for the head of his disciples, as has been plainly shown everywhere.

17,7   Afterwards they came and stayed with him the first day, as I said, they traveled on the second, and on the third day came the first miracle while some disciples were with him—plainly not Andrew, Peter, James or John, but Nathanael and Philip, and some others. (8) And next, after going to Capernaum and returning to Nazareth, and going back to Capernaum from there and working part of the miracles, he returned to Nazareth once more and read the roll of the prophet Isaiah, where it says, "The Spirit of the Lord is upon me, because the Lord hath anointed me to preach the Gospel to the poor,"[75] and so on. This took place some days after the Epiphany.

17,9   And after John's arrest he returned to Capernaum and at last made that his residence; and the final call of Peter, John and their brothers came at this time, when Jesus came [to them] beside the lake of Gennesareth. And thus the entire sequence of events [in the Gospels] is harmonized and contains no contradictions; the whole Gospel account is completely clear and has been truthfully given.

17,10   Then what has gotten into these people < who > have deceived their own minds and spewed this sect out on the world, that they reject the Gospel according to John? I was right to call their sect "Dumb;" they will not accept the divine Word who came from on high, the Word preached by John. (11) Not understanding

---

[75] Luke 4:18

the meaning of the Gospels they say, "Why have the other evangelists said that Jesus fled to Egypt from Herod, came back after his flight and remained at Nazareth, and then, after receiving the baptism, went into the wilderness, and returned after that, and after his return began to preach? (18,1) But the Gospel which was issued under John's name lies," they say. "After 'The Word was made flesh and dwelt among us'[76] and a few other things, it says at once that there was a wedding in Cana of Galilee."

18,2   With their deliberate foolishness these people have not remembered that John < himself >, after saying that the Word was made flesh and dwelt among us—or in other words, became man—said that Jesus went to John [the Baptist] at the Jordan and was baptized by him. (3) < For > John himself testifies that John the Baptist said, "This is he of whom I said unto you,"[77] "I saw the Holy Spirit descending in the form of a dove and remaining on him,"[78] and, "This is he that taketh away the sin of the world."[79]

18,4   You see that none of this is said from forgetfulness; John has omitted the matters Matthew dealt with. There was no more need for them, but there was for the full explanation, in reply to those who believed that Jesus was called Christ and Son of God only from the time of Mary, and was a mere man earlier, but had received the title, "Son of God," as a promotion in rank. (5) Thus in writing his account of Christ's coming from above, John is concerned with essentials—it is all important and essential, but the heavenly things are more so. (6) But these people say that the Gospel according to John is non-canonical because it did not mention these events—I mean the events of the forty-day temptation—and they do not see fit to accept it, since they are misguided about everything, and mentally blind.

19,1   The blessed John came fourth in the succession of evangelists. With his brother James he was the first after Peter and Andrew in the order of calling, but he was the last to issue a Gospel. He was not concerned to give information which had been adequately set down before him, but preferred what had not been said to what had been, and discoursed < along those lines >. (2) For Matthew begins with Abraham, but resumes the narrative after the beginning [of Christ's life], and [again] two years after his birth. Mark, however, begins at the fifteenth year of Tiberius Caesar,

---

[76] John 1:14
[77] John 1:30
[78] Cf. John 1:32.
[79] Cf. John 1:29.

and says < nothing > of < the > intervening years which follow the beginning. And Luke added a beginning before the beginning, his treatment of Elizabeth and Mary before < they > conceived.

19,3 John, however, who was earlier in his calling than they but became an evangelist later, confirms the events before the incarnation. For most of what he said was spiritual, since the fleshly things had already been confirmed. (4) He thus gives a spiritual account[80] of the Gift which came down to us from the Father who has no beginning, < and > of the Father's good pleasure took flesh in the holy Virgin's womb. (5) And he omitted nothing essential; but by the Holy Spirit's inspiration he < introduced > the divine Word who was before all ages, begotten of the Father without beginning and not in time, and told of his coming in the flesh for our sakes. And thus we obtain full and precise knowledge, fleshly and divine, from four evangelists.

20,1 For when all the events of the baptism and temptation were over and then, as I have often said, Jesus had gone to spend a few days in Nazareth and nearby, and near Capernaum—< and > after he had met John at the Jordan < and returned to Galilee* >, taking a few disciples with him on the next day [after his meeting with John]—Jesus performed this first miracle in Cana, the third day after [he had met] John but the twentieth after his return from the temptation, and < began > his preaching. (2) For John does not say that Christ went to a wedding before the temptation, or that he worked any of his miracles < before > he started preaching—except, perhaps, the ones he is said to have performed in play as a child. (3) (For he ought to have childhood miracles too, to deprive the other sects of an excuse for saying that "< the > Christ," meaning the dove, came to him after [his baptism in] the Jordan.[83] They say this because of the sum of the letters alpha and omega, which is [the same as the sum of the letters of] "dove," since the Savior said, "I am Alpha and I am" Omega.")[84]

20,4 This is also why Luke represents Jesus, in his twelfth year, as having asked Mary, "Wist ye not that I must be in my Father's house?"[85] when she came looking for him, and he was engaged in dispute with the doctors at Jerusalem. (5) This refutes the argument of those who claim that he became the Son of God at

---

[80] Clement of Alexandria says that John wrote a "spiritual" Gospel because the fleshly matters had already been reported, Eus. H. E. 6.14.7.
[83] Iren. Haer. 1.14.6.
[84] Rev. 1:8
[85] Luke 2:49
[86] Luke 2:49

the time of his baptism, when the dove, which they say is the Christ, came to him. And it makes it clear that the divine Word came from above and was made flesh of Mary at his coming, and that the Spirit descended upon him in the Jordan, (6) to identify the One of whom the Father testified, "This is my Son, the Beloved, hear ye him."[87] It was also a sign, to those who would be enlightened in him, that they would be vouchsafed < the > gift of the Holy Spirit in baptism, and, by the grace he gives, the remission of their sins.

21,1   And then he began to work his perfect miracles, during the time of his preaching— < for > it says, "This *first* miracle did Jesus in Cana of Galilee."[88] (2) As I have said many times, this was not before the baptism. It was after his return from the temptation, the third day after the two days John's two disciples spent with him, the disciples who had heard [John] speak and followed Jesus. (3) Thus, immediately after the two days they spent with him, the Gospel adds, "And he went forth into Galilee and findeth Philip, and saith unto him, Follow me."[89]

21,4   Then immediately, on the third day there was a wedding in Cana of Galilee. Since there was a wedding just after he had left Judaea, he was rightly invited in its honor, as a blessing on marriage. (5) And it says, "On the third day there was a marriage in Cana of Galilee, and the mother of Jesus was there, and both Jesus was called, and his disciples who were with him, to the marriage. (6) And when they wanted wine," it says, "The mother of Jesus saith, They have no wine. And Jesus saith unto her, Woman, what have I to do with thee? Mine hour is not yet come."[90]

21,7   < This was* > after he came from the wilderness following the temptation, and after he had been taken to Jerusalem and had stood on the pinnacle of the temple, and had been borne from Jerusalem to a very high mountain which many say is Mt. Tabor, or Itarbion in translation; this mountain is in Galilee. (8) For Matthew, who said, "Jesus, hearing that John was cast into prison, departed into Galilee,"[91] assumed this order of events. (9) But Luke, who also accurately described the departure from the mountain, spoke first of the mountain and the kingdoms the devil showed the Lord, and later of the pinnacle and Jerusalem, and how Jesus returned to Galilee and Nazareth. But Matthew agrees with him in saying,

---

[87] Matt. 17:5
[88] John 2:11
[89] John 1:43
[90] John 2:1–4
[91] Cf. Matt. 4:12.

"Leaving Nazareth he went unto Capernaum."[92]

20,10 For he went to Nazareth and from there to the Jordan to visit John, and after crossing the Jordan started back to his boyhood home, to his mother at Nazareth, and stayed there (i.e., at the Jordan) for two days, at which time Andrew and the others also stayed with him. Then, for the salvation of mankind, he was moved to begin preaching; (11) and because he had come [there] after an interval he stayed two days, accompanied by the disciples he had taken by then. And dismissing the two who had followed him he went to Galilee at once, to preach and work the first miracle, the one he performed at the wedding.

21,12 For see how the wording assures < us > of this, when John the Baptist gives his testimony, and says as of an event already in the past, "And I *knew* him not, but he who *sent* me to baptize *said* unto me, Upon whom thou seest the Spirit descending in the form of a dove, the same is he."[93] (13) For when the Father sent John to baptize he granted him this sign, so that, when he saw it, he would recognize the Savior and Benefactor of our souls, who had been sent to the world from on high.

21,14 Sectarians like these are confounded by the truth and accuracy of the sacred scriptures, especially by the agreement of the four Gospels. No one in his right mind would reject the fully accurate account the Holy Spirit has given through the sacred Gospels. (15) For even though they say that the evangelists Matthew, Mark and Luke reported that the Savior was brought to the wilderness after his baptism, and that he spent forty days in temptation, and after the temptation heard of John's imprisonment and went to live at Capernaum by the sea—(16) but [then go on to say] that John is lying because he did not speak of this but straight off of the Savior's visit to John [the Baptist], and all the other things John says he did[94]—[even if this is their argument], their entire ignorance of the Gospels' exact words will be evident. (17) John the Evangelist indicates that, *before* the arrest of John the Baptist, the Lord went to him < again* > after the days of the temptation. If John had been imprisoned, how could the Savior still return to him at the Jordan?

21,18 Nor do they realize that the other three evangelists give an accurate account of the time after John's imprisonment by saying, "Jesus, hearing that John was cast into prison, departing from

---

[92] Matt. 4:13
[93] John 1:33
[94] MSS: λέγει; Holl's < διηγεῖται > λέγων appears unnecessary.

Nazareth dwelt in Capernaum which is upon the seacoast." And you see that everything is said truthfully and in agreement by the four evangelists.

21,19   For John is plainly < following > the [other evangelists'] order when he says in turn that, after the Savior had performed the first miracle, gone to Capernaum and performed certain miracles there, and gone back to Nazareth and read the scroll, then finally, when John the Baptist was imprisoned, he went and lived at Capernaum for "not many days."[95] (20) These are the "days" after the Epiphany, and after Christ's journey to Capernaum and Nazareth, his pilgrimage to Jerusalem for the Passover, and < his > return to John, where John was baptizing at Aenon < near > Salim. (21) For the Gospel says, "After this he went down to Capernaum, he and his mother and his brethren, and they remained there *not many days*."[96] He was not yet referring to Jesus' final residence [at Capernaum], of which he said later < that > *after* John's imprisonment he went to live at Capernaum by the sea.

21,22   "And the Passover of the Jews was nigh," as he says, "and Jesus went up to Jerusalem, and found the sellers of oxen, sheep and doves in the temple, and the changers of money sitting."[97] (23) And after expelling these money-changers and dove-sellers and the rest and saying, "Take these things hence and make not my Father's house an house of merchandise"—and after hearing their answer, "What sign showest thou us, seeing that thou doest these things?" and telling them, "Destroy this temple, and in three days I will raise it up"[98]—(it was at this time that Nicodemus came to him)—and after saying a great deal, John says, (24) "Jesus came, and his disciples, to Judaea, and there he tarried with them and baptized. And John also was < baptizing > in Aenon near to Salim, for there was much water there; *for John was not yet cast into prison*."[99]

21,25   And after John has said a great deal—"He that hath the bride is the bridegroom,"[100] [and so on]—the Gospel then says, "When therefore Jesus knew that the Pharisees had heard that Jesus made and baptized more disciples < than > John (though Jesus himself baptized not, but his disciples), he left Judaea and departed again into Galilee. (26) And he must needs pass through

---

[95] John 2:12
[96] John 2:12
[97] Matt. 4:13
[98] John 2:16; 18–19
[99] John 3:22–24
[100] John 3:29

Samaria."[101] This was the occasion when he sat by the well and talked with the Samaritan woman. And the Samaritan woman told the townsmen about him, and the Samaritans came to him and begged him to stay with them, "and he stayed there two days, and many more believed because of his word.[102]

21,27 "Now after the two days he came into Galilee . . . And there was a certain nobleman whose son was sick at Capernaum."[103] This was when Jesus told him, "Go, thy son liveth,"[104] and he believed, and the boy was healed. And the Gospel says, "< This > is again the second miracle that Jesus did when he was come out of Judaea into Galilee."[105]

21,28 "After this there was a feast of the Jews"—I believe he is speaking of another feast of the Jews, Pentecost or Tabernacles—"and Jesus went up to Jerusalem."[106] This was when he came to the Sheep Pool on the Sabbath, and healed the paralytic who had been ill for thirty-eight years. (29) And then the acceptable year was finally over and they began to persecute him, from the time when he healed the paralytic at the Sheep Pool on the Sabbath. John says in turn, "The Jews persecuted Jesus the more, because he not only had broken the Sabbath, but said also that God was his Father, making himself equal with God."[107] (30) How can the sects which make the Son inferior to the Father escape condemnation? "Making himself *equal* with God," says the Gospel.

21,31 "After these things Jesus went over the Sea of Galilee, which is the Sea of Tiberias, and a great multitude followed him because they saw the miracles which he did on them that were diseased. And Jesus went up into the mountain, and there he sat with his disciples. And the Passover, the feast of the Jews, was < nigh >."[108] (32) And now, as the other Gospels say, when John had been imprisoned Jesus came and made his home in Capernaum by the sea, as we find that John himself says in agreement with the others. For as the Passover comes in the month of March or April, it is perfectly plain that the times at which Jesus came to John after the temptation were different times [than this].

---

[101] John 4:1–4
[102] Cf. John 4:39–41.
[103] John 4:43; 48
[104] John 4:50
[105] John 4:54
[106] John 5:1
[107] John 5:18
[108] John 6:1–4

22,1   Again, they also accuse the holy evangelist—or rather, they accuse the Gospel itself—because, they say, "John said that the Savior kept two Passovers over a two-year period, but the other evangelists describe one Passover." (2) In their boorishness they fail to realize that the Gospels not only acknowledge that there are two Passovers as I have fully shown, but that they speak of two earlier Passovers, and of that other Passover on which the Savior suffered, so that there are three Passovers, over three years, from the time of Christ's baptism and first preaching until the cross.

22,3   For the Savior was born during the forty-second year of the Roman emperor Augustus—in the thirteenth consulship of the same Octavian Augustus and the consulship of Silanus, as the Roman consul lists indicate. (4) For these say as follows: "During their consulships," I mean Octavian's thirteenth and the consulship of Silanus, "Christ was born on the eighth before the Ides of January, thirteen days after the winter solstice and the increase of the light and the day."[109] (5) Greeks, I mean the idolaters, celebrate this day on the eighth before the Kalends of January, which Romans call Saturnalia, Egyptians Cronia, and Alexandrians, Cicellia. (6) For this division between signs of the zodiac, which is a solstice, comes on the eighth before the Kalends of January, and the day begins to lengthen because the light is receiving its increase. And it completes a period of thirteen days until the eighth before the Ides of January, the day of Christ's birth, with a thirtieth of an hour added to each day. (7) The Syrian sage, Ephrem, testified to this calculation in his commentaries when he said, "Thus the advent of our Lord Jesus Christ, his birth in the flesh or perfect incarnation which is called the Epiphany, was revealed after a space of thirteen days from the beginning of the increase of the light. For this too must needs be a type of the number of our Lord Jesus Christ and his twelve disciples, since, [added to the disciples], he made up < the > number of the thirteen days of the light's increase."[110]

22,8   And how many other things have been done and are being done because of, and in testimony to this calculation, I mean of Christ's birth? Indeed, those who guilefully preside over the cult of idols are obliged to confess a part of the truth, and in many places deceitfully celebrate a very great festival on the very night of the Epiphany, to deceive the idolaters who believe them into

---

[109] Consularia Constantia, MG Auct. Antiq. IX, 218. Here, however, the date given is the eighth before the Kalends of January, i.e., December 25.
[110] The passage is not extant.

† hoping[111] in the imposture and not seeking the truth.

22,9 First, at Alexandria, in the Coreum, as they call it; it is a very large temple, the shrine of Core. They stay up all night singing hymns to the idol with a flute accompaniment. And when they have concluded their nightlong vigil torchbearers descend into an underground shrine after cockcrow (10) and bring up a wooden image which is seated naked < on > a litter. It has a sign of the cross inlaid with gold on its forehead, two other such signs, [one] on each hand, and two other signs, [one] actually [on each of] its two knees—altogether five signs with a gold impress. And they carry the image itself seven times round the innermost shrine with flutes, tambourines and hymns, hold a feast, and take it back down to its place underground. And when you ask them what this mystery means they reply that today at this hour Core—that is, the virgin—gave birth to Aeo.

22,11 This also goes on in the city of Petra, in the idolatrous temple there. (Petra is the capital city of Arabia, the scriptural Edom.) They praise the virgin with hymns in the Arab language and call her Chaamu—that is, Core, or virgin—in Arabic. And the child who is born of her they call Dusares, that is, "only son of the Lord." And this is also done that night in the city of Elusa, as it is there in Petra, and in Alexandria.

22,12 I have been obliged to prove this with many examples because of those who do not believe that "The Epiphany" is a good name for the fleshly birth of the Savior, who was born at the eighth hour and *manifested*, by the angels' testimony, to the shepherds and the world—but he was *manifested* to Mary and Joseph as well. (13) And the star was *manifested* to the magi in the east at that hour, two years before their arrival at Jerusalem and Bethlehem, when Herod asked the magi themselves the precise time of the star's *manifestation*, and they told him it was no more than two years before. And this very word gave the Epiphany its name, from Herod's saying, "the *manifestation* of the star." (14) Thus when the magi said, "Where is he that is born king of the Jews? For we have seen his star in the east and are come to worship him,"[112] Herod saw that he had not been inquiring about the name of a merely human king.

22,15 For he mulled the matter over and was puzzled because many kings had been born in Jerusalem—Saul of the tribe of

---

[111] Achelis: ἐλπίσαντες; we prefer MSS: ἐλπίσαντας, in agreement with εἰδωλολάτρας
[112] Matt. 2:2

Benjamin first, David of the tribe of Judah second, David's son Solomon, Solomon's son Rehoboam, and Rehoboam's sons in succession—and no star had ever appeared at any of their births, and never, except this once, had magi arrived to come and worship the newborn king. And after giving this his consideration he hit on the knowledge of the truth as well, and understood that this was not the sign of a man, but of the Lord alone. (16) Thus, when he asked the scribes and the priests, "Where is the Christ born?" and heard their answer, "in Bethlehem of Judaea,"[113] he was no longer asking about an earthly king or a mere man, but about Christ. And he learned the place by asking it of them, but the time by asking it of the magi.

22,17 For the magi themselves reached Bethlehem, after a two year interval, on this very day of the Epiphany, and offered their gifts, the myrrh, the gold and the frankincense. For the beginnings of many of the signs of Christ's manifestation came on this day of the Manifestation. (18) As I have said before and am obliged to say over and over, this was the day in the thirteenth consulship of Octavius Augustus and the consulship of Silanus [which fell] on the eighth before the Ides of January, thirteen days after the increase of the daylight. This lasts from the winter solstice, the eighth before the Kalends of January, until the actual day of Christ's birth and Manifestation, because of the type I spoke of—the Savior himself and his disciples, making thirteen.

22,19 Thus the Savior was born in the forty-second year of the Roman emperor Augustus in the consulship I have mentioned, twenty-nine years after Augustus' annexation of Judaea; Augustus had reigned for thirteen years before Judaea was finally annexed to Rome. (20) After Augustus' accession there was an alliance between the Romans and the Jews for about four years of his reign, with the dispatch of an auxiliary force, the appointment of a governor, and the payment of partial tribute to the Romans. < And again, partial tribute was given to the Romans* > for about five years [more], until Judaea was surrendered to them completely and became [fully] tributary to them, (21) because the rulers descended from Judah had come to an end, and Herod had been made king—a gentile, though indeed a proselyte. And then Christ was born in Bethlehem of Judaea and began to preach, after the last of the anointed rulers (χριστοί) descended from Judah and Aaron had come to an end—(their line had continued until the anointed ruler Alexander, and Salina, or Alexandra.) This was the fulfillment

---

[113] Cf. Matt. 2:4–5.

of Jacob's prophecy, "There shall not fail a ruler from Judah and a governor from his loins, till he come for who it is prepared, and he is the expectation of the nations"[114]—a reference to the birth of the Lord.

22,22 All this was fulfilled beginning with Christ's birth in Bethlehem, in the forty-second year of the whole reign of Augustus. Augustus' forty-second year came after [the following]: The fifth year of the governorship of Herod's father Antipater, when there was an alliance between the Romans and the Jews and the payment of partial tribute; Antipater's governorship, from the sixth year of Augustus through his ninth year; Herod's appointment in Augustus' tenth year, and the payment of partial tribute until Augustus' thirteenth, which was the fourth year of the reign of his appointee, Herod; (23) the period from Herod's fourth year, which finally saw the complete surrender of Judaea, until Herod's thirty-third year, when Augustus had reigned for forty-two < and >, as I said, all Judaea had been subdued. [This came] after it had been tributary to the Romans for twenty-nine years; after Herod's father Antipater had been made governor; and after Herod had been made king of Judaea by Augustus in Augustus' tenth year.

22,24 1. These things (i.e., Christ's birth and the fulfillment of Jacob's prophecy) came about in the thirteenth consulship of Octavius Augustus and the consulship of Silanus, as I have often said. The consulships listed below succeeded that consulship in order, as follows.[115] [The consulships] of:

   2. Lentulus and Piso
   3. Lucius Caesar and Paulus
   4. Vindicius and Varus
   5. Lamius and Servilius Nonnius
   6. Magnus Pompeius and Valerius
   7. Lepidus and Aruncius
   8. Caesar and Capito
   9. Creticus and Nerva
  10. Camillus and Quintillian
  11. Camerus and Sabinus
  12. Dolabella and Silanus
  13. Lepidus and Taurus
  14. Flaccus and Silanus

---

[114] Gen. 49:10
[115] Epiphanius' list of consuls is in close agreement with the Christian list given in the Consularia Constantia and the Chronicon Paschale, Monumenta Germanica Auctorum Antiquorum IX, 218–220 and XI, 197–199.

15. The two Sexti
16. Pompeius Magnus and Apuleius
17. Brutus and Flaccus
18. Taurus and Libo
19. Crassus and Rufus
20. Tiberius Caesar for the second time, and Drusus Germanicus for the second time
21. Silanus and Balbus
22. Messala and Gratus
23. Tiberius Caesar for the third time, and Drusus Germanicus for the third time
24. Agrippa and Galba
25. Pollio and Veterus
26. Cethegus and Varus
27. Agrippa for the second time, and Lentulus Galba
28. Getulicus and Sabinus
29. Crassus and Piso
30. Silanus and Nerva

23,1 And you see that this is a period of thirty years. I have done my best to give an accurate list of the successive consulships, so that those who go over it will see that there is no falsehood in the sacred doctrine of the truth, but that everything has been proclaimed with accuracy by the church. (2) For who can count the successive consulships, which cannot be wrong, and not despise those who believe that there is a discrepancy in the number of the years which is celebrated by the evangelists?

23,3 This is also the downfall of the earlier Valentinian sect and certain others, with their fictitious record of the thirty aeons they thought they could compare with the years of the Savior's life, making it possible for them to write the story of their aeons and first principles, if you please. (4) For in fact, it was in the *thirty-third* year of his incarnation that the Only-begotten suffered for us—the divine Word from on high who was impassible, and yet < took > flesh < and > suffered for us to cancel our sentence of death. (5) For after that consulship which came, as I indicated, in Christ's thirtieth year, there was another, called the consulship of Rufus and Rubellio. And then, at the beginning of the consulship after the consulship < of Rufus and > Rubellio—the one which later came to be called the consulship of Vinnicius and Longinus Cassius—the Savior suffered on the thirteenth before the Kalends of April < in his thirty-third year, which was* > the eighteenth year of Tiberius Caesar. (6) And this confounds the deceit of all these sectarians. The accurate teaching is plainly that the Gospels contain not only periods of two times for the celebration of the feast of the Passover, but even of three.

24,1 For Christ was born in the month of January, that is, on the eighth before the Ides of January—in the Roman calendar this is the evening of January fifth, at the beginning of January sixth. In the Egyptian calendar it is the eleventh of Tybi. In the Syrian or Greek it is the sixth of Audynaeus. In the Cypriote or Salaminian it is the fifth day of the fifth month. In the Paphian it is the fourteenth of July. In the Arabian it is the twenty-first of Aleom. < In the Macedonian it is the sixteenth of Apellaeus. >[116] In the Cappadocian it is the thirteenth of Atartes. In the Athenian it is the fifth of Maemacterium. And in the Hebrew calendar it is the fifth of Tebeth. (2) For in this case too the prophet's oracle had to be fulfilled, "There came unto us the ark of the Lord"—but he means Christ's perfect human nature—"on the fifth day of the fifth month."[117] (3) This had to be fulfilled first by the Hebrew reckoning, by the following of which many of the gentiles, I mean the Romans, observe the fifth day in the evening preceding the sixth. But the Cypriotes keep the fifth of the month itself; and the native Egyptians, and the Salaminians, observe that month as the fifth, just as the Hebrews make it the fifth month from their New Year.

24,4 Christ had lived through these twenty-nine full consulships, but in the thirtieth consulship, I mean < the consulship of Silanus and Nerva* >, he came to John in about the < eleventh > month, and was baptized in the river Jordan in the thirtieth year following his birth in the flesh, (5) on the sixth before the Ides of November. That is, he was baptized on the twelfth of the Egyptian month Athyr, the eighth of the Greek month of Dius, the sixth of third Choiak in the Salaminian, or Constantian calendar, the sixteenth of Apogonicus in the Paphian, the twenty-second of Angalthabaith in the Arabian, the sixteenth of Apellaeus in the Macedonian, the fifteenth of Aratates in the Cappadocian, the seventh of Metagitnium in the Athenian, and the seventh of Marcheshvan in the Hebrew. (6) As I have often remarked, the holy Gospel according to Luke bears me out with some such words as, "Jesus began to be about thirty years old, being, as was supposed, the son of Joseph."[118]

24,7 From this day, the twelfth of Athyr, he "preached the

---

[116] Klostermann's restoration, based on 24,5
[117] This may be a faultily remembered version of Zech. 7:3.
[118] Luke 3:23

acceptable year of the Lord" as had been foretold in the prophet
Isaiah: "The Spirit of the Lord is upon me, for the Lord hath
anointed me to preach the Gospel to the poor. He hath sent me
to proclaim liberty to captives and recovery of sight to the blind,
to preach the acceptable year of the Lord and the day of retribution."[119]

25,1   For he indeed preached an acceptable year of the Lord,
that is, a year without opposition. He preached for the first year
after < the > thirtieth year of his incarnation, and everyone accepted his preaching. Neither Jews nor gentiles nor Samaritans
disputed it; all were glad to hear him. (2) In this year he went
up to Jerusalem, after being baptized and passing the forty days
of the temptation, and the twenty days prior to the first miracle,
which I have spoken of, and the choosing of his disciples. (3) It
is plain that, after returning to the Jordan from the temptation,
and crossing the Sea of Tiberias and going to Nazareth, he went
up to Jerusalem and, midway through the feast, cried out, "If anyone
thirst, let him come to me and drink."[120] And then he went to
Nazareth, Judaea, Samaria and Tyre.

25,4   And at the close of the first year he went up to Jerusalem
again, and now they tried to arrest him during the feast and were
afraid to; at this feast he said, "I go not up at this feast."[121] (5) He
was not lying, never fear! It says, "He set out at the middle of the
feast and went up to Jerusalem,[122] and they said, Is not this he
whom they sought to arrest? And lo, he speaketh boldly. Have the
priests, then, learned that this is the Christ?"[123] (6) For because
he was speaking mysteriously with his brethren, and in supernatural terms, they did not know what he meant. He was telling them
that he would not go up to heaven at that feast, or go to the cross
then to accomplish the work of the passion and the mystery of
redemption, and rise from the dead and ascend to heaven. All this
he accomplished at his own discretion.

25,7   And finally after this, at the close of the two year period
which followed his baptism and his birthday, in November and
January [respectively]—in the thirty-third year of his incarnation,
after living through the two consulships I have mentioned, those
of the two Gemini and of Rufus and Rubellio, (8) the impassible
divine Word accomplished the mystery of his passion in the third

---

[119] Cf. Isa. 61:1–2; Luke 4:18–19.
[120] John 7:14; 37
[121] John 7:8
[122] John 7:14
[123] Cf. John 7:25–27.

consulship, in its third month, after January and February. He suffered in the flesh for us while retaining his impassibility, as Peter says, "being put to death in the flesh, but quickened by the Spirit."[124]

26,1 Jesus suffered on the thirteenth before the Kalends of April, the Jews meanwhile having skipped one evening, that is, at midnight on the fourteenth of the month.[125] (2) For the Jews came ahead of time and ate the Passover, as the Gospel says[126] and I have often remarked. They thus ate the Passover two days before its < proper* > eating; that is, they ate it in the evening on the third day of the week, a thing that ought to be done at evening on the fifth day.[127] For on that basis[128] the fourteenth of the month was the fifth day of the week, [when the Passover should have been eaten].

26,3 But Jesus was arrested late on that same third day, which was the nighttime of the eleventh of the month, the sixteenth before the Kalends of April.[129] The dawning of the fourth day[130] of the week was the nighttime of the [Jewish] twelfth day of the month, the fifteenth before the Kalends of April. The daytime of the thirteenth day of the month[131] was the fifth day of the week, but the [ensuing] nighttime *was* the fourteenth of the month,[132]

---

[124] 1 Pet. 3:17

[125] With some modification we follow Strobel's reconstruction (pp. 305–309) of the situation envisaged by Epiphanius, and read the text without Holl's restorations. Epiphanius seems to have believed that the Jews, as a calendar correction, dropped the six hours between 6pm and midnight on the Jewish fifth day of the week, our Wednesday night. Following this alleged calendar correction the Jewish fifth day of the week, and the days following, would begin at midnight, Roman fashion, rather than in the Jewish manner, at nightfall. The resurrection would then be dated at the midnight between the equinox and the day of the equinox, not only by the Roman calendar but also by the now corrected Jewish calendar.

[126] Epiphanius means Matt. 26:2.

[127] Cf. Didascalia 21 (Achelis-Flemming p. 111). Epiphanius' charge that the Jews ate the Passover two days early, and the calendar correction he believes they made, are connected only in the sense that the calendar correction affects the dating of the days of the month; Epiphanius reveals no belief that the two adjustments were made for the same reason.

[128] οὕτως I.e., if all had been done right

[129] Cf. Didascalia 21 (Achelis-Flemming p. 102). In other words, Jesus was arrested on our Tuesday night. However, the "nighttime of the eleventh of the month" should mean Wednesday night; Epiphanius, or the text, is confused here. Epiphanius might have read the phrase, "late on the third day," in his version of the Didascalia, and taken it as synonymous with "nighttime of the eleventh" or "twelfth" (Schmidt, p. 691).

[130] I.e., the period between 6pm and midnight on our Wednesday

[131] I.e., 6am–6pm on our Thursday

[132] I.e, was the fourteenth *until* the Jews made the six hour calendar correction at this point. But when this had been made, the thirteenth day of the week lasted until midnight, and then the fourteenth began.

the fourteenth before the Kalends of April.[133] The daytime of the
fourteenth of the month was the eve of the Sabbath, the thirteenth
before the Kalends of April. The daytime of the fifteenth of the
month[134] was the Sabbath, the twelfth before the Kalends of April.

26,4   The dawning of the Lord's Day was [the end of] the
nighttime of the fifteenth of the month.[135] That was the illumination of hades, earth and heaven and the < time of the equality >
the night and the day, reckoned [both] because of the [Jewish]
fifteenth of the month and because of the course of the sun; for
the resurrection and the equinox < came > [at midnight] on the
eleventh before the Kalends of April. As I said, < the Jews > were
mistaken about this, and made sure that one day was skipped.[136]

26,5[137]   Now the exact computation [of the lunar year] contains
some [double-]hours,[138] and comes out even every third year, making
a difference of one day in their calculations. (6) For they add four
other [double-]hours per year to the moon's course after its 354
days, making one [additional] day every three years. (7) And so
they intercalate five months in fourteen years because the one
[double-]hour is subtracted from the sun's course of 365 days and
three [double-]hours; for, with the hours added, the final result
is 365 days less one [double]-hour.

26,8   And so, because they multiply the fourteen years by six
every eighty-four years, they intercalate one month in the eighty-
fifth year, so that there are thirty-one [intercalary] months every
eighty-five years; but by exact reckoning there ought to be thirty-

---

[133] I.e., the calendar correction has now been made, and the Jewish 14 Nisan
now begins at midnight on the Roman thirteenth before the Kalends, our Friday.

[134] As in the preceding note, the Jewish day is considered to begin at midnight.

[135] I.e., the midnight that ended the "nighttime" of 15 Nisan as it would have
been reckoned after the Jews' alleged six-hour calendar correction.

[136] I.e., if the Jews had not made their (alleged) six-hour calendar correction,
the resurrection and the moment of the equinox would have been dated in
the nighttime of their 16 Nisan, rather than at the beginning of their 15 Nisan.
In this sense, 16 Nisan has been "skipped."

[137] In 26,5 through 27,1 we follow the MSS almost as they stand. Epiphanius
appears to mean that the Jews ate the Passover two days early to allow for a
two-day variance which they perceived to exist between the date of Passover
calculated by an 85-year Paschal cycle (sic!) and the corresponding date calculated by the Julian calendar. He also seems to be saying that the cause of
their misperception was the fact that the Jewish lunar year is 354 days plus eight
hours, requiring the intercalation of a day every third year. However, the text
as it stands does not express these ideas with any clarity, and may be irrecov-
erably corrupt. For a full discussion, see Strobel pp. 309–316.

[138] ὥρας. We assume that Epiphanius means double-hours here, because 3
x 4 hours make only half a day, not the full day with which Epiphanius appears
to be reckoning. Cf. 26,6.

one months, twenty-four[139] days, and three [double]-hours. (27,1)
The Jews were wrong at that time for this reason; not only did
they eat the Passover two days early because they were disturbed,
but they also added the one day they had skipped, since they were
mistaken in every way. But the revelation of the truth has done
everything for our salvation with the utmost precision. (2) Thus
when the Savior himself had finished the Passover he went out
into the mount "with intense desire"[140] after eating it. (3) And yet
he ate that Jewish Passover with the disciples, and did nothing
different. He himself kept it the same as the others, so as not to
destroy the Law but to fulfill it.

27,4 And so, after completing his thirtieth year in which he
was baptized, and after completing his thirty-first by preaching for
an entire "acceptable year" without opposition,but [then] preaching another year with opposition, to the accompaniment of persecution and hatred; and after completing [part of] another year
after it,[141] a full seventy-four days from his birthday,—(the Epiphany,
(5) January 5 at the dawn of January 6 and the eleventh of the
Egyptian month Tybi)—until the thirteenth before the Kalends of
April, as I said, < on that same thirteenth before the Kalends of
April*, > the twenty-fourth of the Egyptian month Phamenoth, he
had attained a full thirty-two years, plus seventy-four days from the
Epiphany. (6) And he rose on the twenty-sixth of the Egyptian
month Phamenoth—(this was the day of the equinox and was
preceded by the night and the equinox)—the day which followed
the twenty-fifth of Phamenoth, the eleventh before the Kalends of
April, < and appeared to his disciples. > This makes liars of all who
are not sons of the truth.

28,1 Valentinus, first of all, is at once < exposed > as a schemer,
since he expects < to prove* > to us, from the years of the Savior's
rearing and coming to manhood, that there are thirty aeons. He
does not realize that the Savior did not live for only thirty years.
(2) He was baptized in his thirtieth year at the age of twenty-nine
years and ten months, on the twelfth of Athyr, as I said, the sixth
before the Ides of November. And then, following his baptism
which was < sixty days > before his birthday, < he passed* > an acceptable year of the Lord in preaching, and another year, of
opposition, after < the first* > year,[142] and [finally] seventy-four days

---

[139] Strobel and Codex Urbinas: κ̅δ̅; Codex Marcianus Venetus: κ̅α̅. Strobel
suggests that both are mis-transcriptions of an original κ̅ς̅, 26.
[140] Luke 22:15; that is, desire to eat the real Passover
[141] Klostermann: μετ' αὐτόν; MSS and Holl: μετὰ τοῦτο.
[142] Holl: μετὰ τὸν < πρῶτον > ἐνιαυτόν; Klostermann: μετὰ τοῦτο

of opposition. (3) Thus all the years of his incarnation, from his
birth until his passion, amounted to thirty-two years and seventy-
four days. But there were two years and 134 days (sic!)[143] from the
start < of his preaching in* > the consulship of Silanus and Nerva.
And Valentinus stands refuted, and the many who are just as foolish.

28,4   The ones who reject John's Gospel have also been refuted. (I may rightly call them "Dumb," since they reject the Word
of God—the Father's Word who was preached by John, and who
came down from heaven and wrought salvation for us < by > his
whole advent in the flesh.) (5) For from the consulships, the years,
the witness of the prophet Isaiah, the Gospel according to Luke,
the Gospel according to John, the Gospel according to Matthew,
the Gospel according to Mark—in short, the misguided people
have been refuted in every way, (6) since Christ did not live to
see just one Passover over the period of a year from the start of
his preaching, but actually lived through the periods of a little less
than three consulships after his baptism by John. (7) And the
nitwits' fallacious argument has failed < because it is* > full of silliness, and of an ignorance that not only fails to recognize its own
salvation, but even futilely makes a lying war on the truth.

29,1   For somewhere < in > these works I have also found a
notation that the Word of God was born about the fortieth year
of Augustus. Either this was a mistake on the writer's part, or else
he wrote only "forty (μ̄) years" because the figure "beta" had been
erased and only the "mu" was left on the page. For Christ was born
in the forty-second year of Augustus.

29,2   It says besides that Christ < was conceived > on the twelfth
before the Kalends of July or June—I cannot say which—in the
consulship of Sulpicius Cammarinus and Betteus Pompeianus.[144]
(3) I have < also > noticed that those who have given a date for
the conception, and Gabriel's bringing of the tidings to the Virgin,
have said < this because of > a conjecture on the part of certain
persons who † have it by tradition[145] that Christ was born after a
term of seven months. (4) For I have found that there is a time
of seven lunar months less four days between the month they
mention[146] and the eleventh of Tybi, the eighth before the Ides
of January, when the Epiphany really took place and Christ was

---

[143] This should be two years and 14 days, cf. 16,1–9.
[144] This name is inaccurate, and ungrammatically placed in the dative while
Sulpicius Cammarinus is in the genitive; it may have been interpolated (Strobel,
Dummer).
[145] Holl: ἐχόντων ἐν παραδόσει; MSS: λεγόντων ἐν παραδόσει
[146] Holl: προειρημένου μηνός; MSS: προπόσων

born. (5) So if you should find < this > in a marginal gloss somewhere, do not be misled by the information. The actual date of
Christ's birth is in fact the eleventh of Tybi.

29,6   Some, however, say that Christ was carried in the womb
for ten months less fourteen days and eight hours, making nine
months, fifteen days and four hours. They are alluding to Solomon's saying, "compacted in blood for a time of ten months."[147]

29,7   In any case, < it has been shown > by every means < that >
the Lord's birth in the flesh took place on < the > eleventh of the
Egyptian month Tybi. And the first miracle in Cana of Galilee,
when the water was made wine, was performed on about the same
eleventh day thirty years later. (30,1) And even to this day this
happens in many places as a testimony to unbelievers because of
the miracle which was wrought at that time, as streams and rivers
in many localities testify by being changed to wine. (2) The stream
at Cibyre, the chief city of Caria, [gives its testimony] at the same
time of day at which the servants drew the water and Christ said,
"Give it to the governor of the feast."[148] And the stream at Gerasa
in Arabia testifies in the same way. < I > have drunk from the < one
at > Cibyre < myself >, and my brethren have drunk from the stream
in the shrine of the martyrs at Gerasa. (3) And even in Egypt many
give this testimony of the Nile. Thus in Egypt itself, and in many
countries, everyone draws water on the eleventh of the Egyptian
month Tybi, and stores it up.

30,4   And so we see that after the twelfth of Athyr, when he
had gone away and been tempted for forty days, and [then] come
to Nazareth and stayed there for about two weeks and three days,
he [next] went down to the Jordan to see John and spent a first
day there, and a second; and [then he] returned to Nazareth, and
likewise stayed there for a first and a second day. (5) And on the
third day he went to Cana of Galilee. This makes a total of sixty
days after the baptism: the forty days of the temptation; the two
weeks < and two days > at Nazareth, and the other two; and on
the third day the miracle of the water was performed at the wedding.[149]

30,6   After that he came to Capernaum and performed other
miracles as I have said many times, and [then] returned to Nazareth again and read the roll of Isaiah the prophet. This is why
[the people of Nazareth] say, "Do also here whatsoever signs we
have heard thou hast done in Capernaum."[150] (7) But later he

---

[147] Wisd. Sol. 7:2
[148] John 2:8
[149] Cf. at 16,3; 21,10; 30,8.
[150] Luke 4:23

returned from there to Capernaum and from there crossed over
to the Lake, or Sea of Gennesareth, and Peter and the others were
chosen for good; and then he went on to do all of his preaching.

30,8   For going in order, as I said: after the forty < days > [of
the temptation], and the other two weeks and two days < at
Nazareth >, Christ went to John on a first day and the day following. But < from > John he started back to Nazareth, and he stayed
in a lodging from the tenth hour until evening, and on the other
day went out and met Philip, (9) making two days. And finally,
< by saying >, "On the *third* there was a marriage in Cana of Galilee,"[151]
the Gospel shows its unvarying accuracy because of the two days
he stayed [at Nazareth] after his arrival.

30,10   This was symbolic of the church. On the third day of
his business in the heart of the earth, which he spent † in hades[152]
after the passion, he arose and contracted marriage with "Cana"—
for "Cana" means "the bride."[153] (11) But who is "the bride" except
the heiress of whom the Psalmist said, "For the heiress,"[154] and so
on, in the fifth Psalm? Blessed indeed is this wedding, for which
that type gave occasion! (12) For there was a real wedding there,
in Cana of Galilee, and water which really became wine, < and
Christ* > was invited for two purposes. [One was] to dry the wetness
of the world's carousers up, < through > marriage, to a state of
temperance and decency. [The other was] to remedy what is wanting
for good spirits through cheering wine, and through grace. (13)
He thus completely silences the opponents of † marriage,[155] and
by providing the vine with water, and tinting it into wine within
the vine to make men glad, shows that, with his Father and Holy
Spirit, he is God. I have discussed this elsewhere at greater length;[156]
here I hurry over the matter as though in passing.

30,14   At all events, the Savior kept two Passovers after the beginning of his preaching and suffered on the third, and this ends
the things I have by now said in great detail about days, months
and consulships. And their erroneous argument has entirely failed;
the Gospels are in agreement, and no evangelist contradicts another.

31,1   But to return to the subject. To witness to what I have
said in a number of different ways, Luke, again, says, "It came to

---

[151] John 2:1
[152] Holl: ἐν τῷ ᾅδῃ; MSS: ἐν τῇ γῃ
[153] So Origen, In Joh. 13.62
[154] Ps. 5, Superscription
[155] Holl: γάμου; MSS: κυρίου; Codex Urbinas: νόμου κυρίου
[156] Anc. 66,2–10

pass on the second Sabbath after the first."[157] This is to show that a "first Sabbath" is the Sabbath the Lord ordained at the beginning and called a Sabbath during the creation, a Sabbath which has recurred at seven day intervals from then till now—but that a "second" Sabbath is the one instituted by the Law. (2) For the Law says, "Thou shalt take to thyself a lamb of a year old, male and without blemish"—a type of the Savior—"on the tenth day of the month, and it shall be kept until the fourteenth day. And ye shall slay it at even on the fourteenth day; and it shall be to thee a Sabbath, an holy day, and ye shall eat unleavened bread seven days, and the seventh day thou shalt declare holy."[158] (3) And see how such a holy day of the lamb is called a second Sabbath after the first Sabbath, and is consecrated as a Sabbath even though it is the Lord's Day, or the second day of the week, or the third day of the week. (4) But a second Sabbath [after this one], if it recurs in the regular seven day cycle, is called a "first" Sabbath—all of which shows that not only John gave indication of a time of two years and three Passover festivals, but that Luke did too, and the others.

31,5   For the Law says as follows: "Thou shalt number unto thee seven weeks from the first [reaping] of the sheaf, and putting of the sickle unto the standing corn, and in the seventh week thou shalt declare an holy day of the Lord,"[159] meaning the feast of Pentecost. (6) For within three days after the slaying of the Passover—that is, three days after [the sacrifice of] the lamb—the Law enjoined the bringing in of the sheaf, meaning the blessed Sheaf which was raised from the dead the third day. (7) For the earth brought the Sheaf forth, and he received it back from her at his rising < from > the tomb, remained for the forty days with his disciples, and at the end of the Pentecost brought it into the heavens to the Father. (8) He is the firstborn of the firstborn, the holy firstfruits, the Sheaf which was reaped from Mary, the Embrace embraced in God, the Fruit of the womb, the firstfruits of the threshing floor. (9) For after Pentecost the sickle no longer offers a firstfruits to God: "The Lord dieth no more, death hath no more dominion over him."[160] as the scripture says.

31,10   And you see how many of God's mysteries the Law prefigured and the Gospel fulfilled. In which passages can I not expound them? But not to go on too long, I must return to our

---

[157] Luke 6:1
[158] Exod. 12:5; 6; 14; 15
[159] Deut. 16:9; Lev. 23:15–16
[160] Rom. 6:9

order of presentation. (11) However, from the ears, the standing grain and the disciples, it is plain that John, Luke and all the evangelists describe all these things *after* the forty day temptation.

32,1   But again, these people are not ashamed to take arms against the things St. John has said, supposing that they can overthrow the truth, but unaware that they are attacking themselves rather than the sound doctrine. (2) For they derisively say against Revelation, "What good does John's Revelation do me by telling me about seven angels and seven trumpets?"—(3) not knowing that such things were essential, and of use to the message's rightness.

32,4   For whatever was obscure and puzzling in The Law and the Prophets, the Lord in his providence revealed by the Holy Spirit "to his servant John"[161] for our salvation. What was obscure there he proclaims spiritually and clearly here; < for he gave physical commandments* > in the Law, but reveals the same ones spiritually to us.

32,5   And in the Law he makes the tabernacle of skins—the skins that were dyed scarlet, blue and so on—to show that the tabernacle there is actually a tent, but that it awaits the perfect Tabernacle of Christ. (6) For skin comes off a body and is something dead, like the shadow of a living body; and this shows that bodies are God's tabernacle, for God dwells in holy bodies in fulfillment of the words of scripture, "I shall tabernacle in thee and walk in thee."[162]

32,7   Thus error would arise among the faithful if the book had not been revealed to us spiritually, teaching us that there is no need for trumpets, but < enabling us* > to know that God's entire activity is spiritual—(8) so that we will not take these as bronze or silver trumpets like the Jewish trumpets, but understand spiritually that they are the church's message from heaven: as he has said elsewhere, "On that day they sound with the great trumpet."[163] (9) For the prophets were trumpets, but the great Trumpet is the Lord's holy voice in the Gospel. For this is why angels were also privileged to make revelations to us; "For the trumpet shall sound," it says, "and the dead will arise."[164]

32,10   But if you people joke about the angels' trumpets because of their being in Revelation, then the trumpet the holy apostle speaks of must be a joke too, for he says, "The Lord shall

---

[161] Rev. 1:1
[162] 2 Cor. 6:16 (Lev. 26:12)
[163] Cf. Nu. 10:10.
[164] 1 Cor. 15:52

descend from heaven at the last trump, and the dead will arise on the last day at the voice of the archangel."[165] (11) What reply is left you, since Paul agrees with the holy apostle John in the Revelation? How can every error not be refuted at once, when God has testified < for > the saints in every book?

33,1   Then again, some of them seize on the following text in Revelation, and say in contradiction of it, "He said, in turn, 'Write to the angel of the church in Thyatira,'[166] and there is no church of Christians in Thyatira. How could he write to a non-existent church?" (2) In fact these people † demolish themselves since they are compelled by their own declarations[167] to confess the truth. For if they say, "There is no church in Thyatira now," they are showing that John foretold this.

33,3   For since these Phrygians settled there, snatched the simple believers' minds like wolves, and converted the whole town to their sect, those who reject Revelation attacked this text at that time in an effort to discredit it. (4) But now, in our time, the church is there thanks to Christ and is growing, 112 years after [its restoration], even < though > there are some others (i.e., sectarians) there. Then, however, the whole church had deserted to the Phrygians. (5) And thus the Holy Spirit was at pains to give us the revelation of how the church would fall into error ninety-three years after the time of the apostles, John and his successors—or in other words, for a time < of 138 years* > from the Savior's ascension until the church's restoration—since the church there would go astray and be swamped by the Phrygian sect.

33,6   For the Lord exposes < them > at the outset in Revelation when he says, "Write to the angel of the church in Thyatira, Thus saith he whose eyes are as a flame of fire, and his feet like fine brass. I know thy works, and thy faith and thy love and thy ministry, and that thy latter works are more than the first. (7) But I have against thee that thou sufferest the woman Jezebel to deceive my servants, calling herself a prophetess, teaching to eat things sacrificed to idols and commit fornication. And I gave her space for repentance, and she will not repent of her fornication."

33,8   Don't you people see that he means the women who are deceived by a false conception of prophecy, and will deceive many? I mean that he is speaking of Priscilla, Maximilla and Quintilla, (9) whose imposture the Holy Spirit did not overlook. He foretold

---

[165] Cf. 1 Thes. 4:16.
[166] Rev. 2:18
[167] Holl: ἀνασκευάζοντες, ἀναγκαζόμενοι; MSS: ἀναγκάζοντες

it prophetically by the mouth of St. John, who prophesied before his falling asleep, during the time of Claudius Caesar and earlier, when he was on the isle of Patmos. Even the people of Thyatira admit that this has come true. (10) John, then, wrote prophetically to those who were living in Christ there at the time, that a woman would call herself a prophetess. And the false argument which is raised against the truth has failed completely, since it can be shown that the prophetic oracle in Revelation is truly of the Holy Spirit.

34,1   Again, in their endless hunt for texts to give the appearance of discrediting the holy apostle's books—I mean John's Gospel and Revelation and perhaps the Epistles as well, for they too agree with the Gospel and Revelation—these people get excited (2) and quote, "I saw, and he said to the angel, Loose the four angels which are upon the Euphrates. And I heard the number of the host, ten thousand times ten thousand and thousands of thousands, and they were clad in breastplates of fire and sulfur and hyacinth."[168]

34,3   For people like these thought that the truth might be < some sort of > joke. If he speaks of the four angels who are seated at the Euphrates, it is to indicate the various peoples there who live by the Euphrates: the Assyrians, Babylonians, Medes and Persians. (4) For these are the four successive kingdoms that are mentioned in Daniel. The Assyrians were the first of them to rule, and in Daniel's time, the Babylonians. But the Medes succeeded them, and after them the Persians, whose first king was Cyrus.

34,5   For the nations have been put under the command of the angels, as God's holy servant Moses testifies by his consistent explanation of the saying: "Ask thy father and he will tell thee, thine elders and they will say it unto thee: when the most High apportioned the nations, when he dispersed the sons of Adam, he set bounds to the nations according to the number of the angels of God. And his people Jacob became the Lord's portion, Israel the lot of his inheritance."[169] (6) Now if the nations are put under the command of the angels, John was right in saying, "Loose the four angels who are upon the Euphrates." They are plainly in charge [of the nations], and prevented from sending the nations to war until the time of [the end of] God's long-suffering, until he orders the avenging of his saints by their agency. (7) The angels in command are restrained by the Spirit and not allowed to attack, because justice does not release them yet, so that the rest of the

---

[168] Rev. 9:14; 16; 17
[169] Deut. 32:7–9

nations may be released because of the harm which has been done the saints. But they are to be released and fall suddenly on the earth, as John and the rest of the prophets foretold. For when the angels are aroused, they arouse the nations to an avenging onslaught.

34,8   And there is no doubt as to the meaning of the sulfur, fiery and hyacinth breastplates. Those nations wear clothing of that color. "Sulfur clothes" means a quince yellow color, as they call it, of wool. "Fiery" means their scarlet clothing, and "hyacinth" means the blue-green wool.

35,1   But since these people have not received the Holy Spirit they are spiritually condemned for not understanding the things of the Spirit, and choosing to speak against the words of the Spirit. This is because they do not know the gifts of grace in the holy church, which the Holy Spirit, the holy apostles, and the holy prophets have expounded truly and soundly, with understanding and a sound mind. (2) One of the apostles and prophets, St. John, has shared his sacred gift with the holy church, through the Gospel, the Epistles and the Revelation. (3) But these people are liable to the scriptural penalty, "Whoso blasphemeth against the Holy Spirit it will not be forgiven him, neither in this world nor in the world to come."[170] For they have gone to war against the words the Spirit has spoken.

35,4   But let us go on once more to the rest, beloved, with the power of God. Now that I have said such things, and so many of them, against such a sect, I think that they are enough. I have trampled it with God's power and truth, like the many-footed millipede or the serpent they call the wood-louse. It is not very strong and its poison is not very painful, but it has lots of feet and its body is long and twisty.

Against Adamians.[1] *32, but 52 of the series*

1,1   The four-footed animal with an underground den which tunnels in the earth and has its burrow deep inside it, is called a mole. All its characteristics are like a small puppy's, for it has the <same> round shape, and no sight at all. (2) It is a destructive creature which roots out people's crops from below, especially every cucumber bed and the sharp-tasting plants—onions, garlic, purse-tassels

---

[170] Matt. 12:32

[1] This sect is reported only by Epiphanius, and by Theodoret, (Haer. Fab. 1.6) who is dependent on Epiphanius. Epiphanius' sources are oral, cf. 1,6–9.

and the like, and lilies and the rest. (3) But if it actually gets onto the surface during its tunneling, in the open air, or if it is hunted and caught by men, it is a ridiculous sight to all who hunt this creature.

1,4   I am trying to say with all this that the sect with which I now have to do is blind at heart and stupid, creates a desolation for itself, undermines the ground it stands on, and does injury to the roots of many, < I mean > the people who have run across it. (5) But if the wise happen to spy it, it gives them a good laugh. As the creature we spoke of is mocked for its blindness, < and > because of its lack of sight can't find its hole, so is this sect.

1,6   For they have named themselves for Adam. I say this because I have heard it reported by many; I have not found it in any treatise, and have certainly not met any such people. (7) And so, since many have spoken of the sect, I consider it worth mentioning. And this is why I was right in comparing it with that blind animal which is not readily seen by men; it is hidden in the earth and does its damage underneath. (8) But it is simply ridiculous, and I considered not including it at all. However, as long as there is even a rumor of it, it can do the wise hearer no harm to know about all the tares the devil has sown in the world. (9) For whether or not there is such a sect, I have heard many say that there is, and I think it makes sense to speak of it for safety's sake and not leave it out, even if it has been dissolved and is no longer in existence. For I am not certain whether it is still in being or not.

1,10   But why should I spend a long time on the prologue to its description? I shall begin my account of the ridicule, or rather, the sorrow. For it is vulnerable to both at once, ridicule and sorrow— < sorrow > at the devil's way of planting contempt for God's creature in the human mind; ridicule for people who neither see nor can conceive of anything sensible.

2,1   In the first place, they say that these people build their churches—or dens and caves; that is what I would call sectarian conventicles—in heated rooms, and that they heat them from below so that there will be hot air to warm the congregation in the chamber inside. (2) And when they come in they have people to watch the clothes, like cloak-room attendants, stationed at the doors. And they each, whether man or woman, undress outside as they come in, and enter with their whole bodies as naked as the day they were born. And their recognized leaders and teachers all sit stark naked, some in front and some in back, here and there in no particular order.

2,3   They are all called "continent," if you please, and make a boast of it—and "virgins," as they delude themselves into thinking they are—and they have their readings and all the rest of their service naked. (4) But if it appears that one of them has "fallen into transgression," as they put it, they do not admit him any more. They say that he < is > Adam after eating from the tree, and condemn him to expulsion from their church as though from Paradise. For they regard their church as Paradise, and themselves as Adam and Eve.

2,5   Why do they heat the room, then—to keep from getting a chill? Adam and Eve didn't live in a house with a furnace and weren't oppressed by any heat, and no cold afflicted them. (6) They had the purest of air, temperately dispensed to them by God < with > all mildness, neither sharpened by the rigor of cold, nor enervated by the extremely unpleasant heat of summer. The land had been designed as an immortal abode very < well > made by God; it was filled with gladness and well-being, and as I said, got neither cold nor hot. Since the Adamians have none of these things, their absurdity is evident.

3,1   Next let us look at another way of disproving their whole imposture. Adam and Eve were not naked for one hour; they were always naked "and were not ashamed."[2] But the nakedness of these people is not from lack of shame, even if they themselves think so; they are naked for the sake of an insatiable pleasure which casts its spell through the pupils of the eyes. (2) The modesty commended in all the sacred scriptures has been taken from them and the words of the prophet are truly fulfilled, "The appearance of an harlot hath been given thee, who hast been shameless with all ."[3]

3,3   But after that hour they resume their clothes outside, and [thus] cannot be Adam. Adam and his wife did not get clothing right away. They sewed fig leaves together first, and then they were given skin tunics, and so, after a considerable part of their lives, "the manifold wisdom of God"[4] endowed them with the knowledge of clothing.

3,4   These people will also be jeered at in every way because, in calling themselves Adam and Eve, they are lying about themselves, and yet at the same time telling the truth. (5) For it is plain from many indications that they are not Adam, as I have shown. But from their false symbolism, nakedness, shame and absurdity, it is plain that they are being mocked by the serpent in the mind.

---

[2] Gen. 2:25
[3] Jer. 3:3
[4] Cf. Eph. 3:10.

3,6   It is not worth my while to make a big thing of their refutation. To kill a beast of their sort one does not need weapons of war or heavy armor; (7) it is dispatched with a little stick. Often, when it has been pulled from its den it is merely left alone and dies of its own accord, an object of jeers and ridicule with nowhere to run to. And when these people are caught, they too are put utterly to shame by their ridiculous absurdity, unseemly behavior and silly religion.

3,8   But now, as we prepare to look into the rest, let us pray the Lord once more for his assistance in finding out the rest and refuting them, and for our salvation and that of our readers.

Against Sampsaeans.[1] 33, but 53 of the series

1,1   There is a sect of Peraean Sampsaeans, the people also known as Elkasaites whom I have mentioned already in my other Sects,[2] in the country called Peraea beyond the Salt, or, as it is called, the Dead Sea. They are < also > in Moabitis near the river Arnon, and on the other side in Ituraea and Nabatitis, as I have often said of them.[3]

1,2   These people boast that Elxai is their teacher, and further, two women of his stock who are alive to this day, and are worshiped as goddesses, if you please, because they are of the blessed seed. (3) But Ossaeans, Ebionites and Nazoraeans use this book, as I have often said.[4] These Sampsaeans, however, actually base their religion on it, and are neither Christians, Jews nor pagans; since they are simply in the middle, they are nothing. But they say that they have another book, which is called the book of Elxai's brother, Iexai.

1,4   They say that God is one, and worship him, if you please, by the administration of baptisms of some sort. They are devoted to the Jewish religion, [but] not in all ways. Some of them even abstain from meat.

1,5   They will die for Elxai's descendants. And I heard recently that the one woman, called Marthus, had died, though, unless she had died too, Marthana was still alive. (6) Any time these women went out anywhere on foot, the crowds would follow them and take the dust of their feet for healing, if you please, and, since

---

[1] Epiphanius is the only heresiologist to discuss the Sampsaeans. Much of his material is based on the contents of Elxai's book, which Epiphanius knew. Cf. Pan. 19,1,4–4,6; Hippol. Haer. 9.13.2–4; Eus. H. E. 6.36, though as a Palestinian Epiphanius might have had some personal knowledge. Sampsaeans are mentioned in conjunction with Ossaeans and others at Pan. 19,2,1; 20,3,2; 30,3,2.
[2] Pan. 19,2,1; 20,3,2
[3] Cf. Pan. 19,1,2; 20,3,2.
[4] Cf. Pan. 19,5,4.

they were woefully defrauded, their spittle too, and use them in phylacteries and amulets. For every error went blind first, and then learned its nonsense.

1,7 They accept neither prophets nor apostles, but all their own ideas are delusion. They honor water and all but regard it as God, for they claim that it is the source of life.[5]

1,8 They confess Christ in name but believe that he is a creature, and that he keeps appearing every now and then. He was formed for the first time in Adam, but when he chooses he takes Adam's body off and puts it on again. (9) He is called Christ; and the Holy Spirit is his sister, in female form. Each of them, Christ and the Holy Spirit, is ninety-six miles high and twenty-four miles wide; and they < talk* > much other < nonsense* >.

2,1 I have often described these people before, and composed refutations of them in other Sects. Hence I don't feel I have to make a big thing of demolishing them in a refutation, since I have already done this with Elxaeus, or Elxai, himself, and his followers, in the other Sects we spoke of. Anyone can tell that he and his sect are off the track. (2) Let us go on to the rest now since we have struck him, like a solar lizard, with the cudgel of hope in Christ and his cross. For the name they have given themselves may appropriately be used as a symbol to explain their false title. Translated, "Sampsaeans" means "Solar;"[6] this is why I mentioned the beast.

(3) For people call this lizard a "solar lizard." But this sect is inferior to the lizard, since it does not even have its momentary advantage. For though the lizard's sight is dim, it sometimes sees clearly with the aid of the sun's orb; < for > in its den, which faces eastward, it strains itself, fasting, towards the east, < and > when it sees the sun its sight loses its dimness. But in my opinion this sect has the lizard's foolishness in everything, and not even this little bit to its credit.

3,4 And so, now that this sect, which we have called a solar lizard, has also been trampled by the truth, < let it remain in* > † its < foolishness* >,[7] for it cannot prevail against God's truth; but let us, as we have said, set off for the rest.

---

[5] With Brandt, Dummer, Amidon, we punctuate with a comma after σχεδόν.
[6] Epiphanius derives Sampsaean from שמש.
[7] Holl: < ἐν τῇ ἀφροσύνῃ > αὐτῆς; MSS: αὐτοῦ

Against Theodotians.[1] *34, but 54 of the series*

1,1   One Theodotus arose in his turn. He was an offshoot of the
"Dumb" sect I have spoken of, which denies John's Gospel and
the divine Word who it < declared > was in the beginning, and
John's Revelation. (2) He was also associated and contemporary
with the other sects we have discussed, and was their successor in
time.[2] The Theodotians, as they are called, derive from him. I do
not know whether the sect is still in existence, but shall say what
I have learned about it from written works.

1,3   Theodotus was from Byzantium,[3] which is now called Constantinople. He was a shoemaker by trade,[4] but very learned. (4)
When a persecution began—I cannot say which one—he was arrested
by the governor of the city with a number of others and subjected
to examination with the rest for Christ's sake. All the other servants
of God won their victory and attained heavenly rewards by their
witness for Christ. (5) But Theodotus fell into transgression by
denying Christ and missing the mark of the truth. And, deeply
ashamed because of his censure by many, he fled his native land,
moved to Rome and lived there.

1,6   But he was recognized by the Christians in Rome, and once
again incurred the same censure there; for he was charged by
those who knew him for his learning with being a very learned
man who had lost his grip on the truth. (7) But as a lame excuse
for himself, if you please, he invented the new doctrine that follows.
He said, "I didn't deny God, I denied man." Then, when they
asked him, "Which man?" he answered, "I denied the man Christ."

1,8   Thereafter he, and the Theodotians whose founder he was,
taught this doctrine of theirs and said that Christ is a mere man[5]
begotten of a man's seed.[6] (9) Next, as a weak defense for himself,
he collected whatever texts he found useful—not that he honestly
thought [this was what they meant], but he amassed them as an
excuse for his defection. He said, [for example], "Christ said, 'But

---

[1] Epiphanius' information about this sect comes from written sources, 54,1,2.
Other accounts of the Theodotians are found at Hippol. Haer. 8.9.35; 10.23;
Ps.-Tert. 8. However, Epiphanius had a digest of Theodotus' arguments, as is
shown by the form of 1,8–9; 2,3; 3,1 etc.
[2] Hippol. Haer. 8.9.35 makes Theodotus "an offshoot of the Gnostics and
Cerinthians, and the school of Ebion."
[3] Hippol. Haer. 7.35.1; Ps.-Tert. 8
[4] Eus. H. E. 5.26.6
[5] Hippol. Haer. 7.35.2; 10.23; Eus. H. E. 5.28.6; Ps.-Tert. 8
[6] Hippolytus reports that Theodotus taught the doctrine of the Virgin Birth,
Haer. 7.35.2. Cf. Pan. 54,3,5.

now ye seek to kill me, a *man* that hath told you the truth.'[7] You see," he said, "that Christ is a man."

2,1　But the wretch does not know that the Lord says in the same verse, "the truth which I have heard *of my Father.*" He is saying that God is his father—not a man. (2) If he had heard the truth from a man he would not have boasted of his witness to the truth by saying that he had heard the truth from men. Instead he boasts of it to show that he is God, begotten of the Father on high but become man for us, and slain in the flesh, but living forever in his Godhead.

2,3　Theodotus says next that he has not committed sin by denying Christ. "For," says he, "Christ himself has said, 'All manner of blasphemy shall be forgiven men,' and, 'Whosoever speaketh a word against the Son of Man, it shall be forgiven him; but he that blasphemeth the Holy Ghost, it shall not be forgiven him here or in the world to come.'"[8]

2,4　And the unfortunate man does not know that the Lord is saying this prophetically in the extremity of meekness and lovingkindness, since he desires to ensure the salvation of those who have blasphemed him at one time and turned to repentance, and not pass sentence on them. (5) [He is] also [saying it] because he knows that certain persons will blasphemously attack the Holy Spirit and declare that he is in a menial position and a creature, and is different from God's essence. (6) And so he said, as a precaution, "He that blasphemeth against the Holy Spirit, it shall not be forgiven him here or in the world to come." He is not commending his own blasphemers, but showing his foreknowledge, and his lovingkindness which assures the salvation of those who repent of their blasphemy of him. (7) For he himself says, again, "He that hath denied me before men shall be denied before my Father,"[9] and, "I will deny him,"[10] and again, "He that confesseth me I will confess before my Father."[11]

3,1　And again this same Theodotus says, "The Law too said of him, 'The Lord will raise up unto you a prophet of your brethren, like unto me; hearken to him.'[12] But Moses was a man. Therefore the Christ whom God raised up was this individual, but [still] a man. For he was descended from them, just as Moses was a man."

---

[7] John 8:40
[8] Matt. 12:31–32
[9] Matt. 10:33
[10] Matt. 10:33
[11] Matt. 10:32
[12] Deut. 18:15

3,2 Because of his lapse into transgression Theodotus has no understanding of the way in which each text has its safeguard. (3) The Lord raised Christ "from among his brethren" in the sense that he was born of Mary, as the scripture says, "Behold, the Virgin shall conceive and bear a son."[13] While still remaining a virgin "she shall conceive"—not from a man's seed—"and bear a *Son*;" it is plain that the Virgin's offspring was born in the flesh. But "They shall call his name Emmanuel which being interpreted, is God with us."[14] (4) For he is God and man: God, begotten of the Father without beginning and not in time; but because of the incarnation, man, born of Mary.

3,5 Next Theodotus says, "And the Gospel itself said to Mary, 'The Spirit of the Lord shall come upon thee;'[15] It did not say, 'The Spirit of the Lord shall enter into thee.'" (6) The stupid man is thus deprived of the truth from sheer contentiousness. For the scripture is protecting our salvation in every way. To show that the Trinity is altogether and entirely co-existent and co-operant, and make sure that no one will echo the evil allegations which many make (7) and separate the Holy Spirit from Christ and < the > Father, the angel says to Mary, "The Holy Ghost shall come upon thee and the power of the highest shall overshadow thee," and afterwards, "Therefore also that which is born of thee shall be called holy, the Son of God."

3,8 And he did not say merely, "that which is born," but, "*therefore also* that which is born < [shall be] holy >,"[16] to show that < the > divine Word from above also entered the womb and formed his own human nature in his image as he pleased. And because of his human nature which he provided for our salvation, the scripture adds, "Therefore also *that which is born of thee* shall be called holy, the Son of God." (9) For if the angel had said, "The Holy Spirit shall enter into thee," it would not be possible to think that the Son of God had come in the flesh, but [instead] that the Holy Spirit had come in the flesh.

3,10 But since he is the Word come from on high, John said, to clarify the angel's words in the Gospel, "In the beginning was the Word, and the Word was with God, and the Word was God. All things were made by him, and without him was not anything

---

[13] Isa. 7:14
[14] Matt. 1:23
[15] Luke 1:35 Hippolytus reports that Theodotus taught the Virgin Birth, Haer. 10.23.1.
[16] Klostermann: < ἅγιον >

made."[17] (11) Then, after this, "And the Word was made flesh."[18]
And he did not say, "The Spirit was made flesh;" nor did he say,
"Christ was born as a man." (12) On its guard at every turn, the
sacred scripture knows him as God and man: God come from God
on high, man born of Mary without a man's seed. Whoever departs
from these two truths is not of the truth.

4,1 The wretched Theodotus makes another allegation and says,
"Jeremiah too said of him, 'He is a *man*, and who will know him?'"[19]
(2) Because < he > had estranged himself from the truth < he >
did not know that each verse, as I said, has its own force of interpretation. One who is a man is surely known by many acquaintances—I mean by his father and mother, brothers and kin, friends
and neighbors, fellow townsmen, household servants. (3) But here,
to describe the marvel of Christ's whole work, the scripture called
him "man" because of the incarnation, but gave token of his
incomprehensible Godhead by saying, "Who will know him?" (4)
For since "No man knoweth the Son save the Father, neither knoweth
any man the Father save the Son, and he to whomsoever the Son
will reveal him,"[20] no one will know Christ unless < Christ himself >
reveals it to him. (5) But by the Holy Spirit he reveals his own and
his Father's Godhead and glory to his servants, and his eternal life to
come, his mysteries, his teaching, and his true advent in the flesh for
our sakes; for he is God from on high, and man from Mary.

5,1 Theodotus says next, "Isaiah too called him a man, for he
said, 'A *man* acquainted with the bearing of infirmity; and we knew
him afflicted with blows and abuse, and he was despised and not
esteemed.'"[21] (2) But the oaf does not know that he is confuted
once again. In that very passage Isaiah said the following: "He was
brought as a lamb to the slaughter, and as a lamb before its shearer
is dumb so he opened not his mouth. In his humiliation his judgment
was taken away"[22]—(3) then he says, "Who can declare his generation, for his life is taken from men?"[23] And he didn't say, "His
life was taken < from > *him*," but, "from *men*." (4) For the Word
is forever living and in being, has life of himself, and gives life
to those who love him. His life was taken *from men*, but < as God
he lives* > and is life of himself. For "The Word is living,"[24] and

---

[17] John 1:1; 3
[18] John 1:14
[19] Jer. 17:8
[20] Matt. 11:27
[21] Isa. 53:3
[22] Isa. 53:7–8a
[23] Cf. Isa. 53:6b
[24] Heb. 4:12

provides life to all who have hoped in him.

5,5   And "Who can declare his generation?" < cannot apply to a man* >. If he were a mere man born of Mary, it would be easy to declare his generation. But since he is before David, < and > before Abraham—he says, (6) "Your father Abraham desired to see my day, and he saw it and was glad."[26] And then, when they said in astonishment, "Thou art not yet fifty years old, and hast thou see Abraham?"[27] to refute Theodotus and the unbelieving Jews who deny God he said, "Verily, verily I say unto you, before Abraham, I am."[28] (7) For he was indeed before Abraham, and before Noah, Adam, the world, heaven, the time of the universe, and the time of all creatures, for he is not in time. (8) And this is why, through Isaiah, he is declared incomprehensible by the Holy Spirit: "Who can declare his generation? For his life is taken from the earth."[29]

5,9   Theodotus, however, says, "The holy apostles called him 'a *man* approved among you by signs and wonders;'[30] and they did not say, 'God approved.'" (10) But Theodotus, you are foiled again. On the contrary, the same apostles [said that he was God] in the same Acts, as the blessed Stephen said, "Behold, I see heaven open, and the Son of Man standing on the right hand of God."[31]

6,1   His next allegation is that "The apostle called him the mediator between God and man, the *man* Christ Jesus.'"[32] (2) And he does not realize how he is attacking himself once more. The apostle who said, "mediator between God and man, < the man > Christ Jesus," clarified this himself by saying, "declared to be the Son of God with power, according to the Spirit of holiness, by the resurrection from the dead, our Lord Jesus Christ;"[33] and again, "made of a woman, made under the Law."[34] (3) And to confirm these statements he says, "If there be that are called gods many and lords many, yet to us there is one God, of whom are all things, and one Lord Jesus Christ, by whom are all things < and we for him >."[35] (4) But if "All things are by him and we are for him," the Only-begotten cannot be a mere man < who dates > from Mary, or the product of a man's seed. If he was a mere man, how could

---

[26] Cf. John 8:56 and Matt. 13:17.
[27] John 8:57
[28] John 8:58
[29] Isa. 53:6b
[30] Acts 2:22
[31] Acts 7:56
[32] 1 Tim. 2:5
[33] Rom. 1:4
[34] Gal. 4:4
[35] 1 Cor. 8:5–6

all things be by him when, as you say, they were before him? Or how could all things be for him, when they were known and made before him? And Theodotus' foolishness fails completely.

6,5 During the debate itself I have both said what I know of Theodotus, and given the refutation of each of his arguments. In the manner of the series I shall pass him by as though, with the hope and faith of the truth, I had struck and demolished part of a still wriggling snake. Let me investigate the rest, and hurry on to inspect the sects in their brutal savagery.

Against Melchizedekians.[1] 35, but 55 of the series.

1,1 In turn, others call themselves Melchizedekians; they may be an offshoot of the group who are known as Theodotians. (2) They honor the Melchizedek who is mentioned in the scriptures and regard him as a sort of great power.[2] He is on high in places which cannot be named, and in < fact > is not just a power; indeed, they claim in their error that he is greater than Christ.[3] (3) Based, if you please, on the literal wording of, "Thou art a priest forever *after the order* of Melchizedek,"[4] they believe that Christ has merely come and been given the order of Melchizedek. Christ is thus younger than Melchizedek, they say. For if his place were not somehow second in line,[5] he would have no need of Melchizedek's rank.

1,4 Of Melchizedek himself they say that he < has come into being > "without father, without mother, without lineage"—[6] as they would like to show from St. Paul's Epistle to the Hebrews. (5) They also fabricate spurious books for their own deception.

1,6 Their refutation comes from the texts themselves. When David prophesies that the Lord will be a priest after the order of Melchizedek, the sacred scripture is saying in the same breath that

---

[1] The Qumran Melchizedek fragments (11QMelch), 2 Enoch 71–72, Pistis Sophia, and the Nag Hammadi tractate Melchizedek (CG IX,*1*) all witness to the importance of Melchizedek in many ancient circles. Patristic parallels on the Melchizedekian heresy, independent of Epiphanius, are Eus. H. E. 5.28.8–10; Hippol. Haer. 7.36; Ps.-Tert. 8; Jer. Ep. 73. Cf. Pan 67,7.

[2] In Pistis Sophia the heavenly Melchizedek is the "paralemptor of the light," whose function is to restore the imprisoned light to the treasury of light and assist in the rescue of worthy souls, PS 34–36; 194–195; 197; 291; 324–326; 333–334; 363. NHL Melchizedek implies a heavenly origin of Melchizedek, 6,16–19. At "QMelch Melchizedek conducts the last judgment, and is termed "el."

[3] Hippol. Haer. 7.36; Ps.-Tert. 8

[4] Ps. 109:4

[5] The translation is problematic.

[6] Heb. 7:3

Christ will be a priest. (7) But we find that < Paul > says at once, "Made like unto the Son of God, [Melchizedek] abideth a priest continually."[7] Now if he is made *like* the Son of God, he is not *equal* to the Son of God. How can the servant be the master's equal? (8) For Melchizedek was a man. "Without father, without mother," is not said because he had no father or mother, but because his father and mother are not explicitly named in the sacred scripture.

1,9   The profundities and glories of the sacred scripture, which are beyond human understanding, have confused many. The natives of Petra in Arabia, which is called Rokom and Edom, were in awe of Moses because of his miracles, and at one time they made an image of him, and † mistakenly undertook[8] to worship it. They had no true cause for this, but in their ignorance their error drew an imaginary inference from something real. (10) And in Sebasteia, which was once called Samaria, they have declared Jephthah's daughter a goddess, and still hold a festival in her honor every year. (11) Similarly, these people have heard the glorious, wise words of the scripture and changed them to stupidity. With over-inflated pride they have abandoned the way of the truth, and will be shown to have fabricated stories of their own invention.

2,1   In fact Melchizedek's father and mother are mentioned by some authors, though this is not based on the canonical, covenanted scriptures. Still, some have said that his father was a man called Heracles, and his mother was Astarth, the same as Astoriane. He was the son of one of the inhabitants of the country at that time, who lived in the plain of Save. (2) And the city was called Salem, and various authors have given different accounts of it. Some say that it is the city now known as Jerusalem, though it was once called Jebus. But others have said that there was another Salem in the plain of Sicimi, opposite the town which is now called Neapolis.

2,3   But whether it was the one location or the other—the places are not far apart—in any case the passage tells what happened. It says, "He brought forth bread and wine for Abraham, and at that time he was the priest of God Most High."[9] And he blessed Abraham, and took a tithe from him. (4) For the priest of God Most High had to be honored by a servant of God, and—since the circumcised priesthood would stem from Abraham himself— Abraham had to offer first to the priest who served without cir-

---

[7] Heb. 7:3
[8] Holl: ἐπεχείρουν; MSS: προσεκύνουν
[9] Cf. Gen. 10:18.

cumcision, so that "Every high thing that exalteth itself against the knowledge of God"[10] would be humbled. (5) Thus the circumcised, who boast of priesthood, could not dispute the priesthood of God's holy church, which observes neither bodily circumcision nor the absence of it, but possesses the greater and more perfect circumcision, the laver of regeneration.

2,6   For if Abraham offered a tithe to Melchizedek but Abraham's descendants offer it to Aaron and Levi, and next, after the priesthood had become circumcised through Aaron and his sons, the scripture says through David that the priesthood is vested in Melchizedek—says this twelve generations after Levi's birth and after seven generations from the succession of Aaron—it has shown that the priestly rank does not remain with the ancient circumcised priesthood. (7) It was transferred to [a priesthood] before Levi and before Aaron, the priesthood after the order of Melchizedek, which now, since the Lord's incarnation, resides in the church. The seed is no longer chosen [for priesthood] because of a succession; a type is looked for, because of virtue.

3,1   For the first uncircumcised priesthood is reckoned through Abel; after that, moreover, through Noah. But a third [such priesthood] is reckoned through Melchizedek, who did not serve God by circumcision but by perfect righteousness and virtue, and with body uncircumcised. (2) And that Melchizedek was a man, God's holy apostle himself will show in his epistle. For he says, "He whose descent is not counted *from them* received tithes of the patriarch."[11] It is plain that his descent is not traced *from them*, but from others.

3,3   And of how many others is the ancestry not expressly given? Daniel, Shadrach, Meshach, Abednego, Elijah the Tishbite—neither their fathers nor their mothers are found anywhere in any of the covenanted scriptures. But so that no error arises from this, it will do no harm to say what I have learned from tradition myself. (4) For I have found that Daniel's father was a man called Sabaan. And I have likewise actually found Elijah's lineage, and shall trace it in order: (5) Elijah the Tishbite was the brother of Jehoiada the priest. He too was of priestly descent, if you please, and was the son of Ahinaam. But Ahinaam was the son of Zadok, and Zadok the son of Ahitub the son of Amoriah. Amoriah was the son of Razaza, Razaza of Ahaziah, and Ahaziah of Phineas. Phineas was the son of Eleazar, and Eleazar was the son of Aaron, plainly Aaron

---

[10] 2 Cor. 10:5
[11] 2 Cor. 10:5
[12] Cf. 1 Chron. 6:3–5.

the [high]-priest. Aaron was the son of Cohath, Cohath of Levi, and Levi was the third son of Jacob. But Jacob was the brother of Esau and the son of Isaac, and Isaac was the son of Abraham.

3,6   But the genealogies of these persons are by no means plainly set forth in the canonical scriptures—just parts of the subject as it pertains to Elijah, in Chronicles.[12] However I have simply not found the fathers of the three children, Shadrach, Meshach and Abednego, either in traditions or in apocryphal works. (7) What about that? Will they too—Shadrach, Meshach and Abednego— delude us into drawing wrong inferences, wondering far too much about each [one's] lineage, and concluding that they have no fathers and mothers? Let's hope not! (8) Apostolic traditions, holy scriptures and successions of teachers have been made our boundaries and foundations for the upbuilding of our faith,[13] and God's truth has been protected in every way. No one need be deceived by worthless stories.

4,1   But to return to the subject, the things they imagine about Melchizedek. It is plain that this righteous man was holy, a priest of God, and the king of Salem, but he was no part of the < order > in heaven, and has not come down from heaven. (2) "No man hath ascended up to heaven save he that came down from heaven, the Son of Man,"[14] says the holy divine Word who tells no lies.

4,3   For when the sacred scripture proclaimed, and the Holy Spirit expressly taught, the order of Melchizedek, they indicated the removal of the priesthood from the ancient synagogue and the < physical* > nation to a nation which is the finest and best, and which is not united by a common physical descent. (4) For this holy Melchizedek had no successors, but neither did he have his priesthood abolished. He remained a priest himself throughout his life and is still celebrated as a priest in the scripture, since no one either succeeded him, or abolished the priesthood during the time of his service. (5) So our Lord—though he was not a man but the holy divine Word of God, God's Son begotten without beginning and not in time, and was with the Father but became man for our sakes, of Mary and not of a man's seed—our Lord took the clay from his manhood, < received* > the priesthood, and makes his offering to the Father. He had taken his substance from man so as to be made a priest for us after the order of Melchizedek, which has no succession. (6) For he abides forever to offer gifts for us—after first offering himself by the cross, to abolish every

---

[13] καὶ οἰκοδομή Holl: εἰς οἰκοδομήν: Codex Urbinas, Codex Marcianus, Delahaye
[14] John 3:13

sacrifice of the old covenant by presenting the more perfect, living sacrifice for the whole world. (7) He himself is temple, sacrifice, priest, altar, God, man, king, high-priest, lamb, sacrificial victim— become all in all for us that life may be ours in every way, and to lay the changeless foundation of his priesthood forever, no longer allotting it by descent and succession, but granting that, in accordance with his ordinance, it may be preserved in the Holy Spirit.

5,1 Others in their turn imagine and say < other things > about this Melchizedek. (Since they lack a spiritual understanding of the things the holy apostle said in this same Epistle to the Hebrews, they have been condemned by a fleshly sentence.) (2) The Egyptian heresiarch Hieracas believes that Melchizedek is the Holy Spirit[15] because of "made like unto the Son of God he abideth a priest continually,"[16] (3) as though this is to be interpreted by the holy apostle's "*The Spirit* maketh intercession for us with groanings that cannot be uttered." But one who understands the Spirit's mind, knows that he intercedes for the elect with God.[17]

But Hieracas too has departed entirely from the prescribed path. (4) The Spirit never assumed flesh. And not having assumed flesh, he could not be king of Salem and priest of anywhere. (5) In time, however, when I compose the refutation of Hieracas and his sect, I shall discuss this at length; for now, I shall take up the order of presentation.

6,1 But how many other fancies others have about this Melchizedek! Samaritans believe that he is Noah's son Shem,[18] but it will be found that they too are absurd. (2) The sacred scripture, which safeguards everything with due order, has confirmed the truth in every way; not for nothing has it listed the time periods, and enumerated the years of each patriarch's life and succession.

6,3 For when Abraham was eighty-eight or even about ninety, Melchizedek met him and served him loaves and wine, prefiguring the mysteries through types: (4) types < of the Lord's body >, since our Lord < himself > says, "I am the living bread;" and of the blood which flowed from his side for the cleansing of the defiled, and the sprinkling and salvation of our souls.

---

[15] So at Jer. Ep. 73.1.1–2; also at 2.1, where Jerome attributes the idea to Origen and his follower Didymus. Cf. Chrysost. De Melch. 3; Cyr. Alex. Glaph. in Gen. 1.2.7.

[16] Heb. 7:3

[17] Rom. 8:26 and cf. 8:27.

[18] Jer. Ep. 73.5.4; Quaest. Hebraicae in Gen. 1 MSL 23, 961A; Comment Ad Isa. 41 MSL 24, 414B. At 2 En. 71–72 Melchizedek is the son of Noah's brother Nir.

6,5   Now when he became the father of Abraham, Abraham's father Terah was seventy years old, and that made about 160 years. Nahor fathered Terah at the age of seventy-nine, and that made 239 years. Serug fathered Nahor at the age of 130, and that made 369 years. (6) Reu fathered Serug when he was 132, and that came to the five hundred and first year. Peleg fathered Reu when he was 130, and that made 631 years. Eber fathered Peleg in the hundred and thirty-fourth year of his life, and that made 765 years.

6,7   Shelah fathered Eber when he was 230, and that made 895 years. Kainan fathered Salah in the hundred ninth year of his life, and that made 1004 years. Arphaxad was 135 when he fathered Kainan, and that made 1139 years. (8) And the Shem we spoke of, whom the Samaritans imagine to be Melchizedek, fathered Arphaxad in the hundred second year of his life, and altogether there were 1241 years until the time of Abraham, when he met Melchizedek on his return from the slaughter of the kings Amraphel, Arioch, Chedorlaomer and Tidal.

6,9   But Shem did not live that many years, as their foolish imagination would have it. He was 102 when he became the father of Arphaxad, in the second year after the flood. "And after that he lived 500 years," as the sacred scripture says, "and begat sons and daughters, and died."[19] (10) Now then, if he lived for 602 years and then died, how could he reach the age of 1241 so that, after ten generations and 1241 years, they can call Shem the son of Noah, who lived ten generations before Abraham, Melchizedek? How much human error there is!

6,11   But if we go by the figure in other copies, there are about 628 years from the date of Shem's birth until the time of Abraham's meeting with Melchizedek, in the eighty-eighth or ninetieth year of Abraham's life. Thus on no account can Shem have lived until Abraham's time, to be thought of as Melchizedek. And the Samaritans' jabber is likewise all wrong.

7,1   In their turn, the Jews say that Melchizedek was righteous, good and the priest of the Most High, as the sacred scripture says. But they say that his mother's name is not recorded because he was the son of a harlot, and his father is unknown. (2) But their silly assertion too has failed. Rahab was a harlot, and she is in scripture. Zimri's name is recorded although he committed fornication, and Cozbi's with his, even though she was a foreigner and not of Israelite descent. < For the Savior receives harlots, if only they repent through him* >. And as the holy Gospel said,

---

[19] Cf. Gen. 11:11.

"Whoso entereth not by the door is a thief and not a shepherd."[20]

7,3   But some who are members of the church, make various asssertions about this Melchizedek. Some suppose that he is the actual Son of God,[21] and that he appeared to Abraham then in the form of a man. (4) But they too have left the path; no one will ever become "like" himself. As the sacred scripture says, "made *like unto* the Son of God he abideth a priest continually."[22] (5) Indeed "He whose descent is not counted *of them* received tithes of Abraham;"[23] for since his descent is not counted from the Israelites themselves, it is counted from other people. (6) Since I have listed all these errors < which > come to mind because of this sect, I describe these, as though in passing.

8,1   This sect makes its offerings in Melchizedek's name, and says that it is he who gives access to God,[24] and that we must offer to God through him because he is the archon of righteousness[25] ordained in heaven by God for this very purpose, a spiritual being and appointed to God's priesthood. (2) And we must make offerings to him, they say, so that they may be offered through him on our behalf,[26] and we may attain salvation through him. (3) Christ too was chosen, they say, to summon us from many ways to this one knowledge. He was anointed by God and made his elect, for he turned us from idols and showed us the way. For this reason the apostle was sent and revealed Melchizedek's greatness to us, and that he remains a priest forever. (4) And see how great he is, and that the lesser is blessed by the greater. (5) And thus, they say, Melchizedek also blessed the patriarch Abraham, since he was greater [than Abraham]. And we are his initiates, so that we too may receive his blessing.

9,1   And how worthless all the sects' notions are! See here, these too have denied their Master who "bought them with his own blood"[27]—(2) whose existence does not date from Mary as

---

[20] John 10:1
[21] Cf. NHL Melch. 25,4–26,4, "And [you crucified me] from the third hour [of the Sabbath-eve] until [the ninth hour]. And after [these things I arose] from the dead. My body] came out of [the tomb] to me. [. . . they did not] find anyone . . . They said to me, Be [strong, O Melchizedek], great [High Priest] of God [Most High]." See also the fragmentary chapters 26 and 26, and 2 En. J 71.37, where Christ seems to be identified with Melchizedek.
[22] Heb. 7:3
[23] Heb. 7:6
[24] Perhaps cf. note 2.
[25] ἄρχων ἐστὶ ὁικαιοσύνης. At 2 En. J 71.29 Melchizedek is "the priest to all holy priests, the head of the priests of the future."
[26] For a comparable idea about offering see Pan. 26,9.7.
[27] Cf. Rev. 5:9.

they suppose, but who, as every scripture says, is the divine Word ever with the Father and begotten of the Father, without beginning and not in time. It was to him, not to Melchizedek, that the Father said, "Let us make man in our image and after our likeness."[28]

9,3 For even though Melchizedek was priest of God Most High in his own generation and had no successors, he did not come down from heaven. (4) The scripture said, not that he brought bread and wine *down*, but that he brought them *out*, as though from his palace,[29] to Abraham and his companions, when he † received[30] the patriarch as he passed through the country. And he blessed Abraham for his righteousness, faithfulness and piety. (5) For though the patriarch had been tried in everything, in nothing had he lost his righteousness, but here too he had God's assistance against the kings who had attacked Sodom † like bandits[31] and carried off his nephew, the holy Lot. And he brought him back, with all the booty and spoil.

9,6 Where can we not find proof that < the > Son was always with the Father? For "In the beginning was the Word, and the Word was with God, and the Word was God;"[32] it did not say, "In the beginning was Melchizedek," or, "And Melchizedek was God." (7) And again, "The Lord came to Abraham, and the Lord rained fire and brimstone from the Lord upon Sodom and Gomorrah."[33] And the apostle himself said, "One God, of whom are all things, and one Lord Jesus Christ, by whom are all things."[34]

9,8 And lest someone says, "Well then, where is the Spirit, since he speaks of 'one' and 'one'?"—the Spirit shouldn't be the one to commend himself.[35] The sacred scripture is always preserved to be an example for us. The apostle spoke *in the Holy Spirit* and said, "One God, of whom are all things, and one Lord Jesus Christ, by whom are all things." He was saying this *in the Holy Spirit*; his point is not to make the Trinity deficient. (9) But the Lord himself plainly says, "Go baptize all nations in the name of the Father and of the Son and of the Holy Spirit."[36] And the apostle says in his

---

[28] Gen. 1:26

[29] Klostermann: βασιλείων; MSS, Holl: βασιλέων

[30] Klostermann, Codex Marcianus: ἀποδεξάμενος; Holl and other MSS: ἀποδεξόμενος

[31] Holl: λῃστρικῶς; MSS: ἀληθῶς

[32] John 1:1

[33] Gen. 19:24

[34] 1 Cor. 8:6

[35] I.e, as the Speaker in the scriptures (see below) the Holy Spirit should not expressly commend himself, since this would be a bad example to humankind. Cf. 57,5,8.

[36] Matt. 28:19

turn, "One is the Spirit, dividing to every man as he will to profit withal."[37]

9,10   See, then, the Father! See, the Son! See, the Holy Spirit— and nowhere does it say that Melchizedek † has his dwelling among the gifts or in the heights.[38] It is useless for these people to repeat the falsities and artificialities of the stumbling blocks which come to them, not from the truth but from the hissing of the dragon itself, with its ability to deceive and mislead each sect.

9,11   Again, I have heard that some, who are the furthest afield of all and are incited by further pride of intellect, have dared to resort to an unthinkable idea and arrive at a blasphemous notion, and say that this same Melchizedek is the Father of our Lord Jesus Christ. (12) What careless minds men have, and what deceived hearts, with no place for truth! Since the apostle says that Melchizedek has no father and mother and is without lineage, these people have gone wrong because of the sublimity of the expression, have < foolishly* > supposed < that what is said of Melchizedek* > corresponds with the Father of all, and have imagined a blasphemous imposture.

9,13   For because God the almighty, the Father of all, has no father, mother, beginning of days or end of life—everyone admits this—they have fallen into the foolish blasphemy of likening Melchizedek to him because the apostle has spoken of Melchizedek like that, but have not noticed the other things that are said about him. (14) For it is said of Melchizedek that "He was *priest of* God Most High."[39] Now assuming that Melchizedek is the Most High and the Father, then, as the priest of another "Most High," he cannot be the Father of all himself. He serves another Most High as priest.

9,15   Such confusion on people's part, that will not perceive truth but is bent on error! To give the final solution of the entire problem, the holy apostle said, "He whose descent is not counted from them"—obviously not; but it was counted from others— "received tithes of Abraham."[40] And again, he said, "who, *in the days of his flesh,* offered up supplications and prayers to him that was able to save him"[41]—but it is plain that < the > Father did not assume flesh.

9,16   But now that we have discussed them sufficiently too, let

---

[37] 1 Cor. 12:11; 7
[38] Holl: ἐμπολιτεύεται; MSS: δωρεῖται
[39] Gen. 14:18
[40] Heb. 7:6
[41] Heb. 5:7

us leave this sect, for we have struck it with the firm faith and its foundation, as though we had hit a mousing viper with a rock and avoided its deadly poison. For they say that the mousing viper does no immediate harm to the one it bites, but that in time it destroys his body and infects its victim with leprosy in every limb. (17) Similarly, if this heresy is < implanted* > in their minds it < does* > people no apparent < harm > when they first hear of these things. But the long-term effect of the words is to sink into their minds, raise questions, and, as it were, cause the destruction of those who have not happened on the remedy of this antidote—the refutation of this heresy, and the counter-argument to it which I have given.

9,18   The mousing viper is not readily seen; it is active at night and does its harm at that time, especially in Egypt. Thus those who do not know the beast must realize that, when I compared it with the harm that is done by this sect, I did not bring up the subject of the beast lightly, or as a slander; it does this sort of injury. (19) But I shall move on to the others next, so as to thank God for the privilege of keeping my promise in God.

Against Bardesianists.[1] 36, but 56 of the series

1,1   Their successor was a person named Bardesanes. This Bardesanes, the founder of the Bardesianist sect, was Mesopotamian and a native of the city of Edessa.[2] (2) He was the finest sort of man at first, and while his mind was sound he composed no few treatises.[3] For originally he belonged to God's holy church, and he was learned in the two languages, Greek and Syriac.[4]

1,3   At first he won over the ruler of Edessa, Abgar, a very holy and learned man, and assisted him while taking a hand in his education. He survived after Abgar's death until the time of Antoninus Caesar—not Antoninus Pius, but Antoninus Verus.[5] (4) He argued at length against fate < in reply to > the astrologer Abidas, and there are other works of his which are in accord with the godly faith.[6]

1,5   He defied Antoninus' companion Apollonius besides, by

---

[1] Other accounts of Bardesanes are found at Eus. H. E. 4.30.1; Praep. Ev. 6.9; Hippol. Haer. 7.31.1; Jer. Adv. Jov. 2.14.

[2] Hippolytus makes him an Armenian, Haer. 7.31.1; Julius Africanus, a Parthian, 29; Porphyrius, a Babylonian, De Abst. 4.17.

[3] Cf. Eus. H. E. 4.30.1.

[4] At H. E. 4.30.1 Eusebius says that Bardesanes wrote in Syriac and others translated his writings into Greek.

[5] Epiphanius means Marcus Aurelius, but the emperor under whom Bardesanes flourished would have been Caracalla or Elagabalus.

[6] Portions of the Book of the Laws of the Lands, which is apparently Bardesanes' work against astrology, seem to be preserved at Eus. Praep. Ev. 5.9.

refusing to say that he had denied his Christianity. He nearly became a martyr, and in a courageous defense of godliness replied that the wise do not fear death, which was bound to come, < he said >, even if he did not oppose the emperor. (6) And thus the man was loaded with every honor until he came to grief over the error of his own sect and became like the finest ship, which was filled with a priceless cargo and [then] wrecked beside the cliffs of its harbor, losing all its freight and occasioning the deaths of its passengers as well.

2,1 For he unfortunately fell in with Valentinians, drew this poison and tare from their unsound doctrine, and taught this heresy by introducing many first principles and emanations himself, and denying the resurrection of the dead.[7]

2,2 He uses the Law and the Prophets and the Old and the New Testaments, besides certain apocrypha. (3) But he too, like all his predecessors and successors, will be confounded because he has separated himself from the truth and, as it were, turned himself from a brightly shining lamp into soot.

2,4 I have already spoken of the resurrection of the dead in many Sects; however, it will do no harm to say a few words once more in my refutation of this man. (5) For if you accept the Old Testament, Mister, and the New Testament too, how can you not be exposed as corrupting the way of the truth and separating yourself from the Lord's true life?

2,6 For < it is plain > that the Lord himself first died for us and rose again, to become the earnest of our resurrection and the firstborn from the dead. (7) And he did not suffer simply in appearance; he was buried, and they bore his body to the grave. Joseph of Arimathea bears witness that this was no phantom or apparition, and the women who brought the unguents to the tomb, and the hundred pounds' weight of ointment. (8) The angels who appeared to the women are also witnesses that "He is risen, he is not here; why seek ye the living among the dead?"[8] (9) And they did not say that he had not died, but that he had risen— he who suffered in the flesh but lives forever in the Spirit, and who, in his native Godhead, is impassible; he who is eternally begotten of the Father on high, but in the last days was pleased to be made man of the Virgin Mary, as St. Paul testifies by saying, "made of a woman, made under the Law."[9]

---

[7] Eusebius says that Bardesanes was an ex-Valentinian who later wrote against this view, though he never abandoned it altogether, H. E. 4.30.3.

[8] Cf. Luke 24:5–6.

[9] Gal. 4:4

2,10   Haven't you yet heard the text, "This corruptible must put on incorruption, and this mortal must put on immortality?"[10] Hasn't the prophet Isaiah convinced you by saying, "And the dead shall arise, and they that are in the graves shall be raised up?"[11] And the Lord himself, by saying, "And these shall be raised to life eternal, and these to everlasting punishment?"[12]

2,11   Or don't you remember Abel's conversation with God after his death, and how it doesn't say that his soul intercedes and cries out to God, but that his blood does? But blood is not soul; the soul is in the blood. (12) For the visible blood is body, but the soul resides invisibly in the blood. And your wrong belief is completely confounded, Bardesanes, for it is demolished by the truth itself.

3,1   But since I have spoken at length on the topic of many first principles, against those who say that there are such things, I shall not make the discussion of this here a long one. As though in < passing >, however, I shall mention how the holy apostle says, "To us God the Father is one, of whom are all things and we in him; and the Lord Jesus Christ is one, by whom are all things and we by him."[13] (2) How can there be a plurality of gods and many first principles if "Our Lord Jesus Christ, by whom are all things and we by him, is one?" Thus there is one creator, not many gods or many aeons. For Paul said, "If there be many *so-called* gods;"[14] (3) but he pronounced them "so-called" as though speaking < of > beings which have no existence. But he made this declaration because of the so-called gods of the Greeks, the ones they have made gods of—the sun and moon, the stars and the like—and ruled out the notion of all who have fallen into error.

3,4   Now since the sound faith is preserved in every way as the support and the salvation of the faithful, the nonsensical inventions of all the sects have been overthrown. So has Bardesanes, who has been overthrown, shown himself to be a pitiable object, and banished himself from life. (5) For the prophet tells God's holy church, "I will make thy stone a coal of fire, and thy foundations sapphire, and thy walls precious stones, and thy battlements jasper."[15] Then, afterwards, he says, "Every voice that rises up against thee, thou shalt overcome them all. Against thee it shall

---

[10] 1 Cor. 15:53
[11] Isa. 26:19
[12] Cf. Matt. 25:46.
[13] 1 Cor. 8:6
[14] 1 Cor. 8:5
[15] Isa. 54:11–12

not prevail."[16] (6) Nothing will prevail against the true faith, since "She is founded on the rock," and, as her king, bridegroom, Lord and Master, the holy divine Word, has promised her, "The gates of hell shall not prevail against her."[17] To him, the Father in the Son with the Holy Spirit, be glory, honor and might forever and ever. Amen.

3,7 But since this sect too has been trampled underfoot, < let it lie* >, struck by the wood of life, like a head [cut off] from a piece of a snake and still wriggling. < But > let us ourselves give thanks to God, beloved, and proceed once more to the examination of the rest.

Against Noetians.[1] 37, but 57 of the series.

1,1 Another one, whose name was Noetus, arose in his turn after Bardesanes, though not many years ago; it was about 130 years before our time.[2] Noetus was Asian, and a native of the city of Ephesus.[3] (2)[4] By the inspiration of a strange spirit, he chose to say and teach things on his own authority which neither the prophets nor the apostles < had proclaimed >, and which the church from the beginning had neither held nor conceived of. On his own authority he dared to say, with manic elation, that the Father suffered. (3) But from further delusion and derangement he called himself Moses, and his brother, Aaron.[5]

1,4 In the meantime, however, the blessed presbyters of the church sent for Noetus because of the rumor about him, and questioned him about all these things, and whether he had advanced this blasphemy of the Father.[6] (5) At his appearance before the presbytery he at first denied it, since no one before him had belched out this frightful, deadly bitterness. (6) But later, after infecting certain others, as it were, with his madness and winning about ten men over, he was inspired to greater pride and insolence < and > finally grew bold enough to teach his heresy openly. (7) The

---

[16] Cf. Isa. 54:17.
[17] Matt. 16:18

[1] Epiphanius' source for this Sect is Hippolytus' tractate, Contra Noetum. Noetus is also discussed at Filast. Haer. 53; Hippol. Haer. 9.2.7–10; 10.27.
[2] "Not many years ago" comes from Hippol. C. Noet. 1; Epiphanius has inserted the rest.
[3] Hippol C. Noet. 1; Filast. Haer. 53
[4] 1,2 is paraphrased from Hippol C. Noet. 1.
[5] Cf. Hippol. C. Noet. 1; Filast. Haer. 53.
[6] Noetus' examination before the "blessed presbyters"—terminology which

same presbyters summoned him once more, and the men who unfortunately had become acquainted with him, and asked again about the same things. (8) But now, with his followers in error, Noetus struck his forehead and openly opposed them. "What wrong have I done," he demanded, "because I glorify one God?[7] I know one God and none other besides him, and he has been born, has suffered, and has died!"[8]

1,9　Since he held to this they expelled him from the church, with the men he had instructed in his own doctrine. He himself has died recently (sic!) as has his brother, but not in glory like Moses; nor was his brother buried with honor like Aaron. They were cast out as transgressors, and none of the godly would lay them out for burial.

1,10　Those whose minds he had corrupted confirmed this doctrine afterwards under the influence of the following texts, which had influenced their false teacher to begin with. (11)[9] For when he said under questioning by the presbytery that he glorified one God, they told him truthfully, "We too glorify one God, but in the way we know is right. (12) And we hold that Christ is one, but as we know the one Christ—the Son of God who suffered as he suffered, died as he died, has risen, has ascended into heaven, is at the right hand of the Father, will come to judge the quick and dead. We say these things because we have learned them from the sacred scriptures, which we also know."

2,1[10]　Those who are offshoots of Noetus himself, and those who derive from them, make much of this doctrine, and try to establish their insane teaching from the following texts. Among them are God's words to Moses, "I am the God of your fathers. I am the first and I am the last. Thou shalt have none other gods," and so on.[11] (2) They said accordingly, "We therefore know him alone. If Christ came and was born, he himself is the Father; he himself is the Son. Thus the same God is the God who < is > forever, and who has now come—(3) as the scripture says, 'This is thy God, none other shall be accounted God besides him. He hath found out every way of understanding and given it to Jacob his servant and Israel his beloved. Afterwards he appeared on earth

would have been archaic in Epiphanius' day—comes from Hippol. C. Noet. 1.
　　[7] With all of this cf. Hippol. C. Noet. 1.
　　[8] The formula, and the excommunication of Noetus, are taken from Hippol. C. Noet. 1.
　　[9] 1,11–12 closely follow Hippol C. Noet. 2.
　　[10] 2,1–3 closely follow Hippol. C. Noet. 2.
　　[11] Cf. Exod. 3:6; Isa. 44:6; Exod. 20:3.

and consorted with men.'[12] (4) Again," they say, "do you see how, by saying that God himself is < the > only God and appeared later himself, the sacred scriptures give us the wisdom not to believe first in one God and then in another?"

2,5[13] Again, they employ this further text: "Egypt hath wearied and the merchandise of the Ethiopians, and the lofty men of Saba shall pass over unto thee and be thy servants. And they shall walk behind thee bound with chains, and shall bow down to thee and pray through thee—for in thee is God and there is no God beside thee—Thou art God and we knew it not, O God of Israel, the Savior."[14] (6) "Do you see," they say, "how the sacred scriptures state that God is one, and declare that he < has become > visible? And he is admittedly one, forever the same. (7) We therefore say that there are not many gods but one God, the same Impassible, himself the Father of the Son and himself the Son, who has suffered to save us by his suffering. And we cannot say that there is another"—because, if you please, they have learned this confession of faith, and this impious conjecture and ruinous madness, from their master.

2,8[15] Next they cite other texts in support of their position— as their teacher said, "The apostle also bears witness in the following words and says, 'Whose are the fathers, of whom as concerning the flesh Christ came, who is over all, God blessed for evermore. Amen.'"[16] (9) But their account [of Christ] is as one-sided as Theodotus'. Theodotus actually went to one extreme and described him as a mere man. Noetus has one-sidedly described another extreme in his own turn, with his belief that the same God the Father is both the Son and the Holy Spirit, and that he has suffered in the flesh, and been born. (10) Theodotus' followers have not told the truth, then, and neither have this "Brainy" (Νόητος)—"Brainless," (Ἀνόητος) actually—and his followers, since the sacred scriptures refute them both, and all the erring.

3,1 To anyone whose mind is < sound* > in God, and who is enlightened in sacred scripture and the Holy Spirit, their argument will seem easily refutable and full of all sorts of nonsense. (2) The attitude which says that the Father, the Son, and the One who suffered are the same, is the result of impudence and is < full >

---

[12] Baruch 3:36–38
[13] 2,5–7a closely follow Hippol. C. Noet. 2–3.
[14] Isa. 45:14–15
[15] 2,8–10 closely follows Hippol. C. Noet. 2–3.
[16] Rom. 9:5
[17] The first half of this sentence is paraphrased from Hippol. C. Noet. 3.

of blindness;[17] and those who say such things will be judged by right and sound reason. (3) How can the same person be father and son [at once]? If he is a son he must be the son of someone, by whom he was begotten. (4) But if he is a father, he cannot possibly beget himself. And if it is called a son it didn't beget itself; it was begotten by a father. How crazy people are, with their impossible reasoning! (5) For the fact is that the logical conclusion is not as they suppose, but as the truth tells us through the sacred scripture. The Lord states it at once by saying, "Lo, my beloved Son shall understand, he whom I have chosen, whom my soul hath loved. I will put my Spirit upon him."[18] (6) And you see how the Father's voice declares that there is an actual Son upon whom he puts his Spirit. (7) Next the Only-begotten himself says, "Glorify thou me, Father, with the glory which I had with thee before the world was."[19] But someone who says, "Father, glorify me," is not calling himself father; he knows that the "father" is his father. (8) And again, in another passage, "There came a voice from heaven, This is my Son; hear ye him."[20] And it did not say, "I am my Son, hear me," or again, "I have become a Son," but, "This is my Son; hear him."

3,9   And when he said, "I and the Father are one,"[21] he did not say, "I and the Father *am* one," but, "I and the Father *are* one."[22] "I and the Father," with the definite article, and with "and" in the middle, means that the Father is actually a father, and the Son actually a son.

4,1   And of the Holy Spirit he says in turn, "If I depart he shall come, the Spirit of truth."[23] This statement, "*I* am going and *he* is coming," is by far the clearest. Christ did not say, "*I* am going and *I* shall come." He showed with "I" and "he" that the Son is an entity and the Holy Spirit is an entity. (2) And again, "The Spirit of truth which proceedeth from the Father and receiveth of the Son"[24] is intended to show that the Father is an entity, the Son is an entity, and the Holy Spirit is an entity. (3) And again, at the Jordan the Father spoke from above, the Son stepped into the Jordan, and the Spirit appeared between them in the form of a dove and came upon the Son, even though the Spirit has not taken flesh or assumed a body. (4) But to avoid giving the impression

---

[18] Cf. Isa. 42:1; Matt. 12:18.
[19] John 17:5
[20] Matt. 17:5
[21] John 10:30
[22] Hippolytus uses this argument at C. Noet. 9.
[23] Cf. John 16:7; 3.
[24] John 15:26; 16:13; 14

that the Spirit is identical with the Son, the Holy Spirit is represented in the form of a dove, so that the Spirit is seen as truly an entity. (5) But where else can I not find other arguments against these people who have infected themselves with insanity? If there is any truth in their notion, and in their worthless argument with no proof or force and no coherent reasoning or meaning, the scriptures will have to be discarded.[25] For on every page they know the Father as a father, the Son as a son, and the Holy Spirit as a holy spirit.

4,6   But what are you talking about, Mister? Are the true worshipers of the Trinity, the sons of the truth and the only apostolic and catholic church, polytheists? No way! (7) Who will not say that the God of truth is one, the Father almighty, the Source of the Only-begotten Son who is truly the divine Word, a Word subsistent, truly begotten of the Father without beginning and not in time? Hence the church proclaims with certainty that God is one, a Father and a Son: (8) "I am in the Father, and the Father in me, and we two are one"[26]—that is, one Godhead, one will, and one dominion.

4,9   From the Father himself the Spirit also proceeds—subsistent and truly perfect, the Spirit of truth, who enlightens all, who receives of the Son, the Spirit of the Father, the Spirit of Christ. (10) The church, then, knows one Godhead. There is one God, the Father of truth, a Father who is perfect and an entity; and a Son who is a perfect Son and an entity; and a Holy Spirit who is a perfect Holy Spirit and an entity—one Godhead, one sovereignty, one dominion. (11) Thus the sacred scriptures have everywhere plainly declared that God is one—that is, a co-essential Trinity, forever of the same Godhead, the same dominion.

4,12   And your brainless argument has completely collapsed, Brainy! And now that this has been said, and in direct contradiction to Brainy's allegations, it is time to examine these from the beginning and to counter his propositions, as follows.[27]

5,1   First, since he advanced the proposition, "'God is one, of whom are all things and we in him, and the Lord Jesus Christ is one, for whom are all things and we by him,'"[28] don't you see how, to avoid directing our attention to many first principles and a plurality of gods and leading the erring human mind back to the

---

[25] ἀποβλητέαι, not an Epiphanian word. Epiphanius is paraphrasing Hippol. C. Noet. 3.

[26] John 14:10; 10:30

[27] This transition is paraphrased from Hippol. C. Noet. 3.

[28] 1 Cor. 8:6

nonsense of polytheism, Paul points out the oneness of the first principle by saying, "God is one, of whom are all things and we for him?"[29] (2) For do you see how he has used one name and one title, but without denying the Only-begotten God? For he knows that he is Lord and knows that he is God; and he says, to certify this, 'And one *Lord* Jesus Christ, by whom are all things.'"

5,3 However, by saying this of the Lord he did not mean that the Father and the Son are the same, but showed that the Father is truly a father and the Son truly a son. (4) For when he said "one God" of the Father, < he did > not < say it > to deny the Godhead of the Son. (For if the Son is not God he is not "Lord" either; but as he is "Lord," he is also God.) Though the holy apostle was compelled by the Holy Spirit to refer to one title, he explained the faith for us by stating clearly that Christ is "one Lord," and so must surely be God.

5,5 But because he says, "one," and [then] "one" [again, but does not say "one" a third time], no one need think that he has left the number of the Trinity unmentioned by failing to name the Holy Spirit. When he named the Father and the Son "God" and "Lord," he named them *in* the Holy Spirit. (6) For by saying, "*God* is one, of whom are all things," of the Father, he did not deny the Father's Lordship; nor, again, did he deny Christ's Godhead by saying, "and one *Lord* Jesus Christ." (7) As he was content with the one title in the Father's case, and said "one God" although it is plain that "Lord" is implied by "God"—so, in the case of the Son, he was content with "one Lord," but "God" is implied by "Lord." (8) Thus he did not jettison the Holy Spirit by mentioning [only] "Father" and "Son;" as I said, he spoke *in* the Holy Spirit. The Holy Spirit never < speaks* > in commendation of himself, or he might set us an example < of speaking* > of ourselves and commending < ourselves >. (9) Thus "God the Father, of whom are all things, is one, and the Lord Jesus Christ, by whom are all things, is one." And the Holy Spirit is one, not different from God and still an entity, because he is Spirit of God, Spirit of truth, Spirit of the Father, and Spirit of Christ.

6,1[30] But I suppose we also need to speak of "Egypt hath wearied, and the merchandise of the Ethiopians. And the lofty men of Saba shall pass over unto thee and be thy servants. They shall walk behind thee, bound with chains. They shall bow down to thee and pray through thee—for in thee is God and there is no God

---

[29] 1 Cor. 8:6
[30] 6,1–2 closely follow Hippol. C. Noet. 4.

beside thee—For thou art God and we knew it not, O God, the God of Israel, the Savior."[31] (2) Noetus will say, "From the many texts I've shown you, don't you see that God is one?" But not understanding what has been said, he villainously mutilates the scriptures, interprets ambiguous texts, cites the lines out of sequence and does not quote them consistently and exactly—he or the Noetians who stem from him—or expound them in order. (3) As some < will name > a bad dog "Leo," call the totally blind keen-sighted, and say that gall is candy—and as some have termed vinegar honey, and some have named the Furies the Eumenides—so it is with this man and his followers. (4) He has been named Brainy, but he is brainless and his followers have no brains, and he has no idea of the consequences of his statements and their propositions. The holy apostle's words, "Understanding neither what they say nor whereof they affirm,"[32] are applicable to them.

7,1[33] For you see what the sacred scriptures said earlier on, brothers, or rather, what the Lord himself says, as we read at the beginning of the passage. It is from this that we must explain the whole of the truth in the passage itself, and the whole of the subject of it. We read, (2) "Inquire of me concerning my sons and my daughters, and < concerning > the works of my hands command ye me. I made the earth and man upon it; with my hand I stablished the heavens. I gave commandment to all the stars; I raised up a king with righteousness, and all his paths are straight. He shall build my city and restore my captivity, not with ransoms nor with gifts; the Lord of hosts hath spoken."[34] (3) Only then does he say, "Egypt hath wearied and the merchandise of the Ethiopians," and so on [until] "that God is in thee."[35]

7,4 But in whom, should we say? In whom but the Father's Word? For the divine Word is truly the Son, and the Father is known in him, as he says, "He that hath seen me hath seen the Father,"[36] and, "I have glorified thy name on the earth."[37]

7,5[38] Then again, "I have raised up a king."[39] Don't you see that this is the Father's own voice, which raised up the true Word from itself to be king over all—the Word truly begotten of him, without

---

[31] Isa. 45:14–15
[32] 1 Tim. 1:7
[33] 7,1–4 closely follow Hippol C. Noet. 4.
[34] Isa. 45:11–13
[35] Isa. 45:14
[36] John 14:9, cf. Hippol. C. Noet. 4.
[37] John 17:4
[38] 7,5–7a closely follow Hippol. C. Noet. 4.
[39] Isa. 45:13

beginning and not in time? (6) And it raised him up again, this very king, as the holy apostle says, "If the Spirit of him that raised up Christ dwell in you, he that raised up Christ from the dead shall also quicken your mortal bodies."[40] (7) Thus the prophet's words agree with the apostle's, and the apostle's with the Gospels', and the Gospels' with the apostle's, and the apostle's with the prophet's; for Isaiah says, "I have raised up a king," and Paul says, "He that raiseth up Christ from the dead."

7,8[41] But the words, "God is in thee," < show > how mysteriously and marvelously the sacred scripture describes everything. The Godhead's < dwelling > in the flesh as in a temple was foreseen and foretold to the hope of mankind in its return to God. (9) For the Son of God, the divine Word who dwells as God in his holy humanity and human nature as in a sacred city and holy temple, says of this holy temple, "Destroy this temple and in three days I will raise it up."[42] (10) For < the > divine Word who has been sent from the Father in the flesh mystically reveals all things. To show a bond of spiritual love he embraced the flesh, shrinking himself despite his divine vastness—the Word himself, born of a virgin through the Holy Spirit; the Son of God who is one and has made himself one, in flesh and in spirit, as the scripture says, "He that descended is the same also as he that ascended, the Son of Man who is in heaven."[43]

8,1[44] What will Brainy say, then, in his brainlessness? Was there flesh in heaven? Obviously not. Then how can the One who descended from heaven be the same as the One who ascended? This is meant to show that the Word who has come is not from below but has descended from on high, since he was made man in the flesh, not by a man's seed but by making his complete human nature of spirit and flesh. (2) And so, to show the oneness of the union of the Word and his manhood, he said that He who came from on high has ascended on high in the perfection of Godhead. (3) For now the Word, which once was not flesh but spirit, has been made flesh of the Spirit and the Virgin—He who was offered to the Father as a perfect Word, though before this, in heaven, he was not flesh.

8,4 What was the One who was in heaven, then, but the Word who was sent from heaven? To show that he was the same divine

---

[40] Rom. 8:11
[41] 7,8–10 are freely paraphrased from Hippol. C. Noet. 4.
[42] John 2:19
[43] Cf. Eph. 4:9; John 3:13.
[44] 8,1–7 closely follow Hippol C. Noet. 4.

Word on earth and < in > heaven, changeless and unalterable, he
possessed his oneness with the one Godhead, united with it by the
Father's might. (5) For he was Word, was God forever, was spirit,
was might; and he adopted the name which was common and
comprehensible to men, and was called Son of Man,[45] though he
was Son of God. (6) And the name was mentioned beforehand
in the prophets because it would apply to him, though it was not
yet in the flesh.Thus Daniel said, "I saw one like unto a Son of
Man coming upon the clouds."[46] (7) And the prophet was right
to give the Word this name < when he was > in heaven, and call
the One he saw by the Holy Spirit Son of Man, since he scrutinized
the future before its arrival and named the Word Son of Man
before he was made flesh. (8) And thus, although he reverses the
order of events, the Only-begotten says, "No man hath ascended
up to heaven save he that came down from heaven, the Son of
Man."[47] He did not mean that he was flesh in heaven, but < that >
he descended from heaven, and was to be known by this name.

9,1[48]   But what are you going to say, Mister? "'This is our God,
and none can be accounted God besides him?'"[49] And that was
quite right! The apostle affirms it by saying, "Whose are the fathers
and of whom, according to the flesh, came Christ, who is God over
all."[50] (2) < And > he expounds it marvelously: Christ is "He Who
Is (ὁ ὤν), God over all." (ἐπὶ πάντων θεός) Since Christ teaches
us this himself by saying, "All things are delivered unto me of my
Father,"[51] this makes him God over all. (3) For John testifies to
this by saying, "*That which was from the beginning,* which we have
seen with our eyes and our hands have handled."[52] And again, in
Revelation, he says, "*he who is from the beginning* and is to come,
the Almighty."[53] He was absolutely right; for when he said, "All
things are delivered unto me of my Father," he appended < the
Father > precisely as he should have. Though he is God over all,
he has a Father of his own. And < this is evident* > when he says,
"I go unto my Father."[54] To which Father could he go, Brainless,
if he were the Father himself?

---

[45] Cf. Hippol. C. Noet. 7.
[46] Dan. 7:13
[47] John 3:13
[48] 9,1–3 closely follows Hippol. C. Noet. 5.
[49] Bar. 3:36
[50] Rom. 9:5
[51] Matt. 11:27
[52] 1 John 1:1
[53] Cf. Rev. 1:8.
[54] John 20:17

10,1[55]   Or again, he says, "That they may be one, as thou and
I are one."[56] The scripture always guards against men's falls into
extremes, and recalls their minds from all places to the middle
way of the truth. (2) To those who think that the Son is different
from the Father—I mean as Arius and other sects do—it says, "I
and the Father are one."[57] (3) But to those who think that the
Father and the Son are the same because it has said, "I and the
Father are one," the scripture says, "Make *them* to be one as I and
thou are one,"[58] shaming Noetus and his school by his reference
to the disciples' oneness. (4) For how could Peter, John and the
rest be identically one? But since he [is one with the Father] in
one unity of Godhead and in purpose and power, < he indicated
as much* >, to allay any suspicion that arises against the truth from
either standpoint. (5) And the holy apostle Philip < witnesses to
this* > by saying, "Show us the Father." And the Lord replied, "He
that hath seen me hath seen the Father."[59] But he did not say,
"*I am* the Father." (6) He meant himself when he said, "me," but
did not mean himself when he said, "hath seen the Father." "The
Father" is one thing, "me" is something else, and "I" is something
else. (7) If he himself were the Father, he would say, "I am." But
since he is not the Father himself but the Son, he truthfully says,
"He that hath seen me hath seen the Father," to refute the blasphemy of Arius, which separates the Son from the Father.

10,8   And so, since every scripture has plainly laid down our
way with regard to the truth, let us halt < here >. Along with the
other sects we have maimed Noetus and his sect, I mean of Noetians,
like the so-called agate dragon, which cannot turn either right or
left when it pursues someone. (9) < And > since we have escaped
his unsound teachings and his school's, let us focus on the rest
by the power of God, to describe and refute the heretical sayings
against the truth which they have invented.

Against Valesians.[1] *38, but 58 of the series.*

I have often heard of Valesians, but have no idea who Vales < was >,
where he came from, or what his sayings, admonitions or decla-

---

[55] 10,1–5 closely follow Hippol. C. Noet. 7.
[56] Cf. John 17:22.
[57] John 10:30
[58] Cf. John 17:21–22. Hippolytus argues against Noetus from this text at C.
Noet. 7.
[59] John 14.8–9. Hippolytus argues against Noetus from this text at C. Noet. 7.

[1] This group is mentioned only by Epiphanius. His sources are clearly oral.

rations < were >. (2) The name, which is Arabic, leads me to suppose that he and his sect are still in existence, < and I also > suspect— < for* >, as I said, < I cannot say this for certain* > —that there are some at Bacatha, in the land of Philadelphia beyond the Jordan. (3) The locals call them Gnostics, but they are not Gnostics; their ideas are different. But what I have learned about them is the following:

1,4 Most of them were members of the church until a certain time, when their foolishness became widely known and they were expelled from the church. All but a few are eunuchs, and they have the same beliefs about principalities and authorities that < the Sethians, Archontics* > and others do. (5) And when they take a man as a disciple, he does not eat meat while he is still un-castrated; but when they convince him of this, or castrate him by force, he may eat anything, because he is out of the struggle and runs no more risk of being aroused to the pleasure of lust by what he eats.

1,6 And not only do they impose this discipline on their own disciples; it is widely rumored that they have often made this disposition of strangers when they were passing through and accepted their hospitality. (7) They seize them [when they come] inside, bind them on their backs to boards, and perform the castration by force.

1,8 And this is what I have heard about them. Since I know where they live, and this name is well known in those parts and I have learned of no other name for the sect, I presume that this is it.

2,1 But these people are really crazy. If they mean to obey the Gospel's injunction, "If one of thy members offend thee, cut it off from thee. It is better for thee to enter into the kingdom of heaven halt or blind, or crippled"[2]—how can anyone be maimed in the kingdom? (2) For if the kingdom of heaven makes all things perfect, it can have no imperfection in it. And since the resurrection is a resurrection of the *body*, all the members will be raised and not one of them left behind. (3) And if any member is not raised, neither will the whole body be raised. And if just the one member that causes offense is left behind, none of the members will be raised at all, for they have all caused us to offend. (4) Who is going to tear his heart out? And yet the heart is the cause of offenses at every turn, for scripture says, "From within proceed fornication,

---

[2] Cf. Matt. 5:29–30.

adultery, uncleanness and such like."³ All right, who will tear his heart out?

2,5   But if, as some people say in their stupidity and impiety, the body is not raised, how will this Valesian rule make any difference? If none of the members enter the kingdom of heaven, what further need is there to be short one member, when other people do not do this? (6) But if the body is raised—and it is—how can there be bodily mutilation in the kingdom of heaven? How can a kingdom of heaven containing damaged bodies not be unfit for the glory of its inhabitants? (7) And if the offending member must be cut off at all, it has been cut off without having sinned! But if it has been cut off without sinning, since it didn't sin it ought to rise first of all.

3,1   But by their audacity in performing this rash act they have set themselves apart and made themselves different from everyone. Because of what has been removed they are no longer men; and they cannot be women because that is against their nature.

3,2   Besides, the crown and prize for the contest have already been designated, and these people will not appear in any of the three categories of eunuch the Lord mentions. (3) He says, "There are some eunuchs which were so born from their mother's womb."⁴ Those eunuchs are not responsible for their condition, and certainly have no sin, because they were born that way. On the other hand there is nothing to their credit either, since they cannot do < anything like that > —I mean anything sexual—because they lack the divinely created organs of generation. (4) But neither can they have the kingdom of heaven as their reward for being eunuchs, since they have no experience of the struggle. (5) Even though they have felt desires, since they lack the ability to do anything wrong, neither do they have a reward for not doing it. They haven't done the thing, not because they didn't want to but because they couldn't. This is the way of the first eunuchhoood the Lord mentions, the one that is born in eunuchhood. Because of their operation the Valesians cannot be any of these.

4,1   "And there are eunuchs," the Savior says, "which were made eunuchs of men." Valesians are none of these either. They—the eunuchs who are "made eunuchs of men"⁵—are made in the service of a king or ruler. (2) From jealousy and suspicion of their wives, some barbarian kings or despots take boys when they are only children and make eunuchs of them so that they can be entrusted

---

³ Mark 7:21–22
⁴ Matt. 19:12
⁵ Matt. 19:12

with their wives, as I said, when they are grown. (3) And this has been the usual reason for these eunuchs. I imagine that this is < the origin of > the term, "eunuch." The "eunuch" can be "well-disposed" (εὐνοῦς) because his members have been removed, and with his organs removed he cannot have sexual relations. (4) So this is another cataegory of eunuch, the kind that is taken in childhood and made eunuchs by men, but not for the kingdom of heaven's sake.

4,5 "And there be eunuchs," says the Savior, "which have made themselves eunuchs for the kingdom of heaven's sake."[6] Who can these be but the noble apostles, and the virgins and monks after them? (6) John and James, the sons of Zebedee, who remained virgin, surely did not cut their members off with their own hands, and did not contract marriage either; they engaged in the struggle in their own hearts, and admirably won the fame of the crown of this contest. (7) And all the millions after them who lived in the world without spouses and won the fame of this contest in monasteries and convents. They had no relations with women, but competed in the most perfect of contests.

4,8 So it is with Elijah in the Old Testament, and with Paul, who says, "To the unmarried I say that it is good for them if they remain even as I am; but if they cannot contain, let them marry."[7] (9) Now in what state did he "remain?" For if he was a eunuch, and his imitators remained like him in obedience to his "Remain as I"—how could a eunuch marry if he could no longer contain himself, in accordance with "Let them marry and not burn?"[8] You see that he is speaking of continence, not of the mutilation of one's members.

4,10 But if they claim to have made themselves eunuchs for the kingdom of heaven's sake, how can they distinguish themselves from [the case covered by] the text, "There are eunuchs which were made eunuchs of men?"[9] (11) For if one makes himself a eunuch with his own hands, he is a man, and his hands have done this infamous thing. And even though he could not do it himself but was made a eunuch by others, he still cannot be a eunuch "for the kingdom of heaven's sake" because he was "made a eunuch by men," whether by his own hand or the hand of others.

4,12 He will be deprived of his crown and prize as well, however, and have no further credit for abstaining from sexual relations.

---

[6] Matt. 19:12
[7] 1 Cor. 7:8–9
[8] Cf. 1 Cor. 7:9.
[9] Matt. 19:12

With the members which are needed for them removed, he cannot engage in them. (13) But for one who injures his own member, and one who cuts down another person's vineyard, the sentence is one and the same. He has not lived as God wills, but has conspired to rebel against his creator, the Lord and God.

4,14 But such a man will still feel desire. The eunuch in the sage's proverb is not exempt from desire, < but desires* > because he cannot gratify his desire, as it says, (15) "The desire of a eunuch to deflower a virgin."[10] And < their silliness has* > all < come to nothing* >. How much nonsense of all sorts has been invented in the world!

4,16 And this is what I know about them. And so, since I have spoken briefly of them and, as I said, believe that they are the ones, let us leave them behind and laugh at < them >, (17) like a two-stinged scorpion which is the opposite of its ancestors because it has horns and claws, and which, with its sting, resists the norm of God's holy church. Trampling them with firmly placed sandal— that is, with the Gospel's exact words—let us end our discussion of their foolishness here, and go on as usual to the rest.

Against the impure "Purists"[1] *(Cathari). 39, but 59 of the series*

1,1 A group called the "Purists" arose after these, founded, as it is commonly said, by one Navatus. Navatus was at Rome during the persecution before Maximian's—I believe Decius' came then, or Aurelian's. (2) Because of those who had lapsed during the persecution he, along with his followers, became proud, would not communicate with persons who had repented after persecution, and adopted this heresy by saying that such people > cannot be saved. There is one repentance, but no mercy for those who transgress after baptism.

1,3 We ourselves say that there is one repentance, and that this salvation comes through the laver of regeneration. But we do not ignore God's lovingkindness, (4) since we know the message of the truth, the Lord's mercy, nature's pardonability, the soul's fickleness, the weakness of the flesh, and how everyone's senses

---

[10] Sir. 20:4

[1] Contemporary information about the Novatian schism is found at Cyprian of Carthage, Epp. 40–51; Ep. 51 gives Cyprian's arguments against Novatian in detail. Novatian's own Epistle, Clergy of Rome/Cyprian Ep. 30, written before the schism, shows hostility to lapsi. Cf. also Eus. H. E. 6.43 (Dionysius of Alexandria); Basil of Caesarea Ep. 188, Canon 11; Ep. 190 Canon 47; Chrysost. Hom. 6 In Heb..

teem with sins. "No man is sinless and pure from spot, not if he liveth even a single day upon the earth."[2]

1,5 The decisive repentance consists of baptism; but if someone falls [afterwards] God's holy church does not lose him. She gives him a way back, and after repentance, reform. (6) For God said, "Thou hast sinned, be silent!"[3] to Cain, and the Lord told the paralytic, "Lo, thou art made whole; sin no more."[4] The Lord recalls Peter too after his denial, and in the place of the three denials, challenges him three times to confession—"Peter, lovest thou me? Peter, lovest thou me? Peter, lovest thou me?"—and says, "Feed my sheep."[5]

2,1 But the apostle's exact words are their downfall. He says, "It is impossible for those who were once enlightened, and have tasted the good word of God and the powers of the world to come, if they shall fall away, to renew them again to repentance, seeing they crucify to themselves the Son of God afresh, and put him to an open shame. (2) For the earth which drinketh in the rain that cometh oft upon it, and bringeth forth herbs meet for them by whom it is dressed, receiveth blessing. But that which beareth thorns and briers is rejected, and is nigh unto cursing; whose end is to be burned."[6] (3) And it is in fact not possible to renew those who have been renewed once and fallen away. Christ cannot be born any longer to be crucified for us, nor can anyone again crucify a still uncrucified Son of God, or receive a second baptism; there is one baptism, and one renewal. (4) But to heal the church and care for its members, the holy apostle at once prescribes the cure for them and says, "But, beloved, we are persuaded better things of you, and things that accompany salvation, though we thus speak. For God is not unrighteous to forget your good work."[7]

2,5 And you see how he has declared once and for all that there can be no second renewal; but he has not cut those who are still penitent off from salvation. Indeed, he has shown them the accompaniments to salvation, and that God is their helper because of their good works, and that he is the Lord of those who, even after transgressions, perform full penance and turn and reform.

2,6 The holy word and God's holy church always accept repentance, though not to weaken those who are finishing their

---

[2] Job 14:4–5
[3] Gen. 4:7
[4] John 5:14
[5] John 21:15; 16; 17
[6] Heb. 6:9–10
[7] Heb. 6:9–10

course, or to make them lax; still, she does not block God's grace
and lovingkindness, but knows the nature of every case. (7) For
as one who has lost his virginity cannot < recover > it physically
since nature does not permit this, so it is with one who has fallen
into major sins after baptism. (8) And as one who has fallen from
virginity has continence for a second dignity, so he who has fallen
into major sin after baptism has < reform > for a second healing—
not as virtuous as the first, but he has the second healing he has
been given, one that is not kept from salvation. God's word, then,
does not deny the reward of those who grow weary in penance.

3,1   And next, the same people go on once more from this to
invent some other doctrines. For they too say that they have the
same faith which we do, but they will not communicate with the
twice-married.[8] For if someone marries a second wife after baptism,
they never admit him again.

3,2   But this is perfectly silly. It is as though someone saw a man
swimming in the water, and plunged into the water without knowing
how to swim, and drowned because he had no experience or
understanding of the technique of those who keep afloat with their
hands and feet, but thought that the water simply buoys the man
up without his hands. (3) Or suppose that someone heard that
a ruler punishes the doers of < evil > deeds right down to the
smallest, and thought that the same penalty applies to all, so that
the punishment for murder is the same as the punishment for
someone who slanders or has a < serious* > quarrel with his neighbor.
(4) Or suppose that one were only a private citizen and saw someone
with a governor's authority to punish criminals draw his sword
against sorcerers and blasphemers, or the impious, and after seeing
people punished supposed that all are authorized to punish such
guilt and chose to mimic the same behavior and kill people himself
under the pretense of condemning malefactors. (5) But he would
be arrested and punished himself, since he had no such authority
from the emperor to do such things, and because he supposed
that the same sentence applied to all by law, thus condemning
himself to death as a wrongdoer through his own ignorance and
lack of understanding. (6) The Purists have similarly lost everything by mixing up everyone's duties. From not understanding the
exact nature of God's teaching they have mistakenly taken another
path, unaware that † this[9] is not the teaching and the following
of the sacred scripture.

---

[8] This is mentioned in Canon 8 of the Council of Nicaea.
[9] Klostermann: οὐχ᾽ αὕτη; MSS: οὐκ αὐτή

4,1   For they have assumed that what is enjoined upon the priesthood because of the priesthood's preeminence applies equally to everyone. They have heard, "The bishop must be blameless, the husband of one wife, continent; likewise the deacon[10] and the presbyter," but not understood the limitation of the ordinances. (2) Since Christ's incarnation, in fact, because of the priesthood's higher rank, God's holy Gospel does not accept men for the priesthood after a first marriage, if they have remarried because their first wife died. And God's holy church observes this with unfailing strictness. (3) She does not even accept the husband of one wife if he is still co-habiting with her and fathering children. She does accept the abstinent husband of one wife, or a widower, as a deacon, presbyter, bishop and subdeacon, [but no other married men], particularly where the canons of the church are strictly enforced.[11]

4,4   But in some places, you will surely tell me, presbyters, deacons and sub-deacons are still fathering children [while exercising their office.] This is not canonical, but is due to men's occasional remissness of purpose, and because there is no one to serve the congregation.

4,5   Since, by the Holy Spirit's good appointment, the church always sees what is fittest, she knows to take great care that God's services be performed "without distraction,"[12] and that spiritual functions be fulfilled with the best disposition. (6) I mean that because of the offices and business which arise unexpectedly, it is appropriate that the presbyter, deacon and bishop be free for God. (7) If the holy apostle directs even the laity to "give themselves to prayer for a time,"[13] how much more does he tell the priest the same—I mean to be unencumbered, leaving room for the godly exercise of the priesthood in spiritual employments?

4,8   But < this > can be tolerated in the laity as a concession to weakness—even remarriage after the first wife's death by those who cannot stop with the first wife.[14] (9) And the husband of [only] one wife is more highly respected and honored by all members of the church. But if the man could not be content with the one wife, who had died, < or > if there has been a divorce for some reason—fornication, adultery or something else—and the man

---

[10] 1 Tim. 3:2; 6
[11] For other statements of the requirement of clerical continence see Eus. Demon. Ev. 1.9.31; Cyr. Cat. 12.25; Council of Elvira, Canon 26.
[12] 1 Cor. 7:35
[13] 1 Cor. 7:5
[14] Lay widows and widowers are permitted to remarry at Hermas Mand. 4.41; Clem. Alex. Strom. 3.84.2; after a period of continence at Council of Laodicea, Canon 1; Bas. Caes. Ep. 188, Canon 4.

marries a second wife or the woman a second husband, God's word does not censure them or bar them from the church and life, but tolerates them because of their weakness.[15] (10) The holy word and God's holy church show mercy to such a person, particularly if he is devout otherwise and lives by God's law—not by letting him have two wives at once while the one is still alive, but < by letting > him marry a second wife lawfully if the opportunity arises, after being parted from the first.

4,11   [If this were not the case] the apostle would not tell the widows, "Let them marry, bear children, guide the house."[16] Nor, to the man who had his father's wife and had been delivered "to Satan for the destruction of the flesh that the spirit might be saved in the day of the Lord,"[17] would he say in turn, "Confirm your love toward him, lest such a one be swallowed up with overmuch sorrow."[18] (12) For he went on to say, "To whom ye forgive anything, I forgive also. Therefore if I forgave anything, for your sakes forgave I it in the person of the Lord lest Satan should get an advantage over us. For we are not ignorant of his devices."[19] And see how he allows repentance even after a transgression.

5,1   And again the Lord says, "Forgive one another your trespasses, that your Father which is in heaven may also forgive you."[20] (2) Moreover, he says in another passage, "And I shall bewail many among you that have transgressed and not repented"[21] as though to indicate that, even though they have transgressed and repented,

---

[15] Because this apparently lax attitude toward divorce is surprising in Epiphanius, Riggi ("Nouvelle lecture") returns practically to the text of Petavius, though with re-punctuation: καὶ ὁ μὲν μίαν ἐσχηκὼς ἐν ἐπαίνῳ μείζονι καὶ τιμῇ παρὰ πᾶσιν τοῖς ἐκκλησιαζομένοις ἐνυπάρχει, οὐ[instead of ὁ] δὲ μὴ δυνασθεὶς τῇ μίᾳ ἀρκεσθῆναι τελευτησάσῃ. ἕνεκέν τινος προφάσεως ἢ πορνείας, ἢ μοιχείας, ἢ κακῆς αἰτίας χωρισμοῦ γενομένου, συναφθέντα δευτέρᾳ γυναικί, ἡ [instead of ἢ] γυνὴ δευτέρῳ ἀνδρὶ οὐκ αἰτιᾶται. ὁ θεῖος λόγος οὐδὲ ἀπὸ τῆς ἐκκλησίας καὶ τῆς ζωῆς ἀποκηρύττει, ἀλλὰ διαβαστάζει διὰ τὸ ἀσθενές, "The husband of only one wife is held in higher respect and honor by all members of the church [but] not [if he] could not be content with the one wife who died. If there has been a divorce for some reason, for adultery, fornication, or an evil charge, the woman [who has married] a second husband cannot blame [her ex-husband] who has married a second wife. Neither does the word of God bar them from the church and life, but bears with their weakness." However, Epiphanius' scriptural citations at 4,11–5,2 suggest that leniency is indeed his point, and stylistically, abrupt asyndeta in this sort of context are unusual in Epiphanius.
[16] 1 Tim. 5:14
[17] Cf. 1 Cor. 5:1; 5.
[18] 2 Cor. 2: 8; 7
[19] 2 Cor. 2:10
[20] Matt. 6:14; Mark 11:25
[21] 2 Cor. 12:21

they are acceptable and will not be cast off. For the Lord knows how to deal with each.

5,3   And anyone can see that the rule of the truth is of this nature. After the first repentance through the laver of regeneration, by which everyone is renewed, there is no second similar repentance. (4) For there are not two baptisms but one, Christ was not crucified twice but once, and he did not die for us and rise twice. And this is why we need to take care, or we may lose the crown of our renewal by transgression. (5) But if someone transgresses and is "overtaken in a fault," as the apostle says, "ye which are spiritual, restore such an one in the spirit of meekness, considering thyself, lest thou also be tempted."[22] Therefore if anyone is overtaken < in > a fault, no matter which, he should repent. (6) God accepts repentance even after baptism, if one goes astray. How he deals with such a person, he alone knows—"Unsearchable are his judgments, and his ways past finding out."[23] (7) We must not judge before the [second] advent, "until the Lord come, who both will bring to light the hidden things of darkness, and then the praise of every man will be manifest;"[24] "For the day will declare it, for it is revealed in fire."[25]

6,1   Thus to those who have sinned after baptism we neither promise freedom unconditionally, nor deny life. For God is "merciful and pitiful,"[26] and "hath given a way of return to the penitent."[27] (2) The first is obvious; as for the second, we know that God is merciful, if we repent of our transgressions with our whole souls. He holds life, salvation and lovingkindness in his hand, and what he does is known only to him; but no can lose by repentance, and no one who repents of all his faults has been refused.

6,3   How much more, surely, [must this apply to] one who is lawfully married to a second wife! The first wife is a divine ordinance; the second, a concession to human weakness. And even if one marries a further wife [after the second], his weakness is still tolerated. (4) For scripture says, "A wife is bound by law so long as her husband liveth. But if her husband be dead she is at liberty to be married to whom she will, < only in the Lord >."[28] Scripture declares her unquestionable freedom from sin [if she remarries] after her husband's death, and with its addition, < that

---

[22] Gal. 6:1
[23] Rom. 11:33
[24] 1 Cor. 4:5
[25] 1 Cor. 3:13
[26] Ps. 110:4; 111:4
[27] Sir. 17:24
[28] 1 Cor. 7:39

is* >, "in the Lord," sets < the limit* > [to this] freedom. (5) Thus
the woman is not cut off from the Lord if she marries another
husband after her husband's death; nor is the man if he marries
a second wife after his wife's death—"only in the Lord," as the
apostle says. (6) And he indeed says, "But she is happier if she
so abide,"[29] < but he does not command this. He does, however,
command* >, "in the Lord." And this means, "not in fornication,
adultery or an illicit love affair, but with a good will, openly, in
lawful wedlock, abiding by the faith, the commandments, good
works, piety, fastings, good order, almsdeeds, zeal, the doing of
good. (7) When these accompany and remain with them, they do
not render them worthless or unfruitful at the Lord's coming.

6,8   The priesthood ranks first and has the strictest requirements in everything, but moderation and forbearance are shown
the laity, so that all may be taught and all shown mercy. (9) For
the Lord is merciful, and mighty to save all, by their orderly behavior
and true faith in the purity of the gospel. For only he is pure. (10)
These people who call themselves "pure" make themselves impure
on just these grounds; whoever declares himself pure has condemned himself outright for impurity.

7,1   It is the height of stupidity for people like this to think
they can pass such a judgment on the entire laity for one thing—
even if it were true. But we should realize that no soul is charged
for this reason alone. And < one does not > become virtuous in
this way alone, (2) but also by not being abusive; not swearing any
oath true or false but saying, "Yea, yea," and, "Nay, nay;" not being
treacherous, not slandering, not stealing, not trafficking. (3) The
filth of our sins accumulates from all of these, for "As a peg will
be sharpened between two stones," says scripture, "so will sin between
buyer and seller."[30] (4) And < who can doubt* > that, out of the
whole body of Purists, < some > < must be* > drunkards, traffickers,
covetous, or usurers? [Who can doubt] that < they too >, surely,
have such faults and others like them, < and > that each of them
is characterized by lies? (5) How can they call themselves pure,
as though they were sure of the full divine forgiveness of all their
faults for this one reason? They do not know the exact provisions
of the Gospel, or for whom it has reserved this strict rule against
second marriage.

7,6   Those too who have fallen away through persecution, if
they show full repentance, sit in sackcloth and ashes and weep

---

[29] 1 Cor. 7:40
[30] Sir. 12:24

before the Lord—the Benefactor has the power to show mercy even to them. No ill can come of repentance.

7,7 Thus the Lord and his church accept the penitent, as Manasseh the son of Hezekiah returned and was accepted by the Lord—and the chief of the apostles, St. Peter, who denied for a time (8) and [still] became our truly solid rock which supports the Lord's faith, and on which the church is in every way founded. (9) This is, first of all, because he confessed that "Christ" is "the Son of the living God,"[31] and was told, "On this rock of sure faith will I build my church"[32]—for he plainly confessed that Christ is true Son. For when he said, "Son of the living God," with the additional phrase, "the living," he showed that Christ is God's true Son, as I have said in nearly every Sect.

8,1 Peter also makes us certain of the Holy Spirit by saying to Ananias, "Why hath Satan tempted you to lie to the Holy Ghost? Ye have not lied unto man, but unto God,"[33] for the Spirit is of God and not different from God. (2) And Peter also became the solid rock of the building and foundation of God's house, because, after denying, turning again, and being found by the Lord, he was privileged to hear, "Feed my lambs and feed my sheep."[34] (3) For with these words Christ led us to the turning of repentance, so that our well founded faith might be rebuilt in him—a faith that forbids the salvation of no one alive who truly repents, and amends his faults in this world.

9,1 Thus the bride herself said to the bridegroom in the Song of Songs, "My sister's son answereth and saith unto me, Arise and come, beloved, my fair one, my dove, for the storm is past"—the wretched darkness of the overcast sky is past, and the great frightfulness < of the storms* >, as it were, < of our sins* >—(2) "and the rain is over and gone. The flowers appear in our land, the time of pruning has come, the voice of the turtle-dove is heard in our land. The fig tree putteth forth her fruits. Our vines blossom, they have yielded their fragrance."[35] (3) She means that all the past is behind us. Spring is now in bloom, the sea is calm and the fear of rain is past. The old < shoots* > of the vine have been cut off, the grass is no longer merely green but in flower as well, (4) and the voice of the Gospel has cried out "in the wilderness"[36]—that

---

[31] Matt. 16:16
[32] Cf. Matt. 16:18.
[33] Acts 5:3–4
[34] John 21:16; 17
[35] Song of Songs 2:10–13
[36] Mark 1:3

is, "in our land." The fig tree, which once was cursed, has borne "figs"—the fruits of repentance, visible now on its twigs and branches—and vines,[37] now in bloom with the fragrant message of the faith of the Gospel.

9,5   For Christ has even now called his bride and said, "Arise and come."[38] "Arise," < that is* >, from the death of sins, and come" in righteousness. "Arise" from transgression "and come" with confidence. "Arise" from sins, "and come" with repentance. "Arise" from palsy, "and come" whole; "arise" from maiming "and come" sound; "arise" from unbelief "and come" in faith. "Arise" from the lost, "and come" with the found!

9,6   But since the sacred oracle knew that men can fall into many transgressions after their first repentance, their first call and, as it were, their first healing, the bridegroom, again, says, "Arise and come, my beloved, my fair one, my dove, and come thou, my dove!"[39] (7) He calls her this second time and not merely once, but the second time is not like the first. In his earlier call he says, "Arise and come, beloved, my fair one, my dove." The first time he said, "Arise and come," and not, "Come *thou*." (8) And he adds the article the second time (ἡ πλησίον)[40] to show that his call is not a second call, changed after the first, but the same divine right hand of lovingkindness [that was offered] in the first, extended once more after [there have been] transgressions.

9,9   "And come < thou >, my dove," he says, "in the shelter of the rock, nigh unto the outworks."[41] "In the shelter of a rock"— < that is >, in Christ's lovingkindness and the Lord's mercy, for this is the shelter of the rock, the shelter of hope, faith and truth. (10) [And] "nigh unto the outworks" means before the closing of the gate—before the king has gone inside the walls and admits no one further. In other words, after our departure and death, when there is no more "nigh unto the outworks," the gates are closed, and amendment is no longer possible.

10,1   For after one's departure there is no opportunity to fast in the world to come, no call to repentance, no giving of alms. There are no blameworthy deeds either—no war, adultery, licentiousness—but neither is there righteousness and repentance. (2) As

---

[37] ἀμπέλους. Because the vines twine on the fig trees planted in the vineyards?
[38] Song of Songs 2:10; 13
[39] Song of Songs 2:
[40] I.e., the article specifies this call as *the* call issued to the same person who has already been called.
[41] Song of Songs 2:14

the seed cannot thicken or be blasted by the wind after the reaping of the ear, so < after a man's death there can be no increase of his store* > and nothing else to his benefit. (3) But don't tell me about the things that spoil the store, that is, the worms and moths. Scripture says this about the condition of affairs in eternity; but the point of comparison, and what we lock away behind gates and store safely in a barn, is a symbol and type of faith, [which is kept] "where neither thieves break through nor moths corrupt,"[42] as God's word says.

Thus < there is no decrease of our store* > after death, but certainly neither is there any opportunity for godliness, nor, as I said, any < call > to repentance. (4) For Lazarus does not go to the rich man in the next world, and the rich man does not go to Lazarus. Nor does Abraham inconvenience the poor man who has since become rich, and send him [to the rich man]. And the rich man who has become poor does not obtain his request, though he begs and pleads with the merciful Abraham. (5) The storehouses had been sealed, the time was up, the contest finished, the ring emptied, the prizes awarded, and the contestants at ease. Those who had not arrived had left, those who had not fought had no more chance, those who had lost in the ring had been ejected. All is plainly over after our departure from this life.

10,6 But while we are still in this world there is still arising even after a fall, still hope, still a remedy, still confession—even if not for everyone, still < by those who are repenting for the second time* >. And surely < even > the salvation of the others is not ruled out.

11,1 But every sect which has been drawn from the truth in the dark is blind and shortsighted, and makes one supposition after another. For these people are like simpletons who do not understand the character and purpose of any member of the body, or how to clothe it. (2) In a way—(what I propose to say is ridiculous, < but > it bears a resemblance to their stupidity)—they put their shoes on their heads but their wreaths on their feet, and golden collars round their tummies. And they wind what we might call our other footgear, which we have because we wear himatia and which some call drawers or pants, around their hands, but put rings on their feet.

11,3 These ignorant people's ordinance is just as ill-founded and clumsy. They have assumed that the prohibitions of second marriages and the rest, which are reserved for the priesthood,

---

[42] Matt. 6:20

< are enjoined* > upon all the laity; and they have attributed the particularly stringent injunctions, which God has made to keep certain persons from straying through laxity, to cruelty on God's part. (4) It is as though one were to tear a sleeve off an himation and cover himself only to the elbow or to what is called the wrist, but always hold the sleeve in front of his eyes and jeer at the rest, without noticing that his whole body was bare. (5) So these people pride themselves on not receiving the twice-married, but < make light of > all the commandments that are like this and much better in the keeping, but are deadly if not kept. They < needlessly* > forbid the one [sin], but have ignored the others. (6) Forgetting that their whole bodies are bare, they have ceased to obey all the ordinances, and disingenuously retained the one.

12,1   How much nonsense people can think of! Every pretext, however trivial it was, drew each sect away from the truth and impelled it to a prolific production of evils. (2) It is < as though > one found a break in a wall beside a highway, thought of going through it, left the road and turned off < there >, in the belief that a place where he could turn and pick up the road again was right close by. But he did not know that the wall was very high and ran on for a long way; (3) he kept running into it and not finding a place to get out, and in fact went for more than a signpost, or mile, further without reaching the road. And so he would turn and keep going, tiring himself out and finding no way to get back to his route; and perhaps he could never find one unless he went back through the place where he had come in. (4) So every sect, as though it meant to find a shortcut, has gotten into trouble because of the length of the journey, but its entanglement with ignorance and stupidity has made an unbreachable barrier for it. (5) And no sect can reach the true road unless it turns back to the original of the road, that is, to the king's highway. (6) The Law declared this in so many words, when Moses in his holiness said to the king of Edom, "Thus saith thy brother Israel. I shall pass by thy borders to the land which the Lord hath sworn to our fathers to give us, a land flowing with milk and honey, the land of the Amorites, the Pherizzites, the Girgashites, the Jebusites, the Hivites, the Canaanites and the Hittites. (7) We shall not swerve to the right hand or to the left, we shall drink water for money and eat food for money. We shall not swerve this way or that, we shall go by the king's highway."[43] (8) For there is a king's highway, the church of God and the journey of the truth. But each of these

---

[43] Cf. Nu. 20:14; 17; 19; Deut. 7:1.

sects which has abandoned the king's highway, turned to the right or to the left, and ended by getting more lost, will be drawn out of its way, and will never reach the end of the wrong road of its error.

13,1   Now then, servants of God and sons of God's holy church, you who know the sure standard and are on the path of the truth! Let's not be drawn in the wrong direction by voices, and led by the voice of every false practice. (2) For their roads are perilous, and the path of their false notion runs uphill. They talk big, and don't know even the little things; they promise freedom, but are the slaves of sin themselves. They boast of the greater things, and have not even attained to the lesser.

13,3   But I think that this will be enough about these so-called "Pure" people—who, if the truth must be told, are impure people. (4) Let us toss this sect aside like the face of a basilisk—which, from the sound of the name, has a very grand title, (βασιλικός) but which it is death to meet. Striking it with the power of the wood of the cross, let us once more start off for the rest, (5) bringing our prayer to God that he will travel with us, abide with us, be with us, assist us, preserve us, chasten us, and make us worthy to speak the truth, so that we may not tell any falsehoods ourselves and thus get into the same position as the sects, which have taught the world nothing true.

13,6   And further, the people in Africa and Byzicania who are named Donatists for one Donatus, have ideas similar to these and are rebels themselves because, if you please, they will not communicate with those who have lapsed in the persecution. They will be refuted by the same arguments as the Navatians, or so-called Purists, who are unequally yoked with them. (7) I therefore do not need to discuss them any further, but have put them together with those who are like them. (8) However, these latter have fallen again in a more serious way. They believe in the Arian version of the faith and, as Arius was refuted, they likewise will be refuted by words of truth about the faith which they hold incorrectly; for Arius agrees with them and they with him. (9) And once more, we shall pass this sect by as though we had trampled on horrid serpents in the Lord, and go on to the rest.

Against Angelics. 40, but 60 of the series

1,1   I have heard that < there is* > a sect of Angelics and have been told nothing but their name. But I am not sure which sect this is, perhaps because it arose at some time, but later came to an end and was altogether brought to an end.

1,2 But why it got its name I don't know. It may have been because of some people's saying that the world was made by angels—even if it was given this name for saying that, I can't say [so for certain.] Or it may have been because they boasted of having the rank of angels and leading particularly exemplary lives—I cannot make this affirmation either. Or they might even have been named for some place; there is a land called Angelina on the other side of Mesopotamia.

2,1 But if you are reminded of something now, reader, you will harbor no suspicion to my discredit. I promised to report the roots and the nourishment of some sects, or some of the things they do, but just to mention others by name;[1] (2) but as the divine power has equipped and aided me, until this sect I have gone right through them all and left none unexplained, except this one. (3) But perhaps it is because it was puffed up with pride for a short while and later came to an end, that I have no understanding of it.

2,4 But I shall name it with the mere quick mention of its name as though as that of an untimely birth, pass its place [in the series] by, and embark on the investigation of the others. (5) I likewise entreat the Lord of all to disclose himself to me, show my small mind what the sects do, and give it all the exact facts, (6) enabling me to correct myself and my neighbors so that we may avoid what is evil, but gain a firm foundation, in God, in what is good, and absolutely true.

Against Apostolics. 41,[1] but 61 of the series

1,1 Others after these have termed themselves Apostolics. They also like to call themselves Apotactics, since they practice the renunciation of possessions. (2) They too are an offshoot of the doctrines of Tatian, the Encratites, the Tatianists and the Purists, and they do not accept marriage at all. Their mysteries also are different.[2]

---

[1] Pan. Proem. II 2,3–5. But if the text of this Proem is correct as we have it, Epiphanius says nothing there about mentioning some sects "only by name."

[1] Though several authors speak of Apotactics, only Epiphanius uses the term, Apostolics. 2,1 suggests that he has one particular group, in a specific geographical area, in mind. Other authors tend to give such rigorist groups several related titles: "Encratites, Apotactics and Eremites" (Mac. Mag. 3.43); "Cathari, Encratites, Hydroparastatae and Apotactics" (Bas. Caes. Ep. 199, Canon 7); "Encratites, Saccophori and Apotactics" (Code of Theodosius 16.5.7) et al. Below at 1,2 Epiphanius says, "Encratites, Tatianists and Cathari;" at 7,1, "Apostolics, Apotactics and Encratites."

[2] This presumably means that they celebrated the eucharist with water instead

1,3   They boast of having no possessions, if you please, but they divide and harm God's holy church for no good reason, by depriving themselves of God's lovingkindness through their willful sort of worship. (4) For they allow no readmission if one of them has lapsed, and when it comes to matrimony and the rest they agree with the sects we mentioned above. (5) And the Purists use only the canonical scriptures, but these people rely mostly on the so-called Acts of Andrew and Thomas, and have nothing to do with the ecclesiastical canon.

1,6   [But they are wrong]; for if marriage is abominable, all < who > are born of marriage are unclean. And if God's holy church is composed only of those who have renounced marriage, (7) marriage cannot be of God. And if it is not, the whole business of procreation is ungodly. And if the business of procreation is ungodly so are they, since they have been begotten by such behavior.

1,8   But what becomes of scripture's, "What God hath joined together, let not man put asunder?"[3] † < To satisfy > the necessities † < of nature >[4] is human, but deliberate continence exhibits, not the work of man but the work of God. (9) And the necessity of nature is often open to censure because the necessity is not satisfied in a praiseworthy manner, but has overstepped the rule. For godliness is not a necessity; righteousness is by choice.

1,10   The things that must naturally < contribute* > to godliness are obvious, and are over and above nature. For example, not committing fornication, not committing adultery, not being licentious, not have two spouses at once, not plundering, not being unjust, not getting drunk, not being gluttonous, not worshiping idols, not committing murder, not practicing sorcery, not cursing, not reviling, not swearing, being annoyed and quickly appeased, not sinning when angered, not letting the sun go down on one's wrath. (11) But that lawful wedlock < is godly* >, nature, which God has created and permitted, will show; and the other things of this sort have each their measure of permission.

2,1   But as I was saying of them, they live in a small area, around Phrygia, Cilicia and Pamphylia. (2) Now what does this mean? Is the church exterminated from one end of the earth to the other? Will "Their sound is gone out unto all lands, and their words unto the ends of the world,"[5] no longer hold? Or is the Savior's "Ye shall

---

of wine. See p. 4.
  [3] Matt. 19:6
  [4] Holl: τὸ ... ἐπάναγκες < τῆς φύσεως ἐπιτελεῖν >; MSS: τὸ ... ἐπανάγκες χωρίζειν

be witnesses unto me unto the uttermost part of the earth"[6] no
longer in force? (3) If marriage is not respectable, godly and worthy of eternal life, they < themselves* > should be born without
marriage. But if they are born of marriage, they are unclean because
of marriage. (4) If, however, they alone are not unclean even though
they are the products of marriage, then marriage is not unclean—
for no one will ever be born without it. (5) And there is a great
deal of human error which harms humanity in various ways and
for many reasons, and which, by pretense, leads everyone astray
from the truth.

3,1   The church too believes in renunciation, but it does not
consider marriage unclean. It also believes in voluntary poverty,
but it does not look down on those who are in righteous possession
of property, and have inherited enough from their parents to suffice
for themselves and the needy. (2) Many [Christians] have enough
to eat, but they are not contemptuous of those who do not. "Let
not him that eateth despise him that eateth not, and let not him
which eateth not judge him that eateth. For to the Lord he eateth
and drinketh, and to the Lord he eateth and drinketh not."[7] (3)
And you see that there is one harmony and one hope in the church,
and one faith, given to each in accordance with his ability and the
particular difficulty of his labor.

3,4   God's holy church is like a ship. A ship, though, is not
made of one kind of wood, but of different kinds. Its keel is made
of one kind of wood, though not all in one piece, and its anchors
< of > another. Its beams, planks and ribs, its frame-timbers, the
stern, sides and cross-rods, the mast and the steering paddles, the
seats and the oar-handles, the tillers and all the rest, are an as-
semblage of different kinds of wood. (5) But none of these sects
exhibits the character of the church, for each is made of only one
kind of wood.

God's holy church holds marriage sacred and honors the married,
for "Marriage is honorable and the bed undefiled."[8] (6) < But >
it regards continence as extremely admirable, and commends it
because it is in the contest and has still more power [than the
world] and, since it is still stronger than the world, and has despised
the world. And the church sanctions virginity and accords it the
highest praise, because it is a thing of virtue and is fitted with the
lightest wing. (7) The church has members who have renounced
the world and yet are not contemptuous of those who are still in

---

[6] Acts 1:8
[7] Rom. 14:3; 6
[8] Heb. 13:4

the world; they rejoice in the very great piety of such persons, as did the apostles who owned nothing themselves, < and yet did not look down on the others* >. (8) And the Savior himself owned no earthly possessions when he came in the flesh, though he was Lord of all—and yet he did not reject the women who assisted his disciples and himself. The Gospel says, "women which followed him from Galilee, ministering unto him of their substance."[9]

4,1   [If no one may own property], what is the point of "Hither to my right hand, ye blessed, for whom my heavenly Father hath prepared the kingdom before the foundation of the world. For I was an hungered, and ye gave me meat; thirsty, and ye gave me drink; I was naked, and ye clothed me?"[10] (2) How could they do these things except with the [fruits of] their honest labor, and their righteously acquired possessions?

4,3   And if these people < who > have made their own renunciation and live like the apostles would mix with the rest [of us], their ways would not seem strange, or different from God's ordinance. (4) And if they renounced wives for continence' sake their choice would be praiseworthy, provided that they did not call marriage unclean, and provided that they treated the < still > married as comrades, knowing the limitation and the rank of each.

4,5   For God's ship takes any passenger except a bandit. If it finds that someone is a robber and bandit it does not take him on board—or a runaway, in rebellion against his owners. (6) Thus God's holy church does not accept fornication, adultery, the denial of God, and those who defy the authority of God's ordinance and his apostles. (7) But it takes the man on important business, the experienced seaman—the pilot and < helmsman* >, the bow lookout, the man in the stern (the one most used to command), the one who knows even a bit about cargo and lading—and someone who just wants to cross the ocean without drowning. (8) And there is no question of the ship's not giving safety to someone who does not have a particular amount of property; it knows how to save all, and each in his own profession. Why are the members of Caesar's household greeted in the Epistles? (9) Why the apostle's "If any man think that he behaveth himself uncomely toward his virgin, and need so require, let her marry; she sinneth not."[11]

4,10   But without baptism, "sinneth not" cannot apply to him. For if "All have sinned and come short of the glory of God, being

---

[9] Luke 8:3
[10] Matt. 25:24–35
[11] 1 Cor. 7:36

justified freely by his grace,"[12] this is plainly through the laver of regeneration. Baptism has adorned the soul and the body, washing away every sin through repentance. (11) Thus the gift of baptism both enfolds the virgin and, because of her sinfulness, hastens to seal the non-virgin.

5,1   But though I have said that the apostle directed the virgin to marry, no one need get the silly notion that he gave this direction to dissuade the woman from her course once she had vowed virginity to God. (2) He did not mean these women, but marriageable women who had remained virgins in their prime, not for virginity's sake but because they of their inability to find husbands. (3) The apostles, who were Jewish and had begun their preaching after lives lived by the Law, were still bound by the provisions of the Law, not for any fleshly justification but out of regard for the Law's fitting sureness and strictness. (4) The Law admirably forbade the Israelites to give their daughters to gentiles, who might seduce them into idolatry. Thus a believer at that time was ordered not to give his virgin daughters to Jews any longer, but to Christians, whose beliefs and opinions were the same theirs. (5) But as the Gospel was new there was not yet a large number of Christians in every place, and not a great deal of Christian teaching. Hence the fathers of virgin daughters would keep their virgins at home for a long time if they could not give them to Christians, and when they were past their prime they would fall into fornication from the necessity of nature. (6) So because the apostle saw the harm that resulted from this strictness he permitted [marriage to Jews], and said, "he who would < give > his virgin in marriage"[13]—and he did not say, "*his own* virgin," for he was not speaking of the man's own body, (7) but of the father guarding a virgin [daughter]. But even if "his virgin" means his own body, there is nothing to prevent [the man from giving his daughter]. (8) Thus he says, "< He > that standeth steadfast in his intention and ought so to do, let her marry! She sinneth not."[14] "Let her marry anyone she can; she is not sinning." (9) And this is why < he says >, "Art thou bound unto a wife? Seek not to be loosed. Art thou loosed from a wife? Seek not a wife."[15] The apostle who says, "I would that all

---

[12] Rom. 3:23–24
[13] Cf. 1 Cor. 7:36.
[14] Cf. 1 Cor. 7:37; 36.
[15] 1 Cor. 7:27

men be even as I,"[16] also < said >, "If they cannot contain, let them marry."[17]

6,1 And again, when he was urging the < un >married [to remain as they were], he said, "I say therefore to the unmarried and widows, It is good for them if they abide even as I."[18] (2) But in this case how could he go on to say, "Art thou bound unto a wife? Seek not to be loosed?"[19] Why will he not be guilty of contradicting his Lord, who said, "Whoso forsaketh not father, and mother, and brethren, and wife, and sons and daughters, is not my disciple?"[20]

6,3 But if Christ means that one must forsake his lawful wife, and his father, how can say in turn, "He that honoreth father or mother, this is the first commandment among the promises,"[21] and, "What God hath joined together, let not man put asunder?"[22]

6,4 However, none of the sacred words need an allegorical interpretation of their meaning; they need examination, and the perception to understand each proposition's force. (5) But tradition must be used too, for not everything is available from the sacred scripture. Thus the holy apostles handed some things down in scriptures but some in traditions, as St. Paul says, "As I delivered the tradition to you,"[23] and elsewhere, "So I teach, and so I have delivered the tradition in the churches,"[24] and, "If ye keep the tradition in memory, unless ye have believed in vain."[25] (6) God's holy apostles, then, gave God's holy church the tradition that it is sinful to change one's mind and marry after vowing virginity. And yet the apostle wrote, "If the virgin marry she hath not sinned."[26] (7)[27] How can the two statements agree? By that virgin he does not mean the one who had made a vow to God, but < the one on whom* > virginity has been forced by the scarcity, at that period, of men who believe in Christ.

6,8 And that this is the case the same apostle will teach us by saying, "Younger widows refuse. For when they have begun to wax wanton against Christ, they will marry, having damnation, because

---

[16] 1 Cor. 7:7
[17] 1 Cor. 7:9
[18] 1 Cor. 7:8
[19] 1 Cor. 7:27
[20] Cf. Luke 14:26.
[21] Eph. 6:2
[22] Matt. 19:6
[23] 1 Cor. 11:2
[24] Cf. 1 Cor. 11:2; 7:17.
[25] 1 Cor. 15:2
[26] Cf. 1 Cor. 7:36.
[27] We supply a paragraph number missing from Holl.

they have cast off their first faith."[28] (9) If even a woman who has
been widowed after knowing the world will be condemned for
abandoning her first faith because she has vowed to God and then
married, how much more will a virgin, if she marries after devoting
herself to God without having known the world? (10) < For > why
has she, indeed, not waxed far more wanton against Christ, and
abandoned the greater faith? Why will she not be condemned for
relaxing her own godly resolution?

7,1 "Let them marry, bear children, guide the house"[29] is a
concise and temperate retort to those who think evil of every subject of the church's preaching. (2) It is the repudiation of those
who call themselves Apostolics, Apotactics and Encratites; also of
the soft-headed churchmen who persuade women to shirk the
running of a full course, and to refuse to finish the race because
of its length. (3) And whoever spurns virginity for God's sake and
dishonors the contest, is a sinner and liable to judgment. If an
athlete cheats in a game he is flogged and put out of the contest;
and anyone who cheats on virginity is banished from a race, crown
and prize of such importance.

7,4 But judgment, not condemnation, is the better alternative.
Those who do not commit their fornication < openly > for fear of
being shamed before men, < but > do it in secret, < have a further
sin because* > they do this < under the pretense > of virginity, celibacy
or continence. (5) < For > they do not have to confess to men—
but they do to God, who knows secrets and at his coming convicts
all flesh of its sins. (6) It is better to have the one sin, then, and
not more. If one drops out of the race it is better to take a wife
openly, and in place of virginity do penance for a long time, and
be readmitted to the church as one who has strayed and wept,
and is in need of reinstatement—and not be wounded every day
by the secret darts of wickedness which the devil launches at him.

8,1 This is the preaching which the church knows. These are
her healing medicines. These are her ways of preparing unguents.
This is the compounding of the holy oil in the Law. This is the
noble faith with its sweet fragrance, which steels the athlete for
the contest by reminding him that, to be crowned, he must stay
the course. (2) And this is the work of God, gathering all things
for royal disposal: purple from the sea, wool from the flock, linen
from the earth and flax and silk, skins dyed scarlet and precious
stones, emeralds, pearls, agates—stones with different colors but

---

[28] 1 Tim. 5:11–12
[29] 1 Tim. 5:14

of equal value. (3) Moreover, it gathers gold, silver, petrified wood, bronze and iron, and does not disdain goat skins. (4) And this was the tabernacle then; but now, in place of the tabernacle, it is the house made firm in God, founded on the power < of the truth* >. And every sect should stop attacking the truth, or rather, stop driving itself away from the truth.

8,5   And let this be enough. I have struck this haughty viper with the wood of the cross and left it dead, like the quick-darting snake, as they call it, or the blind-snake or mouser. These snakes do not have as much venom, but they may well be compared with the Apostolics as nuisances because of their movement, pride and stroke. Let us disdain them, beloved, and go on to the rest.

Against Sabellians.[1] 42, but 62 of the series

1,1   Sabellius did not arise very long ago in ancient times—his date is recent—and the so-called Sabellians derive from him. (2) He < taught > very similarly to the Noetians, except for a few further doctrines of his own. (3) Many in Mesopotamia[2] and Rome are of his persuasion, due to some sort of stupidity.

1,4   For he, and the Sabellians who derive from him, hold that the Father is the same, the Son is the same, and the Holy Spirit is the same, so that there are three names in one entity.[3] (5)[4] Or, as there are a body, a soul and a spirit in a man, so the Father, in a way, is the body; the Son, in a way, is the soul; and as a man's spirit is in man, so is the Holy Spirit in the Godhead. (6) Or it is as in the sun, which consists of one entity but has three operations, the illumining, the warming, and the actual shape of the orb. (7) The warming, or hot and seething operation is the Spirit; the illumining operation is the Son; and the Father is the actual form of the whole entity.[5] (8) And the Son was once sent forth like a ray, accomplished the entire dispensation of the Gospel and men's salvation in the world, and was taken up to heaven again, as though a ray had been sent by the sun and had returned to the sun. (9) But the Holy Spirit is sent into the world both once and for all, and in individual cases to each person so privileged. He quickens this person and makes him fervent, and, as it were,

---

[1] Sabellians are discussed at Hippol. Haer. 9.3.11–13.

[2] The Mesopotamian bishop Archelaus mentions Sabellius as a heretic, Act. Arch. 41.

[3] The same phraseology is attributed to Sabellius by Dionysius of Alexandria apud Athanasius, De Sententiis Dionysii (Routh III p. 373).

[4] We supply a paragraph number not found in Holl.

[5] Roughly the same comparison is used at Justin Dial. 128.5; Tert. C. Prax. 10.4.

warms and heats him by the power of the Spirit and his communion with him.[6] And these are their doctrines.

2,1   They use all the scriptures of the Old and New Testaments, but [especially] certain texts which they select themselves in keeping with the idiocy they have introduced. (2) First, God's words to Moses, "Hear, O Israel, the Lord thy God, the Lord is one."[7] "Thou shalt not make to thyself other gods."[8] "There shall not be unto thee new gods,"[9] for "I am God, the first and the last, and beside me there is no other."[10] (3) And whatever of this sort < they find, < they alter* > to suit themselves, and advance it as proof of these doctrines. Again, [they use] the saying from the Gospel, "I am in the Father and the Father in me, and we two are one."[11]

2,4   But they have taken all of their error, and the meaning of their error, from certain apocryphal works, especially the so-called Egyptian Gospel, as some have named it.[12] (5) There are many such passages in it, purporting to be delivered privately as mysteries in the person of the Savior, as though he is telling his disciples that the Father is the same, the Son is same, and the Holy Spirit is the same.[13]

2,6   Then, when they encounter simple or innocent persons who do not understand the sacred scriptures clearly, they give them this first scare: "What are we to say, gentlemen? Have we one God or three gods?" (7) But when someone who is devout but does not fully understand the truth hears this, he is disturbed and assents to their error at once, and comes to deny the existence of the Son and the Holy Spirit.

3,1   Man's ancient adversary has inspired all these sectarians in order to deceive people—one in one way and one in another, but deceive most of them and deflect them from the way of the truth. (2)   That God is truly one God, and that there is no other, is plainly confessed in God's holy church, and it is agreed that we do not inculcate polytheism, but proclaim the sovereignty of one God. (3) However, we do not proclaim this sovereignty in a mistaken way, but confess the Trinity—Unity in Trinity and Trinity in Unity,

---

[6] Cf. Athenagoras Leg. 10.
[7] Deut. 6:4
[8] Cf. Exod. 20:3–4.
[9] Ps. 80:10
[10] Isa. 44:6
[11] Cf. John 10:38; 30.
[12] Hippolytus quotes a passage about souls from a "Gospel according to the Egyptians" at Haer. 5.7.8–9.
[13] Perhaps cf. NHL Gr. Seth 59,18, where Christ is made to say, "The Father, who is I."

and one Godhead of Father, Son and Holy Spirit. (4) For the Son did not beget himself, and the Father was not changed from his fatherhood < into being > a Son. Nor did the Holy Spirit ever call himself Christ; he called himself Spirit of Christ and given through Christ, proceeding from the Father and receiving of the Son. (5) The Father is an entity, the Son is an entity, the Holy Spirit is an entity. But the Trinity is not an identity as Sabellius thought, nor has it been altered from its own eternity and glory, as Arius foolishly held. (6) The Trinity was always a Trinity, and the Trinity never receives an addition. It is one Godhead, one sovereignty and one glory, but is enumerated as a Trinity, Father, Son and Holy Spirit, and not as one entity with three names; the names are truly perfect and the entities are perfect.

3,7   But nothing has been changed. The Father is always a father and there was no time when the Father was not a father. Because he is perfect, he is forever an actual Father. And the Son is forever perfect, forever actual, truly begotten of the Father without beginning, not in time, and ineffably. He is not brother to the Father. (8) He has had no beginning and will never come to an end, but co-exists with the Father forever as his true Son, begotten of the Father outside of time, the equal of the Father—God of God, light of light, very God of very God, begotten, not made. But he is not the Father himself, and the Father is not the Son himself; there is one God, Father, Son and Holy Spirit.

4,1   For the Spirit is forever with the Father and the Son—not brother to the Father, not begotten, not created, not the Son's brother, not the Father's offspring. He proceeds from the Father and receives of the Son, and is not different from the Father and the Son, (2) but is of the same essence, of the same Godhead, of the Father and the Son, with the Father and the Son, forever an actual Holy Spirit—divine Spirit, Spirit of glory, Spirit of Christ, Spirit of the Father. For < scripture says >, "It is the Spirit of the Father that speaketh in you,"[14] and, "My Spirit is in the midst of you."[15] He is third in name but equal in Godhead, not different from the Father and the Son, bond of the Trinity, seal of the confession of it.

4,3   For the Son says, "I and the Father, < we two > are one."[16] He did not say, "I am one;" by saying "I" and, "the Father," he shows that the Father is an entity and the Son is an entity. And

---

[14] Matt. 10:20
[15] Hag. 2:5
[16] Cf. John 10:30.

he said, "the two," not "the one;" and again, he said, "*We are* one," not, "*I am* one."

4,4   < He > likewise < says >, "Go baptize in the name of the Father, and of the Son, and of the Holy Spirit."[17] But by inserting the conjunction, that is, the syllable "and" between the names, he refutes Sabellius, with his futile introduction of an identity. (5) For by < inserting > "and" he shows that there is truly a Father, truly a Son, and truly a Holy Spirit—but since the Trinity are of equal rank, and are called "Trinity" by one name, he refutes Arius, with his notion of a subordination, difference or change in the Trinity.

4,6   For even though it is declared that the Father is greater than the Son who glorifies him, the Father, with perfect propriety, accords < equal > glory to the Son. For who else but the true Son should glorify his < own > Father? (7) But when it is his desire in turn to state his equality [with the Father], to prevent certain persons from going wrong by thinking less of the Son he says, "Whoso honoreth not the Son as he honoreth the Father hath not life in himself,"[18] and, "All things that the Father hath are mine."[19] But what can "All things that the Father hath are mine" mean but, "The Father is God; I am God. The Father is life; I am life. The Father is eternal; I am eternal. All things that the Father hath are mine?"

5,1   See and understand, Sabellius! Open the eyes of your heart, and do not fail to see! Let your mind, and the minds of your dupes, go with St. John to the Jordan. (2) Open your ears and hear the prophet's voice say, "I am the voice of one crying in the wilderness."[20] Hear the Lord's fore-runner, privileged to be called "angel," who received the Holy Spirit in his mother's womb and leaped when Mary entered Elizabeth's dwelling. (3) While still in the womb he knew his Master's coming in and leaped for joy. To him was given the preparatory announcement of the Gospel, and the readying of the way of the Lord. Believe him, and you cannot miss the mark of the truth.

5,4   See here, John himself testifies by saying first, "I have need of thee, and comest thou to me?" because he recognizes his Lord. And when the Savior said, "Suffer it to be so now, that all right-eousness may be fulfilled,"[21] (5) and was baptized by him, "John bare record," as the holy Gospel says, and said, "The heavens were

---

[17] Matt. 28:19
[18] Cf. John 5:23–24.
[19] John 16:15
[20] John 2:23
[21] Matt. 3:14

opened. And I saw the Holy Spirit in the form of a dove descending and coming upon him. And a voice from heaven, This is my
beloved Son, in whom I am well pleased."[22] (6) The Father was
in heaven, you trouble-maker, the voice came from heaven! If the
voice came from above, expound your false notion to me! To
whom was the Father saying, "This is my beloved Son, in whom
I am well pleased?" And who was it?

5,7   But why did Spirit descend in the form of a dove, although
he had no body? For the Only-begotten alone assumed a body,
and was made perfect man of the ever-virgin Mary, by the Holy
Spirit, (8) not by a man's seed. The Word, the Master Builder,
formed his own body from Mary, took the human soul and mind
and everything human, all in its perfection, and united it with his
divinity. It was not as though he inhabited a man,[23] nothing like
that! He himself is the holy Word, the divine Word incarnate.

6,1   But why does the Spirit appear in the form of a dove? Why
but to convince you not to blaspheme, you would-be sage without
a correct idea in your head, to keep you from thinking that the
Spirit is identical with the Father or the Son? (2) Although the
Spirit himself has never had a body, he is portrayed in the form
of a dove to point out and expose your error. For the Spirit is
an entity in himself, and the Father is an entity, and the Only-
begotten is an entity, but there is no division of the Godhead, or
subordination of its glory. (3) And you see how the Trinity is
enumerated, with the Father calling from on high, the Son baptized in the Jordan, and the Holy Spirit also coming in the form
of a dove.

6,4   Tell me, who was it that said, "Behold, my beloved Son
shall understand, in whom I am well pleased, he whom my soul
hath chosen. I shall put my Spirit upon him, and he will declare
judgment to the gentiles. He will not strive nor cry, nor will his
voice be heard in the streets. A bruised reed shall he not break
and smoking flax shall he not quench until he bring forth judgment into victory,"[24] and so on? (5) Can't this mean the Trinity,
you trouble-maker? Did the Father say all this through the prophet
about himself?

6,6   Who is it of whom scripture says, "The Lord said unto my
Lord, Sit thou on my right hand?"[25] And it didn't say, "Enter into

---

[22] John 1:32; Matt. 3:17
[23] Cf. NHL Gr. Seth 51,21–24, "I visited a bodily dwelling. I cast out the one
who was in it first, and I went in."
[24] Cf. Isa. 42:1–4.
[25] Ps. 109:1

me." (7) Or again, why does the Gospel say, "And he ascended into heaven, and sat down at the right hand of the Father, and will come to judge the quick and the dead?"[26] (8) Or again, why have the two men who appeared in white garments not convinced you by telling the disciples, "Ye men of Galilee, why stand ye gazing up into heaven? This same Jesus, which is taken up from you into heaven, shall so come in like manner as ye have seen him taken up?"[27] (9) And at whom was the blessed Stephen looking when he said, "Behold, I see the heavens opened and the Son of Man standing on the right hand of God?"[28] But you, you utter boor—you have harmed yourself and your followers the more by not understanding the voice of the holy scriptures, and have been deprived of the holy faith in God's truth.

7,1   Certainly he said, "I am the first and I am the last, and beside me there is no other."[29] (2) For of course there are not many gods! There is one God, the first and the last, Father, Son and Holy Spirit—and the Trinity is not an identification, and not separated from its own identity. It is a Father who has truly begotten a Son; and a Son truly begotten of the Father as an entity, without beginning and not in time; and a Holy Spirit truly of the Father and the Son, of the same divinity, proceeding from the Father and receiving of the Son, forever < an entity >, "one God, the first and the last."[30]

7,3   But this oracle in its turn is given to serve a different purpose, and in the person of Christ himself. Long ago in the time of the prophets our Lord Jesus Christ often appeared and foretold his incarnation—though some have not received him, but await someone else instead. (4) And it is meant for those who have a superstitious regard for idols and have introduced polytheism, to keep the children of Israel from being struck with fear and turned to [the worship of] the idols of the Amorites, Hittites, Canaanites, Perizzites, Hivites, Girgashites, Jebusites, Arucaeans, and Asanaeans, as they had been prophetically warned. (5) For they worshiped Baal Peor, Chemosh, Astarte, the Mazzuroth, the Neastho, Baal Zebub, and the rest of the idols of the heathen. And this is why the Lord told them, "I am the first and the last"—to turn them from the error of the polytheists' heathen mythology.

7,6   And because they would spurn the advent of the Son himself,

---

[26] Cf. Mark 16:19.
[27] Acts 1:11
[28] Acts 7:56
[29] Isa. 44:6
[30] Isa. 41:4; 44:6

our Lord Jesus Christ, he told the Jews, "I am the first and the last"—the One who sojourned here first in the flesh, and will come at the last to judge the quick and the dead. He suffered on the cross, was buried and arose, and was taken up in glory in his body itself, but a body united in glory with his Godhead, and made radiant—no longer tangible, no longer mortal, for "Christ is risen,"[31] as the scripture says; "Death," says the apostle, "hath no more dominion over him."[32]

7,7   And see how exact knowledge guides one, to protect him from error about either part of the truth. Whenever his mind is inclined to construct a pantheon, he hears, "The Lord is thy God, the Lord is one."(8) But when the children of Israel await a Christ other than the Christ who has come, they hear, "I am the first and I am the last,"[33] and, "I am alpha and omega"[34]—the alpha which looks down, and the omega which looks up, in fulfillment of scripture's, "He that descended is the same also that ascended up far above all rule and authority and dominion, and every name that is named."[35]

7,9   And < to show what the truth is* > when < someone > supposes < that > < only the Father is the true God* > because he has said, "I am the first and the last," "I am alpha and omega," "The Lord thy God is one Lord,"[36] and "I am he who is,"[37] (10) Christ says, "My Father is greater than I,"[38] and, "that they may know thee, the only true God, and Jesus Christ whom thou hast sent."[39] Thus no one will deny the Son and the Holy Spirit. This is not [said] because the Son is not the true God, but to reduce the name of the Trinity to oneness, and redirect men's thinking from many divinities to one Godhead.

8,1   But if the blunderer Arius gets the notion that only the one, that is, only the Father, is called the "*true*" God, while the Son is God but not "*true* God," Christ refutes him in his turn, in another way. He says [of himself], "I am the *true* light, that lighteneth every man that cometh into the world,"[40] but of the Father, "God

---

[31] Luke 24:6
[32] Rom. 6:9
[33] Isa. 41:4; 44:6
[34] Rev. 1:8
[35] Eph. 4:10; 1:21
[36] Deut. 6:4
[37] Exod. 3:14
[38] John 14:28
[39] John 17:3
[40] John 8:12; 1:9

is *light.*"[41] (2) And he refrained from saying, "true light," so that
we would realize the equality of the Father's Godhead with the
Son's and the Son's with the Father's because of "*true* God" and
"*true* light," and not be < misled* > because of the Father's being
"light" and the Son's being "God" without the addition of "true"
in those instances. (3) There was no need to say "true" [in these
two latter cases], since there was no doubt about it. The one perfection of the same relationship—the Father's to the Son and the
Son's to the Father—was made plainly evident from the words,
"God" and "light."

8,4   And that demolishes the entire idiocy of your error. The
Father is a father, the Son is a son, and the Holy Spirit is a holy
spirit. They are a Trinity—one Godhead, one glory, one sovereignty, < one God >, to whom be glory, honor and might, the Father
in the Son, the Son with the Holy Spirit in the Father, forever and
ever. Amen.

8,5   And we have now shaken this sect off, and trampled it in
its turn by the power of the Holy Trinity, like a libys or molurus
or elops, or one of those snakes which look very alarming but can
do no harm with their bites. Let us once more go on to the rest,
calling on him to come to the aid of my poverty and mediocrity,
< so that > I may have his help in < giving* > a proper < account* >
of each sect's teachings and activities, < and* > composing the
refutations of them.

Against the first type of Origenists,[1] *who are shamefully behaved as*
well. 43, but 63 of the series

1,1   There are people called Origenists, but this kind of Origenist
is not to be found everywhere. I think, though, that the sect we
are now discussing < arose > next after these [others]. (2) They
are named Origenists, but I am not sure after whom. I do not know
whether they < are derived > from the Origen who is called
Adamantius the Author,[2] or from some other Origen. Still, I have
learned of this name.

1,3   Their heresy might have been modeled on the heresy of
Epiphanes, whom I described earlier in the Gnostic Sects.[3] But
these people read various scriptures of the Old and New Testa-

---

[41] 1 John 1:5

[1] Only Epiphanius mentions this group; his sources of information are plainly
oral.
[2] συντάκτης; cf. Suidas 2.1; Jer. C. Ruf. 1.9.
[3] Pan. 32,3,1–5,1

ments. And they reject marriage, although their sexual activity is incessant. Some have said that the sect originated in the region of Rome and Africa.

1,4 They soil their bodies, minds and souls with unchastity. Some of them masquerade as monastics, and their woman companions as female monastics. But they are physically ensnared because they satisfy their appetite but, to put it politely, by the act of Onan the son of Judah. (5) For as Onan satisfied his appetite with Tamar, but did not finish the act by planting his seed for the God-given [purpose of] procreation and did himself harm instead, thus, as < he > did the vile thing, so these people commit this infamy when they use their supposed < female monastics >. (6) They strive, not for purity but for a hypocritical purity in name. But their effort is merely to make sure that the woman the seeming < ascetic* > has seduced does not get pregnant—either so as not to cause child-bearing, or to escape detection, since they want honor for their supposed celibacy. (7) In any case, this is their act; others endeavor to get this same filthy satisfaction, not with women but by other means, and pollute themselves with their own hands. (8) They too are imitators of the son of Judah, and soil the ground with their forbidden practices and drops of filthy fluid. And they rub their emissions into the earth with their feet, so that their seed will not be snatched by unclean spirits for the impregnation of demons.

2,1 But as I said, they use various scriptures of the Old and the New Testaments and certain apocrypha, especially the so-called Acts of Andrew and the others. Indeed, they themselves have often freely boasted of doing this thing. (2) But they accuse the members of the church, if you please, who have beloved "adoptive wives," as they call them, of doing this too—but secretly from respect for public opinion, so as to engage in the wickedness < in fact* >, but in pretense preen themselves on the name ["virgin"] from regard for the public.

2,3 But some have told me about certain persons who are dead by now, and that they did this too, if you please, and have [alleged] that they had heard it from the women these people had forced into it. (4) Among them they mentioned a bishop who had exercised the episcopate for a number of years in a small town in Palestine, but had had women of this sort, I mean adoptive wives, to wait on him. Indeed, I have learned even from confessors that he was that way. (5) All the same, I do not believe the persons who have said this and claim to have heard it from the women. For distress at the malice of the speakers inclined me sometimes to believe, but sometimes to disbelieve their evil report of the old bishop after his death. (6) For the charge against him was something like this: "So-and-so was caught in sin with a woman, and his defense when we confronted him was that his partner in pollution had told him about the vicious practice"—although she was already along in years and in her old age!—"and taught him to use her but scatter his dirty fluids outside, on the ground."

3,1   And this is their filthy act, which deceives their own minds and is blinded by the devil. (2) I see no need for me to cite the texts which have been their downfall.[4] Otherwise I might give the impression that I use the texts I mean as criticisms, to discourage each sect's evil practices, to encourage the purpose of those whose minds are unstable and always vain, and who seek evil rather than desiring good. (3) Instead I shall offer a few sample arguments as protection against this frightful, snake-like sect.

3,4   What made you people think of your vile act? For to begin with, who cannot see that your teaching is all demons' teaching, and that the mischief you have contrived is deluded, corrupt people's behavior? (5) If conception is in any way evil, this is not because of childbearing but because of carnal relations. Then why do you give in to lust and have carnal relations?

3,6 And if carnal relations are not evil, neither is it evil for one who has them to consummate them. Or < must > an ascetic not cultivative the fruits of the soil, as "Abel was a keeper of sheep, but Cain was a tiller of the ground?"[5] (7) But if one tills the ground, like Noah who "became an husbandman and planted a vineyard"[6] —Noah did not plant a vineyard in order for it not to yield vintage. He planted it and "drank of the fruit thereof and was drunken,"[7] as scripture says.

3,8   But the aged man is excus< able >; he was pleasing to God, and did not fall to drink from intemperance. Perhaps he was overcome with grief and fell into a stupor, and succumbed to weakness from infirmity and old age because he could not bear them; [in any case] it was not to be mocked by his son. (9) But his mocker received the curse, for the punishment of those who offer insult to their parents, and of thoughts in us that rebel against the knowledge of God and his rightly decreed ordinance.

4,1   For even though marriage is not as highly honored as virginity and virginity is superior to it—for true virginity is called glorious and virtuous, not unclean—marriage is respectable too,

---

[4] Contrast Pan. 26,8,4–9,2.1.
[5] Gen 4:2
[6] Gen. 9:20
[7] Gen. 9:21

< if one > † employs[8] God's good creatures for procreation, not shame, and does not misuse God's appointed method of conjugal intercourse. (2) For in fact, virginity is the state the apostle commends because he says, "The virgin, and the unmarried woman, careth for the things of the Lord, how she may please the Lord, that she may be holy in body and soul"[9]—showing that even though the unmarried state is open to suspicion, it is no cause of faults.

4,3   Indeed, < propriety must be preserved in marriage* >. We know that Abraham sired children although he was dear to the Lord, and Isaac, Jacob and their successors. And they did not sully themselves with vile acts by touching filth and < slime* >, or oppose God's good ordinance of procreation through lawful wedlock. (4) Nor did those of them who practiced chastity and virginity spoil the contest and make a different thing of it, as though to evade by trickery the virtuous mode of competing. (5) Elijah too never lightly entered towns or associated with women, but lived in deserts. Elisha, John, and all who < exhibited > this great mark of the imitation of the angels, made themselves eunuchs in the right way for the kingdom of heaven's sake, in accordance with the Lord's ordinance in the Gospel.

4,6   And although I have a great deal to say about them, and could expose the devil's mockery of their minds with many proofs from scripture, I rest content with these few. (7) For anyone can see that their practice is not sensible, and that such knowledge is not from God; their mockery, and the disaster of their infamous practice, are diabolically inspired.

4,8   And now that we have maimed this sect too—like the horrid snake we call the viper, which has a short body but breathes a breath which is fearful for its venom, and blows destruction at those who come near it—let us go on to the rest since we have crushed it, calling on God to help us keep the promise of our whole work in God.

Against Origen,[1] *also called Adamantius. 44, but 64 of the series*

1,1   After these comes Origen, who is also surnamed Adamantius.[2]

---

[8] Holl; μεθοδεύει; MSS: ἀπαγορεύει
[9] 1 Cor. 7:34

[1] Eus. H. E. 6,1–39 (with some interruptions) contains an admiring account of Origen's life. Epiphanius' more hostile treatment is not based on Eusebius, but probably upon oral tradition which may, however, be itself influenced by Eusebius. See also Jer. Vir. Ill. 54.
[2] Eus. H. E. 6.14.10

He was the son of the holy and blessed martyr Leonidas,[3] and in his youth suffered a very great deal of persecution himself.[4] He was well schooled in the Greek education[5] and brought up in the church, and became known at Alexandria in the Emperor Decius' time.[6] (2) He was a native Egyptian, but lived and was brought up in Alexandria, and perhaps also went to the schools at Athens[7] at some time.

1,3   It is said that he suffered a great deal for the holy word of the faith and the name of Christ, and indeed was often dragged around the city, insulted, and subjected to excruciating tortures.[8] (4) Once, the story goes, the pagans shaved his head, set him on the steps of the temple of their idol which they call the Serapeum, and ordered him to hand out palm branches to those who went up the stairs for the vile act of worshiping the idol. (The priests of their idols take this posture.) (5) Taking the branches he cried out without fear or hesitation, with loud voice and a bold mind, "Come get Christ's branch, not the idol's!" And many accounts of his brave deeds are handed down to us by the ancients.

2,1   But his deeds did not remain worthy of the prize till the end. He had been an object of extreme envy for his superior learning and education, and this further provoked the authorities of his day. (2) With diabolical malice the workers of iniquity thought of mistreating him sexually and making that his punishment, and they secured a black to abuse his body. (3) But Origen could not bear even the thought of this devil's work, and shouted that if these were his choices he would rather sacrifice.[9] (4) Certainly, as is widely reported, he did not do this willingly either. But since he had agreed do to it at all, he heaped incense on his hands and dumped it on the altar fire. (5) Thus he was excluded from a martyr's status at that time by the confessors and martyrs who were his judges, and was expelled from the church.[10]

2,6   Since he had consented to this at Alexandria and could not bear the ridicule of those who reproached him, he left and

---

[3] Eus. H. E. 6.1.1

[4] Eus. H. E. 6.3.4–7; 4.1

[5] Eus. H. E. 6.18–19; 1.7

[6] Eusebius says that Origen was tortured during the Decian persecution (H. E. 6.39.5) but began his career in the tenth year of Septimius Severus, our 209 A.D. (H. E. 6.1.2).

[7] Eus. H. E. 6.32.4; Jer. Vir. Ill. 54

[8] Eus. H. E. 6.3.4–7; 4.1; 39.5

[9] This appears to be a variation on the story of Origen's pupil Potimiaena, who is threatened with rape by gladiators, answers defiantly, and is put to death, Eus. H. E. 6.5.1–5.

[10] At Photius Bibl. 11 Eusebius is inaccurately reported as saying that a synod

elected to live in Palestine, that is, in Judaea. (7) On arriving at Jerusalem he was urged by the priesthood, as a man with such skill in exegesis and so highly educated, to speak in church.[11] (They say that the presbyterate had been conferred upon him earlier, before his sacrifice.)[12] (8) And so, as I said, since those who were then serving as priests in the holy church in Jerusalem urged him to speak in church and strongly insisted on it, he stood up and simply recited the verse of the forty-ninth Psalm, omitting all the intervening verses, "But unto the ungodly saith God, Why dost thou preach my laws and takest my covenant in thy mouth?"[13] And he rolled the scroll up, gave it back, and sat down in floods of tears, and all wept with him.

3,1 A while later, at the urgent request of many, he made the acquaintance of Ambrose, a prominent imperial official. (Some say that Ambrose was a Marcionite, but some, that he was a Sabellian.)[14] At any rate, Origen taught him to shun and abjure the sect and adopt the faith of God's holy church, for at that time Origen was of the orthodox, catholic faith. (2) Since Ambrose was from a different sect and, < being > an educated man, was a zealous reader of the sacred scriptures, he asked Origen to explain them to him because of the profundity of the ideas in the sacred books. (3) Because he owed him this, and at his urging, Origen was willing to become the interpreter of all the scriptures, as it were, and[15] made it his business to expound them. It is said that < he spent* > twenty-eight years in Tyre in Phoenicia[16] (4) < devoting himself* > to a life of extreme piety,[17] and to study and hard work. Ambrose provided support for him and his stenographers and assistants,[18] and papyrus and his other expenses;[19] and Origen carried his work

---

expelled Origen from Alexandria after this incident.

[11] Origen is urged to preach at Caesarea, but this gives scandal because he is a layman, Eus. H. E. 6.8.4–5.

[12] Eusebius places Origen's ordination to the presbyterate at Caesarea, H. E. 6.8.4–5.

[13] Ps. 49:16. At In Psalmos 12.348 Origen says, "A sinner should not preside in the office of a teacher."

[14] Eusebius makes Ambrose a Valentinian, H. E. 6.18.1.

[15] Holl: ἑρμηνεὺς γενέσθαι [καί] ἐξηγήασθαι ἐπετήδευσε; Dummer retains the καί.

[16] Jerome says that Origen died at Tyre, Vir, Ill. 54. Epiphanius locates Origen's literary activity there, and seems not to know of his headship of the catechetical school at Alexandria, which Eusebius emphasizes at H. E. 6.3–8.

[17] Origen's austerities are mentioned at Eus. H. E. 6.3.9–12.

[18] Holl: ὀξυγράφοις [καί] τοῖς ὑπηρετοῦσιν αὐτῷ; Dummer retains the καί. Eus. H. E. 6.23.1–2

[19] Eus. H.E. 6.23.1–2

on the scripture through by burning the midnight oil, and with
the most intense study.

3,5   First, making a painstaking effort to collect the < books* >
of the six [Old Testament] versions—Aquila, Symmachus, the
Septuagint, Theodotion, (6) and a fifth and a sixth [version]—
< he issued them* > setting each Hebrew expression next to them,
and the actual < Hebrew > letters as well. But right beside these,
in a second column next to the Hebrew, he made still another
parallel text, but in Greek letters. (7) Thus this is, and is called
a Hexapla.[20] But besides the Greek translations < there are > two
parallel texts, of the Hebrew actually in < Hebrew > letters, and
of the Hebrew in Greek letters. It is thus the whole Old Testament
in the version called the Hexapla, and in the two Hebrew texts.

3,8   Origen had laboriously contrived this entire work but he
did not preserve his fame untarnished till the end; his wealth of
learning proved to be his great downfall. (9) Precisely because of
his goal of leaving no scripture uninterpreted he disguised himself,
as an allurement to sin, and issued mortally dangerous exegeses.
(10) The so-called Origenists < took their cue* > from this—not
the first kind, the practitioners of* > the obscenity. As I have already
remarked, I cannot say whether they originate with this Origen
who is also called Adamantius, or whether they have another founder
whose name was < also > Origen.

3,11   It is said, however, that our Origen also thought of < a >
way of dealing with his body. < For > some say that he severed a
nerve so that he would not be disturbed by sexual pleasure or
inflamed and aroused by carnal impulses.[21] (12) Others say no, but
that he invented a drug to apply to his genitals and dry them up.
But others venture to ascribe other inventions to him—that he
discovered a medicinal plant to assist memory. (13) And though
I put no faith in the exaggerated stories about him, I have not
neglected to report what is being said.

4,1   The sect which sprang from him was in Egypt first, but < it
is > now < to be found > among the very persons who are the most
eminent and appear to have adopted the monastic life—who have
really retired to the deserts and elected voluntary poverty. But this
is a dreadful sect and worse than all the ancient ones, and indeed,
has beliefs like theirs. (2) For though it does not train its disciples
to perform the obscenity, it imposes an † evil meaning,[22] worse

---

[20] Cf. Eus. H. E. 6.15.1–4; Jer. In Tit. 3.9 (MSL 26, 595B).
[21] Eusebius (H. E. 6.8.1–3) says that Origen did something serious to his
body, but does not specify what.

than the obscenity, upon the Godhead itself. For Arius took his cue from Origen, and so did the Anomoeans who succeeded him, and the rest.

4,3   For Origen claims, and dares to say at once,[23] if you please, first that the Only-begotten Son cannot see the Father, and neither can the Spirit behold the Son;[24] and angels surely cannot behold the Spirit, nor men the angels. (4) And this is his first downfall. For he does not believe that the Son is of the Father's essence, but represents him as entirely different from the Father, and created besides. But he holds that he is called "Son" by grace.

4,5   But he has other downfalls too, which are more serious. He says that the human soul is preexistent, and that souls are angels and celestial powers, but have sinned and so been shut up in this body as a punishment. (6) They are sent < down > by God as a punishment, to submit to a first judgment here. And so the body is called a "frame" (δέμας), says Origen, because the soul has been "bound" (δέδεσθαι) in the body—but he is picturing the ancient Greek fabrication. And he tells other stories about this as well. He says that we speak of a "soul" (ψυχή) because it "cooled off" (ἐψύχθαι) in coming down.[25]

4,7   He spreads proof-texts from the sacred scriptures around to suit himself, though not as they stand or with their real interpretation. He claims that the words of the prophet, "Before I was humbled, I offended,"[26] are the words of the soul itself, because it "offended" in heaven before it was "humbled" in the body. (8) And "Return unto thy rest, O my soul,"[27] means that one has been valiant in good works here, and because of the righteousness of his behavior is returning to his rest on high.

4,9   And he says many other things of the sort. He says that Adam lost the image of God. And this is why the scripture speaks of the skin tunics, for "He made them tunics of skin and clothed them"[28] refers to the body. And he talks a great deal of widely repeated nonsense.

4,10   He makes the resurrection of the dead defective, and

---

[22] Holl: κακήν; MSS: δεινήν
[23] [Marcianus, Urbinas, the Georgian, Delahaye: κατ᾽ αρχήν; Venetianus, Holl: περὶ ἀρχῶν, "concerning first principles."
[24] Orig. Princ. 1.1.8; Cf. Justinian, Ep. Ad Mennam, Mansi IX 489C.
[25] Orig. Princ. 2.8.3. Cf. Paschal Epistle of Dionysius of Alexandria for 401 A.D.=Jer. Ep. 96.15.1; for 402=Jer. Ep. 98.1.10; for 404=Jer. Ep. 100.12.1–3.
[26] Ps. 118.6–7. Cf. the attribution of the penitential and supplicatory Psalms to the fallen Pistis Sophia, PS 52–56 et al.
[27] Ps. 114:7
[28] Gen. 3:21

sometimes nominally supports it, sometimes denies it altogether; and at other times < he says > that there is a partial resurrection. (11) Finally, he interprets whatever he can allegorically—Paradise, its waters, the waters above the heavens, the water under the earth. He never stops saying these ridiculous things and others like them. But I have already mentioned things of this sort about him, and discussed them at length, in some of my other works.[29]

5,1   But even now, in the sect that deals with him, it will do no harm to describe them again for the same reason and purpose, and make his refutation out of his own insinuations. (2) For there is a great deal of later nonsense of his, and cultivation of a notion that is false and departs from the truth. (3) For he appeared to speak against every sect before him and refute each one, but later he spat this sect up into the world, one of no small importance.

5,4   And in refutation of his false and bogus notion I shall quote his own words first; then I shall show what I, in my mediocrity, intend to say against him. And here are the things he told the world in *The First Psalm* ; (5) for though he is always on slippery ground in every scripture, in the essential parts he erred in so many words.

But since < his writings are* > very bulky—as I mentioned, he is said to have written a long work on every scripture— < it is impossible to quote all of it; but Origen never* > refused to say what he thought < in his expositions of the scripture* >. (6) And he has a modest reputation for what he said about ethics, types of animals and so on in his sermons and prefaces, and often gave clever expositions. (7) But in his position on doctrines, and about faith and higher speculation, he is the wickedest of all before and after him, except for the shameless behavior in the sects. (8) (For as I indicated above, he chose to adopt even an ascetic style of life. Some say that his stomach was ruined by his excessively severe regimen, and fasting and abstention from meat.

5,9   Well then, I shall quote his own words from the *First Psalm*[30] < along with > his doctrinal speculations in it—word for word, so that no one may call my attack on him vexatious. (10) Not, by any means, that he strayed from the truth only in the *First Psalm* ; as I have often said, he did it in every exposition. But because of the extent of his work let me select some things from his *Psalm* here, and show the whole of his unsoundness in the faith from one, two or three expressions, of course taking care to speak against

---

[29] Epiphanius means Anc. 54–64. See also the later Epiph./John of Jerusalem=Jer. Ep. 51.5.1; 7.
[30] Eusebius mentions this commentary at H. E. 6.25.1.

them. (11) And here, at once, is the text of every word, to show you, scholarly hearer, that Origen plainly held that the Son of God is a creature, and also show you, from his impudence about the Son, that he taught that the Holy Spirit is the creature of a creature. (12) Let us take a part of the *Psalm*, from the beginning until the actual expression [in question], in Origen's own words.

The beginning of Origen's commentary on the first Psalm

6,1 *God's oracles tell us that the sacred scriptures have been locked away and sealed with the "key of David"*[31]*—also, perhaps, with the seal of which it said, "an impression of a seal, hallowed to the Lord."*[32] *They are sealed, in other words, by the power of the God who gave them, the power which is meant by the seal. (2) In the Book of Revelation John instructs us further about this locking away and sealing and says, "And to the angel of the church in Philadelphia write, These things saith he that is holy, he that is true, he that hath the key of David, he that openeth, and none shall shut, and shutteth, and none shall open. I know thy works; behold, I have set before thee an open door, and no man can shut it."*[33] *(3) And a little further on, "And I saw in the right hand of him that sat on the throne a book written within and on the backside, sealed with seven seals. And I saw another strong angel proclaiming with a loud voice, Who is worthy to open the book and to loose the seals thereof? (4) And no man in heaven, nor on earth, neither under the earth, was able to open the book, neither to look thereon. And I wept, because no man was found worthy to open the book, neither to look thereon. (5) And one of the elders saith unto me, Weep not. Behold, the Lion of the tribe of Judah, the Root of David, hath prevailed to open the book and the seven seals thereof."*[34]

6,6 *And, of the sealing alone, Isaiah says the following : "And all these words shall be unto you as the words of this book that is sealed. The which, if it be given to any man that is learned, saying, Read this, he shall say, I cannot read it, for it is sealed. And this book shall be given into the hands of a man that is not learned, and one shall say unto him, Read this. And he shall say, I am not learned."*[35]

6,7 *We must take it that this is said not only of John's Revelation and Isaiah, but of all of sacred scripture—admittedly, even by those capable of a fair understanding of the oracles of God. For scripture is filled with riddles, parables, difficult sayings and manifold other forms of obscurity,*

---

[31] Rev. 3:7
[32] Exod. 28:36; Sir. 45:12
[33] Rev. 3:7–8
[34] Rev. 5:1–5
[35] Isa. 29:11–12

and is hard for human comprehension. (8) In his desire to teach us this the Savior too said, "Woe unto you lawyers!"—as though scribes and Pharisees held the key but made no effort to find the way to open the door. "For ye have taken away the key of knowledge. Ye entered not in yourselves, and them that were entering in ye suffered not to enter."[36]

7,1 *I have said this by way of preface, holy Ambrose, since I am compelled by your great love of learning and my embarrassment at your kindness and humility, to embark on a struggle of the utmost difficulty, and admittedly beyond me and my strength. (2) And since I was hesitant for a long time, knowing the danger not only of speaking of holy things but, far more, of writing of them and leaving one's work for posterity, you will be my witness before God of the disposition with which I have done this—even though, with all the world, I too inquire into these matters. For with all sorts of friendly blandishment, and with godly encouragement, you have brought me to it. (3) And I sometimes hit the mark, but sometimes argue too vehemently or < otherwise* > appear to say something < too daring* >. I have, however, investigated the text without despising the aptly put, "When thou speakest of God, thou art judged of God," and, "It is no small risk to speak even the truth of God."*

7,4 *Now since without God there can be no good thing, especially an understanding of the inspired scriptures, I ask you to approach the God and Father of all through our Savior and High Priest, the originated* (γενητός) *God, and pray that he will grant me, first, to seek as I ought. For there is a promise of finding for those who seek; [but] it may be that there is no promise at all for seekers if God deems them to be proceeding by a road that does not lead to finding.*

So far the excerpt from Origen

8,1 And first I need to discuss the term, "originated God," with this braggart with his illusory wisdom, the searcher out of the unsearchable and exhibitor of the heavenly realms, who, as a greater man than I has said, has filled the world with nonsense. (2) And anyone can see that there are many equivalents and synonyms. (3) If the term were used by someone else, one might say that this too had been said with right intent. But since I have found in many instances that Origen wrongly distinguishes between the Only-begotten God and the Father's Godhead and essence—and the same with the Holy Spirit—it is plain that by saying "originated God" he is pronouncing him a creature.

8,4 For though some would like to outwit me and say that "originated" is the same thing as "begotten," < this > is not admis-

---

[36] Luke 11:52

sible. < The latter may be said only of God, but the former* > may not be said of God, but only of creatures. "Originated" is one thing, "begotten," another.

8,5   Now as to Origen's statement that God is created or originated, let me ask first, "How was the person created whom, by this expression of yours, you honor as God? And if he is created, how can he be worshiped?" (6) Set aside the holy apostle's censure of those who make gods of created things; grant that a creature can be worshiped as God by the principles of the godly faith, which worships the creator, not the creature! Then it will be reasonable for you to derive your erroneous argument from the piety of the fathers. But there is no way you can prove this. (7) And even if you ventured to steal it from somewhere and distort it—even so, you nut, you cannot change the good sense of the godly into judgment as poor as this! Both your intent and your argument are against you; (8) as I said, no created thing is worthy of worship. But if it is worthy of any worship, then, since there are many other created things, it will not matter that we worship them all along with the one creature; they are its fellow servants, and in the same category.

9,1   But let us see by the four Gospels through which the divine Word, when he came, revealed our whole salvation, whether Christ has ever said, "God created me," or, "My Father created me!" And let us see whether the Father declared in any of the Gospels, "I have created the Son and sent him to you." (2) But enough of this for now; as to proof-texts, I have often cited them at length against people who introduce the notion of the Son's creaturehood.

9,3   Even here, however, it will do no harm to show the ease with which the term can be refuted and ask the would-be sage, "Mister, how can he be a creature when he says, "I am in the Father and the Father in me, and we two are one?"[37] (4) How can he be different from the Father when he has equal honor? For "No man knoweth the Son save the Father, nor the Father, save the Son,"[38] and, "He that hath seen me hath seen the Father?"[39]

9,5   And now to resume the thread and speak likewise of all his doubts about resurrection, again from his own words. But let me exhibit the whole of his opinion and expose the infidelity of his doctrinal position from one passage. (6) < For > even though he has spoken extensively of this and talked nonsense about it in many books, I shall still make this disclosure from his argument

---

[37] John 14:10; 10:30
[38] Matt. 11:27
[39] John 14:9

in *The First Psalm* against the sure hope of us believers in resurrection.

10,1   And it is as follows. He says, *"Therefore the ungodly shall not arise in the judgment."*[40] Next he says, *"Theodotion, Aquila and Symmachus agree"*—(he is fond of using the versions to astonish.) Then he goes on scornfully against the sons of the truth:

10,2   *Thus the simpler believers suppose that the ungodly do not attain the resurrection and are not held worthy of the divine judgment; but they have no way of explaining what they think resurrection is, and what sort of judgment they imagine. (3) For even if they think they have expressed their opinion of these matters, examination will show that they cannot defend the consequences of their beliefs, and have no grasp of the nature of resurrection and judgment.*

10,4   *Thus if we ask them what it is a resurrection of, they reply, "Of the bodies we have now." If we then ask further whether or not there is a resurrection of our whole being, before we examine them they say, "Of our whole being."' (5) But if, allowing for the naivete of those who do not even < understand* > the mutability of nature, we raise further questions and inquire whether all the blood that has been lost in bleedings will rise with our bodies—and all the flesh that has wasted away in illness, and all the hair we have ever had, or only the hair we had at the last, towards our end—(6) they are distressed and sometimes take offense at the questioning, since they believe we must allow to God to deal with these things as he wills. But sometimes, since they believe that our hair at the end of this life goes down to the grave with the body, they say that it will rise with it. (7) The better of them, however, say that it is our body at the end that rises, to avoid having to take account of the blood which has flowed from our bodies on many occasions, and the flesh which changes < to > sweat or something else in illness.*

11,1   These are the would-be sage's worthless objections to truth; for those who wish to know the full intent of his disbelief in the resurrection, I was obliged to quote them as proof. Indeed, he makes many other < fool remarks* > in the course of the *Psalm*, one after another. (2) For he says, *Therefore the ungodly shall not arise in the judgment.*[41] From here on he attacks those who declare the certainty of the resurrection, and who believe in the sure hope of the resurrection of the dead, for their naivete. And by adding many weak arguments, inculcating a fallacious opinion, (3) < and presenting > nothing reliable, but any old argument from logic for the ruin of his followers, he tried to overthrow the confession of

---

[40] Ps. 1:5
[41] Ps. 1:5

our true hope in the resurrection by referring to the accidents of our nature.

11,4   But with my limited ability, I wouldn't dare hope to improve on those who have done good work already and replied with full justice to all the rhetorical villainy Origen has thought of. I believe I may rest content with the blessed Methodius' remarks against Origen on account of the resurrection. I shall present these here, word for word; Methodius' words as he composed them are as follows:

An epitome of Origen's arguments, from the writings of Methodius

12,1   *Thus the simpler believers suppose that the ungodly do not attain the resurrection < and are not held worthy of the divine judgment; but they have no way of explaining > what they think resurrection is, < or what sort of judgment they imagine >. (2) For even if they think they have expressed their opinion of these matters, examination will show that they cannot defend the consequences of their beliefs < and have no grasp of the mode of the resurrection and judgment >.*

12,3   *Thus if we ask them what it is a resurrection of, they reply, "of the bodies we have now." If we then ask further whether or not there is a resurrection of our whole being, before we examine them they say, "of our whole being." (4) But if, allowing for the naivete < of those who do not even understand the mutability of nature >, we raise further questions < and inquire > whether all the blood that has been lost in bleedings will rise with our bodies—and all the flesh and hair we have ever had, or just what we had toward our end—(5) they will be distressed and take refuge in the answer that God < may > do as he will. The better of them, however, will say that it is our body at the end that rises, and thus not have to take account of the same blood which flows from our bodies on many occasions, < and the flesh which changes to sweat or something else in illness >.*

12,6   *But because of the natural mutability of bodies and points of this sort, we have raised further questions. As foods are taken into the body and change their appearances, (7) so our bodies too are changed in birds of prey and wild beasts, and become parts of their bodies. And when they in turn are eaten by men or other animals, they undergo corresponding changes and become the bodies of men and other animals. (8) And as this continues for a long time, the same body must often become a part of more men. In the resurrection, then, whose body will it be? And in this way we become immersed in senseless drivel.*

13,1   *And after these objections they resort to the reply that all things are possible with God, and cite texts from the scriptures which, if taken at their face value, are capable of supporting their opinion. (2) For example, Ezekiel's "And the hand of the Lord was upon me, and he brought me forth in the spirit and set me in the midst of the plain, and it was full of men's bones. And he brought me about them round about, and lo, there were very many upon the face of the plain, and lo, they were very dry. (3) And he said unto me, Son of man, can these bones live? And I said, Lord God, thou knowest these things. (4) And he said unto me, Prophesy, son of man. And thou shalt say unto them, Ye dry bones, hear the word of the Lord. Thus saith Adonai, the Lord, unto these bones: Lo, I will bring into you the breath of life, and I will put sinews upon you and cover you with flesh, and I will stretch skin upon you and put my Spirit within you, and ye shall live. And I will place you in your own land, and ye shall know that I am the Lord."[42]*

13,5   *They use this passage < as > a quite convincing one. But they < gather > others too, from the Gospels, such as, "There shall be wailing and gnashing of teeth,"[43] and, "Fear him that is able to destroy both soul and body in hell,"[44] and Paul's, "He shall raise up your mortal bodies through his Spirit that dwelleth in you."[45]*

14,1   *But every lover of truth, who is just as determined as they to contend for the resurrection, must both preserve the tradition of the ancients and guard against falling into the tomfoolery of contemptible notions which are both impossible and unworthy of God. (2) And here it must be understood that no body ever has the same material substratum. A body is controlled by nature, which puts something such as food into it from without, and as this food is eliminated, further things such as vegetable and animal products in place of the other materials it has put there. (3) Thus the body has not inaptly been called a river. For strictly speaking, the first substratum in our bodies is scarcely the same for two days, even though, despite the fluidity of the nature of a body, Paul's body, say, or Peter's, is always the same. (Sameness does not apply just to the soul, whose nature is neither in flux like our [body's], nor ever added to.) (4) This is because the form which identifies the body is the same, just as the features which characterize Peter's or Paul's bodies remain the same—characteristics < like > childhood scars, and such peculiarities < as > moles, and any others besides.*

14,5   *This form, the bodily, which constitutes Peter and Paul, encloses the soul once more at the resurrection, changed for the better—but surely not this extension which underlay it at the first. (6) For as the form is < the same > from infancy until old age even though the features appear*

---

[42] Ezek 37:11
[43] Matt. 8:12
[44] Matt. 10:28
[45] Rom. 8:11

to undergo considerable change, so we must suppose that, though its change for the better will be very great, our present form will be the same in the world to come.

14,7   *For souls which are in bodily places must have bodies to suit the places. (8) And just as, if we had to become water creatures and lived in the sea, we would surely need gills and the other features of fish, so, as we are to inherit the kingdom of heaven and live in places superior to ours, we must have spiritual bodies. (9) But despite its change to greater glory the form of the previous body does not vanish, just as, at the transfiguration, the forms of Jesus, Moses and Elijah were not different from what they had been.*

15,1   *Therefore do not be offended if someone should say that the first substratum will not be the same then. For to those who can understand the matter, reason shows that, even now, the first substratum is not the same two days running. (2) It is also a consideration worth grasping that one thing is sown, but a different thing comes up; for "It is sown a natural body; it is raised a spiritual body."[46] (3) And Paul, practically teaching us that we will discard < every > earthly characteristic at the resurrection but that our form will be preserved, adds, "This I say, brethren, that flesh and blood cannot inherit the kingdom of God; neither doth corruption inherit incorruption."[47] (4) The form will likely be preserved in the holy < body > by Him who once gave form to the flesh. It will be flesh no longer, but whatever was once characteristic of the flesh will be characteristic of the spiritual body.*

15,5   *Now < as to > the sayings of the scriptures which our brethren cite, there is this to be said. First, Ezekiel's, since the simpler sort prefer to < rely > on it. According to these lines there will be no resurrection of flesh, but only of bones, skin and sinews. (6) At the same time they must be shown that they are too hasty, since they have not understood the passage spiritually. Simply because bones are mentioned we need not take them to mean the bones we have—just as it is obvious that, in "Our bones were scattered beside Hades,"[48] "All my bones were scattered,"[49] and, "Heal me, for my bones were troubled,"[50] "bones" in the common acceptation of the word are not intended.*

15,7   *Now to this tally Ezekiel adds, "They say, Our bones are dried up."[51] Are they really saying, "Our bones are dried up," with the intent that the bones be reassembled and rise? But this cannot be. (8) They might*

---

[46] 1 Cor. 15:44
[47] 1 Cor. 15:50
[48] Ps. 140:7
[49] Ps. 21:15
[50] Ps. 6:3
[51] Ezek. 37:11

*say, "Our bones are dried up," however, because they are in captivity and
have lost all their living moisture. And so they add, "Our hope is perished,
we are lost."*[52] *Thus the promise of the people's resurrection is a promise
of their rising from their fall and the death which, in a way, they have
died for their sins by being abandoned to their enemies.* (9) *And the Savior
calls sinners "sepulchers full of dead men's bones and all uncleanness."*[53]
*And it is fitting that God open the graves of each of us, and bring us
forth from the graves quickened, as the Savior brought forth Lazarus.*

16,1   *But as to "There shall be wailing and gnashing of teeth,"*[54] *we
must confront them with the objection that, as in this life the creator has
made every member of the body for some purpose, so he has made the teeth
to chew solid food. Why do the damned need teeth, then? Our brethren
do not claim that they eat in hell.* (2) *And it must be pointed out that
not everything in scripture is to be taken at its face value. Scripture says,
"Thou hast broken the teeth of sinners,"*[55] *and, "The Lord hath crushed
the teeth of the lions,"*[56] *but who is so foolish as to suppose that, while
preserving sinners' bodies, God breaks only their teeth?* (3) *Just as whoever
wanted the lines to read like that was obliged by his discomfort with them
to resort to allegory, so one must look for the gnashing of the teeth of the
damned. The soul has the faculty of "chewing [on things]," and when
convicted of its sins will "gnash its teeth" by the clash of its † thoughts.*[57]

16,4   *But "Fear him which is able to destroy both soul and body in
hell"*[58] *might be meant to teach that the soul is incorporeal. However, it
might also mean that it will not be punished apart from the body. I have
already spoken of the form and first substratum of the body from a naturalist's
perspective.*

16,5   *And the apostle's saying, "He shall also quicken your mortal
bodies,"*[59] *even when the body is mortal and incapable of true life, can be
a proof that, although the bodily form of which we have spoken is by nature
mortal, it will itself be changed from a "body of death,"*[60] *be quickened by
the life-giving Spirit "when Christ who is our life shall appear,"*[61] *and from
< fleshly > become spiritual.* (6) *And "Some man will say, How are the
dead raised up, and with what body do they come?"*[62] *is also plain proof
that the first substratum will not be raised.* (7) *For if we have understood*

[52] Ezek. 37:11
[53] Matt. 32:27
[54] Matt. 8:12
[55] Ps. 3:8
[56] Ps. 57:7
[57] Holl: φρονημάτων; MSS: ὀδόντων
[58] Matt. 10:28
[59] Rom. 6:11
[60] Rom. 7:24
[61] Col. 3:4
[62] 1 Cor. 15:35

the illustration properly, we must hold that when the generative principle in the grain of wheat has laid hold of the matter which surrounds it, has permeated it entirely < and > has taken control of its form, it imparts its own powers to what was formerly earth, water, air and fire, and by prevailing over their characteristics transforms them into the thing whose creator it is. And thus the ear of grain comes to maturity, vastly different from the original seed in size, shape and complexity.

Proclus' own words[63]

17,1   *So much by way of summary of the points which Origen endeavored to make in his treatise on resurrection, in proof of a very complex hypothesis. But consider too the points which follow these. (2) It remains to take up the additional texts from scripture so that, like an image < with > all parts of it in proportion, this presentation may < thereby > gain < symmetry > and be fully framed as a whole, lacking nothing that contributes to its shape and beauty. (3) We must therefore explain why the scriptures which enable one to perfect a better proof agree with the above. For if one is capable of a precise understanding of this and falls short in nothing that is needed, he will realize that the resurrection may not be taken to apply to this body which cannot remain unchanged forever, but that it must apply to the spiritual body, in which the very same form that is even now preserved in this body will be retained—so that, as Origen said too, each of us will be the same even in appearance.*

17,4   *For he proposed that the resurrection will be as follows : Since the material body is mutable, he says, and since it never remains even briefly the same but is increased and diminished in the form characteristic of the man, by which his appearance is preserved, we must of necessity expect the resurrection to be reserved for the form alone. (5) And lest you say, "I don't understand"—Origen's treatment of this was difficult—I shall explain the sense of this more clearly to you here. (6) You have surely seen an animal skin, or something else of the sort, filled with water in such a way that, if it is emptied of a little of its water and then filled with a little, it always shows the same shape ; for the container's contents must conform to the shape of the container. (7) Well then, suppose the water is leaking out. If one adds an amount of water equal to that which is spilled and does not allow the skin to be entirely emptied of water, unless the skin is emptied the added water must look like the water which was there before, since the container of the inflowing and the outflowing water is the same.*

17,8 *Now if one chooses to compare the body to this, he will not be put to shame. For the food which is ingested in place of the flesh which has*

---

[63] The Origenist speaker Proclus has been summarizing Origen's teaching on resurrection. Now he begins to speak for himself.

*been eliminated will likewise be changed to the shape of the form which
contains it. And the part of it that is dispersed to the eyes looks like the
eyes, the part that is dispersed to the face looks like the face, and the part
that is dispersed to the other members looks like them. Thus everyone looks
the same, though the flesh in them is not their original flesh, but the flesh
of the form whose shape the incoming food was given.*

17,9   *Now if we are not the same in body even for a few days but are
the same in the form of the body—only this is stable from its creation—
all the more will we not be the same in the flesh then either. But we shall
be the same in the form which is preserved in us now < and > which always
remains in us. (10) For as, although the body is not the same now, its
appearance is kept the same because it has the same form, so, though the
body will not be the same then either, the form will be manifest, grown
more glorious—no longer in a perishable, but in an impassible and spiritual
body as Jesus' was at the transfiguration when he ascended the mountain
with Peter, and as were the bodies of Moses and Elijah who appeared to
him.*

18,1   *So much for this; this, in sum, is the sense of Origen's doctrine.
(2) But suppose that one who doubts this urges the body of Christ—for
he is called "the firstborn from the dead"[64] and the "firstfruits of them that
slept"[65]—and says that we must expect the resurrection of everyone's <bod-
ies> to be like the resurrection of Christ, so that "God will bring them which
sleep in Jesus with him"[66] in the same way that Christ was raised. But,
[he will go on to say], Jesus' < body > has risen even with the flesh it had,
and with its bones, as Thomas was convinced. We [for our part] shall
say, (3) "But Christ's body was not 'by the will of a man,'[67] 'of pleasure
accompanying sleep,'[68] 'conceived in iniquities and begotten in sins.'[69] It
was 'of the Holy Spirit, the power of the Highest and the Virgin,'[70] while
yours is the product of sleep, pleasure and dirt. (4) And thus the sage,
Sirach, said, 'When a man dieth it is said, He shall inherit creeping things,
snakes and worms.'[71] And < David > in the eighty-seventh Psalm said,
'Wilt thou do wonders for the dead, or shall physicians rise up and confess
thee? Will thy mercy be told in the grave and thy faithfulness in destruction?
Will thy wondrous works be known in the dark, and thy righteousness in
the forgotten land?'"[72] (5) And for one who cares to gather them from the*

---

[64] Col. 1:18; Rev. 1:5
[65] 1 Cor. 15:20
[66] 1 Thes. 4:14
[67] John 1:3
[68] Wisd. Sol. 7:2
[69] Ps. 50:7
[70] Cf. Luke 1:35.
[71] Sir. 10:11.
[72] Ps. 87:11–13

scriptures, there are other passages of the same kind. < Let us omit them* >,
lest, by mentioning them all, I make my discourse many times longer than
what has been said.

For the rest, the words of Methodius

19,1   *Proclus, then, came to a reluctant halt and the hearers were silent*
for some time, for they had fallen into entire unbelief. And I saw that he
had really finished, raised my head unnoticed by the rest, and heaved a
sigh like sailors when the swell subsides, though I was still trembling slightly,
and giddy—(I had been hit, I can tell you, and was overwhelmed by the
frightfulness of the words.) (2) I turned to Auxentius and addressed him
by name. "Auxentius," I said, "I believe that the line, 'Two proceeding
together,[73] *was not spoken in vain, since we have two opponents. Therefore*
'Let the both of us become as strong as the both of them.[74] *(3) I choose*
you for my ally and fellow combatant in the battle against them to keep
Aglaophon, in alliance with Proclus and armed against us with Origen's
objections, from sacking the resurrection. (4) Come then, let us stand our
ground against their sophisms, fearing none of the counter-arguments by
which the cowardly are struck. For there is no soundness or firmness whatever
in them, but merely a specious show of words rehearsed for the purpose
of awing and swaying the hearers, not for the sake of the truth and for
the hearers' benefit, but so that the words will sound wise to the audience.
(5) Thus probable propositions, embellished for the sake of beauty and to
give pleasure, are sometimes thought better by the masses than the results
of precise investigation—though the teachers are not striving for improve-
ment and still more, for holiness, but to please and succeed, like the sophists
who take money for what they say, and cut the price of their wisdom for
applause.
19,6   *"Anciently, expositions were always brief, and were given by persons*
who were at pains, not to please, but to benefit the audiences of their day.
But latterly, ever since, from carelessness, anyone has been permitted to
interpret the scriptures, they have all been filled with conceit and lost their
keenness for doing good, but have prided themselves on their progress in
debating, as though they were clever enough to know everything—ashamed
to admit that they needed teaching, but < ambitious* > to contend, like their
teachers, and to seek to surpass . . .[75] *(7) Thus from over-confidence they*
have lapsed from piety, meekness, and the belief that God can do all that

---

[73] Iliad 10.244
[74] Iliad 21.308–9
[75] Some material has fallen out at this point.

he has promised, and have come to meaningless, blasphemous disputations, unaware that deeds were not performed for the sake of words, but words [were spoken] for the sake of deeds—as < in > medicine, whereby the sick must be cured by the putting of set words into application—so that, once we have been tuned, our minds may be in full accord with our best words, and, like lyres, provide behavior in tune with our speech, but not discordant and inharmonious. (8) *To attain to righteousness we must truly struggle to practice it—not struggle in appearance, setting foot on the path of wisdom with a limp, and in place of a real effort making an apparent one, disguised with pretexts, pretenses, and all the trappings of hypocrisy.*

20,1　*For there are indeed persons who, like women artfully made up for deception, < beguile the simple* > with the embraces of words showily adorned, unless someone examines them with a concern for those even younger in the faith, and in a sober manner.* (2) *One must take care, then, before he learns to accept this sort of talk with trust. Deceivers often overtake the wavering, just as the Sirens overtake those who flee from them by disguising their hatred of humanity with beautiful singing from afar.* (3) *Or what do you < think > of this situation, Auxentius?" I said.*

"The same as you," he replied.

20,4　*"Mustn't we say, then, that the heretical sophists are no more than forgers of images of truth, who, like painters, know nothing of truth? For painters attempt to portray shipwrights, boats and pilots without knowing how to build or pilot ships.*

20,5　*"Now then, let's scrape their paint off, < if > you will, to convince the children who admire such paintings that neither is this ship a ship, nor this pilot a pilot. It is a wall with its surface decorated for pleasure's sake with paint and pictures, and the artists who made these things with their paints are imitators, not of a ship but of the image of a ship and pilot."*

20,6　*"For one who longs to hear you, your introduction is lengthy."*

"Lengthy, my friend, but useful. If one were to remove the words of inspired scripture which these people have daubed on their opinion with bright colors for their own deception, and have arrogantly called righteousness and truth when they know nothing about righteousness, how scornfully do you think they would be treated if they were stripped of such names?"

"Very," replied Auxentius.

20,7　*"Would you like to be the leader on this journey, Auxentius," I said, "or should I lead?"*

"By rights you should," he said, "since you're initiating the discussion."

21,1　*"All right, it was said—come on, let's examine Aglaophon's mind a bit, going in order from the beginning. It was said that the soul has assumed this body of ours because of its transgression, though long ago it lived in bliss without a body.* (2) *For < he said > that the skin tunics are the bodies in which it has been the souls' lot to be shut up, to be punished for their deeds* *by carrying corpses. Or wasn't this what you said first, Doctor, at the beginning? Come, if you think I've forgotten something, remind me."*

21,3 *"There's no need to remind you of it; this was exactly what I said at the beginning."*

21,4 *"Oh? As you went on, didn't you also say repeatedly that, because of its preoccupation with adornment, comfort, and the other temptations that accompany the craving of the belly, the body is a hindrance to our understanding and knowledge of the true reality? And further, that it is the cause of blasphemies and all sorts of sins, since by itself, apart from a body, a soul cannot sin at all? (5) And therefore the soul must remain free and devoid of a body after its departure, so that it may be without sin and transgression in the heavens, where, too, it will hold converse with the angels. For this body is the soul's accessory and abettor in pollution and sin; (6) there is no way a soul can sin without a body. Hence, for its preservation without sin forever, the soul will never again receive the body, to sway it to corruption and unrighteousness here below."*

21,7 *"Yes, this was also said."*

"Oh?" I said. "And do you think you've said this well and rightly?"

"What do you care what I think?" said Algaophon. "But you aren't refuting my argument."

21,8 *"I don't care," said I, "but I want to see your argument tested by your own words."*

"I spoke well and rightly," he said.

"But if someone contradicts and disagrees with himself, do you think his case is put well and rightly?"

"Indeed not!"

21,9 *"Do you think he's clumsily pretending to the truth?"*

"The worst of anyone," he said.

"Then you don't approve of someone who plays the tune of his words with a false note?"

"I sure don't!"

21,10 *"Then you can't possibly approve of yourself, because you're speaking discordantly. You've allowed that souls have strayed from God's commandment and sinned without bodies, and said that God gave them the skin tunics later because of their wrongdoing, so that they would be punished by carrying corpses—interpreting 'tunics' to mean the bodies. But in the course of your argument you forget your original proposition and say that, by itself, the soul can't sin. (11) Sinning is in no sense its nature; the body is its accessory in evils of all sorts. Thus it will be without a body for all eternity, so that it may never again be incited to wickedness as it was before by the body. (12) And yet you had first said that the soul had sinned in Paradise before it had a body, when it was still blessed and free from pain. For once its sin had been strengthened because of its obedience to the serpent, the soul was given the body as a prison in punishment for its transgression of the commandment.*

21,13   *"Thus either your former or your latter statement is incorrect. Either the soul sinned before it had a body and won't be any more of a sinner even if it doesn't get one, and your blather about the body's not rising is worthless. Or else it sinned with a body, and the skin tunics can't be regarded as bodies. (14) For the man clearly broke the divine commandment before the tunics were made; indeed, the tunics were made to cover the nakedness which had resulted from their sin. (15) But do I convince you, and do you see that you've offered contrary propositions? Has this been made clear to you, Aglaophon,"* I asked, *"or don't you understand what I mean yet?"*

21,16   *"I understand,"* he said, *"and don't need to hear anything twice; I failed to notice that I spoke incorrectly. If I allowed that the skin tunics are bodies, I was obliged to admit that the soul had sinned even before it entered a body, (17) for the transgression came before the making of the tunics. For the tunics are made for them because of the transgression, the transgression isn't committed because of the tunics. And because of this admission I had to agree that this body is not an accessory to evil, but that the soul in itself is responsible.*

21,18   *"Thus the soul will sin even if it doesn't get the body, since even before it did, it sinned without a body. And it is foolish to say that the body cannot come back to life for fear of its becoming the soul's accessory in sin. (19) For just as the soul sinned even before it had a body, so it will sin after discarding the body, even if it doesn't receive a body again. On these grounds, then, I must not approve of my or anyone else's saying that the skin tunics are our bodies. For if I did, I would have to admit the truth of your argument."*

22,1   *"But Aglaophon,"* I said, *"don't you think you've made another error?"*

"What error?"

"You said," I replied, *"that the body is designed as a prison and bond for the soul, and this is why the prophet called us 'prisoners of earth,'*[76] *and David called us 'bound.'"*[77]

22,2   *"I can't answer you offhand,"* said Aglaophon. *"But why not discuss it with someone else?"*

22,3   *And I—I saw that he was embarrassed, and afraid of losing the argument. "Do you think I'm trying to refute you from envy,"* I said, *"and am not eager to clear the matter up? Don't flag under questioning, friend. (4) You see that we aren't talking about unimportant things, but about*

---

[76] Lam. 3:34
[77] Ps. 145:7

the way we are to believe. I doubt that anything does a man as much harm as the essentials of the faith, if he has a false idea of them.

22,5 [78] *"Come on, face my questions willingly! Explain yourself, and correct me if you feel I am speaking an untruth, thinking more of the truth than of me. For I believe that to be refuted is better than to refute, to the same degree that to be saved from harm oneself is better than to save someone else from harm. (6) Well then, let's compare our statements and see if there is any difference between them. The things we are arguing about are no small matters, but things which it is better to know about, and a disgrace not to. Well then, you don't believe that the body returns to life, but I do."*

"Precisely," he said, *"and the reason I have spoken."*

22,7 *"And,"* I went on, *"you said that the body is a prison, dungeon, tomb, burden and chain, while I disagree."*

"You're right," he said.

22,8 *"In fact, you've said that the body is an accessory to licentiousness, error, pain, anger, and in a word, all the other evils that hinder the soul's improvement and do not allow us to attain the understanding and knowledge of true reality. (9) For even if we attempt a search for some of it, darkness always falls and obscures our reason, and does not permit us a clear view of the truth. For perception by our ears is full of deceit, as you said, and perception by our sight and other senses."*

22,10 *"Eubulius,"* he said, *"do you see that I'm ready to compliment you whenever you explain my words correctly?"*

23,1 *"All right, to let you compliment me some more—if you people think that the body is a prison, it cannot be blamed for the evil, and further, the unrighteousness of the soul, but on the contrary, must be considered the cause of its moderation and discipline. (2) Look here, you can follow me better in this way. Where do we take people with bodily ailments? To the doctors, don't we?"*

"Obviously," said Aglaophon.

23,3 *"And where do we take criminals? Isn't it to the magistrates?"*

"Of course!"

"Is this so that they will be punished justly for what they have done?" I said.

"Yes."

"But justice is the finest thing there is?"

He agreed.

"But is one who gives a just judgment right—for he is judging righteously?"

He assented.

---

[78] From here till the end of the chapter we renumber the paragraphs, to correct what appears to be a typographical error in Holl.

"But is the right thing beneficial?"

"Plainly."

23,4 *"Then those who are judged are benefited. Their wickedness is removed because it is prevented by their torments, just as illnesses are removed by surgery and pharmacy at the doctor's. For the punishment of the criminals is the correction of the soul, which throws off the severe disease of wickedness."*

He agreed.

23,5 *"Oh? Wouldn't you say that the punishments which are proportionate to their crimes are imposed on criminals with justice, just as surgery proportionate to their hurts is applied to patients?"*

He nodded.

23,6 *"Then one whose crimes deserve death is punished with death, one whose crimes deserve the lash is punished with the lash, and one whose crimes merit imprisonment is punished with prison?"*

Aglaophon agreed.

23,7 *"And the offender incurs the penalty of prison, blows, or some other punishment of the sort, so that he will reform and abandon his wickedness, like bent wood straightened by hard blows?"*

"You're quite right," he said.

23,8 *"The judge isn't punishing him for his past crime but for the future, so that he won't do it again?"*

"Plainly," he said.

23,9 *"For it is plain that prison eliminates his criminal tendencies by not permitting him to do as he pleases?"*

"True."

23,10 *"Then he is prevented from misbehaving, since his imprisonment does not leave him free to enjoy his pleasures. It confines him and teaches him respect for what is right, until such time as he is chastened and learns good sense."*

"That is plain," said Aglaophon.

23,11 *"In that case imprisonment is not the cause of wrongdoing."*

"Evidently not."

"Instead, it teaches good sense and makes men better. It is the prophylactic of the soul, harsh and bitter but medicinal."

"Plainly so," he said.

23,12 *"Now what? Come, let's examine the consequences once more. Didn't you grant that the body is the prison of the soul because of its transgression?"*

"I did and I do," he said.

23,13 *"But that the soul sins with the body—if you think that adultery, murder and impiety, which the soul commits with the body, are sin?"*

He nodded.

23,14 *"But we have agreed that a prisoner cannot commit crimes?"*
"We have," he said.
"He is prevented from committing them because he is loaded with chains?"
"Yes."
"And the flesh is the soul's prison?"
Aglaophon nodded agreement.
23,15 *"And yet we sin while we are in the flesh, with the consent of the flesh?"*
"We do," he said.
23,16 *"But a prisoner in bonds can't sin?"*
Here, too, he nodded.
"For he is restrained?"
"Yes."
"His bonds don't permit him to sin?"
"Obviously not."
23,17 *"But the body is an aid to sin?"*
"Yes."
"While the prison prevents it?"
He agreed.
23,18 *"Then, Aglaophon,"* I said, *"the body is not a prison on your premises or anyone else's. It is the soul's aid either way, for good or evil."*
He agreed.
24,1 *"Then, Aglaophon, if this is the case, defend your first proposition. You said previously that the body is the prison, dungeon and bond of the soul. And do you see that what you said does not agree with what we are saying now? (2) How could it, my friend, if, on the one hand, we must suppose that the flesh is a prison, but on the other, that the soul has it as its partner in crime and its fellow prisoner? This isn't possible. (3) If the body was given to the soul as a place of torment because of its sins, so that the soul may be taught by its pain to honor God, how can the body be the soul's accomplice and partner in crime? Imprisonment, confinement, chains, and, in a word, all such corrective devices are punitive measures, meant to restrain the prisoners from crime and sin. (4) Prison is not prescribed for the wrongdoer as an aid in wrongdoing, so that he will do further wrong, but so that he will be tortured by his chains and stop. It is for this reason that judges put malefactors in chains. (5) Even against their will they are kept from evildoing by their shackles; evil is an option, not for prisoners but for free men who live unguarded.*
24,6 *"Man first committed murder like Cain, and he went on to unbelief, began to heed idols, and abandoned God. And why was the body given to him for a prison? Or, after man had transgressed before he had a body, why would God give him the body as an aid to greater wickedness? (7) Why does God say, 'Lo, I have set before thee life and death; choose life!*

I have set before thee good and evil; choose good!'[79] *after the making of
the prison, and 'If ye be willing and hearken unto me?'*[80] *These things
were said to a person free to choose, not a prisoner under restraint.*

24,8   "*It is fully established, then, that < we must > not regard the body
as a chain, imprisonment or incarceration, or souls as therefore 'prisoners
of earth,*[81] *with God condemning them to be bound in chains of clay. (9)
How can this be, when there is no proof of it? But it is also plainly absurd
to suppose that the body will not join the soul in eternal life because it
is a prison and a bond, to prevent our becoming prisoners forever, as they
say, sentenced to corruption in the kingdom of light. (10) For once the
expression through which they declared the flesh to be the 'prison of the
soul' has been refuted and discredited, the statement, 'The flesh will not
rise lest we become prisoners in the kingdom of light'—and may this kingdom
be ours!—is discredited as well.*

25,1   "*Well, what other truth, clearer than what has been said and
acceptable to them, must I demonstrate to convince the captious? This
contention of theirs can be refuted by these arguments and many more.
(2) As the argument progresses I shall prove next, with real truths and
not with conjectures, that Jeremiah did not call us 'prisoners of earth'
because of our fellowship with the body, and that this is not why David
called us 'bound.' (3) As to the skin tunics and the fact that our first
parents had bodies before the tunics were made and still enjoyed immortality,
and further, that the body cannot be regarded as a prison and dungeon,
I have made the appropriate remarks, gentlemen of the jury. (For I summon
you to be the judges of my argument, 'most excellent Theophilus.')*[82] *As
I promised I turn now to the sequel, to give us a clearer view of the things
we would like to see.*"

26,1   *God, the creator of all, brought all into being in good order like
a great city, and regulated it by his decree. Each element had been joined
in harmony by his will, and all had been filled with various living things,
so that the world would grow to perfect beauty. He therefore gave life to
all sorts of forms—stars in the sky, birds in the air, beasts on earth and
fish in the water—and finally, after preparing the universe as a wonderfully beautiful home for him, God brought man into the world (2) as a
likeness answering to his own image. He made him with his own hands
like a glorious image in a noble temple.*

26,3   *For it was understood that whatever God fashioned with his own
hand must be immortal, since it was the work of immortality. (4) Immortal*

---

[79] Deut. 30:15
[80] Isa. 1:19
[81] Cf. Lam. 3:34.
[82] Luke 1:3

things are made immortal by immortality, as evil things are made evil by evil, and unrighteous things unrighteous by unrighteousness. For unrighteous deeds are not the work of righteousness, but of unrighteousness. Nor, on the contrary, is righteous behavior the work of unrighteousness but of righteousness—just as corruption is not the work of incorruption but of corruption, and immortality not the work of corruption but of incorruption.

26,5   *And in a word, whatever the maker is like, the product must necessarily be made like, on the same principle.* (6) *But God is immortality, life and incorruption, and man is God's product. Anything made by immortality is immortal; man is therefore immortal. This is why God created man in person, but ordered earth, air and water to bring forth the other kinds of living things.*

26,7   *It is said with entire truth that man is by nature neither a soul without a body nor a body without a soul, but is a composite of the union of soul and body in one form, the form of the good. Hence it is plain that man was made immortal, free of decay and diseases.*

26,8   *One may also learn all of this from the scripture. Of the other creatures which are changed at intervals of time by being young and growing old, it is said, "Let the waters bring forth creeping things with living souls, and birds flying over the earth in the firmament of heaven;"*[83] *and "Let the earth bring forth living souls according to their kind, four-footed creatures and creeping things and beasts of the earth according to their kind."*[84] (9) *But "Let the earth bring forth" is no longer said of man as it was of them, nor "Let the waters bring forth," nor "Let there be lights."*[85] *Instead [we read] "Let us make man in our image and after our likeness, and let them have dominion over the fish of the sea, and over the birds of the sky, and over all cattle,"*[86] *and "God took dust from the earth and formed man."*[87]

27,1 *Now then, so that you too may further understand the difference < in > whole and in part between man and the other creatures, and how man ranks next to the angels in honor because of his immortality, let us take this up once more from the standpoint of the true and orthodox reasoning.* (2) *Animation and life were given to the others by their inhalation of the wind in the air, but to man by the immortal and all-excelling essence itself, for "God breathed into his countenance the breath of life, and man became a living soul."*[89] (3) *The others were commanded to serve and be ruled, but man to rule and be the master. The others are given various natural shapes and forms, as many as their tangible, visible nature engendered*

---

[83] Gen. 1:20
[84] Gen. 1:24
[85] Gen. 1:14
[86] Gen. 1:26
[87] Gen. 2:7
[89] Gen. 2:7

*at God's bidding. (4) Man, however, is given God's image and likeness,
and all conformed to the original image of the Father and the Only-begotten.
"For God created man; in the image of God created he him."*

27,5 *Thus, as sculptors are concerned for their images, God was concerned for the preservation of his own image, lest it be easily destroyed. (6)
Sculptors not only think of < the > beauty and loveliness of their pieces,
to make them wonderfully beautiful, but also plan for their immortality
as far as they can, so that they will be preserved for a long while without
being broken. So with Phidias. (7) After he had finished the Pisaean
image—it was made of ivory—he had oil poured in front of the image
around its feet, to keep it as nearly immortal as possible. (8) Now if this
is so with the makers of human handiwork, did not the supreme craftsman,
God, who can do all things and can create from nothing, see to it of every
necessity that man, his own rational image, was wholly indestructible and
immortal? Did he allow what he had seen fit to make in a distinctive way,
and had fashioned with his own hands, in his image and after his likeness,
to be most shamefully destroyed and consigned to ruin and corruption—
the ornament of the world, for the sake of which the world was made? This
cannot be said! Away with anyone foolish enough to think so!*

28,1 *But you people will probably not back off because of what I just
said, Aglaophon, and will reply, "If the creature was immortal from the
beginning, as you say, how has he become mortal? An immortal thing must
remain unalterably what it is, without changing or degenerating into something
inferior and mortal. This cannot be, since < it is not possible* > for an
immortal < thing to come to die.* >*

28,2 *[But it did], I shall say, because the enemy of all good came,
and from envy bewitched the man who had been created free to choose the
good, and had received this ordinance. (3) "For God created man for
immortality and made him an image of his own eternity."*[90] *Indeed, "God
made not death, nor doth he rejoice in the destruction of the living,"*[91]
"but through envy of the devil death entered the world,"[92] *as Wisdom
testified through Solomon.*

28,4 *"Where did death come from, then?" If God did not make death,
this has to be asked again. "If it came from envy, why was envy stronger
than God's purpose?" But this last is blasphemy, we shall say.*

28,5 *"Where did envy come from, then?" our antagonist will say. "If
from the devil, why was the devil made? If he was made, is his maker
then responsible for the existence of evil? (6) But God is in no way responsible
for anyone's evil. Thus the devil must be uncreated—and if uncreated,*

---

[90] Wisd. Sol. 2:23
[91] Wisd. Sol. 1:13
[92] Wisd. Sol. 2:24

also impassible, indestructible and in need of nothing.

An uncreated thing must necessarily possess all these attributes, and yet the devil is brought to nothing and chastised. Now whatever is chastised undergoes change and suffers, while an uncreated thing cannot suffer. The devil, therefore, is not uncreated but created.

28,7 But if the devil is created, and every created thing has had its origin in a particular beginning and has a creator, the devil has a creator. And is the creator uncreated or created? But it must be realized that there is only one uncreated, God. Nor can there in any conceivable way be any creator whatever other than he. *"I am the first and I am the last,"* he says, *"and besides me there is no God."*[93]

28,8 Nor can anything be changed or created against God's will. Even the Son acknowledges that *"He can do nothing of himself, but what he seeth the Father do. What things soever the Father doeth,"* he says, *"the Son doeth likewise."*[94] (9) Surely God can have no antagonist, opponent or rival god. If anything were to oppose God it would cease to exist, for its being would be destroyed by God's power and might. For only the Maker can destroy—even the things that are immortal.

29,1 *"Then what is the devil?"* you will say. A spirit asigned to matter, as Athenagoras has also said.[95] He was created by God like the other angels, and entrusted with the oversight of matter and material forms. (2) For this was the origin of the angels—their creation by God for the care of his created order. Thus God has the general and universal care of the universe, has attached the supreme authority and power over all to himself, and guides the whole on a straight course, like a ship, with the rudder of his wisdom; but angels who have been assigned to it have the care of the various parts.

29,3 The other angels kept to the tasks for which God had made and appointed them, but the devil mocked at his and became evil in the management of the things which had been entrusted to him. He conceived envy of us, like the angels who later became enamored of flesh and consorted for pleasure with the daughters of men. (4) For as in man's case, so to the angels God has allotted a will free to choose good or evil, either to obey his command, be with him and enjoy beatitude, or else to disobey and be judged.

29,5 The devil too was a *"morning star"*—*"How hath the morning star fallen from heaven, that riseth in the morning!"*[96] He once rose with the angels of light, once was a morning star, but he fell, was dashed to the earth, and is [now] the governor of the forces hostile to man. For the

---

[93] Isa. 44:6
[94] John 5:19
[95] Athenagoras Legatio 24.2
[96] Isa. 14:12

Godhead is angry with the proud and balks their arrogant purposes. (6)
But it occurs to me to say in verse,
   Thou serpent, source and end of ills for all,
   Thou bearer of a grievous store of woes,
   Thou false guide of a blind world's ignorance,
   That joyest in the wails and groans of men!
   'Twas ye that armed the fratricidal arms
   Of kin to deeds of lawless violence.
   By your contriving Cain first fouled the soil
   With secret bloodshed, and the first-formed man
   Fell to the earth from realms unblemished.

30,1   *So much for the devil. But death was devised for conversion's sake, just as blows were devised for the correction of children beginning to read. For death is nothing but the severance and separation of soul from body.*

30,2   *"What then," you will say, "is God the cause of death?" Again the same answer comes to me, "No indeed! Neither are teachers primarily responsible for children's being hurt by the blows. (3) Death is a good thing, then, if, like blows for children, it was devised for conversion. A word to the wise—[I do not mean] the death of sin, but the death of the sundering and separation of the flesh [from the soul]."*

30,4   *The man was responsible for himself and his own master, and as I said, had received a free will and the liberty to choose the good. And he had been told, "From every tree in the garden ye may eat, but from the tree of the knowledge of good and evil ye may not eat thereof. For in the day wherein ye eat of it, ye shall surely die."*[97] (5) *But he yielded to a wisdom which had been entrapped by the devil and which incited him to all sorts of disobedience, and set God's command aside. And this became a stumbling block, snare and hindrance for him.*

30,6   *For God did not make evil, and is absolutely not responsible, in any way at all, for any evil. But it is called evil when any creature which God has created free to observe and keep the law he has justly enjoined, fails to keep that law. To disobey God, however, by overstepping the bounds of righteousness of one's own free will, does the most serious harm.*

30,7   *Thus, because the man was spotted and sullied by his rejection of God's decree, and was smeared with the stains of the great evils the prince of darkness and father of deceit had brought forth—and because, as the scripture says, he was sentenced to hard labor so that the devil could keep deceiving him and inciting him to unrighteousness—God the almighty, seeing that, as the devil was a deceiver, man had been made an immortal evil by the devil's plot, (8) made the skin tunics, as though to clothe the*

---

[97] Gen. 2:16–17

man with mortality, so that all the evil which had been engendered in him would die with the destruction of his body.

31,1   *These questions have already been raised, and it has been shown that the skin tunics were not Adam's and Eve's bodies. Still, let us explain it once more—it is not a thing to be said only once.* (2) *The first man himself acknowledged that he had bones and flesh before the tunics were made, when he saw the woman brought to him and cried, "This is now bone of my bones and flesh of my flesh. She shall be called, Wife, for she was taken out of her husband. For this cause shall a man leave his father and mother and cleave unto his wife, and the two shall be one flesh."*[98]

31,3   *For I have no intention of putting up with certain chatterboxes who do violence to the scripture without a blush, suggest that they were "intelligible bones" and "intelligible flesh," and turn things topsy-turvy with allegories in one passage after another, as their excuse for saying that the resurrection is not a resurrection of flesh.* (4) *This though Christ confirms the fact that the scripture should be taken as written, when he answers the Pharisees' question about the divorce of a wife with "Have ye not read that in the beginning the creator made them male and female, and said, For this cause shall a man leave his father and mother,"*[99] *and so forth? How can "Be fruitful and fill the earth?"*[100] *be taken merely of souls? Or* (5) *"God took dust from the earth and formed the man,"*[101] *which is plainly said of the body proper? The soul was not made of earth and the heavier materials.* (6) *Thus it is established with full certainty that the man was provided with a body before the skin tunics were made. For all these things are said before his fall, but the making of the tunics is described after the fall.*

31,7   *Let us thus return to the investigation of the matter in hand, since we have given sufficient proof that the skin tunics were not [Adam's and Eve's] bodies, but the mortality which was made for beasts because of the beasts' want of reason—for only this explanation remains.* (8) *Rest assured, the man was exiled from Paradise for the following reason. God did not expel him because he did not want him to pick fruit from the tree of life and live—for he could have lived forever if he had eaten once more, [a fruit] from [the tree] of life. It is our opinion that God did this to keep evil from becoming immortal.*

31,9   *For if it was at all God's will that man die without ever tasting life, why did God sent Christ from heaven to earth?* (10) *If my opponent should say that God did this because he had changed his mind, he would have a feeble argument and be introducing a changeable God. But God is neither ignorant of the future nor malignant; he is even supremely good,*

---

[98] Gen. 2:23–24
[99] Matt. 19:4–5
[100] Gen. 1:28
[101] Gen. 2:7

and foreknows what is to come. (11) Thus God did not expel the man to prevent his eating from the tree of life and living forever, but so that sin would be killed first, by death. Then, with sin withered away after death, the man would arise cleansed and taste life.

32,1 *And no idiot should gamble that these things are meant in some other sense. For whoever decides that this flesh is incapable of immortality is indeed responsible for the ailment of his stupidity, and is a blasphemer. (2) If it were simply impossible for man to live forever without a body, why is Adam cast out after the making of the skin tunics, and kept from eating of the tree of life and living? (3) The prohibition is predicated on the assumption that, if he takes fruit from the tree of life and tastes it, he can avoid death. For scripture says, "And the Lord God made tunics of skin for Adam and his wife, and clothed them. And God said, Behold, Adam hath become as one of us, to know good and evil. And now, lest he put forth his hand and take of the tree of life and eat and live forever. And the Lord God sent him forth from the delight of Paradise to till the ground whence he was taken, and he cast Adam out."*[102]

32,4 *Thus the body could have lived forever and been immortal if it had not been prevented from tasting life. But it was prevented so that sin would be put to death with the body and die, but the body would rise washed clean of sin. (5) As I said, God made the body mortal by clothing it with mortality to keep man from being an immortal evil with the conquering sin alive in him forever—as it would be if it had sprouted in an immortal body and had immortal nourishment. (6) Hence the skin tunics—so that, through the body's destruction and its separation [from the soul], the sin underneath it would perish entirely, from the root up, leaving not even the smallest bit of root for new shoots of sins to sprout from again.*

33,1 *If a fig tree < has > taken root and grown tall and broad in the beautiful buildings of a temple, and has covered all the joints of the stones with intricate roots, its growth cannot be halted until it is uprooted altogether, and the stones in the places where it sprouted are destroyed. (2) For the stones can be set back in the same places once the fig tree is removed, so that the temple will be preserved and no longer harbor any of the ills that were destroying it. But as the fig tree has been uprooted altogether, it will die. (3) Thus, with the temporary visitations of death, God, the architect, destroyed his temple, man, who had sprouted sin like a wild fig—"killing and making alive,"*[103] *as the scripture says—so that, once the sin had withered and died, the flesh would rise again from the same places like a temple restored, immortal and unharmed because the sin had perished altogether from the ground up.*

---

[102] Gen. 3:21–24
[103] Deut. 32:39

33,4   *While the body is still alive before death, sin of necessity lives within us and conceals its roots within us, even though it is checked on the outside by the cuts of cautions and admonitions. For after his enlightenment no one can do further wrong; sin has simply been removed from us altogether.* (5) *However, we often find ourselves in sins even after coming to faith and the water of purification. For no one will boast that he is so free of sin that he never even thinks of wrong at all.*

33,6   *Thus, as matters stand, sin is reduced and lulled to sleep by faith, and cannot bear harmful fruit; but it has certainly not been destroyed roots and all.* (7) *Here we remove its flowerings—evil thoughts, for example— "lest any root of bitterness trouble us,"*[104] *and we do not let them open, opening their closed pores to suckers. For like an ax the word chops sin's roots off as they grow below. Then, however, even the thought of evil will be done away.*

34,1   *Nor does the text of scripture fail to witness to this, for those who sincerely desire to hear the truth. The apostle knows that the root of sin is still not entirely removed from men, and declares, "I know that in me, that is, in my flesh, dwelleth no good thing. For to will is present with me, but how to perform what is good I find not. For the good that I would, I do not; but the evil which I would not, that do I. If, then, I do that which I would not, it is no more I that do it, but sin that dwelleth in me."*[105] (2) *And "I delight in the law of God after the inward man. But I see another law in my members, warring against the law of my mind, and bringing me into captivity to the law of sin which is in my members."*[106]

34,3   *Thus sin has not yet been entirely dug out by the roots, but is alive. (For it is not wholly dead; how can it be, before the man is clothed with death?) [It is alive], to wither and fade with the man, and to be utterly destroyed and perish—like a plant, when < the stone > is destroyed in < the place > where, as I said, it preserved its roots by concealing them. But the man will rise again, with no further "root of bitterness"*[107] *lurking within him.*

34,4   *For death and destruction were employed as an antidote by our true protector and physician, God, for the uprooting of sin. Otherwise evil would be eternal in us, like an immortal thing growing in immortals, and we ourselves would live like the diseased for a a long time, maimed and deprived of our native virtue, as persons who harbor the severe diseases of sin in everlasting and immortal bodies.* (5) *It is a good thing, then, that God has devised death—this cure, like a medicinal purgative, of both soul and body—to leave us altogether spotless and unharmed.*

---

[104] Heb. 12:15
[105] Rom. 7:18–20
[106] Rom. 7:22–23
[107] Heb. 12:15

35,1   *Now then, since a number of illustrations of such matters are
needed, let us by all means look for them, and not leave off until our
argument ends with a clearer explanation and proof.* (2) *It is plainly just
as though the best of artists were to remelt a lovely likeness he had made
of gold or another material with all its limbs in proportion for beauty's
sake, because he suddenly realized that it had been mutilated by some
vicious person, who injured the piece because, from malice, he could not
bear that it be beautiful, and reaped the empty fruit of envy.* (3) *With
your great wisdom, Aglaophon, observe that if the artist did not want the
piece he had created with so much zeal and care to be completely ruined
and an eyesore, he would be well advised to melt it down again and make
it as it was before.* (4) *If he did not remelt and refashion it, however,
but < merely > patched and repaired it and left it as it is, the piece, which
was hardened in the fire and cast in bronze, could never be kept the same,
but would be altered, and diminished in value.*

35,5   *Thus if he wanted his work to be entirely good and flawless, he
must break it up and recast it, so that the flaws, and all the alterations
produced in it by treachery and envy, would be done away by its destruction
and recasting, but the sculpture restored undamaged and unblemished to
its own form, once more exactly like itself.* (6) *For even if it is dissolved
back into its raw material, in the hands of the same artist the statue cannot
be destroyed, but can be restored. Its blemishes and mutilations can be
destroyed, however, for they are melted. They cannot be restored, for in every
art the best craftsman looks, not to the ugliness of his work or its accidental
flaws, but to its symmetry and rightness.*

35,7   *For it seems to me that God has dealt with us in the same way.
He saw his handsomest work, man, spoiled by the malicious plots of envy,
and in his lovingkindness could not bear to leave him like that, or he would
be flawed forever and marred with an immortal blemish. He has reduced
him to his raw material again, so that all his flaws may be melted and
done away with by the refashioning.* (8) *For the remelting of the sculpture
in my metaphor stands for the death and dissolution of the body; and
the remodeling and reshaping of the material stands for the resurrection.*
(9) *The prophet Jeremiah himself has already made the same recommen-
dation in the following passage:* "And I went down to the house of the
potter, and lo, he was making a work upon the stones. And the vessel he
was making broke in his hands, and again he made it another vessel,
as it pleased him to do. And the word of the Lord came unto me saying,
"Can I not make you as this potter, O house of Israel? Behold, as the potter's
clay are ye in my hands."[108]

36,1   *Observe that, after the man's transgression, the great hand of God*

---

[108] Jer. 18:3–6

did not choose to abandon its work forever, like a counterfeit coin, to the evil one who had unjustly harmed it by the [malicious introduction] of flaws. Instead it melted and reduced it to clay once more, like a potter reshaping a vessel to remove all its flaws and cracks by the reshaping, but make it once again entirely flawless and acceptable. (2) *"Or hath not the potter power over the clay, of the same lump to make one vessel unto honor, and another unto dishonor?"*[109] *In other words—for I am sure that this is what the apostle means—does God not have the power to reshape and refashion each of us from the same raw material of which each is made and raise us each individually, to our honor and glory or our shame and condemnation? To the shame of those who have lived wickedly in sins, but to the honor of those who have lived in righteousness.* (3) *This was revealed to Daniel also, who says, "And many of them that sleep in the dust of the earth shall arise, some to eternal life, some to shame and everlasting contempt. And they that are wise shall shine as the brightness of the firmament.*[110]

36,4 *We are not expected to remove the root of wickedness entirely, but to prevent it from spreading and bearing fruit. Its full and complete destruction, roots and all, is accomplished by God, as I said, at the dissolution of the body; but its partial destruction, so that it will not bud, is accomplished by ourselves.* (5) *And thus whoever fosters the increase and growth of wickedness instead, but does not make it as barren as he can and reduce its size, must pay the penalty. For though he had the ability and the right to do this, he chose to prefer the harmful to the helpful.*

37,1 *Thus no one may blame the Godhead, with wagging tongue, for not giving each his just reward for vice or virtue; the man himself is at fault. "Who art thou, O man, that repliest against God? Shall the thing formed say to him that formed it, Why hast thou made me thus?"*[111] (2) *How can it? The man chose evil of his own free will! He may not ask the God who judges < with > unvaryingly righteous decrees, "Why hast thou made me to be thus condemned to torment?"*

37,3 *For note how, by deftly darting brief quotations, like a spearman, into the body of his words, Paul makes the interpretation of the readings unclear and extremely difficult, though they are entirely true and orthodox and contain nothing careless or evil.*[112] (4) *To those who look into the words with no zeal but mean-spiritedly, they sometimes seem disjointed and inconsistent; but to those who do this zealously and with sober reason, they are correspondingly full of order and truth.* (5) *Only a treatise in itself would be enough for a full and accurate discussion of this at this*

---

[109] Rom. 9:21
[110] Dan. 12:2–3
[111] Rom. 8:20; Isa. 29:16
[112] The quotation Methodius means is that of Isa. 29:16 at Rom. 9:20. The

time. Indeed, it would be ridiculous to abandon the inquiry from you which has led me to compose this, and shift to other subjects.

37,6   *For I have said this because of the justice which punishes willful evildoers. But now that we have made it abundantly clear that death was not devised for man's harm but < for his good* >, whoever opens this book with a good will must have an understanding of the resurrection of the body. (7)*[113] *How can death not be beneficial, when it destroys the things that prey upon our nature? Even though it is unpleasant at the time, while it is being administered, it < is > plainly a medicine, of a very bitter sort, for the patient. (8) But now then! Not to make the same points time and again about the same things, let us further confirm what we have said from the Song in Deuteronomy, and then go on to take up the rest.*

38,1   *For when God says, "I shall kill, and I shall make alive ; I shall smite and I shall heal, and there is none that shall deliver out of my hand,"*[114] *what does he mean to teach but that the body is first killed and dies, so that it may rise and live again? (2) It is struck and shattered first, so that it may be remade sound and whole. (3) And nothing has any power whatever to take it from God's great and mighty hand for ruin and destruction—not fire, not death, not darkness, not chaos, not corruption. (4) "Who shall separate us from the love of Christ?" says scripture— ("Christ" means the Father's Hand and Word.) "Shall tribulation, or distress, or persecution, or famine, or nakedness, or peril, or sword? As it is written, For thy sake are we killed all day long ; we are counted as sheep appointed to be slain. Nay, in all these things we are more than conquerors through him that loved us."*[115]

38,5   *Absolutely true! This serves as the fulfillment of "I shall kill, and I shall make alive"—as I said—"I shall smite and I shall heal." And there is no one to "take us," for our destruction, "from the love of God that is in Christ Jesus." Thus we are "reckoned as sheep for the slaughter," "to die to sin and live to God."*[116] *So much for this line of inquiry ; here, once again, we must take up the next question.*

39,1   *Suppose that, as my opponent proposes, every procreated thing is ill in its origin and diet—for it increases in size from what is added to it, and becomes smaller because of what is subtracted from it. But whatever is not procreated is in good health, since it is not ill and has no needs or desires. Procreated things, however, desire both sex and food, but to have desires is illness, while to have no needs or desires is health. And procreated*

---

subject he declines to discuss is presumably that of predestination.

[113] The next two paragraphs are renumbered to correct a numbering error in Holl.

[114] Deut. 32:19

[115] Rom. 8:35–37

[116] Rom. 6:10

things are ill because they have desires, while things not procreated are not ill. And things that are ill suffer from a surplus or deficiency of the things which are added to them or taken away from them. Now anything that suffers both withers and perishes, since it is procreated. But man is procreated. Therefore man cannot be impassible and immortal.

39,2   *But even as stated, the argument fails. If everything must perish if it either comes to be or is procreated—we may as well say it this way, because the first man and woman were not procreated, but did come to be—but angels and souls came to be, for the scripture says, "He maketh his angels spirits,"*[117] *then, on their premises, angels and souls must perish!* (3) *But neither angels nor souls perish; they are immortal and indestructible as their maker intended them to be. Man too, therefore, is immortal.*

39,4   *No more satisfactory is the argument that all things will be destroyed completely and there will be no more earth, air and heaven. The whole world will be overwhelmed with a deluge of fire, and burned to ashes for its purification and renewal, but will certainly not come to entire destruction and dissolution.* (5) *If the non-existence of the world is better than its existence, why did God make the poorer choice and create the world? But God made nothing to no purpose or inferior.* (6) *Thus God ordered the creation in such a way that it would exist and endure, as Wisdom proves [by saying], "God hath created all things to exist, and sound are the origins of the world; in them is no poison of destruction."*[118] (7) *And Paul plainly testifies to this [with his words], "The earnest expectation of the creature waiteth for the manifestation of the sons of God. For the creature was made subject to vanity, not willingly, but by reason of him who hath subjected the same in hope, because creation itself also shall be delivered from the bondage of destruction to the glorious liberty of the children of God."*[119] (8) *Here he chooses to call this world a "creature," and says that "the creature was made subject to vanity," but that it expects to be set free from such bondage. For it is not the invisible things that are enslaved to corruption, but these, the visible ones.*

39,9   *The "creature," then, endures, renewed once more and in a comelier form, and is joyous and glad for the sons of God at the resurrection, though now it groans for them and shares their travail, while it too awaits our redemption from the perishability of the body.* (10) *Then, when we are raised and have shaken off the mortality of our flesh—as scripture says, "Shake off the dust, rise and sit down, O Jerusalem"*[120]—*and when we are set free from sin, it too will be set free from corruption and no longer enslaved to "vanity," but to righteousness.* (11) *"For we know," says scripture, "that all creation groaneth and travaileth together in pain until now.*

---

[117] Ps. 103:4
[118] Wisd. Sol. 1:14
[119] Rom. 8:19–20
[120] Isa. 52:2

*And not only they, but ourselves also, which have the firstfruits of the Spirit,
even we ourselves groan within ourselves waiting for the adoption, to wit,
the redemption of the body.* "[121]

39,12   And Isaiah says, *"For as the new heavens and the new earth
which I make remain before me, saith the Lord, so shall your seed and
your name be.* "[122] And again, *"Thus saith the Lord that created the heavens, this God that formed the earth and made it. He established its bounds,
he created it not in vain, but to be inhabited.* "[123] (13) Indeed God has
not created the world to no purpose or in vain, for destruction, as those
who think vain thoughts would have it. He has made it to be, to be
inhabited and to abide. Therefore heaven and earth must once more be,
after the burning up and boiling away of all things. (14) To explain the
necessity of this would require an even longer discussion. For after its
dissolution the universe will not be reduced to inert matter, and its state
before its establishment. Nor, again, will it be reduced to total destruction
and decay.

40,1   But suppose our opponents say, *"If the universe will not be destroyed, why did the Lord say that heaven and earth would pass away?
And why did the prophet say that the heaven would perish like smoke, and
the earth grow old like a garment?"*

40,2   *"Because,"* we shall reply, *"scripture's way is to call the world's
change from its present state to a better and more glorious one a 'destruction,' like the change of anything to a more glorious form when its previous
form is done away with ; there is no contradiction or anomaly in the sacred
scripture. (3) [Scripture says that] 'The form of this world passeth away,'
but not that the world does. Thus the scripture's habit is to call the change
of a form to a better, and sometimes a lovelier one, a 'destruction,' (4)
as one might call the change from one's form in babyhood to maturity a
'destruction' because the stature of the infant is changed in its size and
handsomeness. For when I was a child, I spake as a child, I understood
as a child, I thought as a child ; but when I became a man, I put away
childish things."* "[124]

40,5   We would expect the creature to be troubled because it is to die
in the conflagration and be created anew, but we would not expect it to
perish. Thus we, the newly created, shall dwell free from sorrow in the newly
created world—as the hundred and third Psalm says, *"Thou shalt send
forth thy Spirit and they shall be made, and thou shalt renew the face of
the earth* "[125]—at last in the arms of God, the regulator of its mild climate.

---

[121] Rom. 8:22–23
[122] Isa. 66:22
[123] Isa. 45:18
[124] 1 Cor. 13:11
[125] Ps. 103:30

(6) *For if there is to be an earth even after this age, there is every necessity that it also have inhabitants, who will never again die, marry and be born, but like the angels will unchangingly perform the best of works in immortality.* (7) *Thus it is silly to ask how there will be bodies then, where there will be no air or earth or the rest.*

41,1   *But if we are to discuss such important matters with confidence, Aglaophon, something beyond what we have said is worth our looking into, since it occasions a great deal of error.* (2) *After saying that, when the Sadducees tested him, the Lord declared that those who attain the resurrection will be like angels, you added, "But the angels, who have no flesh, are in the highest state of beatitude, and therefore also of glory. Thus if we are to equal the angels, we, like them, must be without flesh."* (3) *But, Sir, you have not understood that He who created the universe from nothing and set it in order, did not adorn it by allotting the nature of immortals to angels and ministers only, but to principalities, authorities and thrones as well.* (4) *The angels are one species and the principalities and authorities are another, for there is not [just] one rank, condition, body and family of immortals, but different species, bodies and varieties. The cherubim cannot relinquish their own nature and be changed into the form of angels ; nor, in turn, can angels be changed into some other form. They must be the same as they are and have been.*

41,5   *But man too, who was charged < at > the first ordering of the universe to inhabit the world and rule all its denizens—man is immortal and will never be changed from his manhood into the form of the angels or any of the others. For no more can the angels be changed from their original form and turned into that of the others.* (6) *Christ did not come to announce the remaking or transformation of human nature into some other, but its change into its original nature before its fall, when it was immortal.* (7) *Each created thing must remain in its assigned place, so that all may be filled with all : the heavens with angels ; the thrones with powers ; the luminaries with ministering spirits ; the most sacred places and the pure and undefiled lights with the seraphim who stand beside the great Will which controls the universe ; and the world with men.* (8) *But if we grant that men are changed into angels, it is time to say that the angels can also be changed into powers, and the powers into one thing and another, until the account reaches a risky stage.*[126]

42,1   *But it is not as though God made man inferior or slipped up in the process of fashioning him, and like the poorest of workmen later changed his mind and decided to make him an angel ; or that he meant to make an angel at first and could not, but made a man. This is incompetence.* (2) *If he wanted the man to become an angel and not a man, why ever*

---

[126] I.e., reaches the point of suggesting that something may become God

did he make him a man and not an angel? Because he couldn't? < This >
is blasphemy! (3) But did he put off doing the better thing and do the
worse? This too is absurd. God neither makes mistakes nor puts off doing
a good thing, nor lacks the power [to do it]. He has the power to do both
as he wills and when he wills, for God is Power.

42,4   *Very well, God created the man at the first and willed that he*
be a man. But if he willed it, and he wills what is good—and if man
is good—and if man is said to be composed of soul and body—then man
will not be bodiless at the [resurrection] but embodied, or man will be other
than man. (5) For the immortal species must all be preserved by God. But
man too is immortal, for Wisdom says, "God created man for immortality,
and made him by his own eternity."[127] *The body does not perish, then,*
for man is a composite of body and soul.

43,1   *Understand, then, that the Lord meant to teach these same things,*
because the Sadducees did not believe in the resurrection of the flesh. This
is Sadducean doctrine, and so, to decry the doctrine of the resurrection of
the flesh, they made up the parable of the woman and the seven brothers,
and came to him. (The evangelist, of course, added "came to him" himself,
when he said, "Likewise Sadducees, which say that there is no resurrection,
came to him.")[128] *(2) Now if there were no resurrection of flesh but only*
the soul were saved, Christ would have agreed that their opinion was good
and right. But he refutes them instead by saying, "In the resurrection they
neither marry nor are given in marriage, but are as angels in heaven[129]—
(3) not by having no flesh, but by neither marrying nor being married
but finally being immortal, and among the luminaries. They will be very
like the angels in this respect—that, like the angels in heaven, we in Paradise
will not spend our time in weddings and banquets, but in seeing God and
enjoying eternal life under Christ's headship.

43,4   *For Christ did not say, "They shall be angels," but, "They shall*
be like angels"—as [in the scriptural text], "crowned with glory and honor
and but a little different from the angels,"[130] *and nearly angels. (5) It*
is as though one were to say that on a balmy, calm night when all was
illuminated with the moon's heavenly radiance, the moon shone "like" the
sun. We would certainly not say he was testifying that the moon "was"
the sun, but that it was "like" the sun, (6) just as a material which is
not gold but < almost > gold< en > is not said to be "gold," but "like gold."
For if it is not gold, but is < almost > gold and looks like gold, it is not
called "gold" but "golden."

43,7   *Thus, when Christ says that the saints will be as angels in the*

---

[127] Wisd. Sol. 2:23
[128] Matt. 22:23
[129] Matt. 22:30
[130] Ps. 8:6

resurrection, we do not understand him to be promising that the saints will actually be angels in the resurrection, but that they will nearly be angels. (8) And it is the height of absurdity to deny the resurrection of bodies because of Christ's statement that the saints will look like angels in the resurrection, although the word itself clearly indicates the actual nature of the event.

43,9 *For "rising" is not said of a thing that has not fallen, but of one that has fallen and gotten up, as when the prophet says, "And I will raise up the tabernacle of David that is fallen."*[131] *But the beloved tabernacle of the soul has collapsed and fallen "to dusty earth"*[132] *for it is not the undying that declines, but the dying. It is flesh that dies, for soul is immortal. (10) Now then, if the soul is immortal and the dead man is a body, those who say that there is a resurrection, but not a resurrection of flesh, are denying that there is a resurrection. For it is not the thing that has been standing that rises, but the thing that has fallen and dropped, as scripture says, "Doth that which falleth not rise, or shall that which turneth away not turn back?"*[133]

44,1 *But the Lord has taught openly that the soul is immortal, both in his own words and through the mouth of Solomon. He has taught it in his own words in the story of the rich man and the poor man Lazarus, by showing the one at rest in Abraham's bosom after the discarding of his body, but the other in torments of which he told Abraham in talking with him. (2) And he taught it through Solomon in the book entitled Wisdom, where it is written that "The souls of the righteous are in the hand of God and there shall no torment touch them. In the sight of the unwise they seemed to die and their departure was taken for misery, and their going from us for utter destruction. But they are in peace, and their hope is full of immortality."*[134] *(3) Thus resurrection is of a body, not a soul. One does not raise a person who is on his feet but a person who is lying down, just as not a healthy individual, but a sufferer is doctored.*

44,4 *And if anyone insists that resurrection will apply to the soul and not the flesh, this is a lot of foolishness and nonsense. One must first prove a corresponding decay and dissolution of the soul to prove its resurrection as well, and not by talking nonsense but by the clear statement of a plain fact. (5) But no matter, let us allow him to declare the soul mortal. Here we must make one of two assumptions. Either the Lord's declaration is untrue when he teaches that the soul is immortal, and whoever says that it does not perish is lying; or else it perishes, and Christ is < telling > a lie by teaching, both in his story of the rich man and the poor man and*

---

[131] Amos 9:11
[132] Dan. 12:2
[133] Jer. 8:4
[134] Wisd. Sol. 3:1–4

*in the vision of Moses and Elijah, that it is indestructible and immortal.
(6) But the Lord has never contradicted himself or lied. He did not show
an image or simulacrum of Elijah and Moses on the mount, with the intent
of deceiving the apostles ; he showed truthfully what Moses and Elijah were.
So even the slowest learner, as it were, can learn that he is immortal, and
affirm the indestructibility of the soul.*

45,1   *Resurrection, then, is a resurrection of the flesh and not of the
soul, so that the tabernacle of David which has fallen into decay may arise,
and, risen and rebuilt, remain undamaged and unfallen for all eternity.
(2) For God was not concerned that David's stone house be built to give
him a fine home in the kingdom of heaven, but that his flesh, the tabernacle
of the soul, be built, which he had fashioned with his own hands.*

45,3 *With your immense wisdom, Aglaophon, you should look at it in
this way. You are sure to understand it very easily if you think of the image
of going to sleep and getting up. If going to sleep follows waking, and
getting up follows sleeping, and this is a rehearsal for death and resurrection—"to the twins, sleep and death!"*[135]*—then, since rising follows [the
sleep of] sleepers, the quickening to life of the flesh must be the result of
death. (4) For if waking issues from sleep, and the sleeper certainly does
not just go on sleeping in the same posture but gets up again, so life will
issue from death ; and the dead man surely does not remain dead because
he dies. (5) For if waking issues from sleep, rising from falling, and
rebuilding from destruction, how can we possibly not expect the resurrection
of the fallen and the quickening of the dead?*

45,6   *And observe, if you will, not only from sleeping and rising but
from seeds and shoots as well, how the resurrection is proclaimed in them
all. Note how seeds are put into the ground "bare, "*[136] *as the scripture says,
without any flesh, and rendered back again mature. If seeds died and
decayed, but there were no more revival and sprouting of the seeds, why
would it not be the lot of all things to be dissolved in death?*

46,1   *But for now, "most excellent Theophilus"*[137] *and you other judges
of the debate, I shall forbear to say more about this. Let us take up his
next points, since they are far from satisfactory. (2) For again, in my
opponent's forced, unnatural interpretation of the prophecy in the sixty-fifth
Psalm, God takes sinners' actual souls, and as punishment for their sins
puts them < into > the flesh as into a "snare."*[138] *But this is absurdity,
not orthodoxy. (3) If the souls had possessed bodies before the transgression,
as I have pointed out, how could they be put into bodies later, after their*

---

[135] Iliad 16.672
[136] 1 Cor. 15:37
[137] Luke 1:3
[138] Ps. 65:11

transgression, < as > into a snare? There was no time for them to sin before they got their bodies.

46,4   *It makes no sense to say one minute that the souls have sinned because of the body, and the next that the body was made for condemnation as a prison and a snare, because they sinned. (5) If their sin was due to the body, the body was with them from the first, even before the sin. For how could they sin because of something not yet in existence? (6) But again, if the body itself is regarded as a snare, chains and a prison, the combination [of body and soul] cannot be responsible for the sin; it must be the soul alone. For bonds, snares and chains are made for the sinner after his sin.*

46,7   *But we have agreed that the body cannot be the prison of the soul, since the body cooperates with either sort of behavior, right or wrong, but a prison prevents wrong behavior. (8) So as I say, one of two alternatives must be true. Either we sinned with a body from the first, and can find no time when we were without a body; and the body shares the responsibility for good and evil actions with the soul. Or else we sinned when we lived without a body, and the body is not responsible for evil at all. (9) And yet the soul cannot be overcome by irrational pleasure without a body; but our first parents were caught and overcome by irrational pleasure. Thus even before its sin, the soul was accompanied by a body.*

46,10   *As to the unthinkability of the body's being made as a prison to punish the transgression, leaving the soul, as our opponents say, with the unmitigated, constant torture of carrying a corpse, I believe I have now given a full demonstration of this with every possible proof. (11) Thus it is untenable and unacceptable to make of the body a snare and chains, and say that God brings the souls into the snare as punishment, after casting them down from the third heaven for their transgressions of his commandment.*

46,12   *For what could one be thinking of to believe the things they have so rashly said? And this although, despite their forced interpretation of it, the psalm does not have this meaning. I shall quote its actual words to show what fiction their exposition is, since they have no desire to understand the scriptures correctly.*

46,13   *The psalm goes something like this: "Thou hast proved us, O God, thou hast tried us like as silver is tried. Thou broughtest us into the snare, and laidest tribulations upon our back. Thou sufferedst men to ride over our heads. We went through fire and water, and thou broughtest us out to refreshment."[139] (14) And they add at once, "This is said by souls which have been cast down from the third heaven, where Paradise is, into the snare of the body." For they say that "We went through fire and water" may mean either the soul's passage from the womb into the world, since*

---

[139] Ps. 65:10–12

it has its dwelling in the midst of much fire and moisture—or else it may mean the soul's fall from the heavens into the world, when < it > passes into the world through the fire, and the waters above the firmament.

46,15   *I have decided to stand up to these people. Now then, Aglaophon, answer for them yourself [and tell us] what they will say.* (47,1) *For in the first place, Paradise, from which, in the person of our first ancestor, we were expelled, is obviously a particular place on this earth, set apart for the untroubled rest and residence of the saints. < This > is plain from the fact that the Tigris and Euphrates, and the other rivers that issue from it, can be seen here inundating our land with their flooding.* (2) *They do not pour down in a cataract from the sky; the earth could not even sustain such a weight of water pouring down all at once from on high.*

47,3   *Nor, to those who can recognize the nuances of words, is the apostle suggesting that Paradise is in a third heaven. He says, "I know < such a man > caught up to the third heaven; and I know such a man, (whether in the body or out of the body, God knoweth), that he was rapt away to Paradise."*[140] (4) *He is declaring that he has seen two great revelations and been taken up visibly twice, once to the third heaven and once to Paradise. "I know such a man caught up to the third heaven" is proof that a particular revelation was shown him in the third heaven, when he was caught up.* (5) *And the next sentence, "And I know such a man, (whether in the body, or out of the body), < rapt away > to Paradise," proves that one more revelation was shown him in Paradise.*

47,6   *It is jabber and rant, then, to speak of the souls' being cast down from the heavens, passing through the sources of fire and the waters above the firmament, and falling into this world.* (7) *Besides, Adam was not expelled from the heavens, but from the Paradise planted in the east, in Eden. For his transgression did not precede his embodiment, as I have shown sufficiently already, and this body is not a snare. The transgression came after the soul's union with the body, for man is a composite of the two; and the fall from Paradise took place here.* (8) *But he did not examine the passage with any care at all, Aglaophon. He employed his skill in things which are not without risk, and set out to interpret the psalm in accordance with the opinions of low people; of whom I forbear to say more.*

48,1   *But now that I have come to the point of correcting their depravity, I should also like to explain to them the reason for this prophecy, "Thou hast proved us, O God. Thou hast tried with fire as silver is tried."*[141] (2) *The martyrs, during their trials, were amply tested by the assaults of their tortures—for the most part, the prophecies are fulfilled in our faith. They thank God that they have fought the battle out honorably and with*

---

[140] 2 Cor. 12:2–4
[141] Ps. 65:10–11

great courage, and say to him, "Thou hast proved us, O God. Thou hast
tried us with fire as silver is tried," as though God, bent on victory in
the true Olympics, tested them with many sufferings, enabling them to win
greater glory in his eyes.

48,3   *And see how Solomon calls out in praise of martyrs, in plain*
agreement with these words—for the line does not go uncorroborated by the
testimony of other scriptures. "God proved them and found them worthy
of himself. As gold in the furnace he tried them and received them as an
whole burnt offering of sweet savor. And in the time of their visitation < they
shall shine >." (4) And before that he had said, "And though they are
punished in the sight of men, their hope is full of immortality. And being
a little chastened they shall be greatly rewarded."[142]

48,5   *Moreover, in the hundred and twenty-third Psalm it is the martyrs*
who sing, "If the Lord had not been in our midst when men rose up against
us, they had swallowed us up alive. The water had drowned us, our soul
had passed through a torrent, our soul had passed through bottomless
water. Blessed be the Lord, who hath not given us for a prey unto their
teeth. Our soul was delivered as a sparrow from the snare of the fowlers.
The snare is broken and we are delivered."[143]

48,6   *There are two choirs of victorious martyrs, one of the New Testament*
and the other of the Old, who with one accord sing their antiphonal hymn
to God, their champion and the King of all : "Thou hast proved us, O
God, thou hast tried us with fire as silver is tried. Thou broughtest us
into the snare, thou laidest crushing burdens upon our backs."[144] *Those*
[burdens] were the tribunal of the heathen, or the tortures in which they
were hard pressed by crushing and burning. (7) For scripture says, "Test
me, O Lord, and prove me, try my reins and my heart."[145]

48,8   *Well might Abraham say, "Thou hast proved us, O Lord ; thou*
hast tried us by fire as silver is tried," after hearing, "Abraham, spare thy
son,"[146] *and throwing his sword away. (9) His heart had ached for his*
only son, though he honored God's command above < his child >. After
Job's flesh had run with filth and his friends had reproached him, and
after his body was in pain, well might Job say, "Thou hast set tribulations
before us, O Lord, that thou mayest try us as gold in the furnace,"[147] *on*
hearing God ask him from the whirlwind, "Or thinkest thou that I have
dealt with thee otherwise than that thou mightest be found righteous?"[148]
(10) *And well might the three children in the furnace, sprinkled with dew*

---

[142] Wisd. Sol. 3:4–7
[143] Ps. 123:2–7
[144] Ps. 65:10–11
[145] Ps. 25:2
[146] Cf. Gen. 22:11–12.
[147] Ps. 65:10
[148] Job 40:8

to prevent their consumption by the fire, say, "Thou hast proved us, O God, thou hast tried us with fire as the silver is tried. We went through fire and water, and thou broughtest us out to a place of refreshment."

48,11   *Grant, O almighty God, the great, the eternal, the Father of Christ, that in thy day I too, Methodius, may pass unharmed through the fire and the waters turned to fuel, escape their onslaughts, and say, "I went through fire and water, and thou broughtest me out to refreshment." (12) For thy promise to those who love thee is, "If thou passest through the water I am with thee, and the rivers shall not overwhelm thee. If thou passest through the fire thou shalt not be burned; flame shall not scorch thee."*[149] *But so much for the exposition of the psalm.*

49,1   *But further, we must examine the argument in which, like sleepers dreaming many impostures, they declare that Paul said, "I was alive without the Law once,"*[150] *and loudly insist < that > by his life "before the commandment" he meant his life in the first man < in Paradise >, before the body. And the words he adds, "But I am fleshly, sold under sin,"*[151] *confirm this. (2) For the man could not have been ruled and mastered by evil, and sold to it for his transgression, if he had not become fleshly; in itself, the soul is immune to sin. And thus, after first saying, "I was alive without the Law once," Paul acutely added, "But I am fleshly, sold under sin."*

49,3   *Awe and consternation overcame the masses when they said these things, but now that the truth has come to light it is plain, not only that they have gone far wrong, but that they have reached even the height of blasphemy. (4) By granting that the souls had lived without bodies before the commandment, and supposing them completely immune to sin in themselves, they have once more demolished their own argument—or, far more, their own selves. For they make it out that the bodies < were given > to the souls later, as a punishment, because they had sinned before they had bodies. And indeed they have been moved to abuse, and compare the body with a prison and chains, and < set about* > to say other silly things.*

49,5   *In fact, as has been said, the precise opposite is true; before the sin the soul must have a body. For if the soul in itself were immune to sin, it would not sin at all before it had a body. (6) But if it sinned, it cannot in itself be immune to sin, but must even be susceptible and prone to it. And therefore—again—it will sin even without getting the body, just as it sinned before it got it.*

49,7   *But why did it get a body at all later on, after it had sinned? Why did it need a body? If it was for torture and pain, why does it revel with the body instead, and behave licentiously? (8) And why does it plainly even have the freedom to make choices in this world? For here it is in our*

---

[149] Isa. 43:2
[150] Rom. 7:9
[151] Rom. 7:14

power to believe and not to believe, to do right and to sin, to do good and to do evil.

49,9   *Moreover, how can the judgment still be awaited, in which God rewards everyone according to his works and behavior? Why not suppose that it is here already, if the soul's birth and entrance into a body is its judgment and retribution, whereas its death and separation from the body is its liberation and refection? For in your view it was put into a a body as judgment and condemnation, for sinning before it had a body.* (10) *But my argument has more than amply shown that it is inadmissible to regard the body as the soul's torture chamber and chain.*

50,1   *To end our discussion of this here, one would need only to show from the scripture itself that, < even > before his transgression, the first man was composed of body and soul. I too shall go over the heads of this now, trying < only* > to correct the bases of their arguments, and thus not exceed the length suitable for speeches.*

50,2   *For you can see at once, gentlemen of the jury, that as the words which follow it indicate, the verse from Romans, "I was alive once without the Law," cannot apply to the life they claim the soul had before the body— even though, because he suffers from a completely incurable childhood ailment, this good physician of the texts forcibly changed the sense as he saw fit by removing the next lines.* (3) *For instead of keeping bodies' limbs next to their natural junctures and joints, and leaving the appearance of the body just right, as nature intended, he mutilated it, like a Scythian mercilessly hacking an enemy's limbs off for his destruction, by ignoring the order of scripture.*

50,4   *"All right," they will say, "if you have proved that this is not what they mean, why did the apostle make these statements?"*

"Because he regarded the 'commandment' as a law," I would reply. "(Let us grant first that, as you suppose, he called the commandment an actual 'law.') But Paul did not suppose because of this that, before the commandment, our first parents also lived without bodies; he supposed that they lived without sin. (5) *Indeed the time between their creation and the commandment, during which they lived without sin, was short—[this time during which] they lived, not without bodies but with bodies. Thus they were expelled directly after the commandment, after a very short youth in Paradise."*

50,6   *But suppose that someone seizes on the line which says, "When we were in the flesh, the motions of sins which were by the Law did work in our members,"*[152] *and believes that Paul is accusing and repudiating the flesh; and suppose that he brings up all the other things of this kind that Paul said,* (7) *such as, "that the righteousness of the Law might be*

---

[152] Rom. 7:5

fulfilled in us, which walk not after the flesh but after the Spirit."[153] *Or,*
"For they that are after the flesh do mind the things of the flesh, but they
that are after the Spirit, the things of the Spirit. For to be fleshly minded
is death; but to be spiritually minded is life and peace. Because the fleshly
mind is enmity against God, for it is not subject to the law of God, neither
again can it be. < So then they that are in the flesh cannot please God >.
But ye are not in the flesh but in the Spirit."[154] (8) *We should ask him*
whether the apostle, and the persons he wrote this to, had already departed
this life, if he was here decrying, not life lived in fleshly terms, but the
flesh itself—or whether he was still in the flesh.

50,9   *But it cannot be said that he sent this when he was not in the*
flesh. Both he and the addressees were plainly in the flesh. But in that
case how can he say, "When we were in the flesh the motions of the sins
that were by the Law did work in our members," as though neither he
himself, nor the addressees, were still in the flesh? (10) *He is speaking,*
not of the flesh itself but of a dissolute life. It is his habit to call a person
who lives such a life "fleshly," just as he calls one who is hardened to
the beholding of the truth and the light of the mystery, "soulish."

50,11   *For [on their premises] they should say that neither can the soul*
ever be saved! Scripture says, "The soulish man receiveth not the things
of the Spirit of God, for they are foolishness unto him. But he that is
spiritual judgeth all things."[155] (12) *< Thus > in that case a soulish and*
a spiritual man are introduced, and the spiritual < is adjudged* > as saved
while the soulish < is adjudged* > as lost, but this does not mean that
the soul perishes and everything besides the soul is saved. So here, (I.e.,
at Rom. 5:8-9) *when Paul says that the fleshly, and those who are in*
the flesh, must perish and cannot please God, he is not striving for the
destruction of the flesh, but the destruction of the fleshly mode of life.

50,13   *And further on, when he says, "They that are in the flesh cannot*
please God," he adds at once, "But ye are not in the flesh, but in the Spirit,
if so be that the Spirit of God dwelleth in you."[156] (14) *And shortly after*
that, "But because the Spirit of him that raised up Jesus from the dead
dwelleth in you, he that raised up Christ from the dead shall also quicken
your mortal bodies by his Spirit that dwelleth in you. Therefore, brethren,
we are debtors, not to the flesh to live after the flesh. For if ye live after
the flesh ye shall die; but if ye, through the Spirit, do mortify the deeds
of the body, ye shall live."[157] *As we must note, he maintained that the body's*
appetite for pleasures is put to death, and not the body itself.

---

[153] Rom. 8:4
[154] Rom. 8:5–9
[155] 1 Cor. 2:14–15
[156] Rom. 8:8–9
[157] Rom. 8:11–13

51,1 *But if they argue, "Then why is it said that 'The mind of the flesh is enmity against God, for it is not subject to the law of God, neither indeed can it be?'"*[158] *we must reply that here too they are mistaken.* (2) *Paul was not suggesting that the flesh itself cannot be subject to the law of God, but that the "mind" of the flesh cannot be, and this is different from the flesh.*

51,3 *It is as though he were to say, "The impurity in poorly refined silver is not subject to the craftsman for manufacture as a household vessel. It cannot be; it must be removed from the silver first, and melted out."* (4) *And he was not claiming because of this that the silver cannot be wrought into a serviceable vessel, but that the copper in the silver, and its other impurities, cannot be.* (5) *Thus when he spoke of the "mind of the flesh," he did not mean that the flesh cannot be subject to the law of God, but that the "mind" that is in the flesh cannot be—its impulse to incontinence, for example. Elsewhere he sometimes called this the "old leaven of malice and wickedness,"*[159] *and urged that it be entirely removed from us. But sometimes he called it the "law which warreth against the law of my mind and bringeth it into captivity."*[160]

51,6 *For in the first place, if he meant that the flesh itself cannot be subject to the law of God, no just judge could blame us for licentious behavior, banditry, and all the other deeds we perform or do with the body— for the flesh cannot be subject to the law of God! How could the body be blamed for living up to its own nature?*

51,7 *But besides, neither could the body be brought to purity or virtue, if it were not in its nature to be subject to the good. For if the nature of the flesh is such that it cannot be subject to the law of God, but righteousness is the law of God, and prudence, then no one at all could ever be a virgin, or continent.* (8) *But if there are virgins and continent persons, but continence is achieved by the subjection of the body—there is no other way of refraining from sin—then it is not true that the body cannot be subject to the law of God.* (9) *How did John subject his body to purity? Or Peter to sanctity? And why does Paul say, "Let not sin therefore reign in your mortal body, that ye should obey it in the lusts thereof. Neither yield ye your members as instruments of unrighteousness unto sin : but yield yourselves unto God, as those who are alive from the dead, and your members as instruments of righteousness unto God."*[161] *And again, "For as ye have yielded your members servants to uncleanness and to iniquity*

---

[158] Rom. 8:7
[159] 1 Cor. 7:8
[160] Rom. 7:23
[161] Rom. 6:12–13

unto iniquity; even so now yield your members servants to righteousness unto holiness."[162]

52,1   *Thus he knew that this tabernacle can be put to rights and assent to the good, so that the sins in it can be put to death.* (2) *Even with us, how can a man be the servant of righteousness if he does not first subject his fleshly members so that they will obey not sin but righteousness, and live worthily of Christ? Sinning and refraining from sin are accomplished through the body, and the soul employs it either as an instrument of virtue or as an instrument of wickedness.*

52,3   *For if "Neither fornicators, nor idolaters, nor adulterers, nor effeminate, nor abusers of themselves with mankind, nor thieves, not covetous, nor drunkards, nor revilers, nor extortioners can inherit the kingdom of God"*[163]—(4) *and if these things are accomplished by the body and derive their strength from the body, and no one is justified without overcoming them first—and if the one who overcomes them is the one who inclines to prudence and faith—then the body is subject to the law of God. For prudence is the law of God.*

52,5   *Thus the apostle did not say that the flesh is not subject to the good, but that the mind of the flesh is not, removing, as it were, the flesh's desire for immoderations just as he removed the soul's desire for evil.* (6) *In his earnest effort to purge even the intemperance of gluttony, teaching us that such desires and pleasures must be utterly destroyed,* (7) *and shaming those who believe that luxury and feasting are life—persons "who regard their belly as God,"*[164] *who < say >, "Let us eat and drink, for tomorrow we die,"*[165] *and who spend their time like greedy cattle in nothing but feeding and dining—he said,* (8) *"Meats for the belly, and the belly for meats: but God shall destroy both it and them."*[166] *And he added, "Now the body is not for fornication, but for the Lord; and the Lord for the body. And God hath both raised up the Lord, and will raise up us by his power. What? Know ye not that your bodies are the members of Christ? Shall I then take the members of Christ and make them the members of an harlot? God forbid! What? Know ye not that that which is joined to an harlot is one body? For two, saith he, shall be one flesh. But he that is joined to the Lord is one spirit. Flee fornication. Every sin that a man doeth is without the body; but he that committeth fornication sinneth against his own body. What? Know ye not that your body is the temple of the Holy Ghost which is in you, which ye have of God, and ye are not your own?*

---

[162] Rom. 6:19
[163] 1 Cor. 6:9–10
[164] Phil. 3:19
[165] 1 Cor. 15:32
[166] 1 Cor. 6:13

For ye are bought with a price: therefore glorify God in your body."[167]

53,1   *Note that the apostle made these statements because the body can
< be subject > to the law of God, and can be immortal if it is kept free
of the fuel of intemperance, and never soiled by forbidden stimulations of
the passions.* (2) *For what else "is joined to an harlot,"*[168] *has relations
with her, becomes one flesh with her by the junction and union of their
members, but this external body with which all sins of sex and passion
are committed?* (3) *This is why Paul said, "Every sin that a man doeth
is without the body; but he that committeth fornication sinneth against
his own body."*[169] (4) *Vanity, unbelief, anger and hypocrisy are sins of
the soul, but fornication, passion and luxury are sins of the body. With
these the soul can neither take refuge in the truth nor the body be subject
to the teachings of prudence; both will slip away from the kingdom of Christ.*

53,5   *And therefore if our bodies, when kept holy, are the "temple of
the Spirit that dwelleth in us,"*[170] *and "The Lord is in the body,"*[171] *and
the members of the body are the members of Christ, the body is subject to
the divine law and "can inherit the kingdom of God."*[172] (6) *For "He that
raised up Christ from the dead shall also quicken your mortal bodies by
his Spirit that dwelleth in you,"*[173] *so that "This mortal shall put on immortality and this corruptible shall put on incorruption, and death will
be swallowed up in victory."*[174] (7) *For the apostle was not discussing some
other body here on earth, but this body which dies and is put to death,
and with which fornication and other sins can be committed.*

54,1   *But what if they surmise that there is a difference between "body"
and "flesh"—to allow them this argument as well—and suppose that "body"
is something different and invisible, < the property > of the soul, as it were,
but "flesh" is this external, visible body? We must reply that it is not only
Paul and the prophets who understand this flesh as "body." Others do as
well, < pagan > philosophers, who are the most particular about the accuracy of terms.* (2) *If our opponents will also make a scientific investigation
of this, "flesh" is the right word—certainly not for the whole mass of our
tabernacle, but for some part of the whole, like the bones, sinews and veins.
The whole, though, is "body." And physicians, who deal with precision
with the nature of bodies, understand "body" to mean this visible body.*

54,3   *Plato too, moreover, understands "body" to mean this actual < body >.
Thus Socrates said in the Phaedo, "Do we suppose that death is anything*

---

[167] 1 Cor. 6:13–20
[168] 1 Cor. 6:16
[169] 1 Cor. 6:18
[170] 1 Cor. 6:19
[171] Cf. 1 Cor. 6:13.
[172] 1 Cor. 6:15
[173] Rom. 8:11
[174] 1 Cor. 15:53–54

other than < the > soul's departure from the body? And when the body has begun to exist separately by itself, apart from the soul, and the soul apart from the body, this is death."[175]

54,4   *Did not the blessed Moses—we come now to the Lord's scriptures—understand "body" to mean the body we see, and say in the purifications that whoever touches something unclean "shall wash his clothes and bathe his body in water, and be unclean until even?"*[176] (5) *And what about Job? Did he too not understand "body" to mean this thing that dies, when he said, "My body is sullied with the rottenness of worms?"*[177] (6) *Solomon too said, "Wisdom will not enter into a soul that deviseth evil, nor make its abode in a body guilty of sin."*[178] *And in Daniel it is said of the martyrs, "The fire had no power upon their bodies, nor was an hair of their head singed."*[179]

54,7   *The Lord said too, in the Gospel, "Therefore I say unto you, Take no thought what ye shall eat or what ye shall put on. Is not the soul more than meat, and the body than raiment?"*[180] (8) *And the apostle proves that he understands "body" to mean this body of ours when he says, "Let not sin therefore reign in your mortal body."*[181] *And again, "If the Spirit of him that raised up Jesus from the dead dwell in you, he that raised up Christ from the dead shall quicken your mortal bodies."*[182] (9) *And again, "If the foot shall say, Because I am not the hand, I am not of the body, is it therefore not of the body?"*[183] *And again, "And being not weak in faith, Abraham considered not his own body now dead."*[184] *And again, "For we must all appear before the judgment seat of Christ : that everyone may receive the things done in his body according to that he hath done."*[185] (10) *And again, "His letters are weighty and powerful ; but the presence of his body is weak."*[186] *And again, "I knew a man in Christ fourteen years ago, whether in the body, I cannot tell,*[187] *or whether out of the body, I cannot tell." And again, "So men ought to love their wives as their own bodies."*[188] *And again, "And the very God of peace sanctify you wholly; and I pray God your whole spirit and soul and body be preserved blameless*

---

[175] Plato Phaedo 64C
[176] Lev. 14:9; 47
[177] Job 7:5
[178] Wisd. Sol. 1:4
[179] Dan. 3:94
[180] Matt. 6:25
[181] Rom. 6:12
[182] Rom. 8:11
[183] 1 Cor. 12:15
[184] Rom. 4:19
[185] 2 Cor. 5:10
[186] 2 Cor. 10:10
[187] 2 Cor. 12:2
[188] Eph. 5:28

unto the coming of our Lord Jesus Christ."[189]

54,11   *But our opponents have surely realized none of this. They supposed the apostle adrift on a stormy sea, as though his thoughts had no harbor and anchorage, but sailed back and forth making contradictory statements, sometimes that the flesh rises, but sometimes that it does not.*

55,1   *And so, to omit none of their propositions and hew < the > hydra all to pieces, I shall return to the subject. For next, as I promised, I shall put the other questions that they raise and show how to answer them, and prove that even our opponent has said things that are themselves in accord and agreement with our faith in the resurrection of the flesh.* (2) *Let us see, then, what we were led at the outset to say of the apostle. As we originally suggested, his words, "I was alive without the Law once,"*[190] *mean our former life in Paradise in our first parents—not without a body but with a body—before the commandment.* (3) *For "God took the dust of the earth and fashioned the man"*[191] *before the giving of the commandment. We lived free from desire and knew no onslaughts of the senseless lust which, with the enticing distractions of pleasures, impels us to intemperance.* (4) *For if one has no rule to live by, and no control over his own reason, what life can he choose to live, to merit just praise or blame? He must be pronounced immune to all charges, since one cannot covet things that are not forbidden.* (5) *But even though he does, he will not be held responsible. "Coveting" does not apply to things which are accessible and at one's command. How can one desire and itch for a thing which is not withheld from him, and which he does not need? Thus < Paul said >, "I had not known lust if the Law had not said, Thou shalt not covet."*[192]

55,6   *But after our first parents were told, "Of the tree of the knowledge of good and evil ye shall not eat, and on the day ye eat thereof, ye shall surely die,"*[193] *they conceived and were infected with desire. For one who "desires" does not desire the things that he has, controls and uses, but the things which are forbidden and barred to him, and which he does not have.* (7) *Thus Paul was right to say, "I had not known lust if the Law had not said, Thou shalt not covet"—that is, if "Ye shall not eat thereof," had not been said. This is the way in which sin gained the opportunity and occasion for its entry, to mock me and pervert me.*

56,1   *For once the commandment had been given, the devil got his opportunity to produce covetousness in me through the commandment, and cunningly urged and provoked me to descend to the desire for the forbidden.*

---

[189]   1 Thes. 5:23
[190]   Rom. 7:9
[191]   Gen. 2:7
[192]   Rom. 7:7
[193]   Gen. 2:17

(2) *"For without a law sin is dead"*[194]—*that is, there was no way to commit sin when the commandment had not been given and was not yet in existnence. "I was" blamelessly "alive"*[195] *before the commandment, because I had no rule and ordinance to live by, from which it would be sinful for me to fall away.* (3) *"But when the commandment came, sin revived and I died. And the commandment, which was ordained to life, I found to be unto death,"*[196] *because once God had given a law and specified what should and should not be done, the devil produced covetousness in me.* (4) *For though God's counsel and the commandment he gave me were meant for life and immortality, so that, if I obeyed the commandment and lived by it, I would have an untroubled life of the highest eternal beatitude, flourishing forever in immortality and joy, its result, because I transgressed it, was my death and condemnation.* (5) *For the devil—whom the apostle called "sin" in this instance because he is the artificer and originator of sin— took occasion from the commandment, deceived me into disobedience, and after deceiving me, killed me by bringing me under the sentence of, "In the day that ye eat thereof ye shall surely die."*[197]

56,6 *"Wherefore the law is holy, and God's commandment holy, and just, and good,"*[198] *because it was not given to harm, but to save. Let us not for a moment suppose that God does anything useless or harmful!* (7) *What, then? "Was that which was good"—the commandment I was given to be the cause of my greatest good—"made death unto me? God forbid!"*[199] *God's commandment was not the cause of my enslavement to corruption and the writing of the tablets of destruction. It was the devil, to make it clear that he had made evil ready for me by means of something good, so that the inventor and architect of sin would become "exceeding sinful"*[200] *and be exposed as such, and the < wicked > overseer of the opposite of God's commandment would be distinguished from the good.*

56,8 *"For we know that the law is spiritual,"*[201] *and thus can be the cause of harm to no one; spiritual things have their dwellings far from senseless lust and sin.* (9) *"But I am fleshly, sold under sin."*[202] *That is, since I am fleshly and placed as a free agent between good and evil, so that it is in my power to do what I will—for scripture says, "I have set before thee life and death"*[203]—*then, if I have consented to disobey the*

---

[194] Rom. 7:8
[195] Rom. 7:9
[196] Rom. 7:9–10
[197] Gen. 2:17
[198] Rom. 7:12
[199] Rom. 7:13
[200] Rom. 7:13
[201] Rom. 7:14
[202] Rom. 7:14
[203] Deut. 30:15

spiritual law, or commandment, but to obey the material law, or the counsel of the serpent, because of this choice I have fallen under sin and am sold to the devil.

56,10   *And therefore, after laying siege to me, the evil settles, makes its home and lives in my flesh, like a drone in a beehive which often hovers buzzing around it. For because I broke the commandment, the punishment of being sold to evil was laid on me. (11) And thus, when I think of things I want not to do, "I allow not what I do." For "I allow not what I do" and "What I hate, that do I"[204] are not to be taken of actually doing evil, but of merely thinking of it. For unseemly thoughts often catch us off guard and cause us to imagine things we want not to, since the soul is very much perplexed by thoughts.*

57,1   *For whether or not we think wicked thoughts is not entirely our choice, but we can choose whether or not to implement the thoughts. We cannot prevent the thoughts from occurring to us, since they are insinuated into us from without to test us ; but we can refrain from obeying them or putting them into practice. (2) How did the apostle do the evil he disliked the most, and least of all do the good he liked—unless he was speaking of the peculiar thoughts which, for some unknown reason, we sometimes entertain even without intending to? (3) These must be combated and curbed, or they will spread and possess the farthest bounds of our souls. For while these linger in us, the good cannot show itself.*

57,4   *The apostle was right, then, to say, "That which I do, I allow not ; for what I would, that do I not, but what I hate, that do I."[205] We want not even to think of things that are unseemly and infamous, for perfect good is not merely refraining from doing such things, but even from thinking of them. (5) And yet this good which we want does not materialize; the evil we do not want, does. Countless < thoughts > on countless subjects haunt our hearts and often enter them even against our will, filling us with curiosity and senseless meddlesomeness. (6) And thus we are capable of wanting not to entertain these thoughts, but < not > of banishing them, never to return to our minds. For as I said, we do not have the power to do this, but only the power to comply with the thoughts or not.*

57,7   *Thus the sense of the line, "For the good that I would, I do not,"[206] is something like this : "I want not to think of what is harmful to me, since [not even to think of this] is irreproachable good, 'built foursquare without blemish by hands and heart,'"[207] as the saying goes. And "The good that I will, I do not : but the evil that I would not, that do I,"[208]*

---

[204] Rom. 7:15
[205] Rom. 7:15;19
[206] Rom. 7:19
[207] Plato Protagoras 339B
[208] Rom. 7:19

means, "I do not want to conceive of them, yet I conceive of the things I want not to."

57,8   *And the question < must > be raised whether David besought God for the same reason—his own disgust at thinking thoughts he did not choose to—[and said], "Cleanse thou me from my secret thoughts, and spare thy servant strange thoughts. If they get not the dominion over me, then shall I be innocent and cleansed of the great sin."*[209] *(9) And the apostle himself says elsewhere, "Casting down thoughts, and every high thing that exalteth itself against the knowledge of God, and bringing every thought into captivity to the obedience of God."*[210]

58,1   *But suppose someone still ventures to speak up and reply that the apostle is teaching that we do the evil we hate and do not want to do, not only by thinking, but also by actually doing it. (2) For Paul has said, "The good that I would I 'do' not : but the evil which I would not, that 'do' I." I shall require the one who says this to explain, if he is telling the truth, what the evil was that the apostle hated and wanted not to do, but still did—and < what > the good was that he wanted to do but did not do, but on the contrary, as often as he wanted to do this good, he did not do the good he wanted, but the evil he did not want. (3) When Paul wanted not to worship idols but to worship God, was he unable to worship God as he wanted to, but able to worship idols as he wanted not to? Or did he not live the sober life he wanted, but a licentious life that was vexatious to him? (4) And in a word, did he drink too much, squander his money, grow angry, do injury, and all the rest of the evil he wanted not to, but not practice righteousness and holiness as he wanted to?*

58,5   *Indeed when, in his effort to see righteousness practiced among us with no admixture of evil, he urgently exhorts all the members of the churches not to transgress, he orders not only that active wrongdoers be reserved for destruction and wrath, but their sympathizers as well. (6) In his Epistles he often plainly teaches us to turn our backs on these very things and hate them, and says, "Be not deceived : neither fornicators, nor idolaters, nor effeminate, nor abusers of themselves with mankind, nor thieves, nor drunkards, nor covetous, nor revilers, nor extortioners shall inherit the kingdom of God."*[211] *(7) And as his last word, to urge us to shun and reject all sin completely, he makes the pronouncement, "Be ye imitators of me, as I am of Christ."*[212]

58,8   *Thus the lines we have quoted suggest, not Paul's actual doing of the things he wanted not to, but his mere thinking of them. Otherwise, how could he be an exact imitator of Christ? Since savage thoughts often*

---

[209] Ps. 18:13–14
[210] 2 Cor. 10:5
[211] 1 Cor. 6:9–10
[212] 1 Cor. 11:1

occur to us, however, filling us time after time with desires and senseless curiosity "like many swarms of buzzing flies,"[213] *Paul said, "What I would not, that do I."*[214] *We should frighten these things away from our souls with a good courage, and not even incline to the carrying out of their suggestions.*

58,9   *For this troubling of our minds with many thoughts is meant to ensure our admission to the kingdom of heaven after being tested with all sorts of pleasures and pains—provided that we do not change, but like pure gold tried by fire, never depart from the virtue that becomes us.* (10) *We must therefore resist heroically, like shock troops who pay no heed to their arrows and other missiles when they see themselves under siege by enemies, but who eagerly charge them, with zeal unflagging, in the defense of their city, till they put their band to flight and drive it beyond their borders.* (11) *For you see how, because of our indwelling sin, these thoughts from without band together against us like mad dogs or fierce, savage bandits, always urged on by the despot and chief of wickedness, who tests our ability to withstand and resist them.*

59,1   *At them, my soul, or you will yield and be made prisoner, and I will have nothing to give in exchange for you! For "What shall a man give in exchange for his soul?"*[215] (2) *It would be a good thing—indeed, a most happy thing—if we did not have our adversaries and opponents. But as this cannot be—it would amount to salvation without effort—and we cannot have what we want, for we want not to have allurements to passion ; and what we want does not materialize, but what we do not want does, since, as I said, we need to be tested ; let us never, never yield to the evil one, my soul!* (3) *Let us "take the whole armor of God" to protect and fight for us, and "Let us put on the breastplate of righteousness, have our feet shod with the readiness of the Gospel of peace, and above all take the shield of faith, wherewith we shall be able to quench all the fiery darts of the evil one, and the helmet of salvation, and the sword of the Spirit, which is the word of God, that we may be able to stand against the wiles of the devil"*[216] *and "cast down thoughts and every high thing that exalteth itself against the knowledge of God;"*[217] *"for we wrestle not against flesh and blood."*[218]

59,4   *I say this because this is the character of the apostle's writings. There is a great deal to say in proof of the orthodoxy and circumspection even of every line in this Epistle; but to go over each one from this stand-*

---

[213] Iliad 2.469
[214] Rom. 7:19
[215] Matt. 16:28
[216] Eph. 6:13–17
[217] 2 Cor. 10:4–5
[218] Eph. 6:12

point would take too long. Here I prefer to show simply his character and purpose, (5) for his purpose is orthodox when he says, "What I would, that do I not; but what I hate, that do I. < If then I do that which I would not >, I consent unto the law of God that it is good. Now then it is no more I that do it, but sin that dwelleth in me. For I know that in me, that is, in my flesh, the good dwelleth not."[219] (6) *For you remember the limits we set for ourselves earlier. Even though I am eager to run quickly over it all I am moving slowly instead, for the time it would seem desirable to take for this discourse has grown longer than I anticipated. Besides, we are not yet finished with the matter in hand.*

60,1 *Very well, we were saying, if you will recall, that at the moment when the man erred and broke the commandment, sin came into being because of his disobedience, and made its abode in him. (2) We first experienced a clash of impulses in this way, and were filled with unseemly thoughts. Because we had taken a shortcut past God's commandment we were emptied of God's inspiration, but filled with the material desire with which the coiling serpent infused us. (3) And so, for our sakes, God devised death for the destruction of sin, to keep it from being immortal, as I said, since it had appeared in us while we were immortal.*

60,4 *Thus in saying, "I know that in me, that is, in my flesh, the good dwelleth not,"*[220] *the apostle means the sin that, since the transgression, has made itself at home in us through desire, and the pleasure-loving thoughts of which keep springing up around us like new shoots and twigs. (5) For there are two kinds of thoughts in us. The one kind arises from the desire which lurks in the body, and has been caused, as I said, by the inspiration of the material spirit. The other has come from our regard for the commandment, which we have been given to have as an innate natural law, and which urges and restores our thoughts to the good. (6) Hence we "delight"*[221] *in the law of God in our minds—this is what the "inner man" means—but with the desire that dwells in the flesh we delight in the devil's law. For the law which "warreth against and opposeth the law of God"*[222]*—that is, which opposes our impulse to the good, the desire of our mind—is the law which is forever fostering lustful, material diversions to lawlessness, and is nothing but a temptation to pleasures.*

61,1 *For it seems plain to me that Paul here assumes the existence of three laws. One corresponds to the innate good in us, and he plainly called this the "law of the mind." One results from the evil one's assault and often draws the soul to sensual imaginings; Paul said that this "law" is at war with the "law of the mind." (2) Another is the law which cor-*

---

[219] Rom 7:15–18
[220] Rom. 7:18
[221] Rom. 7:22
[222] Cf. Rom. 7:23.

responds to the sin that has become habitual in the flesh because of its lust; this, Paul called the "law of sin which dwells in the members." Mounted on this as his steed, the evil one often spurs it against us, driving us to wickedness and evil deeds. (3) For the law which is infused into us from without by the evil one, and which pours, through the senses, into the soul itself like a stream of pitch, is strengthened by the law in the flesh which corresponds to its lust.

61,4   *For it is plain that the better and the worse are within ourselves, and that, when that which is by nature better becomes stronger than that which is worse, the mind as a whole is swayed to the good. But when the worse is larger and weighs us down—the thing which is said to be at war with the good in us—the man, again, is led to all sorts of fantasies and to the worse sort of thoughts.*

62,1   *Because of this law the apostle also prays for rescue; like the prophet who said, "Cleanse thou me from my secret sins,"[225] he regards it as death and destruction. (2) His words themselves prove as much; he says, "I delight in the law of God after mine inner man, but I see another law in my members, warring against the law of my mind and bringing me into captivity to the law of sin, which is in my members. O wretched man that I am! Who shall deliver me from this body of death?"[226] (3) Paul has not termed the body "death," but the law of sin in the members < of the body >, which lurks in us because of the transgression and is always urging the soul, in its imagination, to the "death" of wickedness.*

62,4   *At once, no doubt undone by the sort of death from which he yearned for rescue, he also adds who his rescuer was: "I thank God through Jesus Christ."[227] We must note, Aglaophon, that if, as you people suppose, he meant that this body is death, he would not have invited Christ to rescue him later from an evil such as this. What more peculiar, or more than peculiar result could we have from Christ's coming?*

62,5   *And why ever did the apostle say that he could be freed from this "death" by God through the coming of Christ, when, in fact, everyone died even before Christ entered the world? (6) Everyone was "rescued," from their bodies by their separation from them on departing this life. And all the souls likewise—of faithless and faithful, of unjust and just—were separated from their bodies on the day of their death. (7) What more than the others— who had lived in unbelief—was the apostle anxious to receive? Or if he supposed that the body is the death of the soul, why did he pray for deliverance from the body, which he would surely get even against his will, just as death and the separation of their souls from their bodies is the lot of everyone?*

---

225   Ps. 18:13
226   Rom. 7:22–24
227   Rom. 7:25

62,8   *And so, Aglaophon, he does not mean that this body is death,
but that the sin which lives < within > the body through lust is death—
the sin from which God delivered him by the coming of Christ. (9) "For
the law of the Spirit of life in Christ Jesus hath made us free from the
law of sin and death,"*[228] *so that "He that raised up Jesus from the dead
may also quicken our mortal bodies because of his Spirit that dwelleth in
us,"*[229] *(10) "with the sin in the body condemned" to destruction, "so that
the requirement of the law"*[230] *of nature, which attracts us to the good as
the commandment directs, may be set alight and made visible. For before
Christ's coming, when the flesh was controlled by sin, this smoldered feebly
under a heap of material cares. (11) For God gave new strength to "the
impotence of the natural law within us, while it was feeble"*[231] *from its defeat
by the lust in our bodies. For he sent his Son to take a flesh like our sinful
flesh—that which appeared was real, not an illusion—(12) so that, with
sin condemned to destruction so as to "bring forth" no more "fruit"*[232] *in
the flesh, the requirement of the law of nature would be fulfilled. It would
have grown, through obedience, in those who followed, not the desire of
the flesh, but the desire and the guidance of the Spirit. (13) For "the law
of the Spirit of life," which is the Gospel and is different from the other
laws and was meant to foster obedience and the forgiveness of sins through
its preaching, "hath set us free from the law of sin and death,"*[233] *and
entirely conquered the sin which rules the flesh.*

62,14   *I have said these things, Theophilus, to clarify the passages
which they cite even from the words of the apostle, but do not expound
correctly. But I shall turn to the rest, provided that I can find someone
to help me through to the end of my discourse. For the material which follows
this is abstruse, and by no means easy to master. (15) So I undertake
the more difficult part of it, though I can see that the demonstration will
be long and hard unless a breeze of understanding suddenly blows on us
from heaven as though we tossed in mid-sea, and restores us to a calm
harbor and a more reliable proof.*

So far the excerpt from Methodius

63,1   This is the < selection* > of consecutive passages < which I
have made* > < from > Methodius', or Eubulius', < comments* >
on Origen and the heresy which, with sophistical imposture, Origen
puts forward in his treatise on resurrection. I believe that my quotation

---

[228] Rom. 8:2
[229] Rom. 8:11
[230] Rom. 8:3–4
[231] Cf. Rom. 8:3–4.
[232] Rom. 7:4
[233] Rom. 8:2

of these passages here will take care of his silly teachings, and
refute his < destruction* > of men's < hope* > for life with a malignant growth which has been taken from pagan superstition and
plastered over. (2) For many other things—surely even as many
more—were also said in his followup of the subject by Methodius,
a learned man and a hard fighter for the truth. (3) But since I
have promised to say a few things in its refutation about every
sect—there are not few of them!—I am satisfied with quoting
Methodius' work [only] this far. (4) And I, of my poverty, shall
add a few more comments of my own on Origen's nonsense and
conclude the contest with him, awarding the prize to God who
gives us the victory and, in his lovingkindness, adorns his church
at all times with the unfading wreaths of the teachings of the truth.
So, as best I can, I too shall speak against him.

63,5   As I indicated earlier, Mister, you scornfully say, "Was God
a tanner, to make skin tunics for Adam and Eve when no animals
had yet been slaughtered? And even if animals had been slaughtered, < there was no tanner there. What the scripture meant, then,
was* > not skin tunics, but our body of earth." (6) And this is full
proof that you are a follower of the devil's < inspiration > and the
guile of the serpent, who brought the corruption of unbelief on
mankind, deceived Eve, and continues to corrupt the minds of
simple people with the villainy † of his inspiration.[234]

63,7   Let's see whether your arguments can stand, then, since
you've worked so hard and carried the struggle of writing so many
books to such useless lengths. (8) For if the story that you composed 6000 books is true,[235] you with your wasted energy, then,
after expending all that futile effort on lampoons and useless tricks
and rendering your work of no value, you robbed the toil of your
expedition of its profit by being mistaken in the main points with
which you falsified the resurrection.

63,9   For if the body does not rise, the soul will have no inheritance either. The partnership of the body and the soul is one
and the same, and they have one work. But faithful men exhaust
themselves in body and soul in their hope of the inheritance after
resurrection—and you say there will be none! Our faith is < of no
value >, then; and there is no value in our hope, though it is in
accordance with the apostolic and true promise of the Holy Spirit.

---

[234] Holl: τῆς αὐτοῦ ἐπιπνοίας; MSS: ἐν ταῖς αὐτῶν διανοίαις
[235] Origen's admirer Rufinus attacked Epiphanius for stating publicly that
Origen had written 6000 books, and that he, Epiphanius, had read them.
Epiphanius denied the charge in a lost letter to Jerome. Cf. Jer. C. Rufin. 2.21–
22; 3.23.

63,10   But though you, on the contrary, confess a resurrection
yourself, since what you have is an illusory appearance and nothing
real, you are compelled to say only the name. How can we speak
of a soul's "rising," when it doesn't fall and isn't buried? (11) It
is plain from the name that the *resurrection* of the body, which has
fallen and been buried, is proclaimed, everywhere and in every
scripture, by the sons of the truth. But if the body doesn't rise,
the resurrection proclaimed by all the scriptures isn't possible. (12)
And if there is no resurrection, it is no use awaiting the resurrection of the dead. For there is no resurrection of souls, which have
not fallen; but there is a resurrection of bodies, which have been
buried. (13) And even if a portion of the body is raised while a
portion is laid to rest, how can there be any such portion? There
cannot be parts of the body which are raised, and parts which are
laid to rest and left behind.

63,14   < Anyone with a sound mind can see* > that, because
there is a spiritual body and an ensouled body, the spiritual body
is not one thing and the ensouled body something else; the ensouled
and the spiritual body are the same. (15) We have ensouled bodies
while we are in the world and doing the corruptible deeds of the
flesh; for in the world we are enslaved to the soul in its wicked
deeds, as you yourself have said in part. (16) When we are raised,
however, there is no more enslavement to the soul but there is
a following of the Spirit, for from that time on they have the
Earnest[236] as scripture says, "If we live by the Spirit, let us also walk
by the Spirit; and if we walk by the Spirit, by mortifying the deeds
of the body we shall live."[237] (17) There will be no more marriages,
no more lusts, no more struggles for those who profess continence.
There will be no more of the transgressions which run counter
to purity, and no more of the sort of deeds that are done here;
as the Lord says, "They that are accounted worthy of that resurrection neither marry nor are given in marriage, but are as the
angels."[238]

64,1   And thus Enoch was translated not to see death, and was
not found. But he didn't leave his body, or part of his body behind
at his translation. If he had left his body behind he would have
seen death; since he was translated with his body, he did not see
death. For he is in a living body, and because of his translation
his state is spiritual, not ensouled, though, to be sure, he is in a
spiritual *body*.

---

[236] Cf. 2 Cor. 5:5.
[237] Cf. Gal. 5:25; Rom. 8:13.
[238] Cf. Luke 20:35.

64,2   The same < has been said* > of Elijah, moreover, because he was taken up in a chariot of fire and is still in the flesh—but in a spiritual flesh which will never again have needs, < as > it did when it was in this world and needed to be fed by ravens, drink from the brook of Kerith, and wear a fleece. It is fed by another, spiritual nourishment supplied by God, who knows secrets and has created things unseen, and has food which is immortal and pure.

64,3   And you see that the ensouled body is the same as the spiritual body, just as our Lord arose from the dead, not by raising a different body, but his own body and not different from his own. But he had changed his own actual body to spiritual fineness and united a spiritual whole, and he entered where doors were barred, (4) as our bodies here cannot because they are gross, and not yet united with spiritual fineness.

64,5   What was it, then, that entered where doors were barred? Something other than the crucified body, or the crucified body itself? Surely, Origen, you cannot fail to admit that it was the crucified body itself! (6) It refutes you by Thomas' careful investigation, and told him, "Be not faithless, but believing."[239] For Christ displayed even the mark of the nails and the mark of the lance, and left those very wounds in his body even though he had joined his body to a single spiritual oneness. (7) He therefore could have wiped the wounds away too, but to refute you, you madman, he does not. Therefore it was the body which had been buried for the three days in the tomb, and which had arisen with him in the resurrection. For he displayed bones, skin and flesh, as he said, "See that a spirit hath not flesh and bones, as ye see me have."[240]

64,8   Then why did he enter where doors were barred? Why but to prove that the thing they saw was a body, not a spirit—but a spiritual body, not a material one, even though it was accompanied by its soul, Godhead, and entire incarnate humanity. (9) It was the same body, but spiritual; the same body, once gross, now fine; the same body, once crucified, now < brought to life* >; the same body, once conquered, now unconquerable. It was united and commingled with his divine nature and would never again be destroyed, but would abide forever, never again to die. (10) For "Christ is risen from the dead, the firstfruits of them that slept."[241] < But once risen > "He dieth no more; death hath no more dominion over him."[242]

---

[239] John 20:27
[240] Luke 24:39
[241] 1 Cor. 15:20
[242] Rom. 6:9

65,1   But also to let you know why Christ is called "the firstfruits of them that slept"[243] even though he was not the first to rise— Lazarus and the widow's son arose before him by his aid, and others by the aid of Elijah and Elisha. (2) But since they all died again after rising, Christ is the firstfruits of them that slept. For after his resurrection "He dieth no more,"[244] since, through his life and lovingkindness, † he is to be our resurrection.[245]

65,3   Now if he is the firstfruits of them that slept, and if his body arose in its entirety together with his Godhead, his human nature < must appear in its entirety > after its resurrection with none of it left behind, its body or anything else. "For thou shalt not leave my soul in hades, neither shalt thou give thine holy one to see corruption."[246] (4) And the remark about the soul in hades means that nothing has been left behind; but "holy one" is said to show that the holy body has not seen corruption, but has risen uncorrupted after the three days, forever united with incorruption.

65,5   But you claim, Mister, that the skin tunics are these bodies.[247] No subsequent scripture says so, but you say it because of the seeds of the Greeks' heathen teaching which were sown in you to begin with, and because of the perverse attitude of disbelief in the resurrection which was aroused in you at that time—I mean the attitude of the Greeks, which brought you to this way of thinking, and taught it to you. (6) "For the natural man receiveth not the things of the Spirit; for they are foolishness unto him, because they are spiritually discerned."[248]

65,7   If Adam and Eve had been given tunics before their disobedience, your falsehood would be a plausible one, and deceptive. But since it is plain that < the flesh is already in existence* > at the time of the making of Eve, < how can it not be an easy matter to refute your foolishness?* > What was Eve fashioned from? From a body, of course; scripture says, "God cast a deep sleep upon Adam and he slept, and God took one of his ribs."[249] (8) But a rib is simply a bone; for God built up "flesh in its place." If flesh is mentioned [at this point], how can its creation still be in prospect?

65,9   And it says earlier, "Let us make man in our image and

---

[243] 1 Cor. 15:20
[244] Rom. 6:9
[245] Holl: ἡμῶν μέλλων ἀνάστασις εἶναι; MSS: ἡ μέλλουσα ἀνάστασις εἶναι
[246] Ps 15:10
[247] Cf. Odes of Solomon 25,6; Iren. Haer. 1.5.5; Hippol. Haer. 10.13.4; Clem. Alex. Exc. Theod. 55.11.
[248] 1 Cor. 2:14
[249] Gen. 2:21

after our likeness."[250] "And he took dust of the earth," it says, "and fashioned the man."[251] But dust and flesh are simply body. (10) Then later "Adam awoke from his sleep and said, This is bone of my bones and flesh of my flesh."[252] (11) The skin tunics were not in existence yet—and neither was the falsehood you have created by allegorizing. "Bone of my bones and flesh of my flesh," plainly means that Adam and Eve were bodies, and not bodiless.

65,12 And "She took of the tree and ate"[253] when she was seduced by the serpent and fell into disobedience; and Adam heard the voice of God walking in the garden in the evening, and Adam and Eve hid themselves among the trees." And God said to Adam, "Where art thou?" But because he was found out, Adam answered, "I heard thy voice and hid, for I am naked."[254] (13) What did he mean by "naked?" Did he mean the soul or the body? And what did the fig leaves cover, the soul or the body?

65,14 Then God said, "And who told thee that thou art naked, if thou hast not eaten of the tree of which I commanded thee that of it alone thou must not eat?" And Adam said, "The woman whom thou gavest me gave unto me and I did eat."[255] Now where was the woman "given" from if not from the side, that is, from Adam's body—*before* the tunics were given to Adam and Eve!

65,15 And God said to the woman, "What is this that thou hast done?" And she said, "The serpent beguiled me and I did eat, and gave unto my husband also."[256] And God laid the curse on the serpent, the pangs of childbirth on the woman, and the eating of bread by his sweat on the man.

65,16 "And afterwards God said, Behold, Adam hath become as one of us. [And now] lest he put forth his hand and touch the tree of life and live forever."[257] (17) And do not suppose, hearer, that the Lord said, "Behold, Adam hath become as one of us," as a statement of fact. He said it in reproof, to reproach Adam's vanity for being won round by the deceit of the serpent. What Adam had thought would happen, had not happened; that is, Adam had not "become as one of us." From the desire to rise higher, Adam had fallen lower.

---

[250] Gen. 1:26
[251] Gen. 2:7
[252] Cf. Gen. 2:23.
[253] Gen. 3:6
[254] Gen. 3:8–10
[255] Gen. 3:11–12
[256] Gen. 3:13
[257] Gen. 3:22

65,18   And it was not from envy that God said, "Let us cast him out, lest he put forth his hand to the tree of life, and eat, and live forever," but to make sure that the vessel which had been damaged by its own fault would not always remain damaged. (19) Like a master potter he reduced the vessel with its self-inflicted damage to its raw material, the earth, [to] remold the righteous at the resurrection, completely undamaged, immortal in glory, capable of enjoying the kingdom—and remold the unrighteous at the final resurrection, with the ability to undergo the penalty of damnation. (20) For God planted nothing evil, never think it! He planted just the tree, and by his own decree permitted Adam to take its fruit at the proper time, when he needed it.

65,21   But you will retort, "What becomes of 'In the day in which ye eat thereof ye shall surely die,'[258] if Adam could eat from it? 'Ye shall surely die' would apply to him, surely, no matter when he ate from it!"

65,22   But to one who says this I reply, "God decreed Adam's death for the transgression he would commit, since, even before giving the commandment God, < who > knows the future, knew that Adam would be deceived and eat of the tree." (23) Because they are mistaken in this point the sects blaspheme God and say, "Some God of the Law! He envied Adam, cast him out and said, 'Let us cast him out, lest he put forth his hand and take of the tree of life and live forever!'"[259]

65,24   But their stupid idea stands exposed for the quibble it is. Not only did God not forbid them to eat from the tree of life in the beginning; he even encouraged them by saying, "Of every tree in the garden thou mayest eat for food." But the tree of life too was one of "all the trees in the garden," right before Adam's eyes. (25) Only from the tree of the knowledge of good and evil did God forbid them to eat. But Adam's greed instead disobeyed the commandment, from simplicity and < from listening > to Eve his wife, after the devil had deceived her.

65,26   Since Adam, then, had become defective by his own doing, God did not want him to live forever defective. Like a master potter God chose to change the vessel, which had been spoiled by its own doing, back to its raw material, and again change it from its material, as though on the wheel, at the regeneration, remaking and renewing it with no defects so that it could live forever. (27) Hence the first time, he threatens death. But the second time he

---

[258] Gen. 2:17
[259] Epiphanius means the Manichaeans; he quotes this as a Manichaean argument at Pan. 66,83,2. Cf. also NHL Testim. Truth 45,23–47,30.

no longer says "death," but, "Dust thou art, and unto dust shalt thou return,"[260] without consigning the man to death . . . "[261] (28) And after some other material, "And God made tunics of skin and clothed Adam and Eve, and cast them out of the garden."[262] And you see, Origen, that your silly innovation is worthless. How long Adam and Eve had had bodies!

66,1 But if this shows your guilt, you unbeliever and worse, and if you cannot receive the grace of the Spirit because of your soulish thinking, then tell me how wonderful and astonishing everything is that God has done. (2) How has the heaven been spread out from nothing and hung in mid-air? How was the sun made bright, and how were the moon and the stars created? From which primal matter was the earth taken, when it was made from nothing? From which materials were the mountains hewn?

66,3 What was the origin of the whole world, which God brought forth from nothing? How were the clouds formed, which cover the sky in an instant? (4) Where were the gnats and fleas provided from by God's command, for his servant Moses? How did God change Moses' wooden rod into a living serpent that crawled? How was Moses' hand changed to snow? (5) And in Adam's time too, you unbeliever, God willed, and made actual skin tunics without animals, without human craft and any of the various sorts of human work— < and > made them for Adam and Eve at the moment of his willing them, as he willed at the beginning, and the heaven, and all things, were made at that very moment.

66,6 And for those who care < to choose* > life, salvation can be put in a few words and heresy is an easy matter to refute. But for those who are unwilling to receive the doctrine of salvation, all the time there is would not be time enough for discussion, since, as the sacred oracle says, "Their hearing is ever deaf, like the < deaf > adder that stoppeth her ears, refusing to receive the voice of the charmer and the spell cast by the wise."[263] However, although what I say here is not extensive, I believe that it is of no little value to the sons of the truth.

67,1 But I shall pass on to the discussion of resurrection which you base on the first Psalm. For when you deceive the ignorant, you effort-waster, by palming your ideas off on them, and say that some "simple" people believe that the impious do not attain resurrection—and when you show later how you ask these "simple"

---

[260] Gen. 3:19
[261] A scriptural citation has fallen out before this one.
[262] Gen. 3:21–23
[263] Ps. 57:5–6

people which body will be raised, and < mock them by replying* >
in your own words for the people you call "simple"— < you are
compelled >, for I must say this plainly, to call your so-called "simple" people "good."[264] (2) < For > you are not saying this of yourself, and no grace is being given to your speech; you say it because
of the truth, which compels you to give the indications of the
superiority and goodness of the servants of God!

67,3   Even the heathen proverb says, "Simple is the speech of
the truth." We are accustomed to call the harmless persons, whom
the Savior praises at many points, "simple." < For example >, [he
says], "Be simple as doves,"[265] and, "Suffer the little children"—that
is, the simplest of all—"to come unto me, for of such is the kingdom
of heaven."[266]

67,4   Now the "simple," as you say, gave you the answer that
the resurrection is a resurrection of our current body. And when
you raise a difficulty in reply to this and ask them, "Is it a resurrection of the whole body or of a part of it?" they answer, "of the
whole body." (5) But when, in your very silly way, you say that this
is no good because of the blood that is drained from our bodies,
and the flesh, hair, and other things that are voided through our
spittle, nostrils and excrement, there is a great deal of trickery in
your poor diagnosis. A better man than I, the venerable and most
blessed Methodius, has already countered your fabrication with
many arguments.

67,6   But you will also hear a bit from my modest self. Anything
we want, we want perfectly clean; we do not require the excess
material which is removed from a thing that is clean. (7) Once
a garment has been woven on the web it is complete and that is
what is cut from the warp, with < nothing > added to or removed
from it. If it is given to a fuller it will not be expected back from
the fuller reduced in size; even from the fuller we get it back
perfectly whole. (8) Thus it is plain to everyone that it is entirely
the same garment, and has become a smaller body in no way but
by the removal of the spots and dirt. And surely, since he has
removed the dirt, we will not demand the garment back from the
fuller dirty; we shall want the garment itself, untorn, in good
condition, and perfectly clean.

67,9   But here is another illustration. You have raised the question of the fluid which is drained away by bleedings, illness, excretion,
and the dribbling of our spittle and nostrils; but you will be refuted

---

[264] Cf. 64,10,7; 12,5.
[265] Matt. 10:16
[266] Matt. 19:14

from the very things you have said. (10) For not just this is in the
body; vermin—lice and bugs—grow from us, as it were, and are
not considered either apart from the body or part of the body.
(11) And no one has ever hunted for a bug shed by the body,
or a louse bred from the flesh itself, to keep it, but to destroy it.
Nor would anyone see its destruction as a loss. (12) <Just so > we
shall not make a foolish search for the fluids we excrete—though
it is † often as you say[267]—nor would God return these for our
reconstitution. He would leave them behind the second time, like
dirt which is the garment's dirt but has been removed from the
garment itself for neatness' sake. The creator would plainly return
the whole garment by the goodness of his skill, with nothing missing
or added; for all things are possible to him.

67,13   But if it were not that way—you, with your brains damaged by your long-winded notion! [If it were not that way], our
Savior and Lord, the Son of God, who came to make our salvation
entirely sure, and who illustrated our hope mostly in his own person
to prove his truthfulness to us, could have discarded part of himself
and raised part of himself, you trouble-maker, in keeping with your
destructive fiction and accumulation of a host of worthless arguments.

67,14   For to refute your sort of thing, he himself says at once,
"Except a grain of wheat fall into the ground and die, it abideth
alone; but if it fall and die, it beareth many grains."[268] And whom
was he calling a "grain?" (15) It is plain to everyone, and the whole
world agrees, that he was speaking of himself—that is, of the body
of the holy flesh which he had received from Mary, and of his
whole human nature. (16) But he said "fall" and "die" of the three-
day sleep of his body itself as he says, "Where the fallen carcass
is, there will the eagles be gathered together"[269]—and you yourself
will admit it. For his Godhead can never sleep, fall, be mastered,
or be changed.

67,17   And so the grain of wheat died and rose. Well, did the
grain rise whole, or did a remnant of it rise? Did another grain
rise in place of the original grain, or did He Who Is himself arise
into being? You will surely not deny < that the body* > arose, which
Joseph had wrapped in a shroud and laid in a new tomb. (18)
Then who did the angels tell the women had risen?—as they say,
"Whom seek ye? Jesus of Nazareth? He is risen, he is not here.

---

[267] Holl: πολλαχῶς; MSS: οὕτως
[268] John 12:24
[269] Matt. 24:28

Come, see the place!"[270] This was as much as to say, "Come, see
the place, and let Origen know that there is no question of a
remnant's lying here; the body has risen whole." (19) And to show
you that it has risen whole, < scripture says > in refutation of your
nonsense, "He is risen. He is not here." For no remnant of him
was left behind; the very same body < had risen > which had been
nailed [to the wood], pierced with the lance, seized by the Pharisees, spat upon. (68,1) And why should I give the multitudes of
arguments that demolish this pitiable wretch and the nonsense
that has been generated in him? As Christ has risen and has raised
his own body, so he will raise us.

68,2   For the holy apostle demonstrated our hope on this basis
by saying, "How say some of you that there is no resurrection of
the dead? If there is no resurrection of the dead, neither is Christ
risen. And if Christ be not risen, then is our preaching vain and
your hope is vain. And we are also found false witnesses of God,
for we have said that he raised up Christ, whom he raised not
up,"[271] and so on. (3) And later he adds, "This corruptible must
put on incorruption, and this mortal must put on immortality."[272]
And he didn't just say "mortal," or just say "corruptible," or, "the
immortal soul." He said "*this* corruptible," with the addition of
"this;" and "*this* mortal," with the addition of "this." (4) His grain
has risen itself, whole. A part of him has not risen; he has risen
whole, and not as a grain different than the first. The very grain
that fell in the tomb has risen whole.

68,5   And how can your nonsense have any validity? The sacred
scripture knows of two "grains," one in the Gospel and one in the
Apostle. (6) And the one gives the full explanation because of the
process that has been carried to completion in it, which is the
pattern of < our > resurrection. For by giving this teaching and
putting it into practice, the Savior has surely done everything to
prove it to us. (7) No sooner did he speak of the grain than he
raised the grain, as a true confirmation of the faith of our hope
for our resurrection.

68,8   Here the apostle takes over by the Holy Spirit's inspiration, once more using a grain of wheat to tell us of the saints'
glory after the resurrection, and displays their < hope > for the
enjoyment of good things. (9) He denounces unbelievers with,
"But thou wilt say unto me, How are the dead raised up? With

---

[270] Matt. 28:5–6
[271] 1 Cor. 15:12–15
[272] 1 Cor. 15:53

what body do they come?"[273] And to anyone who says such things he replies, "Fool!" For anyone with any doubt of resurrection is a fool and has no understanding. (10) Then he says, "Thou fool, that which thou sowest is not quickened except it die. And that which thou sowest, thou sowest not the body that shall be, but bare grain, it may chance of wheat or of other seeds, and it is not quickened except it die. But God giveth it a body as he hath willed, and to every seed its own body."[274]

68,11   And you see that the body is not changed. No one sows barley and looks for wheat, and no one has sown cummin and gotten barley; the thing that is sown is the same as the thing that is raised. (12) But if—here, in the case of this perishable wheat which is not under judgment— < some > of it is left below in the ground and its shoot comes up, the part that is left behind is of no use, but the thing that comes up from it is better.

68,13 But because of the unbelief of those who do not look for the hope of God, Paul chose to display its splendor. In fact, the grain of wheat is a very tiny thing. Where are the roots, the bottom parts of it, the stems and the joints, in so tiny a grain? Where is such a number of quills, heads, sheaths, ears, and grains multiplying?

69,1   But to put this more clearly by describing things that are like it—how could Moses, the son of Jochabed and Amram, pierce the rock with his staff, bring water from its impenetrable matter, change something dry to something wet? How could he strike the sea, and part it into twelve highways in the sea, by < God's > command? (2) How could he gather so many frogs in an instant? How could he send the lice upon the Egyptians? How could he mingle the hail with fire? How could he make the blackness of a moonless night even darker for the Egyptians? How could he slay the Egyptians' first-born with pestilence?

69,3   How could he lead the people whose shepherd he was with a pillar of fire? How could he bring the bread of angels by prayer and supplication? How could he provide the flock of quails, and glut so many myriads by God's command?

69,4   How could he hear God's voice? Why was he, among so many myriads, privileged to hear God's voice and talk with God? How could he not need the requirements of human nature for forty days and forty nights? How could his flesh be changed to the brightness and shining ray of the sun, making the people so

---

[273] 1 Cor. 15:35
[274] Cf. 1 Cor. 15:36–38.

giddy that the children of Israel could not look him in the face?
How could his hand, though flesh, be changed to snow? (5) How
could he bid the earth open its mouth and swallow Korah, Dathan,
Abiram and Onan (sic!)? (6) Why was he told at the end of his
life, "Ascend the mount and die there?"[275] Why does no man know
his sepulcher? Holy writ suggests that Moses' body was not buried
by men but, as may reasonably be supposed, by holy angels. (7)
And all this was while Moses was still in this world and still in this
ensouled body—which had, at the same time, become fully spiritual.

69,8   Taking this as the earnest < of our hope, let us use it >
as the model of the perfect sprouting then, when "It is sown in
dishonor, it is raised in glory; it is sown in weakness, it is raised
in power"[276] is fulfilled. (9) For how can something sown without
knowing where be anything but "weak?" How can something dumped
in a grave and heaped with dust, something torn, decomposed,
and without perception, be anything but "dishonored?"

69,10   How can a thing be anything but "honored," when it is
raised, abides forever, and obtains a kingdom in heaven by its hope
in God's lovingkindness—where "The righteous" shall shine "as
the sun;"[277] where they shall be "equal to the angels;"[278] where they
shall dance with the bridegroom; where Peter and the apostles
"shall sit on twelve thrones, judging the twelve tribes of Israel;"[279]
where the righteous shall receive "what eye hath not seen and ear
hath not heard, neither hath entered into the heart of man, the
things which God hath prepared for them that love him?"[280] (11) Our
resurrection, then, rests with God, and so does any man's—righteous and unrighteous, unbeliever and believer, some raised to eternal
life but some to eternal damnation.

70,1   Quiet, Babel, you ancient confusion who have been brought
to life again for us! Quiet, Sodom, and your loud, awful clamor
that ascends to God! (2) "For the redeemer shall come from Zion,
and turn away iniquities from Jacob,"[281] "The trumpet shall sound,
and the dead shall arise,"[282] and "We shall be caught up to meet
him in the air"[283] as < my > better, the < venerable and > blessed

---

[275] Cf. Deut. 32:49–50.
[276] 1 Cor. 15:43
[277] Matt. 13:43
[278] Luke 20:36
[279] Matt. 19:26
[280] 1 Cor. 2:9
[281] Isa. 59:20
[282] 1 Cor. 15:52
[283] 1 Thes. 4:7

Methodius, has said, and I myself have added by building on the same words.

70,3   For from the context of each expression one can see what the wages are. Though the holy apostle distinguished the natures of the two kinds [of saved persons], he united them in one hope with his words, "We shall be caught up in the clouds to meet him"—showing that it is actually this body < that rises > and not something else; for one who is "caught up" has not died. (4) And by indicating that "We shall not precede the resurrection of the dead"[284] as proof that what is impossible for men is easy and possible for God—"For we, the living, shall not precede them that are asleep and their resurrection"[285]—he made it plain that the living are caught up as well. This shows, from the living, that the bodies of the dead will be raised whole; and from the fact that the dead precede those who are alive and remain, it shows what is possible to God. (5) "For the dead shall arise, and they that are in the graves shall be raised up,"[286] says the prophet.

But since I do not want to omit what the prophet Ezekiel says about resurrection in his own apocryphon,[287] I shall give it here. (6) To give a symbolic description of the just judgment in which the soul and the body share, Ezekiel says, *A king had made soldiers of everyone in his kingdom and had no civilians but two, one lame and one blind, and each < of these > lived by himself in his own home. (7) When the king gave a marriage feast for his son he invited everyone in his kingdom, but despised the two civilians, the lame man and the blind man. They were annoyed however, and thought of an injury to do the king.*

70,8   *Now the king had a garden. The blind man addressed the lame man from a distance and said, "How much did we have to eat with the crowds who were invited to the celebration? Come on, let's get back at him for what he did to us!"*

70,9   *"How?" asked the other.*

And the blind man said, "Let's go into the garden and ruin the plants there."

But the lame man said, "And how can I, when I'm lame and can't [even] crawl?"

And the blind man said, "Can I do anything myself, when I can't see where I'm going? But let's figure something out."

---

[284] Cf. 1 Thes. 4:15.
[285] 1 Thes. 4:16
[286] Isa. 26:19
[287] Epiphanius is the sole authority for this fragment of the Apocryphon of Ezekiel, Fragment 1 in the translation of J. R. Mueller and S. E. Robinson, in Charlesworth I pp. 487–495. Jewish versions of the story are found at T. Sanhedrim 91ab; Mekhilta Exod. 15:1.

70,10   *The lame man plucked the grass nearby him, braided a rope, threw it at the blind man, and said, "Grab it, and come here to me by the rope." He did as he was told, and when he got there, the lame man said, "Here, you be my feet and carry me, and I'll be your eyes and guide you from on top, to the right and to the left."*

70,11   *By so doing they got into the garden, and whether they did it any damage or not, their tracks were there to be seen in the garden afterwards.* (12) *And the merry-makers who entered the garden on leaving the wedding were surprised to see the tracks in the garden. They told the king and said, "All are soldiers in your kingdom and no one is a civilian. Then why are there civilians' tracks in the garden?"*

70,13   *The king was surprised*—as the parable in the apocryphon says, obviously speaking to men in a riddle. God is not unaware of anything. But the story says, *The king sent for the lame man and the blind man and asked the blind man, "Didn't you go into the garden?" but the blind man answered, "Oh, Sir! You see my handicap, you know I can< 't > see where I'm going!"* (14) *Then he went to the lame man and asked him, "Did you go into my garden?" But he replied, "Sir, do you want to make me miserable over my handicap?" And then judgment was stymied.*

70,15   *What did the righteous judge do? Seeing how the two had been put together he put the lame man on the blind man and examined them both under the lash, and they couldn't deny the charge.* (16) *They incriminated each other, the lame man by saying to the blind man, "Didn't you pick me up and carry me?" and the blind man by saying to the lame man, "Weren't you my eyes?"* (17) Thus the body is linked with the soul and the soul with the body, for the exposure of their joint work, and there is a full judgment of both, the soul and the body; < they are jointly responsible* > for the things they have done, whether good or evil.

70,18   And see—you who care for your salvation—how all the attackers of the truth have added to their own wickedness, as the prophet David says, "He hath conceived labor and brought forth wrongdoing."[288] (19) For whoever induces labor with heretical notions within him also gives birth to wickedness, his own and his followers': "He hath digged a cistern and shoveled it out, and shall himself fall into the pit."[289]

70,20   But if anyone can reply to all this, let him come on! If anyone < cares > to oppose God, let him make the venture! For God is mighty and "will not tire, or hunger, or thirst, and there

---

[288] Ps. 7:15
[289] Ps. 7:16

is no finding out of his counsel"[290] by which he raises decayed bodies, saves what is lost, quickens what is dead; by which he clothes the corruptible with incorruption, brings the fallen seed to resurrection, by his renewing of it brings what has been sown and has died to a radiance more glorious. So we find in many scriptures where there are hints of our resurrection.

71,1   In David< 's > Psalm on the rededication of the house of David, the prophet aptly said of resurrection—[speaking] as one who awaited what was to come and saw it by the Holy Spirit's inspiration—"I will exalt thee, O Lord, for thou hast lifted me up and renewed mine house"—that is, the fallen body—"and not made my foes to rejoice over me."[291]

71,2   By holding every part of the hope [of resurrection] ready, Solomon too urged us in riddles to prepare for the next life. He says, "Prepare thy works for their end"—by "end" he means departure from this life—"and make ready for the field."[292] [And yet] he directed the admonition to all alike—countrymen and townsmen, the learned and the artisans, from whom no agricultural labor is expected. (3) Why should linen-weavers, silversmiths, poets and chroniclers prepare to farm? But his cry summoned all together without distinction, and said further, "Make ready for the field." < What > can it be suggesting but that the interment of the body, its end by burial, is a "field" for everyone, townsmen and countrymen alike? (4) And then he says next, meaning the same hope of resurrection, "And thou shalt *rebuild* thine house."[293] He didn't say, "Thou shalt *build* thine house;" it was built once by its formation in the womb, when our mothers conceived us all at our formation. The resurrection will come from the earth, or "field," to a house that is no longer being "built" but, because of its cleansing in the entombed corpse, *rebuilt.*

71,5   And as the Savior said, "Destroy this temple, and in three days I will raise," or build, "it."[294] For he is wisdom, and < excels* > by a "counsel which there is no" human "finding out."[295] By it < he gathers* > our < remains* > from inaccessible places, since some of our bodies have been scattered as ashes and some in the sea, while some have been destroyed by birds of prey, wild beasts, or worms—[gathers us] and brings us < whole to regeneration* >. (6)

---

[290] Isa. 40:28
[291] Ps. 29:2
[292] Prov. 24:27
[293] Prov. 24:27
[294] John 2:19
[295] Cf. Isa. 40:28.

For if God brought the < existent > from non-existence to existence, how much more easily can he restore the existent to the
state which is proper to it? In this way he gives a just judgment,
and will not judge one in another's place, depriving me of what
is mine.

71,7   For if the enjoyment and inheritance of the kingdom of
heaven are [only] the soul's, let the body have what it wants! Gideon
and his men may live at ease and not be afflicted "in sheepskins
and goatskins."[296] John, with his garment of camel's hair, need not
labor in vain. Nor need we mortify the flesh in holy retirement,
master our bodies through purity. (8) But if the body is the soul's
partner in its disciplines, purity, fasting and other virtues, "God
is not" [so] "unrighteous"[297] [as] to deprive the laborer of the fruit
of his labor, and award no recompense to the body which has
labored with the soul.

71,9   [If there is no resurrection of the body], judgment will
plainly be suspended. For if the soul appears all by itself it can
reply to its sentence, "The responsibility for the sin is not mine.
Fornication, adultery and wantonness are caused by that corruptible body of earth. For I have done none of these things since it
left me"—and it will have a good case, and undo God's judgment.

71,10   And even if God should bring the body to judgment by
itself—for he can, as I have already shown through Ezekiel.[298] For
even though the action was set in a parable, that kind of thing
was done as an allegory of the truth that was expressed in the
[other] parable, when bone was joined to bone and joint to joint,
and, although the bones were dry and there was no soul or spirit
in them yet to move them, the bodies were put together at once,
and made firm by the prophet's command. (11) And if God so
wills, he has the power to make this body appear and be moved
without a soul, as Abel's blood, which is body, not soul, spoke after
his death. (For the blood is not soul; anything that can be seen
is a body.)

71,12   But the body cannot be judged without a soul. It too
could retort, "I didn't sin, the soul did! Since it was separated from
me have I committed adultery, fornication, idolatry?" And the body
would dispute God's righteous judgment, and with reason. (13)
For this and many other cogent reasons God in his wisdom brings
our dead bodies and our souls to regeneration by his kindly promises,

---

[296] Heb. 11:37
[297] Heb. 6:10
[298] Cf. Pan. 64,70,13 and Ezek. 37:4–6.

so that one who has grown weary in holiness may receive his whole good reward from God; and those whose deeds were worthless may be judged as well, body with soul and soul with body.

71,14   And as a further assurance of our salvation < the Word himself* > came in the flesh, took perfect manhood and < appeared among us* >, to strengthen his faith within us—foreknowing your future unbelief, Origen, and desiring < to confirm* > the doctrine which you doubt more, and which is doubted in many sects, the Manichaeans and Marcionites whose unbelief is similar to yours. And finally, when he had accomplished everything to confirm and establish his faith and truth in his own person, he did [the same things] for all to see. (15) For after rising from the dead [himself] he raised many bodies of the saints with him, and they entered the holy city with him, as I have also described elsewhere.[299] (16) And to leave no opportunity for an unfair stratagem, the scripture did not say, "the saints arose." It hastened < to confirm* > that very thing which is doubted by unbelievers, and to confirm what we know of salvation said, "the *bodies* of the saints." (17) And it wasn't just that he raised them, but that they showed < themselves > to many in the city when the words, "bringing forth prisoners in manhood"[300]—that is, bringing the souls of the risen bodies—had been fulfilled in them by his power. For these were the prisoners of the camp, who had been confined in hades. (18) And it says, "Likewise them that embitter, the dwellers in graves"[301] to mean the bodies of the risen. And he did not say, "them that have been embittered," or "are embittered," but, "them that embitter."

71,19   For when the newly dead, together with the most ancient, appeared to many in the city—(I presume that he began the resurrection with Adam. And the newly dead < had been buried in the same place, Golgotha, and their bodies laid to rest above Adam's, so that Christ, who* > had been crucified < there, raised*> those buried above Adam on Golgotha < together with Adam* [himself] >, fulfilling the scripture, "Awake, thou that sleepest, and arise from the dead, and Christ," who was crucified above thee, "shall give thee light."[302] [When the recently dead appeared] and other members of their families recognized < them >, at first they astonished the beholders. (20) For if a father met a child who had risen, or a brother met a brother, or a < kinsman > met a kinsman who had died ten or twenty years before, and asked in amazement,

---

[299] Anc. 100,2; Pan. 46,5,10
[300] Ps. 67:7
[301] Ps. 67:7
[302] Eph. 5:14

"Aren't you so-and-so, whom we buried here? How have you risen and come back?" (21) the newly risen would ask in reply, "What happened here among you three days ago, when the earth was shaken?"

And when the first said, "We arrested a fraud named Jesus who deceived the people and crucified him, and that put a stop to the deception," (22) the risen would at last confess the Lord's grace and truth and say, "Woe to you! You have denied and crucified the Author of the world's salvation! He has raised us by the mighty power of his Godhead and manhood." This at last would provide the fulfillment of the sacred scripture, "likewise them that embitter, the dwellers in the graves." (23) For when they heard from the risen that they had risen through the Lord Jesus, they would feel bitter as death because they had ventured to deny and crucify the Author of life. (24) And perhaps the kindly Lord did even this for the benefit of those who saw the risen. For I presume that many who were pricked in their consciences by seeing the risen, were benefited by it, and became believers. You be converted and believe too, you Origenists, and stop destroying many with your imposture!

72,1   But this will be enough about the would-be sage, Origen, who named himself Adamantius for no good reason, and his outrage against the truth in many points of the faith, the destructive doctrine of his clumsy invention. (2) I shall pass his sect by too, beloved, and investigate the others next, with my usual plea for God's aid to my lack of education, which will enable me to resist and overcome every voice that is raised in vain against the truth, as the holy prophet Isaiah said, (3) "Every voice that is raised against thee, all of them shalt thou overcome, but they shall be guilty."[303] I shall thus carry out my promise in God to those who are willing to read attentively for exercise in truth, and as a medicine, like an antidote, for each wild beast and poisonous snake—I mean these as symbols of the sects—and for this sect of Origenists, which looks like a toad noisy from too much moisture which keeps croaking louder and louder.

72,4   Taking the Lord's resurrection for a preventive draught, as it were, let us spit out the oil of the toad's poison, and the harm that has been done by the noxious creature. (5) For this is what has happened to Origen with all his followers, and I mourn him on this account. Ah, how badly you have been hurt, and how many others you have hurt—as though you have been bitten by a baneful

---

[303] Isa. 54:17

viper, I mean secular education, and become the cause of others' death.

72,6   Naturalists say that a dormouse hides in its den and bears a number of young at once, as many as five and more, but vipers hunt them. (7) And if a viper finds the den full, since it cannot eat them all it eats its fill of one or two then and there, but punctures the eyes of the rest, and after they are blinded brings them food, and feeds them until it is ready to take each one out and eat it. (8) But if simple people happen upon such creatures and take them for food, they poison themselves with < the > animals that have been fed on the viper's venom. (9) And you too, Origen, with your mind blinded by your Greek education, have spat out venom for your followers, and become poisonous food for them, harming more people with the poison by which you yourself have been harmed.

ANACEPHALAEOSIS V

Here, too, are the contents of the second Section of this same second Volume; in the system of numeration we have indicated, it is the fifth Section. It contains five Sects, as follows:

65   65. < Paulianists, who derive > from Paul the Samosatian, who was made bishop of the metropolis of Antioch. He almost maintained that there is no Christ, for he described him as a spoken word that has existed only since the time of Mary, and said that the statements about him in the sacred scriptures are predictive. But he maintained that Christ was not preexistent, but that he < came into existence > in Mary's time, through the incarnation.

66,1   66. Manichaeans, also called Acvanites, the disciples of Mani the Persian. They pretendedly speak of Christ but worship the sun and the moon, and invoke stars, powers and daemons. They introduce two first principles, a good one and an evil one, [both of them] eternal. (2) They say that Christ has been manifest [only] in appearance, and that he suffered [only] in appearance. They blaspheme the Old Testament and the God who spoke in it, and declare that not the whole world is God's creation, but [only] part of it.

67,1   67. Hieracites, who derive from Hieracas of Leontopolis in Egypt, an expositor of scripture. Although they use the Old and the New Testaments, they deny the resurrection of the flesh. And they entirely forbid marriage, though they accept monks and virgins, and the continent and widows. (2) They say that children who have not reached the age of puberty have no part in the kingdom, since they have not engaged in the struggle.

68   68. Melitians, who live in Egypt and are a schism—though not a sect—because they would not pray with persons who had fallen away during the persecution. Now, however, they have become associated with the Arians.

69,1   69. Arians, also called the Arian Nuts, who say that the Son of God is a creature and that the Holy Spirit is the creature of a creature, and maintain that the Savior took only flesh from Mary and not a soul. (2) Arius was a presbyter of Alexander, the bishop of Alexandria.

This is the summary of the five Sects of the second Section of Volume Two—though counting from the beginning of the series, it is the fifth Section.

Against Paul the Samosatian.[1] *45, but 65 of the series*

1,1   Their successor[2] is Paul, called the Samosatian, who was born after Navatus and Origen. (Origen is at last counted as a heretic because of the deliberate arrogance with which he exalted himself against the truth, through his boastful nonsense and diabolically inspired notion. (2) He must be mourned as one who has indeed come to grief "through envy of the devil"[3] and fallen from a height; for the saying, "The fascination of evil obscures what is good, and the roving of desire perverteth the innocent mind,"[4] fits him exactly.)

1,3   Now this Paul the Samosatian whom it is in my mind to discuss, whose name I mentioned at the start and whose sect I am < now > describing, was from Samosata, which is off towards Mesopotamia and the Euphrates. (4) He was made bishop of the holy catholic church at Antioch at this time, during the reigns of the emperors Aurelian and Probus.[5] But he grew proud and was deprived of the truth, and revived the sect of Artemon,[6] who had lived many years before, at the beginning of it, and had been snuffed out.

1,5   Paul says that God is Father, Son and Holy Spirit,[7] one God. But God's Word and Spirit are always in him, just as a man's own word is in his heart. (6) The Son of God is not an entity but is within God himself—just what Sabellius, Navatus, Noetus and others have said. Still, Paul does not say the same as they, but something

---

[1] The most significant ancient accounts are collected at Loofs, *Paulus von Samosata.* Most derive ultimately from the Epistle of the Council of Antioch, which deposed Paul in 268, and the Hypomnemata, or minutes of the debate between Paul and the presbyter Malchio which was held at that council. Notable are Eus. H. E. 5.18.1–2; the fifth century monk Leontius' Contra Nestorianos et Eutychianos, Appendix to Book III; and the Scholia of Leontius preserved in Theodore, De Sectis, MSG 1213D–1216B.

Though Epiphanius has read Eusebius, his information appears to be independent of the Council of Antioch. It may be oral, and represent the sort of thing the Paulianists of his own day were saying.

[2] I.e., the successor of Navatus and Origen

[3] Wisd. Sol. 2:24

[4] Wisd. Sol. 4:12

[5] Eusebius mentions Probus' having been made emperor *after* Aurelian, H. E. 7.30.22.

[6] Cf. Eus. H. E. 5.28.1. As other authorities say "Artemas," and Eusebius himself says Artemon only here, it is probable that Epiphanius is using Eusebius at this point.

[7] Contrast Loofs p. 85 (Leontius, Scholia), "Paul did not say that the Father, the Son and the Holy Spirit are the same. He said that the Father is God the creator of all, the Son is the mere man, and the Holy Spirit is the grace which was present in the apostles."

different. (7) The Word came, dwelt in Jesus who was a man, < and ascended again to the Father after doing his work* >. (8) And therefore, Paul says, God is one. The Father is not a father, the Son is not a son, and the Holy Spirit is not a holy spirit; the Father, and his Son in him like a word in a man, are one God. (9) Paul bases his heresy on the following texts, if you please: the words of Moses, "The Lord is thy God, the Lord is one."[8] (10) But he does not claim, as Noetus did, that the Father suffered. He says, "The Word came, acted alone,[9] and returned to the Father." And he teaches a great deal of absurdity.

2,1   But let's see whether the deluded man's own words can be proved. For he reminds us that Christ said, "I am in the Father and the Father in me."[10] (2) Now we ourselves say that the divine Word is of the Father, and is with him eternally and begotten of him; but we deny that the Father is without a subsistent Word. (3) On the contrary, the Father's Word is the only-begotten Son, the divine Word, as he says, "Whosoever shall confess me, him will I confess before my Father."[11] And by saying, "me before my Father," he showed that the Father is a true entity < and that the Son is an entity also* >.

2,4   These people, with their covert introduction of Judaism, have nothing more to say than the Jews do. They must be termed neo-Jews, and Samosatians, for they profess [Christianity] simply in name < and > theory. (5) By denying the God of God, the only-begotten Son and the Word, they have become like those who denied him when he was here—God's murderers, the murderers of the Lord, and the deniers of God. Actually, however, < they are neither Christians nor Jews* >, since they do not have circumcision or keep the Sabbath, but < hold* > Jewish < views* > on everything else.

3,1   Now we too, in fact, maintain that there are not two Gods or Godheads, but one Godhead. For since we say that there are not two Fathers, two Sons or two Holy Spirits, but a Father, a Son and a Holy Spirit, < we say* > that there is one Godhead < and* > one glory. (2) Paul, however, does not call the Father the only God because he is the source [of the Trinity]. When he < says that he > is the only God, he is doing his best to deny the divinity and reality of the Son and the Holy Spirit. He holds[12] instead that the

---

[8] Deut. 6:4
[9] Bardy, Diekamp, MSS: μόνος; Loofs, Holl: μόνον
[10] John 14:10
[11] Matt. 10:32
[12] Hübner and MSS: ἕνα θεὸν ἄγονον υἱοῦ; Holl: insert < ποιεῖ αὐτόν >

Father is one God who has begotten no Son, (3) so that there are the two Imperfects, a Father and a Son—the Father who has not begotten a Son, and the Word of the living God and true Wisdom who is not the fruit[13] [of the Father].

3,4   For they believe that the Word is like the word in a human heart, and the sort of wisdom everyone has in his human soul if God has given him understanding.[14] They therefore say that God, together with his Word, is one Person, just as a man and his word are one. As I said, they believe no more than the Jews do; they are blind to the truth, and deaf to the divine word and the message of eternal life.

(5) For they do not respect the true word of the Gospel, "In the beginning was the Word, and the Word was with God, and the Word was God. All things were made through him, and without him was not anything made that was made."[15] (6) For if the Word was in the beginning and the Word was with God, his existence is not just as an utterance but as an entity. And if the Word was *with God*, the One he was with is not the Word—for the One he was with is not a word. For if God [merely] has a word in his heart, and not a Word he has begotten, how can "was," and "The Word was God," mean anything? (7) A man's word is not a man with a man, for it is neither alive nor subsistent. It is only a movement of a living, subsistent heart,[16] and not an entity. It is spoken, and is at once no longer existent, although it stays said.[17] (8) But < this is not the case with* > God's Word, as the Holy Spirit says by the mouth of the prophet, "Thy word endureth *forever.*"[18] And in agreement with this the evangelist says—confessing that God has been made manifest and come, but not including the Father in the incarnation of the Word—(9) "*The Word* was made flesh and dwelt among us."[19] And he didn't say, "The Word-and-Father was made flesh." And he also says, "In the beginning was the Word, and the Word was with God, and the Word *was* God"[20]—not, "The Word was *in* God."

4,1   And lest people ill-advisedly alter the words of life and light

---

[13] Conjectural rendering of ἄκαρπον
[14] Cf. Loofs pp. 77–78 (Leontius Contra Nestorios), "For wisdom was in the prophets, and more so in Moses, and more so in Christ, as in a temple of God."
[15] John 1:1; 3
[16] Hübner and MSS: ἔχει, καὶ οὐ γεγεννημένον; Holl: < προφερόμενον μονόν > καὶ οὐ . . .
[17] Hübner and MSS: λαλούμενος διαμένει; Holl: < ἀφανίζεται καί οὐ > διαμένει
[18] Cf. Ps. 118:89.
[19] John 1:14
[20] John 1:1

to their own disadvantage and harm, and suppose—"From his youth the heart of man is bent on the pursuit of" one sort of "evil"[21] or another. (2) Suppose they begin to argue, "As you say yourself, John didn't say, 'The Word was *in* God,' but 'The Word was *with* God.'[22] Therefore the Word is not of the Father's essence but outside of God." [If they say this] the truth turns around to set her sons straight and confound the ideas that are unfaithful to her, (3) and the Only-begotten himself says, "I came forth from the Father and am come"[23]—and again, "I am in the Father and the Father in me."[24]

4,4   But for our understanding of the proof, the One < who speaks > of the Son in the prophets stoops to human weakness— not < by > bearing physical burdens but < by > providing understandable words—and < proves > in terms familiar to us that the Son is truly begotten of him, God of God, very God of very God, not outside of him but of his essence. (5) And so he says in David, "Before the morning star have I begotten thee from the womb,"[25] as the Seventy rendered it. And in the words of the other versions—Aquila: "The dew of thy youth is of the womb of the morning;" Symmachus: "As in the dewy dawn is thy youth;" Theodotion: "From the womb, from the dawn of thy youth;" the fifth version: "From the womb, from the dawn is thy dew in thy youth;" the sixth: "From the womb they seek thee, dew of thy vigor."[26] (6) But in the Hebrew it is *merem messaar laktal ieldecheth,*[27] which plainly and unambiguously means, "From the womb before the morning star have I begotten thee." For *merem* is "< from > the womb," and *messaar* means, "before the earliest dawn," or in other words, "before the morning star." *Laktal* is "and before the dew;" *ieldecheth* is "child," or in other words, "I have begotten thee." (7) And so the verse will show that the subsistent divine Word was actually begotten of the Father, without beginning and not in time, before anything existed.

4,8   For by the star he did not mean just the morning star— though indeed there are many stars and the sun and moon, and they were made on the fourth day of creation. (And the sea, the trees and their fruit had been created earlier—and the firmament

---

[21] Gen. 8:21
[22] John 1:1
[23] John 16:28
[24] John 14:10
[25] Ps. 109:3
[26] This is almost exactly as at Origen, *Hexapla*, ed. Field, Vol. II, p. 266.
[27] מֵרֶחֶם מִשְׁחָר לְךָ טַל יַלְדֻתֶךָ Epiphanius' version ignores personal pronouns and confuses ילד with ילדות, suggesting that Epiphanius knew the verse only in Origen's Greek transliteration.

and earth and heaven, and the angels, who were created together
with these. (9) For if angels had not been created together with
heaven and earth, God would not have told Job, "When the stars
were brought forth, all the angels praised me aloud.")[28] (10) And
so < he wrote* >, "before the morning star," meaning, "before
anything was in existence and had been created." For the Word
was always with the Father: "Through him all things were made,
and without him was not anything made."[29]

5,1   But someone might say, "You've shown that the angels were
before the stars, but you've said they were created together with
heaven and earth. Tell me, how have you proved this? Weren't
they, surely, created *before* heaven and earth? For scripture nowhere
plainly indicates the time of the angels' creation. (2) And you've
< clearly > given a good proof that they were before the stars; for
if they hadn't been, how could they sing God's praises at the stars'
creation?"

5,3   I cannot give the answer to any question with my own reason,
but I can with a conclusion from scripture. (4) The word of God
makes it perfectly clear that the angels were not created after the
stars, and that they were not created before heaven and earth; for
the statement that there were no creatures before heaven and
earth is plainly a firm one. For "God made the heaven and the
earth *in the beginning*,"[30] because it is the beginning of < the > creation and < there are > no created things before it.

5,5   And so, as I have indicated, the word in a man cannot be
called a man, but must be called a man's word. But if the Word
of God is God, it is not a word with no subsistence but a subsistent
divine Word, begotten of God without beginning and not in time:
(6) for "The Word was made flesh and dwelt among us, and we
beheld his glory, the glory as of an only-begotten of a Father, full
of grace and truth."[31] John testified to him and cried out, "This
is he of whom I said unto you, He that cometh after me is preferred before me, for he was before me."[32] "He came into the
world, that through him the world might be saved."[33] "He was in
the world, and the world was made by him, and the world knew
him not."[34]

---

[28] Job 38:7
[29] John 1:3
[30] Gen. 1:1
[31] John 1:14
[32] John 1:15
[33] Cf. John 3:17.
[34] John 1:10

5,7   Do you see that the Word is only-begotten? Do you see that he came into the world among men, and yet with the full "glory of the only-begotten of a Father?"[35] It is not as though the Father is a Word, or that he appears as a Father [only] in combination with a Word, like a man appearing with his word, < where > his word cannot even appear in the absence of the word's speaker.

5,8   Now then, whom should I believe? With whom should I agree? From whose teachings am I to receive life? From the holy, inspired evangelists, who have said that the Word was sent from the Father? Or from these disciples of Paul the Samosatian, who claim that God is combined with the Word and the Word with God, and declare that there is one Person—[the person] of the Father including the Word and the person of the Word including the Father? (9) If there is [only] one Person, how can the one send and the other be sent? For the prophet says, "He shall send forth his Word and melt them; he shall breathe forth his Spirit, and the waters shall flow"[36]—and again, "I came forth from the Father and am come,"[37] and, "I live, and the Father that sent me liveth in me."[38]

5,10   Now how can the One who has been sent be sent, and appear in flesh? "No man hath seen God at any time; the only-begotten God, which is in the bosom of the Father, he hath declared him."[39] And he says, "the only-begotten God." The Word is begotten of the Father but the Father was not begotten—hence, "only-begotten God."

6,1   For the safety of our souls the divine knowledge proclaimed its own truth beforehand, because of its precognition. It knew the Samosatian's nonsense, the Arians' heresy, the villainy of the Anomoeans, the downfall of the Manichaeans, and the mischief of the rest of the sects. (2) And therefore the word of God makes us certain of every expression. It does not call the Father "only-begotten;" how can One who has never been begotten be "only-begotten?" But it calls the Son "only-begotten," to avoid the supposition that the Son is a Father, and the comparison of the divine Word with a word in a human heart.

6,3   For if he is called a "Word," he is so called for this purpose: to keep it from being supposed that he is different from the essence of God the Father. And because of the words, "only-begotten, full

---

[35] John 1:14
[36] Ps. 147:7
[37] John 16:28
[38] Cf. John 6:57.
[39] John 1:18

of grace and truth,"⁴⁰ he cannot be a word without subsistence, but must be an entity. (4) And you see how much there is to make our salvation sure. "No man hath seen God at any time" is a statement of the Father's invisibility and Godhead; but < "only-begotten God" >⁴¹ affirms the manifestation of his Godhead through the flesh.

6,5   But how many other texts, and more, might one select in our support and to counter the Samosatian's stupidity? If the Word was in the Father like the word in a human heart, why did he come here and appear in his own person? (6) To describe himself to his disciples he says, "He that seen me hath seen the Father."⁴² And he didn't say, "I am the Father;" "me" means that < he himself is an entity in the Father* >. (7) And he didn't say, "I am he," but, "I am come in my Father's name, and it is he that beareth witness of me."⁴³

6,8   And again, he says of the Holy Spirit, "< I will pray the Father > and he shall send you another Advocate."⁴⁴ See how < he says >, "he shall send," "another," < and > "I," to show that the Father is an entity, < the Son is an entity >, and the Holy Spirit is an entity. (9) For besides saying, "He shall glorify me," of the Holy Spirit, he [also] < says >, "He shall receive of mine."⁴⁵ And what is he talking about? The Spirit who proceeds from the Father and receives of "me."

6,10   Moreover, he says, "Two testimonies of men will be established, and I bear witness of myself, and the Father that sent me beareth witness of me."⁴⁶ (11) But how many other texts are there to be found* >, as many as these and more? Look here! He says, "I thank thee, O Father, Lord of heaven and earth, because thou hast hid these things from the wise and prudent, and hast revealed them unto babes. (12) Even so, Father: for so it seemed good in thy sight. All things are delivered unto me of my Father: and no man knoweth the Son save the Father: neither knoweth any man the Father save the Son, and he to whomsoever the Son will reveal him."⁴⁷ "Thou hast revealed them unto babes" and, "All things are delivered unto me of my Father" are said to uproot the heresy which these people have invented.

7,1   But see what men's perennial opponent, the devil, has

---

⁴⁰ John 1:14
⁴¹ John 1:18
⁴² John 14:9
⁴³ John 5:43; 37
⁴⁴ John 14:16
⁴⁵ John 16:14
⁴⁶ John 8:17–18
⁴⁷ Matt. 11:25–27

spawned in them, as though by the diabolic inspiration of their speech. (2) For because of the holy Gospels' plain statement of the their teaching, the flunkies of the sect of Jews are ashamed of this, and not to seem entirely at odds with the true knowledge of the Gospel, defend themselves, if you please, against these charges. (3) They say, "Jesus was a man, and yet God's Word from on high was alive in him,[48] and the man says these things about himself. The Father together with the Son is one God, but the man makes his own person known below, and in this sense there are two persons."[49]

7,4   Now how can a man be God, you stupidest man in the world, with your mind turned away from the heavenly doctrine? How can someone who says, "He that hath seen me hath seen the Father,"[50] be a mere man,[51] as you claim? (5) If the man is like the Father, the Father is not different from the man. If, however, the divine Word, who is perfect and has become perfect man, is God begotten of the Father on high, then he is speaking clearly and correctly of himself when he says, "He that hath seen me hath seen the Father." (6) And the Jews say the same of him. "Not only did they seek to kill him," says the scripture, "because he did these things, but because he said he was the Son of God, claiming equality with God."[52] (7) For once more, in saying, "He that hath seen me hath seen the Father,"[53] he is claiming that God the Father is his equal. Now a man is not equal to God or like God; but < the One who > is truly begotten of God the Father is God the only-begotten Son.

7,8   For Paul says of him, "who being in the form of God thought it not robbery to be equal with God: but made himself of no reputation, and took upon him the form of a servant."[54] (9) < By* > "He was in the form < of God* >," < Paul indicated > his Godhead; but as to the form of the servant, he made it clear that this was

---

[48] Cf. Loofs p. 79 (Leontius, Contra Nestorianos), "What does he mean by saying that the constitution of Jesus Christ is different from ours? As we maintain, he differs from us in one way—although it is of the utmost importance—that the divine Word is in him what the inner man is in ourselves ..."

[49] This is somewhat comparable to Loofs pp. 84–85 (Theodore's Scholia from Leontius), "Paul the Samosatian did not say that the self-subsistent Word had entered into Christ. He said that the word was the bidding and commandment, that is, the Father commanded what he would through that man, and performed it."

[50] John 14:9

[51] Cf. Loofs p. 64 (Formula Macrostichus of Sardica), "The followers of Paul the Samosatian deny that Christ was God before the ages, and say that later, after the incarnation, deification by promotion came to him who had been a mere man."

[52] Cf. John 5:18.

[53] John 14:9

[54] Phil. 2:6–7

something added to him, and did not say that this had ever been < native > to him.

7,10 Our Savior and Lord Jesus Christ, the divine Word, often communicates with us in even human terms, and frequently speaks like a human sufferer. (11)[55] But not when he says, "I came forth from my Father and am come;"[56] this cannot be the utterance of human nature. (12) When, however, he rightly testifies, "If I bear record of myself my record is not true,"[57] this is meant to show his humanity. When, on the contrary, he testifies of his Godhead, "Though I bear record of myself, yet my record is true,"[58] this is to show that his divine nature is true divine nature, and his human nature true human nature.

8,1 And so there are not two Gods, because there are not two Fathers. And the subsistence of the Word is not eliminated, since there is not one [mere] combination of the Son's Godhead with the Father. For the Son is not of an essence different from the Father, but of the same essence as the Father. He cannot be of an essence different from his Begetter's or of an identical essence; he is *of the same essence* as the Father.[59]

8,2 Nor, again, do we say that he is not the same in essence as the Father; the Son is the same as the Father in Godhead and essence. And he is not of another sort than the Father, or of a different subsistence; he is truly the Father's Son in essence, subsistence and truth. (3) But the Father is not the Son; and the Son is not the Father, but truly a Son begotten of the Father. Thus there are not two Gods, two Sons, or two Holy Spirits; the Trinity is one Godhead, Father, Son and Holy Spirit, and co-essential. (4) For when you say, "of the same essence," < you > do not mean an identification. "Co-essential" does not indicate one [single] thing; neither does it differentiate the true Son's essence from his lawful Father's, and distinguish his nature [from the Father's] because of the co-essentiality.

8,5 For sacred scripture does not proclaim two first principles, but one; it says, "The house of Judah shall join with the house of Israel, and they shall agree upon one first principle" (ἀρχή).[60] Therefore whoever preaches two first principles, preaches two Gods; and whoever denies the Word and his subsistence betrays his Judaism.

---

[55] This is paragraph 12 in Holl's numbering, which omits paragraph 11.
[56] John 16:28
[57] Cf. John 8:13.
[58] John 8:14
[59] ἑτεροούσιος, ταυτοούσιος, ὁμοούσιος
[60] Hos. 2:2

(6) Marcion intimates that there are two first principles—or rather, three—in opposition to each other. But these neo-Jews, these Samosatians, do away with the subsistence of the Word, showing that they too are murderers of the Lord and deniers of our Lord's salvation.

8,7 Thus there is one first principle and the Son [begotten] of it—its exact image, the natural replica of his Father, and like him in every way. For he is God of God and the Son of the Father, very God of very God and light of light, one Godhead and one rank. (8) Thus scripture says, "Let us make man in *our* image and after *our* likeness."[61] It says neither, "in thine image," creating a division, nor, "in my image," implying unlikeness and inequality, but, "in *our* image." And "let us make" is said to show that the Father is not strange to his creatures, nor the Only-begotten strange to creation. (9) The Father creates with the Son, and the Son, by whom all things were made, is co-creator with the Father. And since the Son is begotten of the Father there is one Son, the perfect Son of a perfect Father; and there is a perfect Father of a perfect Son, who is in the image of his Father's perfection. [He is] "the image of the invisible God"[62]—not the model of an image, not the image of an image, not unlike the Father, but the Father's image, showing the exact likeness [to the Father] of his true generation from him who has no beginning and is not in time.

8,10 Thus the Son is the image of the Father. It is the same with emperors. Because the emperor has an image there are not two emperors; there is one emperor, with his image. [And] there is one God. He is not one imperfect thing, made of two parts; the Father is perfect, the Son is perfect, the Holy Spirit is perfect. (11) For < the Son does > not < say >, "I am in the Father,"[63] as a word is in a man's heart; we know a supernal Father with a Son, and a Son begotten of a Father. (12) The word of God < does > not < declare > that a Word entered a man for a dwelling, appeared in him after his birth, and is on high in God once more, like a word in a human heart. This is the demon's madness and bears the marks of the entire denial of God.

9,1 < I come to a close* > because I believe that these few remarks which I have made about this sect will do. Their power is not formidable, or such that it cannot be overcome by all wise persons. (2) And we have now uprooted Paul's thorns by preach-

---

[61] Gen. 1:26
[62] Col. 1:15
[63] Cf. John 10:38.

ing the doctrine of the truth, have, as it were, quenched his poison, and pointed its deadliness out. Calling for aid on the Father with the Son—on the truly existent God and the truly subsistent Son he has begotten, and on his Holy Spirit, who subsists as a Spirit— (3) and < arming ourselves* > with the salvation of the work of the incarnate Christ, we have broken the van of this assault of the neo-Jews with the sign of our victory over death, I mean the cross. Let us go on to the rest, beloved.

9,4   For there is a viper called the dryinas which is like this heresiarch. It is said that a dryinas is a viper, and that its den is very often near grass or, also, oaks. This is why it is called a dryinas— from its preference for trees, and its camouflaging of itself among the fallen leaves with the color of each leaf. (5) The beast does not have a particularly painful bite, but if it remains [undetected] it causes death. (6) In the same way this man, with his sect, pretends to belong to the faithful by bearing Christ's name while adopting Jewish doctrine. He confesses that Christ is the Word but does not believe that he is; and he is not ashamed to make a parade of himself in many ways.[64] (7) But now that we have trampled his seeming doctrine, which is actually imposture, with the sandal of Christ, and have scratched the victims of his bites with the healing scalpel of the Gospel and drawn the poison out of them, we shall go on to describe the rest, beloved, as I said.

Against Manichaeans.[1] 46, but 66 of the series

1,1   The Manichaeans < are > also called Acvanites after a veteran from Mesopotamia named Acvas[2] who practiced the profession of the pernicious Mani at Eleutheropolis. (2) They began to preach to the world at that time, and brought a great evil on the world

---

[64] Paul's ostentatious behavior is described at Eus. H. E. 7.30.8–11; Epiphanius may be alluding to this passage. See also the Epistle of the Council of Antioch, 268 A.D., translated at Loofs pp. 4–9.

[1] Epiphanius' main literary source for this sect is the Acta Archelai cum Manete Disputantis. At 23,3 he mentions eight other anti-Manichaean works, of which he has very likely used Titus of Bostra's Adversus Manichaeum and possibly some others. 12,4, 21,4 and especially 36,4 show that he and his acquaintances had personal contact with Manichaeans.

[2] For Zacō, one of Mani's early disciples who died about 301 A. D., see Asmussen p. 106 (M 6, Parthian: MM III pp. 865–867) and pp. 31–32 (M 6, Parthian, MM III pp. 865–867, Cat. p. 2); Fihrist al-ʻUlūm at Flügel, Mani p. 104. Acvas might, however, have been some local Manichaean missionary at Eleutheropolis.

after the < sect > of Sabellius. For they arose in the time of the
emperor Aurelian, about the fourth year of his reign.[3] (3) This
sect is widely reported and is talked of in many parts of the world,
and as I said, owes its worldwide spread to a man named Mani.

1,4   Mani was from Persia, and was originally named Cubricus.
But he changed his name to Mani (Μάνης)[4] to call himself mad,
I suspect by God's providence. (5) And as he thought, he was
calling himself "vessel," in Babylonian[5] if you please; "vessel" (μάνη)
translated from Babylonian to Greek, suggests the name. But as
the truth shows, he was named for the madness which caused the
wretch to propagate his heresy in the world.

1,6   Cubricus was the slave of a widow who had died childless
and left him an incalculable wealth of gold, silver, spices and other
goods. (7) She herself had inherited the property from a Terbinthus
who had also been a slave, whose name had been changed to
"Buddha,"[6] in Assyrian. And Terbinthus himself had been the slave
of a Scythianus,[7] who was a Saracen but had been brought up on
the borders of Palestine, that is, in Arabia.

1,8   Scythianus had been taught the language and literature of
the Greeks there, and had become proficient in their futile worldly
doctrines. (9) But he made continual business trips to India, and
did a great deal of trading. And so he acquired worldly goods[8]
and as he traveled through the Thebaid[9]—there are various harbors
on the Red Sea, (10) at the different gateways to the Roman realm.
One of these is at Aelan—Aelon in sacred scripture. It was perhaps
there that Solomon's ship arrived every three years, bringing gold,
elephant's tusks, spices, peacocks and the rest. (11) Another harbor

---

[3] Epiphanius' information comes from Eusebius by way of Jerome's Chronicle, 223,25. Jerome dates Mani from the time of "Aurelian and Probus," as do
Act. Arch. 31,8; Cyr. Cat. 6.20, and Epiphanius himself at 19,9; 20,3, 78,1.

[4] Cf. Act. Arch. 62–64; Cyr. Cat. 6.20–24. The scurrilous biography of Mani
which follows would have been an attempt to combat the Manichaean deification of him. Contrast Klimkeit p. 163 (*A Bema Liturgy*, Persian and Parthian)
"We would praise the God, Mani, the Lord! We honor thy great, bright glory,
we bow down before thy Holy Spirit," with Cyr. Cat. 6.6, which asks if anyone
would wish to worship such a disreputable person.

[5] Mani describes himself as "a man of Babylon" at Asmussen pp. 8–9 (M 4,
2 V, Parthian: *HR* II, pp. 51–52); M 566 I, Parthian: *HR* II, p. 87.

[6] Cf. Act. Arch. 63.2; Cyr. Cat. 6.23. "Buddha" is named with Zoroaster and
Jesus as one of the three apostles who preceded Mani, Keph. 7,34; 12,15 et al.

[7] Cf. Act. Arch. 62.2–7; Cyr. Cat. 6.22.

[8] Manichaean writings often use the metaphor of a merchant with a wealth
of goods. E.g., Keph. 11,18–20, "like a merchant who comes from [a country]
with the doubling of his large cargo and the wealth of his goods."

[9] With Holl, Drexl we leave the clause before the parenthesis incomplete.
Oehler, Dummer punctuate after διών, giving better grammar but a rather un-
Epiphanian sentence.

is at Castrum in Clysma, and another is the northernmost, at a place called Bernice. Goods are brought to the Thebaid by way of this port called Bernice, and the various kinds of merchandise from India are either distributed there in the Thebaid or to Alexandria by way of the river Chrysorroes—I mean the Nile, which is called Gihon in the scriptures—and to all of Egypt as far as Pelusium. (12) And this is how merchants from India who reach the other lands by sea make trading voyages to the Roman Empire.

2,1   I have been at pains to convey this in full detail for your information, so that those who care to read this will not go uninformed even of the remote causes of every affair. For whoever embarks on a narrative must start it the best way he can, and introduce it from the very beginning. This is how the truth comes to light too, (2) and even though the speaker has no command of polished speech and elegant language the wise will still be told what they should be by the truthful account.

2,3   To begin with, then, Scythianus was puffed up by his great wealth, and his possessions of spices and other goods from India. (4) And in traveling over the Thebaid to a town called Hypsele, he found a woman there who was extremely depraved though of evident beauty, and made a deep impression on his stupidity. Taking her from the brothel—she was a prostitute—he grew fond of the woman and set her free, and she became his wife.[10] (5) After a long while, because of the extreme luxury in his possession, nothing would do the sinner but that, like an idle person accustomed to evil by the extreme wantonness of his luxury, he must finally think of something new, in keeping with his taste, to offer the world. (6) And out of his own head he made up some such words as these—for he did not take them from the sacred scripture and the utterance of the Holy Spirit, but said, on the basis of wretched human reasoning, (7) "What is the reason for the inequalities[11] throughout the visible vault of creation—black and white, flushed and pale, wet and dry, heaven and earth, night and day, soul and body, good and evil, righteous and unrighteous—unless, surely, these things originate from two roots, or two principles?"[12] (8) But

---

[10] Cf. Act. Arch. 62.4. The story comes from the heresiologists' account of Simon Magus, cf. Iren. 1.23.2; Epiph. Pan 21,22 et al.

[11] Klimkeit pp. 273–274 (Uighur Chuashtuanift): "If we ... should have called him the origin and root of Light as well as Darkness, and of God as well as the Devil; If we should have said, 'If anybody quickens, it is God that quickens; if anybody slays, it is God that slays...'"

[12] Cf. CM 132,11–13, "I showed them the distinction between the two natures."

to employ him for further warfare against the human race, the devil spawned the horrid supposition in his mind that non-being does not know being.[13] This was meant to start a war in the minds of the dupes who believe that there is something more than Him Who Is, and that all things are products of two roots,[14] as it were, or two principles. This [last] is the most impious and unsound idea of all.

2,9   But I shall speak of this another time. Scythianus, whose mind was blind about these things, took his cue from Pythagoras[15] and held such beliefs, and composed four books of his own.[16] He called one the Book of the Mysteries,[17] the second the Book of the Summaries,[18] the third the Gospel,[19] and the fourth the Treasury.[20] (10) In them he contrasted and < exhibited* > the personae, in every respect perfectly balanced and evenly matched, < of the > two principles. Pathetically he supposed and imagined that he had made a great discovery about this. And he had indeed discovered a great evil, for himself and the people he misleads.

3,1   Scythianus was busy with this, but had heard how the prophets and the Law spoke prophetically of the creation of the world, of the one, sovereign, everlasting Father who will have no end, and of his Son and the Holy Spirit. (2) Since he lived in greater luxury [than they], made fun of them in his boorish mind, and was egged on by the haughty arrogance within him he chose to travel to Jerusalem,[21] about the apostles' time, (3) and dispute there, if you please, with the preachers of < God's > sovereignty and the [creation of] God's creatures.

3,4   On his arrival the unfortunate man began to challenge the elders there—who were living by the legislation which God had given to Moses and < confirmed* > by the inspired teaching of every prophet—(5) with, "How can you say that God is one, if he made night and day, flesh and soul, dry and wet, heaven and earth,

---

[13] Cf. Tit. Bost. Man. 1.17, "That very writing from which we have produced the doctrines of Manes says that (the powers of darkness) neither knew that God was living in the light . . ."

[14] Cf. Keph. 35,34, "(The first Father is) the root of all the lights."

[15] Scythianus' teachings are identified as Pythagorean at Act. Arch. 62.3.

[16] Keph. 5,22–25, "I have written them in my books of light, in the Great Gospel and the Treasury of Life, and the Pragmateia and the Book of the Mysteries, the scripture I have written for the Parthians, as well as all the Epistles, and the 'Psalms and Praises.'" Cf. Act. Arch. 62.3; Cyr. Cat 6.22.

[17] This is called "Mysteries of Wisdom" at Man. Hom. 43,17.

[18] The Kephalaia, rediscovered by Carl Schmidt in 1929

[19] CM 66,4–70,9 are a long excerpt from the Gospel.

[20] This is called the Treasury of Life at Keph. 230,20–22.

[21] Act. Arch. 62.7; Cyr. Cat 6.22

darkness and light?"[22] (6) They gave him a plain explanation—the truth is no secret—but he was not ashamed to contradict them. And though he could not achieve his aim, he still behaved with stubborn shamelessness.

3,7   But since he met with no success but was worsted instead, he produced an illusion with the magic books he owned. (He was a sorcerer too, and had obtained the horrid, pernicious arts of magic from the heathen wisdom of the Indians and Egyptians.) (8) < For > he went up on a housetop and conjured,[23] but still achieved nothing—instead he fell off the roof and ended his life.[24] He had lived in Jerusalem for some years.

3,9   He had had just one disciple with him,[25] the Terbinthus we mentioned earlier. He had entrusted his possessions to this disciple, as to a very faithful servant who obeyed him with a good will. (10) When Scythianus died Terbinthus buried him with all kindness but once he had buried him planned not to return to the woman, the former harlot or captive who had been married to Scythianus. Instead he took all the property, the gold, the silver and the rest, (11) and fled to Persia. And to escape detection he changed his name as I have said, and called himself Buddha[26] instead of Terbinthus.

3,12   For his evil inheritance he in his turn obtained Scythianus' four books and his implements of magic and conjuring—for he too was very well educated. (13) In Persia he lodged with an elderly widow and in his turn debated about the two principles with the attendants and priests of the idol of Mithra, with a prophet named Parcus, and with Labdacus, but < accomplished nothing* >. Since he could not even dispute with the promoters of idolatry but was refuted by them and disgraced, (14) he went up on the housetop with the same intention as Scythianus—to work magic, if you please, so that no one could answer his arguments. But he was pulled down by an angel and fell, and so died from the same magic that he had intended to work.[27]

---

[22] Cf. Keph. 267,13–18, "All ugly evils and defilements, archons and demons, witches and Satans have said that they come from God and that it is he who made them . . . they do not come from him, and they are bearing false witness against him."

[23] At CM 138,9–13 one of Mani's opponents, the head of a synagogue, attempts to cast spells against Mani.

[24] Like Scythianus' marriage, this detail is influenced by the Christian account of Simon Magus. Cf. Epiph. Pan. 21,5,2.

[25] Act. Arch. 63.4, "no disciple having joined him except an old woman"

[26] Act. Arch. 63.1–2; Cyr. Cat. 6.22

[27] Act. Arch. 63.4–6

3,15 The old woman saw to his burial, and came into possession of his property. Having no children or relatives, she remained
alone for a long while. (16) But later she purchased Cubricus, or
Mani, to wait on her. And when she died[28] she left the evil inheritance to him, like poison left by an asp, for the ruin and destruction of many.

4,1 In his turn Cubricus, who had taken the name Mani, lived
in the same place and conducted discussions there. And no one
believed him; everyone who heard Mani's teaching was annoyed,
and rejected it for its novelty, shocking stories, and empty imposture.[29] (2) Seeing the defeat of his own mischievous formularies,
the feather-brain looked for some way of proving the truth of this
dreadful fabrication of his.[30]

4,3 It was rumored that the son of the king of Persia had fallen
victim to some disease and was confined to his bed in the capital
city of Persia—Mani did not live there, but in another place, a long
way from the capital. (4) Blinded by his own wickedness, and thinking that he might be able to work cures on the king's son from
the books he had acquired of Scythianus' successor, his own master
Terbinthus or Buddha, Mani left his place of residence and
ventured to introduce himself, claiming that he could be of service.[31]

4,5 But though he administered various drugs to the king's
ailing child, his expectation was disappointed. The boy finally died
under his ministrations, to the confusion of all empty claims falsely
made.[32] (6) After this outcome, Mani was imprisoned by royal decree.[33]
(7) (The kings of Persia do not execute persons guilty of major
crimes at once; they find ways of inflicting a further sentence of

---

[28] Act. Arch. 63.1–4; Cyr. Cat. 6.24
[29] CM 87, 6–90,7 chronicles sharp hostility toward Mani's teachings on the
part of the "baptists" with whom he broke. Keph. 186,25–187, 25 tells of a series
of rejections of Mani in various lands.
[30] At CM 36,13–21 Mani prays, "[And] further, that the church may grow,
I [beg of thee all the] power of [the signs], that I may perform [them] by my
hands, [in] every [place, and all villages] and towns.
[31] At CM 121,11–123,13 Mani heals a sick girl. Cf. Asmussen p. 9 (M 566
I, Parthian: *HR* II, p. 87) where he performs what appears to be the same
healing before the king of Persia.
[32] At Asmussen p. 54 (M 3, Middle Persian, W. B. Henning, "Mani's Last
Journey," BSOAS 10, 1942, pp. 949–952) Bahram I accuses Mani, "But perhaps
you are needed for this doctoring and this physicking? And you don't even do
that!"
[33] At Man. Hom. 48,19–25 Mani is loaded with chains and threatened. Man.
Ps. 18,30–19,26 says that the imprisonment lasted 26 days.

death, by torture, on those who are [already] faced with that threat.)[34] And so much for that.

5,1   Thus Mani, or Cubricus, remained < in > confinement, visited by his own disciples. (2) For by now the scum had gathered a band, as it were, already about twenty-two,[35] whom he called disciples. (3) He chose three[36] of these, one named Thomas,[37] and Hermeias, and Addas,[38] with the intention < of sending them to Judaea* >.[39] For he had heard of the sacred books to be found in Judaea and the world over—I mean < the > Christian books, the Law and Prophets, the Gospels, and the Apostles.

5,4   Giving his disciples money, he sent them to Jerusalem. (5) (But he had done this before his imprisonment, when he found himself unable to sustain his doctrine in discussion with many. (6) Having heard of the name of Christ, and of his disciples, I mean the Christians, he had determined to deceive his dupes with the name of the Christian religion.)

5,7   They went off and purchased the books, for they made no delay. But when, on their return, they found Mani no longer at liberty but in the prison, they entered even that and showed him the books. (8) He took and examined them, and fraudulently combined his own falsehood with the truth wherever he found the form of a word, or a name, which could show a resemblance to this doctrine. In this way he finally provided confirmation for the sham of his sect.

5,9   In the meantime, however, he escaped by importuning his jailer and bribing him heavily,[40] and he left Persia, and arrived at the Roman realm. (10) But when he reached the border between Mesopotamia and Persia[41] and was still in the desert, he heard of an eminent man named Marcellus[42] who was famous for piety of

---

[34] At CM 100,1–12 Mani is beaten, though by the "baptists" rather than the king.
[35] Act. Arch. 64.4 mentions only the three named at Pan. 66,5,3; Aug. Haer. 46.8 gives Mani twelve disciples. The number 22 may come from Act. Arch. 14.2, where Mani brings 22 disciples to Marcellus' home.
[36] CM 106,7–23 gives Mani three original disciples, named Simeon, Abizachaeus and Patticius. Cf. Cyr. Cat. 6.31.
[37] A division of the Manichaean Psalms, Allberry pp. 203–227, are the "Psalms of Thom," presumably meaning Thomas.
[38] Man. Ps. 235,13–14, (Allberry p. 34) "Glory to Addas, our [Lord];" cf. CM 165,6.
[39] Act. Arch. 65.2–4; but there Mani sends for the books from prison.
[40] Cf. Act. Arch. 65.7, where Mani escapes in obedience to a dream; Cyr. Cat. 6.26–27 mentions his escape without giving details.
[41] At CM 140,11–14 Mani and Patticius come to Pharat; CM 144,4 says, "a town in Pharat named Og[?]."
[42] Act. Arch. 1.1–3; 3.5–7. Cf. CM 144,4, "In Pharat (in the town?) named

the finest sort and lived in the Mesopotamian city of Caschar.[43] Marcellus was a thoroughgoing Christian and remarkable for his righteous works, and supplied the needs of widows, the poor, orphans and the destitute.

5,11   It was Mani's intent to attach himself to Marcellus, to gain control of him and be able not only to rule Mesopotamia through him, but the whole region adjacent to Syria and the Roman Empire. (12) But he sent him a letter[44] from the boundary of the river Stranga, from a place called Fort Arabio, by Turbo, one of his disciples, and this is what it said. Read it, and have a look at the instrument of the fraud's wickedness![45]

6,1   *Mani, an apostle of Jesus Christ,[46] and all the saints and virgins who are with me, to my beloved son, Marcellus : Grace, mercy, peace from God the Father and our Lord Jesus Christ. And the Light's right hand preserve you from the present evil age and its mischances, and the snares of the evil one. Amen.*

6,2   *I am overjoyed to hear that your love is very great, but grieved that your faith is not in accord with the right reason. (3) I therefore feel impelled to send you this letter, since I am sent for the correction of the human race, and care for those who have given themselves over to imposture and error. (4) [I write], first for the salvation of your own soul, and then for the salvation of those who are with you, so that you may not have an undiscerning mind, as the guides of the simple teach, who say that good and evil are brought by the same [God], and introduce a single first principle. (5) As I have said, they neither distinguish nor differentiate darkness from light, good from wicked and evil,[47] and the outer man from the inner, but never cease to confuse and confound the one with the other.*

6,6   *But do you, my son, not combine the two as most men do, absurdly and foolishly in any chance way, and ascribe them both to the God of goodness.[48] For those "whose end is nigh unto cursing"[49] trace the begin-*

Og, (there was) a man famous for his [power] and authority."

[43] Kaskar (variously spelled) is sometimes called a city by the Arab geographers, and sometimes a district. It was under Persian, not Roman rule. See Flügel, *Mani*, pp. 20–25.
[44] An Epistle to Kaskar is mentioned in a list of Manichaean Epistles, Fihrist al-'Ulūm, Flügel, p.103, Item 6.
[45] This letter is quoted from Act. Arch. 5.
[46] At CM 66,4–7 Mani begins his Gospel, "I Manichaeus, apostle of Jesus Christ by the will of God the Father of truth, from whom I spring." "Apostle" is his regular title in Manichaean literature.
[47] Keph. 191,1–3, "He shall believe, and call on him and the physician whom I have brought, and distinguish light from darkness, good from evil."
[48] Cf. Man. Ps. 248,3–6, (Allberry p. 57) "If it was God who created the evil and the good and Christ and Satan . . . then who sent Jesus, that he might work among the Jews until they slew him?"
[49] Cf. Heb. 6:8.

ning, end and father of these evils to God. (7) Neither do they believe what is said in the Gospels by our Savior and Lord Jesus Christ himself, "A good tree cannot bring forth evil fruit, nor, assuredly, can an evil tree bring forth good fruit."[50] (8) And how they dare to say that God is the maker and artificer of Satan and his ills, is amazing to me.

6,9 *And would that their vain effort stopped with this, and they did not say that the Only-begotten, the Christ who has descended from the bosom of the Father, was the son of a woman, Mary, born of blood and flesh and women's ill-smelling effluent![51] (10) And since I have no native eloquence I shall rest content with this, not to abuse your forbearance by writing at length, for a considerable time, in this letter. (11) You shall know the whole when I come to you—if, indeed, you are still tender of your salvation. For I put a noose on no one, in the manner of the senseless [teachers] of the multitude. "Mark what I say,"[52] most honored son!*

7,1 The most distinguished, godfearing and eminent Marcellus was surprised and shocked when he read this letter. For as it happened, the bishop of the town, Archelaus, was in his home with him the day the servant of God received Mani's letter. (2) When Archelaus found what the matter was and had read the letter, he gnashed his teeth like a roaring lion and with godly zeal made as to rush off to where Mani was and arrest him for a foreigner come from the barbarians, from whom he was hastening to destroy the human race.

7,3 But Marcellus in his wisdom begged the bishop to calm down, but told Turbo to terminate his [return] journey to Mani, [who was] at Fort Arabio, where he would be awaiting Turbo. (This fortress is on the border between Persia and Mesopotamia.) (4) Marcellus declined to go to Mani, and not to compel Turbo to do so sent one of his own runners, and wrote Mani the following letter.

Marcellus' Letter to Mani[53]

7,5 *Greetings from the distinguished personage, Marcellus, to Manichaeus, who is made known by the letter.*

I have accepted the letter you have written, and of my kindness given

---

[50] Matt. 7:18. At Keph. 17,2–9 this text is used to introduce the teaching of the two contrasting realms, though the verse quoted there is Luke 6:43–44. Cf. Act. Arch. 15.6; Aug. Adeim. 26; Fel. 2.2; Theodoret Haer. Fab. 1.26.

[51] Man. Ps. 254,23–26, (Allberry p. 52) "He was not born in a womb corrupted; not even the mighty were counted worthy of him for him to dwell beneath their roof, that he should be confined in a womb of a woman of low degree."

[52] 2 Tim. 2:7

[53] 7,5 to 8,3 is quoted, in slightly expanded form, from Act. Arch. 14.

hospitality to Turbo. But I have no way of understanding the sense of
your letter unless you come, as you promise in your letter, and explain each
point in detail. Farewell.

8,1   When Mani learned of this he thought that the absence
of the detained Turbo boded no good. (To confirm his own notion,
Mani often deceived even himself by drawing wrong conclusions.)
All the same, he took the letter as an occasion for hurrying to
Marcellus.

8,2   Now as well as being intelligent the bishop Archelaus had
a zeal for the faith. His advice was to have Mani executed at once,
if possible—as though he had trapped a leopard or wolf, or some
other wild beast—so that the flock would not be harmed by the
onslaught of such a predator. (3) But Marcellus asked for the
< exercise > of patience, and that there be a restrained discussion
between Archelaus and Mani. (4) Archelaus, however, < had > by
now learned the whole essence of Mani's opinion, for Turbo had
told them—him and Marcellus—all of the sect's nonsense.

8,5   Mani teaches that there are two first principles without
beginnings, which are eternal and never cease to be, and are opposed
to each other. He names one light and good, but the other, darkness
and evil, which makes them God and the devil.[54] But sometimes
he calls them both gods, a good god and an evil god.[55]

8,6   All things stem and originate from these two principles.
The one principle makes all good things; the other, likewise, the
evil things. In the world the substances of these two principles are
mixed together,[56] and the one principle has made the body, while
the soul belongs to the other. (7) The soul in human beings, and
the soul in every beast, bird, reptile and bug is the same; and not
only this, but Mani claims that the living moisture in plants is a
movement of the soul which he says is in human beings.[57]

---

[54] Asmussen p. 73 (Chuashtuanift VIII A), "(Ever) since we have recognized
the true God (and) the pure sacred doctrine, we know 'the two principles'
(roots, origins). We know the light principle, the realm of God, and we know
the dark principle, the realm of Hell."
[55] This does not occur in any published Manichaean writing. Uighur
Chuashtuanift VII A (Asmussen p. 72) "And if one should ever ask, 'Who comes
to the road that seduces, to the beginning of the two poison roads (and) to
the gate of Hell,' (then) it is . . . the one who worships the devil and addresses
him as God," perhaps suggests that some Manichaeans were guilty of this. Contrast Aug. Faust. 21.1, "It is indeed (true) that we acknowledge two first principles, but we call (only) one of these God, and the other matter, or, if I may
use the common parlance, the demon."
[56] Keph. 131.16–17, "They were cast in a mixture with each other, the light
with the darkness and the darkness with the light." In NHL, light is mixed with
darkness at Apocry. Jn. 25,4.
[57] Man. Ps. 246,25–30, (Allberry p. 54) "I am in everything. I bear the skies,

9,1   But he teaches as much other mythology when he says that whoever eats meat eats a soul, and is liable to the punishment of becoming the same himself [58]—(2) becoming a pig in his own turn if he ate a pig, or a bull, or bird, or any edible creature. Manichaeans therefore do not eat meat. And if one plants a fig tree, an olive, a grapevine, a sycamore, or a persea, his soul at his own death is entangled in the branches of the trees he planted and unable to get by them.[59] (3) And if one marries a woman, he says, he is embodied again after his departure and becomes a woman himself, so that he may be married. (4) And if someone killed a man his soul is returned to the body of a leper after departing the body, or a mouse or snake,[60] or else will in his own turn become something of the kind that he killed.

9,5   Again, he claimed that since it desires < to draw up > the soul which is dispersed in all things, God's heavenly wisdom[61]—(6) (For he and his Manichaean followers say that the soul is a part of God and has been dragged away from him and < is held > as the prisoner[62] of the archons[63] of the opposing principle and root. < And > it has been cast down into bodies in this way, because it is the food of the archons who have seized it and < eaten it as* > a source of strength for themselves,[64] and parceled it out among bodies.) (7) And therefore, he says, this wisdom has set these luminaries, the sun, moon and stars,[65] in the sky, and has made

---

I am the foundation, I support the earths, I am the light that shines forth, that gives joy to the souls. I am the life of the world. I am the milk that is in all trees: I am the sweet water that is beneath the sons of Matter."

[58] Asmussen p. 72 (Uighur Chuashtuanift V C), "If we ever, my God, somehow . . . should have killed (living beings) (then) we to the same degree owe life to living beings."

[59] A Manichaean confession of sin translated by Henning, in "Ein Manichäisches Gebet- und Beichtbuch," Türk. Turf. VIII, APAW 1936, No. 10, p. 142, reads ". . . in grosser Unzüchtigkeit Bäume abzukauen oder zu pflanzen (scheue ich mich nicht), am Frühlingsmorgen der Bäume Sprossen und (überhaupt) der Elemente Notlage beachten (bedenke) ich nicht; mit dem Leibe erstreben wir (ja alle) zu pflanzen und zu säen, einen Garten oder ein Grundstück."

[60] Klimkeit p. 174 (Confessional text for the elect, Sogdian with Persian citations), "why was I not (reborn) in the class of pigs, dogs or yakshas?"

[61] Cf. Tit. Bost. Man. 1.17.

[62] Keph. 29,18–20 "The first hunter is the king of the realm of darkness, who hunted the living soul with his net at the beginning of the worlds."

[63] Keph. 50,22, "archons, the enemies of the light"

[64] Klimkeit p.172 (Confessional Text for the Elect, Sogdian with Persian citations), "For the (demon of) Greed . . . that has formed this body . . . constantly provokes contention through these five 'gates.' (Through them) it brings the internal demons together with the external ones, in the courses of which a small part (of the soul) is destroyed day by day."

[65] Keph. 168,1–12 sharply distinguishes between the "five stars" (i.e., the planets)

a mechanical contrivance through what the Greeks call the twelve signs of the zodiac.[66]

9,8   He affirms that these signs draw the souls of dying men and other living things upwards, because they shine. But they are carried to the ship—Mani says that the sun and moon are ships.[67] And the smaller ship loads for fifteen days, till the full moon. And so it carries them across, and on the fifteenth day stows them in the larger ship, the sun.[68] (9) And the sun, the larger ship, ferries them over to the aeon of light and the land of the blessed.[69]

9,10   And thus the souls which have been ferried over by the sun and moon < are saved* >. For of those who < have become > acquainted with his vulgar chatter, he says that they have been purified and deemed worthy of this mythical crossing of his. And again, he says that a soul cannot be saved unless it < shares > the same knowledge. And there is much sound and fury in this fabrication.

10,1   Now these were Mani's teachings, and Archelaus had been made familiar with < them by Turbo >, and because of his extensive knowledge of God and his advance < information > was fully prepared for the debate. For he had obtained precise knowledge of all of Mani's charlatanry from Turbo. And lo and behold, here came Mani, with his companions!

10,2   < Marcellus and Archelaus > came then and there to a public debate in Caschar. They had previously chosen a man named Marsipus, and Claudius, and Aegeleus and Cleobulus as judges of their disputation. One was a pagan philosopher, one a professor of medicine, another a professional teacher of grammar, and the other a sophist. (3) And after many words on both sides, with Mani advancing his fabricated teachings and Archelaus, like the bravest of soldiers, destroying the enemy's weapons by his own strength, and when Mani was finally beaten and the judges had awarded the prize to the truth—(4) that was no surprise. The truth is self-authenticating and cannot be overthrown even if wickedness shamelessly opposes the precept of the truth. For like the shadow

---

which are evil, and the sun and moon which rule over the planets and "oppress" them.

[66] At Klimkeit p. 306 (*Apocryphal Words of the Historical Jesus*), unsatisfactory catechumens ascend to the zodiac and descend again to be reborn.

[67] Klimkeit, p. 68 (*A hymn to the Third Messenger*, Parthian) "Full of joy are the divine abodes, The noble ships, the ferries that are created by the word."

[68] Man. Ps. 267,7–9, (Allberry p. 85) "... now in thy gifts of light ... from ship to ship unto the Envoy in whom ... who will ferry me across in ..."

[69] Keph. 158, 31–32, "(The greater luminary) is the gate of light and the vehicle of peace to this great aeon of light."

of darkness, like the slippery footing of a snake's onset, like the snake's lack of support without feet, falsehood has no ground or foundation.

11,1   And then Mani escaped,[70] though the people would have stoned him if Marcellus had not come forward and shamed the mob with his venerable presence—otherwise, if he had stayed, the miserable dead man would have died a long time earlier. Mani withdrew and came to a village < in the neighborhood* > of Caschar called † Diodoris,[71] (2) where the people's presbyter at the time was a very mild man named Trypho.[72] Mani lodged with Trypho and confused him in turn with his boasts, for he realized that Trypho, while a good man in other respects and a marvel of piety, was lacking in eloquence. (3) Even here, however, he was not able to mock Christ's servant as he had supposed he could. God's way is to prepare the gifts of the Spirit and supply them to those who hope in him, as the One who never lies has promised, "Take no thought what ye shall speak. For it is not ye that speak, but the Spirit of my Father which speaketh in you."[73]

11,4   And so Mani chose to debate once more, with the presbyter Trypho. Trypho answered him at many points and wrote to Archelaus about this matter, (5) "A man has come here like a fierce wolf and is trying to destroy the fold. I beg you to send me instructions on how to deal with him or in what terms I should reply to his heresy. And if you should see fit to come yourself, you would relieve the minds of Christ's fold, and his sheep." Archelaus sent him two books < for > the ready understanding of Mani, and told him to expect him in person.

11,6   At early morning Mani came into the middle of the village, pretending to challenge Trypho to debate as a colleague. And after Trypho had made his appearance, (7) and with his God-given understanding had answered Mani's questions point by point to the fraud's discomfiture—[though] somewhat softly where he felt doubtful—Archelaus turned up like a powerful householder protecting his property, confidently attacked the would-be plunderer, and took him to task.

11,8   As soon as Mani saw Archelaus he said, with fawning hypocrisy, "Allow me to debate with Trypho. Since < you are > a bishop, you outrank me." (9) But along with the refutation of the

---

[70] Cf. Act. Arch. 43.1–2, Cyr. Cat. 6.30.
[71] Holl: εἰς κώμην τινὰ τῆς Καλχάρω < περιοίκιδος > Διοδωρίδα καλουμένην; MSS: . . . τῆς Καλχάρων εἰς Διοδωρίδα καλουμένην
[72] At Act. Arch. 43.4 both the presbyter and the village are named Diodorus.
[73] Matt. 10:19–2074.

remark Archelaus silenced Mani by exposing him as an [even] greater hypocrite, and again put him to shame by answering his arguments, so that he could say nothing further. And the people once more grew angry and tried to lay hands on the offender. He, however, escaped the mob and < returned* > once more to Fort Arabio.

12,1   And then, when the king of Persia learned of Mani's hideout, he sent and arrested him in the fortress. He dragged him ignominiously back to Persia and punished him by ordering that he be flayed with a reed.[74] (2) They still have his skin in Persia, flayed with a reed and stuffed with straw.[75] And this is how he died; Manichaeans themselves sleep on reed mattresses for this reason.

12,3   After he had died like that and had left his disciples whom we have mentioned, Addas, Thomas and Hermeias—he had sent < them > out before he was punished as we described—(4) Hermeias < went > to Egypt. Many < of us* > met him. For the sect is not an ancient one, and the people who had met this Hermeias, Mani's disciple, described him to me. (5) Addas, however, went north[76] and Thomas to Judaea, and the doctrine has gained in strength to this day by their efforts. (6) Mani, however, said that he was the Paraclete Spirit,[77] and calls himself an apostle of Christ on some occasions, and the Paraclete Spirit on others. And there is a great variation of the heresies in his blindness.

13,1   Now at length, beloved, I need to say < something > about the sect and its nonsense; all that precedes, I have described for your information. (2) Now then, the savage Mani begins his teaching, speaking and writing in his work on faith. (3) For he issued

---

[74] This appears only in anti-Manichaean sources, e.g., Theodore Bar Khouni (Pognon p. 184); Cyr. Cat. 6.30. Manichaean sources say oftenest that Mani was crucified, Man. Hom. 44,17–20; 45,9; 71.15; Man. Ps. 226,19–231 (Allberry p. 19) etc. Some say that Mani died in prison, cf. Asmussen p. 57 (M 5, Parthian: *MM* III: 863–865) "On the fourth of the month of Shahrevar, on the Monday and at the eleventh hour, when he had prayed, he shed the wonted garment of the body.

[75] This is scurrilous, but Manichaean sources say that Mani's head was cut off and exhibited to the populace, e.g. at Man. Ps. 19,29–31.

[76] Perhaps cf. Asmussen p. 21 (M 216b, Parthian: *MM* II p. 301, n. 2 and p. 302, n.3), "When the apostle was [in] Veh Ardashir (Seleuceia, on the west bank of the Tigris) then he sent the Teacher, Addas the Bishop . . . [and] other scribes to Byzans . . ." At p. 300 Addas goes to the east.

[77] Keph. 14,31–15,24, "In this year, the year in which Ardashir the king [was ready? to receive] the crown, the living Paraclete descended to me, spoke with me, and revealed to me the hidden mystery . . . In this way all that has come to pass and will come to pass was revealed to me by the Paraclete . . . all that the eye beholds, the ear hears, and the thought considers . . . I knew all and saw all, and became one body and one spirit . . ."

various books, one composed of < twenty-two sections* > to match < the > twenty-two letters of the Syriac alphabet.[78] (4) (Most Persians use the Syrian letters besides < the > Persian, just as, with us, many nations use the Greek letters even though nearly every nation has its own. (5) But others pride themselves on the oldest dialect of Syriac, if you please, and the Palmyrene—it and its letters. But there are twenty-two of them, and the book is thus divided into twenty-two sections.)

13,6   He calls this book the *Mysteries of Manichaeus,* and another one the *Treasury.* And he makes a show of other books he has stitched together, the *Lesser Treasury,* as one is called, and another on astrology. (7) Manichaeans have no shortage of this sort of jugglery; they have astrology for a handy subject of boasting, and phylacteries—I mean amulets—and certain other incantations and spells.

This is how Mani begins his book:

14,1   *There were God and matter, light and darkness, good and evil, all in direct opposition to each other, so that neither side has anything in common with the other.*[79] And this is the scum's prologue; (2) he begins his mischief there. And broadly speaking, that is the book, which contains certain bad propositions of this sort, the difficulty of which, and the contradiction at the very outset between the words and their aim, must be understood. (3) For even though the rest of his nonsense and fabricated religion is extensive, the whole of his wickedness will be shown by its introduction.

For the words, "There were God and matter," taught nothing less than the futile speculation of the Greeks. (4) But it is easy to detect, understand and refute this valueless sophistical notion. < It is plain* > to anyone with good judgment that the conclusion that there are two contemporaneous eternals cannot be reached by correct reasoning and well-intended intelligence. And anyone with sense must find this out. (5) If the two [eternals] are contemporaneous they cannot be different, even in name. For anything that is contemporaneous [with one of them] is also co-eternal. But this co-eternal and ever existent thing is God, particularly as he has no cause. For nothing is eternal but God alone.

14,6   But with your barbarous mind and enmity toward the human race you have referred to these principles by different names. You have spoken of one as "light," but the other as "darkness," and

---

[78] Holl: τῶν κατὰ τὴν τῶν Σύρων στοιχειωσιν < ἐκ κβʹ τόμων > συγκειμενην; MSS: τῶν κατὰ τὴν τῶν Σύρων στοιχείωσιν δἰ ἀλφαβήτου συνγκειμένην. Other suggestions for emendation at Holl.

[79] Tit. Bost. Man. 1.5 gives this as a summary of Mani's teaching. A variation

again, of the one as "good" and the other as "evil." But you claim
that they are in total opposition in every respect, so that neither
has anything in common with the other. You separate them, then;
for it is plain that they are opposites, as you have said. (7) (If they
are partners, however, the partners will be found to be friendly
and in agreement, because they live together in fellowship and
from their profound affection never leave one another.[80]

14,8   However, if [Mani's first principles] are separate from each
other, each of them is surely bounded. But nothing that is bounded
is perfect; it is limited by its boundedness. (9) Besides, a boundary
will be needed for the delimitation of both, or both territories will
touch at the ends, be in contact with each other through the ends,
have something in common, and violate the rule of their opposition.[81] And if you grant that there is a divider between the two,
(10) the divider cannot be like them, but neither can it be different from both. (11) For if the divider can be called comparable
to one of the two eternals we mentioned [even] in one part of
it, then, because of the comparable part, the divider cannot be
different from [the eternal]. Instead it will be connected with the
one with which it is comparable, there will be a junction at the
part that matches, and [the divider] will no longer be bounded
where it parts the two substances from each other.[82]

14,12   If, however, it is not like the two and has no share of
a part of either, there cannot be two eternals and everlastings;
there must, in the last analysis, be three.[83] And there can no longer
be two principles, and two primordials opposed to each other.
There must be another, third thing, which is opposed to both and
unlike both, and which divides the two and, because of its foreign-
ness to them, has nothing in common with either and no likeness
to either.[84] And in the end there are no longer two, but these three.

14,13   And besides, another will also be required, a fourth, to
mediate and set this boundary. For the two could not set the boundary
or partition without another to be the umpire who put the divider
between them—a skillful, wise and fair umpire, what is more, with
higher rank [than either] so that he can persuade them both to
a peaceable reconciliation. (14) Thus there will be one to set the

---

on it is found at Aug. Ep. Fund. 13.
   [80] Epiphanius may here be influenced by Tit. Bost. Man. 1.5.
   [81] The thought and wording here are close to that of Tit. Bost. Man. 1.7.
   [82] Cf. Serap. Thm. 32.13.
   [83] Titus of Bostra argues at Man. 1.7 that Mani's thesis requires at least three
principles. Cf. Alex. Lycop. Man. 8.
   [84] Cf. Tit. Bost. Man. 1.7; Alex. Lycop. Man. 8; Act. Arch. 24.7.

boundary, one to divide, and two to be bounded, and there cannot be only two first principles; there must even be three and four. And in this way one can think of many first principles, ignoring real things and imagining unreal ones.

15,1 In the offender's effort not to allow evil, of all things, to touch God—in fact, to ascribe < evil > to God is an absurdity. In the standard form of the church's teaching it is agreed that the Godhead has nothing to do with evil and no admixture of it. (2) For God made nothing evil; he made "all things very good,"[85] since God is by nature good and of an incomprehensible essence, and contains all things but is himself contained by none. Evil, therefore, did not always exist, nor was evil made by God.

15,3 Since evil does not always exist, then, and was not made by God, it remains to examine the nature of this thing that does not always exist but has a beginning, and that is coming to its end and perishing, and has no permanence— < and > how it began. (4) And in examining this we must first consider the sort of thing that evil is and the sort of thing in which evil arises, and whether it is an object or, as it were, has a body or substance, or whether it can even have a root. (5) And when we think this through we shall find that evil is without substance and has no root, but is limited to the deeds of human activity at work. (6) While we are doing it, evil exists; while we are not doing it, it does not. It is our good judgment that discovers what it means to do evil—to do the thing that does not please God, and can neither contradict God nor resist the Godhead. For when anything can be rooted out and destroyed by men, all the more can it not hold out against God.

16,1 At the same time we must understand that the devil was not made evil by nature at the creation but discovered evildoing for himself later, and not without the knowledge of what he would become. With all creatures he was created well, with the utmost serviceability because of superior righteousness. (2) For though God in his supreme goodness willed that all persons and creatures be < good >, and though he offered his good gifts to all, he still, by allowing the freedom to choose, permits all creatures to undertake whichever action each chooses by its own will. Thus God cannot be responsible for the evils, though there will be a separation of those who progress to virtue and win the rewards of goodness.

16,3 But though this madman Mani (Μάνης) means to exempt

---

[85] Gen. 1:31; with the argument in general, cf. Tit. Bost. Man. 2.1.

God from evil, he has instead set evil over against God on equal terms. (4) And at the same time, while he is abusing all creation, he is not ashamed to use our human errors as his excuse for interweaving < a mixture of the two* > evenly matched < principles* > with all created being. He has in fact become the champion and defender of the evil he claims to forbid. And when he grants its existence and declares its eternity, and that, together with God, it always is and never ceases to be, he is embracing a sort of fondness for evil and fellowship with it instead of a hatred toward it.

16,5   And Mani's departure from the truth can be detected from his use of certain terms for evil in every subject [he discusses]. For the goodness of God's whole creation is proved by the texts Mani himself cites. (17,1) First of all he has called evil, "matter," and holds matter to be corruption in the same sense [as evil].[86] And to begin with, if matter is corruption, what can it be the corruption of? If it is the corruption of other things, but matter itself is enduring, then matter would have destroyed everything long ago; and after putting its power into operation for so long without being extirpated, only it would exist.

17,2   But if matter is the corruption of itself, and if it corrupts, assails, consumes and destroys itself, it is on its way to destruction and cannot endure, since it is the source of its own destruction and corruption.[87] (3) How could it have lasted for so long, as the scum claims, but at the same time have nothing at all to do with life, and not in fact < have a share > of life or goodness?

17,4   But since there is also goodness in each of the creatures Mani abuses, his account of evil is altogether mistaken; each of the principles he speaks of has something in common with the other. (5) All that is has been made for a purpose, but the things that Mani abuses by name contain the opposite of evil. Take snakes, for example and the other < poisonous reptiles >. (6) The sources of deadly poison also † contain[88] an antidote to do away with death and suffering. And the daytime is indeed for human labor, as well as for illumination and vision; but the night, which Mani disparages by name,[89] is also a rest which God has given to

---

[86] At Keph. 31,10, and often in the Kephalaia, matter is "the thought of death." Cf. Keph 31,15–16, where matter forms the body of "the king of darkness and smoke," and 131,4–5, ". . . from the time at which death, that is, matter, is eliminated . . ."

[87] A similar argument is used at Tit. Bost. Man. 1.11; cf. Serap. Thm. in Tit. Bost. 79.21.1.

[88] Holl: καὶ κακώσεως < εὑρίσκεται >; MSS καὶ κακώσεως κακιζομένων

[89] Keph. 161,20–25, "The night reveals the sign of the darkness of its father, from whose essence it comes. For the night came from the first darkness and

man.[90] (7) And so it is evident that each thing individually is good, and cannot be termed evil, or given a name synonymous with evil, because of our sins.

18,1   For all things are good and pleasant, and nothing is rejected by the God < who says >, "And behold, all things are very good."[91] And nowhere is there a root of evil. (2) This is why, when God was making the whole world by his goodness, he ascribed goodness to each of his creatures at the outset, and said, "And God saw that it was good"[92]—testifying to its goodness and confounding the shrewdness of the plotters against mankind, who want to conceal the truth from men with their evil stories. (3) For God made heaven and earth, the light, and the things on the earth, on the first day, "And he saw, and behold it was good,"[93] says the scripture. (4) Didn't he know he would make something good, then, since he says, "Behold, it is good," after it was made? And so, in succession, of the waters, the sea, vegetation, trees, the heavenly luminaries, cattle, birds, reptiles and fish. (5) For scripture said, "And God saw, and behold, it was good," in every case—but not because God did not know this beforehand or because he < learned > it after the thing was made, as though he had acquired his knowledge of its goodness by experience. Because of the opinion of the injudicious he declared in advance that all things are good, and that evil has no existence anywhere. (6) Since all things are good, and since their goodness is attested by the absolutely true testimony of the Good, < the > Privation of all that is evil and of all wickedness said, "Behold, it is good", for the refutation of men's whole artificial opinion of evil, and the demolition of the entire notion of those who introduce this mischievous teaching.

18,7   Then, when he came to man, God did not say that man is "good," and did not say that man is "bad." And yet man is the most excellent of all earthly creatures, created by God, with his ineffable wisdom, to rule the world—and God would give him dominion over all his creatures as he says, (8) "Let us make man in our image, after our likeness, and let them have dominion over the fish of the sea and over the fowl of the air, and over the creeping things of the earth, and cattle and beasts, and over all

---

appeared in the world. Look at the night, the shadow of the first darkness which is made fast and bound in all things above and below." And see the entire passage, Keph. 160,18–161,25.

[90] Cf. Tit. Bost. Man. 2.18.
[91] Gen. 1:31
[92] Gen. 1:4; 10; 12; 18; 21; 25
[93] Gen. 1:4

that is on the earth."[94] (9) Since man had been made in God's
image, holy writ was content with such a great dignity, which needed
no further addition. (10) For if man possessed the image of Goodness
itself at his creation—I mean the image of the Lord God, the
artificer, and good artificer, of all creatures, the wellspring of all
goodness and the source of the good in all—why would man need
the further testimony of "Behold, it is good?" He had received the
image of the Good himself.

18,11   But later at the end of the whole account, after the making
of all of God's handiwork, the word of God, in conclusion, bore
the same witness for all and said, (12) "And God saw all that he
had made, and behold, it was very good,"[95] adding the word, "very."
This was the sixth day, and the seventh day of rest. The point was
to remove the root of [Mani's] < opinion > of evil, so that never
again would anyone find an excuse for daring to believe that evil
is eternal. (13) For this same account of evil had been demolished.
There was no evil anywhere, for all things were very good, and
had been made and witnessed to by a good God.

19,1   "Matter" can mean two things. On the one hand, in the
offender's sense of the word, it is the name of an activity, as I said,
and a consuming corruption. But we ordinarily say "matter" of the
material < consumed* > by craftsmen in the production of every
article—wooden matter, for example, ceramic matter, the matter
of gold, the matter of silver. The result of the bodily process which
is caused by the decomposition of † food[96] is also called "matter."
All right, let's have the newly arrived diviner (μάντις), who claims
to have been before the ages, tell us < which kind of matter he
meant* >. (2) For he even dared to say he was the Paraclete Spirit—
though on other occasions he calls himself an apostle of Jesus
Christ, as I said. And yet he never took the form of a dove, or
put on the Paraclete Spirit who was sent to the apostles from heaven
to be their garment of immortality < and* > the power <of their
testimony* >. (3) The Only-begotten promised to send this Spirit,
and set the time for it "not many days hence"[97] but directly after
his ascension—as he said, "If I depart, he will come."[98] And on their
return from the Mount of Olives, "they were filled with the Holy
Spirit" at once in the upper room[99] (4) as the scripture says, "There

---

[94] Gen. 1:26
[95] Gen. 1:31
[96] Holl: βρώσεως; MSS: κακώσεως.
[97] Acts 1:5
[98] Cf. John 16:7.
[99] Sic! Acts 2:4 combined with 1:13

appeared to them cloven tongues of fire."[100] And the house was filled as with a violent blast of wind, and the Spirit settled on each of them, and they spoke of God's wonders in tongues, and all heard them in their own languages. (5) For they came from every people under heaven and yet each of them was comforted by the Spirit—the apostles by the gift, and all the nations by the sound of God's wondrous teaching.

19,6   For if the Paraclete Spirit the Lord promised his disciples was this scum—this true Maniac, and bearer of the name by his own self-designation— < the > apostles went to their rest cheated of the promise, though the Lord who does not lie had told them, "Ye shall receive the gift of the Holy Spirit after these few days."[101]

19,7   And it will be found that the fraud is falsely accusing Christ of failure to keep his word. For the apostles' generation is gone— I mean the generation from Peter until Paul, and until John who even lived until the time of Trajan. And James is gone, the first to exercise the episcopate in Jerusalem. (James was called the Lord's brother but he was Joseph's son, born, like the rest of his brothers, of Joseph's real wife. (8) Because the Lord Jesus Christ, who was born in the flesh of the ever-virgin Mary, was brought up with them, < they > were in the position of brothers to him, and he was called their brother.) And all the saints who shared James' throne are gone, and Symeon, the son of James' uncle, with them—Symeon, the son of Cleopas the brother of Joseph.

19,9   I subjoin their successive episcopates one by one, beginning with the episcopate of James— < I mean the successive > bishops who were appointed in Jerusalem during each emperor's reign until the time of Aurelian and Probus, when this Mani, a Persian, became known, and produced this outlandish teaching.

The list follows:[102]

20,1   James, who was martyred in Jerusalem by beating with a cudgel. [He lived] until the time of Nero.

2.   Symeon, was crucified under Trajan.
3.   Judah
4.   Zachariah
5.   Tobiah
6.   Benjamin
7.   John, bringing us to the ninth [or] tenth year of Trajan.[103]

---

[100] Acts 2:3
[101] Acts 1:5; 2:38
[102] The following list appears to be derived from a series of references in Eusebius' Chronicle. For a discussion in detail see Holl, *Panarion* II, pp. 44–47.
[103] MSS: ἐὼς δέκα ἐννέα ἔτους. Holl suggests that this is dittography.

8. Matthias
9. Philip
10. Seneca
11. Justus, bringing us to Hadrian.
12. Levi
13. Vaphres
14. Jose
15. Judah, bringing us to the † eleventh year of Antonius.[104]
The above were the circumcised bishops of Jerusalem.
The following were gentiles:
16. Mark
17. Cassian
18. Puplius
19. Maximus
20. Julian. These all exercised their office up until the tenth year of Antoninus Pius.
20,2   21. Gaian
22. Symmachus
23. Gaius, bringing us to the time of Verus, in the eighth year of his reign.
24. Julian
25. Capito
26. Maximus, bringing us to the sixteenth year of Verus.
27. Antoninus
28. Valens
29. Dolichian, bringing us to Commodus.
30. Narcissus
31. Dius, bringing us to Severus.
32. Germanio
33. Gordius, bringing us to Antoninus.
34. Narcissus, the same person, bringing us to Alexander the son of Mamaea—not Alexander of Macedon, but a different one.
35. Alexander, bringing us to the same Alexander.
36. Mazabanus, bringing us to Gallus and Volusian.
37. Hymenaeus, bringing us to Aurelian.
20,3   According to some annalists there are 276[105] years altogether from Christ's ascension until the time of Mani, Aurelian and Probus. According to others, there are 246.
And there have been eight other bishops from that time until

---

[104] MSS: μέχρι ἐνδεκάτου Ἀντωνίου. Holl tentatively suggests μέχρι Ἱεροσολύμων ἁλώσεως.
[105] This figure is obtained by adding the thirty years of Christ's life to the 246.

the present: Bazas, Hermo, Macaris, Maximus, Cyril, Herennis, Cyril once more, and Hilarion, the present occupant of the see, who is accused of consorting with the Arians.

20,4   And the successive emperors whose reigns coincided [with these last eight episcopates] are: The remaining one year of the remaining part of Aurelian's reign; Tacitus, who reigned for six months; < Probus, six years >; Carus, Carinus and Numerian, two years. Diocletian, twenty years. Maximian, Licinius, Constantine, Constantius, Julian, Jovian, Valentinian, Valens, Gratian, < 73 years altogether >. (5) Thus there are 101 years from Mani until the present, that is, till the thirteenth year of Valens, the ninth of Gratian, the first of Valentinian the Younger and the ninety-third of the Diocletian era.[106] (6) < In other words the Holy Spirit waited for 276 years in Mani* >, so that he could be sent to the world as [his] emissary in the fourth year of Aurelian and the episcopate of Hymenaeus at Jerusalem, < and > deprive and cheat his followers of the truth through the working of imposture and delusion by the devil who inhabited him.

21,1   Hence his trickery is altogether confounded, since, with their accurate knowledge of everything, the minds of the wise will condemn his false notion. (2) And all his other beliefs are sophisms, filled with foolishness—perverse, uncertain and, to all the wise, ridiculous. < Since I intend > to analyze them phrase by phrase, and set down the arguments against them all, I am going to make the refutatory part of my work against him very bulky. (3) However, marvelously good replies to him have already been composed by great men—by Archelaus the bishop, as has been said; and, I have heard, by Origen; and by Eusebius of Caesarea and Eusebius of Emesa, Serapion of Thmuis, Athanasius of Alexandria, George of Laodicea, Apolinaris of Laodicea, Titus, and many who have spoken in opposition to him.

21,4   Still, even in my poverty it will do no harm to make a few remarks to the wretched man's shame, in refutation of what I have already called his entirely false notion. (5) And I would prefer not to put his refutation in harsh terms but as gently as possible, except that, in his impudence, he does not hesitate to blaspheme the Lord of all and deny at the outset that he is the creator—this though he made this whole body of heaven, earth, and everything in them, and everything in the world. But in imagining another God who does not exist, Mani has abandoned the

---

[106] I.e., 377 A.D. Epiphanius has been at work on the Panarion for approximately two years, cf. Pan. Proem II 2,3.

One who does. (6) He has been deprived of the truth, and has had the experience in the comic proverb, where the crow had food in its mouth and saw the reflection of the food in the water, and wanting to get something else to eat, lost the food it had and still didn't get the food it didn't.

21,7 But who can put up with the blasphemer? If we have fathers of flesh and blood and cannot bear to hear them criticized, how much more if we hear the Lord God of all blasphemed by the savage Mani?

21,8 When, in the divine goodness, storms are sent by the mercy of God, Mani is not ashamed to say blaspehmously that storms do not come from God, but from the effluent of the archons.[106] (22,1) But who would not laugh out loud to say the rest, since the tales of Philistion probably carry more conviction than Mani's mimes? (2) He teaches about a mythical porter who supports the whole world,[107] and says that every thirty years the porter's shoulder gets tired, and he shifts the world to the other shoulder, and < this is why > we have earthquakes.[108]

22,3 But if this were so, the thing would be a fact of nature and not supernatural. (4) The Savior's words refute the charlatan, however, for he said, "Become good like your Father in heaven, for he maketh his sun to rise on the just and on the unjust, and sendeth his rain on the evil and on the good,"[109] and, "There shall be earthquakes in divers places, and famines and pestilences."[110] (5) If earthquakes were natural or normal, < but > perhaps there were frequent quakes in a country and the earth happened to shake many times a night for a whole year, would that be because the porter's shoulders hurt, and he was uncomfortable and made the quake continuous? And who can put up with this sort of nonsense?

22,6 But what else < in >credible has he not dared to say? For

---

[106] Keph. 116,29–31 is more dignified: "(The archons) and also the tyrants, in whose heart it is to rule in the clouds, the storms (?), the winds, the pneumata and the storm-winds." With Epiphanius' version, (a parody?) cf. Act. Arch. 9.3; Cyr. Cat. 6.34; Tit. Bost. Man. 8.2.

[107] Man. Ps. 2,18–20, " The Omophorus, the great burden-carrier, who treads upon the . . . with the soles of his feet, supporting the earths with his hands, carrying the burden of the creations." Cf. Act. Arch. 8.2.

[108] At Keph. 93,16–19 the earthquake "in the watch of the Porter" is a primordial one, and is caused by a rebellion in the depths: "Again, during the watch of the Omophorus who humbles . . . there was a rebellion of the depths below . . . bowed, and the fastenings beneath came loose . . . in the foundation below. Cf. NHL Orig. Wld. 102,25–31. Outside of Epiphanius, the shifting of the porter's pole is found only at Timothy Presbyter MSG 86, 21A.

[109] Matt. 5:45

[110] Cf. Mark 13:8.

he claims that souls which have become acquainted with his imposture are taken up into the moon, since the essence of the soul is luminous. (7) This is why the moon waxes and wanes, he says; it becomes filled with the souls which have died in the knowledge of his unbelief. (8) Then, he says, they are transferred from the moon—the smaller ship, < as > he calls it—to the sun. And < the sun > takes them aboard and deposits them in the aeon of the blessed.

22,9   But wickedness is always blind, and unaware of its own shame—how it is refuted by its own words, because it cannot make its lies consistent. (23,1) For one man was formed to begin with, Adam, and had sons and daughters. But in the beginning of the creation, around Adam's hundredth year, Abel was killed at roughly the age of thirty.[111] (2) The first man, Adam, died after this first victim of murder, at about the age of 930. But the sun, moon and stars had been fixed and established in the sky on the fourth day of creation. (3) Now what should we say, Mister? Should we agree that your stupidity has been revealed? How could 930 years go by without the moon's waning and waxing? (4) With which departed souls was the sun filled and loaded? Well? But Mani did not know that there are wise persons who cannot be convinced by lying words, but [only] by the most authentic proofs.

23,5   But if we do grant that this is so—heaven help us, it can't be! [But if we grant that it is so], and the moon, in growing full, is crammed with the souls of Manichaeans, still what proof is there of such a proposition? (6) If no Manichaean died after the fifteenth of the month, and it was fore-ordained that Manichaeans would die up until the fifteenth, but no more after the fifteenth until the moon's cargo had been unloaded to start loading again at the new moon, their lie would be convincing. As it is, it is unpersuasive. (7) Manichaeans die every day, and the heavenly bodies which God has ordained know their course.[112] And once more, the slop[113] about the souls in the moon won't do.

24,1   Again, some of them < concoct another story* > with villainous intent, < and* > say that the Mother of all[114] allowed her

---

[111] Jub. 2.10

[112] At Man. 22, Alexander of Lycopolis bases his anti-Manichaean argument on the fixed periods of the moon's waxing and waning.

[113] Epiphanius is apparently punning on γόμος, which can mean either "cargo" or "soup."

[114] In Manichaean theology the Mother of all is usually the first emanation from the Father. She does not ordinarily interact directly with earthly beings. Cf., however, Keph. 71,21–23, "If (the Mother of Life) had descended and come down, by [her own will alone], from the Father's height to the earth, [she would

power to come down from heaven to steal < from > the archons[115]
and rob them of the power they had taken from on high. (2) For
Mani says that the principalities and authorities made war on the
living God and seized < his* > great and incomprehensible < essence* > from him, as a power which Mani calls the soul.

24,3   How very absurd of him! Whoever is seized and handled
with violence has been bested. If the principalities oppressed the
good God and took power from his armor, they must be more
powerful than he. (4) And if he gave in to them to begin with,
he does not have the ability to take the power, or armor, which
they stole from him back from them[116]—not when he was unable
to resist his enemies in the first place.

24,5   To put it another way, suppose that he could win a victory
at some time, prevail over his antagonists, and take back the power
they had stolen from him. Since the root of evil, its first principle
with no beginning, would still be in existence and impossible to
destroy altogether, it would win in another war, prevail by the
exercise of some power, and again take more power from the good
God, as well as his power which he had taken back.[118] (6) And evil
will always be ranged against the good God and never controllable,
so that it will be forever seizing and being seized.

24,7   But even though these entirely deluded half-wits say that
if the good God frees the part of his armor that has been seized
from him, he will then do away with the principalities and authorities of the opposing power and destroy them altogether—even if
this will still happen, and the good God will indeed get rid of them
entirely and destroy them, the scum's argument is wrong. For he
claims that the "good" God is not "just" and does not condemn
the sinner, either by consigning him to torments or by putting him
to death. (8) For if he makes any attempt to do away with the
devil, or opposing power, and destroy him, either he cannot be
good in himself, as he is said to be; or, if he is good and still
destroys evil, then this Lord who made heaven and earth must be
< just >, as in fact he is, since he "rendereth to every man according
to his deeds."[118] For with extreme goodness he provides the good

---

have spent a thousand] years, and ten thousands..."
[115] Keph. 124,28–29, "Thus when the matter that is in them is oppressed . . . and
robbed . . ." Cf. PS IV.136 (MacDermot pp. 354–355), "But the base of the moon
was of the type of a boat, and a male dragon and a female dragon steered it, while
two white bulls drew it. And the likeness of a child was at the back of the moon,
and guided the dragons as they stole the light of the archons from them."
[116] Cf. Tit. Bost. Man. 1.23; 30.
[117] Cf. Tit. Bost. Man. 1.30
[118] Rom. 2:6

man, who has grown weary in well-doing, with good, and metes out justice to the evildoer. (9) And it has been shown in every way that Mani's talk gradually turns men's hearts to the opposites [of his teachings].

25,1   But next I appropriately insert Mani's doctrine word for word as Turbo himself revealed it, one of Mani's disciples whom I mentioned earlier, taking this from Archelaus' arguments against Mani in the debate with him. (2) When the bishop Archelaus, and Marcellus, questioned Turbo about Mani's teaching, Turbo replied in the words I quote from the book. They are as follows:[119]

25,3   *The beginning of Mani's godless teachings*

If you would like to learn the creed of Mani, hear it from me in a concise form. Mani believes in two gods, unbegotten, self-engendering, eternal, and each other's opposites. And he teaches that one is good and the other evil, and calls the one Light, and the other, Darkness.[120] The soul in human beings is part of the light, but the body is part of the darkness and the creature of matter.[121]

25,4   *Now < Mani > says that there has been a mixture or confusion of these in the following way—likening the two < gods > to the following illustration: Suppose two kings were at war with each other, and they had been enemies from the first, and each had his respective territory. But in the battle the darkness sallied forth from its territory and assailed the light. (5) Now when the good Father found the darkness had invaded his land he emitted a power from himself called Mother of life,[123] and she emitted First Man < and clothed him* > with the five elements.[124] These are wind, light, water, fire and † matter.[125] (6) Putting these on as battle gear, he went below and did battle with the darkness.[126] But as they fought against*

---

[119] 25,3–31,8 are quoted from Act. Arch. 7.13.

[120] Keph. 286,127–30, "[the] two essences which are primordial . . . light and darkness, good and evil, [life and] death . . ."

[121] Cf. Henning, "Ein Manichäischer kosmogonischer Hymnus," NGWG 1032, pp. 251–253, ". . . matter is distributed which (in) itself is seven she-demons. The first one is the skin . . . (. . . she, i.e., Greed, Az) took, and she made this carrion, the microcosm, in order to be made joyful through it . . ."

[122] Keph. 4,1–2, "the darkness made war on the light, because it desired to rule over an essence that was not its own." In the NHL, cf. Tri. Trac. 84,6–17.

[123] Keph. 71,19–20, "at the time when the Mother of Life was called forth from the Father of Greatness"

[124] Keph. 153,23–24, "[At] the time when the First Man put on the elements and (stood firm) against the first enmity that originated in the darkness"

[125] "Matter" is never a Manichaean element; Epiphanius appears to misunderstand Act. Arch. 82.17; 83.18; 23. The fifth Manichaean element is either air or ether.

[126] This key episode in the Manichaean story is continually alluded to in

him the archons of the darkness ate part of his armor,[127] *that is, the soul.*

25,7 *Then First Man was dreadfully hard pressed there below by the darkness, and if the Father had not heard his prayer*[128] *and sent another power he had emitted, called Living Spirit, and if Living Spirit had not descended and given First Man his right hand and drawn him out of the darkness,*[129] *First Man might well have been captured long ago.*

25,8 *Thereafter First Man abandoned the soul below. And when Manichaeans meet they give each other their right hands*[130] *for this reason, as a sign that they have been saved from the darkness. For Mani says that all the sects are in the darkness. Then Living Spirit created the world;*[131] *and he himself descended clothed with three other powers, brought the archons up and crucified them*[132] *in the firmament, which is their body, the sphere.*

26,1 *Then in turn, Living Spirit created the luminaries, which are remnants of the soul,*[133] *and made them circle the firmament. And he created the earth in its turn, in eight forms.*[134] *But beneath it < is* > the Porter, who bears < it on his shoulders* >; and whenever he gets tired of bearing it he shivers, becoming the cause of an earthquake out of its time. (2) This is why the good Father sent his Son from < his > bosom to the heart of the earth and its lowest depths, to give the Porter his due punishment.*[135] *For*

Manichaean literature. Treatments at length are found, among others, at Keph. 38,8–40,16; 271,30–273,9.

[127] Cf. Asmussen p. 121 (Fragments M 1001, M 1012, M 1015, Middle Persian; Ed. W. Sundermann, lines 113–133), "Thus [it was] that God, [the First] Man, appeared. And again, to all these powers it (i.e., the Light) was like a sweet meal before hungry ones; When it stands before them, they all devour it;"

[128] Cf. Asmussen p. 122 (M 21, Parthian: *MM* III: 890–891), "The God Ormizd prayed to his mother, and his mother prayed to the righteous God: 'Send a helper to my son, for he has carried out your will, and he has come into oppression.'" This is comparable to the prayer of the Logos at Tri. Trac. 81,26–82,14, and of Sophia in other Valentinian documents.

[129] Keph. 39,19–21, "The second right hand is the one that Living Spirit gave to First Man after drawing him from the contest . . ." At NHL Gosp. Tr. 30,14–23, "the Spirit" gives his right hand to (Adam ?).

[130] This, and similar gestures, are discussed at length in Chapter 9 of the Kephalaia, Keph. 38,1–41,34.

[131] Cf. Asmussen pp. 122–123 (T III 260e II= M 7984 II, Middle Persian: *MM* I 177–181) for a lengthy account of the creation by Living Spirit. There are frequent references to this in the Kephalaia.

[132] Keph. 26,28–31, "This is the second night . . . which was brought up by Living Spirit and put in the [mixed world] below and above;" 27,10–12, ". . . the second night which the Living Spirit has crucified in the [mixed world] below and above"

[133] The luminaries are made from the remains of the soul only at Alex. Lycop. 19 and Bar Khouni in Pognon p. 189. But note Keph. 269,21–23, "The second image (in man) is the remnant and remainder of the new man, the psychic image which is bound in the flesh."

[134] Keph. 118,23–25, "The second part is the eight earths beneath, the four that are mixed and the four places of darkness."

[135] At Keph. 9,6–11 Jesus comes to the Porter's aid: "Again, since the earth

whenever there is an earthquake he is either trembling from fatigue or shifting the earth to his other shoulder.

26,3   *Next, matter too created growing things from herself. And since they were being stolen by certain archons, she called all the chief archons, took power from each,*[136] *made man as we know him in First Man's image,*[137] *and bound the soul in him.*[138] *This is the reason for the mixture.*

26,4   *But when Living Father saw the soul squeezed into the body, in his mercy and compassion he sent his beloved Son for the soul's salvation— for he sent him for this reason and because of the Porter.*[139] *(5) And when the Son arrived he changed his appearance into a man's and appeared to men as a man, though he was not one; and people supposed that he had been begotten [like a man].*[140] *(6) And when he came he made the handiwork intended for the salvation of souls,*[141] *and a device with twelve water jars which is turned by the sphere and draws up the souls of the dying. And the greater luminary takes these with its rays, cleanses them and transfers them to the moon, and this is how what we call the disk*

---

beneath the porter escaped the making fast . . . for this reason Jesus came below, putting on Eve until he arrived at that place. He ordered and fastened the fastenings that were below, and returned and ascended to his rest." At NHL Orig. Wld. 102,25–103,2 Pistis sends her breath to bind the "trouble-maker" below, who is making the heavens shake.

[136] Klimkeit p. 41 (*Verses from a hymn on the Third Messenger and the Archons*, Parthian) "Filth and dross flow from (the Demon of Wrath) to the earth. They clothe themselves in manifold forms and are reborn in many fruits." Cf. NHL Orig. Wld. 114,24–30, "And at that time, the prime parent then rendered an opinion concerning man to those who were with him. Then each of them cast his sperm into the midst of the navel of the earth. Since that day, the seven rulers have fashioned man . . ."

[137] At Keph. 138,6–14 Matter sees the image of the third Messenger (not of First Man), and then enters the tree of life and becomes its fruit. The archons eat the fruit and then make man.

[138] Keph. 95,15–17, "But his [soul] [he] took from the five splendid gods [and bound] it in the five members of the body. He bound the mind . . ."

[139] Keph. 267,28–268,1, "Jesus has not come and saved the world only on man's account . . . He has come and appeared on earth . . . But after he was through working outside, in the great cosmos, he came . . ." and 1) revealed himself to Adam and Eve; 2) dispatched apostles in every generation to preach the Manichaean message of salvation.

[140] Cf. Asmussen p. 103 (M 24 R 4–8=M 812 V 1–4 Parthian: W. B. Henning, "Brāhman" TPS 1944, p. 112) "Grasp, all believers, the truth of Christ, learn and wholly understand his secret: He changed his form and appearance;" Man. Hom. 11,5–6, "[Jesus] was [sent] to it; he came and took the form (?) of a body . . . ;" Man. Ps. 191,4–11, "Amen, I was seized; Amen again, I was not seized. Amen, I was judged; Amen again, I was not judged . . . I mocked the world, they could not mock me."

[141] Keph. 61,22–24, "until he went and descended into the plasma (!) of the flesh, and set up the earths and all plants."

of the moon gets full—for Mani says that the two luminaries are ships, or ferry-boats.[142]

26,7   Then, if the moon is filled [with souls], it ferries them across to the east wind, and thus gets its load dislodged and is lightened, and begins to wane.[143] And it fills the ferry-boat again, and again discharges its cargo of the souls which are drawn up by the water jars, until it has saved its part of the soul. For Mani says that all soul, and every living and moving thing, partake of the essence of the good Father.

26,8   When the moon has delivered her load of souls to the aeons of the Father, they remain in the pillar of glory, which is called the perfect air.[144] But this air is a pillar of light, since it is full of souls being purified. This is the reason the souls are saved.

27,1   But this, in turn, is the reason why people die.[145] A lovely, beautifully dressed Virgin with a very winning manner is attempting to rob the archons who have been brought up by Living Spirit and crucified in the firmament. She appears as a lovely women to the males and as a handsome, desirable youth to the females.[146] (2) And when the archons see her with all her adornment they go mad with love; and because they cannot catch her[147] they become frightfully hot, and their minds are ravished with desire.[148] (3) Now when they run after her the Virgin disappears. Then

---

[142] Man. Ps. 10,30–11,2, "The sun and the moon he founded, he set them on high, to purify the soul. Daily they take up the refined part to the height, but the dregs however they erase ... they convey it above and below;" Keph. 159,25–26, "(The sun) removes the darkness with its light and sweeps it away." At NHL Treat. Res. 45,9–46,2 the departed "are drawn to heaven by him like beams of the sun;" this constitutes the "spiritual resurrection." See also note 65.

[143] Keph. 108,20–22, "through the manner of the garment of the wind, in which he appeared, [Living Spirit] has swept out and scraped out all the shadows of destruction and dirt, and poured it down on the earth."

[144] The pillar of glory is regularly called the "perfect man," (ἀνήρ) not the "perfect air (ἀήρ)." However, in Manichaean poetry the ideas approach one another, cf. Man. Ps. 83,25–27, "Hail, Perfect Man, holy path that draws to the height, clear air, mooring-harbor of all that believe in him."

[145] The Virgin of Light is often associated with death, cf. Man. Ps. 84,30–32, "Draw not the veil of thy secrets until I see the beauty of the joyous image of my Mother, the holy Maiden, who will ferry me until she brings me to my city." At Keph. 244,9–13 and regularly in Pistis Sophia, the Virgin of Light is a judge and assessor of departed souls.

[146] Klimkeit p. 68 (*A hymn to the Third Messenger*, Parthian) "The mighty powers, the giants eager for battle, Withdraw light from all creatures. In two bright forms they seduce the demons of wrath." For a longer version see Theodore bar Khouni, (Pognon p. 190).

[147] Cf. NHL Apocry. John. 19,18–20,5; Nat. Arc. 87,33–88,15; Orig. Wld. 115,3–116,8.

[148] Cf. Asmusssen p. 132 (M 741 Mary Boyce, "Sadwēs and Pēsūs," BSOAS, Vol. 13, No. 4 (1951); pp. 911–913) "Bright Sadwēs shows her form to the Demon of Wrath; by her own (nature) she seduces him. He thinks she is the essence (of light). He sows ... he groans when he no longer sees the form.

the chief archon emits the clouds to darken the world in his anger; and if he is extremely vexed he perspires and is out of breath, like a man. But his sweat is the rain.[149]

27,4 *At the same time, if the archon of destruction*[150] *is robbed by the Virgin, he sheds pestilence on the whole world to slay human beings.*[151] *For this body of ours may be called a < miniature* > world which answers to < this > great world,*[152] *and all people have roots below which are fastened to the realms on high.*[153] *Thus, when the archon is robbed by the Virgin, he begins to cut men's roots. (5) And when their roots are cut a pestilence sets in and they die. But if he shakes the heavens by [tugging at] the cord of their root, the result is an earthquake, for the Porter is moved at the same time. This is the reason for death.*

28,1 *But I shall also tell you how the soul is reincarnate in other bodies.*[154] *First a little of it is purified, and then it is put into the body of a dog or camel, or another animal. But if a soul has committed murder, it is put into the bodies of lepers.*[155] *If it is found to have reaped grain, it is put into stammerers. (These are the names of the soul: reason, mind, intelligence, thought, understanding.)*[156]

28,2 *But reapers, who reap grain, are like the archons who were in the darkness*[157] *at the beginning, when they ate some of First Man's armor. Thus they must be reembodied in grass, beans, barley, wheat or vegetables,*[158] *so that < they too > may be reaped and cut down. (3) Again, if someone*

Light is born in the sphere; she gives it to the higher Powers. The dirt and dross flows from him to the earth. It clothes itself in all phenomena, and is reborn in many fruits. The Dark Demon of Wrath is ashamed, for he is distraught and had become naked. He had not attained to the higher, and had been bereft of what he had achieved."

[149] Cf. Tit. Bost. Man. 2.32. At Keph. 240,19–243,8, clouds are formed in the image of the Virgin of Light. The archons steal power from them and the angels pursue the archons; this is the cause of lightning. And see the note preceding.

[150] Keph. 153,29, "archon of death;" 153,34, "warrior of destruction"

[151] Keph. 169,5–8, "but when the robbery is on the side of Gemini, Libra and Aquarius, there is loss and diminution everywhere in the seal (?) of mankind."

[152] Keph. 169,29–170,1, "this whole world above and below answers to the form of the human body, while the fashion of this body of flesh answers to the form of the cosmos."

[153] Keph. 124,15–17, "but the root of man . . . is not in the whole earth, but only in this southern world."

[154] Cf. Keph. 223,29–31; 225,8–11; 27–28; 249,32–250,3 et al.

[155] Cf. Tit. Bost. Man. 2.35.

[156] These are regularly called the "limbs" of the soul; cf. Keph. 76,16–25.

[157] Keph. 26,13, "the whole band of archons, which is in the world of darkness"

[158] Henning, "Gebet- und Beichtbuch," APAW 1936, No. 10, pp. 32–33, "Wenn (ich zulasse, das) . . . (er) die fünf pflänzlichen Geschöpfe oder die fünf fleischlichen Geschöpfe, seien sie feucht oder trocken, entzweitritt oder zerstückelt, verletzt oder zerreisst . . ."

eats bread[159] he must become bread himself and be eaten. If one kills a bird, < he too > will be a bird. If one kills a mouse, he will also be a mouse[160] (4) And again, if one is rich in this world, he must be reembodied in a poor man when he leaves his tabernacle, so that he may go begging, and after this go away to eternal punishment.[161]

28,5 Since this body belongs to the archons and matter, whoever plants a persea must pass through many bodies until that persea is planted. But if anyone builds a house,[162] bits of him will be put into all the kinds of bodies there are. Whoever bathes[163] plants his soul in the water. (6) And whoever does not give his alms to the elect will be punished in the hells and reincarnate in the bodies of catechumens until he gives many alms. And for this reason they offer the elect whatever food is their choicest.[164]

28,7 And when they are about to eat bread they pray first, and tell the bread, "I neither reaped you, nor ground you, nor pounded you, nor put you into an oven; someone else did these things, and brought you to me. I eat without guilt." And whenever [an electus] says this for himself, he tells the catechumen, "I have prayed for you," and the catechumen withdraws.[165] (8) For as I told you a moment ago that whoever reaps will be reaped, so whoever throws wheat into a thresher will be thrown in himself— or if he kneads dough he will be kneaded, or if he bakes bread he will be baked. And for this reason they are forbidden to do work.[166]

---

[159] At CM 97,11–17 Mani says that Elxai, the founder of the "baptists," at the bidding of the bread itself, forbade his followers to bake bread.

[160] Klimkeit p. 169 (*Confessional Text for the Elect* Sogdian with Persian citations) "If (I should have allowed) the weight of my body, the cruel [self . . .] to beat or hurt (that Light) . . . by injuring . . . the five (types of) fleshly beings . . . "

[161] Keph. 116,22–25, "Before the dregs and sediment (?) of the darkness were swept out of creation, [Hells] were established for them to be the receptacle of the dregs until the dissolution of the world."

[162] Klimkeit, p. 169 (*Confessional Text for the Elect*, Sogdian with Persian citations) "If (I should have allowed) the weight of my body, the cruel [self] to bear or hurt that light . . . by digging or shoveling, building or constructing a wall in the dry cracked, injured, oppressed and trodden earth . . ."

[163] At CM 25,8 Mani says that a face appeared in the water to Elxai, the founder of the "baptists," and forbade him to bathe.

[164] Keph. 166,13–16, "But whoever loves (the elect) and deals with them through his alms, will live and be victorious with them and will be delivered from this dark world"

[165] Cf. Asmussen p. 50 (T II E = 6020 I, Parthian: Henning, "A Grain of Mustard," *Annali, Ist. Or. Napoli* Sc. 2 Line 6 (1965) pp. 29–30), "(The elect) himself will be saved, he will also save him who gave the alms-food, and it (i.e., the Living Soul, self) will reach the dome of the gods unharmed." Cyr. Cat. 6.32 calls this prayer a curse on the catechumens, cf. Tit. Bost. Man. 2.32.

[166] CM 93,2–11, "See how the disciples of the Savior . . . did not work in the tillage and husbandry of the soil . . ."

28,9   *And again, < they say that > there are other worlds, since the luminaries set from this world †and rise in those.*[167] *And whoever walks on the ground injures the earth*[168]—*and whoever moves his hand injures the air, because the air is the soul of men, animals, birds, fish, reptiles and everything in the world. < For > I have told you that this body does not belong to God but to matter, and that it is darkness and must itself be made dark.*[169]

29,1   *But as to Paradise, which is a name for the world : Its plants are lusts and other impostures which destroy men's reasonings. But that plant in Paradise through which the good is recognized is Jesus,*[170] *< and > the knowledge of him in the world.*[171] *One who takes [its fruit] can distinguish good from evil. (2) The world itself, however, is not God's ; it was made from a part of matter, and all things are therefore destroyed.*[172]

The thing the archons stole from First Man is the very thing that fills the moon, and is cleaned out of the world every day. (3) And if the soul departs without knowing the truth, it is given to the demons to subdue in the hells of fire.[173] *And after its punishment it is put into < other > bodies to be subdued, and so it is thrown into the great fire until the consummation.*[174]

30,1   *Now this is what he says about your prophets. There are spirits*

---

[167] Holl: καὶ ἐκείνοις ἀνατελλόντων; MSS: ἐξ ὧν ἀνατέλλουσι

[168] Klimkeit p. 169 (Confessional text for the elect, Sogdian with Persian citations) "If (I should have allowed) the weight of my body, the cruel [self . . .] to beat or hurt that Light while walking or riding, ascending or descending, (walking) quickly or slowly . . ."

[169] Man. Hom. 6,1–8, "I shall (judge?) my body and pronounce its condemnation, 'Cursed art thou, O [body] . . . Thy lust is condemned in thee . . . Thy demons shall enter . . . Thou hast tormented me . . . Thou hast caused [me] to weep . . . year after year I show thee no reverence . . . thou hast brought them upon me. Cursed art thou . . . cursed is he that made thee."

[170] Perhaps cf. Keph. 53,26–28, "Afterwards he planted his good plantings, the tree of life which bears good fruit. So it is with the likeness of the coming of Jesus the Splendor."

[171] Cf. CM 84,9–16, "the purity which has been spoken of is the purity that comes by knowledge, the distinction of light from darkness, death from life, and the living waters from the astonied," and many other Manichaean praises of knowledge.

[172] Man. Hom. 39,22–27, "Then, after Jesus, comes the destruction of the world . . . the flesh shall vanish altogether and be uprooted from the world. If the . . . flesh is destroyed and perishes and . . . [the All] is cleaned up. The world . . . and it shall remain waste . . ."

[173] Cf. Fihrist al-'Ulūm (Flügel, p. 101) "wenn aber dem sündigen Menschen...der Tod erscheint, so nahen sich ihm die Teufel, packen und quälen ihn . . . Dann irrt er in der Welt unaufhörlich umher von Peinigungen heimgesucht bis zu der Zeit, wo dieser Zustand aufhört und er mit der Welt in die Hölle geworfen wird."

[174] Keph. 29,12–14, "Blessed is anyone who is perfect in his works, that, at his end, [he may escape] the great fire which is prepared for [the world] at the end of time."

*of impiety or iniquity which belong to the darkness that arose at the beginning,
and because the prophets were deceived by these they did not tell < the
truth >. For < that > archon has blinded their minds.*[175] (2) *And anyone
who follows their words will die forever, imprisoned in the clod [of earth],
because he did not learn the Paraclete's knowledge.*[176]

30,3   *Mani has commanded only his elect, of whom there are no more
than seven,*[177] *"When you finish eating, pray and put oil on your heads
which has been exorcized with many names, as a support for this faith."
The names have not been revealed to me; only the seven employ them.* (4)
*And again, < he says > that the name of Sabaoth, which is revered and
of great importance among you, is human in nature and a father of lust.
And so, he says, the foolish worship lust, thinking it is God.*

30,5   *This is what he says about the creation of Adam. The person
who said, "Come, and let us make man in our image and after our
likeness"*[178]—*that is, "in accordance with the form which we have seen"—
is the archon who told the other archons, "Give me the light which we have
taken and let us make a man in the form of us archons < and > the form
we have seen, which is First Man."*[179]

And so they created the man. (6) *But they likewise created Eve and
gave her some of their lust for Adam's deception. And the fashioning of
the world from the archons' handiwork was done through Adam and Eve.*

31,1   *God has nothing to do with the world itself and takes no pleasure
in it, because it was stolen from him by the archons at the beginning and
became a burden to him.*[180] *This is why he sends emissaries and steals his
soul from them (i.e., the archons) every day through these luminaries, the
sun and the moon, by which the whole world, and all creation, is taken
away.* (2) *Mani says that the god who spoke with Moses, and with the
Jews and their priests, is the archon of darkness; thus Christians, Jews
and pagans are one and the same,*[181] *since they believe in the same god.*

---

[175] At Aug. C. Faust. 16.6 Faustus says, "Moses' tradition is so dissimilar to
Christ's, and so very different, that if the Jews believed one of them they must
certainly repudiate the other." In contrast, both CM 62,9–63,1 and Man. Hom.
75,22 appear to praise the prophets.

[176] Keph. 233,25–27, "one (portion of his sins will be forgiven him) because
he knows the knowledge and has distinguished light from darkness . . ."

[177] This might be a misunderstanding of the Greek version of Act. Arch. 63.5,
where the Latin reads, "nomina quaedam invocare coepit quae nobis Turbo
dixit, solos septem electos didicisse," which means that only seven of the elect
knew the names.

[178] Gen. 1:26

[179] In the Kephalaia the archons usually make man, in the likeness of Third
Messenger. Cf. Keph. 133,5–134,7; 135,14–26; 157,7–9; 158,3–5.

[180] Evodius De Fide Contra Mani 13: "Mani's God . . . is in mourning after
losing a part of himself."

[181] At Aug. C. Faust. 18.5 Faustus argues that on Christian premises, to become
a Christian one must be a Jew. Cf. 1.2; 16.10 and Ut. Cred. 10.14.

(3) *For as that god is not the God of truth, he deceives them with his lusts. Therefore all who hope in that god, the god who spoke with Moses and the prophets, must be imprisoned with him, since they have not hoped in the God of truth. For that god spoke with them in accordance with his lusts.*

31,4   *After all this he finally says, as he himself has written,*[182] *When the † elder*[183] *makes his image*[184] *manifest, the Porter will drop the earth*[185] *outside. Then the great fire will be let loose and consume the whole world.* (5) *Next he will drop the clod < that is interposed > between [the world and] the new aeon, so that all the souls of sinners may be imprisoned forever. These events will take place when the image arrives.*

31,6   *But all the emanations—Jesus, who is in the smaller ship, Mother of Life, the twelve steersmen, the Virgin of Light, the third Elder, who is in the larger ship, Living Spirit, the wall of the great fire,*[186] *the walls*[187] *of the wind, the air, the water, and the living fire within—have their dwellings < on high* > near the lesser luminary, until the fire destroys the whole world over a period of years whose length I do not know.*[188] (7) *And after this there will be a restoration of the two natures, and the archons will occupy their own realms below, while the Father will occupy the realms above, and have received his own back.*[189]

31,8   *Mani imparted this entire teaching to his three disciples and told each of them to make his way to his own area : Addas was assigned the*

---

[182] Neither the identity of the document alluded to, nor the extent of the quotation, is clear.

[183] This is Third Messenger, cf. 31,6. The Greek should be πρεσβεύτης rather than πρεσβύτης; the error is presumed to have originated in the archetype, and persists throughout Sect 66.

[184] Keph. 54,12–19 "until the time of the end, when he shall waken and arise in the great fire, and shall gather his own soul and form himself into the last image . . . he gathers the life and light which is in all things, and builds it on his body."

[185] Fihrist al-'Ulūm (Flügel, *Mani*, p. 90), "während dieses geschieht, erhebt sich der Engel, dem das Tragen der Erden obliegt, und der andere Engel steht von dem Nachsichziehen der Himmel ab, so dass sich das Höchste mit dem Untersten vermischt und es lodert ein Feuer auf und frisst sich fort in diesen wirren Dingen, und hört nicht eher zu brennen, bis das, was sich in ihnen noch vom Licht befindet, aufgelöst ist."

[186] Keph. 108,25–29, "By his splendor, by his might, he has poured the fire of the darkness out from all the archons, cast it on this earth, and again, swept if off the earth and bound in the vehicle that encompasses the whole world, and so is called the wall of the great fire."

[187] Le Coq, Türk. Man. II, APAW 1904, pp. 38–39, "Fahrzeuge zwei, Jesus der Sonne . . . mit fünf Mauern, einer ätherischen, windigen, leuchtenden, wassrigen und einer feurigen . . ."

[188] At Müller, Handschriftliche Reste aus Turfan II, APAW 1904, p. 19, the number of years is given as 1468. So in the Fihrist al-'Ulūm Flügel p. 90.

[189] More typical is Keph. 52,17–19, "The light goes to its own land but the darkness remains in bonds and chains forever."

east, Syria fell to Thomas, but the other, Hermeias, journeyed to Egypt. And they are there to this day for the purpose of establishing the teaching of this religion.

32,1   These are the passages I have quoted from the book by Archelaus that I mentioned, and his is how Mani organiz< ed > his school of tares' seed, by belching out the tares of his teaching. (2) But everyone must see how much one could offer to counter an equal amount of slander from this mime. Even though the counter-arguments are not polished, the mere knowledge that this is what they believe will be enough to put them to shame, for their tenets are shaky and have no cogency. (3) For Mani overturns his earlier statements with his later ones, and says things later that are different from what he has said earlier. He sometimes would have it that the world is God's creation, but sometimes that it comes from the archons and that God bears no responsibility for it, but that it is slated to perish. And sometimes he says that the firmament is the archons' hides, but sometimes that they are crucified up above in the celestial sphere— < and > that they chase people, and make clouds, and get excited and wild at the sight of the virgin and the handsomeness of the youth.

33,1   What a disgrace! What could be worse, more disgusting, and more shameful than for the Spirit of truth to change himself into a female, though sometimes appearing to the archons in male form? It is disgraceful for a man to get drunk and act and look like a woman. But for women to act like men and dress in men's clothes is the most disgraceful of all. (2) And if this spirit is the Spirit of virtue, and divine, why will it not have been insulted rather [than glorified] by Mani, its creator? And how can the archons go wild after having been skinned? Tell me that, Mister! How were they skinned after being crucified? And if they had indeed been crucified, how can they run after the power when it disappears?

33,3   Who can put up with the blasphemer, with his declaration that we draw our nourishment from the archons' sweat, and that the rain pours down on us from their dirty fluids? How can Mani drink himself—since he, along with his disciples, draws his water from the rain? What else can he be but absurd, to be so mastered by bodily needs that he drinks sweat?

33,4   There are various degrees of sin, and the unintentional sinner will not be punished as severely as the one who commits the sin deliberately. (5) Even if this were true—and perish that thought, it's the nut's imagination! [But if it were true], then people who draw and drink sweat and dirty fluids without knowing it < are > excusable, and more entitled to mercy than someone who succumbs to his own frailty and is moved, with full knowledge, to draw and drink water, for no good reason, from the archon's drinks and other bodily functions.

34,1 And there are many ways in which he has deceived his followers with his lying mouth. Which of his notions is not absurd? The idea that seeds of herbs, produce and pulse are souls! (2) To venture < a > joke, to refute him in terms of his own mythology I may say that if the seeds of lentils, beans, chick-peas and the rest are souls, but the soul of a bull is the same, then, on his premises, people who eat meat have more to their credit than ascetics do. (3) For as his rigmarole goes, he is afraid that if he eats living things—(4) animals and the rest—he will become like them. < But > [the truth is] the opposite! Sure, in his worthless quibble if fifty, or even a hundred men assemble and they all dine on one bull, < they are all guilty of murder together* >. But still, we must say in refutation that the fifty, or the hundred, become guilty [of the murder] of one soul, while someone who eats the grains of seeds will be guilty of ingesting thirty or forty souls at one gulp! And all his teachings are worthless and absurd.

35,1 For to everyone whose mind < stands fast > in the Lord, the signs of the truth must surely be apparent from the true teaching itself; as a revelation of men's salvation, nothing is more reliable than the Savior. (2) This barbarian who has come to us from Persia and has the mind of a slave—being a slave in body never bothered him—says that all souls are alike and that the one soul is in all: people, domestic animals, wild beasts, birds, reptiles, creatures that fly and swim, bugs and the seeds of produce, trees and all other visible things. (3) But our Lord didn't tell us this. When he came to save human beings, did he also see to the cure of cattle, and < initiate* > the healing and resurrection of dead beasts by gathering < their bones* >? He neither described this nor taught this to us, (4) far from it, but he knew about saving human souls, as he said concisely in the riddle, "I am not come but for the lost sheep,"[190] meaning all humankind.

35,5 And what does scripture say? "He healed all whom they brought unto him, that were lunatick and were taken with diverse diseases."[191] They brought him the blind, the deaf, the lame, the palsied, the maimed, and he extended his benefaction and healing to all of them; but scripture nowhere says that they brought him animals.

---

[190] Cf. Matt. 15:24.
[191] Matt. 4:24

35,6 Then again, "He came to the parts of Gergestha,"[192] as
Mark says—or, "in the coasts of the Gergesenes," as Luke says;[193]
or "of the Gadarenes," as in Matthew,[194] or "of the Gergesenes"
as some copies [of Matthew] have it.[195] (The spot was in between
the three territories.) (7) "And behold two possessed with devils,
exceeding fierce, coming out of the tombs, and they cried out,
saying, Let us alone, what have we to do with thee, Jesus thou Son
of God, that thou hast come before the time to torment us? We
know thee who thou art, the holy one of God. And there was an
herd of swine there feeding and the devils besought him saying,
If thou cast us out of the men, send us into the swine. And they
ran violently into the sea and perished in the waters. And they
that kept them fled and told it in the city."[196]

35,8 And in Matthew we are told of two possessed, but it simply
mentions swine and does not give the number. (9) But Mark even
reported the exact number of the swine and said, "He came unto
the parts of Gergestha, and there met him one possessed of a devil,
and he had been bound with iron chains and plucked the chains
asunder, and he had his dwelling among the tombs and cried out,
Let us alone, what have we to do with thee, Jesus thou Son of God?
Thou hast come before the time to torment us. And Jesus asked
him, What is thy name? And he said, Legion, for many devils had
entered into him. And they besought him not to be sent out of
the country, but to enter into the swine. For there was there an
herd of swine feeding, and he gave them leave to enter into the
swine. And the herd ran violently down a steep place into the sea
(for they were about two thousand) and were choked in the sea.
And they that fed the swine fled, and told it in the city."[197]

35,10 Did the divine Word who had become man for us ask
in ignorance, and not know the demon's name before he asked?
No, it is the Godhead's way to make the causes of each event clear
through the words of people who are questioned. (11) And here
too, to show the frightfulness and the great number of the demons, he asks the question, so that the marvelous deed will be
made known out of their own mouths. "And the devils besought
him saying, Send us not into the abyss, but give us leave to enter
into the swine. And he gave them leave. And the devils went out

---

[192] Cf. Mark 5:1, but this reading is found only in Epiphanius and Theophylact.
[193] Luke 8:26
[194] Matt. 8:28
[195] Matt. 8:28 as read in ℵ[c], L, W, X, et al.
[196] Matt. 8:28–33
[197] Mark 5:2–14

and entered into the swine, and the herd ran violently down a steep place into the sea, and perished in the waters."[198]

36,1 What great kindness on God's part! How he confounds falsehood but shows his servants the truth, through his deeds, his words, and all of his care! For he has shown through a deed that it is not the same soul in people, cattle and beasts. (2) If the soul were the same, why did he not refrain from destroying two thousand souls at once when his aim was to purify one person or save one soul, the demoniac's? If it were the same, why did he purify the one man or < save > the one soul, but permit the demons to enter the other bodies, or indeed, the other souls?

36,3 Are the deeds of the light not plain to see? Are these words not "performed in the light?"[199] Is the truth's face not radiant? Are "all things" not "plain to them that understand, and right for them that find knowledge?"[200] Who can hear and look into these things without convicting Mani of stitching things together that he should not have, to divert men's minds from what is real?

36,4 But the offenders < try to evade the truth* > in their turn. I have even heard one argue like this: I had used this argument with him, and the oaf twisted and turned and thought he might get somewhere against God's truth. He offered an absurd defense, † dared[201] to make it out that the truth < agrees > with falsehood, and said, "But he had reserved death for the swine; their souls escaped from their bodies and were saved!"

37,1 The stupidity of the people who can't see, and who blind their minds, and don't even listen to what they say themselves! (2) If he had any idea that the deliverance of souls from the body is salvation, the Savior should have killed the demoniac for the salvation of the soul by its deliverance from a human body. He must have loved the souls in the swine more than the man's soul! (3) Why didn't he let the man plunge into the sea with the pigs and die too, so as to purify and save all of the souls, the man's and the pigs'?

37,4 But we have seen nothing of the kind. The Savior calls Lazarus from the tomb on the fourth day following his death, raises him and restores him to the world, and not to do him a disservice or cause him harm. The scripture says, "Jesus *loved*

---

[198] Mark 5:12–13
[199] Cf. John 3:21.
[200] Prov. 8:9
[201] Holl: ἐτόλμησεν; MSS: ἐνόμισε, "expected to"

Lazarus."[202] (5) If flesh is evil, why did Jesus make the man he loved return to the flesh? Why didn't he leave him alone instead, once he had died and been delivered from the body?

37,6   And no one should suppose that Lazarus immediately died again. The holy Gospel makes it clear that Jesus reclined at table and Lazarus reclined with him. Besides, I have found traditions which say that Lazarus was thirty years old when he was raised. (7) But he lived another thirty years after < the Lord > raised him and then departed to the Lord. He lay down and fell asleep with a good name, and like all the rest < awaits* > the hour of the resurrection—when, as he promised, the Only-begotten will restore the body to the soul and the soul to the body and "reward every man according to that he hath done, whether it be good or bad."[203]

38–39,1[204]   If there were no resurrection of bodies, how could there be "gnashing of teeth?"[205] And don't anyone make that half-witted remark again, "Teeth are made for us to chew with; what food will we eat after the resurrection of the dead?" (2) If Jesus ate again after his resurrection, and [took] "a piece of a broiled fish and an honeycomb,"[206] and lived with his disciples for forty days, will there be no food? (3) And as to food, it is plain that "Blessed is he who shall eat bread in the kingdom of heaven."[207] And it is the Lord's own promise that "Ye shall be seated at my Father's table eating and drinking."[208] (4) And what this eating and drinking is he alone knows, for "Eye hath not seen nor ear heard, neither have entered into the heart of man, the things which God hath prepared for them that love him."[209]

38–39,5   But now that we have reached this point in our description of the differences between souls, < we have explained* > —and on the authority of the truth itself and its perfect Example —that a man's soul is one thing, and a beast's is another. And Christ did not come to save the soul of the beast but the soul of the man, since beasts are not judged. (6) For human beings inherit the kingdom of heaven, and human beings are judged. "These

---

[202] John 11:5
[203] 2 Cor. 5:10
[204] Numbered as in Holl
[205] Matt. 8:12
[206] Luke 24:42
[207] Luke 14:15
[208] Luke 22:30
[209] 1 Cor. 2:9

shall go away into everlasting judgment and these to life eternal,"[210] says the Only-begotten.

40,1   And what do the people who hunt for problems accomplish? Whenever they find them, and do not grasp the interpretation of the text, they distress themselves by thinking of contradictions instead of looking for things that are of use to them. Matthew says that there were two demoniacs, but Luke mentions one.

40,2   And indeed, < besides this > one evangelist says that the thieves who were crucified with Jesus reviled him; but the other disagrees, and < not > only shows that both did not revile him, but presents the defense of the one. (3) For "He rebuked the other and said, Dost not thou fear God seeing that we are in the same condemnation? But this holy man hath done nothing < amiss >." And he exclaimed besides, "Jesus, remember me when thou comest into thy kingdom." And the Savior told him, "Verily I say unto thee, today shalt thou be with me in Paradise."[211]

40,4   This makes it appear that there is contradiction in the scripture. But everything is straightforward. (5) Even though there are two demoniacs in Matthew the same ones are in Luke. Luke does not mention the two, but [only] the one, because it is the scripture's way to give the causes of events. (6) There were two men healed of demon possession, but one persevered in the faith while the other came to grief. And so, because of his perseverance in the faith, he followed Jesus "whithersoever he went,"[212] as the Gospel says. This is why Luke omitted the one thief and mentioned the one who is the kingdom of heaven. And nothing can be contrary to the attainment of the truth.

41,1   But the Gospel now gives another reason, one that resembles this instance, [for speaking of more than one person] as though of one. The Lord had cleansed ten lepers and the nine had gone away without giving glory to God. But the one had turned back and remained—the one the Lord commended, as he said, "Ten lepers were cleansed. Why hath not one of them returned to give glory to God save only this stranger?"[213] (2) And you see that, because of this man's perceptiveness and his demonstration of gratitude, the Gospel mentions the one in place of the ten. It is a comparable case, since the same evangelist spoke of the thieves.

41,3   For we are accustomed to speak of singulars in the plural,

---

[210] Matt. 25:46
[211] Luke 23:40–43
[212] Cf. Luke 8:38; 9:57.
[213] Luke 17:17–18

and plurals in the singular. We say, "We have told you," and, "We have seen you," and, "We have come to you," and there are not two people speaking, but the one who is present. And yet by customary usage the one says this in the plural, as though he were many. (4) Thus the Gospel's[214] narrative included [many persons] by its use of the plural; but the other [Gospel] tells us that one was the blasphemer, while one confessed and found salvation.

41,5   And you see that every part of the truth is plain, and there is no contradiction in the scripture. (6) But I suppose I've made my statement of the argument lengthy by going over all this scriptural material. Let me get tired from the time the argument takes, but let me confound < the enemies* > of the truth and, with the truth's healing remedies, bring joy to her sons.

42,1   Next, let's look at the scum's other teachings. He claims that the two Testaments contradict each other[215] and that the god who spoke in the Law is different from the God of the Gospel.[216] The former god he terms "the archon;" but in the latter.case, < where he posits a good God, he calls him Father, just as the Son* > says that his < Father* > is a good God.

If he would only tell the truth, and not blaspheme himself by mistake! (2) We ourselves agree with the same proposition, that the good Offspring of a good Father—light of light, God of God, very God of very God—has come to us to save us. "He came unto his own" property, not someone else's, "< and > his own received him not. (3) But as many as received him, to them gave he power to become the sons of God, who were born, not of blood, nor of flesh, but of God."[217] (4) And yet, surely no one in the world has been born without flesh and blood; all people are flesh and blood. What were they before they were born in the flesh? What can we do without flesh? (5) But since the world is God's creation and we are creatures of flesh and born of fathers and mothers, the Lord came to beget us "of Spirit and of fire."[218]

For we have been born, and that is true, and no one can deny his first birth, or his fleshliness. (6) But our second birth is not of flesh or blood, that is, it is not by the commerce of flesh and blood. In the Spirit we possess a flesh and soul that are no longer

---

[214] I.e., Matthew's
[215] Man. Ps. 57,11–14, "[He] cries out in the Law saying: I am God . . . who then led Adam astray and crucified the Savior?"
[216] Cf. Asmussen p. 14 (M 28 I, R II, 24–26; V I, 32–34; *MM* II, p. 314), "If he (Adonay) is the Lord of everything, why did he crucify the Son?"
[217] John 1:11–13
[218] Cf. Matt. 3:11.

carnal, but are blood, flesh and soul in a spiritual union. (7) In other words, "To them gave he power to become the sons of God"[219]—those who had been converted, and had pleased God with flesh, blood and soul.

42,8 Thus He who came to "his own" is no stranger, but is Lord of all. And this is why he says, "Lo, here am I that speak in the prophets." And he told the Jews, "Had ye believed Moses ye would have believed me; for he wrote of me;"[220] and, "Your father Abraham rejoiced to see my day, and he saw it and was glad;"[221] (9) and, "Thus did your fathers unto the prophets;"[222] and, "Blessed are ye when men shall revile you and say all manner of evil against you falsely. Rejoice and be glad, for great is your reward in heaven. For so persecuted they the prophets before you."[223] And in another passage he says, "Jerusalem, that killest the prophets and stonest them that are sent, how often would I have gathered thy children?"[224]

42,10 Now the words, "how often" show that he had taken care to "gather" Jerusalem through the prophets. For if he says "killing the prophets" as a reproof, then he takes care of the prophets. But in taking care of the prophets he was not caring for strangers, but for his own. (11) He says, "And the blood that has been shed shall be required, from the blood of Abel unto that of the righteous Zacharias, which was shed between the temple and the altar."[225]

< And see how he takes care of the temple too; in another passage he says* >, (12) "And he took them all away, and overthrew the tables of the money-changers, and said, Make not my Father's house an house of merchandise."[226] And to Mary and Joseph he said, "Why is it that ye sought me? Wist ye not that I must be in my Father's house?"[227] And the Gospel is quick to add, "Make not my Father's house an house of merchandise," as it says, "And the disciples remembered that it was written, The zeal of thine house hath eaten me up."[228] (43,1) And how much there is to say, using < words of the* > Gospels and Apostles such as these, in refutation and < rebuttal > of Mani's madness, with his desire to divide and separate

---

[219] John 1:12
[220] John 5:46
[221] John 8:56
[222] Cf. Luke 6:23.
[223] Matt. 5:11–12
[224] Matt. 23:27
[225] Cf. Luke 11:50–51; Act. Arch. 32.6.
[226] Matt. 21:12–13; John 2:16
[227] Luke 2:49
[228] John 2:17

the Old Testament from the New, even though the Old Testament testifies to the Savior and the Savior acknowledges the Old Testament.

43,2   And not only that, but † the Savior testifies that he is the son of David, as he says,"[229] The Lord said unto my Lord, sit thou on my right hand. If David then call him Lord, how is he his son?"[230] (3) And again in another passage, when the children cried Hosannah to the son of David and "He did not rebuke them"— < and when > the Pharisees say, "Hearest thou not what these say? Bid them be silent," he replies, "If these were silent, the stones would have cried out."[231] (4) For he is David's son in the flesh but David's Lord in the Spirit, and both statements are cogent and accurate. There is no falsity < in > the truth.

43,5   But not to lengthen this argument I shall content myself with these texts and go on to the others, for the scum's full refutation. If the body belongs to one god, Mister, and the soul belongs to another, what association can the two have? (6) And I am afraid that this modest person's small mind is trying to peer into some pretty deep thoughts. So, not to give the readers a great deal of heavy reading, I shall hold myself in check and confound the charlatan with one item of evidence. (7) Common partnership is not to be found in those who differ; it is the work of one friend, and the business of two. Now if the body and the soul are together, this is the work of one God. For there is no distinction, since both work duly together and are in agreement.

43,8   But if, after eating the soul as Mani claims, the archons made this body as a prison for it, how can they lock it up in a body again after it is eaten? Whatever is eaten is consumed, and whatever is consumed also ceases to exist. But something that ceases to exist and has no more being isn't confined in a place; there neither is, nor can be, prison for a non-existent thing.

44,1   But Mani often loses track of his own notion, forgets what he has said, and unknowingly again breaks down what he once built up. He sometimes claims that the soul has been eaten < and has vanished, even though* > he declares that it is shut up in the bodies that presently exist. But sometimes he decides that it has been snatched from on high from the good God's armor by the

---

[229] Holl: ἑαυτὸν υἱὸν Δαυὶδ διαμαρτυροῦντος, ὡς λέγει Δαυίδ; MSS: οὐ μόνον, ἀλλὰ καὶ οἱ ἀπόστολοι, ὡς λεγει Δαυίδ

[230] Matt. 22:44–45. At Aug. C. Fort. 19, Fortunatus calls attention to the apparent discrepancy between the Davidic sonship and the Virgin Birth; cf. Aug. C. Fort. 22.1.

[231] Cf. Luke 19:39–40

archons, so that it has not been eaten yet but is being held prisoner.

44,2   But at times he says in disagreement with this that the soul has been taken prisoner and < defeated* >, but tells its story in a different way. (3) Then he claims that it has been set out as bait, of its own free will, by the power on high[232]—like a kid thrown into a pit to catch a beast of prey, which is excited and leaps down get the kid, < with the result that* > the beast itself is caught.

44,4   Now suppose that the power on high—that is, the good God, or the "light," as Mani calls it—did send the "kid," < a bit of > its own power. In the first place, even though he catches the beast, the kid will be eaten up in the meantime. And rather [than helping itself], the power on high will harm itself by offering part of itself as food for the beast, to catch the beast with the part it sees fit to lose. (5) And it will no longer conquer the beast because of its power and supremacy, and the might of its reason and will; to enable itself to master the beast it employs all sorts of schemes, and plays the knave. (6) And even if the beast is caught, the good God will still have lost the kid that got eaten, from a part of himself—assuming that he can catch the beast at all.

44,7   For if the power on high sent the soul here to catch and bind the principalities and authorities, he has not achieved the goal he planned on. (8) Although he sent the soul to catch, it has been caught. Although he sent it to trap, it has been trapped. For it came from a pure essence and was subjected, first to the prison of the material body, and then to many enormities of sins. And the fraud's argument, and the offender's teaching, are all wrong.

45,1   Now then, let's also see about Mother of Life. Mani says that she too was emitted < from the > power < on high >, and that Mother of Life herself < emitted > both First Man < and > the five elements which, as he says, are wind, light, water, fire and matter. (2) Putting these on as battle gear, First Man went below and made war on the darkness. But during their battle with him the archons of darkness ate part of his armor, that is, the soul.

45,3   What low comedy on the scum's part! What † efforts to prove an unintelligible joke and an absurd story![233] Mani positively

---

[232] Man. Ps. 9,31–10,7, "Like unto a shepherd that shall see a lion coming to destroy his sheep-fold: for he uses guile and takes a lamb and sets it as a snare that he may catch him by it; for by a single lamb he saves his sheep-fold. After these things he heals the lamb that has been wounded by the lion: this too is the way of the Father, who sent his strong son." And cf. Act. Arch. 28.2.

[233] Holl: ἐπιχειρήματα; MSS: τὰ ἐπίχειρα

attributes powerlessness to God, absolutely ascribes ignorance to God the omniscient! (4) For the God who, as Mani says, emitted Mother of Life, is to be blamed either for not knowing what would be produced from Mother of Life, or for not knowing that the things which had happened contrary to his expectation < had* > turned out other than < he thought they would* >. (5) For who-ever expects things to happen, but finds that something else has happened later against his wishes, must be charged with ignorance.

45,6   For Mother of Life, whom Mani calls a power, < is born of God* > as his emanation, something it is "a shame even to say."[234] No one whose mind is sound can suppose that there is anything female in the Godhead. (7) And this female, says Mani, emitted First Man < and the five elements as a mother bears a child >. And in a word, Mani imagines the First Man † he speaks of,[235] and Mother of Life, in terms of our experience. By "man" we mean [the first man] on earth, and by the "mother † of life"[236] who bore us, the woman God created for Adam.

45,8   But on the basis of his own reasonings the oaf imagines that there are the same sorts of thing in heaven that there are on earth—though as the sacred scripture everywhere teaches, this cannot be. (9) For scripture says, "There are celestial bodies and bodies terrestrial: but the glory of the celestial is one, and the glory of the terrestrial is another."[237] And < the apostle > had not yet given any description of the things above the heavens, but only of these visible things, which are body—I mean < the bodies of > the sun or moon, or the creatures on earth and the bodies of the saints—or so, with all humility, I suppose. (10) I have no way of deciding whether, because of the apostle's profound capacity for knowledge, there was also to be a discussion < of > the realms above the heavens. But in any case it has been said that < heavenly things > are very < different > from earthly; how much more the things above the heavens? < All right >, Mister, how can they be compared with things on earth?

46,1   And what else can you be doing but < imagining* > First Man < as well* >—who, you say in turn, made wind, light, fire, water and matter for his armor < to fight with the darkness* >? (2) If First Man is from on high, and has still come here in order to make his armor[238] and emit it to protect and strengthen himself,

---

[234] Eph. 5:12
[235] Holl: ὃν φησίν; MSS: τὴν φύσιν
[236] Holl: τῆς ζωῆς; MSS: ἐκ τῆς γῆς
[237] 1 Cor. 15:40
[238] Epiphanius assumes that First Man must obtain the elements from the

the things in this world must be more powerful than the one who
came down < from > the heavens. (3) For "water" is the water we
can see, "light" is visible light, "matter" is what you claim is in
decay; "wind" is what sounds in our ears, and "fire" is the thing
we all use for our needs with nothing to stop us.

46,4   And if he fights the archons with such things, tell us, how
shall the battle be fought? Who is to be our commanding officer
and blow the trumpet? Should we break through the ranks, should
we combine to oppose the wings? (5) Who should cast the first
spear—going by the raving maniac's < talk > —at the stuff of the
archons and authorities? (6) Mister, does the wind fight? Does
matter, which you say is in decay? Does fire, which the Lord has
made for our use? Does light, which gives way to darkness at the
successive intervals ordained by God? Does water? How? Explain
your vaporings!

46,7   In fact we see that, really, [both] good and evil deeds are
done with these elements. Sacrifices are offered to idols by fire,
and the fire does not object, or prevent the sin. Daemon-worshipers
pour libations of sea water, and no one attempting folly with water
has ever been stopped. (8) How many pirates have committed
murders with sea water? If anything, water is not opposed to the
archons of wickedness, as you call them. Instead, water is their ally,
though the water is not responsible; every human being is responsible for his own sin. And how much you talk!

46,9   What good did manufacturing armor and wearing a breastplate made of the elements do your First Man who came down
to fight and was swamped by the darkness? For you claim that the
Man was oppressed there below. (10) But the Father heard his
prayer,[239] you say, and sent another power he had emitted, called
Living Spirit. (11) Raise your mask, Menander, you comedian! That
is what you are, but you hide yourself while you recite the deeds
of adulterers and drink. For you say nothing original—you mislead
your dupes by introducing the Greeks' works of fiction in place
of the truth. (12) Hesiod, with his stories of the theogony, probably
had more sense than you, and Orpheus, and Euripides. Even though
they told ridiculous stories, it is plain that they are poets and made

---

earth. Manichaean teachings make these elements heavenly: Keph. 69,27–31,
"At this very same time the First Man drew near to his clothing, the shining
gods, and spoke with them, (saying) that he would surrender them . . . He [ap-
peared] to them and made them aware of everything . . . He clothed himself
with them and put them in order . . ."

[239] Keph. 38,32–39,2, "He bowed his [knee as he prayed] to the God of truth
and all the aeons of light who belong to the house of his people and as he

things up that were not real. But to compound the error, you tell them as though they were.

47,1 You claim that this Living Spirit came below, offered his right hand, and drew First Man, as you call him, out of the darkness, because he was in danger down in the depths. First Man had descended to save the soul[240] that had been eaten, and could not save it but fell into danger himself. (2) Though he was sent on a mission of rescue he was endangered, and somebody else had to be sent to rescue him! (3) In how much more danger must the soul be because of which the messenger, First Man, fell into danger when he came?

But there was a second messenger sent to the rescue, which you say was Living Spirit. (4) Did the Father change his mind, then, and send someone still more powerful to be the savior of First Man? Or was he at first unaware that First Man lacked the power, and did he think that he would save the soul? < But > did he find this out by experience later when First Man fell into danger, and emit [Living Spirit] and send [him]? (5) What a lot of nonsense, Mani! Your silly statement of your whole teaching is incoherent gibberish.

47,6 He claims in turn that Spirit descended, offered his right hand, and drew up the endangered First Man. This is why he taught his disciples to offer their right hands as a mystery when they meet, as a sign that they have been saved from darkness. (7) For he says that everyone, with the sole exception of himself, is in darkness. Well, to make a joke, blind men avoid bad words better than the sighted, and see a great deal by hearing.

48,1 And next, to make other artworks and furnishings for us, Mani claims—as though he had been there, and yet he is imagining things with no existence—that this Living Spirit then made the world. Clothed with three powers himself he too descended, brought the archons up, and crucified them in the firmament, which is their < body >, the sphere. (2) And yet the oaf does not realize how he contradicts himself with his "brought them up," and how he finds fault with things he commends and makes the things he finds fault with commendable—like a drunkard who goes staggering around and babbling one thing after another.

48,3 For he claims that the archons in the darkness below are made of evil stuff, and that < the realms below* > are the place

---

petitioned for a power to accompany him when he would withdraw..."

[240] Keph. 76,34–36, "Again (the First Man) [is like a man] whose two sons have been taken from him ... [he] came to them to save them."

of corruption. (4) Now if, when Spirit overpowered the archons, he brought them up from this corruption and dark realm to < the > heights—as a punishment, if you please!—if he brought about their departure from evil places and drew them aloft for a punishment, the realms above cannot be good, and made of the stuff of life. They must be made of the stuff of death; and the realms below cannot be a punishment, but must be of a nature somehow good. (5) And because Spirit meant to move the archons as a punishment, as a way of punishing them he took them from pleasant, familiar places to a place of punishment.

48,6   And here is a different argument. If Spirit made the world, why do you say, on the contrary, that the world was not made by God? And if the firmament is the archons' body, to which cross did Spirit fasten the archons? For you sometimes say that they are fastened in the firmament, but sometimes declare that the firmament itself is their body.[241] (7) And your arguments show a great inconsistency, with no correspondence with the truth. < You are defeated* > everywhere you have assailed us—assailed yourself, rather, and those who have adopted your opinion.

49,1   The same teacher says yet again that after crucifying the archons in the sphere Spirit made the luminaries, which are remnants of the soul. (2) What confused doctrine, and what false and incoherent statements! Any "remnant" is a part of a whole, but the whole is larger than the remainder. (3) All right, if the luminaries are the remnants Mani should show us < something > larger than the luminaries, so that we can see the soul! (4) But if the whole has been eaten and consumed, and the luminaries are its remnants, since they are beneath the crucified archons they will get eaten too, because the archons have the position on top. (5) But if they can no longer remain in possession of the soul and luminaries because of being crucified, then, Mani, your silly account is wrong!

49,6   Then in turn the same person teaches that after rebuking the Porter, Matter created all growing things for herself. And when the archons stole them the great archon called all the archons and chief archons, took one power apiece from them, made a man in First Man's image and imprisoned the soul in him. This is the reason for the combination [of soul and body]. (7) But Living Father is kind and merciful, says Mani, and sent his beloved Son

---

[241] Cf. Bar Khouni at Pognon p. 188, "Alors l'Esprit ordonna à ses trois fils que l'un tuât, que l'autre écorchat les Archontes, fils des ténèbres, et qu'ils amenassent à la Mère de la Vie. La Mère de la Vie tendit le ciel de leurs peaux; elle fit onze cieux, et ils jetérent leurs corps sur la tierre de ténèbres."

to the soul's rescue when he saw the soul oppressed in the body. For Mani claims that he was sent for this reason, and because of the Porter. (8) And on his arrival the Son changed himself into the likeness of a man and appeared to men as a man, and men supposed that he had been begotten [like a man]. (9) Thus he came and did the creating which was intended for men's salvation, and made a device with twelve water jars, which is turned by the sphere and draws up the souls of the dying. And the greater luminary takes these with its rays, and purifies them, and transfers them to the moon; and this is how what we call the moon's orb becomes full.

50,1   And do you see how great this charlatan's silly nonsense and drunken forgetfulness are? For he consigns his own words to oblivion, revises and reverses whatever he seems to say, and refutes his own doctrines by describing them in a whole series of different ways. His later teachings destroy his earlier ones and he rebuilds the things he originally destroyed, (2) as though to show that they are not his own but that, like the delirious, he is driven by an unclean spirit to tell one story after another.

50,3   For he either means that the advent of our Lord Jesus Christ < came before the creation of the stars, or that the stars were made long after the creation of the world. But it is obvious* > that the advent came many years after the creation of the luminaries and the thing Mani calls the "device" of the twelve water jars. (4) The stars have been in the sky ever since their creation. Whether they prefer to call them "elements" or "intervals and measurements of the sky," they have all been put in place since the fourth day of creation, properly, and not to the harm of God's subjects. (5) But Christ's advent < came* > in the fifteenth year of Tiberius Caesar. < For* > he began his preaching < at this point* >, thirty years after his birth, coincidentally with the 5509th year of creation and the thirtieth of his age—but the crucifixion came in his thirty-third year.

50,6   Now [if Christ came and made them], why were these in the sky from the beginning, the luminaries and stars? But if he says that Christ came before this to make them, his nonsense is confused. What he calls elements, and the twelve "water jars" as he futilely terms them, and the "device" † by which[242] he wants to deceive his dupes with nice names, were made before man was on earth.

51,1   For it is plain to anyone with sense, from the scripture

---

[242] Holl: δἰ ἧς; MSS: ἤν

itself and the sequel to it, that all the stars and luminaries were made on the fourth day of creation, before the making of Adam the first man. (2) But Mani says, "He came in the form of a man to make the twelve water jars, and appeared to men < as > a man." Since he does not even know God's original provision he thinks he has something to say. Like a blind man serving as his own guide he tells the people he has blinded whatever lies are handy. (3) But when the truth arrives and gives < clear > vision to the wise it makes a joke of his nonsense. To which men did Christ "appear" when there weren't any? If he hadn't taken a body, how could he "appear in the form of a man?" (4) And if he performed any works during his advent in the flesh, when he "appeared" to be a man but wasn't one, his works were appearance. In that case he neither appeared nor came!

51,5 For if he was not real when he came, neither did he come at the beginning. If he was supposed to be a man but was not a man, what impelled God's Word to appear as a man when he was not one? Unless he was being hounded by money-lenders, and wanted to disguise himself to escape his creditors! (6) But if he indeed appeared and yet wasn't there, what sort of "truth" was this? There can be no lie in truth, as the Only-begotten says of himself, "I am the truth and the life."[243] But life cannot die and the truth cannot be subject to change, or it would jumble the truth up and no longer be truth. (7) And Mani's dramatic piece is a failure for every reason. The stars were not created after Christ's advent, and there were no people before the creation of the stars. And as I have just shown, the fraud Mani is confounded, both by the latter fact and by the former.

52,1 But on the subject of the moon, he says that its orb is filled with souls. Now how could the moon's orb get full before anyone on earth had died? How could the one soul, the first person to die after the nine hundred and thirtieth year of Adam's life,[244] fill the moon's orb? (2) Or why were the 930 years also called "< the > times," if the moon did not wax, wane and run its appointed course, not because it had been flooded with souls but because it had God's wise ordinance? (3) But Mani says that all living things are filled with the same soul—thus equating the souls of a man, a mouse, a worm, and the other bodies with nasty origins.

52,4 But now for the rest of his nonsense—how [he says that] the Virgin appears, sometimes in a man's form and sometimes in

---

[243] John 14:6
[244] Epiphanius overlooks, for the moment, the death of Cain.

a woman's, to the archons, and is probably explaining the passions of his own lusts, since he resembles his daemon in bisexuality. (5) Then he says that when the chief archon is robbed by this so-called virgin he emits his clouds, causes pestilence and begins cutting the roots, with death resulting. (6) And yet the oaf has not seen that what he disparagingly calls "death" he ought to call "life" instead, because of the souls' deliverance from bodies. (7) But if the archons have any inkling that the soul's residence in a body is an imprisonment, the chief archon will never do such a thing as to release the soul, which Mani claims he holds captive, from prison. And how much absurdity is there in this tricky teaching?

53,1   But their other absurdities, such as their so-called "elect."[245] They have been "chosen," all right—by the devil for condemnation, in fulfillment of the words of scripture, "and his choice meats."[246] (2) For they are drones who sit around and "work not, but are busybodies,"[247] "knowing < neither what they say nor whereof they affirm* >."[248] The holy apostle denounces them because of his prophetic knowledge that certain idle, stubbornly evil persons will be making their rounds,[249] not in obedience to God's teaching but because the devil has driven them insane. (3) < For > in contempt for these idlers' occupation he says, "Let the non-worker not eat!"

53,4   Manichaeans instruct their catechumens to feed[250] these people generously; they offer their elect all the necessities of life, so that < whoever > gives sustenance to elect souls will appear pious, if you please! (5) But silly as it sounds, after receiving their food the elect all but put a curse on the givers under the pretense of praying for them, by testifying to their wickedness rather than to their goodness. For they say: "*I* did not sow you. *I* did not reap you. *I* did not knead you. *I* did not put you into the oven. Someone else brought you to me and I eat. I am guiltless." (6) And if anything, they have stigmatized the people who feed them as evildoers—

---

[245] Keph. 166,4–9, "At the time when I leave the world and enter the house of my people, all my elect will be drawn to me, and I will gather them in that place, and draw each one of them to me at the time of their departure. I will not leave one of them in the darkness."

[246] Hab. 1:16

[247] 2 Th. 3:11

[248] 1 Tim. 1:7

[249] Manichaean sources indicate that the behavior of the elect sometimes gave scandal; cf. the chapter, "The Catechumen Who Found Fault with the Elect (and Asked) Why He Was Irritable," Keph. 219,2–221,7. Augustine portrays the elect as unpleasant people at Mor. Man. 2.29–31.

[250] Keph. 189,6–11, "He who shall [give] bread and a cup of water to one of my disciples in God's name, in the name of the truth I have revealed, he shall become great before God and surpass the four great kingdoms in their greatness."

which, indeed, is true. No one who denies that God is the maker of all should take nourishment from God's creatures < except > in mockery.

53,7 The elect do not cut the cluster themselves but they eat the cluster, which shows that they are out-and-out drunkards and not persons with a grasp of the truth. (8) For which is the worse? The harvester cut the cluster once, but the eater tormented and cut it many times over, with his teeth and by the crushing of each seed. There can be no comparison between the one who chewed it up and the one who cut it once. (9) < But they do this* > merely to give the appearance of < abstaining from God's creatures* >, and < show, by their* > fabrication of false doctrines, how much evidence Mani has of the truth.

54,1 Then again he is impudent about Paradise, which is what he calls the world. The trees in it are < evils* >, he says—for anything we approve of, he denies, to show that he is truly the serpent's dupe. Just as the horrid serpent corrupted the ear of the blameless Eve, so he corrupts Mani's ears. (2) For Mani says that what we call trees in Paradise are the deceits of lusts, which corrupt men's reason. But the tree in Paradise whereby they learn to know the good is Jesus, the knowledge in the world. But anyone who takes that fruit can tell good from evil.

54,3 And you see how he perverts whatever is right, although the apostle expressly and emphatically teaches, "I fear lest by any means, as the serpent beguiled Eve through his subtlety, so your minds should be corrupted from the simplicity and innocence that is in Christ."[251] And see how he pronounced him a fraud and villain, and the deceiver of Eve. (4) And once more, the same apostle says in another passage, "A man ought not to have long hair, forasmuch as he is the glory and image of God."[252] And you see how he called hair the glory of God, though it is grown on the body and not in the soul. (5) And afterwards he says, "Adam was not deceived, but the woman sinned by falling into transgression. Notwithstanding, she shall be saved by childbearing, if they continue in the faith."[253] And see how the real truth is proclaimed in the sacred scripture, while Mani makes futile boasts—or rather, makes himself ridiculous in the eyes of persons of sound mind.

54,6 Then again he explains here that the world is not God's but has been made from a part of matter. But because he is not

---

[251] 2 Cor. 11:3
[252] 1 Cor. 11:7
[253] 1 Tim. 2:14–15

consistent, but goes back and forth plastering over the places he pulls down and builds up, it is perfectly plain to everyone that this is fool's doctrine.

55,1   He describes transmigrations of souls from body to body, most likely borrowing this lie from Plato, Zeno the Stoic, or some other victim of delusion. (2) For how can a soul go from one body into another? If bodies came ready-made and received souls under those circumstances, his pompous fiction would have some credibility. (3) But since the embryo develops from a tiny drop, how did the soul find such a broad passage into so small a body? For this is how bodies are formed; what Mani says cannot be proved.

55,4   Neither do souls migrate from body to body; no body is formed in any living thing without the intercourse of female with male and male with female. Now, is this how the soul has come to be, climaxing the scum's tragic piece with the union of two bodies? And people who even think such things are very strange.

55,5   But not to plow up things that deserve respect, I am content just to give a glimpse of the subject, as though from a distance. I shall pass on from such a degrading idea; all suppositions of this sort are outrageous. (6) For if there is a migration of souls from body to body, and someone who was once a man later < becomes > a dog, why isn't a dog born from a man or an ox? Why isn't a bird? If, indeed, some monster happens to be born during the immensely long course of history, this is for a sign. (7) Even nature knows its own boundaries. It does not change a man's nature and make him, contrary to nature, into something else. Nor does it change the nature of any beast; the like is born of its like. (8) And if a different kind of body is never born from a body, how much more does a human soul not migrate into a different body?

55,9   And why is the body changed, does he say? So that, if it did not have the knowledge of the truth while it was in a man, it will be born in a dog or horse and be disciplined,[254] return to a human body knowing the truth, (10) and be taken up into the moon's orb, now that it has come to knowledge. It is a surprise to see that the soul was ignorant when it was born in a man although men have schools, grammarians, sophists, innumerable trades, and speech, hearing, and reason—but it came to knowledge when it was born in a pig! This shows that, if anything, Mani's promise of knowledge is for pigs, because of his imposture and impiety.

56,1   As to Adam's creation, Mani gives a substitute version and

---

[254] A long passage at Keph. 249,1–250,30, explains that, if catechumens are not perfected, their souls undergo transmigration as a remedial discipline.

combines it with his error. He says that the person who said, "Let us make man in our image and after our likeness,"[255] < is the archon, who said it to the other archons* >. And Mani adds to this by saying, "*Come*, let us make man." That is not the text; it is, "*Let us* make man in our image and after our likeness."

56,2 But the holy apostle refutes him by saying, < "The man is the image and glory of God."* >[256] So does the Lord himself, in the Gospel. The Pharisees told him that it is not good for a man to be by himself, and that Moses said he should give his wife a certificate of divorce and dismiss her. (3) And the Lord said to confute the Pharisees, "Moses wrote because of the hardness of your hearts. But from the beginning it was not so,[257] but he which made them male and female"—and he said, "For this cause shall a man leave his father and his mother and cleave unto his wife, and they twain shall be one flesh." (4) And he immediately added, "What therefore God hath joined together, let not man put asunder."[258] For he confessed that God, that is, his Father, had made Adam and Eve, and that lawful wedlock is God's institution.

56,5 And the holy apostle, the herald of the truth, says in the same vein, "This is a great mystery, but I say it of Christ and the church,"[259] using the comparison < to confirm the truth of* > God's creation of Adam and Eve* > —(6) < and confirm at the same time* > that God created < Eve* > and that Adam said, "This is bone of my bones and flesh of my flesh, therefore shall a man leave,"[260] < and so forth >. And God shaped his side into a wife for him. (7) And the apostle says nothing else † on the subject[261] that is different, but [simply], "It is a great mystery." And if < the apostle confirms the divine creation* > in the man and the woman and this is treated anagogically in an allegory, why does Mani, speaking blasphemy and ignoring the truth, suppose that God's creatures are abominable and foreign to God's truth, and < say that they were made* > by an archon?

56,8 Next, he says, it troubled the power on high that the soul had been torn away from it at the beginning. And so it sent someone once and for all and stole the remnant of itself—the soul, that is—from the archons through these luminaries. (9) What high

---

[255] Gen. 1:26
[256] Holl assumes that the citation which has fallen out here is 1 Cor. 11:7.
[257] Matt. 19:8
[258] Matt. 19:5–6
[259] Eph. 5:32
[260] Gen. 2:23–24
[261] Holl: οὐκετι ἕτερον ὁ ἀπόστολος εἰς αὐτὸ φάσκει; MSS: οὐκέτι ἕτερον αὐτῷ φάσκει

hopes we have, and what a great expectation! God the good, living and mighty is powerless to save—never mind his own power which has been dragged away from him—he can't save the creature he has made and fashioned! He can't save it except in some other way, or by the banditry of secretly stealing the power that has been torn away from him out of the heavens—or so the scum says.

57,1   But why am I still tiring myself by spending time on his absurdity in its exact wording? For instance, neither is the wretch ashamed of the blasphemy that it was the archon of darkness who spoke in the Law and the Prophets. (2) What blessed hopes we have, since Christ came and compelled us to offer gifts to the archon of darkness! For after cleansing the leper < he commands > him to offer the gift which is prescribed in the Law by the very person who spoke in the Law. "Go and offer thy gift as Moses commanded,"[262] says he to the leper he has cleansed. (3) But in leprosy's case the "gift" was a bird for a sacrifice, and fine flour for a burnt offering. (4) If the archon of darkness were < the God of the Law* >, the Word from on high—the Son of God who, as Mani says, came to turn humankind from the error of the archons— would not have encouraged the leper he had healed to become their subject. He would have encouraged him to escape instead, by teaching him not to do this.

57,5   But he had not come to destroy the Law or < the > Prophets—he had given the Law himself—but to fulfill them, to show us himself that unwavering adherence to the Gospel is the fulfillment of the Law and the Prophets. For the prophets worshiped the same God, and the Law was given by him. Today, however, the worship is not offered to the same God with the same gifts; (6) God gave burdensome commands, as though to slaves, to followers of the Law, since that was the way they could obey. But to the hearers of the Gospel he gave lighter commands as though to free men, in the excellence of his lovingkindness. (7) But since the God of the Law and the God of the Gospel are equivalent, and the worship of neither period has been abolished, this same God is one God, ruler of the entire world, worshiped by his servants—but worshiped as befits his lovingkindness in each generation.

57,8   And Mani's imposture is altogether refuted, since the Savior orders that the Law's commandments be kept. And [then], after ordering the keeping of the Law's commandments, he breaks the Law's commandments, not by destroying them but by fulfilling them. For in place of the Law's commandments he permits the

---

[262] Luke 5:14

offering of other sacrifices—the sacrifices of piety, goodness, purity and ascetic discipline.

58,1 But again, Mani claims that in the last days the Elder will come and make his image manifest; and then, when he sees his face, the porter will drop the earth and the eternal fire will consume the earth. (2) The oaf did not notice that he was once again making the earth material, although he had said a while before that it was created by the Spirit of life. For simultaneously with this he supposes that the whole world will be consumed by fire.

58,3 And then, he says, after this, the restoration of the two natures at once will pass into the original state. What a lot of trouble, and after the trouble no improvement! (4) For if everything is to be used up and consumed after it has been created and made, so that the originals of the two natures, the good and the evil, will remain as they were, this will serve as provocation for the evil nature to come back, start a war and seize some more power, so that there will be another world.

58,5 But if this is no longer so, then evil will learn sense and not be provoked at goodness any more; and [so will] the evil god, who will declare no more wars on the good God. (6) But if he is ever taught sense he will no longer be evil, since he has been changed and altered from his original evil nature. But if the nature of the evil god is indeed changeable, this is surely because it is changed from evil to good, and the nature which can be changed to goodness cannot be evil. For it can also be changed today, and evil can be turned to good while the world is still going on. (7) And if he is to be changed, why is he not changed already? And if the evil god is changed by God's contriving and can no longer do evil, the evil god cannot be responsible for himself. The responsibility must lie with the good God, since he is capable of suppressing the bad god's evil but will not to do a work whose time has been set, before the time.

58,8 However, if evil is altogether unchangeable it can never stop warring and being warred on, and there can never be a restoration of the two natures. Evil will remain unchanged, and be provoked into doing evil to the good and declaring war on goodness.

58,9 And yet, if evil is always nagged by some desire for the good, it cannot be evil.[263] In its yearning for the good it desires to draw the good to itself, so that, by acquiring power from the nature of the good and its armor, it can feel it is honoring, illu-

---

[263] A similar argument is found at Alex. Lycop. 9 and Tit. Bost. Man. 1.17.

minating, emboldening and strengthening itself. (10) For < the* >
notion < of the good* > is surely present in anyone who wants the
good, because † he expects[264] < to be benefited* > by good < itself* >. And evil cannot be altogether evil, since, as it turns out,
it yearns for the good. For anything [really] evil is hostile to the
good, just as the good has no desire for evil.

58,11   But if the power is made of both principles jumbled
together, and the good God can steal what belongs to him, and
can attack the principalities and authorities and skin them—can
sometimes destroy and do away with the matter made by the evil
god, sometimes making things from it but sometimes doing away
with it—then < there can be no difference between good* > and
evil. < And* > < the > chatter this offender has offered us < will be
simple > wickedness, and incapable of proof.

59,1   Come on, buddy, talk! Take up your account of the nature
of evil again! You arrived in the Emperor Aurelian's time, and yet
are telling us what was before all ages, though no prophet had
ever foretold this, and neither the Savior himself nor any of the
apostles had taught it—unless you play the fool by writing some
forged books yourself in the names of saints,[265] and palming them
off! Tell us where you come from, you with your primordial principle
of evil!

59,2   If I ask him whether he claims that evil is changeable or
unchangeable, < he talks incoherent nonsense* >. But I have already been told that he describes it [both] as [altogether] changeless, and as changeable at some times but not changeable at others—
[that is], changeless in evil but changeable in good—so that he
deserves the world's contempt for both terms. (3) For if evil was
changeless over immense ages of time, and had only this very name
and no other name but "evil," who changed the changeless nature
of evil many ages later, into something not suitable to it?

59,4   For who made it change, if it had not yet seized power
and gone to war, and if it had not yet taken armor to strengthen
itself and for food, but had gone for many ages without food or
the need of food—[who made] this thing that had never needed
food begin to eat, seek what it had never sought, need what it had
never needed?

59,5   But if its nature was changed, how can you prove the
changelessness of evil that you teach? And even if he reverted to

---

[264] Holl: < αὐτοῦ ὠφεληθήσεσθαι > ὑπονοεῖ, < ἡ τοῦ ἀγαθοῦ >; MSS: ἀγαθοῦ
ὑπονοίας ἔγκειται διάνοια
[265] I.e., the Acts of Thomas. Cf. Aug. C. Faust. 27.9; Adeim. 17.2.5; Serm.
Dom. Mont. 1.20.65; Cyr. Cat. 4.36; 6.31.

his normal condition when he found nothing more to eat, how could a wicked, or evil [god] bear to go on without food for all time to come, once he had become used to eating and having food? (6) For if, when he was used to not eating, he could not bear it, but acquired the new habit of eating and got hold of the soul for his food by stealing it, he will be harder to restrain when he is used to foods. And once he has become greedy and acquainted with food, nothing could induce him to go on without these things, as your incoherent account would have it.

60,1   But I shall pass this by, and once more apply the discussion to other parts of his foolishness. Once again, he claims that the archons will be in their own territory then, (i.e., at the restoration) and the Father will regain his own. (2) Now who is this person so equitable that he can survey the boundary of each territory from either side? Why will [the bad god] obey [him] when he disobeyed the truth and the good God at the outset? If the good God is to prevail on the wicked god, through the use of force, to be satisfied with his property and not encroach on the good God's, why couldn't he do this in the first place, before any parts of it were stolen?

60,3   But why will the two co-exist, each with his respective possessions? If God has any territory, and the other territory is not his, the Almighty cannot be called almighty or God of all. Nor can the evil god be subject to the good God; each one has his own realm.[266]

60,4   But then, what can the evil god be the master of, when there is still no world, and no animals or people under his sway? And if he is in any way evil, matter and corruption, why hasn't he decayed? If evil has always been corruption, and corrupts other things but not itself, it cannot be in decay—not when it corrupts other things, but is perennial [itself] and does not disappear. (5) But if it remains stable itself, but corrupts other things and not itself, it cannot leave anything unaffected; the corruption of some things must surely corrupt others. But if it is the < only* > thing < left* > in existence, and it will no longer leave anything untouched but only it will remain, the things it corrupts must disappear. (6) However, if it is also bad for itself and the cause of its own decay, its existence cannot continue. I should not say only in the future; it would disappear < as soon as > it was in being, and would in itself already be the cause of its own decay and disappearance.

60,7   But all these are the yarns which go to make up the fool's

---

[266] A comparable argument is found at Tit. Bost. Man. 1.30.

nonsense. Take note of them, you wise sons of God's holy church and the Lord's faith, judge the scum, and laugh at his drivel! But he will return to the misconceived bases for it and resemblances to it in the sacred scriptures— < false ones* > which do not bear that interpretation, but which he misunderstands in that sense. (8) All right, let's give the exact words of the texts which, as I said, he steals from the sacred scriptures and explains in his own way— though I have often discussed the same ones < already >, and refuted them perfectly well.

61,1   In the first place, because he had found something about the name "Paraclete" in the sacred scriptures and did not know the power of the Holy Spirit, he insinuated himself in on the supposition that he was the Paraclete. (2) And he claims that St. Paul's words defer to him, since the holy apostle said, "We know in part and we prophesy in part; but when that which is perfect is come, that which is in part shall be done away."[267]

61,3   But though St. Paul was counted worthy of the Holy Spirit himself, as were the apostles who were like him, he never says this of the Paraclete. Paul explained the two worlds, this world and the world to come, as he told those who want < an advance > knowledge of the times, "Let no man affright you by word < or > by letter, as that the day of the Lord is at hand. For except the son of sin be revealed, the man of iniquity,"[268] and so on.

61,4   And again, when the disciples were assembled with the Savior they asked him about the consummation, and he told them, "It is not for you to know the times and the seasons, which the Father hath put in his own power. But ye shall receive power after that the Holy Ghost is come upon you."[269] (5) And again he said, "Depart not from Jerusalem, while ye await the promise of the Spirit, which ye have heard."[270] This means the Paraclete Spirit, as he said, "If I depart, he shall come and shew you all things."[271] (6) But < he said* >, "He shall show you all things," because of the gift that was to be vouchsafed them; < for* > the Holy Spirit < would* > dwell in them to give them a clear explanation of all that they could understand in this world.

61,7   And as vessels of the Paraclete Spirit, they prophesied here in this world, as < the scripture says > that Agabus prophesied

---

[267] 1 Cor. 13:9–10. Mani is said to use this argument at Act. Arch. 15.3; cf. Aug. C. Faust. 15.6; 32.17; Fel. 1.9.
[268] 2 Th. 2:2–3
[269] Acts 1:7–8
[270] Acts 1:4
[271] Cf. John 16:7; 13–15.

an impending famine, and that "Prophets came down from Jerusalem,"[272] and that "Philip had four daughters which did prophesy."[273]

61,8 But when these prophets prophesy, they prophesy in part and know in part; however, they hopefully await what is perfect in the ages to come, "when the corruptible is changed to incorruption and the mortal to immortality."[274] But < "When this mortal shall have put on immortality, >[275] then shall we see face to face." (9) For things are shown to us "darkly"[276] now; but there "what eye hath not seen here" is prepared. There perfection is revealed, the things that "ear hath not heard" here. The greatest grace for the saints is there—a thing "that hath not entered into the heart of man"[277] here.

61,10 And you see that no further knowledge was held in reserve for Mani. How could Mani know it when < he > fell short of his own goal? He undertook to master Marcellus; he came to Archelaus with the intent of worsting him, and could not. (11) Since he has no knowledge of recent events, how can he know about the greater things? When he was caught and punished, for example, why did he not escape from the king of Persia—except to show all people with understanding that he was a complete liar?

62,1 Again, he uselessly cites a text to prove the existence of the dyad he believes in and distinguish between the two first principles: the Savior's words, "A good tree cannot bring forth evil fruit, neither can a corrupt tree bring forth good fruit; for by its fruit the tree is known."[278] (2) And notice his shallow mind, which does not understand the contents of sacred scripture in any depth! If there are trees they have a cultivator; trees are growing things, and must have been planted by someone. But nothing planted is beginningless; it has its beginning. But since it has a beginning, it will have an end as well. (3) The corrupt tree was not always there, then; it had been planted. And this "good tree" is not a reference to all the goodness on high—for < there is* > goodness unfeigned there, changeless, of ineffable dignity—< and* > the thought is < not about* > the true holy God.

62,4 But let's see whether Mani is right about the capacities

---

[272] Acts 11:27
[273] Acts 21:9
[274] 1 Cor. 15:53
[275] MSS: ὅταν τότε; Holl: ὅταν ... τότε γὰρ βλέπομεν. We adopt Dummer's suggestion, which follows Diekamp, that Epiphanius quoted 1 Cor. 15:54 after ὅταν.
[276] 1 Cor. 13:12
[277] 1 Cor. 2:9
[278] Matt. 7:18; 20. Keph. 17,1–23,13 treats this as the fundamental principle of Manichaeism. Cf. Aug. Fel. 2.2.

of trees, and take it from there. If we are to discuss the devil, I have already often proved that he was not created evil; God made nothing evil, and this is plain to the wise. (5) For if we are going over the same ground, it will do no harm to give our account of the truth even now. The devil was not wicked to start with; he proved to be wicked. Look here, the point about the tree won't be proved like that!

62,6 We see too that Saul was a persecutor, but was later persecuted for the name he once persecuted. We see that Judas was chosen with the twelve apostles but later proved to be < evil >, and is counted as evil. (7) We see that Rahab the harlot was not of Israelite stock, but that she repented later and received God's mercy. We see that the thief was apprehended in a crime and hanged on the wood, and yet he confessed and entered Paradise with the Lord. We see that Nicolaus was a good man and had been chosen—but that he proved to be evil afterwards and was counted as an heresiarch.

62,8 And why give all these examples? What is this evil tree from which no good can come? † Plainly,[279] it is people's actions. No good can come of fornication, no righteousness of the wickedness of envy,[280] nothing commendable of adultery. (9) The tree of sin itself cannot grow through goodness—that is, an evil tree does not bear good fruit, nor < can > the fruit of a good tree < be > evil. (10) The good tree which does not bear evil fruit < is the human heart which is firmly established in God and from which, like good fruit, there spring such good works* > as hospitality— (< hospitality is never evil* >. However many < evils > result from hospitality, charity does not for < this > reason have the force of wickedness. [Nor does] purity for God's sake, continence for the Lord's, righteousness for the Law's.)

62,11 These two trees are figurative expressions for righteousness and sin; but in this barbarous Mani's opinion, [one] means God and [the other] means the devil. (12) And yet, it is plain that no one can dare to say that God will ever create evil—perish the thought!—or that the devil does good. (13) All good things are made by God, and nothing evil has been created or made by him. But if certain evils come from the devil, look here! < In this case too we have found that God fights on the side of the faithful* >, weaves a wreath for the saints, awards the victors a prize.[281] (14)

---

[279] Holl: δηλόν; MSS: πάλιν

[280] φθόνου πονηρίας. Dummer, following Drexl, suggests that one of these two nouns should be deleted.

[281] This is probably a reference to martyrdom, which is normally regarded

And Mani's argument has failed. The evil and good trees refer to good and evil works and not to the Old and the New Testaments, the position Mani takes.

63,1   Moreover, wanting to present the basis of the two first principles, he ferrets out and employs the texts he thinks apply, though they do < not > have this meaning. (2) He says that the Savior told the Jews, "Ye are sons of the devil; he was a murderer because his father was a liar."[282] He likes to say blasphemously that the maker of heaven and earth is the devil's father, though the text cannot possibly refer to this.

63,3   For if the Jews are in any sense sons of the devil, the argument about the devil has been defeated, and Mani is contradicting himself without knowing it. For if their souls are made by the devil it follows that they are distinct [from the others] and cannot come from Mani's mythical power on high, or be a part of the light or its armor, or the pillar of light, or the Mother of Light. (4) But if < they are > in any sense the devil's children, it follows from Mani's argument that their father Abraham, whose offspring the Jews are, is the devil's son too.

63,5   Well then, why does the Savior say to them in accusation, "Ye are no children of Abraham, but children of your father, the devil. If ye were children of Abraham, ye would do his works. For ye seek to kill me, a man that hath told you the truth. This did not Abraham."[283] (6) And you can see that this is colloquial language. The Jews are Abraham's children, and yet separate themselves from the Lord by their works, not their nature or creation—I discussed this earlier.[284] How can the part of Abraham's descendants at one moment be unrelated to him and the devil's portion, and be God's portion at the next? (7) The Savior means this as an accusation. By his activity and his teaching a man is the slave of the one to whom he submits, as Paul says, "Though ye have many instructors, yet have ye not many fathers. For in Christ Jesus I have begotten you through the Gospel."[285] (8) And do you see that he means teaching? And if Mani accepted Abraham, we would say that Abraham was the son of the God of light, but that his children were someone else's!

63,9   But here is the truth of the matter. The Jews imitated the

---

as combat with the devil. So at Cyprian of Carthage, Treatise 11.2; NHL Apoc. Jas. 4,32–36, etc.

[282] Cf. John 8:44.
[283] Cf. John 8:39–41.
[284] Pan. 38,4,2–9; 40,5,5-8a; 6,1–8
[285] 1 Cor. 4:15

murderer, imitated the betrayal of Judas, hearkened to the slander of the betrayer, became the children of his denial of God. He was a liar, for he "had the bag and stole,"[286] and said, "Hail, master," to the Savior, and heard his reproach, "Friend, wherefore art thou come?"[287] (10) Since he became a murderer this Judas was the imitator of Cain, for Cain was a murderer who lied to the Lord's face and said "Am I my brother's keeper? I know not where he is."[288] And Cain himself became the son of < the devil >, by imitation and by paying heed to the lying voice that spoke in the serpent and said, "Ye shall be as gods, knowing good and evil."[289]

63,11   This is what the Savior says in the Gospel, "Ye are sons of the devil."[290] For he says, "Have I not chosen you twelve, and one of you is a devil?"[291] "Devil" because he was "a liar and a murderer from the beginning, for his father was a liar."[292]

63,12   And this question has been resolved. The Jews were not the devil's children, far from it! The Samaritan woman says to the Savior, "Here in this mountain our fathers worshiped; and ye say that in Jerusalem is the place where men ought to worship"—(13) and later, after much discussion, the Savior told her, "We speak that we do know, for salvation is of the Jews."[293] And the apostle said in his turn, "It is plain that the Lord sprang from Judah."[294] And there is a great deal to say about this in refutation of Mani's imposture.

64,1   Again, he seizes on the following text: "The light shineth in the darkness, and the darkness overcame it not."[295] This means that the darkness pursued the light, he says, since the evil archons pursued the Godhead and fought against it.

64,2   But if the light is under attack and pursued by the darkness, the darkness must be stronger than the light—since the light runs away from the darkness and seemingly cannot bear to make a stand, since darkness is the stronger. (3) But that is not so. The light does not flee from the darkness, for "The light shineth in the darkness and the darkness overcame it not."[296] But if the dark-

---

[286] John 12:6
[287] Matt. 26:49–50
[288] Gen. 4:9
[289] Gen. 3:5
[290] John 8:44
[291] John 6:70
[292] Cf. John 8:44.
[293] John 4:20; 22; 3:11
[294] Heb. 7:14
[295] John 1:5
[296] John 1:5; cf. Act. Arch. 27.11.

ness did not overcome the light, this is very different from what
Mani means. He says not only that the darkness overcame the light,
but that it seized armor from it as well. Now how can it be possible
that < the > darkness did not overcome the light, when Mani declares
that it has seized armor? However, if the light is being pursued,
why does it shine in the darkness by its own choice?

64,4   But because people's minds had been blinded by the
muddiness of sin, God sent the Law first, giving them light as when
a lamp appears, (5) as Peter says in his Epistle, "Taking heed unto
the word of prophecy, as unto a light that shineth in a dark place,
until the day star arise, and the day dawn in your hearts."[297] For
that is the source of the light which shines in the darkness—the
Law which was given "by the hand of a mediator,"[298] through God's
faithful servant Moses.

64,6   Because the Law had always shone like a spark in the law
of nature, Enoch, who saw it, pleased the Lord; Abel pleased the
Lord by its guidance. Noah saw his way by it, and found favor
before God; Abraham believed God by it and it was reckoned to
him for righteousness. (7) Then the light outgrew the dimensions
of a spark, and was added to the luster of "the lamp that shineth
in a dark place." This is the meaning of "The light shineth in the
darkness:"[299] God's commandment, and the intent of goodness,
which gives light in the hearts of the faithful, among the minds
which have been muddied < by > the wicked, evil deeds of men—
idolatry, the denial of God, murders, adultery and the rest.

64,8   But when the great Light came, "the true light which lighteth
every man that cometh into the world, he was in the world, and
the world was made by him, and the world knew him not—this
light that came unto his own, and his own received him not—but
as many as received him, to them gave he power to become the
sons of God."[300] (9) And do you see the kind of darkness in which
this light shines, and the kind of darkness that has not overcome
it? For the good which is constantly sent by God to the human
mind, and which gives light in the world, has not been vanquished
by sin.

65,1   Once more, Mani similarly seizes on the Savior's words,
"The kingdom of heaven is like unto a man that is an householder,
which sowed good seed < in > his field. And while men slept an
enemy came and sowed tares. (2) Then his servants said unto him,

---

[297] 2 Pet. 1:19
[298] Gal. 3:19; Heb. 3:5
[299] John 1:5
[300] John 1:9–12

Didst not thou sow good seed in the field? He said, Yea. They said, Whence then the tares? He answered and said, An enemy hath done this. His servants said unto him, Wilt thou that we go and root the tares out? (3) But he said unto them, Nay, lest while rooting out the tares ye root out also the wheat. Leave them until the time of harvest, and I shall say to the reapers, Gather up the tares and bind them in bundles, but store the wheat in the barn, and make the tares ready to be burned with fire unquenchable."[301]

65,4   But when his disciples asked him in the house, "Tell us the parable of the tares," he explained it without concealment, for fear of providing the cheat with an opening against the truth. (5) The Lord answered them plainly and said, "He that sowed the good seed is God. The field is the world; the tares are the wicked men; the enemy is the devil; the reapers are the angels; the harvest is the consummation of the age; the wheat is the good men. (6) < The consummation will come > when the Lord sendeth his angels and gathereth the sinners out of his kingdom and delivereth them to be burned."[302]

65,7   Sons of the truth, see that this man who has become the replacement for Jannes and Jambres employs his own arguments against himself. He himself denies that the world is God's; yet the Savior has said here that the world is the field, that the householder and owner of the field < is God > —that is, his Father; and that it is he who has sown his good seed. (8) And the Savior did not distinguish souls from bodies or bodies from souls, but said that the enemy had sown the tares, which are the evil men. And he does not call men just bodies < or just souls > but said, "evil men," [meaning both] together. (9) But he similarly said in turn that the good men are the good seed < which > the householder sowed in his field. And he didn't say their souls, but "good < men >," with body and soul. (10) God thus sows the good in men by his teaching, and the devil sows the evil deeds in men secretly, by his mischief.

65,11   But we shall not find a root of wickedness in this place or in that, but works done by ourselves. And God is in no way responsible for the tares which have been sown. Christ makes this clear at once by saying, "while men slept;" he didn't say, "while the householder slept." Whenever we doze off from good works, whenever we neglect righteousness, whenever we do not alert our minds to God's commandment, sins are sown < in us >.

---

[301] Cf. Matt. 13:24–30 and Act. Arch. 15.7.
[302] Cf. Matt. 13:36–42.

65,12 Do you see that the reapers get the bundles ready for the eternal fire? Tell me, Mani, do they bind up souls there? Or do they burn bodies without souls, or burn the souls too? Your description of the purification of souls cannot stand up, because they will be consigned to punishment and condemnation. But so much for this. For the wise, the utterances of the truth are plain.

66,1 He seizes on yet another text and cites it without realizing its implications, but with a wrong interpretation of its saving teaching. I mean the words of the Savior, "The prince of this world cometh, and findeth nothing of his in me;"[303] < and again, " The prince of this world shall be cast down >;"[304] and again, in the apostle, "The god of this world hath blinded the eyes of them that believe not, lest the light of the glorious Gospel of Christ should shine."[305]

66,2 Let's see < whether > the ruler of this world, of whom the Lord speaks, will be cast down—for Christ adds, "And if I be lifted up, I will draw all men unto me."[306] Whom does he mean by "the ruler of this world?" And if he means the devil, why does John say of the Savior in his Gospel, "He came unto his own?"[307]

66,3 For we can see that the two following sayings are contradictory. The apostle says, "The whole world lieth in the evil one,"[308] and yet the Savior "was in the world."[309] How can both of these allow for each other? And if the whole world lies in the evil one, where is there room in the world for the Savior, so that he can be "in the world?" (4) And if the world's contents are the Son of God's "own,"[310] what "ruler" exercises control over God's own? But if the contents of the world are not the Son of God's "own," what "ruler of the world" would allow the world's contents to be the Savior's own? And if the world is the Son of God's, why would he allow a "ruler" to hold his own world prisoner?

66,5 But all the words of the sacred scripture are spoken with wisdom, as the Lord himself says, "John came in the way of righteousness, neither eating nor drinking, and they say, He hath a devil. The Son of Man came eating and drinking, and they say, Behold,

---

[303] Cf. John 14:30.

[304] Cf. John 12:31.

[305] 2 Cor. 4:4. Cf. Man. Ps. 172,26–27, "He that ate the sheep is the devouring fire, the God of this aeon that led the world astray." The "god of this world" is identified with the evil god at Act. Arch. 175.7; cf. Aug. C. Faust. 20.1; C. Fel. 2.2.

[306] John 12:32

[307] John 1:11

[308] Cf. 1 John 5:19. This is from "The Apostle" in the sense that it is an Epistle quotation.

[309] John 1:10

[310] John 1:11

a man gluttonous and a winebibber, the friend of publicans and
sinners. And wisdom is justified of her children."[311] (6) And how
was wisdom justified by her children? How but by those who
understand wisdom's words, as it also says in the prophet, "Who
is wise, and he shall understand these things? For the ways of the
Lord are right, and whoso hath the word of wisdom shall likewise
understand these things; but the impious shall faint in them."[312]

67,1   < Mani > has indeed fainted in the sacred and heavenly
words, and been impious with the impious. For the Savior said
shortly before this, "I beheld Satan as lightning fall from heaven;"[313]
and here again, he says, "The ruler of this world shall be cast
down."[314] (2) And if he was speaking of a Satan who had already
fallen, why did he need to be cast down again?

But you will surely say, "[He had to be cast] into the abyss." All
right, where was the Lord to be "lifted up?" If he was to be lifted
from the abyss, < he needed to go there first. But he spoke while
he was on earth, and was to be lifted up from there* > — < for >
the comparison of like with like assures equivalence of expression.

67,3   But when was he lifted up on earth? He was speaking of
his lifting on the cross, and his ascent to heaven to draw all to
himself. (4) And why didn't he draw them while he was [still] in
heaven, but came to earth instead? He had to come and assume
the form of men, in order to < exalt > the holy vessel < in himself >
first of all—[the holy vessel] he had taken from Mary and formed
as his own holy body, the divine Word from on high, come from
the bosom of his Father. Then, when he had been exalted in his
own body, he could draw the persons who were like him to himself.

67,5   But who is the ruler of this world? When scripture says,
"The whole world lieth in the evil one," it does not mean heaven,
earth, the sun, the moon, vegetation, the sea, mountains, the air,
clouds, the wind, stars, winged things—it does not mean any part
of the creation, perish the thought! "The world" < is* > human
< lust* >, the arrogance of the human mind, the insolence of human
vanity, the boastfulness of human pride. (6) This, arrogance, was
the "ruler of this world" who was cast down. For the Savior says,
"Ye receive honor one of another, but I seek not mine own glory."[315]

67,7   How could arrogance not fall, how could the ruler of the
world not be crushed, when Herod kept the Judge and Lord of

---

[311] Matt. 11:18–19; cf. Luke 7:35.
[312] Hos. 14:10
[313] Luke 10:18
[314] John 12:31
[315] John 5:44; 8:50

the quick and dead under guard and judged him? When Pilate sat in judgment on him, a servant struck his jaw, Judas betrayed him, Caiaphas sentenced him, the Jews spat on him, and soldiers struck his head though he could have crushed heaven and earth with a nod? (8) This was the arrogance, insolence, and vainglory of the men of the world; this was the ruler of the world, who fell to the earth. In this world all the persons of high rank exercise their authority by shouting, insolence, reputation and arrogance, none of which are to be found in the Savior. For "a smoking flax shall he not quench, and a bruised reed shall he not break."[316]

68,1   And I have a great deal to say about this. But once more, Mani also says that "The god of this world hath blinded the minds of them that believe not, lest they should shine in the light of the Gospel."[317] (2) If there is any "god of this world," what was the Savior doing, coming to someone else's territory? And if he coveted someone else's possessions, this is no way for a good or a just person to behave. (3) But if he came to save things which were not his but someone else's, this is the behavior of a flatterer whose object is to make his neighbor's slaves more impertinent than they are.

68,4   And if he did come to save the possessions of the god of this world, he was doing the favor for the god of this world himself, by trying to save his vessels. And if the god of this world assents in any way to the rescue of his property by the Savior, then he is good even if he cannot save it himself, since he is pleased with the rescue of his possessions.

68,5   And then there will be a single mutuality of goodness. For the One who can, saves, while the one who cannot save his own is pleased with those who are saved, and feels that he gains by receiving his own, saved, from the One who can really save them. (6) And if he offers no opposition to the One who wants to save his possessions, he will be grateful too.

But if he is grateful to him, < the Savior > will first save the owner of the saved—to display his goodness in the rescued owner, and < because > of his unwillingness to save the less important persons and overlook the essential one, from whom the saved come.

68,7   Or again, from another viewpoint: If he prefers not to save him (i.e., the god of the world) and yet saves < the persons > he < has made >, he does not complete his task, and is unable to do good in the fullest sense of the word. But if he cannot save

[316] Isa. 42:3
[317] Cf. 2 Cor. 4:4.

him because of his unsaveability, but still saves the persons he
made—if anything, the ones he made are worse than he, and
incapable of salvation.

68,8   But to put it in still another way: If he had no possessions
of his own to save and came to someone else's for show, < to >
make a display of his assistance—what a desperate plight, that cannot
save anything of its own, and goes to foreign territory to demonstrate the act which it could not show in its own!

68,9   And Mani's argument about the Savior and the ruler of
this world has failed already. In fact the "god of this world" cannot
be another god different from the real one, or a real other god,
perish the thought! God the Lord of all, the maker of the world,
is one God, the Father of our Lord Jesus Christ, and never fails.

69,1   The god the apostle says the unbelievers have chosen for
their god—I don't mean that there is only one "god of this world,"
far from it! There are many. The unbelievers have submitted to
them and gone mentally blind, as the apostle says in another passage,
(2) "whose god is their belly and whose glory is in their shame."³¹⁸
And the Lord says in the Gospel, "Ye cannot serve two masters;"
and then a good while later, to show who the two masters are,
he says, "Ye cannot serve God and mammon."³¹⁹

69,3   Very well, God is God, and "the god of this world" is
mammon. For most people are caught by mammon and the belly,
these two, and go blind, not at God's instigation but by their own
mischief—for in their unbelief they each desire everything and
submit to everything. (4) Thus the apostle says, "The love of money
is the root of all evil."³²⁰ And he curses their wicked propensity for
god-making for this reason, and to curse the lusts of the belly says,
"Meats for the belly, and the belly for meats; but God shall destroy
both it and them."³²¹

69,5   The god of this world, then, has blinded the unbelievers'
perceptions. The scribe in the Gospel † at first³²² says a good thing,
"What shall I do to inherit eternal life?"³²³ but the Lord said, "Honor
thy father and thy mother as it is written." For the commandments
of the Law were not strange to him, and thus the Lord himself
teaches that to observe the Law is to inherit eternal life.

69,6   Then the scribe says, "All these things have I done from

---

³¹⁸ Phil. 3:19
³¹⁹ Matt. 6:24
³²⁰ 1 Tim. 6:10
³²¹ 1 Cor. 6:13
³²² Holl πρῶτον καλῶς; MSS πρῶτος καὶ δεύτερος
³²³ For this and the next three citations, cf. Mark 10:17–21.

my youth." And the Lord "rejoiced" to hear this, showing that the Law's commandments are not strange to his Godhead; for by saying that he "rejoiced," scripture expressed the agreement of the Old Testament with the New Testament.

69,7 But the scribe said, "What lack I yet?"[324] and the Lord told him, "If thou wilt be perfect sell that thou hast and give to the poor, and take up thy cross and follow me, and thou shalt have treasure in heaven. But he went away sorrowing, for he was very rich."[325] (8) Then the Lord said, "It is easier for a camel to go through the eye of a needle than for a rich man to enter into the kingdom of heaven."[326] < The rich > cannot enter because they have been blinded by the god of this world, and have taken mammon for their god and submitted to the "god of this world," that is, to covetousness. (9) As Christ says, "Beware of the leaven of the Pharisees, which is hypocrisy,"[327] and elsewhere, "which is covetousness."[328]

And to show the effect and consequence of covetousness he says, "They be blind leaders of the blind. And if the blind lead the blind, both shall fall into the ditch."[329] (10) For since covetousness, the god of this world, had blinded them, neither had "The light of the Gospel shone in their hearts,"[330] for they had gone blind from covetousness. (11) Covetousness blinded Judas, killed Ananias, has destroyed many. Here is "the god of this world." By their choice of him for their god men have taken up his honor and despised the Lord, as he says, "He will hold to the one and despise the other; ye cannot serve God and mammon."[331]

69,12 And there you see a literal and plain explanation of the matter. There cannot be any other god, not in heaven, not on earth, not anywhere. There is "one Father, of whom are all things, and one Lord Jesus Christ, by whom are all things,"[332] and one Holy Spirit, in whom are all things—forever the Trinity, one Godhead, receiving no addition and admitting of no subtraction.

70,1 Let us go on again to something else, beloved, and tear the nets of this beast, enemy and criminal apart by comparing his heresies with the speech of the truth, for the benefit of those

---

[324] For this and the next citation cf. Matt. 19:20–21.
[325] Luke 18:23
[326] Matt. 19:24
[327] Luke 12:1
[328] This is a variant reading of Luke 12:1.
[329] Matt. 15:14
[330] Cf. 2 Cor. 4:.4.
[331] Matt. 6:24
[332] 1 Cor. 8:6;3

whose aim is to learn the truth and turn their minds away from every sect's wicked teaching. (2) For once more he seizes on the Law and the Prophets, though he is the enemy of the truth, and of the Holy Spirit who has spoken in the Law and the Prophets. Characteristically, he has given free rein to his tongue against the God who made all things and has spoken in the Law and the Prophets, "the Father of our Lord Jesus Christ, of whom all the family in heaven and earth is named."[333]

70,3   Mani says, "From him (i.e., the God of the Law) comes lust, from him come murders and all the rest. For he ordered the Jews to take the Egyptians' clothing and that sacrifices be offered to him, and the rest of the Law's provisions—but ordered the murder of the murderer, so that he is still not satisfied with the first murder,[334] but even commands a second to revenge the first, if you please. And he puts lusts into people's minds by his descriptions < of > women and other things; but he constrains himself to make a few prophecies of Christ, to establish his credibility by these few plausible remarks."

70,4   And these were the words of the insolent Mani, which he impudently utters against his own Master. In considering them one must realize that there is nothing to be seen in them but the behavior of a delirium patient. For as a delirious man with a sword draws his sword against himself, cuts his own flesh in his fit in the belief that he is fighting enemies, and does not know it, so Mani is at war with himself because he does not understand the texts he applies against himself. (5) For if lust comes from God and he is its cause, why does the God who puts lust in people's heads write against lust all over the scriptures? It is he who says, "Thou shalt not covet thy neighbor's goods, nor his ox nor his ass nor his maidservant nor his field nor his wife, nor anything that is thy neighbor's."[335] If he prohibits lust, it cannot be he who provides it.

71,1   Why, Mani asks, did he order the spoiling of the Egyptians when the Israelites went out of Egypt? Yes, he did—he is a just judge, as by now I have often said of him. (2) And to show that he himself has no need of sacrifices, he says through the prophet, "Have ye offered unto me sacrifices forty years, O house of Israel? saith the Lord."[336] (3) To whom were the < sacrifices > offered, then? To him, proportionately to the understanding of the offerers; but God had commanded this, not because he needed the

---

[333] Eph. 3:15
[334] Cf. Act. Arch. 44.8.
[335] Exod. 20:17
[336] Amos 5:25

sacrifices, but to wean them away from polytheism to the recognition of one God. [He commanded it] because they had seen sacrifices offered to the gods of the Egyptians, so that their minds would not be changed because of the polytheism, and desert the one and only God. (4) But when God had dissuaded them from polytheism over a long period of time and weaned them away from such a thing, he began to get rid of the things that were not his will, and said, "To what purpose bring ye me incense from Saba, and spices from a land afar off?"[337] "Will I eat the flesh of bulls and drink the blood of goats?"[338] "I have not required this at your hands,"[339] "but to do righteousness each man to his neighbor, and truth each man to his brother."[340]

71,5   And you see that the substance of the sacred < oracles' > meaning is revealed over time. God himself tells Samuel, "Anoint Saul as king,"[341] but later he accuses them with the words, "Ye have anointed a king but not by me, and rulers, and I did not command you."[342] (6) But since their minds were set on this God consoled[343] the prophet Samuel with, "They have not rejected thee, but me, saith the Lord. But anoint for them Saul, the son of Kish." The Godhead was dealing with them as though with little children, to show patience with the feebleness of the weak and coax the infant out of its weakness. (7) Then, at the very last, he says, "The sacrifice of God is a broken spirit; a broken and contrite heart God will not despise,"[344] "Offer unto God the sacrifice of praise,"[345] and whatever else can be said about this.

72,1   Next Mani says that < the God who gave the Law reluctantly* > consented to say something about Christ. < And the cheat does not see how he is confuting himself* >. (2) For if he knows the future he is not devoid of foreknowledge—but it is God who knows the events of the future; he wrote of them to make sure that they would transpire. But if they were repugnant to him, he wrote of them but forbade them, so that we would not be won over by them. (3) But since he guarantees that those future events will be realized in Christ, the Spirit who spoke in the Law and the Prophets, and in the Gospel, is the same, for there is one

---

[337] Jer. 6:20
[338] Ps. 49:13
[339] Isa. 1:12
[340] Cf. Zech. 8:16.
[341] Cf. 1 Kms. 9:16.
[342] Cf. Hos. 8:10.
[343] Cf. 1 Kms. 8:7; 22.
[344] Ps. 50:19
[345] Ps. 49:14

accord. Thus God says through Moses, "The Lord shall raise up unto you a prophet, from your brethren, < like unto me >;"[346] (4) and in his turn the Lord says in the Gospel, "Moses wrote of me."[347] Moses says, "Every soul that shall not hearken unto that prophet, shall be destroyed,"[348] and the Lord, in turn, says, "If ye believe not Moses' writings, how shall ye believe my words?"[349] And it is perfectly plain that the truth is radiant, and "has no spot."[350]

73,1   Again, Mani declares that the testament of the Law is the testament of death, since the apostle has said, "If the testament of death, graven with letters on stones, was given with glory."[351] (2) And the sacred scripture said not only this, but, "The Law is not made for a righteous man, but for murderers of fathers and murderers of mothers, for perjured persons, and if there be anything that is contrary to sound doctrine."[352] (3) Now because the Law is not made for a righteous man, is the righteous man a law-breaker? Of course not! But since the righteous man has already obeyed the Law's commandments, there is no Law against a righteous keeper of the Law; the Law is against the lawless, and condemns law-breakers.

73,4   This, then, is why the testament is a < testament of death >. It said that the murderer should be murdered, the adulterer put to death, the law-breaker stoned. But "It was given with glory," for its glory was great. It prevailed over the glory men gain from injustice to each other; and it was typified by the light of a pillar of fire [and] fearful trumpets with their loud blasts, < was deposited* > in the tent of meeting, and came at that time with great glory.

73,5   For the testament of death had to come first, so that we would "die to sin" first and "live to righteousness"[353] —as Christ "hath borne our griefs and carried our infirmities,"[354] "bearing all in his body on the cross,"[355] so that first what pertains to death and then what pertains to life would be fulfilled in him for our sakes.

73,6   And this is why he died first, to confirm the testament of death. Then he rose from the dead, so that < we would be

---

[346] Deut. 18:15
[347] John 5:46
[348] Cf. Deut. 18:19.
[349] John 5:47
[350] Eph. 5:27
[351] Cf. 2 Cor. 3:7; Act. Arch. 15.12; 32.4.
[352] 1 Tim. 1:9–10
[353] Cf. 1 Pet. 2:24.
[354] Isa. 53:4
[355] 1 Pet. 2:24

"changed > from glory to glory, even as by the Spirit of the Lord."[356] For "He triumphed over principalities and powers"[357] on the cross and "condemned sin"[358] in death. He buried iniquity by his burial, and broke "death's sting"[359] by tasting death. By his descent into hades he despoiled hades, manfully loosed its prisoners, and won the trophy of the cross against the devil.

73,7 And see how this glory continues from Moses until the Lord! How much more should the testament of life be glorious, when a stone has been rolled away, rocks rent, graves opened, angels shine like lightning, women proclaim the good tidings, peace is bestowed, a Spirit is given the apostles by the Lord, a kingdom of heaven is proclaimed, and a Gospel has enlightened the world? "He that descended is the same as he that ascended far above all heavens,"[360] (8) and sits at the Father's right hand. But the testament was not a cause of death, it was a testament against death. The testament of death was given with glory so that the glory that excelled it might be [a testament] against death.

74,1 The next thing this Mani says is, "The Old and New Testaments cannot be the testaments of one teacher. For the one grows older every day, while the other is being renewed every day. For whatever is growing old and aged is nearing disappearance. The former is the testament of one God and one teacher, the latter, of a different God and a different teacher."[361]

74,2 Now what he says might carry conviction if he were able to show that there are two Old Testaments, because two testaments would have been given then. And similarly, if he could show that there are two New Testaments, one could take what he has said to heart.[362] (3) But if the Old Testament is one God's and the New Testament is another's, and the New Testament is the testament of a good God while the Old is the testament of a bad one, the good God would not have known that God should give a testament if he had not seen the bad god giving one. And if anything, he would be taking the cue for his teaching from the bad god. For if he had not seen the bad god giving a testament he would not have imitated him, since he had no practical experience. For if he had not seen this, he would not have imitated it. (4) And, if

---

[356] 2 Cor. 3:10
[357] Col. 2:15
[358] Rom. 8:3
[359] 1 Cor. 15:55–56
[360] Eph. 4:10
[361] Cf. Act. Arch. 15.12.
[362] Cf. Act. Arch. 52.2.

anything, the Old Testament ought to be the good God's so that, if someone must be called an imitator, it is the bad god rather than the actual God.

74,5 For the Lord says in the Gospel, "What things soever the Son seeth the Father do, the Son likewise doeth."[363] And to avoid deferring to a counselor, and keep the devil from boasting that the Savior has done something by his advice—as the devil tells him, "Command that the stones be made bread,"[364] but he will not hear of it. If he agreed he might be suspected of taking the advice from the devil.

74,6 And do you see that he says that the two testaments belong to one God? The apostle says, "The first testament was given at Mt. Sinai and gendereth to bondage. For Mt. Sinai is in Arabia. < But the heavenly Jerusalem is free, which is the mother of us all >."[365] For if there are two wives, there is still only one husband. Thus even though there are two Testaments, there is one God, who gave the two. (7) And this is why he did not call two testaments "New," or two testaments "Old," but called one Old and one New. And he says, "A testament is of force after men are dead; therefore the first testament was not dedicated without blood. For Moses took the blood of goats and sprinkled both the book and the people."[366] Thus the second testament too was given at the death of the Savior. (8) And above all, both Testaments are in agreement. The one says, "There shall not fail a ruler from Judah, nor a governor from out of his loins, until that come for which it is prepared;"[367] but the second says, "God was in Christ, reconciling the world unto himself, not imputing their trespasses unto them."[368] And there is a great deal to be said about this, but for brevity's sake I shall omit it.

75,1 And again, he compares the Law and the Prophets to trees which are withered and old, taking this, if you please, from the text which said, "The Law and the Prophets were until John."[369] (2) And nothing could be sillier. Who does not understand that once < the Law > which the prophets proclaimed was fulfilled, the prophets were finished? If prophets were still coming and announcing a Christ to come from Mary, Christ would not have arrived yet.

---

[363] John 5:19
[364] Matt. 4:3
[365] Gal. 4:24–26
[366] Heb. 9:17; 18; 19
[367] Gen. 49:10
[368] 2 Cor. 5:19
[369] Luke 16:16. Cf. Act. Arch. 15.14.

75,3   For the position is something like this:[370] A king who intends to visit a country sends riders, advance men and heralds before him, and the nearer the king's arrival the more heralds there are of the king's arrival, preceding him and proclaiming his arrival in the cities. (4) But when the king reaches the city, what further need is there for heralds? What further need is there for riders, or the others to proclaim the king's arrival beforehand, since the king himself is in the city?

75,5   And thus "The Law and the prophets were until John."[371] After John had cried aloud in the wilderness and made it known that "This is the lamb of God which taketh away the sins of the world,"[372] there was no more need for prophets, to come and tell us of Christ's advent from a Virgin. But there was a need for those who had previously proclaimed his coming, to confirm the fact that his coming had been previously proclaimed.

75,6   It is as though someone had a pedagogue, as the apostle says, "The Law was our pedagogue until the Lord's coming."[373] When the person grows old enough and obtains a teacher, he surely does not fire the pedagogue as though he were an enemy. (7) So we too were given guidance in the Law and the Prophets until the coming of our Teacher. But now that we have our teacher we do not despise the pedagogue but, indeed, are grateful to him. He has served as the guide of our childhood, and set us on our way to the more advanced studies.

75,8   Or, it is as though a man planned on making a sea voyage and had a big ship, but he sailed over the open roadstead beside the shore in a little boat, and the boat took the man to the big ship. Because he has reached the big ship, he surely does not sink the boat. He boards his larger, safe ship with gratitude for the boat. (9) Or to put it another way, suppose one is exposed in infancy by the mother who bore him, but taken in by a passerby and reared for some time, and recognizes his real father later when he grows up, and his father acknowledges him. Does he despise the man who brought him up because he has recognized his father and gets his own inheritance? Won't he far sooner thank the man who brought him up, because he did not leave him to die? (10) In the same way, we thank the God who has given us the Law and

---

[370] The following series of metaphors may have been suggested by Act. Arch. 15.14.
[371] Luke 16:16
[372] John 1:29
[373] Gal. 3:24

the Prophets, and we thank him < who > has counted us worthy
of his Son's New Testament.

76,1   Once more, Mani says that we are kinds of archons, that
we were made by the archons,[374] and that we are held in reserve
for them for food. But there is a great deal of ignorance in this
sort of talk; (2) we can see that this is not the way things are.
Nothing at all, not even one of < the > more dangerous, fiercer
beasts, attacks its own kind; it attacks other kinds. (3) Lions do
not eat lions, for example, because lions are in their image and
are of the same kind. Even when a severe famine bears hard upon
the beasts in the mountains, and they find no < food > for a long
while because of snow or some other exigency, they live in their
caves and dens, lions with cubs and lionesses, < and do not so
much as touch each other* >. And a beast will not attack a beast,
or a wolf, a wolf, (4) unless the beast goes mad, and in its rage
does not know what it is doing. (5) Very well, if a wolf will not
eat a wolf because they look alike, how can the archons eat us,
if we are of the same < kind >? Won't they treat us gently instead,
with the idea of preserving their own kinds? And the scum's
arguments are altogether refuted.

77,1   Then again, he seizes on the text from the Gospel, "All
cannot receive this saying, save they to whom it is given."[375] And
the Savior was not speaking of teaching here, but of eunuchs. (2)
However, if "Not all can receive it," is here applied to his teaching
by the Savior, then, if they will not receive it, this is by their free
choice. They will be termed praiseworthy or blameworthy by their
own free choice; their reception of the teaching cannot be by
nature. Otherwise, what good would it do the Savior to give his
teaching? (3) So Mani's argument has altogether failed. The Savior
did not make this declaration about teaching, but about eunuchhood.
But even if he had said it about teaching, Mani's argument would
not hold good.

77,4   Again, Mani says, "I knew my own, 'For my sheep know
me and I know my sheep.'"[376] But he lies in everything. He said
this of the audience at the debate, because he wanted to catch
souls by cozening and as it were setting a trap, so that they would
see fit to join him because of the flattery. (5) Then, once they
had joined him, he could begin to boast, and say that he knew
them before they came to him. (6) But the outcome for him was

---

[374] Cf. Act. Arch. 16.10.
[375] Matt. 19:11. Cf. Act. Arch. 28.1.
[376] John 10:14. Cf. Act. Arch. 28.1.

same as the Greek myth about the soothsayer (μάντις) Apollo, who told others' fortunes but could not tell his own, and instead failed in his prediction—(7) for he was in love with Daphne, and because of her discretion failed to win her. Mani too prophesied that he knew his own, and actually came for Marcellus, to obtain his submission. But his oracle failed. Neither Marcellus, nor anyone else who was present on that occasion, obeyed him.

78,1 Next he said that no one was saved in ancient times,[377] but [only] from the fifteenth year of Tiberius Caesar until his own day. (Probus was emperor then, and his predecessor Aurelian, when Mani made his appearance.) (2) And in this too he is altogether refuted, since the Gospel, and the words of the apostles, speak of those who have already been saved. The Lord likewise says, "There shall be required of this generation all the righteous blood that hath been shed upon the earth, from the blood of righteous Abel unto the blood of Zacharias, which was shed between the temple and the altar."[378] (3) How could Abel be righteous, how could Zacharias, unless salvation were already possible, and they had already been saved by the Law and the prophets? < Thus the apostle also* > says, "Death reigned from Adam to Moses,"[379] to show you that death was checked, though not altogether destroyed, in Moses' time.

78,4 For Moses acknowledged the "Finisher"[380] of all things, "Jesus," who, when he gave himself for humankind—when the immortal died, the invulnerable became vulnerable, life endured suffering in the flesh—would, through death, break the one who had control of death, and the sting of sin, and death. Then at last < the words >, "O death,where is thy sting? O grave, where is thy victory?"[381] would come true.

78,5 For there, in Moses' time, the death which had reigned until Moses was restrained and checked. And Abel was righteous before that, and Enoch, "who was taken away that he might not see death, and was not found."[382] (6) But there < was > no written Law yet—only the law which comes naturally to the mind and by tradition, through successive transmission from fathers to sons.[383] When, however, the Law was given for all to see, it became, as

---

[377] Cf. Act. Arch. 32.4.
[378] Matt. 23:35. Cf. Act. Arch. 32.4.
[379] Rom. 5:14. Cf. Act. Arch. 33.5.
[380] Heb. 12:2
[381] 1 Cor. 15:55
[382] Cf. Gen. 5:24.
[383] Cf. Act. Arch. 32.9.

it were, a sword to cut the power of sin in two. But when the Savior came, the sting of death was broken. And again, < when this corruptible puts on incorruption and this mortal puts on immortality* >, then death will be swallowed up in victory.

78,7 And see how God saved by many means, but the fullness of salvation has come and will come in Christ Jesus, our Lord, as the Gospel says, "Of his fullness have we all received."[384] (8) And which "fullness?" "The Law was given by Moses, but grace and truth came by Jesus Christ."[385] There, it was "given;" here, it has "come." If the Law, grace and truth come through Jesus of < his > fullness, the Old and the New Testaments < are from the same Testator, who gives them* > in the Law, in grace, and in truth.

79,1 But Mani has utilized another text, and says that "Christ has bought us free from the curse of the Law, being made a curse for us."[386] (2) Well then, he should tell us how much we were sold for, what it cost to buy us! Paul didn't say "bought," but, "redeemed." However, Mani understands the purchase, but doesn't know the price.

But the truth admits of both expressions. (3) Christ has indeed redeemed us and bought us "free from the curse of the Law by being made a curse for us." And the teacher of the church immediately adds the way in which Christ bought us, and says, "Ye were bought with a price,"[387] "the precious blood of Christ, the lamb without blemish and without spot."[388] Now if we were bought with the blood, you are not one of the purchased, Mani, for you deny the blood.

79,4 Tell me, from whom did he buy us? Did he buy us as someone else's property? If so, was our former owner out of funds and in need of our purchase price, so that he took it and gave us to Christ? And if we were given to Christ, we no longer belong to our former owner.

79,5 If our former owner no longer owns us, however, then he has been deprived of his abundance and has no authority in his own domain. How can he "work in the children of disobedience,"[389] then, as the scripture says? (6) But this utter madman who has opened his mouth without being able to "affirm that whereof

---

[384] John 1:16
[385] John 1:17
[386] Gal. 3:13. The thought is common in Manichaean writings; cf. CM 16, 2–9, "to redeem the captives from the tyrants [?] and free his own members from subjection to the rebels and the power of the governors" et al.
[387] 1 Cor. 6:20
[388] 1 Pet. 1:19
[389] Eph. 2:2

he speaks,"[390] does not understand how Christ ever bought us, does not understand that we were redeemed, how Christ became a curse for us. (7) I can see them addressing Christ at the regeneration and crying, "In thy name we ate, and in thy name cast out devils.[391] And he shall say to them, Depart from me ye cursed, I never knew you."[392] (8) How can they confess him, and he curse them? But what was the curse of the Law? The curse of the Law was the cross, the penalty for sins.

For if someone was caught in a transgression, the Law said, "And ye shall hang him on a tree. The sun shall not set upon him, upon his corpse, but ye shall surely take him down and shall surely bury him before the setting of the sun, for cursed is he that hangeth on the tree."[393] (9) Thus, since the curse had been pronounced because of crucifixion, he himself "bare our sins upon the tree"[394] when he came, by "giving himself for us."[395] His blood has bought us, his body lifted the curse on us—that is, by the penance of the cross, and by his coming, it has done away with the sins. (10) Thus the Law was not a curse, never think it! Neither the Gospel nor the Lord assumed the curse; but because of his death, the death decreed for sin is destroyed.

80,1 Next he says that the Law "was the ministration of death."[396] < But > I have already said a great deal to show that it was not a minister of death. (2) It did not order murder, but commanded, "Thou shalt do no murder."[397] Its ministry was a ministry of death because it murdered the murderer to prevent murder through the murder of one person, so that many would be afraid because of the one person, keep their wickedness in check and commit no more murders. This was not to minister death, but to ensure the death of the murderer so that many would no longer become murderers.

80,3 But since the pedagogue had at last made his charges peaceable for the most of the time, the Savior gave the more advanced lessons when he came, with the agreement of the Law of "Thou shalt do no murder; Thou shalt not steal; Thou shalt not bear false witness."[398] (4) The Savior said, "To him that smiteth

---

[390] 1 Tim. 1:7
[391] Matt. 7:22 (Luke 13:26)
[392] Luke 13:27
[393] Cf. Deut. 21:33.
[394] 1 Pet. 2:24
[395] Gal. 1:4
[396] 2 Cor. 3:7
[397] Exod. 20:13
[398] Exod. 20:13; 15–16

thee on the right cheek turn to him the other also,"[399] to make the ministry a ministry of life, with murder eliminated altogether. For if someone receives a blow on the cheek, he offers no provocation to murder. Instead, by his humility he disarms the murderer's hand, and soothes the wickedness in him. And thus all the ancient laws, and the New Testament, are in agreement.

81,1 Then he seizes on something else, as a covert way of introducing two items of evidence for the dyad he speaks of—the dyad of the natures which I mentioned before, of two principles with no beginnings, and of two roots. In his desire to say something similar about a distinction between things, he ventures to distinguish them as follows, and is not ashamed to say, (2) "The Old Testament said, The silver is mine and the gold is mine;"[400] but the New Testament says, "Blessed are the poor in spirit, for theirs is the kingdom of heaven."[401]

81,3 But he does not know that the Old Testament also says, "The poor and the rich have met together: but the Lord is the maker of them both."[402] And the New Testament agrees, and pronounces a blessing on the poor who are literally poor, and in another passage a blessing on the poor in spirit, so that both pronouncements have force. Thus Peter can point with pride to his literal poverty and say, "Silver and gold have I none, but what I have, I give thee; in the name of Jesus Christ, rise up and walk,"[403] (4) showing that there is no contradiction between the blessing of the literally poor and the blessing of the poor in spirit. The "poor in spirit" are persons in righteous possession of property, while the "poor" are the humble, of whom Christ said, "I was an hungered, and ye gave me meat, thirsty, and ye gave me drink," and so on.[404]

81,5 Next he explains, "These (i.e., the poor in spirit) acted of their abundance;"[405] and you can see one and the same Spirit pointing out the poor and the rich in the Old Testament and the same in the New, just as the Savior praises them both. (6) For as he watched the treasury he saw people putting money into the treasury, and did not refuse the gifts of the rich; but he praised

---

[399] Matt. 5:39
[400] Hag. 2:9
[401] Matt. 5:3. The argument, and this scriptural text, are found at Act. Arch. 44.8.
[402] Prov. 22:2
[403] Acts 3:6
[404] Matt. 25:35, cf. Act. Arch. 44.9–10.
[405] Mark 12:44; Luke 21:4

the widow who had put in the two mites for her [real] poverty, as we have said, in fulfillment of the scripture, "The poor and the rich have met together: but the Lord is the maker of them both."

81,7 And because this is so, and the Spirit of the Old and the New Testaments is the same, see the apostle say of the ancient prophets, "The time would fail me to tell of Gideon, Barak, Samson, Jephtha, David and the other prophets who wandered about in sheepskins, in goatskins, being tormented, straitened, afflicted, of whom the world was not worthy."[406] For I have found that Isaiah wore sackcloth, and Elijah too. And do you see how, in the Old and the New Testaments, the poor are called blessed for piety, and the rich are called blessed for righteousness?

82,1 Then, once more, Mani says, "The Old Testament commands us to keep the Sabbath, and if one did not keep it he was stoned, as one was put < to death > for gathering a bundle of sticks. But the New Testament, that is, the Lord in the Gospel, said, 'I work, and my Father worketh.'[407] And the disciples plucked ears of grain on the Sabbath, and he healed on the Sabbath. And not only this, but He said besides, 'Take up thy bed, and go unto thine house.'"[408]

82,2 What ignorance! There is nothing worse than lack of expertise; ignorance has blinded many. When has the Sabbath not been broken for a good cause? When was not only the Sabbath, but every day not a forbidden day for evil?

82,3 Moses' successor Joshua the son of Nun counts as a prophet, was God's chosen, and stopped the sun and moon by prayer when he said, "Let the sun be still over Gibeon, and the moon over the valley of Ajalon."[409] But it is immediately obvious that he broke the Sabbath to perform a good work. (4) When traveling farther than the prescribed six stades was not allowed on the Sabbath, Joshua circled the walls of Jericho for seven days. But the circumference of Jericho is more than twenty stades; if they circled it for seven days, the Sabbath surely fell on one of the days. (5) But this was a command of God, to show his will to work wonders. For there were no machines or catapults, no battering-rams, no siege engines; the enemy's walls sagged and fell simply at the sound of a ram's horn and the prayer of a righteous man. (6) For their punishment was due, since the tally of the Amorites' sins had been completed.

---

[406] Heb. 11:32; 37
[407] John 5:17
[408] Matt. 9:6. Cf. Act. Arch. 44:9–10.
[409] Josh. 10:12–13

83,1   The Law was a judge of iniquity and rewarded everyone in accordance with his works. I have already said this elsewhere, but to repeat it here will do no harm. The Amorites were in sin, had fallen into transgression, and had violated the oath they had sworn. (2) An example of Mani's frightfulness that comes to mind is, "Some 'good' God of the Law! He spoiled the Egyptians, expelled the Amorites, Girgashites and other nations, and gave their land to the children of Israel. If he said, 'Thou shalt not covet,'[410] how could he give them other people's land?"

83,3   The ignoramus did not know that they took their own land back which had been seized from them, and that retribution was exacted for the pact that was made between them, with a true decision and an oath. (4) For when Noah was saved from the flood—and his wife, with his three sons and their three brides— he alone divided the whole world. As is logical and nothing foolish or false, he distributed it among his three sons, Shem, Ham and Japheth, by casting lots in Rhinocorura.[411]

83,5   For Rhinocorura means Neel, and its inhabitants actually call it that; but in Hebrew it means "lots," since Noah cast the lots for his three sons there. (6) And the land from Rhinocorura to Gadiri fell < to Ham >, including Egypt, the Marean Marsh, Ammon, Libya, Marmaris, Pentapolis, Macatas, Macronas, Leptis Magna, Syrtis, and Mauritania, out to the so-called Pillars of Hercules and the interior of Gadiri. (7) These were Ham's possessions to the south. But he also owned the land from Rhinocorura eastwards, Idumaea, Midianitis, Alabastritis, Homeritis, Axiomitis, Bugaea, and Diba, out to Bactria.

83,8   The same lot sets a boundary between Shem and the lands to the east. Roughly, Shem's allotment was Palestine, Phoenicia and Coele-Syria, Commagene, Cilicia, Cappadocia, Galatia, Paphlagonia, Lazia, Iberia, Caspia, and Carduaea, out to Media in the north. (9) From there this lot assigned the northern lands to Japheth. But in the west < Japheth was assigned > the land between Europe and Spain, and Britain, < Thrace, Europe, Rhodope > and the peoples who border on it, the Venetians, Daunians, Iapygians, Calabrians, Latins, Oscans [and] Megarians, out to the inhabitants of Spain and Gaul, and the lands of the Scots and Franks in the north.

---

[410] Exod. 20:17
[411] Rhinocorura comes from LXX Isa. 27:12, where it is used to translate נַעַל. Epiphanius, who is the first to locate Noah's division of the world here, is thinking of the resemblance between נַחַל and נַחֲלָה, "lot."

84,1   After these allotments, Noah called his three sons together
and bound them with an oath, so that none of them would encroach
on his brother's allotment and be covetous of his brother. (2) But
Ham's son Canaan was covetous and invaded Palestine and took
it; and the land was named Canaan because Canaan settled in it
after leaving his own allotment, which he thought was hot. (3) And
he settled in Shem's land, which is now called Judaea, and fathered
the following sons: Amorraeus, Girgashaeus, Pherizaeus, Jebusaeus,
Hivaeus, Arucaeus, Chittaeus, Asenaeus, Samaraeus, Sidonius and
Philistiaeus. (4) And so, to show that the number of their sins
against the oath was reaching completion, the Lord says in the
Law, "The sins of the Amorites have not yet been completed."[412]
And therefore [Israel] remained in the desert and loitered in the
wilderness, until the Amorites condemned themselves by going to
war with the wronged sons of Shem.

84,5   For Shem was the father of Arphaxad, Arphaxad of Kenah,
Kenah of Selah, Selah of Eber, Eber of Peleg, Peleg of Reu, Reu
of Serug, Serug of Nahor, Nahor of Terah, Terah of Abraham,
Abraham of Isaac, Isaac of Jacob, Jacob of Judah, Judah of Perez,
Perez of Esrom, Esrom of Aram, Aram of Aminadab, Aminadab
of Naason. (6) In the time of Naason the head of the tribe of
Judah and Joshua the son of Nun, the sons of Shem took their
own land. There was no wrong involved, but a righteous judgment.
And so the walls of Jericho fell of themselves, for righteousness
avenges unrighteousness. (7) They circled the walls on seven days,
and the Sabbath was violated so that righteousness would be fulfilled.

85,1   And not only this, but the sacred lampstand in the tent
of the testimony had seven lamps, and the seven lamps were all
lit every day. Not one remained unlit on any day; on every day
there was the same light. (2) For the Sabbath was not instituted
for the stoppage of work, but for a good work. While no member
of the twelve tribes ever worked on the Sabbath, just one thing,
the altar, did not stand idle, as the Lord says in the Gospel, "Your
priests profane the Sabbath in the temple, and are blameless."[413]
(3) But "They profane the Sabbath" means that they break it. But
how do they break it but by offering sacrifice to God, so that the
altar will not stand idle?

85,4   And not only this. The sun rises and sets, the moon waxes
and wanes, winds blow, fruit is produced, mothers give birth, and
it all takes place on the Sabbath. (5) And thus when the Lord came

---

[412] Gen. 15:16
[413] Matt. 12:5

he did not practice carpentry or coppersmithing on the Sabbath, or < do > anything else [of this sort], but as God he did the work of God. And he says, "Take up thy bed and walk,"[414] to make his ongoing work known from the man carrying the bed, so that all will recognize Him who has come from heaven to the aid of the human race.

85,6   For he did in fact come to abolish the Sabbath, but he could not have abolished it if it had not been his. No one destroys someone else's work unless he is a tenant[415] and busybody, whose punishment is well deserved. (7) But since the Sabbath was his own he said, "The Son of Man is Lord of the Sabbath;" and he said, "Man was not made for the Sabbath, but the Sabbath for man."[416] (8) Now if God made the Sabbath for man, and valued man more highly than the Sabbath, then < there is one God, who made the law of the Sabbath* > so that everyone would be aware of the rest < God has given us [now*] >, and the repose of the things to come; for the things here are types of the heavenly things. (9) Here things are partial, but there is all perfection. So the Sabbath of the Law was in force until Christ's arrival. But he abolished that Sabbath and gave us the supreme Sabbath, the Lord himself, our Rest and Sabbath Repose.

85,10   Thus the Old Testament is no different from the New, or the New from the Old. However, if an unschooled, ignorant person sees two ladles draw water from one stream, but supposes because of the difference of the ladles that the kinds of water [in them] are different too, the wise will tell him the truth, "Taste the two ladles, and see that there are two ladles, but one stream." (11) Thus there is one Lord, one God, one Spirit who has spoken in the Law and Prophets, and in the Gospel. This is why there are not two Old Testaments and not two New Testaments. There are not two testators but one, who makes the Old Testament old and the New Testament new—not by reducing the Old Testament to nothing but by bringing the Old Testament to a close and adding the inheritance of abundance through the second Testament.

86,1   Mani introduces yet another text by saying, "I know that spirit is saved without body.[417] For the apostle teaches this," says he, "with the words, 'It is actually reported that there is fornication among you, and such fornication as is not found even among the

---

[414] John 5:8
[415] ἐκλήμπτωρ translates the Latin conductor, or susceptor.
[416] Mark 2:28; 27
[417] Man. Hom. 75,13–14, "their souls went to the heavens, their bodies returned to the ground."

gentiles, that one should have his father's wife. And ye are puffed up, and have not rather mourned, that he that hath done this deed might be taken away from among you. I verily, as absent in body, but present in spirit, have judged already him that hath done this deed, when ye and the Lord are gathered together with my spirit, to deliver such an one to Satan for the destruction of the flesh, that the spirit may be saved in the day of the Lord.'[418] (2) But the destruction of the flesh is its entire reduction to nothing. If the flesh is reduced to nothing by the devil's agency, and the spirit is saved, how can there still be a resurrection of bodies or flesh, and a salvation of spirit?"[419]

86,3   And in his total ignorance he did not know that "The works of the flesh are fornication, adultery, uncleanness"[420] and similar things, and < that > Paul is not speaking of the flesh itself, but of the works of the flesh. (4) When fornication is committed, the flesh commits it. But if one practices continence, the flesh is no longer flesh. The flesh has been turned to spirit as the apostle says, "He who joined both at the beginning said, For this cause shall a man leave his father and his mother and shall be joined unto his wife, and they two shall be one flesh."[421] "Thus he which is joined to an harlot is one body, and he which is joined unto the Lord is one spirit."[422]

86,5   Thus if someone commits fornication he has become "flesh"—and not just his flesh itself, but everything about him, his soul and the rest, becomes "flesh." He became flesh by his union with the harlot, and since he is fleshly the whole of him is called flesh. "But he that is joined to the Lord is one spirit"—that is, his body, his soul and everything in the man, is one spirit in the Lord.

86,6   And the same apostle says in his legislation on the subject, "God hath set the members in the body, every one of them as it hath pleased him."[423] And see how he acknowledges that God is the maker of the body, and the Disposer of our members as he has willed, by his wisdom and goodness.

86,7   Then again, in place of the illustration of our own bodies < he introduces the illustration of the body* > of Christ, < and

---

[418] 1 Cor. 5:1–5
[419] Chapter 13 of the Kephalaia, pp. 45,16–46,12, is entitled "On the Five Saviors Who Raise the Dead, and on the Five Resurrections." The chapter is fragmentary, but the five resurrections are surely "spiritual" or metaphorical.
[420] Gal. 5:19
[421] Eph. 2:14; 5:31
[422] 1 Cor. 6:16–17
[423] 1 Cor. 12:18

says >, "As we are the body of Christ and members † in particular,"[424] and, "the church of God, which is the body of Christ."[425] (8) Now if God's church is a body, < but > it is one spirit when it is joined to the Spirit, that is, to the Lord, then a member who sins ceases to be spirit and becomes entirely flesh, in his soul and body, and everything in him.

86,9 Otherwise, how could part of someone be delivered to Satan, and part not delivered? Paul did not say that the man's *flesh* was delivered to Satan, but ordered the delivery of "such an one." But since he says, "such an one," (10) he has delivered a man whole, with his soul and entire manhood. If he has delivered him whole, however, he has declared that he is entirely flesh. But he said that "the spirit" is saved at the day of the Lord, so that the church would not be held responsible for the fault of the man who fell, and the whole church polluted by the transgression of the one. < Thus > what he means is, "Deliver the one who has fallen, that the spirit, that is, the whole church, may be saved."

87,1 But, says Mani, the scripture says, "Flesh and blood cannot inherit the kingdom of God;"[426] and here he thinks he has a point. In fact, however, *fornication* cannot inherit the kingdom of heaven, nor can adultery, uncleanness or idolatry; that is, "flesh and blood" cannot inherit the kingdom of heaven.

87,2 If you suppose, however, that the "flesh and blood" [mentioned here] is the actual flesh, what application can be left for, "And as many as received him, to them gave he power to become the sons of God, who were born, not of the flesh, but of God?"[427] Who in the world has been born without flesh? (3) But because their *minds* were changed—not the *natures* of those who are born of flesh and blood mothers and fathers, [but their *minds*]—and they were born with the second birth, which is birth from the Lord by Spirit and fire, he gave them the right to become the sons of God.

87,4 Thus, as they were born of flesh and blood here, < so in turn they are born again of spirit* >. And because of their conversion to righteousness their birth is no longer counted as a birth of flesh and blood, although < they live* > in flesh and blood— as he says, "For though we walk in the flesh, we do not war after the flesh."[428] (5) Thus there can be flesh that does not "war after

---

[424] Read ἐκ μέρους with 1 Cor. 12:27. MSS ἐκ μέλους is surely an error.
[425] Eph. 1:22–23
[426] 1 Cor. 15:53
[427] John 1:12–13
[428] 2 Cor. 10:3

the flesh." And this is why he says that flesh and blood cannot inherit the kingdom of heaven. He < is not speaking > of this flesh which has grown weary [in welldoing], been sanctified, pleased God, but of the "flesh" which is counted as sinful. (6) Otherwise what application can there be of "This corruptible must put on incorruption, and this mortal must put on immortality?"[429]

87,7 But so that no one will fall into error and despair of the body's resurrection because of its evil works, the same apostle puts this more clearly and says, "Put to death your members upon earth, which are fornication, adultery, uncleanness,"[430] and so on. < And see that he means the members that do not rise, the passions of the flesh.* > (8) On the other hand, listen to the angels who appeared to the Galilaeans and said, "This Jesus whom ye have seen taken up from you, shall so come *in like manner* as ye have seen him taken up."[431]

88,1 From all that I have said, the sensible can understanding the meaning in all the words of the truth, and in those of this so-called Mani's falsehood. And even if I have overlooked some text, all his lies are detectable by means of the two or three testimonies which I have mentioned.

88,2 We have gone over a long, hard road and many dangerous places, and < have* > with difficulty < crushed the head* > of this amphisbaena and venomous reptile, the cenchritis, which has coils of many illustrations for the deception of those who see it, and conceals beneath it the sting and poisonous source < of the lies of heathen mythology* >. (3) For since Mani is a pagan with the pagans and worships the sun and moon,[432] the stars, and daemons, the man < is heathen* >, and his sect teaches heathen religion. < And besides this* > he knows the lore of the magi and is involved with them, and he praises astrologers and practices their mumbo jumbo. He merely mouths the name of Christ, as the cenchritis too conceals its poison, and deceives people with its tangled coils by hiding in deep woods and matching its background.

88,4 But with the power of God, the cudgel of the truth, the blood of Christ, his body truly born of Mary, the resurrection of the dead, and the confession of the one Divine Unity, we have

---

[429] 1 Cor. 15:53
[430] Col. 3:5
[431] Acts 1:11
[432] Man. Ps. 86,19–21, "Thou madest me worship these Luminaries and the Fathers that are in them, that ferry across them that believe to the Land of the Immortals."

crushed the head of the dragon upon the waters, put this many-headed sect to flight and smashed its head. Let us close with gratitude to God and hurry on to the other sects, calling on God to be the help of our weakness, so that we may keep the promise we have made in God, and give him perfect thanks.

Against Hieracites.[1] 47, but 67 of the series

1,1　After this most wicked and venomous of all sects and the savage attack, like a snake's, of Mani's teaching, came a man named Hieracas, the founder of the Hieracites. (2) He lived at Leontus in Egypt[2] and had quite a bit of education, for he was proficient in the Greek and other literary studies, and well acquainted with medicine and the other subjects of Greek and Egyptian learning. And perhaps he had dabbled in astrology and magic. (3) For he was very well versed in many subjects and, as his works show, < an extremely scholarly > expositor of scripture.[3] He knew Coptic very well—he was Egyptian—but there were few deficiencies in his Greek, for he was quick in every way.

1,4　He was Christian, if you please, but did not persevere in the Christian way of life; for he strayed from it, slipped, and came to grief. He could recite the Old and New Testaments accurately from memory and gave expositions of them, but because of his silliness he privately held whatever doctrines suited his fancy and came into his head.

1,5　Hieracas too believes that the flesh never rises, only the soul.[4] He claims, however, that there is a spiritual resurrection. And he collected whatever texts he could < find > in the sacred scripture to support his position, and so made a pile of them and wickedly concocted any old cheap fictions for proof of his heresy. (6) But he was awesome in his asceticism, and capable of winning souls over to him; for example, many Egyptian ascetics were led astray by him. I suppose he took the cue for his denial that the resurrection of the dead is a resurrection of the flesh from Origen—or spat this up out of his own head.

1,7　He does not allow matrimony, and claims that this is an

---

[1] 1,3, 3,3, and the quotations from Hieracas at 2,2–6;7 and 3,2–3 show that Epiphanius knows a work or works by Hieracas. The Life of Epiphanius, 27, says that Epiphanius had a personal encounter with Hieracas and rebuked him, but had this been the case, Epiphanius would have said so here. In fact, at 68,1,2 Epiphanius dates Hieracas in the time of Diocletian.

[2] So at Vit. Epiph. 27

[3] Holl: ἐν ἐξηγήσει < φιλοκαλώτατος >

[4] Vit. Epiph. 27 says "not this flesh, but another in its place."

Old Testament institution. For he accepts Abraham, Isaac, Jacob, Moses, Aaron, and all the saints alike, Isaiah and Jeremiah too, and regards them as prophets. (8) He says that marriage is allowed in the Old Testament, but that after Christ's coming marriage is no longer accept< able >,[5] (9) and cannot inherit the kingdom of heaven.

For what did the Word come to do, he asks, that was new? What new message did the Only-begotten come to give, and set us straight? If it was about the fear of God, the Law had this. If it was about marriage, the scriptures had proclaimed it. If it was about envy, covetousness and iniquity, all this is in the Old Testament. But Christ came to make only this correction—to preach continence in the world, and choose the pure and the continent for his own; and without continence no < one > can be saved.

2,1   Hieracas collects the warrants for this from all sorts of places—for example, when the scriptures say, "and your consecration, without which no man shall see God."[6] (2) And if they ask him, "Why did the apostle say, 'Marriage is honorable and the bed undefiled, but whoremongers and adulterers God will judge,'"[7] < he replies, "But on the other hand the apostle says, 'It is good for a man not to touch a woman,'*>[8] (3) and adds immediately, < 'It is good for a man so be.'" >[9] And skipping a little he says, "'The unmarried woman careth for the things of the Lord, how she may please the Lord, likewise the virgin. But she that is married careth how she may please her husband, and is divided.'[10] (4) Now if there is division, where there is division how can there be fellowship? And if the married woman does not please God but her husband, how can she have her inheritance with God? (5) < The apostle > doesn't < say >, 'To avoid fornication, let every man have his own wife,'[11] in order to commend matrimony after the incarnation, but in order to bear with it, to prevent falls into further ruin. 'For there be eunuchs, which have made themselves eunuchs for the kingdom of heaven's sake.'[12] And Paul says, 'I will that all men be even

---

[5] At Ps.-Ath. Haer., MSG 28, 516C, it is said that Hieracas will not accept the marriage of Adam and Eve as a precedent for the legitimacy of matrimony, because he rejects the Old Testament.
[6] Heb. 12:14
[7] Heb. 13:4
[8] 1 Cor. 7:26
[9] 1 Cor. 7:26
[10] Cf. 1 Cor. 7:34.
[11] 1 Cor. 7:2
[12] Mat. 19:12

as I myself.'[13] (6) And 'The kingdom of heaven is likened unto ten virgins, five foolish and five wise.'[14] Wise virgins, foolish virgins, are likened to the kingdom of heaven—but virgins! He didn't say, 'married persons.'" And he heaps up a great deal of material of this kind during his repudiation of matrimony, if you please.

2,7   Hieracas does not accept children who die before the age of reason,[15] but excludes them from the hope in which we believe. They cannot inherit the kingdom of heaven, he says, because they have not taken part in the contest. "'For if a man strive, yet is he not crowned except he strive lawfully.'[16] If even someone who strives is not crowned unless he strives lawfully, how much more those who have not yet been summoned to the arena?"

2,8   Again, precisely like Origen, as I said, he does not believe that Paradise is an actual place. Nor, as I said, does he believe that the resurrection of the dead is a resurrection of the flesh. He says that there is a resurrection of the dead but that it is a resurrection of souls, and also tells some fairy story about "spirit." (9) And no one can worship with them without being a virgin, a monk, continent or a widow.

3,1   But Hieracas does not agree with Origen about the Father, the Son and the Holy Spirit.[17] He believes that the Son is really begotten of the Father and < gives his assent to the doctrine > that the Holy Spirit is of the Father. (2) However, as I remarked above in the Sect of the Melchizedekians, he claims that the Holy Spirit is Melchizedek himself[18] because "< The apostle > has said, 'He maketh intercession for us with groanings which cannot be uttered.'[19] And who is this? Who but < 'he that was made like unto the Son of God, who > remaineth a priest forever?' But it says, 'a priest forever,'[20] because of the intercession."

3,3   This Spirit met Abraham at that time, since he is like the Son. "And this," says Hieracas, "is why the apostle < says >, 'without father, without mother, without descent.'[21] 'Without mother'" he says, "because he has no mother. 'Without father' because he had no father on earth, but is 'made like unto the Son of God, and

---

[13] 1 Cor. 7:7
[14] Matt. 25:1–2
[15] Cf. Vit. Epiph. 27. The Greek here is literally, "before knowledge."
[16] 2 Tim. 2:5
[17] Cf. Arius Ep. Ad Al. at Pan. 69,7,6.
[18] Pan. 55,5,2–4
[19] Rom. 8:26
[20] Heb. 7:3
[21] Heb. 7:3

remaineth a priest forever.'" And he talked lots of nonsense about the Holy Spirit, and went to a great deal of trouble over him.

3,4   He likes to derive his clinching proof from the Ascension of Isaiah, as the so-called Ascension tells us, if you please, that Isaiah said, "The angel that walked before me showed me, and he showed me and said, 'Who is that on the right hand of God?' And I said, 'Sir, thou knowest.' He said, 'This is the Beloved. (5) And who is the other, who is like him, that hath come from the left?' And I said, 'Thou knowest.' < He said >, 'This is the Holy Spirit, that speaketh in thee and in the prophets.' And," Isaiah says, "'he was like unto the Beloved.'"[22] Hieracas uses this as proof of the saying [he quotes from scripture], "Made like unto the Son of God, he remaineth a priest forever."

3,6   Now how many things can my mind, in contrast to his great, false intellect, learn even about this? (7) He died in old age. He wrote both in Greek and in Coptic, expositions he had composed < of > the six days of creation, and in which he fabricated certain legends and pompous allegories. But he wrote on any number of other scriptural subjects and composed many latter-day psalms. (8) And many of the † believers[23] in his doctrines abstain from meat. Hieracas himself really practiced considerable asceticism, but his disciples after him do it as a pretense. He himself abstained from all sorts of foods, and denied himself wine as well. (9) But some say that, although he lived past ninety, he practiced calligraphy till the day of his death—he was a calligrapher. For his vision remained unimpaired.

4,1   All right, let's investigate this one's tares too. Which of sacred scripture's ideas shall we get hold of, to scotch this poisonous snake that strikes fore and aft like a scorpion? For he heaped up harmful material from two Testaments, not as the sacred words stand, but as his false thinking formed obscure notions of clear things. (2) Honey is not nasty or bitter, and neither are the nicer foods God has created. But if they are given to a fever patient they seem bitter in his mouth, not because the sweet things have turned bitter, but because the patient's taste imparts bitterness to the things he is given. (3) In the same way, no one who has fallen away from the truth has been deceived by the truth; he tasted the truth with bitter thoughts and it became bitter to him.

4,4   But let's see, what shall we say about the children—the

---

[22] Asc. Isa. 9.33
[23] Holl: τῶν πειθομένων αὐτοῦ τοῖς δόγμασιν; MSS: τῶν ἀληθινῶν αὐτοῦ τῆς δογματος

ones who were killed for Christ straight off, in Bethlehem of Judaea? Have they no part in the kingdom of heaven, or have they one? They have, since they are innocent. (5) For if they have no part in it, the Lord has become an accessory to their murder; they were killed for him. But if they were killed for him and could not enter the contest or gain the prize for that reason, then the Lord's advent, which was intended < for salvation >, has become harmful to the world instead. For it has become the cause of the untimely departure of the babies, who were punished and fell victim to the king's menace, so that they could not enter the contest to gain its rewards.

4,6   But let's look at some other considerations. Call the blessed Solomon, the wisest man of all, as a witness against this Hieracas! Come here, you most blessed of prophets, who "received of the Lord a profusion of heart and wisdom, as the sand upon the seashore."[24] What would you think of the children? (7) And Solomon replies, "Old age is not honorable, nor length of life, nor is the reckoning made by number of years. Wisdom is an hoary head for men, and a spotless life their old age. For in his innocence he was loved by God, and from living among sinners he was translated. He was rapt away, lest wickedness alter his understanding, or guile deceive his soul. For the influence of evil doth weaken things that are good, and the wandering of desire doth undermine an harmless mind."[25] (8) And because he is speaking of children he adds at once, "Being perfected in a short time he fulfilled < long years >"[26]—that is to say, he lived for many years even though he died young. "For his soul was pleasing unto the Lord, therefore he hasted to remove him from the midst of wickedness."[27] (9) And to Jeremiah the Lord says, "Before thou camest forth from the womb I sanctified thee."[28]

5,1   But let's look at the Savior himself, the mouth that cannot lie, the One who knows all things. Come here, Lord, and lend our minds your aid, but confound Hieracas and his rashness! (2) Scripture says, "There came unto him little children, that he might put his hands on them and bless them. But the disciples thrust them away and forbade them. But he said unto them, Suffer the little children, and forbid them not, to come unto me. For of such

---

[24] 3 Kms. 5:9
[25] Wisd. Sol. 4:8–12
[26] Wisd. Sol. 4:13
[27] Wisd. Sol. 4:14
[28] Jer. 1:5

is the kingdom of God."[29] (3) And lest it be thought that the kingdom of heaven is composed solely of children and < seems* > not to < extend to* > all ages, he begins with the children, but has granted those who are like them to possess the inheritance with them. (4) For if those who are like them can reign, how much more the models for those who are like them? And Hieracas' fairy story has fallen flat.

5,5 For the Lord is merciful to all. "The Lord keepeth guard over the little ones,"[30] and, "Praise the Lord, ye children."[31] And the children cried out, "Hosannah in the highest, blessed is he that cometh in the name of the Lord."[32] And, "Out of the mouths of babes and sucklings hast thou perfected praise."[33] And there are any number of other texts like them.

6,1 But as to the resurrection of the flesh, Hieracas you would-be sage, how can there not be a resurrection of flesh? The term itself shows the meaning of the expression. We cannot speak of the "rising" of something that has not fallen. (2) But what is it that fell? What was buried? What was destroyed but the body, and not the soul? A soul neither falls nor is buried. And how much is there to be said about this? We cannot speak of the resurrection of a soul; it is the body that is raised.

6,3 And as to the selection the Savior came to make of virgins, the continent, and the pure—to whom is it not plain that there is a selection, and that < virginity* > is the pride of the holy catholic and apostolic church? < But the Savior accepts* > the partners in lawful wedlock as well; for "every man" is saved "in his own order."[34] (4) How can "marriage" not be "honorable"[35] and possess the kingdom of heaven in God, when the Savior was invited to a wedding to bless marriage? If he had refused to go to a wedding he would have been a destroyer of matrimony, and not the One who accepts each one, from pity for his weakness. Marriage is honorable, then, for he designated it as such. (5) This is why he went to a wedding—to silence those who speak against the truth.

For Jesus performed a first miracle there in Cana of Galilee, by turning the water into wine. (6) As he had dawned from a virgin to show the light that dawned from the virgin to the world, so he

---

[29] Matt. 19:13–14
[30] Ps. 114:6
[31] Ps. 112:1
[32] Matt. 21:9
[33] Ps. 8:3
[34] 1 Cor. 15:23
[35] Heb. 13:4

performed his first miracle at a wedding in Cana of Galilee—to honor virginity by his conception and the ray of light that dawned through her, but honor lawful wedlock by his miracles. For he performed the first at a wedding, by changing the water to un-mixed wine.

6,7   Similarly, if marriage was wrong why does the teacher of the gentiles command it, as he says, "Younger widows refuse. For after they wax wanton against Christ, they will marry, having damnation, because they have cast off their first faith."[36] (8) What does he say then? "But let them marry, bear children, guide the house."[37] If Paul allows these things, how can you, Hieracas, teach that marriage is to be rejected after Christ's incarnation?

7,1   And as to your claim that Melchizedek himself is the Spirit—in that case, the Spirit came and took flesh. It cannot be just the Only-begotten who has been born in the flesh; the Spirit must have been too. But if the Spirit was born in the flesh—well, it was Mary who bore the Savior. Hieracas should say where the mother who bore the Spirit is.

7,2   And in saying, "Made like unto the Son of God he remaineth a priest forever,"[38] the scripture cannot be referring to the Holy Spirit. (3) It didn't say, "*like* the Son of God," but, "*made* like." Now "made like" refers to a thing that came later. But if the Spirit is "made like" Christ after the time of Abraham, there was a time when there was no Spirit, and this is why he was "made like" the Son of God.

And how can he be "without father?" (4) If the Spirit is self-existent and not of the Godhead's own essence, it can fairly be shown that he is "without father." And indeed, the Son is *only*-begotten and has no brother, but is *the* Son of God. (5) But even though we do not call the Spirit begotten, since the Son is only-begotten, Christ still says that the Spirit "proceedeth from the Father and receiveth of the Son."[39] Hence the Spirit who "proceedeth from the Father" and "receiveth of me," cannot be "without fa-ther."

7,6   Even if he means "'without mother' in heaven and 'without father' on earth"—for this can also be said of the Savior—why does the apostle explain this at the end by saying, "He whose descent is not counted *from them* received tithes of the patriarch Abraham."[40]

---

[36] 1 Tim. 5:11
[37] 1 Tim. 5:14
[38] Heb. 7:3
[39] John 15:26; 16:15
[40] Heb. 7:6

(7) "From them" is an indicator of precision [of expression]; for since his descent was not counted from the children of Israel he must surely have been descended from other nations. But because his father and mother are not recorded in the scriptures, those who misrepresent the truth imagine one thing after another. (8) I, though, have found both his mother and his father in traditions; he was descended from the Sidonians and the Canaanites.

Thus his fairy story has crumbled. And his ascetic practice is of no avail; to settle for lifeless things coupled with wrong belief is no school of life and the hope of salvation. Scripture says, "Let *all* things be done to the glory of God."[41]

8,1   But here too, I believe enough has been said about them. We have broken the scorpion's wings and drawn its powers off. For Hieracas is a winged snake and scorpion which has all sorts of wings, which flies, and which mimics the church's virginity but without a clear conscience. (2) For he and people like him exemplify the words, "Having their conscience seared with an hot iron; and forbidding to marry, and to abstain from meats which God hath made to be received. For they are sanctified by the word of the living God and prayer, since all things are good and wholesome, and nothing is abominable with God."[42]

8,3   However, they are a complete laughing-stock because of their adoptive wives, whom they are at pains to have as domestic servants. (4) But as I said, we have pulled his wings off too, and broken his head with the wood of life, the cross of our Lord Jesus Christ. Let us go on to the rest, calling on God himself to aid us, so that we may reply to the remaining sects, and refute the heresies they fruitlessly palm off on the world.

< *Against* > *the Schism of Melitius the Egyptian.*[1] *48, but 68 of the series*

1,1   There is a body of Melitians in Egypt whose founder was Melitius, a bishop in the Thebaid. He had belonged to the catholic church—and the orthodox faith, for his faith never changed from that of the holy catholic church. (2) Melitius was a contemporary of Hieracas, flourished at the same time as he, and became his successor. He was also a contemporary of St. Peter the bishop of

---

[41] 1 Cor. 10:31
[42] Cf. 1 Tim. 4:2–4.

[1] Some of Epiphanius' information comes from Athanasius' *Apologia Secunda,* but Epiphanius has other sources, including oral ones (cf. 3,1; 8). He is far more sympathetic to Melitius than was Athanasius. His account of Arius' death

Alexandria. (3) And all of these lived during the persecution in the reigns of Diocletian and Maximian; but here is Melitius' story.

1,4 He instigated a schism, but certainly not by an alteration of the faith. He was arrested during the persecution, with the holy bishop and martyr, Peter, and the other martyrs, by the officials the emperor had assigned to the task, the governors of Alexandria and Egypt at the time. (Culcianus was prefect of the Thebaid, but Hierocles, prefect of Alexandria.)[2]

1,5 And Melitius was confined in the prison, he and the martyrs we spoke of, with Peter the archbishop of Alexandria. Indeed, Melitius himself was held to be the first < of the bishops* >[3] in Egypt, (6) and second to Peter in the archiepiscopate, in order to assist him; but he was under him and referred ecclesiastical matters to him. (7) For it is the custom for the archbishop in Alexandria to have the ecclesiastical administration of all Egypt and the Thebaid, Mareotis, Libya, Ammon, Marmarica and Pentapolis.

1,8 Now all these had been imprisoned to await martyrdom, but had remained in confinement for some time after their arrest. Others, who had been imprisoned before them, were martyred, received their reward, and fell asleep; but these, as eminent and more important prisoners, were kept for later. (2,1) And since some had been martyred, but others had been deprived of martyrdom by committing the enormity of idol worship, those who had even been forced to partake of sacrifices once they had fallen away, and had offered sacrifice and committed the transgression, applied to the confessors and martyrs for the mercy of penance. Some were soldiers, but others were clergy of various ranks, the presbyterate, the diaconate and others.

2,2 There was a disturbance and no little trouble over this, among the martyrs. For some said that persons who had once fallen away, denied the faith, and failed to maintain their courage or take part in the contest, should not be allowed penance. Otherwise the ones who were still left would have less regard for the penalty, and would be corrupted because of the forgiveness so speedily accorded the others, and come to the denial of God and the enormity of paganism. And the thing that was said by the

---

might be based on Athanasius' *Ad Serapionem, De Morte Arii.*
   [2] In fact Culcianus seems to have been the Prefect of Egypt, and Hierocles his successor. See Holl *ad loc.*
   [3] Or, "was regarded as < responsible for* > affairs in Egypt and < foremost* > in rank," Amidon's rendering of Hall's alternative emendation.

confessors themselves was reasonable. (3) Those who said this were Melitius and Peleus, and most of the other martyrs and confessors with them. And they of course † convinced < many >[4] by saying it, since they had shown their zeal for God.

2,4   They did say, however, "If penance should be allowed them some time after the persecution is over, when peace has been restored—provided that they truly repent and show the fruit of repentance—it certainly should not be to take each one back in his own order. They may be received into the church and its communion after an interval, < but > as < laypersons >, not as clergy." And this showed respect for the truth and was zealous.

3,1   But the most holy Peter, a kindly man and like a father to all, begged and pleaded, "Let us receive them and set them a penance if they repent, so that they will hold by the church, and let us not turn them out of their offices either"—or so I have been told. "Otherwise they < will be > disgraced, and those who, from cowardice and weakness, were once shaken and undermined by the devil, may be perverted entirely because of the delay, and not healed [at all]. As the scripture says, 'Let that which is lame not be turned out of the way; but let it rather be healed.'"[5]

3,2   And Peter spoke for mercy and kindness, and Melitius and his supporters for truth and zeal. Then and there the schism was started, by the appearance of the seemingly godly proposals of both parties;[6] for some said the one thing, and some the other. (3) For when Peter the archbishop saw that Melitius' party opposed his kindly advice, and were carried to extremes by their zeal for God, he himself hung a curtain in the middle of the prison by spreading out an himation—that is, a cloak or pallium—and proclaimed < through > a deacon, "Let those who are of my opinion come here to me; and let those who are of Melitius', join Melitius." (4) And the majority of bishops, presbyters and the other orders sided with Melitius; but a very few, bishops and a few others, < joined > the archbishop Peter. And after that the one group prayed by itself and the other by itself, and in the same way each held its other services separately.

3,5   In the event, Peter was martyred and the blessed man was perfected, leaving Alexander as his successor in Alexandria. For he succeeded to the throne after Peter. (6) But Melitius and many others were sentenced to exile, and banished to the mines at Phaeno.

---

[4] Holl: ἔπειθον < πολλοίς >; MSS: ἔπασχον
[5] Heb. 12:13
[6] Athanasius, in contrast, says that Peter deposed Melitius for cause at a council, and that Melitius retaliated by starting the schism, Ath. Ap. Sec. 59.1.

And then those who were dragged away because of being confessors < went into schism* > with Melitius. Melitius himself ordained clergy—bishops, presbyters and deacons—in prison < and > on his journey as he passed through every country and place, and founded his own churches. And the first group would not communicate with the second, nor the second with the first. (7) But each put a sign on its own church. Those who held the existing, old churches in succession from Peter, labeled theirs, "Catholic Church;" Melitius' succession labeled theirs, "Church of the Martyrs." (8) And so Melitius ordained many clergy that way on his arrival at Eleutheropolis, Gaza and Aelia.

3,9 But Melitius still had to do time in the mines. Meanwhile, however, the confessors were released from the mines, those of Peter's party—for there were still many—and those of Melitius'. For even in the mines they did not communicate or pray with each other.

But it was given Melitius to live in the world a while longer, so that he flourished at the same time as Peter's successor, Alexander, and was friends < with him >. And he was anxious over the state of the church and the faith; for I have frequently said that he held no altered beliefs.

4,1 For Melitius himself detected Arius, after he had come to Alexandria and spent some time there, holding his own assemblies with his own people. And because it was rumored that Arius had gone beyond the prescribed bounds of the faith in his expositions, he brought him to Alexander. (2) Arius was a presbyter at the church in Alexandria which is called Baucalis. There was one presbyter assigned to a church—there were many churches, but now there are more—and the church was entrusted to him, even if there was another presbyter with him. When I need to I shall speak of these things in detail, at the proper place.

Since Alexander in his zeal had detected Arius, he summoned bishops, < called > a council and examined him, inquiring about his faith and demanding < an accounting > from Arius for the corruption of the heresy which had infected him. (3) But Arius denied nothing; indeed, he brazenly replied that it was so. And Alexander excommunicated him, and a large number were excommunicated with him, the virgins and other clergy whom he had polluted.

4,4 Arius fled and made his way to Palestine. And he reached Nicomedia and wrote letters to Alexander from there, but did not go beyond the insane spirit of his heresy. (5) A little later, however, when Alexander, the holy bishop in Alexandria, had taken care to arouse the blessed Constantine, Constantine called a council in the city of Nicaea.

4,6   And Arius' sect was anathematized. < But > after < Alexander died, Arius wished to be received back into the church* >. For he first denied his heresy before the blessed emperor Constantine, and pretendedly professed the orthodox formularies under oath. (7) But the emperor said to him, "If you are swearing with complete sincerity, may your oath be confirmed, and you guiltless. But if you are swearing guilefully, may < God >, by whom you have sworn, take the vengeance on you!"[7] And this happened to him not long afterwards, as I shall say later.

4,8   Arius was acting in concert with Eusebius the bishop of Nicomedia, who held the same beliefs as he; and he was presented to the same emperor as having denied and condemned his heresy, if you please. And so Constantine directed and permitted Eusebius to receive Arius into the church at Constantinople in the presence of the bishop Alexander, who had the same name as the bishop of Alexandria but was the bishop of Constantinople.

5,1   But now, after the death of the confessor Melitius, the blessed Alexander of Alexandria rekindled his anger at the schism in the church, and saw fit to offer every kind of harassment and hindrance to those who assembled by themselves and whom Melitius had left behind him, and forcibly prevent them from rebelling against the one church. But as they were unwilling, they caused trouble and disturbances. (2) And then, because of their oppression and restraint by the blessed Alexander, certain of them, who were the foremost and preeminent for their piety and life, undertook the journey to court with a petition, to request the privilege of assembling by themselves without hindrance. (3) Those who did so were an important man named Paphnutius, an anchorite who was himself the son of a female confessor < and > had nearly been a confessor himself on a number of occasions; one of their bishops, John, also a highly respected man; and the bishop in Pelusium, Callinicus;[8] and certain others. (4) But when they went with their petition for the emperor, they were turned away and rebuffed. (5) For when the court officials heard the name, "Melitians," without knowing what that might be, they would not let them petition the emperor.

6,1   During all this Paphnutius, John and < the > others had to

---

[7] Ath. Ep. Ad Serap. De Morte Arii, MSG 25, 688A
[8] John and Callinicus are numbers 25 and 34 in the list of Melitian bishops Melitius is said to have furnished Alexander, Ath. Apol. Sec. 71.6.

spend some time in Constantinople and Nicomedia. They became friends at this time with the bishop of Nicomedia, Eusebius, told him their story—they knew he had access to the emperor Constantine—and asked for his introduction to the emperor. (2) But after promising to present them to the emperor and do what they asked, he made this request of them—that they receive Arius into communion with them, since, if you please, he had made a false, pretended repentance.[9] (3) They promised him this, and then Eusebius brought them to the emperor and explained their situation to him; and the emperor granted the Melitians permission to assemble by themselves from then on, with no disturbance from anyone.

6,4 If only these Melitians, who had received the absolutely correct form of the truth, had communicated with the lapsees after penance instead of with Arius and his followers! (5) Theirs has been the proverbial fate of fleeing the smoke to fall into the fire. Arius could not have gained a foothold and voice except through this business, which has become an evil alliance for them even now. For the Melitians, who were once simon pure and absolutely correct in their faith, have gotten mixed up with the disciples of Arius. (6) And by now most of them have been defiled by Arius' heresy, and been turned away from the faith in our time. Even though some have continued to hold the true faith, they hold it, but because of their communion with Arius and the Arians they are by no means out of the slimy muck.

6,7 But a little later—as I promised to, I shall report the whole matter here—Alexander the bishop of Constantinople was compelled to receive Arius, although he prayed, groaned, and knelt before the altar about the ninth hour of the Sabbath. And Eusebius said, "If you won't receive him willingly yourself he'll enter the church with me against your will tomorrow"—and it was getting close to the Lord's Day. (8) But as I said, Alexander prayed and besought our Lord either to take him away so that he would not be defiled with the blasphemer of the Lord, Arius, or else to work a wonder, as he does in every generation. And the holy man's prayer was answered with small delay. (9) That night Arius went to the privy to relieve himself, and, like Judas once, burst. And thus his end came in a foul, unclean place.

7,1 Finally, after this, the plot against the church was hatched by Arius' disciples. Alexander of Alexandria died after the council

---

[9] At Apol. Sec. 59.4 Athanasius claims that Eusebius took the initiative in courting the Melitians.

in Nicaea. (2) But Athanasius was not there (i. e., in Alexandria) after Alexander's death; he was a deacon under Alexander at that time, and Alexander had sent him to court.[10] (3) Although Alexander had given orders that no one but Athanasius be consecrated bishop—as he himself, and the clergy testified, and the whole church—the Melitians seized the opportunity and, since there was no bishop in Alexandria (Alexandria has never had two bishops, like the other cities) they consecrated a man named Theonas as bishop of Egypt in Alexander's place. And three months later he died. (4) Not long after Theonas' death, Athanasius arrived. And a council of orthodox bishops was summoned from all quarters. And thus Athanasius' consecration took place, and the throne was given to the man who was worthy of it and for whom it had been prepared, by God's will and the testimony and command of < the > blessed Alexander.

7,5 And then Athanasius began to be distressed and saddened by the church's division, between the Melitians and the catholic church. He pleaded with them, he exhorted them, and they would not listen; he pressed and urged them < and they would not obey* >.

But Athanasius often visited the churches nearby, particularly the ones in Mareotis. (6) And once when the Melitians were holding a service a deacon, together with some laity, came rushing out of the crowd with Alexander and broke a lamp—as the story goes— and there was a fight.[11] (7) This was the beginning of the intrigue against Athanasius, for the Melitians brought charges and false accusations against him, and < told > one story after another. But the Arians plotted and lent their assistance because of their envy of God's holy faith, and of orthodoxy. (8) And they communicated with the emperor Constantine. But Eusebius, who, as I said, was the bishop of Nicomedia, was the servitor of their whole gang, and the one who plotted the injury to the church and Pope Athanasius.

So the accusers went to the emperor and said that the implement which some, as I told you, said was a torch, was a vessel for the mysteries. (9) And they made certain other accusations. They claimed that a presbyter in Mareotis named Arsenius had been struck, and that his hand had been cut off with a sword, either by Athanasius' people or by Athanasius himself.[12] They even brought a hand to court and displayed it—it was in a box.[13]

8,1 On hearing this, the emperor grew angry. The blessed

---

[10] Cf. Ath. Ap. Sec. 6.1–2.
[11] Cf. Ath. Ap. Sec. 63.2–4.
[12] Cf. Ath. Ap. Sec. 65.2–5.
[13] Cf. Theodoret H. E. 1.30; Soc. 1.29.6; Soz. 2.25.10; Rufinus 10.16.

Constantine had a zeal for God; he had no idea that they were
false accusers because of the Arians' anger against orthodoxy, which
we have mentioned. But he commanded that a council be convened in Phoenicia, in the city of Tyre.[14] (2) He ordered Eusebius
of Caesarea and certain others to sit as judges; if anything, however, they had a certain leaning towards the Arians' vulgar chatter.
And bishops of the catholic church of Egypt were summoned, who
< were > under Athanasius—eminent, distinguised men with illus-
trious lives in God. Among them was the blessed Potamon the
Great, the bishop of Heracleopolis and a confessor. But Melitians
were summoned too, especially Athanasius' accusers.

8,3   The blessed Potamon was a zealot for truth and orthodoxy,
a free-spoken man who had never shown partiality. His eye had
been put out for the truth during the persecution. When he saw
Eusebius sitting on the judge's bench and Athanasius standing, he
was overcome with grief and wept, as honest men will. He shouted
at Eusebius, (4) "Are you seated, Eusebius, with Athanasius before
you in the dock, when he's innocent? Who can put up with things
like that? Tell me—weren't you in prison with me during the
persecution? I lost an eye for the truth, but you don't appear to
be maimed and weren't martyred; you stand here alive without a
mark on you. How did you get out of jail, if you didn't promise
our persecutors to do the unthinkable—or if you didn't do it?"[15]

8,5   Eusebius was indignant when he heard this. He rose and
dismissed the court, and said, "If you've come here and answer
me like that, your accusers are telling the truth. If you're playing
the tyrant here, you'd much better do it in your own country."

9,1   Then Eusebius and his fellow judges undertook to send
two Pannonian bishops with Arian views, Ursaces and Valens, to
Alexandria and Mareotis, where they said these things had happened—the affair of the vessel and the other circumstances of the
fight.[16] (2) But although they went they did not bring back the
truth; they perjured themselves with one † falsehood[17] after another, and brought false charges against the blessed Pope Athanasius.
(3) And they fabricated those in writing as though they were true,
and took them and referred them to the council of Eusebius and
the others. Ursacius and Valens showed this later by repenting,
approaching the blessed Julius, the bishop of Rome, with a peti-

---

[14] Cf. Ath. Ap. Sec. 71.2—79.4; Eus. Vit. Const. 4.41–45.3; Socr 1.28–33; Soz.
2.25.10; Rufinus 10.16; Theodoret H. E. 1.28.4; Philostorgius 2.11.
[15] Cf. Nicephorus MSG 100, 561D; Ath. Ap. Sec. 71.2–79.4.
[16] Cf. Ath. Ap. Sec. 72,4.
[17] Holl: παρεισφέροντες; MSS: παραχωρήσαντες

tion, and saying in admission of their fault, "We have accused Pope Athanasius falsely; but receive us into communion and penance." (4) And in repentance they sent their confirmations of this in writing to Athanasius himself.[18]

At Tyre Pope Athanasius saw that the plot he was faced with was in every way a serious one. Before his trial and confrontation with the false charges he fled by night, came to Constantine at court, and gave him his side of the story with an explanation.[19] (5) Constantine was still aggrieved, however, and remained angry because he thought that the accusers might well be telling the truth and Athanasius offering a false defense. But in spite of his anger Pope Athanasius sternly told the emperor, "God will judge between you and me, just as surely as you are in agreement with the traducers of my poor self." (6) And then he was condemned to exile because of the Council's letter to the emperor—they deposed Athanasius *in absentia*—and the angered emperor's displeasure with him. And he lived in Italy for more than twelve or fourteen years.

10,1 Later it was widely reported that Arsenius, whom the traducers had originally reported as dead and whose hand was said to be cut off, had been found in Arabia, and that Arsenius had actually made himself known to Athanasius in exile.[20] And Pope Athanasius sent for him secretly, I have been told, Arsenius came in person to the blessed Athanasius himself, < they came > together to Constantine's sons, Constans and Constantius, Athanasius exhibited Arsenius alive and with two hands, and it became clear that his accusers were guilty not only of slander but of grave-robbing, because of the dead hand they used to carry around.[21] (2) And this made the whole thing ridiculous, and there was astonishment at such fabrication and so much of it, and no one had any idea of what to say of the accusers, the accused, and all the other things— which will take a great deal of time < if I choose > to tell even part of them.

10,3 But Constantine died, and Pope Athanasius < had become > very much at home, esteemed and welcome < at > Rome and all over Italy, and with the emperor himself and his sons, Constans and Constantius. After the death of Constantine the Great he was sent < to Alexandria* > by the two emperors, although Constantius was at Antioch and gave his consent < through > his representatives

---

[18] Cf. their letters to Julius and Athanasius at Ath. Ap. Sec. 58.1–6.
[19] Ath. Ap. Sec. 9.2
[20] Ath. Ap. Sec. 8.4–5; 72.2
[21] Cf. Ath. Ap. Sec. 64.1–69.4.

and by a letter < to Alexandria* >, as I know from the three emperors'
< letters* > to the Alexandrians, and to Pope Athanasius himself.[22]
(4) And once again he occupied his throne after his successor
Gregory, < who > had been sent by the Arians while Athanasius was
in exile.

11,1   But he was informed on again, to Constantius by Stephen,
and was expelled. And after that he was intrigued against once
more, by the eunuch Leontius and his supporters. He was banished therefore, and again recalled. For George was sent [to Al-
exandria] by Constantius, and Athanasius withdrew into hiding for
a while,[23] until George was killed; Julian came to the throne at that
time, and after Constantius' death reverted to Hellenism. (2) For
the Alexandrians had nourished anger at George and they killed
him, burned his body, reduced it to ashes, and scattered it to the
winds. (3) But after Julian had died in Persia and the blessed
Jovian had succeeded to the empire, he wrote to the bishop
Athanasius with great honor and a memorable letter; and he sent
for him, embraced him, and sent him to his own throne, and the
holy church had received its bishop back and was comforted for
a short while.

After Jovian's death the blessed Athanasius was once more assailed
by the same persecutions, defamations and disturbances. (4) He
was not, indeed, driven from the church and his throne; the
Alexandrians had sent an embassy on his behalf, and the entire
city had demanded him after Lucius, < who is > still alive, had been
consecrated in a foreign country as the Arian < bishop of Alexandria >. It is likely that at Antioch, and a number of times, he
had urged the emperor Valens that he be sent to the throne [of
Alexandria], < but that the emperor* >, who was unwilling to expel
Athanasius for fear of a disturbance among the people, < had not
heeded him* >. (5) Indeed, Lucius was finally sent when Pope
Athanasius died, and did much harm to church and city—to the
laity, bishops and clergy who had been under Athanasius and had
received him in every church, and to Peter, who had been consecrated as Athanasius' successor in Alexandria.

11,6   This is still the situation. Some have been exiled—bishops,
presbyters and deacons—others have been subjected to capital
punishment in Alexandria, and others sent to the arena; and virgins
have been killed, and many others are perishing. (7) God's church
is still in this plight because of the affair of the Melitians and

---

[22] Cf. Ath. Hist. Ar. 8.1–2; Ap. Sec. 64.1–69.4.
[23] Cf. Ath. Ap. De Fuga 2–3.

Arians, who have used means of this sort to gain their foothold, and < the opportunity > for the same heretical gang, I mean the gang of Arians, to win out. (8) I shall discuss all this in detail in my refutation of Arius.

But I shall pass this subject by as well and go on to the Arian sect itself, calling on God for aid as I approach this fearful, many-headed serpent to battle with it.

Against the Arian Nuts.[1] 49, but 69 of the series

1,1   Arius and the Arians who derive from him came directly after this time of Melitius and St. Peter the bishop of Alexandria. Arius flourished during the episcopate of Peter's successor, the holy bishop Alexander, who deposed him amid much turmoil and with [the calling of] a great council. For Alexander removed him from office and expelled him from the church and the city, as a great evil which had sprung up in the world. (2) They say that Arius was Libyan, but that he had become a presbyter in Alexandria. He presided over the church called the Church of Baucalis. All the catholic churches in Alexandria < are > under one archbishop, and presbyters have been assigned to each particular church to meet the ecclesiastical needs of the residents whose < homes are* > near each church. These are also called quarters and lanes by the inhabitants of Alexandria.

1,3   Arius was born during the reign of the great and blessed emperor Constantine, the son of Constantius in his old age. Constantius was the son of the emperor Valerian, < who > himself had ruled jointly with Diocletian, Maximian and the others. (4) Everyone knows that Constantine, the father of Constantius, Constans and Crispus, was admirable in the practice of Christianity and the apostolic and prophetic faith of the fathers, which had not been adulterated in the holy churches until the time of Arius himself. But Arius succeeded in detaching a large number [from the church.]

2,1   A spirit of Satan, as scripture says, entered this Arius who was Alexander's presbyter, and incited him to stir up the dust against the church— < just as > no small fire was lit from him, and it caught on nearly the whole Roman Empire, especially the east.

---

[1] The literary sources of this Sect include Arius' letters to Eusebius of Nicomedia (6,1–7) and Alexander of Alexandria (7,1–8,5); the beginning of Constantine's dubious Encyclical against Arius (cf. Ath. Nic. 40.1–2); Athanasius' *Apologia Secunda* and *Epistula Ad Serapionem De Morte Arii*. There may be some debt to Athanasius' *Orationes Contra Arium*. However, if there is another literary source it is probably an Arian tract or some compendium of Arian proof texts. The bulk of Epiphanius' refutation of Arianism clearly bears the marks of his own style and thought.

Even today his sect has not stopped battling against the true faith.

2,2   But at that time Arius was to all appearances a presbyter, and there were many fellow presbyters of his in each church. (There are many churches in Alexandria, including the recently built Caesarium, as it is called, which was originally the Adrianum and later became the Licinian gymnasium or palace. (3) But later, in Constantius' time, it was decided to rebuild it as a church. Gregory, Melitianus and Arianus began it, and the blessed Athanasius, the father of orthodoxy, finished it. It was burned in Julian's time, and rebuilt by the blessed bishop Athanasius himself. (4) But as I said there are many others, the one called the Church of Dionysius, and those of Theonas, Pierius, Serapion, Persaea, Dizya, Mendidius, Ammianus, and the church Baucalis and others.)

2,5   A presbyter named Colluthus served in one of these, Carpones in another, Sarmatas in another, and Arius, who was in charge of one. (6) Each of these plainly caused some discord among the laity by his expositions, when he taught the people entrusted to his care at the regular services. Some were inclined to Arius, but others to Colluthus, others to Carpones, others to Sarmatas. Since each of them expounded the scripture differently in his own church, from their preference and high regard for their own presbyter some people called themselves Colluthians, and others called themselves Arians. (7) And in fact Colluthus < also > taught some deviations, but his sect did not survive and was soon scattered. And if only this were also true of Arius' insane faith, or better, unfaith—or better, wicked faith!

3,1   For in his later years he was inspired by vanity to depart from the prescribed path. He was unusually tall, wore a downcast expression and was got up like a guileful serpent, able to steal every innocent heart by his villainous outer show. For he always wore a short cloak and a dalmatic,[2] was pleasant in his speech, and was forever winning souls round by flattery. (2) For example, what did he do but lure all of seventy virgins away from the church at one time! And the word is that he drew seven presbyters away, and twelve deacons.[3] And his plague immediately spread to bishops, for he convinced Secundus of Pentapolis and others to adopt his error. (3) But all this went on in the church without the knowledge of the blessed Alexander, the bishop, until Melitius, the bishop of Egypt from the Thebaid whom I mentioned, who was regarded as an archbishop himself—the affair of Melitius had not yet reached

---

[2] Both of these were sometimes worn by monks.
[3] Cf. Soc. 1.6.8; Soz. 1.14.7; Gel. 2.3.6; Theod. 1.4.61.

the point of wicked enmity. (4) Melitius was motivated by zeal, then—he did not differ in faith, only in his pretense of would-be righteousness, < because of > which he did the world great harm himself, as I have explained. Well then, Melitius, the archbishop in Egypt but supposed to be under Alexander's jurisdiction, brought this to the attention of the archbishop Alexander. As I have said, Melitius was contemporary with the blessed bishop and martyr Peter.

3,5 When Melitius had given all this information about Arius—how he had departed from the truth, had defiled and ruined many, and had gradually weaned his converts away from the right faith—the bishop sent for Arius himself and asked whether the information about him was true. (6) Arius showed neither hesitancy nor fear but brazenly coughed his whole heresy up from the first—as his letters, and the investigation of him at the time, show. (7) And so Alexander called the presbytery together, and certain other bishops who were there [at the time], and held an examination and interrogation of Arius. But since he would not obey the truth Alexander expelled him and declared him outcast in the city. But the virgins we spoke of were drawn away from the faith with him, and the clergy we mentioned, and a large number of others.

4,1 But though Arius stayed in the city for a long time, the confessor and martyr Melitius immediately died. Arius, then, destroyed many by instigating schisms and leading everyone astray. Later though, since he had been discovered and exposed in the city and excommunicated, he fled from Alexandria and made <his> way to Palestine. (2) And on his arrival he approached each bishop with fawning and flattery in the hope of gaining many supporters. And some received him, while others rebuffed him.

4,3 Afterwards this came to the ears of the bishop Alexander, and he wrote encyclical letters to each bishop, seventy letters in all, which are still preserved by the scholarly. He wrote at once to Eusebius in Caesarea—he was alive—and to Macarius of Jerusalem, Asclepius in Gaza, Longinus in Ascalon, Macrinus in Jamnia, and others; and in Phoenicia to Zeno, a senior bishop in Tyre, and others, along with < the bishops > in Coele Syria. (4) When the letters had been sent reproving those who had received Arius, each bishop returned his explanation to the blessed Alexander. (5) And some wrote deceitfully, others truthfully. Some defended themselves by saying that they had not received him, others, that they had received him in ignorance, and others that they had taken him in for hospitality's sake. And this is a long story.

5,1 Later, when Arius found that letters had been sent to the bishops everywhere, and that afterwards he was turned away from every door and none but his sympathizers would take him in any more—(2) (for the elderly senior bishop of Nicomedia, Eusebius, was a sympathizer of † his[4] together with Lucius, his colleague in Nicomedia. And so was Leontius, the eunuch in Antioch who had not yet been entrusted with the episcopate, and certain others. Since all of them belonged to the same destructive party, Eusebius sheltered him for some time). (3) And so, before he came to Eusebius in Nicomedia, Arius himself sent letters to Eusebius of Nicomedia which were filled with absurdity and contained the whole of his heretical creed. At that time he composed them without putting anything more in them than what he really thought. I feel obliged to offer one of them here which has come into my hands, so that the readers can see that I have neither said, nor say anything slanderous against anyone. Here is the letter:[5]

6,1   *Greetings in the Lord from Arius, unjustly persecuted by Pope Alexander for the all-conquering truth of which you too are a defender, to the most beloved man of God, the faithful and orthodox Master Eusebius.*

6,2   *As my father Ammonius is coming to Nicomedia I feel that it is reasonable and proper to address you through him, at the same time recalling your characteristic love and [kindly] disposition toward the brethren for the sake of God and his Christ. For the bishop is harassing and persecuting us severely, and stirring up every sort of evil against us,* (3) *so that he has driven us from the city as godless men because we do not agree with his public declaration, "Always God, always a Son. If [there is] a Father then [there is a Son], and if [there is] a Son [then there is a Father]. The Son co-exists with God without origination, ever begotten, begotten without [physical] begetting. Not by a thought or a moment of time is God prior to the Son, [but] there is always a God, there is always a Son, the Son is from God himself."* (4) *And as your brother in Caesarea, Eusebius, and Theodotus, Paulinus, Athanasius, Gregory, Aetius and all the bishops in the east say that God is prior to the Son without beginning, they have become anathema—except for the ignorant sectarians Philogonius, Hellanicus and Macarius, some of whom say that the Son is an eructation and others, an uncreated emanation.* (5) *And to these impieties we cannot listen, not if the sectarians threaten us with a thousand deaths.*

6,6   *But what is it that we say and believe, and that we have taught and teach? That the Son is not uncreated or any part of an uncreated being, or made of anything previously existent. He was brought into being by the will and counsel [of God], before time and before the ages, as unbegotten*

---

[4] Holl: ὑπουργός; MSS: λόγος
[5] Cf. Theodoret Haer. 1.5.1–4.

God in the fullest sense, and unalterable; and before he was begotten, created, determined or established, he did not exist. (7) *But we are persecuted because we have said, "The Son has a beginning, but God is without beginning." We are also persecuted because we have said, "He is made from nothing." But we have so said because he is not a part of God or made from any thing previously existent. It is for this reason that we are persecuted; the rest you know.*

I pray for your good health in the Lord, my true fellow Lucianist Eusebius; be mindful of my afflictions.

7,1   Moreover, I subjoin another letter written from Nicomedia by Arius in self-defense, if you please, and sent to the most holy Pope Athanasius. Once again it is filled, to an incomparably worse degree, with the blasphemous utterances of his venom. This is the letter:[6]

7,2   *Greetings in the Lord from the presbyters and deacons to the blessed Pope and bishop, Alexander.*

7,3   *Our faith which we have received from our forefathers and learned from you as well, blessed Pope, is as follows. We know that one God, the only ingenerate, the only eternal, who alone is without beginning, the only true God, who alone has immortality, the only wise, the only good, the sole sovereign, the sole judge with the governance and care of all, immutable and unalterable, just and good, < the Lord* > of the Law and Prophets and of the New Testament—[we know] that this God has begotten an only Son before eternal times, (4) and through him has made the ages and the rest. He has begotten him not in appearance but in truth and brought him into being by his own will, immutable and unalterable; (5) God's perfect creature but not like any other creature; an offspring, but not like any other offspring; (6) and not an emanation, as Valentinus believed the Father's offspring to be; nor as Mani represented the offspring as a co-essential part of the Father; nor like Sabellius, who said "Son-Father" to divide the Unity; nor as Hieracas called him a light kindled from a light, or a lamp become two; (7) nor existent before his begetting and later generated or created anew as a Son. You yourself, blessed Pope, have very often publicly dissuaded those who give these explanations in the church and assembly. But as we say, He is a Son created by the will of God before the times and ages, who has received his life, being and glory from the Father, the Father subsisting together with him. For by giving him the inheritance of all things the Father did not deprive himself of his possession of ingeneracy in himself, since he is the source of all.*

8,1   *Thus there are three entities, a Father, a Son and a Holy Spirit. And God, who is the cause of all, is the sole and only being without*

---

[6] Cf. Ath. Syn. 16.

*beginning. But the Son, who was begotten of the Father though not in time,
and who was created and established before the ages, did not exist before
his begetting, but was alone brought into being before all by the Father alone,
and not in time.* (2) *Nor is he eternal, or co-eternal and co-uncreated with
the Father. Nor does he have a being contemporaneous with the Father's,
as some speak of things [which are naturally] related to something else,
thus introducing two uncreateds. But God is before all as a Unit and the
first principle of all. And thus he is also before Christ, as we have learned
from you when you have preached < in > the church.*

8,3   *Thus, in that the Son has his being from God < who > has provided
him with life, glory and all things, God is his first cause. For God is his
ruler, as his God and—because the Son originates from him—prior to him
in existence.* (4) *And if "out of the belly,"*[7] *and "I came forth from the
Father and am come,"*[8] *are taken by some to mean that he is part of a
co-essential God and an emanation, the Father must be composite, divisible
and mutable—and in their opinion the incorporeal God has a body and,
for all they care, is subject to the consequences of corporeality. We pray for
your good health in the Lord, blessed Pope.* (5) *Arius, Aeithales, Achillas,
Carpones, Sarmatas, Arius, presbyters ; the deacons Euzoeus, Lucius, Julius,
Menas, Helladius, Gaius ; the bishops Secundus of Pentapolis, Theonas
of Libya, Pistus*—the bishop the Arians consecrated for Alexandria.

9,1   Now that matters had been stirred up like that, Alexander
wrote to the emperor Constantine. And the blessed emperor summoned Arius and certain bishops, and interrogated them. (2) But
< with the support > of his co-religionists Arius at first denied the
charge before the emperor, though within himself he was hatching
the plot against the church. And as though he too were partially
inspired < by > the Holy Spirit, the blessed Constantine warned
Arius when he summoned him, "I trust in God that if you are
guilefully denying [guilt] and holding something back, the Lord
of all has the power to confound you speedily, especially since it
is by him that you have sworn." Hence Arius was indeed caught
holding the same opinions, and was exposed before the emperor.

9,3   But he made a similar denial again, and many of his de-
fenders petitioned the emperor for him through Eusebius of
Nicomedia. But meanwhile the emperor was angry, and wrote a
long circular against Arius and his creed to the whole Roman
realm, filled with all sorts of wisdom and truthful sayings. (4) It
is still preserved by the scholarly and begins, "The most high Augustus
Constantine, to Arius and the Arians. A bad expositor is plainly

[7] Ps. 109:3
[8] John 16:28

the image and representation of the devil."[9] (5) Then, after some other remarks and a long refutation of Arius from the sacred scripture, he also indignantly directed a line from Homer against him, which I feel impelled to quote. (6) It goes, "Come now, Ares Arius, there is a need for shields. Do this not, we pray; let Aphrodite's speech restrain thee."[10]

10,1[11] Arius wished to be received back into the church in Constantinople, and Eusebius pressed for this and had great influence with the emperor, and kept pestering the bishop of Constantinople at that time. The bishop did not wish to-be in the same fellowship with Arius or enter into communion with him, and was troubled and groaned, but Eusebius said, "If you won't do it by your own choice he'll come in with me tomorrow at the dawn of the Lord's Day, and what can you do about it?"

10,2 From the time when he heard that, that most pious and godfearing bishop, Alexander, bishop of the best of cities—(he and the bishop in Alexandria had the same name)—spent the whole day and night in groans and mourning, and in beseeching God either to take his life so that he would not be polluted by communion with Arius, or to work a wonder. And his prayer was answered. (3) Arius went out that night from the need to relieve himself, went to the privy, sat down in the stalls inside, and suddenly burst and expired. Thus, just as he had belched out a dirty heresy, he was overtaken and surrendered his life in a smelly place

11,1 When this was over the emperor felt concerned for the church, because by now many members often differed with one another and there were many schisms. He therefore convened an ecumenical council of 318 bishops, whose names are still preserved. And they condemned Arius' creed in the city of Nicaea, and confessed the orthodox and unswerving creed of the fathers, which has been handed down to us from the apostles and prophets. (2) After the bishops had signed this and condemned the Arian sect, < peace* > was restored. They passed certain ecclesiastical canons at the council besides, and at the same time decreed with regard to the Passover that there must be one unanimous concord in the celebration of God's holy and supremely excellent day. For it was variously observed by people; some kept it early, some between [the disputed dates], but others, late. (3) And in a word, there was a great deal of

---

[9] The entire letter, which may not actually be Constantine's, is found at Ath. Nic. 40.
[10] Ath. Syn. 40.6. The Homeric line is apparently a misquotation of Iliad V.31.
[11] For the story that follows see Ath. Ep. Ser. Mort. Ar.

controversy then. But through the blessed Constantine God directed the right ordering of these things for the sake of peace.

11,4   Alexander died that same year after Arius' condemnation and these measures, and Achillas succeeded him but Theonas was consecrated too, by the Melitians. Then the blessed Athanasius succeeded Achillas after he had been bishop for three months.[12] Athanasius was Alexander's deacon at that time, and had been sent by him to court; as Alexander's death approached he ordered that the episcopate be conferred on Athanasius. (5) But the custom at Alexandria is that the consecrators do not delay after the death of a bishop; < the consecration* > is held at once for the sake of peace, to avoid conflicts among the laity with some for one candidate and some for another. (6) Since Athanasius was not there they were forced to consecrate Achillas. But the throne belonged to the one whom God had called and the blessed Alexander designated, and the priesthood was prepared for him.

11,7   Thus Athanasius arrived and was consecrated. He was very zealous for the faith and a protector of the church, and by now there were [schismatic] services everywhere, and a splinter group of laity formed by the so-called Melitians, for the reason I gave in my piece on Melitius. In his desire to achieve the unification of the church Athanasius accused, threatened, admonished, and no one would listen. (8) This was the reason for all the intrigues and plots against him, the extremity of his God-given zeal. And so he was subjected to banishments too because of his excommunication by the Arians with the highly unjust secular power. (9) But enough about the blessed Athanasius. His story has been told in full detail in the above description of Melitius.

12,1   Arius, then, was infused with the power of the devil, and with shameless impudence wagged his tongue against his own Master—at first, if you please, from his desire to expound the words of Solomon in his Proverbs, "The Lord created me a beginning of his ways. Before the age he set me up in the beginning, before he made the earth, before he made the depths, before the springs of waters came forth, before the mountains were settled, before all hills he begot me."[13] (2) This was the introduction to his imposture; < he > and his disciples were not ashamed to call the creator

---

[12] Athanasius was actually consecrated a month and a half after Achillas' death. Epiphanius may be misinterpreting Ath. Apol. Sec. 59.3, which refers, not to the time of Athanasius' consecration, but to the time between the Council of Nicaea and the death of the bishop Alexander. With Epiphanius' account cf. Theod. 1.26.1.

[13] Prov. 8:22–25. Cf. Ath. Nic. 13; C. Ar. 53.

of all things—the Word begotten of the Father without beginning and not in time—a creature.

12,3   But then, because of this one passage, he drove his mischievous mind down many evil paths, < he > and his successors, and they undertook to utter ten thousand blasphemies and more against the Son of God and the Holy Spirit. (4) They broke the front, as it were, and the concord of the holy, orthodox faith and church, [though] not by their own power or wisdom. The deluded people who were [truly] inclined to join them were few, but many gradually came in from hypocrisy; and many, besides, were forced into communion with them because they had < no way to resist* >. And no one < whose faith was sound* > was their patron; it was the care< less >ness of the faithful first, but [also] the protection of emperors.

12,5   The beginning < came with > the emperor Constantius, who was a meek and good man in other respects and who, as the son of the great and perfect Constantine with his piety and unwavering observance of the right faith, was pious himself, and good in many ways. (6) But he erred only in this matter, his failure to follow the faith of his fathers—not by his own doing, but because of those who will give account at the day of judgment, the so-called bishops [who were bishops] in appearance but corrupted God's true faith. (7) These must give account, both for the faith and for the persecution of the church, and the many wrongs and murders that have been committed in the churches because of them; and for such vast numbers of laity who still suffer today under the open sky; and for the blessed Constantius himself who, since he did not know the orthodox faith, was led astray by them and in his ignorance deferred to them as priests. For he was not aware of the imposture of the blindness and heresy which the devil had plotted.

13,1   Their gang of snakes won out yet a second time through Eudoxius, who wormed his way into the confidence of the devout emperor Valens, a very pious man and a lover of God, and once again corrupted his sense of hearing.[14] The reason the Arians could maintain their position was Valens' baptism by Eudoxius. (2) Otherwise < they would have been refuted > long ago even by women and kids—never mind the more mature, who understand all the exact details of godliness and right faith, but also by anyone with any partial glimmer of understanding of the truth. And because of their refutation by the ancients they would have been harried as blasphemers of the Master, second killers of the Lord, and despisers

---

[14] Cf. Socr. 4.1.6; Soz. 4.6.10; Theod. 4.12.4.

of the divine protection of our Lord Jesus Christ. (3) But by the emperor's patronage, that is, his protection, < they won out >, so as to get to work on all the wrongs that have been done and are still being done by them at Alexandria, Nicomedia, Mesopotamia and Palestine, under the patronage of the same, current emperor.

14,1   All the rest of their teachings are contrived from this line in Proverbs, "The Lord created me the beginning of his ways, for his works."[15] And < they collect > every possible agreement and equivalent to this text < from the scriptures >, and everything that could be in accord with it, although neither the text itself nor the other passages say anything of the sort about the divinity of the Son of God. (2) All the same, anything like this—the text in the Apostle, "Receive ye the high priest of your profession, who is faithful to him that made him;"[16] and < the one > in the Gospel according to John, "He it is of whom I said unto you that he that cometh after me *hath come into being* (γέγονε) before me;"[17] and the one in Acts, "Be it be known unto all you house of Israel that God hath made this Jesus whom ye crucified both Lord and Christ,"[18] and others like these—wherever < they find some text* > that needs investigation < they collect it* > as a defense against their foes. (3) For they are indeed foes and conspirators. "Let God arise and let his foes be scattered"[19] might have been written about them and their kind. They appear to be members of our household—there is nothing worse than foes of one's own household, for "A man's foes are all the men of his household."[20] And this probably fits them too.

15,1   For they leap up like savage dogs to repel their foes and say, "What do you say of the Son of God?" (For these are their devices for introducing dangerous teaching to the simple.)

"And what more can there be after this, after one calls him the Son of God, you folks who are 'wise in your own eyes and prudent in their sight,'[21] and give the appearance of knowledgeability? What more can one add to the name of Jesus, other than to say that he is true Son, of the Father and not different from him?"

15,2   Then they scornfully jump right up and say, "How can he be 'of God?'" And if you ask them, "Isn't he the Son?" they

---

[15] Prov. 8:22
[16] Heb. 3:1–2. Cf. Ath. Or. I C. Ar. 53; Or. II C. Ar. 6; 10; De Sent. Dion. 10–11 (MSG 25, 493B, 496B).
[17] John 1:15
[18] Acts 2:36. Cf. Ath. Or. 1 C. Ar. 53; Or. 2 C. Ar. 11–12.
[19] Ps. 67:2
[20] Matt. 10:36
[21] Isa. 5:11

confess the sonship in name but deny it in force and meaning, and simply want to call him a bastard, not a real son. (3) "For if he is of God," they say, "and if God as it were begot < a Son > from himself, from his own substance or his own essence—well then, he swelled, or was cut, or was expanded or contracted in begetting him, or underwent some physical suffering."[22]

And they are simply ridiculous to compare their own characteristics with God's, and draw a parallel between God and themselves.[23] (4) There can be nothing of the kind in God. "God is spirit,"[24] and has begotten the Only-begotten of himself ineffably, inconceivably and spotlessly.

15,5   "If he is of his essence then," they say, "why doesn't he know the day and the hour, as he says, 'But of that day or that hour knoweth no man, neither the angels, neither the Son, but the Father only?'[25] And if he is 'of the Father,' how could he become flesh?' How could that nature which cannot be contained put on flesh, if by nature he were of the Father?"

16,1   And they do not know how disadvantageous to themselves their conclusions are. For if he took flesh, and suffered and was crucified in it because he differed in essence from the Father, they should tell us which other spiritual beings took flesh even though they were creatures. For they cannot help admitting that the Son is superior to all. Even if they call him a creature, they admit that he is superior to all his creatures.

16,2   Indeed, their intention is to flatter him as though they were doing him a favor—as though they were hitting him with one hand but anointing him with the other. For they wish to make this concession to him as though by their own choice, and say, "We call him a creature, but not like any other creature; a product of creation, but not like any other product; and an offspring, but not like any other offspring."[26] In this way they deprive him of the begetting which by nature is proper to him by saying, "not like any other offspring," and declare him a true creature by saying, "not like any other creature."

16,3   A creature is whatever a creature is. Even though its name is any number of times more exalted it is just the same as all

---

[22] Cf. Ath. Or. I 16; 28.
[23] Cf. Ath. Or. I 16; 28
[24] John 4:24
[25] Mark 13:32; Matt. 24:36. Cf. Ath. Or. III C. Ar. 26.
[26] Athanasius quotes this at Or. II 19.

creatures.[27] The sun is no less a creature than a rock because it is brighter than the other creatures. And because the moon out-shines the stars, it is no less a creature on this account. "Behold, all things are thy servants."[28]

16,4   But the Only-begotten is truth, and his word is truth, as he said, "If ye continue in my word ye are truly my disciples, and ye shall know the truth, and the truth shall make you free."[29] But if his word is truth and frees the souls whom he liberates, how much more is he himself free—since he is truth, and frees his believing servants! For all things are his servants, and his Father's, and the Holy Spirit's.

17,1   Then again they say, "How could he come in the flesh, if he was of the Father's essence?" They should tell us why angels, who are his servants [and not of his essence], have not taken flesh. Why not archangels? Why not hosts? Why not all the other spiritual beings? (2) But they say besides that the Spirit is still more inferior, and the creature of a creature, since he is < the product > of the Word. Why didn't the Spirit take flesh then, since, as they see it, his face can be more changeable than the Son's? But since the Son was the Father's wisdom he consented, by his own perfection, to assume our weakness, so that all salvation would come to the world through him. (3) But people who turn good things to bad are ungrateful—ungrateful, unwise, insulters and blasphemers of their own Master.

And whatever else they say, in the last analysis they mean it as detraction of him. "If he was of the Father's essence, why was he hungry? Scripture says that God 'shall not hunger or thirst, nor is there any finding out of his counsel.'[30] But Christ was hungry and thirsty. Why did he tire from his journey and sit down, < when scripture says > that God 'shall not weary?'[31] (4) And why did he say, 'The Father that hath sent me is greater than I?'[32] The sender is one person, the sent, another."

And it is plain that the Father is not the Son, and the Son is not the Father. We do not talk like Sabellius, who says that he is the Son-Father. (5) If he had not said, "Another is he that hath sent me,"[33] and, "I go unto my God and your God, unto my Father

[27] For a similar argument see the Letter of Marcellus, Pan.73,4,6–7; Ath Or. II 20.

[28] Ps. 118:91

[29] John 8:31–32

[30] Isa. 40:28

[31] Isa. 40:28

[32] John 14:28

[33] Cf. John 5:32; 36.

and your Father,"[34] < the disciples would have believed that he himself was the Father. This is why* > he said, < "My God." But he said, "your God," because* > his disciples were begotten < only by grace* >, and not by nature from the essence of God. < This is why > he said, "*your* Father," to them.

17,6   But people who say things like that are just cracked. If the Son is only nominally called the Son and is not the Son by nature, he is no different from all the other creatures, however superior his rank. Because the emperor outranks his governors and generals, this does not mean that he does not have the same limitations as the rest, and is not their fellow servant of the same creation. For he is mortal, just as his subjects are. (7) And because the sun outshines the other stars, and the moon does to an extent, this does not mean that they are not heavenly bodies subordinate [to God], and subject to the ordinance of the one artificer and creator, the Father, the Son and the Holy Spirit. (8) And because angels surpass the visible creatures and, in comparison with the rest, are the greatest of all—for they were created invisible, enjoy the supreme privilege of serving God with continual hymns, are immortal by grace though not by nature, and yet have been vouchsafed a natural immortality by him who in himself is life and immortality—[all] this does not mean that they do not serve with fear and trembling, and that they are not accountable to the holy Godhead, and subject to its interrogation, bidding and command.

18,1   This will help us < understand* > the exact truth we are after: to say, "Son," but say it without considering him a son in name only, but say that the Son is a son by nature. With us too, many are called sons without being sons by nature. But our real sons are called "true;" they were actually begotten by us. (2) And if he was only called a son, as indeed all have been called sons of God, he is no different from the rest. And why is he worshiped as God? On Arius' premises all the other things that have been given the title of sons should be worshiped, since they are termed sons of God. (3) But this is not the truth. The truth at all times knows one only-begotten Son of God whom all things serve and worship, and to whom "every knee shall bow, of things in heaven and things in earth and things under the earth, and every tongue shall confess that Jesus Christ is Lord to the glory of God the Father."[35]

18,4   But neither is the Holy Spirit equivalent to the other spirits,

---

[34] John 20:17
[35] Phil. 2:10–11

since the Spirit of God is one, proceeding from the Father and
receiving of the Son. Arius, however, makes him a creature of a
creature. For they say, "'All things were made by him, and without
him was not anything made that was made.'³⁶ (5) Therefore," they
say, "the Holy Spirit is a creature too, since *all* things were made
by him."

And those who have lost their souls for nothing do not know
that created beings are one thing, and < un >created beings another—Father, Son and Holy Spirit, one God, Trinity in truth and
Unity in oneness. (6) Because there are not two Fathers, two Sons
or two Holy Spirits, because the Son is not different from the
Father but begotten of him, and because the Holy Spirit is not
different [from them], there is one God. But the Son is only-
begotten, without beginning < and > not in time. And as the Father
himself and the Only-begotten know, the Holy Spirit is neither
begotten nor created, nor unlike the Father and Son; he anointed
Christ with the Holy Spirit."³⁷ If the Only-begotten himself is anointed
with the Spirit, who can bring a charge against the Holy Trinity?

19,1   Then again the insane Arius says, "Why did the Lord say,
'Why callest thou me good? One is good, God,'³⁸ as though he
himself denied his own goodness?" (2) Because they are soulish
and fleshly, are discerned by the Holy Spirit and devoid of him,
and lack the gift of the Holy Spirit which gives wisdom to all, they
do not know God's power and goodness, or the revelation of God's
wisdom.

19,3   "Again," says Arius, "the sons of Zebedee asked him through
their mother if one of them might sit at his right and one at his
left in his kingdom, and he told them, 'Ye know not what ye ask.
Are ye able to drink the cup that I shall drink of? And when they
said, Yea, he said unto them, Ye shall drink of my cup, but to sit
on my right hand and on my left is not mine to give, but is for
them for whom it is prepared of the Father.'³⁹ (4) Then the apostle
says, 'God raised him from the dead,'⁴⁰ as though he needed someone to raise him. And it says in the Gospel according to Luke,
'There appeared an angel of the Lord strengthening him when
he was in agony, and he sweat; and his sweat was as it were drops
of blood, when he went out to pray before his betrayal.'⁴¹ (5) And

---

³⁶ John 1:3
³⁷ Acts 10:38
³⁸ Mark 10:18; Matt. 20:28. Cf. Marcellus of Ancyra, Inc. 1.7.
³⁹ Cf. Matt. 20:20–23
⁴⁰ Rom. 10:9. Cf. Marcellus of Ancyra Inc. 1.7.
⁴¹ Cf. Luke 22:43–44; Ath. Or. III 26.54.

again, on the cross he said, 'Eli, Eli, lema sabachthani, that is, My God, my God, why hast thou forsaken me.'[42] And do you see," says Arius, "how he needs help?"

19,6   But in connection with the text, "I am in the Father and the Father in me,"[43] < they cite >, "We two are one, that they also may be one,"[44] < "And do you see," he says, "that we too shall be one *as the Father and the Son are one*?* > Their oneness is no oneness by nature, but the oneness of concord."

19,7   But not only this; they also deny that he has received a human soul, and do so by design.[45] For they confess that he has true flesh from Mary, and everything human—except for a soul. Thus, when you hear of his hunger, thirst, weariness, journeying, sweat, sleep or anger, and say that he needed these because of his human nature, they will tell you afterwards that flesh does not do these things of itself unless it has a soul. (8) And in fact, this is true. "What can this mean," they say, "except that his 'divine nature' had needs?"—so that, when they say that his "divine nature" had needs, they are declaring that he is alien to and different from his Father's essence and true nature.

19,9   I believe, however, that from one, two, or five of their poorly chosen, refuted and exploded proof texts < I can make the whole of their villainy plain* > to someone[46] with understanding. And since the whole truth is proclaimed, and plainly confirmed, in the faith of orthodoxy, < I trust that* > even if they cite a million other texts besides these contrived expositions, the Arians will be confuted by anyone with sense. For since they mean the same, most of these will be refuted in [the refutation of] these few.

20,1   And I shall start with the place where Arius began the planting of their bitter root, the words of Solomon, "The Lord created me the beginning of his ways, for his works."[47] (2) And scripture nowhere confirmed, nor did any apostle ever mention this text in relation to the name of Christ. Solomon is not speaking of the Son of God at all, even if he says, "I, wisdom, have given counsel and knowledge a home, and I have summoned judgment."[48] (3) How many "wisdoms" are loosely called God's? But there is

---

[42] Matt. 27:46; cf. Ath. Or. III.

[43] John 14:10

[44] John 17:22

[45] Cf. Ps.-Ath. C. Apollin. 2.3; Theod. Haer. Fab. 4.1; Eustathius 18.

[46] Drexl and MSS: τῷ σύνεσιν κεκτημένῳ; Holl: < παντὶ > τῷ . . .

[47] Prov. 8:22. This is quoted as an Arian proof text at Ath. Or. I 53, but given no particular emphasis.

[48] Prov. 8:12

one Only-begotten, and he is not given that name loosely, but in truth.

For all things are God's wisdom, and whatever is from God is wisdom. (4) But the unique, supreme Wisdom is different—that is, the Only-begotten, He who is not called wisdom loosely but truthfully, He who is always with the Father, "the power of God and the wisdom of God."[49] But "The poor man's wisdom is despised;"[50] and, "since in the wisdom of God the world knew not God, it pleased God by the foolishness of the Gospel to save them that believe;"[51] and, "God hath made foolish the wisdom of this world;"[52] And, "God gave to Solomon an heart like the sand of the sea, and made him wiser than the sons of Anak;"[53] and, "God gave wisdom to Bezaleel, and God filled Uri with wisdom."[54]

20,5 And there is a great deal to say about wisdom, and "Where is the place of understanding, and where can wisdom be found?"[55] Even though the renowned wisdom says, "I, wisdom, have given counsel and knowledge a home, and I have summoned judgment. By me kings reign, and through me princes are great, rulers write righteousness, and despots possess the earth. (6) I love them that love me, and they that seek me shall find me. Wealth and glory are mine, and the possession of many goods, and righteousness. I walk in the way of righteousness, and I tread in the midst of right paths, to apportion substance to them that love me, and fill their treasures with goods. (7) If I tell you the incidents of each day, I shall remember to recount the happenings from everlasting. The Lord created me the beginning of his ways, for his works. Before the age he established me in the beginning, before he made the earth and before he made the deeps, before fountains of water came forth, before mountains were founded and before all hills he begat me,"[56] and so on—(8) [even so], since there are some who want to dispute the passage, our opponents will obviously reply by citing the term, "wisdom," and the line after it which says, "The Lord created me," as well as the one that says, "I, wisdom, have given counsel a home." "Look here," < they will say >, "wisdom gave her own name at the beginning, and said, 'The Lord

---

49 1 Cor. 1:24
50 Eccles. 9:16
51 1 Cor. 1:21
52 1 Cor. 1:20
53 3 Kms. 4:25; 27
54 Exod. 31:2
55 Job 28:12
56 Prov. 8:12; 15–18; 20–25

created me,' afterwards to mean herself. (9) See, she says, 'I, wisdom,' above; and below she says, 'If I tell you the happenings of each day, I shall remember to recount the things from everlasting.' And what does she say [are the 'happenings from everlasting]? 'The Lord *created* me the beginning of his ways.'"

21,1   I have said that many things which < are > loosely < termed > wisdoms have been given by God from time to time, since God does all things with wisdom. But there is one true wisdom of the Father, the subsistent divine Word. For the word ["wisdom"] itself (i.e., at Prov. 8:22) by no means compels me to speak of the Son of God; < scripture > did not say that, nor did any of the apostles mention it. Neither did the Gospel. (2) But if it were taken of the Son of God—the word [in itself] is not the same [as "Son"], and does not lend itself to an immediate judgment [as to whether it means "Son" at this point].

For the whole book is proverbs. And nothing in a proverb has the same meaning [that it usually does]; it is described verbally in one way, but intended allegorically with another meaning. (3) If Solomon says this, however, and some venture to apply it to the Son of God—never! The word is not a reference to his Godhead. (4) But if it can be applied to Christ's human nature—for "Wisdom hath builded her house"[57]—and if it can therefore be piously spoken in the person of Christ's human nature,[58] as though his human nature were saying, "The Lord created me" of his Godhead—(that is, "the Lord established me in Mary's womb")—"the beginning of his ways for his works," [then wisdom might indeed mean "Son" here.][59] (5) For the beginning of the "ways" of Christ's descent into the world is the body he took from Mary in his "work" of righteousness and salvation.

But some crackbrain who is sick with this frightful plague and has enmity for the Son of God in his heart will be sure to rush forward and say, (6) "He said, 'If I tell you the incidents of each day, I shall remember to recount the happenings from everlasting.'[60] And you see that he says, 'from everlasting.' But according to Matthew God's incarnation came after seventy-two generations; how can 'from everlasting' be said by the human nature?" (22,1) And those who have strayed entirely off the road of the truth do not realize that whatever the sacred scripture wishes to teach, < if >

---

[57] Prov. 9:1
[58] So Athanasius, much more confidently, at Nic. 14.2–4.
[59] Prov. 8:21
[60] Prov. 8:21a

it is beginning an exposition it does not go straight to the oldest
data and, as it were, the main point, but begins with the events
nearest at hand in order to show last of all what came first. (2)
For this is why it said, "If I tell you the incidents of each day,"
[first], but "I < shall > also recount the things from everlasting"[61]
afterwards. So God showed Moses the burning bush first, and the
vision in the first instance was that of a bush on fire. And an angel
spoke to him immediately, but later the Lord spoke to him from
the bush.

22,3   But Moses did not ask him straight off about what he had
seen, but inquired about things in the distant past. For God said,
"Come, I send thee to the children of Israel, and thou shalt say
unto them, The God of your fathers hath sent me, the God of
Abraham, the God of Isaac and the God of Jacob,"[62]—naming
Abraham, who was five or six generations before Moses. And since
he said "the God of your fathers" he declared something ancient
to him. (4) But Moses did not ask about this with God-given understanding, but about something even more ancient: "If I go unto
them and they say to me, What is his name? what shall I say unto
them?"[63] And then he revealed his name: "I am He Who Is."[64] (5)
And he began first with the things nearest in time, but last of all
revealed what was furthest in the past.

Luke too begins with things that are later and nearest in time,
"And Jesus began to be about thirty years of age, being, as was
supposed, the son of Joseph, the son of Eli, the son of Matthan,
the son of Nathan, the son of David, the son of Judah, the son
of Jacob, the son of Abraham, the son of Nahor, the son of Noah,
the son of Lamech, the son of Enoch, the son of Seth, the son
of Adam, the son of God."[65] And you see how he spoke of the
incarnation first, and then the [things he says] last.

22,6   And so when Matthew wanted to remind people of Christ's
human nature in the fleshly genealogy, he did not at once say,
"The birth of Jesus Christ the son of Abraham." He said "son of
David" first and then "son of Abraham," indicating the sight most
lately seen and the most recent happening and [then] one still
further in the past, to show the indispensability of what is still
higher above all creation.

23,1   And so, when the blessed John came and found people

---

[61] Prov. 8:21a
[62] Exod. 3:10; 15
[63] Exod. 3:13
[64] Exod. 3:14
[65] Luke 3:23–38

preoccupied with Christ's human nature on earth, with the Ebionites in error because of the tracing of Christ's earthly genealogy from Abraham < by Matthew > and Luke's carrying of it back to Adam— and the Cerinthians and Merinthians, and the Nazoraeans and many other sects saying that he was a mere man, sexually engendered—(2) John came along behind them, we might say, (he was the fourth evangelist), and began to recall them from their wandering, as it were, and their preoccupation with Christ's earthly human nature. As though he were following behind and saw that some were pointed towards rough, steep paths and had left the straight, true road, he began, as it were, to ask them, "Where are you headed? Where are you going, on that rough road full of obstacles, that leads to a pit? (3) That isn't the truth! Turn back! The divine Word begotten of the Father on high doesn't date only from Mary. He isn't from the time of Joseph her betrothed. He isn't from the time of Shealtiel, Zerubbabel, David, Abraham, Jacob, Noah and Adam. '*In the beginning* was the Word, and the Word was with God, and the Word was God.'"[66]

23,4   The word, "was," followed by "was" and followed by another "was," admits of no "was not." And you see, first of all, how scripture gave the most recent events at once—how Matthew showed the way with the genealogy and still did not give < all > the precise facts himself, though he surely carried the genealogy into the past. And Mark < described > the events in the world, a voice crying in the wilderness, < and > the Lord who was foretold by the Prophets and Law. And Luke traced him from the most recent times back to the earliest. < But > afterwards John, who came fourth, at last made the climax known, and the purity of the heavenly decree and the eternal Godhead. (5) In the same way Solomon in his proverb < indicated* > the beginning of the ways < first* >—if, indeed, some may wish with piety to say that, since his Godhead itself had made the flesh and human nature as "the beginning of its ways for its works"[67] of men's salvation and its own goodness, Christ's human nature itself said of his Godhead, "The Godhead itself hath founded the house."[68] And then, as the topic developed still further, it said, "He founded me in the beginning."

23,6   Was the Son of God really created and later founded in his divine nature? The technicians, the people who spy on heaven, had better tell me the method by which wisdom was created, the

---

[66] John 1:1
[67] Prov. 9:1
[68] Prov. 8:23

tool with which it was founded. But if it is allowable even to conceive of it, let us flee from such profound blasphemy, to keep our hands off the divine nature of the Only-begotten, which is always with the Father and has been begotten of him. (7) For the Word was always with the Father, was always wisdom. < The > Lord was always God of God, was true and not spurious light, always deriving his being from the Father, and always truth and life.

24,1   And why should I say so much about this? He then says, "He founded me in the beginning."[69] The godly can therefore see that he means the human soul. (2) For the incarnate human nature says "The Lord created me,"[70]—if, indeed, it should be taken in this way. "He founded,"[71] however, should be taken in the sense that he was founded in the soul. But "Before all hills he begot me,"[72] means that his begetting is heavenly.

And I have by no means said this as a statement of fact, but as an orthodox way of understanding the passage as a reference to the human nature. (3) Even though I must speak in this way, no one can ever make me say that this passage refers to Christ. But it if is to be said of Christ, there is its meaning—I do not say this by divination but because of the orthodoxy of the thought, so as not to attribute any deficiency to the Son < or > suppose that he is inferior in Godhead to the Father's essence. (4) For indeed, if we must speak in this way of "The Lord created me and founded me,"[73] some of our fathers, who were orthodox,[74] have interpreted this by taking it of the human nature. And < because > this is a pious thought many important fathers have taught it. (5) And if one does not wish to accept the teaching of the orthodox [on this point], he will not be compelled to; it does no harm, however, to those who are strangers to the faith and pagan.

For neither will < the fact that Christ suffered* > for us entail any deficiency in < the Son >; his Godhead is free [from suffering] and is always with the Father. (6) Christ suffered whatever he suffered, but was not changed in nature; his Godhead retained its impassibility. Thus, when he willed of his own good pleasure to suffer for humanity—since the Godhead, which is impassible in itself, cannot suffer—he took our passible body although he is Wisdom,

---

[69] Prov. 8:23
[70] Prov. 8:22
[71] Prov. 8:23
[72] Prov. 8:25
[73] Prov. 8:22; 23
[74] For example, Athanasius?

to consent to suffering in it and take our sufferings upon him in the flesh, accompanied by the Godhead.

For the Godhead does not suffer. (7) How can One who said, "I am the life,"[75] die? God remains impassible but shares the sufferings of the flesh so that, even though Godhead does not suffer, the suffering may be counted as the Godhead's and our salvation may be in God. The suffering is in the flesh and we have, not a passible God but an impassible God who counts the suffering as his own, not of necessity but by his own choice.

25,1 But anyway, neither have these people examined the Hebrew expressions, or found out about them, or < understood > their meaning, and yet they rise up willfully and rashly as deadly foes, looking for a chance to mutilate the faith—or themselves, rather, for they can't mutilate the truth. And since they have found "The Lord created me," they dream reckless dreams like persons under a delusion, although they have contributed nothing useful to mankind, and have disturbed the world. (2) This is not what the Hebrew means; Aquila says, "The Lord got me." Parents always say, "I have gotten a son."

But Aquila did not render the meaning either. "I have gotten a son" sounds as though there is something new in God, but there can be nothing new. (3) Even if one confesses that the Son has been begotten of the Father and not created, he was begotten outside of time and without beginning. (4) For there can be no time between the Father and the Son, or some time will † be longer[76] than the Son's. For if all things are made through him, so is time. (5) But if there is a time before Him who is before all—how can there be? But if there is, then we shall need another Son, through whom the time before the Son has been made.

And there is much to lead the minds of those who "are always busy but do nothing good"[77] into endless perplexity. (6) In the Hebrew it says, "Adonai" (which means, "the Lord") "kanani," which can be rendered both "hatched[78] me" and "got me." In the strictest sense, however, it means, "hatched me." But which hatchling is not begotten from the substance of the parent that sired it? And here, among created bodily things, the young are produced by the pairings of male and female—men, cattle, birds and all the rest. (7) And so, since the Only-begotten was in all respects the Father's

---

[75] John 11:25
[76] Holl: ὑπερτείνων; MSS: ὑπὲρ πλείω
[77] 2 Thes. 3:11
[78] The verb is not elsewhere attested. Is Epiphanius thinking of Hebrew ‎קן, "nest?"

wisdom and willed to do all things for rectification, so that no one would form a false notion of him and be deprived of the truth, he was not conceived from a man's seed when he visited the human race, when he was truly born of a woman and lay in the Virgin's womb during the period of gestation. Otherwise his birth in the flesh might have required pairing and sexual congress. But he took flesh only from his mother and yet made his human nature complete in his own image—not deficient, but true human nature.

25,8   And his not being of a man's seed did not make him deficient. He to whom all things belong took all things in their perfection: flesh, sinews, veins and everything else; a soul, truly and not in appearance; a mind; and all other human characteristics except for sin, as scripture says, "He was in all points tempted as a man, apart from sin."[79] (9) Thus, by being born in the flesh here simply of a mother, as perfect man and without defect [yet] simply of a woman, he showed those who care to see the truth and not blind their own minds that he has been perfectly begotten of the Father on high, without beginning and not in time; and on earth was born simply of a woman, without spot or defilement.

26,1   But to explain the phrase, "Adonai kanani," or, "The Lord hatched me." Whatever begets, begets its like. A man begets a man and God begets God, the man in a fleshly way and God spiritually. (2) And as is the man who begets, so is the man begotten of him. The human begetter, who is subject to suffering, < begets > his own son, and the impassible God begot the Son who was begotten of him without suffering—begot him truly and not in appearance, of himself and not from outside himself, impassible spirit impassibly begetting spirit, impassible God impassibly begetting very God.

26,3   For if he created all things himself—and you, Arius, admit that God has created all things—then he also begot the Son himself. (4) But if you say, "If he begot, he suffered in begetting," we'll tell you that if he suffered in begetting he tired from creating. But all that he wills, he simultaneously possesses fully in himself; the Godhead will not bring suffering on the Son in the process of creating, nor can it be conceived of as suffering because of its spotless begetting of the Son. For the Father is unchangeable, the Son is unchangeable, the Holy Spirit is unchangeable, one essence, one Godhead.

26,5   But you'll surely to ask me, "Did God beget the Son by willing it or without willing it?" And I am not like you, you trouble-maker, to think any such thing of God. If he begot him without

---

[79] Cf. Heb. 4:15.

willing it, he begot him unwillingly. And if he begot him willing it the will came before the Son, and because of the will there will be at least a moment of time between the Son [and the Father]. (6) But in God there is no time to will and no will to think. God begot the Son neither by willing to nor without willing to, but begot him in his nature which transcends will. For his is the nature of Godhead, which neither needs a will nor does anything without a will, but of itself possesses all things at once and is in want of nothing that exists.

27,1 But Arius ferrets out still more texts and keeps wandering all over, wasting his time on unsound arguments—not as the sacred text is, but as he < conceives of it > in his unhealthy preoccupation with controversies and verbal disputes which are good for nothing except for his and his dupes' ruin. < And > he seizes on the text where the Lord blessed his disciples and said, "Father, grant them to have life in themselves. And this is life eternal, that they know thee, the only true God, and Jesus Christ whom thou hast sent."[80] (2) However, I have already dealt with all this in my long work on the faith which, in my mediocrity and feebleness, I have been compelled to write about faith at the urgent request of the brethren, and have called the *Ancoratus*.[81] (3) And as, with God's help, my poor mind was able to gather the truths of God's teaching from every scripture—like an anchor for those who wish < to hold onto > the holy apostolic and prophetic faith of our fathers which has been preached in God's holy church from the beginning until now—I have set it out clearly for our minds to grasp and be sure of, < so that > they will not be shaken by the devil's devices or damaged by the seas that they have raised in the world with all their bluster.

27,4 For the Lord taught his own disciples, "If what ye have heard from the beginning abide in you, and what ye have heard † of me[82] abide in you, ye shall abide in me and I in you, and I in the Father and ye in me."[83] (5) Thus the truths of the faith, which we have heard from the Lord since the beginning, abide in God's holy church. (6) And so God's holy church and orthodox faith abide in the Lord; and the Lord, the Only-begotten, abides in the Father, and the Father in the Son, and we in him through the Holy Spirit, provided we become temples to hold his Holy Spirit. (7) As God's holy apostle said, "Ye are the temple of God,

---

[80] Cf. John 17:2–3.
[81] Cf. Anc. 71,3.
[82] Holl: παρ' ἐμοῦ; MSS: ἀπ' ἀρχῆς
[83] 1 John 1:1; John 15:4; 10; 17:21

and the Spirit of God dwelleth in you."[84] Thus the Spirit is God of God; and through God's Holy Spirit we are called temples, if we give his Spirit a home within us. For as the Only-begotten himself confesses, < the > Spirit is the Spirit of Christ who proceeds < from > the Father and receives of the Son.

28,1   I have discussed all this in that book of mine about faith—the book I wrote to Pisidia and Pamphylia, as I said.[85] But here, since I have come to the expressions we need next, I have had to hurry and make the same points over again, as it were, because of Arius, the heresiarch with whom we are dealing, and the Arians who derive from him—to put a stop to their wicked deeds which turn "sweet to bitter, good to evil, and light to darkness."[86] (2) For through Isaiah "Woe" is definitively pronounced by the Lord upon such people, who turn good to evil. And God is in no way responsible for their kind. From pride, prejudice, would-be wisdom or devilish conceit, each of them has been deprived of the truth and brought an affliction on the world, his unsound teaching.

28,3   All right, to understand the words the Lord has spoken let's begin with this text, as the holy apostle says, "We also have the Spirit of God, that we may know the things that God hath bestowed upon us, which things we likewise speak."[87] (4) For the Lord says, "Grant them to have life in themselves. And this is life eternal, that they may know thee, the only true God, and Jesus Christ whom thou hast sent."[88]

29,1   But this trouble-maker, Arius, and his followers jump up and say, "His praying to God at all, and saying, 'Father, grant them to have life in themselves,' shows that he is not the equal of the Giver of the life. If he were of the Father's essence he would give the life himself, and not ask the Father to give the recipients the gifts he gives in answer to prayers."

29,2   And people who have turned their minds against themselves do not realize that the Only-begotten came to be our example and salvation in every way, and took his stand in the world like an athlete in an arena, to destroy all that, sometimes by idolatry, sometimes by Jewish conceit, sometimes from unbelief, sometimes from the vanity of human prejudice, rebels against the truth—came to teach men humility, so that no human being will think himself important, but will ascribe everything to the Father of all.

---

[84] 1 Cor. 3:16
[85] Cf. Anc. Proem; 2,1; 5,1.
[86] Cf. Isa. 5:20 and Ath. Or. I 1.
[87] Cf. 1 Cor. 2:12–13.
[88] Cf. John 17:2–3.

(3) And so, although he is life—as he says, "I am the life"[89]—and although he has the power to give life, he has no wish to confuse what is right. < As > he came for one sovereignty, one Godhead, one truth, one concord, one Glory, to secure men's salvation and understanding, he also prayed to the Father [for life] in the presence of his disciples. (4) For which son does not ask [for gifts] from his father? And which father does not give [gifts] to his son? But which son is different from his Father's nature? And thus < the > Son, "the only-begotten of a Father, full of grace and truth,"[90] needed no filling, since he was not in want of truth but full of grace and truth. (5) But, being full, he both gives and can give; but his will is to refer all things to the Father.

For the Son glorifies the Father and the Father glorifies the Only-begotten. "I have glorified thee on the earth,"[91] said the Son to the Father, and the Father said to the Son, "I have both glorified thee, and will glorify thee again."[92] (6) The Godhead can have no dispute, no envy: "Grant them to have life in themselves."[93] He who is life, wills to receive life from the Father and give it to his disciples, not to divide the Divine Unity and not to put an obstacle in the Jews' way—so that the Jews would hear him asking of the Father and giving to his disciples.

30,1   In what way does the Son ask the Father, then? By asking because he does not have? No, but by declaring the oneness of the Trinity, which gives with the utmost fullness to him who receives the gifts worthily. But in another passage, to show the oneness of the Godhead, he gives [gifts] no longer by asking for them but by giving his own on his own authority, for he is Wellspring of Wellspring,[94] and God of God; < for > "He breathed in their faces and said, 'Receive ye the Holy Spirit.'"[95] (2) And in another passage "He lifted up his hands and said, 'Receive ye the Holy Spirit.'"[96]

And he has life in himself, to give to anyone he chooses. "For as the Father hath life in himself, so hath the Son life in himself."[97] (3) And you see that he offers the prayer as to the Father, and to honor the Father gives the Father a glory that cannot be taken away, because of their single oneness and one glory, and to keep

---

[89] John 14:6
[90] John 1:14.
[91] John 17:4
[92] Cf. John 12:18.
[93] Cf. John 5:26; 17:2–3.
[94] Perhaps cf. Ath. Or. I 19.
[95] John 20:22
[96] Cf. Luke 24:50.
[97] Cf. John 5:26.

the disciples from thinking that the Only-begotten came to turn believers' minds from the God of the Law and the prophets. (4) Being God, and foreknowing the malice of men, [he offers the prayer] to confound Mani's denial of the Father, to teach the disciples that the Godhead is the same in the Old and the New Testaments, and to shame the Jews because the Only-begotten came not to teach another God, but to reveal his divinity and the divinity of his heavenly Father. (5) "Grant them to have life in themselves," [he says], although he himself proclaimed this life. Why, then, would he ask the Father to give them what he himself taught and gave? For he made the life known afterwards when he said, "This is life, that they may know thee, the only true God."[98]

31,1 Next, because Christ said, "the only true God,"[99] Arius and his followers jump at the phrase and think that they have found an argument against the truth. (2) But let's ask you Arians ourselves, "What do you say? Only the Father is 'true,' but what's the Son? Isn't the Son true? If the Son isn't 'true,' 'Our faith is vain and our preaching is in vain.'[100] (3) And you'll find yourselves blaspheming against your own selves and comparing the Son of < God > with the unspeakable, infamous idols—you people to whom the prophets said, as though to the deluded, < 'Solomon says, The worship of the unspeakable idols is the beginning of all evil.'* >[101] And each of the prophets recalled this text, < like Jeremiah* > who said, < 'Woe unto them that follow after idols,'* >[102] and, 'Our fathers made for themselves false gods, and their high places became false.'[103] (4) [If you don't think the Son is 'true'] the Only-begotten is condemned in your eyes, and you hold this disgusting opinion of 'him who redeemed you'[104]—if, indeed, he did redeem you. For since you deny your Savior and Redeemer, you cannot be of his fold."

For if God is not true, he should not be worshiped; and if he is created, he is not God. And if he is not to be worshiped, how can he be called God? Stop it, you who < make a god* > of one more natural object, (5) who practice Babylonian < worship* > and set up Nebuchadnezzar's image and idol! You who blow this famous

---

[98] Cf. John 17:3 and Ath. Or. III 26.
[99] Cf. Ath. Or. I 6.
[100] 1 Cor. 15:14
[101] Holl suggests that some scriptural citations, including Wisd. Sol. 14:27, have fallen out here.
[102] Cf. Jer. 9:14.
[103] Cf. Jer. 16:19 and 3:32.
[104] Gal. 3:13

trumpet to unite † the worshipers[105] < against > the Son of God* >
and bring the image with music, cymbals and psaltery to overthrow
the peoples with your words of error, and prepare them to serve
an image instead of God and truth. And who else is as true as
the Son of God? (6) "For who shall be likened to the Lord among
the sons of God?"[106] says the scripture, and, "None other shall be
reckoned in comparison with him."[107] And what does he say [next]?
To show you that he means the Son, he describes him next and
says, "He hath found out every way of understanding, and given
it < to Jacob his servant and Israel whom he loveth. > (7) And
thereafter he appeared on earth and consorted with men."[108] How
can this not have been said truly of him? < And how can the Son
not be true God* > when he says, "I am the truth?" [109]

32,1   But you will ask me, "Why did the only-begotten true God
say, 'that they may know thee, the *only* true God,' as a way of
discouraging polytheism and the division of the life-giving knowledge?"[110] If the Father is the only true God, then the Son is true
and truly begotten of the Father! (2) For it was "to honor the
Father"[111] and reveal him alone as "true God," that the Son made
it known that he is "truly begotten of the Father."

And how was this to be made known? (3) Just look at the texts
here! It says here that the Father is the only "true God," but in
the Gospel according to John it says, "He was the true light."[112]
And which "true light" was this but the Only-begotten? And again,
the scriptures say of God, "God is light,"[113] and they didn't say,
"God is true light." On the other hand, they said of God's only-
begotten Son that the Only-begotten is "true light."

32,4   It said, "true God," of the Father, and not that God is
"true light." But of the Son, it said, "God," and didn't add "true"
to the sentence, "The Son is God." And where it said, "God is
light," it didn't add, "true light." Then what should we say of the
Father? We < shall confess* > that God is "true light," and not
make the Godhead defective. (5) And because "true light" is not
[said of God] in the scripture, should we < also > sinfully say that
God is not true light? And since scripture says that the Son is God,

---

[105] Holl: προσκυνούντων; MSS: πολεμούντων
[106] Ps. 88:7
[107] Bar. 3:36
[108] Bar. 3:37–38
[109] John 14:6
[110] Cf. Ath. Or. C. Ar. I 6.
[111] Cf. John 8:49.
[112] John 1:9
[113] John 1:5

and that he was God with the true Father—("The Word was God';"[114] and it didn't say that the Word *became* God, but that he *was* God)— the equivalence [of the Father and the Son] will be shown by the two phrases. From the Father's being "true God" and the Son's being "true light" the equality of their rank will be evident; and from the Son's being "God" and the Father's being "light" the equivalence of their glory will be plain. (6) And there will be no difference, nor can anyone contradict the truth. The Father is true God, and the Only-begotten is true God.

33,1   But I am also obliged to speak further here, about the Holy Spirit, or, if I leave anything out, I may give the enemy, who want < to contradict > us, a chance to hold their < wicked beliefs* >. For it is the same with the Holy Spirit, as the Lord himself testifies by saying "the Spirit of truth" and "the Spirit of the Father,"[115] but the apostle by saying of Christ." (2) Thus, as the Spirit of the Father [and] the Spirit of the Son, the Holy Spirit is the Spirit of truth, the Spirit of God, just as God is true God, just as he is true light. For there is one Trinity, one glory, one Godhead, one sovereignty. (3) The Father is a father, the Son is a son, the Holy Spirit is a holy spirit. The Trinity is not an amalgam, not separate from its own unity, not wanting in perfection, not strange to its own identity, but is one Perfection, three Perfects, one Godhead.

33,4   And the opposition's sword has fallen [from its hand]. Indeed, scripture says, "< Their blows became a weapon > of babes."[116] Even if infants want to take weapons they lack the strength, and cannot do anything with their hands. Even though infants are disturbed they kill and harm themselves rather [than anyone else], since they cannot use weapons on others. Similarly these people have sent their imposture to war with themselves, but will bring no evil on the sons of the truth.

34,1   But once more I shall go on to other texts which they have thought of. To begin with, the deception they use to hoodwink the simple and innocent is amazing. As the serpent deceived Eve in her innocence, so they, if they wish to win their allegiance, first < approach* > those who do not wish to go by their creed with much flattery, and with liberal expenditure, attention, and both promises and threats, such as "You're opposing the imperial decrees and the wrath of the emperor Valens." (2) And what do they say [next]? "Well, what is it that we're saying? It's the faith [itself],

---

[114] John 1:1
[115] For both, see John 15:26.
[116] Ps. 63:8

only you're [too] proud [to admit it]!"

All right, let's see whether this is the faith. They say, "We confess that the Son is begotten of the Father, and do not deny it. (3) But," they say, "we must also confess that he is a creature and a product of creation."

But nothing could be worse. Nothing created is like anything begotten, and nothing begotten is like anything created, especially in the case of that one, pure and perfect essence. (4)[117] For all things have been created by God, but only God's Son has been begotten, and only the Holy Spirit proceeded from the Father and received of the Son. All other things are created beings, and neither proceeded from the Father nor received of the Son. But they received of the Son's fullness, as the scripture says, "By the Word of God were all things established, and all the host of them by the Spirit of his mouth."[118]

34,5   "But we must confess the creaturehood as well," says Arius, "since scripture said 'creature' in a figurative sense, and 'offspring' is meant figuratively. For even though we say, 'offspring,' we shall not mean an offspring like any other."

Well then, they are deceiving the innocent by saying, "offspring," and the offspring isn't a real one. (6) "But we also confess that Christ is a creature," they say. "For Christ is also called door, way, pillar, cloud, rock, lamb (αρνίον), lamb (αμνός), stream, calf, lion, well-spring, wisdom, Word, Son, angel, Christ, Savior, Lord, man, Son of Man, cornerstone, sun, prophet, bread, king, building, husbandman, shepherd, vine, and as many other things of this sort. In the same way," they say, "we use 'creature' in a loose sense of the word. For we are bound to confess [that he is a creature]."

35,1   Such wicked speculation, and such cunning! May the Lord allow no son of the truth to be brought by such dissimulation to accept "creature" as the Son of God's title for such reasons, and agree to confess it. Let them tell us what the use of this is, and we will grant them the result of their reasoning. (2) For all these things are ways of talking and do not impair the Son's divinity, make him defective in comparison with the Father, or < alter him* > out of his essential nature. Though he is called door, it is because we enter by him. Though he is called road it is because we go by him, though pillar, it is because he is the support of the truth. Though he is called a cloud, this is because he overshadowed the children of Israel; though he is called pillar, it is because of the

---

[117] We insert a paragraph number missing in Holl.
[118] Cf. Ps. 32:6.

brightness of the fire which gave them light in the wilderness. Though he is called manna, this is because they denied that he was the bread from heaven; though he is called bread, this is because we are strengthened by him.

35,3   Though he is called "angel," this is because he is a messenger of a great counsel. The word, "angel," is a synonym. Rahab received the "angels," and yet the men who had been sent there were not angels, but persons who *reported* (ἀναγγείλαντες) on the place. And so, because he reported the Father's will to men, the Only-begotten is an "angel of a great counsel," who reports the great counsel in the world.

35,4   Though he is called stone, the "stone" is not inanimate; this is a way of talking, because he has become an obstacle to the Jews, but the foundation of our salvation. And he is called "cornerstone" because he unites the Old and the New Testaments, and the circumcised and uncircumcised, in one body. (5) But he is called "lamb" because of his harmlessness, and because the sin of humankind has been done away by his offering to the Father as a lamb for the slaughter; for the Impassible came to suffer for our salvation. And whatever else in these examples is an aid to human salvation is applied to him by the sacred scripture in some accommodated sense.

36,1   Now what good can "creature" do, or what use is it to our salvation and the divine Word's incarnate glory and perfect divinity? How does calling him "creature" help us? What can a creature do for creatures? How does a creature benefit creatures? (2) Why did God create < a Son > and allow < him > to be worshiped as God, when he says, "Thou shalt not make to thyself any likeness, neither on earth nor in heaven, and thou shalt not worship it?"[119] Why did he create himself a Son and command that he be worshiped, particularly when the apostle says, "And they served the creature rather than the creator, and were made fools."[120] It is foolish to make a god of a creature and break the first commandment, which says, "Thou shalt worship the Lord thy God, and him only shalt thou serve."[121] (3) And thus God's holy church worships, not a creature but a begotten Son, the Father in the Son, and the Son in the Father, with the Holy Spirit.

36,4   "Oh, yes!" says Arius. "Unless I say he is a creature, I attribute diminution to the Father. For the creature does not diminish the

---

[119] Exod. 20:47
[120] Rom. 1:25; 22
[121] Deut. 6:13; Matt. 4:10

creator, but by the nature of things the begotten shrinks its begetter, or broadens or lessens or cuts it, or does it some such injury."[122]

36,5   It is very foolish of those who think such things to imagine Godhead in their likeness—and of those who attribute their frailties to God, since God is wholly impassible, both in begetting and in creating. We are creatures, and as we suffer when we beget, we tire when we create. And if the Father suffers in begetting, then he also tires in creating.

36,6   But how can one speak of suffering in connection with God, and of his tiring if he creates? He does not tire, never think it! The scripture says, "He shall not weary."[123] "God is spirit"[124] and begot the Son spiritual< ly >, without beginning and not in time, "God of God, light of light, very God of very God, begotten, not made."[125]

37,1   But I shall pass this text by too, and once more devote my attention to others which they repeat and bandy about in wrong senses, and which I have mentioned earlier. For again, they confusedly misinterpret this one: "Receive your high priest, who is faithful to him that *made* him."[126] (2) In the first place they reject the Epistle, I mean the one to the Hebrews, remove it bodily from the Apostle and say that it is not his. But they unhealthily < turn > the text to their advantage, as I said, take it in a wrong sense, and covertly introduce the Son's creaturehood, if you please, through the words, "faithful to him that *made* him."[127]

37,3   But a person with sense could ask them when our Lord took the title of "high priest," and they will be at a loss because they have no answer. (4) Christ never adopted these names before his incarnation—stone, sheep led to the slaughter, man and Son of Man, eagle, lamb and all the rest that are applied to him after his coming in the flesh. He came to be called "high priest" for the reason the Law declared of him, "A prophet shall the Lord raise unto you, of your brethren."[128] (5) The oracle thus plainly explains "prophet," "high priest," and "of them" [as titles given] *after* his sojourn on earth, and it can be seen at a glance how God's unconquerable power and foreknowledge foretold and certified all this by its wondrous light, and certified it to the "stopping of every

---

[122] Cf. Ath. Or. C. Ar. I 15; 21.
[123] Isa. 40:28. Cf. Ath. Nic. 7.
[124] John 4:24
[125] Creed of Nicaea, as given, for example, at Ath. Jov. 3
[126] Heb. 3:1–2. Cf. Ath. Sent. Dion. 10–11.
[127] Heb. 3:2
[128] Deut. 18:15

mouth"[129] that rebels against the truth. (6) For he says in the same
connection, "Every high priest taken from among men is ordained
for men to offer gifts and sacrifices, being able to bear with [their
infirmities]. For he hath need < to offer > for his own sins. But
he that had no sin offered himself to the Father."[130] (7) And "of
men" is said because of the earthly sojourn, but "not of men"
< and > "that hath no sin" are said because of the divinity. And of
his divinity he says, "though he were a son;" but of his humanity,
"He learned by the things he suffered."[131]

38,1   And you see that all of Christ's titles are plain and contain
nothing crooked. "High priest faithful to him that *made* him" describes
neither the making of his body here nor the making of his human
nature. It does not speak of creation at all, but of the bestowal
of his rank after his sojourn on earth, in the same sense as "He
gave him a name which is above every name."[132] (2) And this was
not done long ago in the divine nature, but in his present human
nature. For it was the human nature he took from Mary that received
the name above every name, the title "Son of God" in addition
to "Divine Word." (3) And again, he said here for this reason, and
through the apostle himself, "We see Jesus, who for a little was
made lower than the angels, crowned with glory and honor."[133]
Thus the angels' Master and Maker would appear lower than the
angels; he who inspires the angels' dread and fear and who, with
the Father and the Holy Spirit, made the angels from nothing,
would be called "lower." And it would become plainly evident that
he is not speaking of his Godhead here, but of his flesh.

38,4   For the suffering of death was not counted as the Word's
before his flesh, but after his incarnation. For this reason the same
Word is both passible and impassible—impassible in Godhead but
suffering in his human nature, just as both of his natures were
all there in one [person]—[that of] the Son of Man in the same
person, and [that of] the Son of God in the same person. For
Christ is called the "Son" in both alike.

39,1   What did God "make" him, then? From all that has been
said the trouble-makers should learn that nothing in this text
corresponds to the divine nature; [the text] corresponds to the
human. And "made him," does not refer to the making or creating

---

[129] Rom. 3:19 (2 Cor. 10:5)
[130] Heb. 5:1; 3; 8:3; 9:14
[131] Heb. 2:9
[132] Phil. 2:9
[133] Heb. 2:9

of him, but to his rank after the advent.

39,2 If someone asks a king about his son, and says, "What is he to you?" the king will tell him, "He is my son."

"Is he your legitimate or your illegitimate son?" The king will say, "He is my legitimate son."

"Then what did you make him?"

"I made him king." Plainly, the son's rank is no different from his father's. (3) And because he has said, "I made him king," this surely does not mean that the king is saying, "I created him." In saying, "I made him," he certainly did not deny begetting—which he had acknowledged—but made that plain; "I made him," however, was a statement of his rank. Thus, by those who wish < to attain > salvation, the Son is unquestioningly believed to be the Son of the Father, and is worshiped.

39,4 But "was made high priest" is said because he offered himself in his body to the Father for mankind, himself the priest, himself the victim, for all creation; but he ascended spiritually and gloriously in his body itself and "sat down at the Father's right hand"[134] after "being made an high priest forever"[135] and "passing through the heavens"[136] once and for all. The same holy apostle testifies to this of him in the lines that follow. (5) And once again the argument from the sacred scripture which they use as their excuse has proved a failure, for scripture is life-giving; nothing in it offers an obstacle to the faithful or makes for the downfall of blasphemy against the Word.

40,1 Then they mention one more passage, when John stood in the wilderness and saw him coming, and said, "This is he of whom I said unto you, a man cometh after me that *was made* (γέγονεν) before me, for he was before me."[137] (2) And first they change the meaning of the words as though they were half asleep and say, "How could this apply to the human nature, when he was not conceived in Mary's womb before the conception of John? The evangelist says instead, 'In the sixth month the angel Gabriel was sent to a city of Galilee, to a virgin espoused to a man whose name was Joseph. And he came in unto her and said, Hail, thou that art highly favored, the Lord is with thee,'[138] and the rest that follows. (3) When the virgin was troubled at his greeting he said to her, 'Behold, thou shalt conceive in thy womb and bear a son, and shalt

---

[134] Heb. 10:12
[135] Heb. 7:3
[136] Heb. 9:14
[137] Cf. John 1:29–30.
[138] Luke 1:26–28

call his name Jesus. And behold, thy cousin Elizabeth hath conceived a son in her old age, and this is the sixth month with her
that is called barren.'[139] And you see," they say, "that John was
already there six months before the annunciation to Mary. (4)
How can 'He was made (εγένετο) before me' apply to Christ's
human nature?"

Can anyone who is innocent and whose mind is not clear and
firmly made up, hear that without being upset? (5) For † indeed,[140]
for those who bring their troubles on themselves, the sacred scriptures' cogent, innocent, life-giving teachings appear to do more
harm then [good]; but the texts are always illumined in the Holy
Spirit. (6) What has been omitted to make the text convincing?
Look here, it says "this"—to indicate something visible and show
it to the onlookers—"is he of whom I said unto you that he cometh
after me." And who is coming but a "man?" But no one with sense
would suppose that our Lord is a *mere* man—only the sects we have
already indicated, the Cerinthians, Merinthians and Ebionites.

40,7　　But besides knowing him as "man" the true believers are
surely bound to know him as Lord. So John testifies, "That which
we have heard from the beginning,"[141] meaning him who is from
the beginning—the invisible divine Word, of whom we have heard
in the sacred scriptures, who is proclaimed in the prophets, who
is hymned in heaven. (8) Thus the intent of < the line >, "We have
heard with our ears from the beginning and have seen with our
eyes," is for the word, "hear," which comes first, to confess that
he is God from the beginning, but for the word, "see," to show
that he is the man of whom John the Baptist said, "After me cometh
a man."[142] And the intent of "our hands have handled" is to show
that he is God from on high and indicate that he is visible man,
born of Mary and raised in his entirety from the dead; and that
he does not lose the sacred vessel he took from Mary and his
perfect human nature, but, through the handling of his side and
the nail-prints, gives a sure acknowledgement of the three. (9) So
please understand here too that "This is he of whom I said unto
you that a man cometh after me"[143] means the human nature, and
"He was before me" means the Godhead "because he was before
me." For "He was in the world," says the holy Gospel, "and the

---

[139] Luke 1:30–31; 36
[140] Holl: ἀληθῶς; MSS: λέγει
[141] 1 John 1:1
[142] John 1:30
[143] John 1:30

world was made by him, and the world knew him not."[144]

41,1 But if he was in the world before the begetting and creation of John he got to (ἐγενόμην) the world before him—not meaning creation or making, but in the sense in which people use the same word to say, "I got to (ἐγενόμην) Jerusalem, I got to Babylon, I got to Ethiopia, I got to Alexandria"—not meaning creation here, but presence and arrival. (2) What does "I got to Babylon" or some other place mean but, "I came [there]?" "He got [here] before me" shows the Word's continual presence on earth, and "He was before me" shows the eternity of the Godhead. "Coming after me" does, however, indicate his conception after John's.

And so "I am the voice of one crying in the wilderness"[145] means a cry to draw attention. (3) When people call they give a loud shout first without any words, to call from a distance to the people who need to hear something from them. And as soon as the people hear the shout [which is] just [a shout], pay attention and get ready to hear, then finally the shouter pronounces whatever words he wanted to say. (4) And thus John was a voice in the wilderness to draw attention. For John himself was not the Word; the Word on whose account the preparatory shout was heard came after him. And this is why he says, "the voice of one crying in the wilderness, Prepare ye the way of the Lord."[146] (5) The voice prepares the ways, but the Lord sets foot on the ways thus prepared. And a voice speaks < to > the ear; but when the ear is open, the word is implanted in the hearer's ears. Thus Arius and his followers will never perceive God's truth. And yet it enlightens the hearts of the faithful at all times to prevent their turning away from the salvation to be found in the Word, the true, uncreated and unoriginate Son of God.

42,1 But again, as I move forward and come to each topic in turn, I shall not omit any point I have previously proposed for solution but shall once more take up the thread.[147] The Arians offer another excuse, St. Peter's words in Acts, "Be it known unto you, all ye house of Israel, that God hath *made* this Jesus whom ye crucified both Lord and Christ."[148] (2) And again they say, "Here we find 'made' in scripture;" and they do not see that by "this Jesus" the wording—for the wording is self-explanatory—means the Lord's human nature. < The meaning* > is clear from "this

---

[144] John 1:23
[145] John 1:23
[146] John 1:23
[147] I.e., the Arian arguments in the order of their appearance at 14,1–15,4
[148] Acts 2:36. Cf. Ath. C. Apol. 2.9.

Jesus *whom ye crucified.*" This is < plainly* > the flesh which they crucified, for they crucified flesh. (3) And thus the Lord says in the Gospel, "But now ye seek to kill me, a *man* that hath told you the truth which I have heard of my Father,"[149] < declaring himself man* > but not separating his Godhead from his manhood. (4) For Christ's Godhead was not separate from his manhood when he was about to suffer, and when he suffered the human nature was not abandoned by the Word. But neither had the impassible Word suffered before this; he suffered < only > in the suffering flesh. For the same name truly applies to both natures and is given to the divine nature and the human. The human nature of the Word himself is Christ, and yet Christ is the Lord in the human nature itself. (5) But the suffering is limited to the flesh, as Peter said, "Christ suffered for us *in flesh*"—to show the divine nature's impassibility—and again, "dying *in the flesh,* brought to life in the Spirit."[150]

Thus Peter said "this *Jesus* whom ye crucified" to show that the sacred human nature was not abandoned by the impassible and uncreated Word, but was united with the uncreated Word on high. (6) And this is why he said, "God hath *made*" the thing conceived by Mary "Lord and Christ,"[151] the thing that had been united with Godhead. For Mary is not divine in nature, and for this reason he adds "made." And so, when Mary asked him, "How shall this be, seeing I know not a man?" the angel Gabriel said, "The Spirit of the Lord shall come upon thee and the power of the highest shall overshadow thee. Therefore also that which shall be born shall be called holy, the Son of God."[152]

42,7   But when he said, "that which shall be *born*," he gave plain indication that the divine Word is unquestionably a *Son*—not created, not made. (8) And as to the human nature which was born of Mary, he showed, by adding "that which is born < shall > also < be called holy, the Son of God >," that he had made < even the thing that was born > Christ and Lord. And as everything in the other passages has been taken care of and leaves no room for difficulty, here everything about his human nature had been taken care of, and for those who are attending to their salvation there is no bypath. (9) For the Word is a living Word from a living Father— the Father's Son, not his creature. But everything in the human

---

[149] John 8:40
[150] 1 Pet. 3:18
[151] Acts 2:36
[152] Luke 1:34–35

nature has been taken care of, so that no one can suppose that he is an apparition, or that his flesh is co-essential with his God-head on high, but everyone [will realize] that the human nature is united in one impassibility, especially after his resurrection from the dead. For scripture says, "He dieth no more, death hath no more dominion over him."[153] (10) There is one Lord, one Christ, one King, seated at the Father's right hand, one union physical and spiritual, one spiritual Godhead, both natures radiant and glorious. (11) But since I feel that the passage has been sufficiently expounded I shall pass it by; and may I resume by < going on* > to † warn my hearers against the other foolishness < of their invention*>.[154]

43,1 For again, they say, "If he is of the Father's essence why does he not know the hour and the day, but by his own admission acknowledges to the disciples that he does not know something the Father is clear about, and says, 'Of that day and of that hour knoweth no man, not even the angels in heaven or the Son, but the Father only.'[155] (2) If the Father knows," they say, "and he doesn't know, how can the Father's and the Son's Godhead be the same, when the Son doesn't know something the Father is clear about?"

43,3 But not knowing their human frailty they seize to their own harm on everything that the Only-begotten, in his divine wisdom, taught mysteriously as an assurance of the truest knowledge—as horrid serpents, when caught by a crafty hunter, take the bait to their own destruction. They do not know that falsehood will never stand, while the truth always sets its own sons right and confounds falsehood. (4) Those who have harbored this evil suspicion of Christ from the first must tell us which is by nature greater and more important to know—God the Lord of all and the Father of our Lord Jesus Christ, or the day which is brought to its dawning by the Father, the Son and the Holy Spirit, and the hour when it dawns. But if they are asked that question, the truth itself will surely oblige them to say that the Father is greater; and so he is.

43,5 Now if the Son says, "Neither knoweth any man the Father save the Son, and no man knoweth the Son save the Father,"[156] how can he not know the lesser thing when he knows the greater thing, the Father? But these words are sacred and spoken by the

---

[153] Rom. 6:9
[154] Holl: παρατροπήν, which construes which the word Holl restores, μωρολογίας. MSS: ἀνατροπήν
[155] Matt. 24:36; cf. Ath. Or. III C. Ar. 26.
[156] Matt. 11:27

Holy Spirit, and are unknowable by those who have not received the gift and grace of the Holy Spirit. (6) For such are the Arians with their wavering spirit and feeble intellect, and even in their minor deviations they slip into hurtful ones.

44,1   For the Lord's own words will step out to meet them, "Be ye ready, < let > your loins < be > girded about and let there be lamps in your hands, and be ye as good servants, awaiting their Master. For like a thief in the night, so will the day come."[157] And the holy apostle says, "Ye are not children of the night but of the day, lest the day should come upon you as a thief."[158] (2) If, however, the children of the day are not hidden by the darkness, but are ready because "Their Master cometh in a day they know not and at an hour they await not,"[159] then won't < He who > gives them being because of his glory and Godhead be different from his servants, the sons of the day? Or will he be caught in ignorance and deficiency like those who do not know the day and are unprepared? (3) Who but the < in >sane could think that the Lord will be like his subjects and disciples—or like those who, from their unpreparedness and ignorance, are inferior to these? That is just silly.

44,4   Now if these things are not possible, but the explanation, when compared with it, turns out to contradict the saying, we need to see what explanation we can find that will leave both saying and explanation uncontradicted and prevent our deviating from the truth. For the Lord cannot lie, and can say nothing for our salvation in vain.

44,5   Thus the Father knows [the day], the Son knows [the day], and the Holy Spirit knows [the day]. Nothing in the Father is different from the Son, and there is no divergence between the Son and the Spirit. In every Sect, when I needed to, I have shown with authentic proofs that the Trinity is one Godhead and has no internal differences but is all perfection—three Perfects, one glory and one sovereignty.

45,1   But you will ask me, "Why did he say this, then?"

And I have already explained the reason for this elsewhere.[160] But nothing need keep me from adding to the same things and telling the same truths; "To me it is not burdensome, but it is a safeguard"[161] for the readers and the refutation of the opposition. The reason for this is as follows. (2) Christ has made incidental

---

[157] Cf. Matt. 24:44; Luke 12:35; 1 Thes. 5:2.
[158] 1 Thes. 5:4
[159] Matt. 24:44; 50
[160] Cf. Anc. 89,2.
[161] Cf. Phil. 3:1.

mention, in the same sentence, of three ranks, the Father, himself, and the angels in heaven. And he has attributed knowing to the Father, implying not only knowledge and personal acquaintance (γνῶσις) but everything that is always unquestionably controlled, brought about and made by the Father and the Son. (3) And the Father indeed knows the day—knows it, has fashioned and made it, and judged < all at once >, as he said in the Gospel according to John, "The Father judgeth no man, but hath given all judgment to the Son."[162] For he has judged by giving [the judgment], and gained person acquaintance [with the day] by judging; and by being acquainted with it he knows when it will come. (4) For "He that believeth not on the Son is judged already"[163]—not in the sense that the judgment is over, but in the sense that what will happen then is already plain, just as any particular thing occurs for a particular reason. For scripture is aware of more than one sort of "knowledge;" and in my frequent returns to the main point I have never failed to clarify and explain each subject with the similes and examples which have already been worked out.

46,1 But let's take this discussion up again < too >, from the beginning. What do you say, people? Did or didn't Adam know Eve his wife even before their disobedience and transgression? And you can't contradict the truth. (2) Even though you prefer not to deal fairly with the sense of this, you will be exposed, for scripture says, "They were naked and were not ashamed."[164] For if they were naked and not blind[165] they saw and knew each other. For neither can you deny this and not admit that they could see; "Eve *saw* that the tree was good for food and goodly to look upon."[166] Thus they had sight and knowledge.

But since they knew (εἰδότες) and could see, they recognized each other. (3) But when scripture said, "And Adam knew (ἔγνω) Eve his wife," it was much later. It speaks of the first knowledge and sight in the sense of knowledge acquired by seeing and intellection, but in the case of the second acquaintance and knowledge it is describing knowledge by experience. (4) The sacred scripture says the same of David in his old age, "And David was old and could not keep warm. And his servants said, Let a virgin be sought for the king. And there was found Abishag the

---

[162] John 5:22
[163] John 3:18
[164] Gen. 2:25; cf. Clem. Hom. III.42.
[165] Drexl and Dummer. Holl: < ἑαυτοὺς εἶδον καὶ ᾔδεισαν >
[166] Gen. 3:6

Shunamite."[167] And it says, "And she warmed him, and he slept by her side, and David knew her not."[168] (5) How could he not know her when she was close to his body and slept beside him? But here scripture is describing, not knowledge by intellection but knowledge by experience.

46,6   Indeed it is the same with Jacob. He served seven years as a shepherd with Leah and Rachel and knew (ᾔδει) them. But when the scripture speaks of their lawful conjugal intercourse it says, "He knew (ἔγνω) Leah his wife."[169] The first knowledge came by intellection and sight, but the second acquaintance and knowing was through experience and activity.

46,7   And thus in the sacred scripture "The Lord knoweth (ἔγνω) them that are his"[170] doesn't mean that he doesn't know those who aren't his, but refers to the activity of the Lord's assistance to them. And [so with] "Depart from me, all ye workers of iniquity. I never knew you."[171] Did he have no intellectual knowledge of them? But because they were not worthy of him he takes his active [help] away from them. And elsewhere he says, (8) "You have I known of all nations."[172] [If we take this literally], all the nations, and the entire human population, have been left out of his knowledge. On the contrary, aren't the hairs of each one's head known < by > him—of those who serve, and those who disobey him? And "God knoweth the ways on the right hand."[173] Doesn't he know the ways on the left? And how much of this sort can be said of the different kinds of knowledge!

47,1   And so with God's only-begotten Son. Since < he says >, "The Father hath given judgment to the Son,"[174] he attributed the knowledge of personal acquaintance and experience to the Father. For "No one knoweth the day save the Father"[175] is meant in two ways. He knows when it comes—indeed, the day and hour come by his authority—and he knows it < through activity >. For there has already been activity on his part, the delegation of the judgment to the Only-begotten.

47,2   And thus the same knowledge is in the only-begotten Son of God, since he is God and no different from the Father. For

---

[167] 3 Kms. 1:1; 2; 3
[168] 3 Kms. 1:4
[169] Cf. Gen. 29:23.
[170] 2 Tim. 2:19
[171] Luke 13:27
[172] Deut. 14:2
[173] Prov. 4:27a
[174] John 5:22
[175] Matt. 24:36

he himself knows the day, he brings it himself, he himself carries it through, brings it to an end, and judges, and without him it cannot come. (3) But he does not know it through activity yet, that is, he has not yet judged. The impious are still impious, the unrighteous covet, fornicators, adulterers and idolaters commit iniquity, the devil is at work, sects arise, and imposture does its work until God's only-begotten Son brings the day itself, and gives each his just due. And < then* > he will know it < through activity* >, that is, [know] it through deed and power. (4) And the Father has full knowledge in two ways, while the Son has knowledge of the day and is not unaware of it, but his knowledge has not yet been completed by activity, that is, he has not yet judged.

47,5 But knowledge has been withheld from the holy angels in two ways— < in that they do not yet have intellectual knowledge [of the day]* >, and < also > that they do not yet know it through activity, that is, through the fulfillment of their function. For they have not yet been told to go out, gather the impious in bundles like tares and prepare them for burning. (6) And you see, beloved and servants of God, that all these people who welcome shocking notions because of some preconception of their own, have gone to war in vain, and directed against themselves their various attempts to blaspheme the Son of God as lesser and inferior.

48,1 But now that we have also discussed this sufficiently, let us once again, by the power of God, devote our attention to their other arguments. Although these fine heretics who are game for anything do not have beliefs like the Manichaeans and many other sects, still, while they believe in the reality of Christ's flesh, they believe even this inadequately and not in the fullest sense. (2) They confess that the Savior had true flesh; but when they learn from the Gospel itself that he tired from his journey, was hungry and thirsty, and went to sleep and got up, they apply all this in a body to his Godhead as though aiming, for reasons like the following, to separate his Godhead from the Father's essence.[176] (3) For they say, "If he is of the Father, but the Father does not tire or thirst or hunger as the sacred scripture says, 'He shall not weary not hunger nor thirst nor sleep, and of his counsel there is no finding out'[177]— (4) if these things are characteristic of the Son," they say, "then he is different from the Father's essence and nature."

And they themselves will admit that these things did not apply

---

[176] Cf. Ath. Sent. Dion. 27.1–2.
[177] Isa. 40:28

to the Only-begotten before the incarnation. However, when they are compelled to admit this, but come to the acts of Christ's human nature and hear that these things were appropriate because he had taken a body, and that he gave in to them for his legitimate needs like a mule giving in to a chariot because he took flesh in reality and not appearance, then they claim that these things are not characteristic of flesh by itself.

49,1 And it is indeed true that [flesh] cannot of itself thirst or grow tired. But those who have left the road and turned off on paths that lead the other way do not know that the Son of God did not simply take flesh at his coming, but also took a soul, a mind and everything human except for sin, and was < truly begotten > —though not of a man's seed, but of the holy virgin Mary by the Holy Spirit. (2) < But if* > they will not admit < themselves* > that he has taken a soul, < they will be made fools of* > by this counter-argument, the simplest of all the replies to their nonsense.[178] (3) The true God— < who > says of himself, "I am the truth"— himself admits, "My soul is troubled,"[179] "My soul is exceeding sorrowful,"[180] and "I have power to lay down my soul and to take it"[181]—[this last] to show that, as God, he has this power, < but that by his incarnation he has truly become man* >. (4) For no [mere] man could say this; no one has the power to lay his soul down and take it. But when Christ speaks of a soul he shows that he has become man in reality, not appearance.

49,5 And again, [he says], "I am the good shepherd who layeth down his soul for the sheep."[182] And to show the reality of these things he said to his Father on the cross, "Into thy hands I commend my spirit;"[183] and when the soldiers came, the scripture says, "They found that he had already given up the ghost."[184] (6) And again, "Crying with a loud voice" he said, "Eli, Eli, lema sabachthani, that is, My God, my God, why hast thou forsaken me?"[185]—I have also explained this way of speaking earlier—and, as the Gospel says, "gave up the ghost." (7) For when the truth says, "He gave up the ghost," "into thy hands," "My soul is troubled," and all the rest, who would be < so > foolish as to believe such a gang of

---

[178] John 14:6
[179] John 12:27
[180] Matt. 26:38
[181] John 10:18
[182] John 10:11
[183] Luke 23:46
[184] Cf. John 19:33.
[185] Matt. 27:46

myopic dreamers and ignore the actual credible statements of the divine Word?

50,1 But in the end, like pirates mutilating sound bodies, they chase down things which have been well and rightly said by each scripture, and appeal to some text which the scripture often uses figuratively. And they have a way of citing what has been said figuratively in a literal sense, and interpreting a literal and un-equivocal statement as an allegory of something else. (2) They jump right up and cite some words from the holy Isaiah which were spoken in the person of the Father, "Behold, my servant shall understand, my beloved in whom I am well pleased, whom my soul loveth,"[186] as though this is the Father talking; and so it is. (3) "Well, now," they say, "has the Father taken a soul too?" But if we say, "Heavens, no! What can this be but a figurative expression?" they reply, "Then what was said by the Son is figurative too." (4) And they think they can get an occasion against the truth in this way, but it won't be given them. The truth stands unadorned on its own feet, undefeated and with no need for decoration.

50,5 For let's see what both of these mean. If the Father had become corporeal, assumed flesh and said these words, he would really have taken a soul. But if the Father did not assume flesh and still said, "my soul," this is a figure of speech referring to God, to safeguard the [Son's] legitimacy and show the legitimacy of the Father's relationship to the Son. (6) But one cannot say the same of the Son in this respect. The Father did not take flesh, while the Son assumed flesh. The Father did not become man, but the Son did.

50,7 Something else of the sort may be said of the Father. As he says, "My soul hath loved him,"[187] in this passage, so he says, "I have found David the son of Jesse, a man after mine heart,"[188] "My heart is far from them."[189] (8) If we take what is said of the soul figuratively because "My soul hath" loved is a figure of speech, then what is said of the heart is also figurative. And clearly, this must be evident to any sensible person. (9) Therefore, if the Father speaks figuratively of a soul and a heart, which he did not take— for he never assumed flesh—things of this sort are applied to the Father in a figurative sense. But the same is not to be supposed of the Son; for the Son took flesh, and the entire human constitution.

---

[186] Isa. 42:1
[187] Isa. 42:1
[188] Cf. 1 Kms. 13:14.
[189] Isa. 29:13

51,1 This will serve as a reply to anyone who speaks figuratively
of the Son in the character of < Christ's > humanity. < There has
been no allegory even* > in a part of a word, because Christ really
took human nature. (2) For if what is said of the Son's soul is
allegory and we must take language about the soul figuratively,
then the same should be said of his heart. And in the end we
would be admitting that everything about him is apparent and not
real. (3) < Therefore >, according to the contentious Arius, when
the Word came he cannot have received a heart either—or a liver,
flesh, entrails, bones, or anything like that. In the last analysis all
of these are allegories and meant figuratively—or else he just received
a blob for a body, without any insides. (4) In that case, how could
he eat and drink? Forget it! If the Father speaks of his soul and
heart but in his case they are allegories and intended figuratively,
then, since the Arians deny that the Son has taken a soul, < they
should also take the heart* > figuratively in the Son's case.

51,5 But if, when pressed, they cannot deny Christ's heart because
they admit that the Lord received the whole bodily frame, therefore—since they < admit > that there are different sorts of "hearts,"
some undeniably real and some allegorical—in the case of Christ's
"soul" the word is accurate, and not allegorical or figurative. (6)
However, since Christ's human nature is perfect in every respect—
body, soul, mind, heart, and everything human except sin—he
naturally could do what men do, and yet have perfect Godhead,
with entire † impassibility.[190] (7) His Godhead cannot be less glorious than the perfect Godhead of the Father, but since his Godhead
is impassible he will be made complete by his human nature and
his thirst, hunger, drinking, eating, sleeping, discouragement. And
again their argument about this has failed, since Christ, though
he is God, became flesh.

52,1 But if they say, "If he was of the Father why did he become
flesh?" our reply would be, "What do you say about the angels?"
Everyone knows that Arians admit that the angels were made by
the Son. (2) Indeed, they also blaspheme the Holy Spirit by venturing
to say that he was created by the Son, although he is an uncreated
being who proceeds from the Father and receives of the Son. (3)
Hence, if they dare to say this of the Holy Spirit, how much more
can they not deny that the angels, who are creatures, have their
being from the Only-begotten?

But if the angels he created were made spiritual but in spite
of that are his creation, and, as his workmanship, are infinitely far

---

[190] Holl: ἐν ἀπαθείᾳ; MSS: ἐν σωτηρίᾳ

below his essence—and yet they have not taken flesh—what about that? (4) Are they greater than the Son even though he created them? Or what about the Holy Spirit? Why didn't he—either the Holy Spirit of God or one of the holy angels—become flesh, and put on flesh and become man? (5) The Son surely did not assume flesh because of an inferiority to the Father. In that case the angels, or even the Spirit, would surely have assumed flesh. But since the Son, who is the Father's wisdom, power and Word, had made all things himself with the Father and the Holy Spirit, he assumed flesh (6) to show that the reason for Adam's transgression or disobedience was not his creaturehood, or that God had made sin. It was his own choice, so that [the Son] could conduct his righteous judgment as Isaiah said, "A bruised reed shall he not break, and smoking flax shall he not quench, till he shall carry the judgment through to victory, and in his name shall the gentiles hope"—[191] as David said of him, "Thou shalt be victorious when thou art judged."[192]

52,7 For he was judged in order to silence his future opponents by judging justly; for no one will be able to oppose his righteous judgment. For he wore the body and kept it undefiled. What was in man, that is, in Adam, from the beginning, did not become sin, for it was surely intended not to by the creator, who is not responsible for Adam's sin; it [did not become sin] and so commit sin. The creator allowed Adam freedom of choice, and everyone is responsible for his own sin. (8) And thus, though he was without guilt, the divine Word, the creator, who with his Father and the Holy Spirit created man, the immortal and undefiled Word, became man of his own good pleasure, by some ineffable mystery of wisdom. And in his extreme lovingkindness, under no compulsion but of his own free will, he assumed all his creature's characteristics for his creature's sake to "condemn sin in the flesh,"[193] annul the curse on the cross, utterly destroy destruction in the grave, and by descending to hades with soul and Godhead make void the covenant with hades and break "the sting of death."[194] (9) But the ungrateful turn good things completely to bad and no longer thank the kind, perfect, good Son of a good Father for the things < they should > thank him for. Instead they show ingratitude by attributing frailties to his Godhead—though they cannot prove them,

---

[191] Isa. 42:3–4
[192] Ps. 50:6
[193] Rom. 8:3
[194] 1 Cor. 15:56

since the truth is evident to everyone.

53,1   And now that I have expounded these, I shall again go on to other arguments. For they quote the text in the Gospel, "The Father who sent me is greater than I,"[195] but interpret it poorly. In the first place it says, "The Father who *sent* me," not, "the Father who *created* me." (2) For all the sacred scriptures show his true sonship to the Father. They say, "The Father begot me,"[196] "I came forth from the Father and am come,"[197] "I am in the Father and the Father in me,"[198] and, "the Father who sent me."[199] And nowhere have they said, "the Father who created me," or, "the Father who made me."

53,3   And why do they keep piling up things that are not so? "The Father who sent me is greater than I"[200]—what could be more proper? More cogent? More necessary? More fitting? Who but his true Son, the One begotten of him, is the proper person to glorify the Father? (4) For the Father glorifies the Son and the Son glorifies the Father. And the Son glorifies the Father both to be an example for us, and < for the sake > of his glorification of the Father as one union and glory [with himself], teaching us that his honor is the Father's honor, as he has said, "He that honoreth not the Son as he honoreth the Father, the wrath of God abideth upon him."[201]

53,5   But how do the Arians think he is "greater?" In bulk? Time? Height? Age? Worth? Which of these is in God, for us to conceive of? Time does not apply to the Godhead, so that < the > Son who is begotten of the Father, but not in time, could be considered inferior to the Father. Nor does the Godhead allow for progress, or the Son might achieve the Father's greatness by progressing to it. (6) For if the Son of God is called the Son of God as a promotion, then he [once] had many equals and advanced by being called higher in rank, but was [once] lower than someone who outranked him. (7) But the scripture says, "Who shall be likened unto the Lord among the sons of God?"[202] since all things are termed sons colloquially, but he alone is Son by nature, not grace—for "He hath found out every path of understanding, and none shall be declared his equal."[203]

---

[195] John 4:34 and 14:28
[196] Cf. Ps. 109:3.
[197] John 16:28
[198] John 14:10
[199] John 4:34
[200] John 4:34 and 14:28
[201] Cf. John 5:23; John 3:36.
[202] Ps. 88:7
[203] Bar. 3:36

But what do Arians say? "The Father surpasses the Son in exaltation." (8) Where is the Godhead located? Or is it bounded by space? Then "bigger around" could be said of it. <Bosh*>, "God is spirit!"[204] And their heretical invention is a complete failure. Let us pass this by too, beloved, and go on to the rest of their arguments.

54,1 For they say that the sender is not like the sent, but that sender and sent differ in power because the one sends, while the other is sent. And if the meaning of the truth were what they say, the whole subject of our knowledge could not be traced to one unity of truth, power and Godhead. (2) For if two were meeting or two were sending, the Son would no longer be a son, but a brother—who had another brother, no longer a father.[205] If they were related by identity or adoption, or if one were to send himself, or if the two sent together or arrived together, they would show that there are two Godheads and not one unity. (3) But here there is a Sender and a Sent, showing that there is one Source[206] of all good, the Father; but next after the Source comes One who—to correspond with his name of Son and Word, and not with any other—is one Source springing from a Source, the Son come forth, ever with the Father but begotten < without beginning and not in time as the scripture says* >, "For with thee is the source of life."[207] (4) And to show the same of the Holy Spirit < it adds >, "In thy light shall we see light," showing that the Father is light, the Son is the Father's light, and the Holy Spirit is light and a Source springing from a Source, [that is], from the Father and the Only-begotten—the Holy Spirit. "For out of his belly shall flow rivers of water springing up unto eternal life; But," says the Gospel, "he said this of the Holy Spirit."[208]

54,5 And again, to teach his disciples his co-essentiality with the Father, he says, "If any man open to me, I and my Father will come in and make our abode with him."[209] And [here] he no longer said, "I shall be sent by my Father," but, "I and my Father will < make our abode > with him," because the Son knocks and the Father enters with him, so that they are always together, the Father is never separated from the Son, and the Son never separated from his Father. (6) And so he says in another passage, "I am the way, and by me shall they go in unto the Father."[210] And

---

[204] John 4:24
[205] Perhaps cf. Ath. Or. I C. Ar. 14.
[206] Perhaps cf. Ath. Or. I 14.
[207] Ps. 35:10
[208] John 7:38; (4:14); 7:39
[209] Rev. 3:20
[210] Cf. John 14:23.

lest it be thought that < he > is less than the Father because they go in to the Father by him, he says, "No man can come unto me unless my heavenly Father draw him."[211] (7) Thus the Father brings him to the Son and the Son brings him to the Father, but brings him in the Holy Spirit. The Trinity exists forever as one unity of Godhead, three Perfects, one Godhead. And their argument is wrong.

55,1   But again, they say, "Why did Christ tell his disciples, 'I go unto my Father and your Father, and unto my God and your God?'[212] If he acknowledges him as his God, how can he be his equal or begotten of him as Son?" This shows that they are entirely ignorant of God, and in no way "illumined by the light of the Gospel."[213]

55,2   Always, and in every generation, one who has examined and investigated will know the meaning of the knowledge of our Savior's truth and his equality with the Father. But these people itch from their immersion in Judaism, and are annoyed with the Son of God just as the Jews said, "For no evil deed do we stone thee, but that thou, being a man, callest thyself Son of God, making thyself equal with God."[214] (3) They are annoyed too because they have gotten into the same state as the Jews[215] and Pharisees, and will not call the Son equal to the Father who begot him.

55,4   For observe the precision of the scriptures, since the sacred scripture never said this (i.e., "my God") before the incarnation. The Father says "Let us make man"[216] to the Son, calling the Son his fellow creator and showing that he is his own Son and equal. (5) Nor did the Son ever say, "my God and your God," < before the incarnation, but* >, "And Adam heard the voice of God walking in the garden,"[217] and < "God said to Noah >, Make to thyself an ark of acacia wood,"[218] and, "The Lord rained from the Lord,"[219] and "The Lord said unto Moses, I am the God of Abraham and the God of Isaac and the God of Jacob;"[220] and David says, "The Lord said unto my Lord, Sit thou on my right hand."[221] And the

---

[211] John 6:44
[212] John 20:17
[213] 1 Cor. 15:34; 2 Cor. 4:4
[214] John 10:33
[215] Cf. Ath. Or. I 8.
[216] Gen. 1:26
[217] Gen. 3:8
[218] Gen. 6:13–14
[219] Gen. 19:24
[220] Exod. 3:6
[221] Ps. 109:1

Lord never said, "my God and your God."

55,6   But when he had taken our body, "appeared on earth and consorted with men,"[222] and become one of us, then he said "my God and your God, and my Father and your Father" to his disciples, whom it was his duty to be like in all respects except for sin. "My Father" in the Godhead, by nature, and "your Father" by grace, by adoption, because of me. "My God" because I have taken your flesh, and "your God" by nature and in truth. (7) And thus everything is crystal clear, and nothing in the sacred scripture is contradictory or has any taint of death, as the Arians pretend in concocting their wicked arguments. But again, I think this has been sufficiently explained, and must now go on to the rest.

56,1   For again, they say that the Holy Spirit is the creature of a creature because of, "By the Son all things were made,"[223] as the scripture says. (For they stupidly seize on certain passages without reading the text correctly, and misinterpreting what the text says correctly in terms of their clumsy speculation.)

56,2   For the sacred Gospel did not say this of the Holy Spirit. It said of all created things that anything which is created was made through the Word and by the Word. If you read further, the line, "All things were made through him, and without him was not one thing made," includes the words, "that was made," to show that all [created] things were made by him, and not a single thing without him.

56,3   Then again it says, "In him was life."[224] For even in this John needed to be consistent, and acknowledge every time that things which had no being † have been made[225] in something which does. For "In the beginning was the Word, and the Word was with God, and the Word was God."[226] (4) Since [he says] "was," and "was," and "In him was life,"[227] and "that *was* the true light,"[228] and "He *was* in the world"[229] and all < the rest* >, the blessed John, by the Holy Spirit's inspiration, is making it plain with this "was" that "All *that was made*, was made through him."[230] But the Maker of all the things that were made is prior to them all.

---

[222] Bar. 3:38
[223] Cf. John 1:3.
[224] John 1:4
[225] Holl: γεγενημένα; MSS: πεπληρωμένος
[226] John 1:1
[227] John 1:4
[228] John 1:9
[229] John 1:10
[230] Cf. John 1:3.

56,5   The scripture, however, says that all things were made through him without saying what the things that were made were. For there was never a suspicion of wickedness, allowing people to suspect untruths and blaspheme God's changeless and unalterable Holy Spirit. (6) It is on their account that the Lord says, : If any man say a word against the Son of Man, it shall be forgiven him. But if any man say ought against the Holy Spirit it shall not be forgiven him, neither here nor in the world to come."[231] For everything they say is ridiculous.

56,7   One ought, however, to answer them in terms of their blasphemous suspicion and say, "You natural born sophists and twisters of the words—you who would like to count God's Holy Spirit as a creature because of the word, 'all,' in the line, 'All things were made through him,' when the Holy Spirit is never counted together with 'all!' (8) You should assume, then, in terms of your blasphemous speculation—if, indeed, there is anyone else who is worse than you—that the Father too was made through the Son." For the line which says that all things were made through him is comprehensive. (9) But if it is blasphemous and foolish to think any such thing of the Father, the like applies to those who suspect it of the Holy Spirit, who belongs with the Father and the Son.

56,10   For if the Holy Spirit were a created thing, he would not belong with the uncreated Father and the uncreated Son. But he does, because he is uncreated; the scripture said, "Go baptize in the Name of the Father, and of the Son, and of the Holy Spirit."[232] And how can the Spirit be created when it is testified of him that "He proceedeth from the Father"[233] and "receiveth of me,"[234] and through him man's full salvation, and everything required for the human nature, was made complete. (11) For scripture says of the Lord, "God anointed him with the Holy Spirit."[235] But the Father would not have anointed Christ's human nature, united in Godhead with the divine Word, with a creature. However, since the Trinity is one, three Perfects, one Godhead, this needed to be done for the Son through God's providence, so that the Trinity would be glorified in every way, and in every way perceived to be < one >. I have cited no [mere] one or two texts against all the sects in my discussions of the Spirit, because he is God's Spirit, glorified with the Father and the Son, uncreated, changeless and

---

[231] Matt. 12:32
[232] Matt. 28:19
[233] John 15:26
[234] John 16:15
[235] Acts 10:38

perfect. And, in its turn, the argument the trouble-makers have concocted against themselves about this has proved a failure.

57,1   But again, let's devote our attention to their other arguments. For they say in turn, though they do not have a sound understanding of the text, that the Savior himself said, "Why callest thou me good? There is one good, God,"[236] thus separating himself from the Father's essence and subsistence.

But this is just foolish. (2) If they do not think that the One who has done so much for us is good, who else is < good? But what > could be worse than this, that the One who gave his life for the sheep; who went willingly to the passion although he was the impassible God; who freely forgave our sins; who worked cures in all Israel; who, of his own goodness, brought such a numerous people, in goodness, to the Father—that the Promoter of goodness and Lord of peace, the Father's good word begotten on high of the good Father, the Giver of food to all flesh, the Author of all goodness for men and all his creatures, is not considered good by the Arians!

57,3   And since they have managed to forget it, they do not know that his reply to the questioner in this was intended to humble his overweening insolence. A scribe was boasting that he had fulfilled the exact requirements of the Law. And to parade his own righteousness and goodness he said, "Good Master, what [more can] I do to inherit eternal life?" (4) And since he thought himself < the possessor* > of such great righteousness, the Lord, whose wish was to ascribe all goodness to God, said, "Why callest thou me good? None is good save God," so that no flesh and blood being would indulge in vanity. For no one but God is good. By saying such a thing when he was what he was, and when he was as great as he was, he meant to humble the arrogance of the speaker who was vain of his righteousness, and show what was in his heart. For with his lying lips he called him a good teacher, but did not abide by his good teaching.

57,5   And that he is good he teaches us himself by saying, "Many good works have I done among you; for which of them do ye stone me?"[237] To whom is this not clear and plain as day, particularly as many of his creatures are, and are called good, as the sacred scripture says? (6) Look here, the sacred text tells of many good things. It says, "Saul, the son of Kish, of the tribe of Benjamin, was a good man, and from the shoulders and upward higher than all the

---

[236] Mark 10:18
[237] John 10:32

people."[238] And "Samuel" was "good with the Lord and men."[239] And "The last word was better than the beginning."[240] And, "Open thy good treasure, the heavenly."[241] (7) But since these are creatures, and are shown by himself and his creatures to be good, how can there be any doubt about the confession that the author of their being is good? But < not > to prolong the discussion of this subject—I have spoken extensively of it everywhere—I shall once again go on to the next, and answer each argument.

58,1   But these people who will try anything cite some other texts to sow the suspicion that there are defects in their Redeemer— if, indeed, they have been redeemed. For when the mother of the sons of Zebedee approached Jesus and begged that the one son should sit on his right and the other on his left when he came in his kingdom, he told them, "Ye know not what ye ask. Are ye able to drink the cup that I shall drink of? And they said, Yea. We are able. And he said to them, Ye shall drink of my cup, but to sit on my right hand or on my left is not mine to give, but is for them for whom it is prepared of my Father."[242] (2) "Do you see," they say, "how he has no authority independent of the Father's, who has the authority to give it to anyone he chooses?"

And who in his right mind would think such a thing? If the Son does not have authority, who does? "For," he says, "the Father giveth life to the dead, and thus he hath granted the Son to give life to whom he will;"[243] and, "All things have been delivered unto me of my Father."[244] (3) Who could have any further doubt? But his sacred, wise saying is meant to show that God gives nothing from respect of persons, but [only] for merit. Giving is the Lord's prerogative, but he gives to each according to his deserts. Each who has done something right receives < from the Lord > in accordance with his labor; and not mere giving can be his alone, but giving to one who has made himself worthy.

58,4   For I venture to say that giving [as such] is not the Lord's prerogative, although he had the power to give but does not wish to. Nor is it the Holy Spirit's although the Holy Spirit has the power to give, as the scripture says, "To one is given wisdom by the Spirit, to another divers kinds of tongues by the same Spirit, to another the interpretation of tongues, to another power, to

---

[238] 1 Kms. 9:2
[239] 1 Kms. 2:27
[240] Eccles. 7:9
[241] Deut. 28:12
[242] Matt. 20:22–23
[243] John 5:21
[244] Matt. 11:27

another teaching, but it is one Spirit that divideth to every man
as he will."[245] And it didn't say, "as he is directed," but, "as he will."
(5) And "The Son giveth life to whom he will,"[246] and "The Father
calleth whom he will to the Son."[247] And again, neither the Father
and the Son, nor the Holy Spirit, calls, gives, provides or awards
from respect of persons, but as each person renders himself
worthy; this is the meaning of, "It is not mine to give, but if you
toil it will be prepared for you by my Father." But < I shall give* >
at the End, for "I am the life."[248] And I shall go right on to the
others.

59,1   They say, "Why do you say that he is of the Father's perfect
Godhead? See here, the apostle says of him that 'God hath raised
him from the dead.'[249] If he needs God's help to raise him from
the dead, then there is one party who raises him by his power;
but the other party, who is raised by the power of the One who
can do this, is inferior."

59,2   And how long must I tire myself with the silly ideas of
the wickedly stubborn? Who raised Lazarus? Who raised the widow's son at Nain? Who told the synagogue ruler's daughter, "Qumi
talitha," "Get up, child?" On whose name did the apostles call, and
the dead were raised?

59,3   I suppose the apostles < said this to show* > that all this
had been done at the Father's good pleasure, by the will of the
Son and with the consent of the Holy Spirit, because the apostles
were in a dispute with Jews who thought that they were preaching
apostasy from the God of the Law, and because they had received[250]
the knowledge from the Holy Spirit that sects would set Christ in
opposition to the will of the Father. (4) But this is not said to show
any defect or weakness, or any difference between the divine Word's
essence and the Father's. There are no differences. See, in the first
instance, how the angel describes him when he asks Mary and the
others, "Why seek ye the living among the dead?"[251] He who was
alive had risen, you see, in his Godhead and flesh; he was not with
the dead. And what does the angel tell them? "He is risen. He
is not here."[252] He didn't say, "'God has raised him' and is he not

---

[245] Cf. 1 Cor. 12:8; 10; 11.
[246] John 5:21
[247] Cf. John 6:44.
[248] John 11:25
[249] Rom. 4:24
[250] Holl: προσ< δεξασθαι > τὸ γνωστόν; MSS: πρὸς τὸ γνωστόν
[251] Luke 24:5
[252] Luke 24:6

here?" but to show the power of the Savior he said that he had risen even living.

59,5 And again, he himself told his disciples before his passion, "Behold, we go up to Jerusalem, and the Son of Man shall be delivered to be crucified, and the third day he shall rise again."[253] (6) And he didn't say, "< God > will raise him." But he plainly showed the extent of his power by saying, "I have power to lay my soul down, and power to take it."[254] (7) If he had the power, however, why couldn't he raise himself? The apostle wrote, "God raised him from the dead,"[255] to show that nothing in the economy of salvation has taken place without the Father's will, for the apostle himself says in another passage, "Even though he died from weakness, he lives by power."[256]

59,8 If I could only pick the brains of those who know the ins and outs of scripture, [and find] which weakness the Only-begotten had—[the Only-begotten] by whom the heaven has been spread out; by whom the sun was made to shine; (9) by whom the stars shone; by whom all things have been made from nothing. Which weakness does the apostle mean? Isn't it the weakness the Word assumed when he came in our flesh, and took it on so as to bear our weakness? As the prophet's oracle about him says, "He took our weaknesses and bare our illnesses."[257] He who is life and the impassible God died because of our weakness in the flesh which we had made weaker [yet], but he lives by power. "For the Word is living and active and sharper than any two-edged sword."[258] (10) Thus he died in weakness, but he lives by the power of his Godhead, and lives in our flesh in which he accepted the passion. And the apostle said, "God raised him from the dead,"[259] because of this dispensation, to give token of the good pleasure of the Father.

60,1 They cite still another text from the Gospel according to Luke, a sacred and remarkable text which is useful in every way. Which text? When the Lord was about to accept the passion by his own will, and took the disciples into the mount at that time, "went apart from them about a stone's cast, and went and prayed and said, Father, if it be possible, let this cup pass from me that I drink it not. Nevertheless, not what I will, but what thou wilt."[260]

---

[253] Matt. 20:18–19
[254] John 10:18
[255] 1 Cor. 15:15; Rom. 4:24
[256] Cf. 2 Cor. 13:4.
[257] Isa. 53:4
[258] Heb. 4:12
[259] 1 Cor. 15:15; Rom. 4:24
[260] Luke 22:41–42

60,2   And first they pretend once more, and say, "Do you see how he coaxes, and how he shows a distinction of wills by saying, 'Not what I will, but what thou wilt?' How can it be the same essence," they ask, "when there is one will in him, but a different will in the Father?"

And they are ignorant of the whole meaning. For this is why the apostle said, "O the depth of the riches and wisdom and knowledge of God!"[261] (3) And how could Christ say that his own will is different from the Father's when he himself tells his disciples, "My soul is troubled, and what shall I say, 'Father, save me from this hour?'"[262] as though he were saying this in preparation for something, and using the words, "What shall I say, 'Father, save me from this hour?'" equivocally? He means, "Shall I say this? For for this cause came I unto this hour."[263] (4) He did not come unwillingly but willingly. For earlier he says, "I have a cup to drink, and how eager I am to drink it! And I have a baptism to be baptized with, and what will I if I were already baptized!"[264] If he is willing and eager, then, and says that he has come for this purpose, how can he be showing that he has one will, and the Father has another? (5) But of his kindness, and to spare Abraham's seed, he was putting in a word for the people, because he would be betrayed by Israel.

However, it was the Father's will that his provision be executed in this way by the children of Israel, who were accessory to their own betrayal of the Son, and were not compelled to it by God; and the Son's will was not different from the Father's. (6) But it was essential that he show this even here to ascribe the whole of the divine unity to the Father, leaving no division between the one unity and human nature.

61,1   And Arius adds next that, < as > we find in the Gospel according to Luke, "Christ was in agony while he prayed and 'He sweat, and his sweat was as it were drops of blood falling to the ground. And there appeared an angel of the Lord strengthening him.'"[265] (2) The nit-pickers rush right out as though they had found an opening against an enemy, and add, "Do you see that he also needed the strength of angels? An angel strengthened him, for he was in agony."

And they don't know that the human nature of Christ would

---

261   Rom. 11:33
262   John 12:27
263   John 4:27
264   Matt. 20:22; Luke 12:50
265   Luke 22:44; 43

have been an illusion if he did not have all these things, including "Not my will, but thine;" and if Christ had not been in agony and sweat had not poured from his body, there would be some sense in the theory of the unreality of the human nature that Manichaeans and Marcionites yap about, < since he would be an apparition > and not real at all. (3) But < he did > all this to ensure our salvation, < because > he assumed everything < that is ours >, and deliberately said certain things, in truth, not deceit, that reflected human weakness. < For example >, [he said] "not my will," to show the reality of his flesh and confound those who deny him a human mind and say he has no flesh.

61,4   For every divine word stands in the midst of the sons of darkness, confounding the darkness but enlightening the sons of the truth. See how much helpful material there is in this saying. Beings with no bodies don't sweat; but by this he showed that his flesh was real and no apparition. And there can be no agony of a flesh that is united to the Godhead without a soul and a mind. By his agony he showed that he had a soul, a body and a mind at once, which is why he could show agony. (5) And again, by saying, "not my will, but thine," he revealed a mind truly human though without sin.

For his Godhead is always in the Father, the Father is in the Son, and the Son is in the Holy Spirit, in perfect possession of all things. And the Son's intent is no different from the Father's or the Father's from the Son's, or the Holy Spirit's from the Father's and the Son's. (6) If the Son desires what the Father does not will, he will be a mere man as you say, and, as his inferior, will be < subject > to the will of the Father. But it is not that way, never think it! By saying things reflective of human frailty he shows the reality of his incarnation and the perfection of his manhood, so that he will be our salvation in every way and we will not perceive one thing after another and be deprived of the truth.

62,1   But as to his being observed receiving strength from angels, what could be more proper? What could be more necessary? Look here, we have found the application of the passage in the great Song written by Moses, "Let my utterance be awaited as the rain."[266] And a little farther on he says, "Let all the sons of God worship him, and all the angels of God strengthen him"[267]—(2) though not in order that the angels would give him strength. He did not need the strengthening of the angels. They "strengthen" him in

---

[266] Deut. 32:2
[267] Deut. 32:43

the sense that they confess him through their acknowledgment to
him of his attribute of strength. (3) Indeed, for all our weakness
we too have often blessed God, often strengthened God—not because God needs our blessing, but we acknowledge the power of
his blessing. And we say in precise detail, "Thine is the power,
thine the might, thine the honor, thine the glory, thine the blessing, thine the strength, thine the power." (4) Not that we provide
God with strength by saying "Thine is the might, thine the power,
thine the blessing," not that we have given God power, have blessed
God. But we have confessed the power of God by corroboration
and confirmation, and ascribed the strength to God.

62,5   Thus the angel too was amazed at that time, and was
astonished at his Master's lovingkindness because, although he was
God and was worshiped in heaven with the Father and served by
his own angels, he endured such a < depth* > [of humiliation] as
to come of his own will and assume flesh. (6) Not only that, but
he submitted < even > to suffering for his own creation, the human
race; < to coming* >, and even being crucified and "tasting death,
even the death of the cross,"[268] so that humanity would win the
trophy over death through him, "destroy him that had the power
of death, even the devil,"[269] and "triumph over every rule and
authority."[270]

62,7   And so, in amazement and awe, to glorify and praise his
Master as he stood in such an arena and with such remarkable
deeds, the angel said to him, "Thine is the worship, thine the
might, thine the power, thine the strength," applying the words
that Moses had written, "Let all God's angels give him strength."[271]

62,8   And you see, servants of Christ and sons of God's holy
church and orthodox faith, that there is nothing obscure or knotty
in the sacred scripture; everything has been written marvelously
and applied marvelously for our salvation. However, in their hostility
to God's only-begotten Son and the Holy Spirit, Arians think up
all sorts of plans and subtleties like enemies. (9) But far be it from
us to rely on human subtleties. We must keep our minds sound
to glorify our Master, but not conceive of any defect in him. For
if the One who came to save all things has any defect, how can
creation be saved from its own defects?

63,1   In their search for proof-texts to attack the Savior, this
new crop of Jews who are springing up again—for they are devoted

---

[268] Cf. Phil. 2:8.
[269] Heb. 2:14
[270] Col. 2:15
[271] Deut. 32:43

to Judaism and no different from Jews except just in name—they seize, like adversaries, on something else "to entangle him in his talk,"[272] as the Gospel has said. (2) They say, "On the cross he said, 'Eli, Eli, lema sabachthani, that is, My God, my God, why hast thou forsaken me?'" And "You see," they say, "that he begged for mercy with sorrow and lamentation, and said, 'Why hast thou forsaken me?'"[273] (3) And those whose minds are torpid from the poison of Arius' madness, and who have no knowledge of God, do not know that we must confess that all the human frailties in the Lord are in his true human nature.

63,4 In the first place, they fail to notice that they jump from one thing to another in their thinking about him and have no settled position. How can they, when their minds are not sound? For they sometimes like to call the Savior himself Lord and Christ, before all ages, Master of the angels and archangels and the One through whom all things were made—principalities and authorities, angels and archangels, the heavens and all things, the earth and all humanity, everything on earth, the sea and everything in it. (5) How foolish of them to say such glorious things of him and not realize that < He who > in his Godhead < is > before the ages cannot say such a thing as, "My God, my God, why hast thou forsaken me?"[274] here in the person of his Godhead—He by whom heaven and earth were made, and angels and archangels, and in a word, all things visible and invisible.

63,6 When was the Son forsaken by the Father, and when was the Son not in the Father and the Father not in the Son? For he came to earth as the Son and the divine Word, and yet he touched heaven, and all his enemies were filled with his glory. And he was in Mary and was made man, and yet filled all things by his power. (7) How could such a person, and One of such greatness, say piteously, "Eli, Eli, lema sabachthani, that is, My God, my God, why hast thou forsaken me?" in his divine nature, though it was he himself who said, "I shall come again and shall not leave you desolate, but I shall come unto you."[275] And he says again in another passage, "Verily I say unto you, All ye shall be offended because of me this night, and ye shall all leave me alone, and yet I am not alone, but the Father who begot me is with me."[276] (8) And again, "I go, and I shall send unto you the Holy Spirit, the Paraclete, who

---

[272] Matt. 22:15
[273] Matt. 27:46
[274] Matt. 27:46
[275] John 16:7; 14:18
[276] Cf. Matt. 26:31; John 16:32.

proceedeth from the Father and receiveth of me."[277] And again, in another passage, he says, "I knock, and if any man open to me, we shall come unto him, I and my Father, and make our abode with him."[278] This is as much as to say that he is not forsaken by the Father, but that the Father is always with the Son, just as the Holy Spirit is always with the Father and the Son.

64,1 "Well then," they say, "what did he mean when he said, 'My God, my God, why hast thou forsaken me?'" But who cannot see that the words are uttered in the person of his human nature, reflecting human frailty? (2) His human nature [said this], though not by itself. (He never spoke from a separate divine nature and a separate human nature, as though < he were > sometimes the one and sometimes the other. He spoke with his manhood united with his Godhead as one holiness and therefore possessed of perfect knowledge in it.) Appropriately for the manhood which had been united with God and joined to one divine nature, but which now saw its Godhead, with its soul, impelled to leave its holy body, it < pronounced the words > in the person of the Lord-man, that is, in the person of his human nature. (3) For the divine nature was about to accomplish all that the mystery of the passion involved and descend to the underworld with his soul, to secure the salvation there of all who had previously fallen asleep, I mean the holy patriarchs. Thus, when it was so impelled, Christ's voice said, in the person of the human nature [speaking] to his divine nature itself, "My God, my God, why hast thou forsaken me?"[279]

64,4 But this had to be, in order to fulfill, through him, the prophecies the sacred scriptures had made of him through his own prophets. And it was in fulfillment of the words against Hades which are said to Hades, seemingly by the man, so that though the archon Hades and Death intended to subdue a man he would unknowingly < seize > the < holy > Godhead < concealed > in the soul, and Hades himself would be subdued and death destroyed, fulfilling the saying, "Thou shalt not leave my soul in Hades, neither shalt thou suffer thine holy one so see corruption."[280]

64,5 For the holy divine Word did not abandon the soul, nor was his soul abandoned in Hades. The holy Trinity unceasingly controls so great a mystery—the Father, the Son and the Holy Spirit, with the Son < made > flesh but the Father incorporeal, and the Son, although unchangeable, incarnate by his own choice and

---

[277] Cf. John 16:7; 14; 15:26.
[278] Rev. 3:20
[279] Matt. 27:46
[280] Ps. 15:10

by the will of the incorporeal Holy Spirit. But all these provisions were made by the holy Trinity for humankind's salvation.

66,1[281] Since he has said, "Why hast thou forsaken me?" he says something further in another passage; and here he says, "I will never leave thee, nor forsake thee."[282] For < his > body had to spend the three days in the grave in fulfillment of the sayings, "And I was free among the dead;"[283] and, "They cast me, the beloved, out like a loathéd corpse."[284] This was also in fulfillment of "Thou shalt not suffer thine holy one to see corruption,"[285] (to show his holiness through his body), and < "Thou shalt not leave my soul in Hades" >, (to show that his soul was not left in hades either). (2) For the divine Word was in it throughout his sojourn in Hades, in fulfillment of the apostle's saying, "It was impossible for him to be holden of hades."[286]

66,3 And why does scripture say, "impossible," except that Death and Hades was eager to detain a soul but that, because of his Godhead, it was impossible that his soul be detained? However, if his soul could not be detained because of his Godhead, how could, "My God, my God, why hast thou forsaken me?"[287] be said in the person of his Godhead? (4) To teach us that Christ was incarnate truly, and not in appearance or imagination, this saying was shown to have originated with the manhood, reflecting human frailty.

66,5 But what arose from the earth, other than the body that had fallen asleep? "He is risen," says the scripture, "he is not here."[288] And what was it that had arisen except a body? Therefore it was the body that was in the grave, while the soul departed with the divine Word. (6) And again, Christ completed his perfect resurrection all together in the same Godhead, the same soul, the same holy body, and finally united his whole self in one spiritual union—one union of Godhead, one self, one perfection. In the ninety-second Psalm it says, "The Lord hath reigned, he hath put on comeliness,"[289] meaning the divine Word's entry from the heavens into the world clothed with comeliness, that is, with the flesh that was born of a Virgin.

---

[281] The chapter numbering in Holl-Lietzmann does not include a chapter 65.
[282] Heb. 13:5
[283] Ps. 87:5
[284] This citation is not identifiable.
[285] Ps. 15:10
[286] Acts 2:24
[287] Matt. 27:46
[288] Mark 16:6
[289] Ps. 92:1

For since he seemed unimportant to his unbelieving beholders but was accounted comely, this was to show his power which, through the seeming weakness of the flesh, overcame the arbiter < of death. For he arose* > after abolishing < the curse* > of sin—death—and after accomplishing the entire provision for our salvation in a comely manner, after doing away with corruption and the curse, annulling the writ against us and the covenant with Hades, and making all the provisions for the salvation of humankind. (7) For directly after it says, "The Lord hath reigned, he hath put on comeliness," the scripture makes a further addition and says in the second place, "The Lord hath put on, and hath been girded about, with strength."[290] This is to show that his first garment came from Mary, but that his further clothing the second time came from the resurrection of the dead; (8) for as the sacred scripture has said, he is "the firstborn from the dead."[291] This is why he adds a further assurance by this second donning of a garment and says, "The Lord hath put on, and hath been girded about, with strength."

67,1   For as a person with his waist belted tightens his garment about his loins, making his appearance trimmer and bringing the garment close to his own skin, so Christ "girded on comeliness" for the first time because of his sojourn here in the flesh. But he "put on strength" the second time, as the scripture says, by rising from the dead. His manhood is no longer subject to suffering, no longer subject to scourging, can no longer be crucified, as the apostle said of him, "He is risen, he dieth no more, death hath no more dominion over him."[292] (2) This is why it says, "He was girded"— [that is], by uniting his flesh with one Godhead, a single oneness, < one > spirit, the divine and the bodily completed as a spiritual oneness never to be destroyed.

And so, at the last, he entered where doors were barred, < to prove > that his grossness was ethereal and his passibility impassible, for he had suffered in the flesh but kept his impassibility. (3) [Even so] he displayed his bones and his flesh after making his entry, the mark of the lance and the marks of the nails, and was felt by Thomas and seen by the disciples. But he entered where doors were barred to show that, for the salvation of us men, he had united the whole [of his human and divine nature] as a single spiritual entity. (4) And why do I tire myself with so much talk? To say "the same things" often "is not grievous to me, but" for

---

[290] Ps. 92:1
[291] Col. 1:18
[292] Rom. 6:9

my readers < "it is safe."²⁹³ Therefore* >, when I think of < the same thing* > for your security I have said it many times, as a way of getting through the savage attack of Arius' thoughts, words and purposes.

68,1   And now that I have likewise discussed this text sufficiently, let me go on to the rest, to give a full explanation of most of their foolishness that comes to my mind and show, from a few texts or even more, that if one has received the Holy Spirit and a sober mind from the Lord, there can be no suspicion of crookedness anywhere in the sacred scripture, and no sort of frailty in the Father, the Son or the Holy Spirit. (2) Though adapted to each need and to the subject of every passage, everything said in truth in the sacred scriptures by the Lord himself and the holy prophets he has sent is exactly right.

68,3   Indeed, the Lord prophesied this when he said, in Hebrew, "Eli, Eli, lema sabachthani." On the cross the Lord duly fulfilled what had been prophesied of him by saying "Eli, Eli," in Hebrew, as had originally been written. And to complete the companion phrase he said, "lema sabachthani," no longer in Hebrew but in Aramaic, so as to begin as had been written of him but to change the remainder of the line to another language < as > he went on. (4) This too he did as a good provision. By saying, "Eli, Eli," he meant to acknowledge that the words had been spoken of him by the prophet. But by saying the rest no longer in Hebrew but in Aramaic, he meant to humble < the pride > of those who boast of Hebrew, and to declare other languages fit for the fulfillment of the oracles about him. (5) For he was now to extend the knowledge of himself to all nations, not just the Hebrews, as this whole series [of phrases] in the twenty-first Psalm²⁹⁴ indicates by setting forth all his human frailties in the person of his human nature.

68,6   But he himself, when he came, answered to every word of this description, just as < everything > in the whole psalm corresponds with the fulfillment in the flesh of this sketch of Christ. It says, "And they parted my garments,"²⁹⁵ and, "They pierced my hands and my feet, they stared and looked upon me."²⁹⁶ And as many other such things are said, which cannot apply to his Godhead, but must be fulfilled in the flesh—although, impassibly and in truth, the Godhead has condescended to them all.

---

²⁹³ Phil. 3:1
²⁹⁴ Cf. Ps. 21:26–32.
²⁹⁵ Ps. 21:19
²⁹⁶ Ps. 21:17; 18

69,1   But they leap up again, like dogs mad with some frenzy which do not know their master because of their madness, and attack him first. When we tell them truly that the Lord in the Gospel said of his disciples, "Those whom thou hast given me, Father, I have kept in the world,"[297] (2) and again, "Make them to be one in me, as I and thou are one,"[298] they reply, "Can't you see from his words, 'I am in the Father and the Father in me, and we two are one?'[299] that he means, not equality but concord? (3) How could the disciples be in him by equality? But they could be in him by concord."

And God's truth entirely refutes them at once, since the disciples could not do this and it could not be said of them, if the Word had not come and shared their flesh, and united them in him for adoption as sons. (4) Thus everywhere in the Song of Songs, he calls his holy church "neighbor," addresses her with his holy voice of arousal and admonition, and says, "Rise up and come, my neighbor, my fair one, my dove!"[300] (5) And do you see how he calls her "neighbor?" But the church could not be called Christ's "neighbor" if he had not come from above and drawn near to her, through the flesh he had taken with its frailties which were like hers, to gather those who had become his neighbors through obedience, and call her his holy and spotless bride.

69,6   And this is why the Word, our Lord the Only-begotten, here prays the Father that his disciples may be in him, so that, when the disciples have been sanctified, they may join in a union of good will and adoptive sonship, the kinship with him which they have by the Father's good pleasure, and that, in the Father's Firstborn, they may have "enrollment with the firstborn in heaven."[301] (7) And lest it be thought that the Son differs from his Father's glory because of the flesh, to confirm their faith and knowledge of his truth < and > see that < no one > suspects his servants and is deprived of his hope, he says, "that as I and thou are one, so these may be one. (8) For I and thou are one"[302]—since < he is > God of God, and co-essential [with the Father] in Godhead.

And "We are one," does not mean, "[We are] a unit." He did not say, "I am one," but, "I and thou." And he said, "We are one," to confound Sabellius and his school, for Sabellius thinks that the

---

[297] John 17:11–12
[298] John 17:21
[299] John 14:6; 10:30
[300] Cant. 2:10
[301] Cf. Heb. 12:23.
[302] John 17:21; 10:30

Son and the Father are identical, and that the Father is likewise identical with the Holy Spirit. This is why Christ says, "We are one," and did not say, "I am one." (9) For there are two Perfects, a Father and a Son, but they are one by equality because of their < one > Godhead, one power, and one likeness. (10) The Father and the Son are one in Godhead, the Son and the disciples are one in manhood, and because of the esteem of their calling the disciples, by his inexpressible lovingkindness, are brought to a single oneness of adoptive sonship at the good pleasure of the Father, the Son and the Holy Spirit. And this, again, will expose the imposture of those who, for no good reason, hold wrong beliefs about their Master.

70,1   But let me pass this text by as well and look at the rest. Since they spend their time on syllogisms and nonsensical reasonings and, although they are men, try to out-argue God, the sophists come rushing forward when they discover some texts. The prophet reproved them by saying, "If one will cheat God, do ye cheat me?"[303]

70,2   Well, what do the great guys have to say now? The other thing I explained and set down above, but which they direct at me in the form of an inquiry, "Did God beget the Son by willing it or without willing it?"[304] I have shown that to God there is no future, (3) but that in him all things are complete at once. He does not will a thing first before doing it; nor does he do it without willing it or will a thing in preparation for it, and his preparation does not require will. (4) Thus his Offspring has always been begotten and did not have a beginning at any time. It is always with the Father as an Offspring begotten, and never ceases to be such. Since I have repeated the argument here, I again make the statement that the Father did not beget the Son either by willing it or without willing it, but in his nature which transcends will. For the Son is < the offspring > of a nature beyond will and above all conception and belief.

71,1   But as I said, these latter day disciples of Aristotle invent another, similar argument. For they have imitated Aristotle's poison and abandoned the harmlessness and meekness of the Holy Spirit, as the Lord says, "Learn of me, for I am meek and lowly in heart, and ye shall find rest for your souls."[305] (2) But these people have abandoned meekness and gone in for cleverness instead, and adopted Aristotle and the world's other dialecticians. They go for the

---

[303] Mal. 3:8
[304] 26, 5–6
[305] Matt. 11:29

dialecticians' fruits in their contentiousness, but they know no fruit of righteousness and have not been privileged to have the gift of the Holy Spirit within them.

71,3   Now here is what they say to us, when we tell them that the Son Who Is was with the Father Who Is—since the Father said to Moses, "Thou shalt say unto them, He Who Is hath sent me,"[306] and again, the Gospel says of the Son that "In the beginning *was* the Word, and the Word *was with* God, and the Word *was* God."[307] If we tell them that He Who Is was with Him Who Is, they ask us, "Well now, was something that is begotten, or was something that isn't? If he 'was,' why was he begotten? But if he was begotten, how come he 'was?'"

71,4   And < this > is typical of their foolishness, which is pre-occupied with philosophical questions, has its head in the clouds, "meddles with things in the heavens, and does no good."[308]

For we shall ask them, "What gave you this idea of thinking these things?" (5) But if they tell us, "Our mind requires us to examine them," we for our part shall say, "All right, people, tell us, are you reasoning about your own affairs, or about God's?"

Then they say, "We're reasoning about God's on our own initiative, as rational beings."

"Well, isn't God different from your condition, state and being?"

"Yes," they reply, "he's different."

"Well, if God's nature is different from yours, then in the first place your nature can't comprehend things about God that are incomprehensible. And in the second, your comparison of God with your own nature is an impiety."

71,6   For in our own case, something that does not exist is begotten [and then it exists]. For at one time we did not exist, but we were begotten by our fathers, who at one time did not exist either; and so it must be understood from the beginning, back to Adam. But Adam was made from the earth, and at one time earth did not exist. But the earth was made from nothing, since it did not always exist.

But God was always a Father.[309] And as he was by nature, so he begot the Son. (7) He begot him as an everlasting [Son]—not as a brother to him but begotten of him as his like in nature—Lord of Lord, God of God, very God of very God. And whatever one concludes of the Father, he must also conclude of the Son; whatever

---

[306] Exod. 3:14
[307] John 1:1
[308] Cf. 2 Thes. 3:11.
[309] Cf. Ath. Or. I C. Ar. 5.

he believes of the Son he must < also > hold of the Father. (8)
For the Gospel says the Son says, "He that believeth not on the
Son as he believeth on the Father, and honoreth < not > the Son
as he honoreth the Father, the wrath of God abideth on him."[310]

And their inference has failed in its turn. (9) For God, who is
incomprehensible, has begotten incomprehensible God before the
ages and before time. And there is no interval between Son and
Father; in perceiving a Father you perceive a Son, and in naming
a Son you imply a Father. For Son is perceived from Father and
Father is known from Son. (10) How can he be Son if he has no
Father? And how can there be a Father if he did not beget the
Only-begotten? When can the Father not be called "Father," or
the Son, "Son," so that people may perceive a Father without a
Son who later, as a sort of improvement, begot a Son, so that after
the Offspring's begetting the Father could be called "Father," with
the perfect God who needs no improvement improving in Godhead?

72,1   In their desire to reject this curative drug and health-
giving antidote, the foundation of the faith of God's holy church,
they pretend something else and say, "Why the term, 'essence?'
Why is the Son called co-essential with the Father? Which scripture
has spoken of co-essentiality? Which apostle said anything about
an 'essence' of God?"

But they do not know that "being" and "essence" mean the same.
(2) Christ is Lord in his "being," and "the brightness of the Father's
glory and the express image of his being."[311] Thus he is [the Father's]
essence—not an extraneous addition (περιουσία) to it but actually
this being, as Moses said when he spoke to the children of Israel,
"He Who Is hath sent me."[312] "He Who Is" means the actual thing,
but the actual thing is the actual essence. (3) But on the other
hand, "co-essential" does not mean "one"; two perfect entities are
to be understood from the "co." Yet the two do not differ from
each other and are not different from their own oneness. But if
we have employed an < unscriptural > expression from motives of
piety, to pin the truth down—(there can be no refutation of heresy
without the confession of the homoousion. (4) As a snake hates
the smell of pitch, the exhalation of hartshorn, the odor of lignite
and the incense of storax, so do Arius and Sabellius hate the statement
of the true confession of the homoousion.) [But even if we have

---

[310] Cf. John 3:36; 5:23.
[311] Heb. 1:3
[312] Exod. 3:14

employed such an expression] we shall still tell them, (5) "Even though the expression is not in the sacred scriptures—indeed, it is plainly implicit in the Law, the Apostles and the Prophets, for 'By two or three witnesses shall every word be established'[313]—all the same, it is permissible for us to employ a useful expression for piety's sake, to safeguard the holy faith.

72,6 "But what do you people say? Tell us, folks, what do you say about the Father? Is the Father uncreated?" Of course they'll say yes. Who is silly < enough > to doubt this? What sort of nut would suppose that the God and Father of our Lord Jesus Christ is not uncreated? You yourselves must surely admit that the Father is unbegotten, uncreated, and unoriginate. For he has no Father before him, no limit to his years, and no "beginning of days,"[314] as the scripture says.

72,7 "Thus, if he has no beginning or end in time, it is agreed and unquestionable that he is uncreated—but nowhere does scripture say this of him.[315] But even though it is not scriptural we are obliged for piety's sake to think and say this of him with all reverence. (8) In the same way, even if it were not scriptural we would need to speak of 'homoousion' in our own language as a summary expression—even though this might seem beyond us, and the discussion of God might appear to be beyond our powers. (9) May the Lord himself pardon us all the same for our wish to defend the Godhead which has no need of our support. But we must speak with piety and think with piety, or we perish.

73,1 "Well then, disciples of Arius, answer us! We all agrée in saying that the Father is unbegotten and uncreated, and the expression is plainly a wonderful one. But where is this in scripture? Show us the passage! The Law has not said it, nor the prophets, nor a Gospel, nor the apostles. Thus if we may use an unscriptural expression with piety, and it is allowable when said for the glory of God, who can accuse us even if the homoousion were not in the scriptures, (2) since we have found a word with which to confess the certainty of our salvation?" But there are texts [which, confirm the homoousion when] used with the help of pious reasoning, the ones I have listed above[316] and many others. I shall also pass this expression by, however, and with God's help tear open the other expressions and devices in their bait for the innocent.

---

[313] Matt. 18:16
[314] Heb. 7:3
[315] Cf. Ath. Or. I C. Ar. 34.
[316] The only text with which Epiphanius has supported the homoousion is Heb. 1:3 (72,2). Holl suggests that some Biblical citations may have fallen out.

74,1   Among all the texts which these people, with evil intent, alter to suit themselves from the Gospels and Apostle, they also cite the following from the Apostle, who says in the Epistle to the Corinthians, in the chapter on resurrection, (2) "Then cometh the end, when he shall have delivered the kingdom to God and his Father, when he shall have put down all rule and authority and power. For he must reign until he hath put all his enemies under his feet. The last enemy that shall be destroyed is death. Now when he saith that all things are in subjection under him, it is manifest that he is excepted that hath put all things in subjection under him. (3) Now when all things are put in subjection under him, then shall the Son himself be subject to him that hath put all things under him, that God may be all in all."[317]

74,4   They seize on this passage, and with their usual hostility toward the Only-begotten take his ineffable, glorious Godhead away and say—carried away by folly, as I have often remarked—"You see that he says, 'Then cometh the end, when he shall have delivered the kingdom to God and his Father, when he shall have put down < every rule and > all authority and power. For he must reign, until he hath put all his enemies under his feet.' (5) But 'must,' 'until,' and, 'when he shall deliver the kingdom,' are the setting of a time." And they blasphemously say that these are indications of the end and dissolution of his reign, < for he remains* > [in power only] until he delivers the kingdom to God and his Father.

74,6   And they do not know the truth's intent to begin with. Because the Only-begotten partakes of our flesh and blood his human frailties are dwelt on and, in connection with his human nature, are mentioned in addition to his glory—but not without his ever perfect and glorious Godhead which needs no further glory, but is possessed of absolute glory and absolute perfection. (7) He himself gives an account of the two natures by saying of the more recent one, "Glorify thou me, Father, with the glory that I had with thee before the world was."[318] But when the Father proclaims the glory of the two natures, he says spiritually of the first, "I have glorified it," to show its infinity; but he says, "And I will glorify it again,"[319] of the newer nature because of the incarnation.

It must be observed, however, that Epiphanius appears somewhat embarrassed about the lack of scriptural support for this doctrine.

[317] 1 Cor. 15:24–28. Cf. Marc. Anc. Inc. 20.
[318] John 17:5
[319] John 12:28

75,1   But now to clarify the things the apostle said when he explained the truth about Christ in two ways < and wrote "Son" because of his divine nature* >, and "until he shall deliver the kingdom unto God and his Father" because of his human nature with its beginning in time. For the divine nature of the Only-begotten was always with the Father—the only-begotten divine Word who has proceeded from the Father without beginning and not in time. (2) Otherwise what is the point of the angel's words, "The Spirit of the Lord shall come upon thee and the power of the Highest shall overshadow thee?"[320] For he told Mary, "Thou shalt bear a son and shalt call his name Jesus,"[321] to show that the divine Word had descended from on high, had taken flesh in this virgin's womb and had become perfect man. (3) < And > not to separate his human perfection from his divine perfection he added "also" and told her, "Therefore *also* that which shall be born of thee shall be called holy, the Son of God."[322]

Next < he says >, "God will give unto him the throne of his father David, and he shall reign over the house of Jacob unto the ages, and of his kingdom there shall be no end."[323] (4) But each of these is the opposite of the other—"He must reign *until*," and "He shall reign over the house of Jacob *unto the ages*." (And he said not merely, "unto the age," but, "unto the ages.") And again, "when he shall have delivered the kingdom unto God and his Father," stands in contrast with "and of his kingdom there shall be no end." But since both have said such things of the Lord and Christ < and > are entirely trustworthy—the angel Gabriel is holy, but the holy apostle is inspired—what should those who do not know the life-giving scripture say? (5) Can the scripture, which is always truthful in every respect, contradict itself? Never think it!

But as I said at the outset, because of the addition of the manhood Christ possesses all the natural concomitants of manhood. (6) For if he ever hands the rule over to anyone, he does not rule now. But if he does not yet rule, why is it that he is worshiped continually by the angels and archangels, before and during his advent in the flesh as the scripture says of him, "When he bringeth the first begotten into the world, it saith, angels of God worship him."[324] And again, "He sat down at the right hand of the Father."[325] And

---

[320] Luke 1:35
[321] Luke 1:31
[322] Luke 1:35
[323] Luke 1:32
[324] Heb. 1:6
[325] Heb. 10:12

again, "Unto him every knee shall bow, of things in heaven, and things in earth, and things under the earth."[326]

75,7　Thus, if he is worshiped < by > all, he always rules. What shall we say then, since, as the Son has not yet handed the rule over to the Father, he rules forever—in the past, now, and in the future? (8) Is the Father left out of the rule? Never think it! The Son is ruler together with the Father, and the Father with the Son and the Holy Spirit.

But what do they say? "'When he delivereth the kingdom to God and his Father' does he himself stop ruling?" Never think it! (9) What would be the point of, "Of his kingdom there shall be no end?"[327] ["He shall deliver the kingdom" is said] to show that nothing that has applied or does apply to the Son is opposed to or different from the unity of the Father, and from < the > one will of the Father, the Son and the Holy Spirit. (10) For even here we see that "When he shall have delivered the kingdom to God and his Father, when he shall have put down all rule and authority and power" is said of the Son himself because the Son delivers the kingdom, and puts down all rule and so on. And "He must reign until he hath put all his enemies under his feet" is said because the Son does all things and possesses all sovereignty and authority, and delivers his subjects, with the kingdom, to the Father.

76,1　Then finally he turns his attention once more to the person of the Father who subjects all things to this Son, and says, "He hath put all things in subjection under his feet. The last enemy that shall be destroyed is death." But he no longer speaks only in the person of the Father, or only in the person of the Son, but in between the persons of the Father and the Son, and says, "The last enemy that shall be destroyed is death."

76,2　"But when he saith that all things have been put under him," < and so on >. If I could only ask them in whose person that "He saith" is said! For the profundity of God's mysteries judges the fleshly by spiritual criteria. "The fleshly man receiveth not the things of the Spirit, for they are foolishness unto him."[328] (3) If the Father is speaking to the Son, the action is not right; the Son made things subject to the Father. But if "when he saith < that > all things are put in subjection under him" is said in the person of the Son, the thought is not right because it assumes futurity in God, either in the Father or in the Son.

---

[326] Phil. 2:10
[327] Luke 1:33
[328] 1 Cor. 15:27

76,4   But who is saying that all things have been made subject? For it has not said, "when *they* say;" if it had said, "when they say," it could apply either to the angels or to the subjects. (5) But since it has been indicated that the Son subjects and hands all things over to the Father, and that the Father subjects all things to the Son, the curious are left with the person of the Holy Spirit. And therefore, after the person of the Father and the person of the Son, the scripture gave unequivocal intimation of the person of the Holy Spirit—since the Holy Spirit always declares and teaches the truths about the Father and the Son—to keep the full knowledge of the Trinity, and of the additional glory of [Christ's] human nature, from being defective. (6) Then he says, "The last enemy that shall be destroyed is death." But one who is destroyed has been curbed and can no longer do what he does, or even be; he is destroyed.

77,1   Well, what have those who do not know the scriptures to say about this? "If this is what the text said, we must conclude that the Son will cease to rule."

But [if we say this] we shall commit an impiety and < venture > to rank him with God's subjects, particularly after he ceases to do what he was doing. (2) Perish the thought! No one who believes and truly hopes in Christ will think of saying or hearing anything unbecoming his glory, as the Arians futilely believe. The sacred scripture teaches everything < when it says >, "When he saith, All things are put in subjection under him, it is manifest that he is excepted who hath put all things in subjection under him. But when all things are put in subjection under him, then shall also the Son himself be subject unto him that hath put all things under him."[329]

77,3   In other words, the angel's original statement, and the statement linked with it here by similarity of language, give a clear, logical explanation of the full meaning of the expression. The angel said a similar thing, first indicating the Son and then intimating the union [of the two natures] with an added reference to the human natures, "Therefore that which shall be born of thee"—and he added, "also"—"shall be called the Son of God."[330] (4) For this and similar reasons it is "Because that which shall be born of thee shall be called the Son of God" that "The Son himself shall be subject to him that hath put all things under him." Thus Christ's flesh will no longer be fleshly in power but will be united

---

[329] 1 Cor. 15:27–28
[330] Luke 1:35

with the Godhead—the flesh joined in one union [with the God-
head]—and will reign with the Father and Holy Spirit, "of whose
kingdom there shall be no end."³³¹

77,5   And "that God may be all in all"³³² began at his resurrection, for his flesh has been spiritually united with his one Godhead.
But since he says, "Do this in remembrance of me until the coming
of the Son of Man,"³³³ and "Ye shall see him in like manner as
ye have seen him taken up,"³³⁴ then, when all things have at last
been fulfilled and nothing left unfulfilled that is † applic< able*>³³⁵
to his Godhead, the prophecy, "that God may be all in all" < will
come true* >.

77,6   < But > the text says, < "God," >³³⁶ to make no distinction
[between the manhood and the Godhead]. To guard against polytheism no distinction is made, for there is one glory. For the Son
is not now out of the Father's control, like a warlord, or under
his control like a slave with no freedom of action; < he > is begotten of the Father, of the same nature and the same Godhead.
And he will not be subject to the Father then from some defect
or inferiority, or by compulsion or the cessation [of his rule], (7)
but as a true only-begotten Son who rules with the Father forever,
and who both elevates the whole creation to a single oneness and
honorable reward and teaches this to his holy church, "so that God
may be all in all."³³⁷ For there is one Godhead, one sovereignty
and one glory of Father, Son and Holy Spirit, with the Father
fittingly honored by the Son as a true son, and by the Holy Spirit
as not different from the Father and the Son. (8) And let this
exclude even the words of those who blaspheme God's Son and
Holy Spirit, and their hostile thoughts towards the Son and the
Holy Spirit. And once more we have detected their evil devices
and thwarted them.

78,1   Once more they choose certain texts from the Gospel and
say, "Why can 'The Son do nothing of himself, but what he seeth
the Father do?'"³³⁸ And they do not realize what is said at the
beginning [of scripture]; although the Father surely [created], he

---

³³¹ Luke 1:33
³³² 1 Cor. 15:28
³³³ Cf. 1 Cor. 11:25–26.
³³⁴ Cf. Acts 1:11.
³³⁵ Holl: ἀναφέρεσθαι μελλόντων; MSS: ἀναφέρειν. We suggest ἀναφέρεσθαι
< δυναμένων >.
³³⁶ 1 Cor. 15:28
³³⁷ 1 Cor. 15:28
³³⁸ John 5:19

did not create something first, and the Son manufacture it afterwards. (2) Which heaven did the Father make all by himself, for the Son to take the example of the first heaven as his model, and manufacture one like it?

But no inventor of evil can prove this. "In the beginning God created the heaven and the earth,"[339] but he says at the same time, in the beginning at the creation, "Let us make man in our image and after our likeness."[340] And he didn't say, "Come here and I'll show you how." (3) And then it says, "And God made the man,"[341] and it didn't say, "God made the man and showed the Son how to make one." The Son was no ignoramus, that he needed to learn a trade first and then put it into practice.

78,4   But when our Lord had come in his turn, put on flesh, become man and lived in our midst, he conversed with the Jews who thought that he was abolishing the Father's commandments and said, "The Son doeth naught but that which he seeth the Father do," to elevate their minds, so that they would not attend to his manhood alone. He meant to show that the work of the Son is the work of the Father, and that the Father is pleased with the Son's execution of all his work.

78,5   And they will be harried like this < about > each of the other texts in its turn, as they blunder into them like beasts and are confounded by the light of the face of the Word, the truth. "Flash thy lightning and scatter them, send forth thine arrows and confound them."[342] (79,1) For we have to deal with the following text, which they select next and quote from the Gospel, "For the Father loveth the Son and showeth him all that he doeth, and greater works than these shall he show him, that ye may marvel;"[343] and again, "The Father raiseth the dead and giveth them life. Likewise also doth the Son give life to whom he will;"[344] and further, "The Father judgeth no man but hath given all judgment to the Son, that all may honor the Son as they honor the Father."[345] (2) But take note, Arius, of the conclusion the discourse has come to at the end of my debate with you. Christ did not say, "that some may say yes and some say no," but, "that *all* may honor the Son as they honor the Father." Stop dishonoring the Son, then, and

---

[339] Gen. 1:1
[340] Gen. 1:26
[341] Gen. 1:27
[342] Ps. 143:6
[343] Cf. John 5:20.
[344] John 5:21
[345] John 5:22–23

you won't be dishonoring the Father! If you choose to think that
there is inferiority in the Son or suspect some defect, does your
thought carry over to the Father? It is part of your impudence that
you think < less > of the Son, and do not honor him as you honor
the Father.

79,3   Why, indeed, does the Father also give him [authority to
judge]? Tell me what he says, wonder man! "That the Son may
give life to whom he will"—he didn't say, "to whom he is told."
There were two particular reasons why the Son needed to receive
all this from the Father, though not to be less than the Father.
(4) First, it was to direct our minds upward to a single oneness
of Godhead, the Father, the Son and the Holy Spirit, and not to
lower the human reason to divisions and a multiplicity of gods,
but to raise it to a single oneness. But second, it was also to transform
the glory of Christ's human nature and unite it with his Godhead.

79,5   For since he came to gladden his disciples with his promise, "There be some standing here that will not taste death till they
have seen the Son of Man coming in his glory"[346] "and on the
eighth day,"[347] as the Gospel says—(6) or, as the other says, "after
six days."[348] For the evangelists do not say one thing first, and then
another. There is one exact truth, but it is protected from time
to time so that people will have no excuse to stumble at the essentials,
since "The mind of man is continually bent on evil from his youth."[349]
(7) This is the reason why one evangelist said, "on the eighth day."
Part of the day on which the Savior said this was left over, and
the evangelist counted from that day and hour—if the day was
declining, at about the ninth hour or from the tenth. And again,
since the promise was kept at about the third or fourth hour of
the eighth day, this day was called the eighth. (8) But the other
evangelist provides a safeguard and says, "after six days." He did
not count on the day when the Savior promised the disciples, or
the day on which he kept the promise, but the six full days in
between.

80,1   But now that I have come this far in my discussion of the
promise, I shall give the quotation. "He took Peter and James and
John and brought them into the mount, and was transfigured, and
his countenance shone as the sun"—his fleshly countenance united
with his Godhead—and "his raiment shone white as snow."[350] Plainly,

---

[346] Matt. 16:28
[347] Luke 9:28
[348] Matt. 17:1
[349] Gen. 8:21
[350] Cf. Matt. 17:1–2.

this means the flesh taken from Mary, which was of our stock. (2) And it was changed to glory, the added glory of the Godhead— the honor, perfection and heavenly glory which his flesh did not have at the beginning, but which it < was > receiving here in its union with the divine Word.

80,3   Understand the words we have quoted, "He hath given all judgment to the Son"[351]—because he has given him authority "to give life to whom he will"—[352] as proof, first of all, of the unity of the divine nature, and its one will which ascribes the whole of goodness to the Father and to one First Principle and Godhead. For there are three perfect entities but one Godhead, the Father, the Son and the Holy Spirit; and in its turn the human nature [of Christ] which, along with the divine nature, receives the gift, authority and perfection of rank which is granted it by the Father and the Son, and which < has been united > in a single supernatural oneness of Godhead.

81,1   And we have barely managed to get past this stormy place and through this whole attack by savage beasts—the wild heaving of the billows and the fearful foaming of the seas. Because, in my inadequacy, I received the power and the grace from God, I have burned my opponents' spears and shields thanks to the right reasoning in my mind, have broken the bows of the opposition, < and have been victorious* > over this serpent, the many-headed ugliness of the hydra, (2) so that I can sing < the > song of triumph in God, "Let us sing to the Lord, for he is gloriously magnified; horse and rider hath he hurled into the sea."[353]

I have broken the dragon's head above "the water that goes softly," which these present day fellow heirs with the Jews would have no part of. The prophet had them in mind when he said, (3) "Because ye refuse the water of Siloam that goeth softly, and prefer to have the king Rezin and Tabeel the son of Remaliah, behold, the Lord bringeth upon you the mighty water of the river, the king of Assyria,"[354] and so on. (4) But we have received help in the Lord, the "saliva spat on the ground" by his true flesh, and with the spittle have received "the clay" smeared "on our eyes,"[355] so that we who were once in ignorance now know the truth, and have gone and washed in "Siloam," which means "the Sent."[356] That

---

[351] John 5:22
[352] John 5:21
[353] Exod. 15:1
[354] Isa. 8:6–7
[355] Cf. John 9:6.
[356] Cf. John 9:7.

is, [we have washed] in his human nature and perfect Godhead, and since we now see we no longer deny the Lord, even though the partisans of Arius and successors of the Jews cast us out of the synagogue. (5) For like the Jews, the Arians have agreed that whoever confesses the Lord must "be cast out of the synagogue,"[357] showing that one who has recovered his sight is a reproach to those who cannot see. For if their synagogue were not all blind, they would not eject someone whose eyes had been opened.

81,6 Let us thank the Lord, then, that we have recovered our sight and confess the Lord and, if we perform the work of the commandments, have healed our hurts; and that we have trod upon the serpent and broken the head of the dragon by the power of God, to whom be glory, honor and might, the Father in the Son, and the Son in the Father with the Holy Spirit, unto the ages of ages. Amen.

81,7 But leaving this hydra we have slain, with its seven heads and many segments, let us go on to the rest as usual, beloved, calling on God, our constant help, to take the same care of us, and of any who desire to read this work, for the cure of those who have been bitten, and the correction of those who have already joined the ranks of the evil.

---

[357] Cf. John 9:22.

Here too are the contents of Section One of Volume Three, Section Six in the system of numbering we mentioned before. It contains seven Sects together with the Schisms, as follows:

70. The rebellion and schism, but not sect, of the Audians. They are orderly in their behavior and way of living, hold the faith exactly as the catholic church does, and most of them live in monasteries. But they make an immoderate use of a number of apocryphal works. They do not pray with us because they find fault with our bishops, and call [some of] < them > "rich," and others by other names. They keep the Passover separately from the rest of us, on the Jewish date. They also have an ignorant and contentious belief, and take the doctrine of our creation in God's image with extreme literalness.

71. Photinians. Photinus of Sirmium, who is still alive, was an itinerant; he held the same beliefs as Paul the Samosatian. But they are somewhat different from Paul, though they too maintain that Christ's existence dates from Mary.

72. Marcellians, < who > derive from Marcellus of Ancyra in Galatia. Originally it was rumored that his views were about the same as Sabellius'. And although he often appeared in his own defense, and explained himself in writing, many accused him of persisting in the same beliefs. But he has perhaps repented and corrected his errors, or his disciples have. For some orthodox authorities have more or less defended him and his disciples.

73. Semi-Arians, who confess Christ as a creature, but deceptively say that he is not a creature like any other. "We call him 'the Son,' they say, "but to avoid attributing suffering to the Father as the result of begetting, we call the Son a creature." They similarly state categorically that the Holy Spirit is likewise a creature, and they reject the Son's homoousion but prefer to say "homoeousion." Others, however, have rejected the homoeousion as well.

74. Pneumatomachi. These have proper views of Christ, but blaspheme the Holy Spirit by terming him a creature and not part of the Godhead, and instead say casually that he has been created for an operation and is only a power of sanctification.

75. Aerians. Aerius was from Pontus; he is still alive to be a trial for the world. He was a presbyter of the bishop Eustathius who was slanderously accused of Arianism. And because Aerius was

not made bishop himself he taught many doctrines contrary to those of the church and was a complete Arian in faith, though he carried his doctrines further. He says we need not make offerings for those who have fallen asleep before us, and forbids fasting on Wednesday and Friday, and in Lent and Paschal time. He preaches the renunciation of the world, but eats all sorts of meat and delicacies without hesitation. But he says that if one of his followers chooses to fast, he should not do it on set days but when he wants to, "for you are not under the Law."[1] He says that a bishop is no different from a presbyter.

76.   Aetians derive from Aetius of Cilicia, who was made a deacon by George, the Arian bishop of Alexandria. They are also called Anomoeans, but some call them Eunomians from one Eunomius, a disciple of Aetius who is still alive. Eudoxius the Arianizer was allied with them too, but he separated from them for fear of the emperor Constantius, if you please, and only Aetius was exiled. Eudoxius continued to be an Arianizer, but not like Aetius.

These Anomoeans, or Aetians, separate Christ and the Holy Spirit from God altogether, maintain that he is a creature, and deny that he has even a likeness to God. For they like to give proofs of God with Aristotelian and geometrical syllogisms, and < determine > by such methods, if you please, that Christ cannot be of God.

The ones named Eunomians after Eunomius rebaptize all who come to them, not only [catholics] but < converts > from the Arians as well. But they turn their candidates upside down to baptize them, or so it is widely reported. And they say that it does not matter if one errs through fornication or another sin; God requires only that one be in none other than this faith which they hold.

These, too, are the seven sects of Section One of Volume Three, which is Section Six of the series.

On the Schism of the Audians.[1] 50, but 70 of the series.

70,1   Audians, or Odians, are a body < of laity* >. They have withdrawn from the world and reside in monasteries—in deserts and, nearer the cities, in suburbs, and wherever they have their

---

[1] Cf. Rom. 6:15.

[1] Audius is discussed at Theodore bar Khouni, Pognon pp. 194–196; Theod. Hist. Eccl. 4.10.1; Haer. Fab. 4.10. The Audians were on Cyprus for a time, and Epiphanius would have had ample opportunity for contact with them. 1,5 and 6,2 contain quotations from Audian sources, and at 8,11 Epiphanius says specifically that he has been quoting them. It is uncertain, however, whether he is using an Audian written source, or retailing scraps of conversation and debate.

residences, or "folds." Audius became their founder in Arius' time, when the council of those who pronounced his sentence of deposition was convened against Arius.

70,2 Audius was from Mesopotamia and eminent in his homeland for the purity of his life, for godly zeal, and for faith. And when he saw what went on in the churches under the noses of the bishops and presbyters, he would often oppose such persons and say in reproof, "This is not how it should be; these things ought not to be done in this way"—like a truth-teller, and as befits persons who speak openly from regard for the truth, particularly when their own lives are exemplary.

70,3 And so, as I said, when he saw such things in the churches he felt compelled to speak in reproof of them, and would not keep quiet. For if he saw a money-loving member of the clergy—a bishop, or presbyter, or any other cleric—he was sure to speak out. And if he saw one < living > in luxury and wantonness, or someone debasing the church's message and ordinance, he could not abide it, and, as I said, would accuse him. (4) And this was a nuisance to those whose lives were not up to standard.

He was insulted and contradicted for this, was hated, and lived a stormy life of rejection and dishonor. He was welcome in the churches for some time until certain persons, in extreme annoyance, expelled him for this reason. He would not consent to this, however, but persisted in speaking the truth and not withdrawing from the bond of the one unity of the holy catholic church.

1,5 But because he, and his companions with him, were subjected to beatings and often very ill-used, he most reluctantly took his mistreatment as decisive. For he separated from the church and many rebelled with him, and this is how he caused the division. It was not by any divergence from the faith; he and his companions were entirely orthodox. Even so, it should be specially mentioned that he and his faction are contentious about a certain small point.

2,1 Besides his admirable confession of the Father, the Son and the Holy Spirit in the sense of the catholic church, and his maintaining of the rest with complete orthodoxy, his whole manner of life < was > admirable. (2) For he earned his living with his own hands, and so did the bishops under him, and the presbyters and all the rest. (He was consecrated bishop later, after his expulsion from the church, by another bishop who had the same complaint and had withdrawn from the church.) (3) < But > as to what I started to say—since I have gotten sidetracked I shall take up the thread again and tell the whole story—I mean about the expression from the sacred scriptures which he harps on, as though to be as stubborn, ignorant and contentious as possible. (4) For he and his adherents stubbornly declare that the gift of being in his image which God granted Adam applies to his body,[2] because, if you please, of the literal wording of "Let us make man in our image and after our likeness."[3] And then the word of God adds, "And God took dust of the earth and made man."[4] (5) "Since scripture has said < that God made > man from the earth," says Audius, "see how it has said with perfect truth that the entire earthy part is 'man.' Therefore it said earlier that the earthy part of man will itself be in the image of God."

And this is stubborn, as I said, and ignorant—this deciding in which part of man, if there is any need to say, "part," God's image is located—because of the many conflicting ideas of this text which occur to people, occasioning a number of disputes. (6) If being "in the image of God" applies literally, and not figuratively, to the body, we shall either make God visible and corporeal by saying this, or else make man God's equal. (7) We should therefore never declare or affirm with confidence which part of man is "in God's image," but, not to make light of God's grace and disbelieve God, we should confess that God's image is in man.

For whatever God says is true, even though, in a few instances, it has eluded our understanding. (8) To deny this doctrine of God's image is not faithful, or true to God's holy church. All people are plainly in God's image and no one whose hope is in God will deny it, unless certain persons, who are expelled from the church and the tradition of the patriarchs, prophets, Law, apostles and evangelists, make up their own mythology.

3,1   And thus, with their quite contentious position on this point, the Audians too depart from the church's form of the tradition, which believes that everyone is in God's image but < makes > no < attempt > to define where in man the image is located. For neither those who discuss this in mythological terms, nor those who deny it, can prove their point.[5] (2) For some say that "in the image" applies to the soul, from a belief that only physical things are susceptible to reasoning. And people like this do not know that

---

[2] Cf. Theod. H. E. 4.10.2; Haer. Fab. 4.10; Theodore bar Khouni, Pognon p. 195.

[3] Gen. 1:26

[4] Gen. 1:27. Cf. Gen. 2:7. Chrysostom argues against an anthropomorphic interpretation of these texts at In Gen. Sermo 2.2., MSG 54, 589.

[5] The discussion which follows is anti-Origenist. Cf. Anc. 55,4; Epiphanius/ John of Jerusalem = Jer. Ep. 51.7.

the soul can be reasoned about—if we must attend to syllogisms and not just rely on God with simple minds and believe that what God has said is truth, but is known only to one who knows the whole truth.

3,3 Others, though, say in turn that "in the image" applies neither to the soul nor to the body, but means virtue. But others say that it is not virtue but baptism and the gift conferred in baptism, from the literal wording, if you please, of "As we have borne the image of the earthly, we shall also bear the image of the heavenly."[6] Others, again, disagree (4) but prefer to say that the image of God was in Adam until he fell into transgression, ate of the tree, and was expelled. But from the time of his expulsion he lost the image. (5) And people do make up lots of stories! We must not "give place" to them "even for an hour"[7]—to the one group or the other, to those who say this, or those who say that—but believe that the image of God is in man, but that, first and foremost, it is in the whole man and not just < in one part >. But where this image is, or to which part of man "in the image" applies, is known only to the God who has graciously granted man the image.

3,6 For man has not lost the image of God, unless he has debased the image by sullying himself with unimportant matters and pernicious sins. Look here, God says to Noah, after Adam's time, "Lo, I have given thee all things as herbs of the field. Slay and eat, but eat not flesh with the life-blood, for I shall require your lives. Everyone that sheddeth a man's blood upon the earth, for the blood of that man his own blood shall be required, for in the image of God have I made man, and I will require your blood from everyone that sheddeth it upon the face of the earth."[8] (7) And do you see that God's image is said to be in man ten generations after the creation of Adam?

David too says, much later, < in > the Holy Spirit, "All is vanity, every man that liveth; < and yet man goeth on in the image. >"[9] Moreover, the apostle after him says, "A man ought not to have long hair, for he is the image and glory of God."[10] (8) Moreover James says that "The tongue is an unruly evil, full of deadly poison. Therewith we bless our God and Father, and therewith curse we men, which are made in the image of God. My brethren, these

---

[6] 1 Cor. 15:49
[7] Gal. 2:5
[8] Cf. Gen. 9:3–6.
[9] Ps. 38:6–7
[10] 1 Cor. 11:7 (15)

things ought not so to be."[11] And see how the argument of those
who say that Adam lost the image has come to nothing.

4,1   But again, the argument and apologia of people who say
that "in the image" means the soul, goes something like this. The
soul is invisible as God is invisible. It is active, a mover, intelligent,
rational—and for this reason it is the image of God, since it mimics
God on earth by moving, acting and doing all the other things
that man does rationally. (2) But they too can be out-argued. If
these are the reasons why the soul is said to be in the image of
God, the soul cannot be in his image. God is more than ten thousand
times more incomprehensible and inconceivable than the soul,
and what is more, he knows all things past and present, visible and
invisible, the ends of the earth and the pillars of the abyss, the
heights of heaven and all that is—and himself contains all things
but is contained by none. (3) The soul, however, is contained in
a body, does not know the pillars of the abyss, has no knowledge
of the breadth of the earth, is unacquainted with the ends of the
world, does not comprehend the heights of heaven, < and does
not know* > all that will be, or when it came to be and all that
came to be before it. And there is a great deal to say about the
soul and this sort of thing.

Besides, the soul has divisions, while God is indivisible. (4) The
apostle says, "For the word of God is living, and quick, and sharper
than any two-edged sword, piercing even to the dividing asunder
of soul and marrow, and is a discerner of thoughts and intents.
And no creature is not manifest in his sight,"[12] and so on. And
you see that their argument too has failed.

5,1   And the argument of those who say that the body is in
God's image has failed in its turn. How can the visible be like the
invisible? How can the corporeal be like the incorporeal? How can
the tangible be like the incomprehensible? (2) We see in front
of us with the eyes we have, but do not know what is behind us.
But in God there is no accident, no defect, never think it! He is
altogether light, altogether eye, altogether glory; for God is spirit,
and spirit above spirit, and light above all light. For all that he
has made is inferior to his glory; only the Trinity exists in incomprehensibility, and in incomparable, unfathomable glory.

5,3   And in its turn, the argument of those who say that virtue
is the image—there can be no virtue without the observance of
the commandments, but many people differ from each other in

---

[11] James 3:8–10
[12] Heb. 4:12–13

virtue. For there are many kinds of virtue. I myself know some who are confessors, who have given their bodies and souls for their Master in the confession of him; who have persevered in purity and held the truest faith; who are outstanding in godliness, kindliness and piety and have persevered in fasting, and in every kind of goodness and the marks of virtue. (4) But they happen to have some failing— < they are > abusive, swear by God's name, are storytellers or irritable, lead a life < covetous* > of gold, silver and the rest—all things that decrease the proportions of virtue. What shall we say? Did they acquire God's image because of their virtue, but suddenly < lose* > God's image because of a few human failings, < so that* > the image of God < is incomplete* >, and the image in them is no longer the full one? And again, their argument has failed.

5,5   Once more, there is a great deal wrong with the argument of those who say that baptism is < the > image of God. Abraham did not have baptism—or Isaac, Jacob, Elijah, Moses, or Noah and Enoch before them, or the prophets, Isaiah and the rest. Well? Don't they have the image? And there is much to say in reply < to > these people, as there is < to > Audius, with his contentious declaration that the image of God is in the body.

6,1   But the Audians cite certain other texts as well. They say, "'The eyes of the Lord look upon the poor, and his ears are open unto their prayer,'[13] and, 'The hand of the Lord hath made all these,'[14] and, 'Hath not my hand made all these, O stiff-necked people?'[15] (2) and, 'Heaven is my throne and the earth is my footstool,'[16] and whatever else of the kind that scripture says of God. 'I saw the Lord of hosts seated upon a throne high and lifted up;'[17] His head was white as wool and his garment white as snow.'[18] And do you see," they say, "how the body is in the image of God?" And even in this they are refractory, and press "The Lord appeared to the prophets"[19] farther than it is in man's power.

6,3   Of course the Lord appeared as he chose since he is mighty in all things, and we do not deny that the prophets saw God— and not only the prophets, but the apostles as well. St. Stephen the Protomartyr says, "Behold, I see heaven open, and the Son of Man standing at the right hand of God and the Father."[20]

---

[13] Ps. 10:4; 33:16
[14] Isa. 41:20
[15] Isa. 66:1
[16] Isa. 66:1
[17] Isa. 6:1
[18] Cf. Dan. 7:9.
[19] This citation is not scriptural.
[20] Acts 7:2

6,4　But in his kindness to his creation God the all-good [reveals himself] by his power, so that no unbeliever may suppose that what is said of God is mere words and not fact, that what is said of God stops with speech, and that the apostle's "He that cometh to God must believe that he is, and that he is a rewarder of them that love him,"[21] is not so. (5) To hearten his creature, man, God reveals himself to his holy and worthy ones, so that they may actually see God, be secure in their minds, hope in truth, preach him truly, and assure the faithful, (6) "Of course the pagans' beliefs about God are nothing but words and imagination. But we really know God, the true and truly existent king, the incomprehensible, the maker of all, one God—and the only-begotten God who is begotten of him and in no way different from the Father; and his Holy Spirit, who differs in no way from the Father and the Son"—as I have said at length, in every Sect, about the godly faith.

7,1　And I have often said, and do not deny, that God has appeared to men. For if I deny the sacred scriptures I am not truthful, but guilty of abandoning the truth—or, if I reject the Old Testament, I am no longer a member of the catholic church.

7,2　But the Gospel has said, "No man hath seen God at any time, let the only-begotten God himself declare him."[22] On the other hand, the same sacred scripture < says >, "God appeared to Abraham when he was in Mesopotamia."[23] And the Lord himself says in the Gospel, "Their angels behold the face of my Father which is in heaven."[24]

7,3　But someone will be sure to say the sacred scripture means that the prophets saw God in their minds, because of the text, "Even their angels behold the face of my Father which is in heaven," and again, "Blessed are the pure *in heart*, for they shall see God."[25] (4) If < someone > has noticed this and put texts together to fit his own conception, < he > might say that each prophet sees God in his mind, for he does not do it with his eyes.

7,5　But the sacred scripture contradicts this by saying through Isaiah the prophet, "Woe is me, for I am stunned, for I, a man of unclean lips, dwell in the midst of a people of unclean lips, and with mine eyes I have seen the Lord of hosts."[26] And he did

---

[21] Heb. 11:6
[22] Cf. John 1:18.
[23] Acts 7:2
[24] Matt. 18:10
[25] Matt. 5:8
[26] Isa. 6:1

not say with his mind or thoughts, but with his eyes, thus confirm-
ing the truth and sureness of the faith.

7,6   What can we say, then, since the Gospel says that no one
has ever seen God, while the prophets and apostles, and the Lord
himself, say that they have? Is there any contradiction in the sacred
scripture? Never! (7) Prophets and apostles did see God, and this
is true. But they saw him as they were able and as it was possible
for them, and God appeared to them as he willed, "for with him
all things are possible."[27] It is plain and universally agreed that God
is invisible and incomprehensible; but on the other hand, he is
able to do what he wills, "For none can resist his will."[28] By his
nature, then, he is invisible, and in his glory he is incomprehensible; (8) but there is nothing to oppose his will if he chooses to
appear to the man he has made. For the Godhead has no frailties
to prevent its doing what it wills or make it do what it does not
will; it has the power to do what it wills. But it does what befits
its Godhead, for there is nothing whatever to oppose God's will
so that he cannot do what he wills in keeping with his Godhead.
(9) And first and foremost, it is not possible for a human being
to see God, and the visible cannot see the invisible. But the invisible
God has accomplished the impossible by his lovingkindness and
power, and by his might has rendered some worthy of seeing the
invisible. And the one who < saw > him saw the invisible and infinite,
not as the infinite was, but as the nature of one who had no power
to see him could bear when empowered to the fullest. And there
can be no discrepancy in the sacred scripture, and no text will
be found in contradiction to another.

8,1   To give an example I have often used, it is as though one
saw the sky through a very small hole and said, "I see the sky."
He would not be lying; he really sees the sky. But someone might
wisely tell him, "You haven't seen the sky," and he would not be
lying. (2) The one who says he has seen the sky isn't lying, and
the one who tells him he hasn't is also telling the truth. For the
man didn't see its extent or its breadth. And the person who had
seen it told the truth, but the one who replied that he hadn't did
not lie, but also told the truth.

8,3   Besides, we often stand on a mountain top and behold the
sea, and if we say we have seen the sea, we have not told a lie.
But if someone replies, "You haven't seen it," he isn't lying either.
< No > human being can know its full breadth, its full length, its

---

[27] Matt. 19:26
[28] Cf. Rom. 9:19.

depth, where the innermost chambers of the deep are, and the furthest bounds of the deep. (4) Now if our knowledge of created things is as limited as this, how much more so with the grace God has granted the prophets and apostles? They truly saw God, and yet did not see him. They saw him as far as their natures could bear, and that by the grace of the power with which, from friendship with the man who is his, He who is mighty in all things has endowed his true servants.

8,5 So if Audians think that God has hands for this reason, or eyes or the rest, because he appeared like that to the prophets and apostles, they are contentious, but are confuted by the truth. (6) Of all that God says in the sacred scripture, we must believe that it is; but how it is, is known only to God. And that he really appeared—yes, but he appeared as he chose, and truly looked as he appeared. For God can do all things, and nothing is impossible for him. But he is incomprehensible, unfathomable spirit, and contains all things but is himself contained by none. (7) And as is the Father in his divinity, so is the Son, and so is the Holy Spirit. But only the Only-begotten came and assumed the flesh in which he also rose, which he also united with his Godhead, < and > [in which] he sat down in glory at the Father's right hand as the scripture says, after uniting it with Spirit. (8) And since God is incomprehensible and unfathomable, all that is said of him is true, but there is no comprehending any of God's attributes, and how he exists in incomprehensible glory.

8,9 And with my human lips I have said these things in praise of God as I was able. For even though I have further ideas about God in my mind I do not have the use of a tongue other than the one God has allotted me. But the mouth cannot say all that is in the mind; it is closed by its limitation and hemmed in by the organs of the body. (10) And so God pardons me and accepts my knowledge of him, and the praise that is beyond my power to give. < Not that I desire > to give God anything, but I desire to glorify the Godhead as best I can, so as to hold godly beliefs, and not be deprived of his grace and truth.

8,11 But in making these points about Audius himself and the Audians I have disclosed the things they say, on which they inappropriately rely through their own ignorant description of them and contentious standing by them. (9,1) But they have certain other positions besides, on which they take a particularly strong stand to aggravate the division of the church, and with which they frighten others, often detach them from the church, and attract them, men and women, to [their fellowship]. (2) For they choose to celebrate the Passover with the Jews—that is, they contentiously celebrate the Passover at the same time that the Jews are holding their Festival of Unleavened Bread. And indeed, < it is true > that this used to be the church's custom—even though they tell churchmen a slanderous thing in this regard and say, (3) "You abandoned the fathers' Paschal rite in Constantine's time from deference to the emperor, and changed the day to suit the emperor." (4) And some, again, declare with a contentiousness of their own, "You changed the Passover to Constantine's birthday."[29]

9,5 And if the Passover were celebrated on the same day each year, and it had been decided to keep it on that day at the council convoked by Constantine, what they say might be plausible. But since the rite cannot fall on the same date each year, their argument is worthless. The emperor was not concerned for his birthday, but for the unity of the church. (6) In fact God accomplished two highly important things through Constantine, the most beloved of God and forever the most blessed. [One was] the gathering of an ecumenical council and the publication of the creed that was issued at Nicaea and confessed < by > the assembled bishops with their signatures—the deposition of Arius, and the declaration to all of the purity of the faith. [The other was] their correction of the Passover for our unity's sake.

9,7 For long ago, even from the earliest days, the Passover was celebrated at different times in the church, occasioning ridicule every year. For some kept it a week early and quarreled with the others, while others kept it a week late. And some celebrated it in advance, others in between, others afterwards. (8) And in a word, as is not unknown to many scholarly persons, there was a great deal of muddle and tiresomeness whenever trouble was stirred up in the church's teaching on the question of this festival. In the time of Polycarp and Victor the east was at odds with the west and they would not accept letters of commendation from each other.[30] (9) But in as many other times—in the time of Alexander, the bishop of Alexandria, and Criscentius,[31] when we find each of them writing argumentatively to the other, and down to our own day. This has been the situation ever since < the church > was thrown

---

[29] Holl III, p. 241: "Die Vicennalia Konstantins sind am 25. Juli 325 (*natalis purpurae*) gefeiert: die Audianer meinen, man habe dem Kaiser die Einigung über den Ostertermin als Geburtstagsgeschenk dargebracht; Epiphanius missversteht das."

[30] Epiphanius may have learned of the controversy between Polycarp and Victor from Eus. H. E. 5.24.1–11.

[31] Criscentius is mentioned on p. 7 of the Chronicon Paschale (Dindorf).

into disorder after the time of the circumcised bishops.[32] And so, when < bishops > gathered from every quarter they determined, precisely and with one accord, that the Passover must be celebrated as befits its date and rite.

10,1   But on this point the Audians cite the Ordinance of the Apostles, which is doubted by many but is not discredited. For it contains every canonical regulation and < there is > no falsification of the faith there—of its confession, or of the church's order, law and creed. (2) But the passage from which, by a bad misinterpretation, they take < their cue > for [their way of celebrating] the Passover, and which they ignorantly misunderstand, is < the following >. The apostles decree in the Ordinance, "Reckon ye not, but celebrate when your brethren of (ἐκ) the circumcision do; celebrate with them."[33] And they did not say, "your brethren *in* the circumcision," but, "your brethren *of* the circumcision," to show that those who had come from the circumcision to the church were the leaders from then on, and so that the others would agree < with them >, and one not celebrate the Passover at one time, and another at another. (3) For their entire concern was for the unity [of the church], so that there would be no schisms and divisions.

But the Audians were not aware of the apostles' intent and the intent of the passage in the Ordinance, and thought that the Passover should be celebrated with the Jews. (4) And there were altogether fifteen bishops from the circumcision.[34] And at that time, when the circumcised bishops were consecrated at Jerusalem, it was essential that the whole world follow and celebrate with them, so that there would be one concord and agreement, the celebration of one festival. (5) Hence their diligence in bringing people's minds into accord with the church.

< But* > since < the festival* > could not be celebrated < in this way* > for such a long time, < a correction > for harmony's sake was made in Constantine's time by God's good pleasure. (6) For what the apostles said was for the sake of harmony, as they testify by saying, "Even though they are in error, let it not concern you."[35]

---

[32] I.e., the first fifteen bishops of Jerusalem. Cf. Eus. H. E. 4.5.5.

[33] The Didascalia in its present form does not contain this line, but Schwartz argues (pp. 104–121) that the Didascalia is a much edited and reedited law book, and that the quotation may have stood in the version known to the Audians and Epiphanius. In fact the version of the Didascalia now extant ties the Easter celebration to the Jewish Passover, in that it directs Christians to begin their fast of of of of of Holy Week on the day of the Jewish Passover, Didascalia 21, Achelis-Flemming p. 110.

[34] Cf. Eus. H. E. 4.5.3.

[35] This is connected with the quotation given above. See the preceding note.

But from the very words that are said there, their (i.e., the Audians') contradiction [of the church] will be evident. For they say that the vigil should be held half way through the [Jewish] Days of Unleavened Bread.[36] But by the church's dating [of the Passover] this cannot always be done.

11,1   For the harmonized date of the Passover is determined by three criteria. The Lord's Day is determined by the course of the sun, and the month by the course of the moon because of the Law's requirement that the Passover be slain on the fourteenth of the month, as the Law said. (2) Thus[37] the Passover may not be celebrated unless the day of the equinox is past, although the Jews do not observe this or care to keep so important a matter precise; with them, everything is worthless and erroneous.[38] But even though so much precision is required in so important a question, the apostles' declaration was not made for the sake of this question and for accuracy's sake, but in the interest of concord. And < if >, as the Audians insist, the apostles' ordinance was that we celebrate with the enemies of Christ, how much more must we celebrate with the church for the sake of concord, so as not to mar the harmony of the church?

11,3   Now how can this (i.e., celebrating on the Jewish date) be done? The same apostles say, "When they feast, mourn ye for them with fasting, for they crucified Christ on the day of the feast. And when they mourn on the Day of Unleavened Bread and eat with bitter herbs, then feast ye."[39] (4) But it sometimes happens that they take the bitter herbs on the Lord's Day. For they may possibly slay the Passover at evening in the hours before the Lord's Day, since they do not work after the evening [which began] the Sabbath which has [just] gone by. Very well, if they wake up feasting after slaughtering [the lamb], how can we mourn and weep on the Lord's Day since, again, the apostles tell us in the Ordinance, "Whoso afflicteth his soul on the Lord's Day is under God's curse."[40]

---

[36] "ihr sollt eifrig sein, um euer Wachen zu erfüllen mitten im Fest ihrer Ungesäuerten," Didascalia 21, Achelis-Flemming p. 114

[37] Because the course of the sun, as well as the course of the moon, must be taken into account

[38] Cf. Didascalia 21, Achelis-Flemming p. 111. This is supplementary evidence that Epiphanius is familiar with a form of the Didascalia.

[39] This is not in the version of the Didascalia now extant. But cf. Didascalia 21, (Achelis-Flemming p. 114), "Ihr müsst also fasten, wenn jenes Volk das Passach feiert, und eifrig sein, um euer Wachen zu erfüllen mitten im (Fest) ihrer Ungesäuerten."

[40] Didascalia 21, Achelis-Flemming p. 114, "Am Sonntag aber sollt ihr allezeit guter Dinge sein, denn der macht sich einer Sünde schuldig, der am Sonntag sich selbst quält."

11,5   And do you see how much scruple and contradiction there
is when the thing cannot be done as directed? But the whole truth
lies in the purpose of their teaching, and < it is plain > from the
apostles' Ordinance itself that the harmonization of the reckoning
was arrived at for the sake of concord. < For > if we < always >
celebrate on the Jewish date, < we shall sometimes celebrate > after
the equinox, as they often do, and we too; and again, we shall
sometimes celebrate before the equinox, as they do when they
celebrate alone.[41] (6) Therefore if we celebrate [then] too, we may
keep two Passovers in one year, [one] after the equinox and [one]
before it; but the next year we shall not keep any Passover at all,
and the whole will turn out to be error instead of truth. For the
year will not be over before the day of the equinox; and the cycle[42]
of the course [of the sun], which God has given men, is not complete
unless the equinox is past.

12,1   And much could be said about the good the fathers did—
or rather, the good God did through them—by arriving at the
absolutely correct determination, for the church, of this all-venerable, all-holy Passover festival, its celebration after the equinox,
which is the day on which the date of the fourteenth of the lunar
month falls. Not that we are to keep it on the fourteenth itself;
the Jews require one day, while we require not one day but six,
a full week. (2) The Law itself says, to extend the time, "Ye shall
take for yourselves a lamb of a year old, without blemish, perfect,
on the tenth of the month, and ye shall keep it until the fourteenth, and ye shall slay it near evening on the fourteenth day of
the month,"[43] that is, the lunar. But the church observes the Paschal
festival, (3) that is, the week which is designated even by the apostles
themselves in the Ordinance, beginning with the second day of
the week, the purchase of the lamb. And the lamb is publicly
slaughtered (i.e., by the Jews) if the fourteenth of the month falls
on the second day of the week—or if it falls on the third, the
fourth, the fifth, the eve of the Sabbath, or the Sabbath; for the
six days are designated for this purpose.[44]

12,4   For we cannot < observe > the Passover on the night before
the sixteenth of the month, or begin the so-called holy week of
dry fare and Passover on the ninth, but must keep it between the
tenth and the night before the fifteenth, in between the two courses

---

[41] I.e., when the Christians cannot observe the same day
[42] Holl: περίμετρος; MSS: ἐνιαυτός
[43] Exod. 12:3; 5; 6
[44] Epiphanius' point is that the Jews really keep a week themselves, as the
Christians do.

of the night and the day. (5) And though their reckoning, of the fourteen days of the lunar month, is included [in ours]—even though it barely reaches to daybreak on the fifteenth because of our necessarily exact calculation of the course of the sun after the equinox, the course of the moon because of the fourteenth, and the full week because of the Lord's Day—[still], we also < observe* > the calculation on the tenth day, which is the taking of the lamb and the initial letter of the name of Jesus.[45] For his antitype, a lamb, was taken in this name, and so is set on the tenth.

But we can no longer have the beginning or end [of the festival] on the night before the sixteenth of the month, or on the ninth. (6) For by growing progressively shorter[46] because of the difference between the courses of the sun and the moon the [lunar] years cause the following inequality, though this is not meant to be a divinely ordained stumbling block. For this exact computation has been set by God in his all-wise governance, which he has granted his world by appointing, of his lovingkindness, the bounds of the luminaries, seasons, months, years and solstices, through his providential care for humankind.

13,1   For though the solar year is completed in 365 days and three hours, there is still a shortage of eleven days, three hours in the course of the moon, since the moon completes its year in 354 days. (2) And the first year has eleven intercalary days, so called, and three hours, the second has twenty-two days and six hours, and the third has thirty-three days and nine hours. This makes one intercalary month, as it is called.

13,3 For the thirty days are intercalated, but three days and nine hours are left over. Added to the eleven days and three hours of the fourth year, these make fourteen days and twelve hours. And when another eleven days and three hours are added, the total is twenty-five days and fifteen hours. And in the sixth year, since another eleven days and three hours are added to the year, there is a total of thirty-six days and eighteen hours, which make one intercalary month. And two months have been intercalated, and (one) every three years. (4) There is one month in the first three years, and another month in the other three.

---

[45] Didascalia 21, Achelis-Flemming p. 107, "am Zehnten (Tage) aber, weil Jod der Anfang meines Namens ist . . ."

[46] ἀνθυπερβάτως ὑστεροῦντες, literally, "by retrogressive deficiency." I.e., because of the greater length of the solar year, the end of the lunar year moves farther back, each year, toward the beginning of the solar year, unless this is corrected by intercalation. Sophocles *Lexicon* 171a suggests ἀνυπερβάτως, "shorten in arithmetical progression."

And six days, plus eighteen hours, are left over from the intercalary days. When these are added, in the seventh year, to the eleven days and three hours of that year, the total is seventeen days and twenty-one hours. And when the eleven days and three hours are again added on the eighth year, this becomes twenty-eight inter-calated days—and twenty-four hours, which make two days. (5) The sum of these hours added to the twenty-eight days is thirty. And so the thirty days < are intercalated > in the eighth year, the one month in two years. (6) And thus ninety days < are interca-lated > over a period of eight years These are a total of three intercalary months, which come one month every three years, and later one month in two. The Jews, the Christians and the others differ in these three intercalations of the three groups [of days].

14,1   Here is where the Audians differ; and they deceive men and women in this regard with their parade of keeping the original tradition and following the Ordinance of the Apostles. But they ignore any exact calculation and are not clear about the apostles' charge in the Ordinance—which was by no means to hold the observance exactly < like > the Jews, but to eliminate the conten-tiousness of those who each wanted to celebrate in their own way, and not in harmony [with the rest]. (2) For Christ desires one Passover, reckons this [one a Passover], and accepts a person who keeps it without contention but with those whose observance is exact, [that is], all the holy church which keeps the festival in many places. (3) And if the Passover had been fragmented after Constantine, the slanderers would have a point. But since the divisions came before Constantine and ridicule arose, with the pagans talking about the disharmony in the church and making fun of it—but by the zeal of the bishops the division was united in one harmony in Constantine's time—(4) what can be more important and ac-ceptable than to reconcile a people to God from [all] the ends of the earth on one day? [What better] than that they agree, hold their vigil and keep exactly the same days, and < serve* > God with watchings, supplications, concord, service, fasting, abstinence, purity and the other good things that please God, on this all-venerable day? But I think this is enough about this matter of the Audians' disagreement.

14,5   Audius suffered exile in his old age and was banished to Scythia by the emperor; < for > he was reported to the emperor by the bishops because of the rebellion of the laity. He lived there for the most part—I cannot say for how many years—and then went further on, even into the interior of Gothia. He instructed many Goths, and besides founded monasteries in Gothia itself, and introduced the religious life, virginity and an ascetic discipline of no mean order. (6) In fact this body is absolutely < outstanding* > in its admirable conduct, and all their customs are well regulated in their monasteries, except for these points of contention, the difference in their Passover and their ignorant profession of the doctrine of the divine image.

15,1   But the worst, most fearful thing of all about them is that they will not pray with someone even if he is plainly respectable and they have nothing against him—no charge of fornication, adultery or covetousness, but simply membership in the church. Besides, this is a fearful thing, to change the name of the Christians—the holy church, which has no additional name, but simply the name of Christ and Christians— < and > be named for Audius, and to make, and be required to make a covenant < against > the human race even though their group † lives[47] pure and entirely righteous lives.

15,2   For even after Audius' death many joined them and became bishops of his faction after him—one Uranius of Mesopotamia, and they got some men from Gothia and consecrated them as bishops, < including. . . >[48] and there was a Silvanus and certain others. But some of these have died, Uranius in particular. For he was proud to be a member of this group.

15,3   But many members were dispersed after the death of these bishops, Uranius and Silvanus of Gothia, and their body dwindled to a small one in Chalcis by Antioch, and the Euphrates region. (4) Indeed, the majority of them were hounded out of Gothia— not only they, but also the Christians of our kind who were there, when a great persecution was launched by a pagan king. He was a dreadful person; besides, he drove all the Christians out of those < territories* > from anger at the Romans, because the Roman emperors were Christian. But neither a root of wisdom nor a shoot of faith is wanting; even if they all appear to have been driven out, there must surely be < faithful > men there. It is not possible for the spring of faith to fail.

15,5   Many Audian refugees from Gothia came even here < to > our country, and lived as resident aliens for four years after that time. But they also withdrew once again < to > their Audian monasteries in the Taurus mountains, and in Palestine and Arabia. For they are widely dispersed by now but are still very few in number, and have few monasteries. But perhaps the group is still in two

---

[47] Holl: διακείμενον; MSS: σεμνύμενον
[48] A name appears to have fallen out at this point.

villages in the outer part of Chalcis, as I mentioned, and beyond Damascus and Mesopotamia, though, as I said, greatly reduced in number.

15,6   But I think that is enough about this group in its turn. Once more, I shall pass them by and investigate the rest, so as to omit nothing about the divisions, splits, differences and schisms which have arisen in the world. For even though they are not that much changed in faith and < different* > in behavior, if I can help it I am still not going to omit any separate group which has its own name.

Against Photinians.[1] 51, but 71 of the series

1,1   Photinus, the founder of the Photinians, flourished in our own time. Though he was consecrated a bishop of the holy catholic church, his insanity was by no means mild—he was crazier than all before him, took a view of the Son of God like Paul the Samosatian's and worse, and belched out incoherent blasphemies. (2) He came from Sirmium,[2] and was a bishop when he introduced this tare to the world in the reign of the emperor Constantius. But he is still alive, and was deposed for his stream of blasphemy by the western council which was assembled at Sardica.[3]

1,3   He claims that Christ did not exist from the beginning but dates from Mary's time—after the Holy Spirit came upon her, he says, and Christ was conceived of the Holy Spirit. But the Holy Spirit is greater than Christ—says he, like a venturesome master builder, and a surveyor of the ineffable heights of heaven.

1,4   Photinus was all talk and glib tongue, but could fool many with his flow of words and readiness of speech. For though he was refuted many times by many opponents < he persisted in his defense of himself* > —even after his defense at Sardica, when he was summoned by the bishops to give an account of the heresy he had put forward. Indeed, on the plea that he had been deposed for nothing, he asked the emperor Constantius for another set of auditors, so as to prove that he had been deposed for no good reason. (5) And so the emperor sent Thalassius at that time, Datianus,

---

[1] Epiphanius' information comes chiefly from the stenographic record of Photinus' debate with Basil of Ancyra at the Council of Sirmium in 351 A. D. See 2,8.

[2] Actually from Ancyra in Galatia

[3] The Council of Sardica did not deal with Photinus. His first condemnation came at Antioch in 344, cf. Ath. Syn. 27.1 and the Ecthesis Macrostichus of the third Council of Antioch, c. 6 (Hahn, p. 194).

Cerealius, Taurus, Marcellinus, Euanthius, Olympius, and Leontius
to be the judges and auditors of his promised defense. Basil of
Ancyra was to cross-examine him and rebut or, indeed, accept the
points he would make in his own defense.

1,6   Photinus engaged Basil in a debate of some length. But
in his speeches during the debate he offered confused formularies
which, like a painted hussy's complexion, < had a sense something
like* > the sense of the truth, but in his own mind were understood in an altered sense. (7) But when Basil and the audience
< were caught > by his deceptive talk and the readiness of his speech
for verbal trickery, the great man claimed, even boastfully, that he
could cite a hundred texts in proof of his position. (8) For despite
the < auditors' > frequent replies to him < he never stopped offering arguments* > —as I have found in the Debate with Basil,[4]
in the parts they had the stenographers take down: Basil's deacon,
Anysius; the governor Rufinus' secretary, Callicrates; the recorders
Olympius, Nicetes and Basil; and the imperial notaries Eutyches
and Theodulus. One volume was sent sealed to the emperor
Constantius, one remained with Basil's council, and another, also
sealed, < was left > with the court officials as the † statements[5] of
Photinus' opinion.

2,1   For any time Basil asked why the sacred scriptures teach
that the Lord, the Word of God, is the Only-begotten before the
ages and is with the Father, Photinus would accept the formula
but, for a distinction, apply it partly to Christ but partly to the
eternal Word, on the analogy < of human nature >. (2) "For the
Father said 'Let us make man in our image and after our likeness'[6]
to his Word," said Photinus. "In what way? The Word was in the
Father, but was not a Son. And 'The Lord rained from the Lord'[7]
means the Word in the Father. (3) And scripture said 'I saw one
like unto a son of man descending on the clouds'[8] in a predictive
sense, and not as though the Son already existed. Because he would
be called a Son after the time of Mary, and Christ would come
forth with flesh after being born by the Holy Spirit's agency and

---

[4] Other accounts of this debate are found at Soc. 2.30–43–35; Soz. 4.6.15.
Both, however, make Photinus the loser.
   [5] Holl: < ῥήματα > προβεβλημένα; MSS: ὑποβεβλμένα
   [6] Gen. 1:26. A doctrine of this kind is condemned by c. 14 of the Anathemas
of Sirmium, Ath. Syn. 27. Cf. Formula Macrostichus.
   [7] Gen. 19:24. An heretical use of this text is condemned at ch. 17 of the
Anathemas of the creed of Sirmium I (351) (Hahn p. 198). Cf. Ath. Syn. 27.3.
   [8] Dan. 7:13. The doctrine that the Old Testament ascribes divinity to the Son
only predictively is condemned by c. 6 of the Ecthesis Macrostichus of the third
Council of Antioch (Hahn p. 195).

of Mary, all this is applied to him at the outset, by anticipation. (4) But he was not < a Son > yet, he was a Word like the word in me." But I have said already that < he expressed* > opinions to some extent like Paul the Samosatian's, but that he expressed others, and went even farther in his thinking than Paul.

3,1   It will be shown, however, that he too has reached the highest degree of the denial of God, and come to an opinion entirely foreign to eternal life. If the Son of God has acquired his divine nature recently, then David is earlier—or rather, David is even to be preferred over his Maker. For Photinus meant this when he < cited* > the sacred scripture—(2) or rather, passed the sacred scripture by with his wrong notion < and > said, "Even the apostle has said, 'The first *man* is of the earth, earthy, and the second *man* is from heaven.'"[9] (3) But the speech of the truth contradicts him at once, and exposes the blindness of his mind. For the holy apostle said, "man," and [again], "man," and that the *first* "man," Adam, is of the earth, while the *second* is from heaven. (4) But Christ's flesh did not descend from heaven, though surely he said "man" [the second time]; even Photinus admits that it comes from Mary. Paul is not carelessly saying that flesh is from heaven, but means that the second man is from heaven, ever since the Word came down from on high and "dwelt among us,"[10] as the scripture says.

3,5   Now if the Lord < came from on high* >, he was pre-existent. < Photinus concedes* >, indeed, < that the scripture says* > that "He which hath found out every path of knowledge"[11] is with us, but that the actual < Finder of every path of knowledge is the Word in the Father; and he wants to prove this from the line following, "Then he appeared on earth." But anyone with sense can see* > that the sacred scripture does not doubt < the Son's preexistence* >, for "then" (μετὰ ταῦτα) and "hath found out every path of knowledge" imply his preexistence. Then "He appeared on earth" < indicates > his coming incarnation.

3,6   And as to their claim that he has brought the man from heaven, the apostle does not say < this >. He calls him "man" because of the union of his human nature [with his Godhead], < but secondly >, because of the amount of time between Adam and the incarnation. (7) But he says that he is "from heaven" because the divine Word has come from on high and < assumed > flesh, as the scripture says, "The Word was made flesh,"[12]—but not as though

---

[9] 1 Cor. 15:47
[10] John 1:14
[11] Bar. 3:37–38
[12] John 1:14

he supposes that the Word has come forth from the Father and been turned into flesh.[13] For this is the explanation that Photinus, with his deluded notion, gave of the passage.

3,8   But if Adam is before the Word, through whom was Adam himself created, and all God's creatures before him? To whom did the Father say, "Let us make man?"[14] (9) No one ever gives advice to the word within him or to his own spoken word;[15] God makes his all-wise statement < of > the coming creation of man to his immanent, holy Word, to teach us that the Son is with the Father from the beginning—so that we will not think that our creator is of recent origin, but that he is always with the Father before the ages. So John testifies by saying, "In the beginning was the Word, and the Word was with God."[16]

4,1   I say too, as the scum himself does, that the Word is from the beginning—but as a Son begotten < of > God. And if he is not God's Son Photinus' labor is for nothing, and so is his devotion, hope and purpose; for he is saying nothing more than the Jews who denied Christ. (2) The Gospel does not say of him, "In the beginning was the Word, and the Word was *in* God," but, "the Word was *with* God."[17] (3) And it does not say only that ["The Word] was in God," but that "The Word *was* God."[18] The immanent word which is always in man and is man's spoken word cannot be called, "man," but must be called, "man's word." (4) < But > if, as Photinus says, there was no Offspring yet [when the Word was "with God"], and if the divine Word was not yet God's Son, through whom were all things made? For the Gospel says, "All things were made *through him*, and without him was not anything made."[19]

4,5   But Photinus says, "As man does what he chooses through his reason, so the Father made all things by his own reason, through the Word that is in him." (6) Then why does the Lord say in the Gospel, "My Father worketh hitherto; I too work?"[20] However, "My Father worketh; I too work" does not mean that the Father is not at work in the work of the Son, or that the Son is separate from him and not at work in the Father's creation. (7) All the works

---

[13] The Anathemas of the creed of Sirmium I (351 A.D.) condemn this doctrine at c. 12 (Hahn pp. 197–198).
[14] Gen. 1:26
[15] The Anathemas of the creed of Sirmium I (351 A. D.) condemn the doctrine that Christ is either of these, ch. 8, (Hahn p. 197).
[16] John 1:1
[17] John 1:1
[18] John 1:1
[19] John 1:3
[20] John 5:17

there are, are performed jointly by the Father, the Son and the Holy Spirit. For all things have been done through the Son by the Father, and the Son himself has done all things with the Father, and with the Holy Spirit. "By the Word of the Lord were the heavens established, and all the host of them by the Spirit of his mouth."[21]

4,8   And so the Lord spoke with assurance in the Gospel, knowing the opinion of those who have gone astray, and spoke with divine foreknowledge, and with < an awareness > of the way in which each would deprive himself of the truth. < For > he told the Jews, "The Son doeth nothing of himself, but what he seeth the Father do."[22] And this is not because he sees first and then does; he has all things within himself and does what he will.

5,1   Well, Photinus, how will it come out? Or again, who is in you to offer us this tare? Who concocted this poison for the world? What gave you the wicked idea of adopting a blasphemous opinion of your Lord? (2) Hasn't Abraham convinced you by speaking to Christ and saying, "Shall not the judge of all the earth do judgment?"[23] Admit defeat, for the Son visited him—and not as an utterance, but as a real divine Word.

5,3   And to show you what happens to those who have spent their time on this, you would-be sage, < hear > how God has closed the subject for us in the sacred scripture by saying, "The Lord rained upon Sodom and Gomorra fire and brimstone from the Lord out of heaven."[24] (4) And he didn't say, "The Lord's word," but, "The Lord, from the Lord," just as David says, "The Lord said unto my Lord."[25] And to < show > that the Son does not date only from the incarnation, he also says of his original [begetting], "From the belly before the morning star I begot thee."[26]

5,5   And no one will accept what you say of the Holy Spirit, you windbag and useless busybody! The Holy Spirit is neither "greater" nor "less;" "Who hath required this at your hands?"[27] says scripture. (6) But the holy Word himself confounds you; to acknowledge the legitimacy of his Godhead the Lord says of the Holy Spirit, "that proceedeth from the Father and receiveth of me."[28]

---

[21] Ps. 32:6
[22] John 5:19
[23] Gen. 18:25. Chapter 15 of the Anathemas of Sirmium condemns anyone who says that the Son did not come to Abraham. Cf. ch. 6 of the Antiochene Symbol.
[24] Gen. 19:24
[25] Ps. 109:1
[26] Ps. 109:3
[27] Isa. 1:12
[28] Cf. John 15:26; 16:14.

6,1   And how many other proof texts are there? But since everyone can see that your nonsense is erroneous and untrue, and that it will be detected not only by the wise but even by those who have a little knowledge of the order of the sacred scripture, and this frees me from the need of a great many proof texts or a long refutation—your tall tale and your wicked belief are easily refutable—(2) < I believe > that what I have said about you will do. I shall leave you behind as though I had squashed < some kind of > feeble bug with no strength that had grown up from the earth, or a worm or a maggot, with the foot of reason and the truth of the Word of God. (3) For this fool's sect has already been dispersed[29] in a short time. Calling on God as usual, I shall go on to the rest.

Against Marcellians.[1] 52, but 72 of the Series

1,1   In his own turn Marcellus was at Ancyra at the same time—all these people came at once. < He > was still < alive > in our day, but he died about two years ago.[2] (2) He too caused a division in the church from the start of his career, and gave a slight adumbration of this when—due to the Arians' irritation with him over his anti-Arian † pamphlet,[3] if you please—he was compared with Sabellius and Navatus. For this reason he is also attacked by < certain orthodox teachers for > believing in Sabellius' nonsense, as I said, up to a point.

Some have said in his defense, however, that this was not so; they maintained that he had lived rightly and held orthodox opinions. There has therefore been a great deal of controversy about him. (3) His secret thoughts are known only to God. But either because they did not know his mind, or because they were giving his actual ideas, his converts and pupils would not confess the three entities, which is what the truth is—that there is one Godhead and one Glory, a co-essential Trinity with no differentiation of its own glory. It is a perfect Trinity and one Godhead, one power, one essence, and neither identity nor subordination.

---

[29] Drexl and MSS: ἐις ὀλίγον χρόνον; Holl: ἐις ὀλίγον ἐλθοῦσα

[1] Much of Epiphanius' information comes from Marcellus' Epistle to Julius of Rome, 2,1–3,1, fragments of Marcellus' writings preserved in George of Laodicea's refutation of Acacius of Galatia, 6,1–9,9, and the creed issued at Ancyra by Marcellus' disciples (11–12,5). But Epiphanius also uses oral sources. 4,4 recounts a conversation between himself and Athanasius.
[2] 376 or 377 A.D. Cf. 66,2.
[3] Holl: τὸ λόγιον; MSS: τοῦ λογισμοῦ

1,4 But when he wanted in the worst way to prove his point to certain persons, he showed that < his > opinions were like those of Sabellius; hence this group too is refuted like a sect and counted as one. But again, I subjoin a copy of the exposition of his argument that Marcellus wrote (5) in his own defense, if you please, for Julius, the blessed bishop of Rome. From his defense [itself], and the document, it will be evident that his beliefs differed from the true faith. For if he did not think otherwise, why did he decide to offer a defense—if he had not said things which were not orthodox, and which served as the occasion for a defense < on his part > because they had disturbed certain people? Very well, here is the copy:

A Copy of a Letter of Marcellus, Whom the Council Deposed for Heresy

2,1 *Greetings in Christ from Marcellus to his most blessed fellow worker, Julius.*

Some who were formerly convicted of heresy, and whom I confuted at the Council of Nicaea, have dared to write your Reverence that my opinions are neither orthodox nor in agreement with the church, thus endeavoring to have the charge against themselves transferred to me. (2) I therefore felt that I must come to Rome and suggest that you send for those who have written against me, so that I could prove, in a direct confrontation, that what they have written against me is untrue, and further, that they persist even now in their former error, and have dared dreadful ventures against the churches of God and us who head them.

2,3 *But they have chosen not to appear, though you have sent presbyters to them and I have spent a year and three full months at Rome. On the eve of my departure, therefore, I feel that, with all sincerity and by my own hand, I must submit a written statement to you of the faith which I have learned and been taught from the sacred scriptures and remind you of the evils they have spoken, to acquaint you with the words with which, for their hearers' deception, they conceal the truth.*

2,4 *For they say that the Son of the almighty God, our Lord Jesus Christ, is not his true and actual Word, but that God has a different word and a different wisdom and power. This person whom he has made is called Word, wisdom and power; and since they hold this opinion they say that he is another entity, separate from the Father. (5) They further declare in their writings that the Father is prior to the Son, < and > that the Son is not truly a son [begotten] of God. Even though they say he is "of God," they mean that he is "of God" just as all things are. And moreover, they dare to say that there was a time when he did not exist, and that he is a creature and a product of creation, and so separate him from the Father.*

It is my conviction, then, that persons who say these things are strangers to the catholic church.

2,6   *Now I, following the sacred scriptures, believe that there is one God and his only-begotten Son, the Word, who is always with the Father and has never had a beginning, but is truly of God—not created, not made, but forever existent, forever reigning with God and his Father, "of whose kingdom," as the apostle testifies, "there shall be no end."[4]*

2,7   *This Son, this power, this wisdom, this true and actual Word of God, our Lord Jesus Christ, is a power inseparable from God, through whom all created things have been made as the Gospel testifies, 'In the beginning was the Word, and the Word was with God, and the Word was God. All things were made through him, and without him was not anything made.'[5] (8) He is the Word of whom Luke the Evangelist testifies, "Inasmuch as they have delivered unto us, which were eye witnesses and ministers of the Word."[6] Of him David also said, "My heart hath burst forth with a good Word."[7] (9) So our Lord Jesus Christ has taught us through the Gospel by saying, "I came forth from the Father and am come."[8] At the end of days he descended for our salvation, was conceived by the Holy Spirit, and assumed manhood.*

3,1   *Therefore I believe in one God the Almighty, and in Christ Jesus his only-begotten Son, our Lord, who was born of the Holy Spirit and Mary the Virgin, was crucified under Pontius Pilate, was buried, on the third day rose again from the dead, ascended into the heavens and is seated at the right hand of the Father, whence he shall come to judge the quick and the dead.*

And I believe in the Holy Spirit, the holy church, the forgiveness of sins, the resurrection of the flesh, and the life everlasting.

3,2   *I have learned from the sacred scriptures that the Godhead of the Father and of the Son cannot be differentiated. For if one separates the Son, that is, the Word, from Almighty God, he must either suppose that there are two Gods, which is agreed to be untrue to the sacred scripture, or else confess that the Word is not God, which likewise is plainly untrue to the right faith, since the Evangelist says, "and the Word was God."[9] (3) But I understand perfectly that the Father's power, the Son, is indistinguishable and inseparable [from him]. For the Savior himself, our Lord*

---

[4] Luke 1:33
[5] John 1:1–3
[6] Luke 1:2
[7] Ps. 44:2
[8] John 8:42
[9] John 1:1

Jesus Christ, says, "The Father is in me and I am in the Father,"[10] *"I and my Father are one,"*[11] *and, "He that hath seen me hath seen the Father."*[12]

3,4   *This faith, which I have both learned from the sacred scriptures and been taught by godly parents, I preach in God's church and have now written down for you, keeping a copy for myself. (5) I also request that you enclose a copy of it in your letter to the bishops, so that none of those who do not know me and my accusers well will be deceived by paying attention to what they have written. Farewell!*

The End

4,1   Those who can read this document, and those who can understand exactly what it says, < must > say whether it is all right. And if it is wrong, they must decide this for themselves. I do not wish to say anything more than I know and have been told. (2) For even though the document is right on the subject, those who read it and hear it read will suspect in their turn that Marcellus was not obliged to defend himself for nothing, or for no good reason, or because of < enmity > towards him—not unless he had belched out words that disturbed some and forced him to undertake his own defense because of things he had said.

4,3   For it may be that, even after falling into error, he defended and corrected himself with this document. Or he may have dressed his words up with the document to hide what he had said, and avoid exclusion by deposition from the college and order of bishops. At any rate, this is what I have learned about Marcellus.

4,4   However, I once asked the blessed Pope Athanasius myself how he felt about this Marcellus. He neither defended him nor, on the other hand, showed hostility towards him, but merely told me with a smile that he had not been far from rascality, but that he felt he had cleared himself.

5,1   But I shall cite the statements which some have found in Marcellus' own writings and felt reprehensible, and so have inveighed against him and written replies of their own. (2) Their replies to him < were brought to light* > by others in turn, for purposes of refutation, since those who had written in reply to him but later changed their minds < preferred to conceal what they had written earlier* >. < Hence >, in refutation of Acacius, these people issued Marcellus' statements and made them known in their own writings, during the disputes between Acacius, Basil of Galatia, and George of Laodicea. (3) It was Acacius who, to refute Marcellus,

---

[10] John 10:38
[11] John 10:30
[12] John 14:9

had quoted passages from Marcellus' writings. < I shall cite them > to show by omitting none of the truth that I neither despise anything that may make for the correction of persons who try to prove untruths, nor wish to agree with such persons. And here are the passages from Acacius' argument against Marcellus:

The following citations are made because of Marcellus:

6,1 *After his misinterpretation of the comments on Proverbs, Marcellus wrote the things which follow and more like them, speaking unrighteously of God and lifting up his horn on high. Past the middle of the book he again quotes the words of Asterius, which say,* (2) *"For the Father is another, who has begotten of himself the only-begotten Word and the firstborn of all creation—Unique begetting Unique, Perfect begetting Perfect, King begetting King, Lord begetting Lord, God begetting God, the exact image of his essence, will, power and glory."*

6,3 *He quotes these words but objects to the "exact image"—that is, to the distinct, clear impress of God's essence, and the rest. Calling this notion a bad one, he appends his dissatisfaction and at this point writes:* (4) *"These words plainly reveal his poor opinion of the Godhead. How can One who was begotten as Lord and God, as he himself has said earlier, still be an 'image' of God? An image of God is one thing, and God is another. If he is an image he is not Lord or God, but an image of a Lord and God. But if he is really Lord and really God, the Lord and God cannot be the image of a Lord and God."*

6,5 *And next, "He does not allow that he is any of the things he has mentioned; he calls him the 'image' of all these things. Very well, if he is the image of an essence, he cannot be self-existence. If he is the image of a will, he cannot be absolute will. If he is the image of power, he cannot be power; if of glory, he cannot be glory. For an image is not an image of itself but an image of something else."*

7,1 *You commended these words earlier, Marcellus, at the beginning of your book. But you have now plainly betrayed your poor opinion of the Godhead by denying that the God of God, the Word, is the Son and is Unique begotten of Unique, Perfect begotten of Perfect.* (2) *You ought to have cut your profane tongue out for understanding the image of the Great King < to be > lifeless and without Godhead, will, power, glory and essence, saying a word against the Lord, and dooming the soul to death that has committed such impiety.*

7,3 *For by limiting the image of God to lifelessness, < you are saying > that it is neither Lord, God, essence, will, power nor glory. You would have it be a motionless image of these things and make it an inert, lifeless image set outdoors, as inert < as though > it were the product of mere human skill. You will not have God's image be a living image of a living God,*

*will not have the image of an essence be an essence, or have the exact image
of will, power and glory be will, power and glory.* (4) *But "exact" does
not mean the same as "unoriginate;" it means that the divinity, and every
action, of the image is expressly and precisely like the divinity, and every
action, of the Father.*

7,5   *And later [Acacius says], "Your lying < lips > should be put to
silence that speak unrighteously against God, haughtily and with contempt."*[13] (6) *For even though you do not care for this and now prefer
something else, the Father begot the Only-begotten as Unique begets Unique.
The Son did not make his appearance because of Valentinus' aeons, but was
begotten of a sole Father; and "Perfect begot Perfect." For there is no imperfection in the Father, and therefore there is none in the Son; the Son's perfection is the
legitimate offspring of the Father's perfection and more than perfection.*

And "A King begot a King." (7) *It is orthodox doctrine that God rules
< before the > [rule] of the Son, who was begotten before the ages and is
a King who himself has a ruler; through him the rest are ruled, and he
gratefully acknowledges his subjection [to the Father]. The Father has not
begotten a subject but a King "whose kingdom hath neither beginning of
days nor length of life."*[14] *For his rank is not a thing external to him but
belongs to his essence, as is the case with the Father who begot him. And
therefore scripture says, "Of his kingdom there shall be no end."*[15] (8) *But
we confess that "Lord begets Lord" in this way, and "God begets God."*

*And in a word, we say he is the image of an essence, a will, a power
and a glory—not inert and dead but essential, possessed of a will, powerful
and glorious.* (9) *For power does not beget powerlessness, but absolute
power. Glory does not beget the absence of glory, but absolute glory. Will
does not beget the absence of will, but absolute will. Essence does not beget
the absence of essence, but self-existence.*

*The divine Word is therefore an image, a living wisdom, subsistent, an
active Word and Son, himself invested with being. This < was > the image
"in which" God "daily rejoiced, when he delighted in his completion of the
world."*[16] (10) *But since you, Marcellus, have "denied these things before
men, you will be denied," by that image itself, "before the Father which
is in heaven."*[17] *You will also, however, be denied before the church which
is under heaven, and which has written of you in all parts of the world,
"Hear the word of the Lord, write of this man, A man rejected; for no
ruler shall grow any more from his seed to sit upon the throne of David."*[18]

---

[13] Ps. 30:19
[14] Heb. 7:3
[15] Luke 1:33
[16] Prov. 8:30–31
[17] Cf. Matt. 10:32.
[18] Jer. 22:29–30

8,1 And later, after Marcellus has mentioned the words of Asterius, he goes on, *You quote these words and persist in your denial of our Savior's image and essence; of his only-begotten sonship to the Father and his status as firstborn of all creation; of the uniqueness of the Only-begotten, his perfection begotten of the Perfect, his kingship begotten of the King, his lordship begotten of the Lord, and his Godhead begotten of God. In a word, [you persist in] your denial of the exact image of the essence, will, power and glory of God. (2) You "deny this before men" in words of no little import—"and therefore will be denied before his Father"[19]—and write next to this, "These words clearly demonstrate his poor opinion of the Godhead of the Father and the Son." But your denial of them has plainly exposed your perverse and mean heresy with regard to the Godhead and essence of Christ.*

9,1 And later he adds some words of Marcellus': *His next addition is worthless: "He will not allow him to be any of the things which he has mentioned, for he says that he is the 'image' of all these. Very well, if he is the image of an essence, he cannot be self-existence. If he is the image of a will, he cannot be absolute will. If he is the image of power, he cannot be power; and if of glory, he cannot be glory. For an image is not its own image, but an image of something else." (2) But these remarks are worthless, Marcellus, and lies. When Asterius says, "A King begot a King; a Lord begot a Lord," he would have him be everything that he has mentioned. And he destroys your lifeless image, which in your view is a product of mere human skill. (3) He is saying that the Son is a living image of all these and the impress of the image of a living Begetter, and is calling him self-existence, the image of an essence; absolute will, the image of will; absolute power, the image of power; absolute glory, the image of glory—and not its own glory, but the glory of another image.*

9,4 *But by not confessing that the Son is God of God, light of light or power of power, you do not let the Son be God, light, power, essence, will or glory. In sum, the [lifeless] body [of your "image"] impiously does away with these things, together with the Son.[20] (5) You also deny that "The Word was God,"[21] and either call him God's Son in name only, or else in the sense that [any] man [can be called God's son]—making God the begetter of something different from himself, who begets the Son by adoption, as in "I have begotten sons and raised them up,"[22] "Ye have received the Spirit of adoption,"[23] and, "Ascribe to the Lord, O sons of God."[24]*

---

[19] Cf. Matt. 10:32.
[20] Holl: τοῦ υἱοῦ (?); MSS: τούτων
[21] John 1:1
[22] Isa. 1:2
[23] Rom. 8:15
[24] Ps. 28:1

9,6   *Thus, in saying that the Son is the exact image of the Father's
essence, power, will and glory, Asterius as good as says that the Father's
attributes inhere in the Son, and that what is conceived of the Father is
impressed in or given to the Son, and is not different from him.* (7) *Thus
he would have the Son be everything he has said. For he does not take
the "image" as a painted image, or introduce a third artist to paint the
qualities of someone different from the Father in some other place, and call
this a "Son." (8) For whether intentionally or not, this is what you are
saying [with your] "Very well, if he is the image of an essence, he cannot
be self-existence; and if of a will, he cannot be absolute will."*

*For in our view, if he is the living image of an essence, he can be, and
is self-existence. And thus we call the image of an essence an essence, because
of its most faithful reproduction of its life and activity. And we call the
image of a will, a will, "the angel of a great counsel;"*[25] *and the image
of power and glory, power and glory.* (9) *And texts which support this
are, "For as the Father hath life in himself, so hath he given to the Son
to have life in himself,"*[26] *and, "As the Father raiseth up the dead and
quickeneth them, < even so the Son quickeneth whom he will >."*[27] *For the
[combination of the words] "as" and "thus" implies the exact reproduction
of the portraiture and likeness which are proper to an image.*

10,1   *And a little later, For the divine Word who provides life, beauty
and form for others, is not to be conceived of as himself without life, beauty
and form, or dead or non-existent. He is informed with the Father's attributes,
and not as though he were different, with attributes different from the form.
His attributes inhere in his existence, and his existence in his attributes.
(2) But because the image—someone else's image as you yourself agree,
and not its own—possesses the attributes of its original, it displays otherness,
but otherness as though it were likeness. For as "the image of the invisible
God,"*[28] *which it is, this image is not an image of itself, but an image
of another person.*

10,3   *In motion, activity, power, will and glory, then, the Son is the
image of the Father, a living image of a living God—not a lifeless or inert
image, which has its being in something else and is drawn on something
else, but is not in motion in and through itself. And it is an exact image,
though the exactitude makes it, not the Father, but a Son in the exact
likeness [of the Father].*

The end of the excerpt from Acacius

10,4   However, orthodox persons, brethren of mine and confessors,

---

[25] Isa. 9:5
[26] John 5:26
[27] John 5:21
[28] Col. 1:15

say that they have received a confessional statement in defense of Marcellus' faith from some of the disciples he left behind him. I publish its subtleties here, since I do not understand it myself. Here is the copy:

A Written Statement of the Faith of Marcellus' Disciples

11,1   *Greetings in the Lord from the presbyters of Ancyra in Galatia, Photinus, Eustathius, another Photinus, Sigerius, the deacon Hyginus, the sub-deacon Heraclides, the lector Elpidius, and the proctor Cyriacus, to the most reverend and holy bishops in Diocaesarea who have been banished for the orthodox faith in our Savior Jesus Christ, Eulogius, Adelphius, Alexander, Ammonius, Harpocration, Isaac, Isidore, Annubio, Pitimus, Euphratius and Aaron.*[29]

11,2   *While we were staying with your Reverences our countrymen, during the visit we fittingly made you, we were asked by your Holinesses how we hold the faith that is in us. Both because we approve of your solicitous inquiry, and particularly because those who so choose are spreading certain lies about us to no purpose, (3) we feel we must assure you, not only through the letter of fellowship your Holinesses have been shown which was addressed to us all by the thrice blessed Pope Athanasius, but also through this written confession of ours, (4) that we neither believe, nor have believed, anything other than the worldwide and church-wide creed determined at Nicaea. We offer this confession † because we can assure you*[30] *that this is our belief, (5) and we condemn those who dare to say that < the Son or > the Holy Spirit is a creature; and the Arian heresy, and the heresies of Sabellius, Photinus and Paul the Samosatian; and those who deny that the Holy Trinity consists of three infinite, subsistent, co-essential, co-eternal and absolute Persons. (6) We also condemn those who say that the Son is an expansion, contraction or activity of the Father, and those who do not confess that the divine Word, the Son of God, is before the ages and co-eternal with the Father, and is subsistent, absolute Son and God.*

12,1   *If anyone says that the Father, the Son and the Holy Spirit are the same, let him be anathema.*

If anyone attributes a beginning or end to the Son and Word of God or to his kingdom, let him be anathema.

If anyone says that the Son or the Holy Spirit is a part of the Father, and does not confess that the Son of God was begotten of the Father's essence before anyone can conceive of it, let him be anathema.

---

[29] These presbyters are referred to at Theod. H. E. 4.22.35; Basil Ep. 265; Facundus v. Hermiane pro Defens. Trium Capitum 42; Palladius Hist. Laus. 46.
[30] Holl, tentatively: δυνάμενοι ὑμᾶς πληροφορεῖν; MSS: δυνάμει ταῦτα φρονεῖν

12,2   *As to the incarnation of the divine Word, the only-begotten Son of God, we confess that < the > Son of God has also become man without sin, by the assumption of all of human nature, that is, of a rational and intellectual soul and human flesh.*

12,3   *We believe in one God the Father Almighty, maker of all things visible and invisible, and in one Lord Jesus Christ the Son of God, begotten as the Only-begotten of the Father, that is, of the Father's essence, God of God, Light of Light, very God of very God, begotten, not made, co-essential with the Father, through whom all things were made in heaven and on earth;*

Who for us men and for our salvation came down and was incarnate and made man, suffered and rose the third day, ascended into the heavens, and will come to judge the quick and the dead; and in the Holy Spirit.

12,4   *But those who say that there was a time when the Son of God did not exist, and that he did not exist before his begetting, and that he was made from nothing, or that he is of another substance or essence, or that he is mutable or alterable, them the catholic and apostolic church condemns.*

12,5   *I, Photinus, presbyter of the catholic church at Ancyra, believe and hold as is written above.*

< I >, Eustathius, presbyter of the catholic church at Ancyra, believe and hold as is written above.

I, Photinus, presbyter of the same, believe and hold as is written above.

I, Sigerius, presbyter of the same, believe and hold as is written above.

I, Hyginus, deacon of the same, believe and hold as is written above.

I, Heraclides, sub-deacon of the same, believe and hold as is written above.

I, Elpidius, lector of the same, believe and hold as is written above.

I, Cyriacus, proctor of the same, believe and hold as is written above.

12,6   This is what they wrote to the confessors and fathers. If the wise can take it to be a commendable statement it should be categorized as such. On the other hand, if there are accidental unorthodoxies even there, in the argument they use in their actual defense of themselves, the scholarly, once more, should put it in that category. But since I have given all the above information about Marcellus, I shall pass him by in his turn and go on to investigate the rest.

Against Semi-Arians.[1] *53, but 73 of the series*

1,1   By God's power we have torn up the abominable doctrines of Arius, which he originally belched out like a man overtaken with drunkenness, and the doctrines of his successors—I mean Photinus, and Marcellus too during the short time in which he seemed to be shaken. May Arius' pupils be set straight, if indeed they can be!

But now that, with the word of God "which is sharper than any two-edged sword,"[2] we have cut down the tares which sprouted from Arius himself, let us survey the tangled woodland which has grown up from Arius, to see how some are halfway Arians, (2) who repudiate his name but adopt the man and his heresy. By some pretense they falsely put on a different mask, as the acting of stage performers is a sham, and they conceal their faces with different masks, and inside the masks recite the shameful, boozy lines of the comedy—a new comedy, or the myths of the ancients, since their poets used to do the same. (3) Thus, though these people would like to mislead the simple, they are the same as Arius and the Arian Nuts—on the surface, in their behavior, and in their heresy. (4) But in the desire to pretty up their perverse doctrine, as a deceitful piece of flattery they call the Son of God a creature but cheaply add, "We do not mean a creature like any other creature or an offspring like any other offspring"—as a piece of deception and to do the Son of God a favor, as well as to soothe those who are frightened by this expression. And yet they altogether reject the homoousion as untrue to the sacred scripture, if you will! (5) I have discussed this with extreme thoroughness in the Sect about Arius.

But to suggest a word similar to "homoousion" they say—I mean the followers of Basil and George, the leaders of this Semi-Arian sect—"We do not say, 'homoousion,' but 'homoeousion.'" (6) These were the members of the Council < at Ancyra >[3] who separated from the sect of the Arian Nuts itself—their leader, Basil of Ancyra, and George of the Laodicea in Daphne by Antioch, or Coele-Syria.

1,7   Their view of the Holy Spirit too is the same as that of the Pneumatomachi. [In the case of the Spirit] they no longer begin as they do with the Son, with a sort of shame or with a word

---

[1] The literary sources of this Sect are the Epistles of Basil of Ancyra (2,1–11,11) and George of Laodicea (12,1–22,8); the encyclical of the Council of Seleucia, 359 A. D. (25–26); and the inaugural homily of Melitius at Antioch, 360 A. D. (29–33).

[2] Heb. 4:12

[3] Held in 358 A. D. See below at 2,1.

expressive of hesitancy. They are ashamed to say that the Son is altogether a creature, though this is what they think, but from fear of men they add the homoeousion, and the doctrine that the Son is a creature < but not > like any other. But with the Holy Spirit, as I said, they do not begin hesitantly, but like ravening dogs pitilessly declare him a creature in every respect, and thus also maintain that he is different from the Father and the Son.

1,8   And lest it be said that I accuse anyone falsely, I shall cite a letter here as each of them wrote it—Basil, one, but George of Laodicea together with Basil and his companions, another. And here are the letters.

2,1   *Greetings in the Lord from the holy council, assembled from various provinces at Ancyra at the approach of Easter, to the most honored Masters, our colleagues in Phoenicia and elsewhere, who are of one mind with us.*

2,2   *After the trial of the church's faith, as though by fire, by the ordeals for the faith which took place in our midst; and < after > the proceedings at Constantinople because of Marcellus;[4] and the issuance of the creed at the council gathered for the dedication of the church in Antioch;[5] and afterwards at Sardica,[6] and the faith that bloomed again there—and further, after the proceedings at Sirmium[7] with regard to Photinus (3) and still further, after the explanations we issued of each article of the creed when questioned by those who differed with the easterners at Sardica,[8] it is our prayer that we may rest at last and, with all stumbling blocks removed and the church from east to west united under the pious rule of our master Constantius, be at peace and attend to the divine services.*

2,4   *But the devil, it seems, does not abandon his utmost endeavors to foment apostasy in every way through his peculiar vessels, < as > was foretold by the Lord and, correspondingly, declared by the holy apostle for the protection of the faithful. (5) For by devising rebellions against the faith of the church he is even now <attempting*> to claim certain individuals*

---

[4] The Synod of Constantinople, 336 A. D., confirmed Arius' deposition and condemned Marcellus for a too close identification of the Word with the Father. Cf. Soc. 1.36.8; Soz. 2.33; Eusebius Contra Marcellum 2.4.29.

[5] The second Council of Antioch, 341 A. D., issued four creeds. Basil probably refers to the second, which calls the Son the "exact image of the Godhead, essence, will, power and glory of the Father," Hahn pp. 184–186; Ath. Syn. 23.3; Soc. 2.10.76; Hilary De Synodis 29.

[6] The Council of Sardica, 343 A. D., split into a council of western and a council of eastern bishops; the easterns reissued the fourth creed of Antioch with anathemas added.

[7] The first Council of Sirmium, 351 A. D., condemned Photinus.

[8] Probably the Ecthesis Macrostichus, an extensive explanation of the creed of the easterns at Sardica, which was presented before the emperor Constantius at the third Council of Antioch in 345. It contains the formula, "like the Father in all respects," which Basil's letter emphasizes. Cf. Ath. Syn. 26.6; Soc. H. E. 2.9.11.

for his own "with a form of godliness,"[9] *and through them has invented < novelties* > and "profane new babblings"*[10] *against the godly truth of [the doctrine of] the only-begotten Son of God.*

When we heard formerly that some were running about in Antioch, but also in Alexandria, and further, in Lydia or Asia, and planting sparks of impiety in the souls of the simple, (6) we hoped that, due to the audacity of the impiety and < the > extent of their shamelessness, the heresy they have invented had been quenched, and the evil suppressed, by the championship of the Masters, our colleagues, in each locality.

2,7   But since persons from the places aforesaid next arrived, and persons from Illyria, and informed us that the inventors of this evil are zealous in the venture of doing harm to a larger number and infecting them with a leaven of wickedness, we could brook no further delay. (8) Since, moreover, we have read the letter, copies of which we subjoin, of our like-minded colleague, George of the church of Laodicea,[11] and since we respect the testimonies of those who have witnessed to us before God, (9) as many of us have gathered as could do so given the season, the approach of the holy day of Easter—the winter was a hindrance to many, as they have indicated by letter—and hastened to set forth the norm of the faith in the following form. (10) As far as the remaining points are concerned, < we are in agreement* > with the council at Antioch, as we have said, and the creed the Council at Sirmium accepted,[12] which was issued at the dedication as well as at Sardica, and with the arguments that were presented at Sirmium. < It is our purpose > to give an accurate description of the catholic church's faith in the holy Trinity, as we said, and of the form of the innovation besides, replying to it only as the Spirit has permitted us.

2,11   And because you, most honored Sirs and colleagues, have stood firm in the faith which has been handed down to us from our fathers, and because our faith, as we believe, is in accord with yours, we urge you, on reading this, to append your signatures. Thus those who dare to introduce this impiety will be assured that we have accepted, and guard as our inheritance, the faith < of the > fathers, < transmitted > from the time of the apostles, through the intervening generations, even to us. (12) Hence they will either be ashamed and submit to correction, or persist in error and be expelled from the church, < for > preparing the falling away, by their own efforts, for the son of iniquity who threatens to venture "to sit even in the temple of God."*[13]

---

[9] 2 Tim. 3:5
[10] 1 Tim. 6:20
[11] This letter is thought to be lost. It is not the letter given at Soz. 4.13.2–3, which says nothing about Laodicea, but reports the situation at Antioch.
[12] The fourth Creed of the second Council of Antioch (341 A. D.), reissued in 341 by the easterns at Sardica, and in 351 by the first Council of Sirmium.
[13] 2 Thes. 2:14

3,1   *Our faith is in a Father, a Son and a Holy Spirit. For so our
Lord Jesus Christ taught his disciples, "Go make disciples of all nations,
baptizing them in the name of the Father, and of the Son, and of the Holy
Spirit."*[14] *(2) Therefore we who are born again into this faith should have
a godly understanding of the meanings of the names. He did not say,
"Baptize them in the name of the Incorporeal and the Incarnate," or, "of
the Immortal and of Him who knew death," or, "of the Ingenerate and
the Generate."*[15] *He said, "Baptize them in the Name of the Father, and
of the Son, and of the Holy Spirit." (3) And thus, since we also hear
< the > names in nature, and < a father* > there < always begets a son
like himself* >,*[16] *we may understand the "Father" to be the cause of an
essence like his. And when we hear the name, 'Son,' we may understand
that the Son is like the Father whose Son he is.*

3,4   *We have therefore believed in a Father, a Son and a Holy Spirit,
not in a creator and a creature. For "creator and creature" are one thing
but "father and son" are another, since these two concepts differ in meaning.
(5) If I say, "creature," I must first say, "creator;" < and if I say* >, "son,"
< I must first say, "father." But even the term, "Son," is not quite right* >,
since it is taken from physical things, and [used] because of the passions
and effluents of flesh and blood fathers and sons. < If we exclude these,
however* >, it does plainly mean the existence of the incorporeal Son of
an incorporeal Father. (6) Thus < our Lord refrained from putting the
term* >, "creature," [into the baptismal formula], because it entailed a
notion of something corporeal. And since the creature the Father makes < is
a "son" >, < God called > him "Son" by borrowing from the notions of
"creator" and "creature" only the creator's impassibility with respect to the
creature, and the creature's stability—the result of the impassibility—and
< its being as the > creator intended, (7) and has plainly taught us the
whole notion of the Father and the Son from the parallels of a physical
father and son, < and > a physical creator and creature.*

*For if we abstract from "creature" its existence as an external object, its
materiality, and all else that the name, physical "creature," implies, all that
remains of "creature" is the notion of impassibility—I mean the impassibility of its creator—and the notion of the creature, and of its being as
its creator intended, is complete. (8) If, again, we then eliminate the rest
from the notion of "creator" and "creature," and take only the notion that
a creature is made by an impassible creator and is perfect, stable and as
its creator intended, it follows—since we have been taught above all to*

---

[14] Matt. 28:19
[15] Such descriptions of the Father and the Son are termed inadequate at Ath.
Nic. 31.3; Or. I C. Ar. 32; Or. II C. Ar. 41; 42.
[16] Athanasius uses a similar argument, but in favor of the homoousion, at
Ath. Or. I C. Ar. 26.

believe in a Father and a Son—that as orthodox Christians believe, we form one particular idea of the terms, "Father" and "Son."

4,1   *Thus, if we eliminate anything in their case that has to do with passion or effluent, < and > understand that the Father is the Father of a Son, and that the Son is one who was not engendered sexually and brought to maturity by natural physical things which, as is characteristic of physical things, are constantly made to grow and decay, only the notion of likeness will be left. (2) For as we shall say once more of a creature < that >, when < all physical features > were eliminated, the < notion > of its creator's impassibility was left, but the < notion > of the creature's perfection, of its being as its creator intended, and of its stability, so we shall say of the Father and the Son that, with all physical features eliminated, only the generation of a living being of like essence will be left—for every "father" is understood to be the father of an essence like his. (3) If, however, along with the elimination of all other physical notions from the terms, "Father," and "Son," the one which enables us to think of the Father as < the cause > of a living being of like essence is also eliminated, our faith will no longer be in a Father and a Son but in a creator and a creature. And the terms, < "Father," and "Son," > will be unnecessary, since they contribute nothing from their own meanings. And thus, as God, he will be a creator < but > in no sense a Father.*

4,4   *For it is plain from natural considerations that the "Father" does not mean the Father of an activity but of an essence like himself, whose subsistence corresponds with a particular activity. God has many activities, and is seen to be a creator from another activity whereby he is the creator of heaven, earth and everything in them, and of things invisible as well. But as the Father of the Only-begotten he is seen to be, not a creator but a Father who has begotten [a Son].*

4,5   *But if, from motives of reverence, < someone > removes the true notion of the relationship of the Father and the Son because of his idea of physical paternity and sonship, and his fear that the Incorporeal may suffer some effect in begetting unless his Offspring, and the effects of physical paternity and sonship, are incomplete, whatever he says, he will be saying that the Son is another creature, and never that the Son is a son. (6) Even if he says that the Son surpasses [other creatures] in greatness as heaven surpasses a mountain or hill, he will in fact be regarding him as a creature[17]— even though the creature is thought to excel in greatness, in utility as the first creature to be made, or as serving for the creation of the rest.[18] Even so he will not remove him from the category of creatures. (7) For just as taking a coal from the altar with tongs rather than with the hand itself*

---

[17] Athanasius himself uses this argument at Or. II C. Ar. 20.
[18] So Arius in his Thaleia, Ath. Or. 1 C. Ar. 26.

is the same thing, even < though > the bronze work, the overlaying of the iron, is done with the hand—for both the tongs and the iron that is overlaid by the hand are creatures—even so, the One through whom all creatures were made will not be different from the creatures unless he is a Son, as the natural concept [of "son"] suggests. Even though he is the Maker's instrument by which the Creator makes all things, he will be the first of the objects made [by the Creator].

5,1   *And may no one produce an ingenious derivation of the notion of "Father" in the proper sense, and "Son" in the proper sense, from the things more commonly called "sons" < as > when scripture says, "I have begotten sons and brought them up, and they have rebelled against me;"*[19] *"Have we not all one Father?"*[20] *"As many as received him, to them gave he power to become the sons of God, which were born, not of the will of the flesh, nor of the will of man, but of God"*[21]—*and also of inanimate objects, "Who hath begotten drops of dew?"*[22] *(2) These texts will prove instead, from the < meaning > common [to all of them], that the Son is not a son just as these things are not, but that as a creature, he is merely named "son" in common with them.*

5,3   *But the church has believed that God is not only a creator of creatures—Jews and Greeks know this as well—but is also the Father of an Only-begotten. He possesses not only his creative activity whereby he is understood to be a creator, but a generative activity peculiar and unique to himself, whereby we understand him to be the Father of a unique Offspring. (4) It is to teach us this that the blessed Paul writes, "For this cause I bow my knees unto the Father, of whom the whole family in heaven and earth is named."*[23] *< For as fathers on earth are termed "fathers" > because they have sons in the likeness of their own essences, so we name the One for whom the fathers on earth were named "fathers" in accordance with their essences, "Father in heaven"—for he surely has the Son begotten of him in the likeness of his own essence.*

5,5   *And the notion of "sons" which applies to things that are loosely and equivocally so called cannot fit the Only-begotten. For as a "box tablet" properly speaking means a tablet made of boxwood, but more commonly and in the colloquial sense of the word, a tablet made of lead, bronze or any other material < is called* > a "box tablet" after the boxwood tablet, < so only the Son begotten of the Father is properly termed "Son of God," while the others are so named in the loose sense of the word.* > (6) Nor < is he named "son" in the sense of, "Who hath begotten drops of dew?"*

---

[19] Isa. 1:2
[20] Mal. 2:10
[21] John 1:12–13
[22] Job 38:28
[23] Eph. 3:14–15; cf. the Fourth Antiochene Symbol.

Properly speaking, God did not "beget" dew >, that is, not in actuality;
here the word for begetting an offspring is colloquially applied to a created
object. And he is not called "Son" in the sense of, "I have begotten sons
and brought them up;" here too the term is loosely applied, because of
[God's] good will and respect towards them. (7) Nor is he called "Son"
< in the sense of >, "He gave them power to become sons of God;" this
too is derived < from > the idea of virtuous creation in his own image.
The Only-begotten is < not > to be understood as Son in these senses but
in the proper one, as an only Son begotten of an only Father, in the essential
likeness of the Father whose Son he is called, and is understood to be.*

6,1   *But suppose that, from the incapacity of his reasoning powers,
someone refuses to accept this line of reasoning on the grounds that the
Father must be subject to some passion, division or effluence if he is to
be conceived as this sort of father—and has [thus] mutilated the godly
conception of the Father and the Son, and requires reasons for it. (2) He
must be required to provide reasons why God is crucified, and why "the
foolishness" of the proclamation of the Gospel—[called "foolishness"] because of its unreasonableness in the eyes of those whom the world counts
as wise—"is wiser than men."*[24] *The blessed Paul did not consider these
persons worthy of notice, since by the unreasonableness of power God has
"made the wisdom" of persons with the ability to reason "foolish."*[25] *(3)
For Paul said, "I came declaring unto you the mystery of God, not with
wisdom of words, lest the cross of Christ should be made of none effect."*[26]
*Anyone who, with wisdom of words, demands < reasons > for the mystery,
should disbelieve the mystery, since his portion is with the wisdom which
has been made foolish. For even though such a person disbelieves from
wisdom of words, Paul < chooses to preach "only in demonstration of the
Spirit and of power"* >*[27] *"lest the cross of Christ should be made of none
effect."*[28]

6,4   *But if he replies in this way he does not do so with wisdom of
words, but by the unreasonableness of power confounds all wisdom which
is based on reasoning, and accepts faith alone for the salvation of those
who receive the Gospel. (5) He does not answer [by explaining] how the
Father begets the Son without passion, or the mystery of the Only-begotten's
sonship to the Father might be robbed of its significance. He confounds
the wisdom of the wise, which is "made foolish"*[29]—*as scripture says, "Where
is the wise? Where is the scribe? Where is the disputer of this world?"*[30]—

---

[24] 1 Cor. 1:25
[25] Cf. 1 Cor. 1:25.
[26] Cf. 1 Cor. 2:1; 1:17.
[27] 1 Cor. 2:4
[28] 1 Cor. 1:17
[29] Cf. Ath. Or. C. Ar. I 28.
[30] 1 Cor. 1:20

(6) *but not with verbal wisdom, so that < the mystery > will not be rendered meaningless by suspicions occasioned by arguments. I mean that < the > godly conception of the Father and the Son—but a Father and a Son with no passions—declares, without deriving the idea from reason, that the Father has begotten the Son of himself without emission and passion, but that a Son like his Father in essence has been begotten of the Father, Perfect of Perfect, an only-begotten entity. [These are] doctrines which are either < believed > by the faithful, or suspected < by the unbelieving >.*

6,7   *For only a fool would hear of Wisdom originating from a wise God, as the Father of the Wisdom begotten of him wisely knows, and attribute passion to the Father < because > Wisdom originated from him—if, [that is], the Wisdom essentially like the wise God is to originate from him.* (8) *For, if we are not to conceive of the wise God as compoundedly wise by participation in wisdom, he is himself wise, himself an essence, without compounding, and the wisdom by which he is known is not the Son. The Wisdom which is the Son is an essence begotten of the essence of the Wise, which is Wisdom. The Son will subsist as an essence like the essence of the wise Father, from whom the Son originated as Wisdom.*

7,1   *And so the blessed Paul, with his excellent training in Hebrew lore, was accustomed, by the inspiration of the same Spirit who spoke in the Old and the New Testaments, to derive the same notions as the ones in the two Psalms, "Thy judgments are a great deep,"*[31] *and "Thy paths are in deep waters, and thy footsteps shall not be known."*[32] *But he altered the language about God's judgments < by replacing > "great deep" with "O the depth of the riches;"*[33] *"Thy paths are in deep waters and thy footsteps shall not be known" with "unsearchable;" and "Thy judgments are a great deep" with "Thy judgments are past finding out."*

7,2   *And because Wisdom itself had taught him its notion of the Father and itself, and of its relation to created things, Paul in his own writings presents us with the idea of the Father and the Son, and the things which have been created by the Father through the Son, in the following manner.* (3) *For Wisdom had said, "I, Wisdom, give counsel a home"*[34] *and so forth, and gone on to explain "by whom?"—for it said, "By me are kings,"*[35] *and "If I shall tell you the things that are by me, I shall remember to recount the things of old."*[36] *It said, "The Lord created me the beginning of his ways, for his works. Before the age he established me, and before all things*

---

[31] Ps. 35:7
[32] Ps. 76:20
[33] The New Testament quotations in 7,1 are taken from Rom. 11:33.
[34] Prov. 8:12
[35] Prov. 8:15
[36] Prov. 8:21a

he begets me;"[37] (4) *but for "beginning" Paul understood "first,"*[38] *and for "begets me," "-born."*[39] *And for the entire sentence, "He created me the beginning of his ways and begets me," the apostle understood "firstborn of every creature." For "he established" Paul understood "In him are all things created;" for "By me are the things of old," "Whether thrones or principalities or powers or authorities, all things were created by him and for him."*

7,5   *Thus all < the > apostle's phrases are word for word equivalents of the things that were said by Wisdom. That is, "beginning" is equivalent to "first," "begets" to "-born," and "He created me the beginning of his ways, for his works," to "firstborn of every creature." "In him were created" is a substitute for "He established me," and "All things are by him" for "By me are the things of old."* (6) *It is thus evident < that > neither did the "image" originate from passion, but that it must be understood in the sense of "I, Wisdom;" and that, as Wisdom is the Son of the Wise, an essence which is the Son of an essence, so the image is like the essence.* (7) *And we have the equivalents for all the words: "God" for "wise," "image" for "wisdom," "first" for "beginning," and "-born" for "first."*

But we can also give the equivalents of whole phrases. "Firstborn of every creature" is the equivalent of "He created me the beginning of his way, for his works, and begets me." "In him were created" is the equivalent of "He established me." "All things are by him and for him" is the equivalent of "by me." (8) *It is thus plain that not only Paul exposes the entire wrongness*[40] *of those who hear that the Son "is the image of the invisible God," and try to quibble shamelessly about the Son's likeness of essence to the Father. John before him, truly the son of thunder, similarly sounded the godly conception of the Son forth to us with his own loud peal—from the clouds, as it were, of the riddles of Wisdom.*

8,1   *For see how he too transmitted the truths he had learned from Wisdom in the Gospel he proclaimed to us.* (2) *Because Wisdom had said, "He created me the beginning of his ways,"*[41] *John used the phrase, "in the beginning," in his "In the beginning was the Word."*[42] *And for "He created me" John substituted "And the Word was God,"*[43] *so that we would not take this to mean the spoken word, but the divine Word < begotten > of the Father without passion, as a stable entity. And for "I was by him"*[44]

---

[37] Prov. 8:22; 23a; 25b
[38] The New Testament citations in 7,4–8 are from Col. 1:15–16.
[39] πρωτό – τοκος: "first*born*"
[40] Holl and MSS: παραπέσοντας; Eltester: lacuna, or παραπεσεῖν
[41] Prov. 8:22
[42] John 1:1
[43] John 1:1
[44] Prov. 8:30

John substituted "And < the Word > was God." (3) *For "Through me are
the things from of old"*[45] *John substituted "All things were made by him,
and without him was not anything made."*[46] *For "She hath founded"*[47]
John substituted "That which was made, in him was life,"[48] *which means
the same as "In him were all things created."*[49] (4) *He said, "The Word
was made flesh,"*[50] *to correspond with "Wisdom hath builded her house."*[51]
*He substituted "The Son can do nothing of himself, but what he seeth the
Father do; for what things soever he doeth, these also doeth the Son likewise"*[52] *for "I was by him in accord with him."*[53] *John thus has < the
confirmatory testimony* > of two or three witnesses to prove the Son's likeness
of essence to the Father.* (5) *For one witness says that the Wisdom of the
wise God is his Son; one, that the Word of God is the only-begotten God;
one, that the Son is the image of God. Thus it is proclaimed by all that
the Word, Wisdom and Image of God is in all respects like him, as we
have said, and that he is the essential Son of his God and Father.* (6)
*Still more, when God's Word says, "As the Father hath life in himself, so
hath he given to the Son to have life in himself,"*[54] *he is educating us,
like Thomas, by contact with the actuality of the likeness of essence.* (7)
*For if "as the Father hath" does not mean what it would in something
else—(the Father is not one thing and the life in him something else, so
that the one thing means the possessor and the other the thing possessed.
The Father himself is uncompoundedly life, and has granted the Son < to
have life > as he does—plainly, to have it uncompoundedly, like the Father.)
[Even so], it is plain that in having life in this way, since he has it neither
without generation nor compoundedly, the Son too, like the Father, has all
things essentially and without compounding.*

8,8   *And yet it is plain that "like" can never be the same as the thing
it is like. For proof < of this we have* > the fact that when the Son of
God "was made in the likeness of men"*[55] *he became man indeed, but not
the same as man in every respect. And when he was made "in the likeness
of the flesh of sin"*[56] *he was made with the passions which are the cause
of sin in the flesh—I mean hunger, thirst and the rest—but was not made*

---

[45] Cf. Prov. 8:23.
[46] John 1:2
[47] Cf. Prov. 8:25.
[48] John 1:3–4
[49] Col. 1:16
[50] John 1:14
[51] Prov. 9:1
[52] John 5:19
[53] Prov. 8:30
[54] John 5:26
[55] Phil. 2:7
[56] Rom. 8:3

the same as the flesh of sin. Thus the Son's likeness of essence to the Father is also proclaimed by the texts from the apostle.

9,1   *For as he was made in the likeness of man and was man, yet not entirely—was man in his assumption of human flesh, for "The Word was made flesh,"*[57] *but not man in that he was not begotten of human seed and sexual commerce—(2) just so, in that he was the Son of God, he was the Son of God before all ages, just as, in that he was a son of man, he was man. But he is not the same thing as the God and Father who begot him, just as he is not the same thing as man, since [he was begotten] without emission of seed and passion, < just as > [he was made man] without human seed and sexual enjoyment.*

9,3   *And < as he was made > in the likeness of the flesh of sin through being subject to fleshly hunger, thirst and sleep, the passions by which bodies are moved to sin, and yet, though subject to these passions of the flesh, he was not moved to sin by them—(4) even so the Son, who was < Son > of God, "in the form of God," and is "equal" to God,*[58] *possessed the attributes of the Godhead in being by nature incorporeal, and like the Father in divinity, incorporeality and activities. As he was "like" the flesh in being flesh and subject to the passions of the flesh, (5) and yet was not the same, < so he is "like" God > in the sense that, as God, he is not "the form" of "the God" but the form of "God,"*[59] *and "equal," not to "the God" but to "God." Nor does he < have the Godhead > with full sovereignty like the Father. For as he was not < moved > to sin < like > a man, and yet behaved like a man, < so, as God, he behaves "like" the Father* >, "For whatsoever the Father doeth, the Son also doeth.*[60]

9,6   *Now he was not moved to sin here on earth, but was moved in ways similar to persons in the flesh. (It would be strange if, after passing from his natural state to a state unnatural to him, that is, after becoming a son of man when he had been God, he should become like those to whom this state was natural—that is, who were human by nature—in a trait that was unnatural to him, but [at the same time] not be like his Father by nature in the trait that was natural to him, since he was God begotten of God. And it is plain that those who deny the Son's likeness of essence to the Father do not call him a son either, but only a creature—and do not call the Father a father, but a creator. For the notion of "like" does not entail the Son's identity with the Father, but his likeness of essence to him, and his ineffable sonship to him without passion.) (7) For, I say again, as he was not made identical with men < by being made > in the*

---

[57] John 1:14
[58] Phil. 2:6
[59] For the distinction between θεός and ὁ θεός see Lampe *Lexicon of Patristic Greek* 643ab.
[60] John 5:19

likeness of men and of sinful flesh, but, for the reasons given, became like the essence of the flesh, so, by being made like in essence to the Father who begot him, the Son will not make his essence identical with the Father, but like [him].

10,1   *And if, through heeding the wisdom of the world which God has made foolish, anyone fails to heed God's wise declaration and confess with faith the Son's likeness of essence to the Father, but gives false names to the Father and the Son and does not truly term them "Father" and "Son" but "creator" and "creature," equating the concepts of the Father and the Son with the [fatherhood and sonship] of other creatures—and if, from a desire to rationalize, he says that the Son < is superior > [only] in utility as the first of < the > creatures < which have been made > through him, or in the excellence of his greatness, thus confessing none of the church's faith in the Father and the Son, as though to preach by deliberate choice a Gospel different from the Gospel the apostles preached to us, let him be anathema.*

10,2   *And—to repeat the blessed Paul's words, "As we said before, so say I now again"*[61]—*we too must say < in our turn >, If, on hearing that the Father is the only wise God and that his only-begotten Son is his Wisdom, anyone says that the Wisdom is the same as the only wise God and thus denies his sonship, let him be anathema.*

10,3   *And if, on hearing that the Father is the wise God and the Son is his Wisdom, anyone says that the Wisdom is unlike the wise God in essence, and thus denies that the wise God is truly the Father of the Wisdom, let him be anathema.*

10,4   *And if anyone regards the Father as "the God" but, in denial of his true sonship, < denies > that the Word and "God" in the beginning existed as "God" with "the God" and that, as Word and "God," he belonged to "the" very "God" with whom he existed as Word and God—and so denies his true sonship—let him be anathema.*

10,5   *And if anyone, on hearing that the only-begotten divine Word is the Son of "the God" with whom the Word and "God" is, says that the Father's divine Word, the "God" who belongs to "the God" and Father, is essentially unlike Him with whom the Only-begotten was at the beginning as [his] divine Word, let him be anathema.*

10,6   *And if, in denial of his true sonship, anyone, on hearing that the Son is "the image of the invisible God,"*[62] *says that the image is the same as the invisible God, let him be anathema.*

10,7   *And if, in true denial of the sonship, anyone, on hearing that the only-begotten Son is "the image of the invisible God," says that, since*

---

[61] Cf. Gal. 1:18.
[62] Col. 1:15

he is the invisible God's "image," the Son is unlike the invisible God in essence even though the Son is held to be the invisible God's "essential" image, let him be anathema.

10,8   *And if anyone, on hearing the words of the Son, "For as the Father hath life in himself, so hath he given to the Son to have life in himself,"*[63] *says that the Recipient of the life from the Father—he who confessed, "And I live by the Father"*[64]—*is the same as the Giver of the life, let him be anathema.*

10,9   *And if anyone, on hearing "For as the Father hath life in himself, even so hath he given to the Son to have life in himself," says that the Son is essentially unlike the Father even though he affirms that the truth is as the Son has stated it,*[65] *let him be anathema. For plainly, as the life which is held to be in the Father means his essence, and as the life of the Only-begotten, who is begotten of the Father, is held to be his essence, thus the word, "so," denotes the likeness of essence to essence.*

11,1   *And if anyone, on hearing the Son's, "He created me," and, "He begets me,"*[66] *does not take "begets me" literally and as a reference to essence, but says that "He begets me" means the same as "He created me," thus denying that the Son is < designated > by the two terms as the perfect < Son > [begotten] without passion, < but >, < on the basis of these two terms >, confessing that he is a mere creature and not a Son—for Wisdom has conveyed the godly meaning by the two terms—let him be anathema.*

11,2   *And since the Son reveals to us his likeness in essence to the Father through his words, "For as the Father hath life in himself, so hath he given to the Son to have life in himself," but reveals his likeness in activity through his teaching, "For what things soever the Father doeth, these also the Son doeth likewise"*[67]—*[therefore], if anyone grants him only the likeness of activity but denies the Son his likeness of essence, the cornerstone of our faith, and denies himself eternal life in the knowledge of the Father and the Son, let him be anathema.*

11,3   *And if anyone who professes to believe in a Father and a Son says that the Father is not the Father of an essence like his, but the Father of an activity, let him be anathema for daring to utter "profane babblings"*[68] *against the essence of the Son of God, and denying the truth of his sonship.*

11,4   *And if anyone who holds that [Christ] is the Son of an essence like his of whom he is held to be the Son, should say that the Son is the*

---

[63] John 5:26
[64] John 6:57
[65] Amidon: "insisting that that is in fact what he has said"
[66] Prov. 8:22;25
[67] John 5:19
[68] Cf. 1 Tim. 6:20.

same as the Father, or is part of the Father, or that the incorporeal Son originated from the incorporeal Father by emission or passion as corporeal sons do, let him be anathema.

11,5   And if anyone who, because the Father is one person and the Son is another, says that the Son differs from the Father since the Father is never conceived of as the Son and the Son is never conceived of as the Father—as the scripture says, "There is another that beareth witness of me,"[69] for "The Father that hath sent me beareth witness"[70]—[if anyone who says this] because of this godly distinction of the persons of the Father and the Son which is made in the church, fears that the Son may be supposed to be the same as the Father, and therefore says that the Son is unlike the Father in essence, let him be anathema.

11,6   And if anyone holds that the Father is the Father of the only-begotten Son in time, and does not believe that the only-begotten Son has originated impassibly from the Father beyond all times and differently from any human thought—thus abandoning the preaching of the apostles, which rejected time with reference to the Father and the Son, but faithfully taught us, "In the beginning was the Word, and the Word was with God, and the Word was God,"[71]—let him be anathema.

11,7   And if anyone says that the Father is prior in time to his only-begotten Son, and that the Son is later in time than the Father, let him be anathema.

11,8   And if anyone ascribes the only-begotten Son's timeless origin from the Father to the unbegotten essence of God, and thus speaks of a Son-Father, let him be anathema.

11,9   And if anyone says that the Father is < the Father > of the only-begotten Son by authority only, and not the Father of the only-begotten Son by authority and essence alike—thus accepting only the authority, equating the Son with any creature, and denying that he is actually the true Son of the Father—let him be anathema.

11,10   And if anyone, though saying that the Father is the Father of the Son by authority and essence, also says that the Son is co-essential, or of identical essence with the Father, let him be anathema.

11,11   The signers are Basil, Eustathius, Hyperechius, Letoeus, Heorticus, Gymnasius, Memnonius, Eutyches, Severinus, Eutychius, Alcimides and Alexander. I too believe as the above articles have stated, and confess them with my signature.

The end of the memorial of Basil, George and his companions

---

[69] John 5:32
[70] John 5:37
[71] John 1:1

< The Letter of George >

12,1   *It is plain that the term, "being,"*[72] *does not appear in the Old and the New Testaments, but the sense of it is to be found everywhere. In the first place, He who owes his origin to none but is the cause of all things < is implied > by God's words when he sent Moses, "Thus shalt thou say unto the children of Israel, 'He Who Is'"*[73]—*meaning him who is regarded primarily as the Father "of whom the whole family in heaven and earth is named."*[74] *(2) Now the Son also "is;" but Paul the Samosatian and Marcellus took advantage of the text in the Gospel according to John, "In the beginning was the Word."*[75] *No longer willing to call the Son of God a true Son, they took advantage of the term, "Word," I mean verbal expression and utterance, and refused to say "Son of God." (3) And so the fathers who tried Paul the Samosatian for this heresy were forced to say that the Son too is a being, to show that the Son has reality, subsists, and is, but is not a word, and to distinguish, by means of the term, "being," between a thing which has no existence of its own, and a thing which does. (4) For a word has no existence of its own and cannot be a son of God, since if it could, there would be many sons of God.*

For it is agreed that the Father said many things to the Son—when, for instance, he said, "Let there be a firmament,"[76] *"Let there be luminaries,"*[77] *"Let the earth bring forth,"*[78] *and, "Let us make man."*[79] *(5) The Father therefore speaks to the Son, and yet God's words, which he says to the Son, are not sons. The Son to whom the Father speaks, however, may with piety be called, among other things, "bread," "life," and "resurrection;" and he is further termed, "Word," since he is the interpreter of the counsels of God.*

12,6   *And therefore lest, to deceive the simple, the heretics should say that the Son is the same as the words which are spoken by God, the fathers, as I say, called the Son a "being," to show the difference between the Son of God and the words of God. They expressed the distinction in this way because God "is," and the words which he speaks < "are" >, and yet they are not God's "beings" but his verbal operations. But although the Son is a Word, he is not God's verbal operation; he is a "being," since he is a Son. (7) For if the Father "is" the Son also < "is" >; but the Son "is"*

---

[72] οὐσία. In the Letter of George it is more convenient to use this rendering than "essence."
[73] Exod. 3:14. Cf. Euseb. Eccl. Theol. 2.20.15; Ath. Dec. Nic. Syn. 22; Or. IV 26.
[74] Eph. 3:15
[75] John 1:1
[76] Gen. 1:6
[77] Gen. 1:1
[78] Gen. 1:24
[79] Gen. 1:26

in such a way that, (8) *since he has his being from God by true sonship, he will not be regarded as a Word like the words God speaks. They have their being in the Speaker; but he has his in virtue of his begetting by the Father, his hearing of the Father, and his service to the Father. The fathers, then, called this entity a "being."*

13,1   *We regard the Son as like the Father in all respects, in opposition to the party that is now growing up as an excrescence on the church.* (2) *This current faction declares that the Son is like the Father in will and activity, but that the Son is unlike the Father in < being >.* (3) *Thus it is the contention of these new sectarians that the will of the Son and the activity of the Son are like the will of the Father and the activity of the Father, but that the Son himself is unlike the Father. And they agree that the Son's will and activity are like the Father's will and activity, but the reason they will not allow that the Son is like the Father is that they maintain that the Son is not begotten of God. He is merely a creature, and differs from the other creatures in that he surpasses them in greatness and came into being before them all, and that God availed himself of his assistance in the creation of the rest.* (4) *Because, say the sectarians, God made the rest through a Son, but made him by no one's instrumentality but personally, and made him superior in greatness and might to all things, God called him an "only-begotten Son."*

14,1   *We of the catholic church, however, have taken our confession of faith from the sacred scriptures, and hold as follows. The Father is the Father of a Son like himself, and the Son is like the Father of whom he is held to be the Son.* (2) *Defining this further, and thus narrowing the sense of it as against the Sabellians and the rest, we hold that the Son cannot be a Father, or the Father a Son.* (3) *(The accurate knowledge of the Persons consists of the following: The Father, who is everlastingly a Father, is incorporeal and immortal, while the Son, who is everlastingly a Son and never a Father, but is called everlasting because of his being's independence of time and incomprehensibility, has taken flesh by the will of the Father, and has undergone death for us.)*

14,4   *Despite the clarity of these distinctions, the strange people who support this sect exert themselves in an effort to achieve two aims. One is never again to say "Father and Son," but "Ingenerate and Generate;" for in this way they hope to foist the sophistry of their sect on the church.* (5) *For those who are wise in the things of God understand that "Ingenerate" < plainly > means less than the term, "Father." Since "ingenerate" means [only] that a thing has not been generated, it does not yet say whether it is also a father—for the term, "father," means more than the term, "ingenerate."* (6) *As I say, "ingenerate" does not carry the connotation of fatherhood, but "father" connotes, both that the father is not a son— provided that he is understood as a "father" in the proper sense of the* *word—and that he is the cause of a son like himself.*

14,7 *This is one aim. Besides, they were the first to portray the Son as unlike the Father in essence, since they supposed, from something they had unearthed in a letter by the venerable bishop Hosius in which the essential unlikeness is mentioned,*[80] *that the church had affirmed it. (8) However, since the easterners who came to Sirmium last year*[81] *exposed this sect's sharp practice, they tried their best, in order to escape punishment for their assaults on the church's faith, to remove the term, "being," which was used by the fathers, from the church's teaching for these reasons, as another way of lending apparent strength to their sect.*

15,1 *For they supposed that, if the word, "being," were rejected, they could say that the Son is like the Father only in will and activity, and gain the right to say, finally, that since "being" was not mentioned, the Son is unlike the Father in being and existence. (2) But God, the vindicator of the truth who "taketh the wise in their own craftiness,"*[82] *openly declared, through the mouth of the pious emperor, that his Only-begotten's relation to himself is the Son's likeness to him in all respects. (3) For this was the emperor's own view, in his piety, of God's only-begotten Son who fought for him. And since this was his belief he declared with pious lips that the Son is like the Father in all respects, as the catholics believe; and that it was not by his doing that this proceeding against the church's faith had been launched, the aim of which was to eliminate the term, "being," so that, with "being" no longer on men's lips, the heresy might make its lair in their hearts.*

15,4 *But let us anticipate them, since they describe [the Son] as like [the Father] in will but unlike him in essence. If, indeed, they candidly and plainly admit his likeness in all things to the Father, the worthlessness of their anxious effort to remove the word, "being," will be exposed. (5) For they gained nothing, since they were compelled to confess that the Son is like the Father in all respects. For if he is like in all respects, as they have confessed him to be—and it is in this way that the Son is like the Father—he is like, not just in will and operation—the distinction they draw—but in existence, subsistence and being, as a son should be.*

And once for all, < the phrase >, "in all respects," is all-inclusive and leaves no room for distinction. (6) This—if it be admitted that the Father himself is not "like" himself, and the Son himself is not "like" himself, but

---

[80] Hosius of Cordova signed the creed of the Second Council of Sirmium, A.D. 357. This creed repudiates both the homoousion and the homoeousion, because they are not in scripture and the manner of the Son's generation cannot be known. It does not mention in so many words the doctrine of the Son's unlikeness to the Father.

[81] I.e., 358 A.D.

[82] 1 Cor. 3:19

is instead a Son who is like his Father; and that, since he is in all respects like the Father, he is not a Father but a Son—[this] provides us with a worthy conception of the Father through our contemplation of him. (7) *For the Son was begotten of this Father, Perfect begotten of Perfect, begotten † in the Father's likeness*[83] *before anyone can conceive and before all reckonings, times and ages—as only the Father knows, who begot the Son of himself without passion; and the Son, who has his being from him; and he to whom the Son will reveal him.*

16,1   *And the word, "hypostases," need trouble no one. The easterners say "hypostases" as an acknowledgment of the subsistent, real individualities of the persons.* (2) *For if the Father is spirit, the Son is spirit, and the Holy Ghost is spirit, < but > "the Son" does not mean "Father"—and since there is also a "Spirit," and this does mean "Son," and he is not the Son—and since the Holy Spirit cannot be the Father or the Son, but is a Holy Spirit given to the faithful by the Father through the Son—and since, in all probability, the Holy Spirit too subsists and is real—the easterners, as I said, call the individualities of the subsistent Persons 'hypostases.' They do not mean that the three hypostases are three first principles, or three Gods, for they condemn anyone who speaks of three Gods.* (3) *Nor do they call the Father and the Son two Gods; they confess that the Godhead is one, and that it encompasses all things through the Son, in the Holy Spirit.*

16,4   *< But > though they confess one Godhead, dominion and first principle, they still acknowledge the Persons in an orthodox manner through the individualities of the hypostases. They perceive the Father as subsistent in his paternal authority and confess the Son, not as a part of the Father, but as a perfect Son plainly begotten without blemish of a perfect Father. And they acknowledge that the Holy Spirit, whom the sacred scripture calls the Paraclete, owes his being to the Father through the Son.* (5) *< For > as the Paraclete, the Spirit of truth, teaches us the truth, which is the Son— "No man can say, Jesus is Lord, but by the Holy Spirit"*[84]—*so the Son, who is truth, teaches the godly knowledge of the true God, his Father, as he says, "He that hath seen me hath seen the Father."*[85] (6) *In the Holy Spirit, then, we have a godly apprehension of the Son; but in the only-begotten Son we piously and worthily glorify the Father. And this is the seal of the faith, the seal with which our Savior and Lord, Jesus Christ, who said, "Go make disciples of all nations, baptizing them in the name of the Father, and of the Son, and of the Holy Spirit,"*[86] *commanded us to be baptized.*

---

[83] Holl: καθ᾽ ὁμοιότητα; MSS: ὁμοιότητος, "of the Father's likeness," which is not really possible.

[84] 1 Cor. 12:3

[85] John 14:9

[86] Matt. 28:19

17,1   *The Son's likeness in all respects to the Father has been more extensively discussed elsewhere. Even now, however, I do not mind noting briefly in passing that the apostle, who called the Son "the image of the invisible God"*[87] *and in this way taught us that the Son is like the Father, has told us in other passages how we are to conceive of the Son.* (2) *In the Epistle to the Philippians he says, "Who, being in the form of God, thought it not robbery to be equal with God, but made himself of no reputation, and took upon him the form of a servant, and was made in the likeness of men;"*[88] *and in the Epistle to the Romans,* (3) *"For what the Law could not do, in that it was weak through the flesh, God, sending his own Son in the likeness of flesh, and for sin, condemned sin the flesh."*[89]

Thus, through the two passages from the two Epistles, we are also taught, through physical examples, the orthodox notion of likeness as it applies to the incorporeal Father and Son. (4) *The words, "took upon him the form of a servant and was made in likeness of men," show that the Son took flesh from the Virgin. Therefore the flesh which the Son of God took is the same as human flesh. But it is "in the likeness" of men, since it was not generated from seed, as men are, or by commerce with a man.* (5) *Similarly the Son, who is spirit and begotten of the Father as spirit, is the same as the Father in that he is spirit begotten of spirit, just as he is < the same as men > in that he is flesh born of Mary's flesh. But in that he is begotten of the Father without emanation, passion and division, he is "like" the Father, and yet not < the Father > himself— < just as > the fleshly Son is in the "likeness" of men, and yet not himself man in all respects.*

18,1   *Through the Epistle to the Philippians, then, Paul has taught us how the hypostasis of the Son is like the hypostasis of the Father. For the Son is spirit, [begotten] of the Father, and, as far as the meaning of "spirit" goes, the same as he—just as he is the same [as man] as far as the meaning of "flesh" goes. And yet he is not the same but like, since "spirit," which the Son is, is not the Father, and the flesh the Word assumed has not originated from human seed and through pleasure, but as the Gospel has taught us.*

18,2   *As I have said, the Son has taught us through Philippians how the Son is entirely like the Father in his being and subsistence.* (3) *But how he is like him in his will, activity and operations he has taught us through Romans, with the words, "In the likeness of the flesh of sin he condemned sin in the flesh." The flesh which the Son of God assumed was the same as the flesh of sin, and was likewise moved to hunger, thirst and sleep like all flesh, but was not moved to sin by them.* (4) *This is why*

---

[87] Col. 1:15
[88] Phil. 2:6–7
[89] Rom. 8:3

scripture says, "in the 'likeness' of the flesh of sin," an expression similar to, "What things soever the Father doeth, the same doeth the Son in like manner."[90] *For the Father, who is spirit, acts on his own authority; the Son, though spirit, does not act on his own authority like the Father, but acts "in like manner."*

18,5   *Therefore, insofar as all flesh is the same, he is the same—just as, insofar as all spirit is the same, he is the same. But insofar as [his flesh was conceived] without seed, he is not the same [as flesh] but like it, just as, insofar as he was begotten, [though] without emission and passion, he is not the same [as the Father], but like him. And he is the same as flesh insofar as all flesh is the same, just as he is the same as spirit insofar as all spirit is the same. But insofar as he is in the likeness of sinful flesh, he is like in the impulses of the flesh and yet not the same, just as the Son [acts, but] in a subordinate role in the likeness of the [Father's] action, and not in the same way that the Father acts, with full sovereignty. (6) From these considerations it is evident that the Son is like the Father in all respects, as a son is like his father if he is truly begotten of him.*

For it would be absurd for Him who was God's Son before all ages, and who was by nature God of God the Father, to become like those who were men by nature, in a way unnatural to him, when he was made man of Mary, contrary to nature—(since he was God, it was not natural for him to become man)—and yet for him not to be like the Father who begot him in a way that was natural to him. (7) If he, unnaturally, is like those who are men by nature, all the more is he by nature like the Father who truly begot him in accordance with his nature. It is thus in keeping with the scriptures that the doctrine of the Son's likeness to the Father in all respects be added to the scriptures. < But > he is like him, < and > has been understood < by us > [to be like him] in the senses in which the apostle has taught us the notion of "likeness" through the above passages. (8) For he is also like [the Father] in that he is life of life, light of light, very God of very God, and wisdom of the wise God. And in a word, according to the scriptures he is not like [the Father] merely in activity and will. In his very being, subsistence and actuality, he is in all respects like the Father who begot him, as a son is like a father.

19,1   *If the new sectarians go on to dispute with us and speak of "ingenerate" and "generate," we shall tell them, "You have disingenuously refused to accept the word, 'being,' although it was used by the fathers, because it is unscriptural. Neither will we accept the word, 'ingenerate,' since it is unscriptural. The apostle says, 'incorruptible,' 'invisible,' 'immortal,' but scripture has never called God 'ingenerate.'"*

---

[90] John 5:19

19,2 *Then, as I have already said, "ingenerate" does not yet mean "Father." And in itself, "generate" does not yet mean "Son," but applies the meaning equally to all things that have origins. (For if one says "generate," he has indicated that the thing had an origin, but has nowhere given indication of One who must forever be regarded as a Son. We, therefore, who forever regard him as the Son of God, shall not accept this term.)*

19,3 *< But > besides, the phrase, "Father and Son," denotes a relation to something. Thus even if we name only a "father," we have the notion of "son" included in the term, "father," for "father" means the father of a son. < And > even though we name only a "son," we have the notion of the "father," for "son" means the son of a father. (4) Each is linked with the other, and the connection cannot be broken. Indeed, either of them mentioned alone implies the notion of the other—and not only the name, but with the name, the natural relationship. (5) In understanding God to be a Father, we understand him to be the Father of God. And in understanding a Son of God to be God, we also understand the said Son of God to be of like nature with Him whose Son he is understood to be. But "ingenerate" does not mean "the ingenerate father of a generate son", nor does "generate" mean "generate son of an ingenerate father."*

20,1 *The terms "ingenerate" and "generate," then, do not imply a relationship between the ingenerate and the generate, or, at the same time, give indication of their nature. Instead they put the individuality of the Son on a level with the rest of created things. Therefore, because of the impious trickery, we shall not accept the terms, but shall persist in our pious use of "Father and Son."*

20,2 *In the first place, we who were called from the gentiles were not baptized in the name of an Ingenerate and a Generate, but of a Father and a Son. And then, the Son is nowhere found to have called his Father "Ingenerate," but to have always called God, "Father," and himself, "Son of God." (3) To mention a few examples in passing, we hear him say, "If ye loved me, ye would rejoice because I go unto my Father;"*[91] *"Are ye angry with me, whom the Father hath sanctified and sent into the world, because I said, I am the Son of God?"*[92] *"I proceeded forth from the Father and am come. I came forth from the Father and am come into the world. Again, I leave the world and go unto the Father."*[93] *And Peter's confession, "Thou art the Christ, the Son of God."*[94] *And the Father says from on high, "This is my beloved Son."*[95]

---

[91] John 14:28
[92] John 10:36
[93] John 16:28 combined with 8:42
[94] Matt. 16:16
[95] Matt. 17:5

20,4 *And therefore, since the Father thus refers to the Son and the Son to the Father, and we—to say it once more—were baptized in these names, we shall always use them, and reject the "profane innovations"*[96] *against the apostolic faith. (5) For the words of the Father, "By the splendors of the saints, from the belly, before the morning star begot I thee,"*[97] *are spoken perforce, and will withdraw the Son from the category of creatures; for by the term which corresponds to the term, "belly," (i.e., "beget") the Father teaches us of the Son he has truly begotten as his own. (6) And when the Son likewise said "The Lord created me,"*[98] *to < keep us from > supposing that his nature is in the same category as the other, created things,*[99] *he perforce added, "Before all hills he begets me,"*[100] *providing us with the notion of his sonship to God the Father that is a godly one and implies no passion. (7) However, the Father has expounded "generate" to us once, and the Son once,*[101] *because of the Son's godly filiation. But the entire New Testament is full of the words, "Father," and, "Son."*

21,1 *But so that the coiners of the heresy may be known by their own words, I note in passing a few examples of the many things they have written on the subject—[no more than a few], because of their length. From these, I presume, the catholics must surely understand the whole purport of their heresy, and make the decision that those who have written these things must abjure them, and to expel both them < and > their doctrines from the apostolic faith, as well as condemning those who believe and teach the same as they. For they write as follows, in these very words:*

21,2 *"Most of all am I eager to convey to you, in brief compass, some of the finest, God-inspired words. Any who suppose that the Son has a likeness of essence to the Father have departed from the truth, for with the title, 'ingenerate,' they impeach the likeness of essence."*[102]

21,3 *And again, they say, "The Son both is, and is admitted to be inferior < to the Ingenerate because of his > generation. He therefore cannot have likeness of essence to the Ingenerate, but does have the likeness by upholding the will of God, unaltered, in his own person. He has a likeness, then—not a likeness of essence but a likeness in respect of will, < for God* > brought < him* > into being as he willed."*

And again, "Why do you yourself not agree with me that the Son is not like the Father in essence?"

---

[96] 1 Tim. 6:20

[97] Ps. 109:3

[98] Prov. 8:22

[99] I.e., "The Lord created me *himself*, and therefore I am different from any creature."

[100] Prov. 8:25

[101] I.e., at Prov. 8:22 and 25

[102] I.e., if the Father is "ingenerate" the Son must be "generate." Therefore they cannot be of like essence.

Further, (4) *"When it is admitted that the Son is everlasting although he does not have life of his own nature but by the authority of the Ingenerate; but it is also admitted that ingenerate nature endlessly transcends all authority; why is it < not > plain that the impious are exchanging the godly doctrine of the heteroousion for 'likeness of essence?'"*

21,5 *And again, "Therefore the word, 'Father,' is not indicative of essence, but of the authority which brought the Son into being before all ages as the divine Word, everlastingly < in possession > of the essence and authority which have been given him, and which he continues to possess."*

21,6 *And again, "< If > they maintain that 'Father' denotes essence but not authority, they should also call the person of the Only-begotten, 'Father.'"*

22,1 *We shall now say to the present day sectarians, "You have written, 'Like in will, unlike in essence.' We have therefore written in reply, 'Like, not merely by imitation, but in essence as well.' (2) You, then, were the first to mention essence, when you said 'unlikeness in essence;' and you are eager for the elimination of the word, 'essence,' so that you can say that the Son is like the Father only in will. (3) Therefore, if you really agree that the Son is in all respects like the Father, condemn those who speak of a distinction in likeness, and write as follows: 'If anyone denies that the Son is like the Father just as [any] son is like his father, but says that he is like him only in will and unlike him in essence, let him be anathema.'" (4) And if they choose < not > to mention the word, "essence," after that, and repudiate even their own signatures by making < no > mention at all of "essence", they should still confess the faith of the fathers that the Son is like < the > Father not only in will, but in essence, subsistence and actuality—in a word, in everything, as a son is like his father, as the sacred scriptures say.'*

22,5 *The signatories of the statement of faith*[103] *in the Son's likeness to the Father in all respects were the following:*

Mark, bishop of Arethusia. I so believe and hold, and < I >, and all here present < am in agreement > with the foregoing.

But Valens subscribed as follows. All here present, and the godly emperor before whom I have testified both orally and in writing, know how I have affixed the above signature on the night before Pentecost.

22,6 *But after this Valens signed the document in his own way. To his signature he added a statement that the Son is like the Father, but*

---

[103] The creed of the fourth Council of Sirmium, May 22, 359 A. D., concludes, "The word, 'essence,'. . . gives scandal, as the scriptures do not contain it. It is our pleasure that it be removed. . . But we affirm that the Son is like the Father in all respects, as the sacred scriptures say and teach." Hahn pp.204–5 (Ath. Syn. 8.70; Soc. 2;37; Nic. H. E. 9.39)

without adding, "in all respects," and making it clear in what sense he
agreed with the above, or how he understood "co-essential." The godly emperor
pointed this out and compelled him to add, "in all respects," which he did.

But Basil suspected that he had added even "in all respects" in a sense
of his own[104] *to the copies < which > Valens was anxious to obtain, to take*
to the council at Ariminum.[105] *So he subscribed as follows:*

22,7   *Basil, bishop of Ancyra. I < so > believe. And I assent to the*
foregoing by confessing that the Son is like the Father in all respects. But
in all! Not merely in will, but, as the sacred scriptures teach, in subsistence,
actuality and essence, as a son is. [I believe that he is] spirit of spirit,
life of life, light of light, God of God, very Son of very < Father >; the Son,
who is Wisdom, of a wise God and Father. And in a word, [I confess]
that the Son is like the Father in all respects, as a son is like a father.
(8) And as has been stated above, if anyone says that the Son is like the
Father [only] in a particular way, he is untrue to the catholic church, since
he is not saying that the Son is the Father in accordance with the sacred
scriptures.

The postscript was read and given to Valens in the presence of the bishops
Mark, George, Ursacius, Germanus and Hypatian, and a larger number
of presbyters and deacons.

23,1   I have inserted these letters to show all studious persons
who are in search of the truths of the faith that I do not accuse
people without reason, but do my best to base what I say on reliable
evidence.

23,2   In turn, the Semi-Arians fell out with their allies; and they
quarreled with each other and competed for leadership because
of the grudges of some of them, and from common jealousy. And
at that time the party of these Semi-Arians—I mean Basil, George,
Silvanus and the rest of them—were in the ascendant. But < the
others* >—Eudoxius, George of Alexandria, and Euzoeus of
Antioch— < opposed them* >, and had on their side an arm of
flesh, the emperor Constantius. (3) And in spite of their great influence the party of Basil and George of Laodicea were humiliated.[106]
Still others of them broke with this faction and confederacy, and
the Arian movement was divided into three groups. (4) For because of his envy and hatred of Cyril of Jerusalem, Acacius of

---

[104] Amidon and MSS: ἰδίῳ νῷ; Holl < μὴ > ἰδίῳ νῷ

[105] The creed of the Council of Ariminum, 359 A.D., was a compromise formula
which said, ". . . like the Father, the Begetter, according to the scriptures, whose
origin no one knows save the Father, who alone begot him. . ." Hahn p. 208
(Jer. C. Luc. 17)

[106] Basil, along with Eustathius of Sebaste and Cyril of Jerusalem, was deprived
of his see at the synod held at Constantinople in 360.

Caesarea in Palestine, along with Melitius, Uranius of Tyre, and
Eutychius of Eleutheropolis opposed Basil, George of Laodicea,
Silvanus of Tarsus, Eleusius of Cyzicus, Macedonius of Constanti-
nople, Eustathius of Sebaste and the newly consecrated bishop of
Antioch, Anianus. < And > by ranging himself against them, Acacius
caused a great deal of confusion.

23,5 [All of] these people, in fact, were of the same opinion,
but because they each confessed it differently they differed, were
divided, and were separated into the three factions I have indicated. (6) For although they were the same as the others, Acacius
and his allies would neither confess the homoousion, nor say that
Christ is a creature < like > any other creature. While < they > kept
quiet about the word, "creature," because of the times, they were
entirely like < the > Arians. But at that time they concealed the
fact that they believed no differently than these, because of the
admixture with them of people who were really orthodox, but were
hypocrites and practiced hypocrisy for fear of the emperor's right
arm.

And what with their mutual hatred, < they could not > stand firm
even though they wanted to. (7) For from enmity towards Cyril,
Eutychius of Eleutheropolis became one of Acacius' supporters,
since he had learned the plain creed of orthodoxy from the blessed
Maximo, the confessor bishop of Jerusalem. He was orthodox for
a while, but dissembled to keep his see, as did many other Palestinian bishops. (8) For their sakes Acacius and his friends, though
they were infected with the same madness and insane heresy, did
not agitate these issues for the time being, and < did not dare >
either to confess or to deny < the homoousion >. But at the Emperor
Constantius' command they met at the town in Isauria called Rugged
Seleucia and issued another creed, if you please[107]—a creed not
in agreement with the one the fathers had drawn up in the city
of Nicaea, which was orthodox and well drawn. Instead, they said
with feigned simplicity, (24,1) *We believe in one God the Father almighty,* and next simply, *And [we believe] in the Son of God,* without
saying anything of weight about him.[108] But later, to give a glimpse
of their device, they said, *We reject the homoousion as untrue to sacred
scripture, but condemn the doctrine of the Son's unlikeness to the Father.*

---

[107] The Council of Seleucia was held in 359 by the eastern bishops, while
the western bishops were holding the Council of Ariminum. For its creed see
below at 25,6.

[108] The creed of Seleucia in fact reads, "And we also believe in our Lord Jesus
Christ, his Son, who was begotten of him. . ." etc. Epiphanius is either misin-
formed, or tendentious, at this point.

24,2   And this was the lure of crafty hunters. In fact, when they were by themselves they would assert and teach that the Son of God is a creature, but that he is "like" the Father in the common understanding of the term. (3) For even sculptors create images and produce likenesses, of gold, silver and other materials or of paint on wood, and they have the likeness of their models, but nothing to equal them. And so their strategy was to confess that the Son is "like" the Father, but without one bit of the Father's Godhead.

24,4   Some of their supporters accepted this < with hesitation* >, but still accepted it because of the misfortune of the time that had befallen them; and at the same time most knew what they were doing, though some were indeed in ignorance, as was shown later. For Patrophilus of Scythopolis was on their side, and after him Philip, who was consecrated there as his successor, and many others who really held this heresy. (5) Now, however, after their deaths, when their heresy has become widespread and they are free to speak because of the arm of flesh, they are stating their thesis plainly with no further hindrance, and are no longer restrained by any shame, or pretending because of an emperor's order. (6) < But > lest it be thought that I am attacking them for no good reason, I shall here give the creed which was issued there by Acacius' faction themselves, over the signature of the participants in the council. It is as follows:

(The synodical letter of Seleucia)[109]

25,1   *The bishops who have assembled at Seleucia in Isauria from various provinces at the command of his Reverence, our most God-fearing emperor Constantius. We, who have assembled at Seleucia in Isauria by the will of the emperor, have passed the following resolution:*

25,2   *Yesterday, the fifth before the Kalends of October, we made every effort, with all decorum, to preserve the peace of the church and, as our emperor Constantius, the most beloved of God, commanded us, produce a sound statement < of > the faith in the words of the prophets < and Gospels >, and add nothing contrary to the sacred scriptures to the creed of the church.*

25,3   *But certain persons abused some of us at the council, silenced*

---

[109] This is the encyclical issued by the Council of Seleucia September 27, 359, and represents the thinking of the Acacians. It is also found at Ath. Syn. 29.3–9; Soc. 2.40.8–17.

others and did not permit them to speak, locked some out against their will, were accompanied by deposed clerics from various provinces, and brought with them persons who had been uncanonically ordained. The session thus became full of clamor on every side, as the most illustrious count Leonas, and Lauricius, the most illustrious governor of the province, saw with their own eyes.

25,4 *< But > since the doctrines of the homoousion and homoeousion have troubled many in the past and do today, and it is further said that the novel doctrine of the Son's unlikeness to the Father is even now taught by some, we reject the homoousion as untrue to the scriptures, but condemn the doctrine of the unlikeness, and regard all who hold it as strangers to the church. (5) However, like the apostle who said, "He is the image of the invisible God,"[110] we plainly confess the likeness of the Son to the Father.*

25,6[111] *We confess and believe in one God, the Father almighty, maker of heaven and earth, things visible and invisible.*

25,7 *And we believe in our Lord Jesus Christ, the Son of God, begotten of him without passion before all ages, the divine Word, only-begotten God of God, light, life, truth, wisdom, power, by whom all things were made, things in heaven and things on earth, whether visible or invisible. (8) We believe that, to take away sin, he took flesh of the holy Virgin at the close of the ages and was made man. He suffered for our sins, rose again, was taken up into heaven, is seated at the right hand of the Father, and will come again with glory to judge the quick and the dead.*

25,9 *And we believe also in one Holy Spirit, whom our Lord and Savior Jesus Christ also termed the Paraclete, and whom he promised to send to the disciples after his ascension; and he sent him, and through him sanctifies the believers in the church, who are baptized in the name of the Father, and of the Son, and of the Holy Spirit.*

The catholic church knows that those who preach anything other than this creed are not her own.

25,10 *The readers will recognize that the creed formerly issued at Sirmium[112] in the presence of his Reverence, our emperor, is of a meaning equivalent to this.*

26,1 *Those who are here have signed this creed: Basil, Mark, George the bishop of Alexandria, Pancratius, Hypatian, and most of the bishops of the west.*

26,2 *I, George, bishop of Alexandria, have issued this creed. My profession is as it is set forth here.*

---

[110] Col. 1:15
[111] Hahn pp. 206–208
[112] I.e., the creed of the Second Council of Sirmium, issued in 351

*I, Acacius, bishop of Caesarea, have issued this creed. My profession
is as it is set forth here.*
Uranius, bishop of Tyre,
Eutychius, bishop of Eleutheropolis,
Zoilus, bishop of Larissa in Syria,
Seras, bishop of Paraetonium in Libya,
(3) Paul, bishop of Emisa,
Eustathius, bishop of Epiphania,
Irenaeus, bishop of Tripoli in Phoenicia,
Eusebius, bishop of Seleucia in Syria,
Eutychianus, bishop of Patara in Lycia,
Eustathius, bishop of Pinari and Sidymi,
(4) Basil, bishop of Kaunia in Lydia,
Peter, bishop of Hyppus in Palestine,
Stephen, bishop of Ptolemais in Libya,
Eudoxius, bishop of . . .
Apollonius, bishop of Oxyrynchus,
Theoctistus, bishop of Ostracine,
Leontius, bishop of < Tripoli in > Lydia,
(5) Theodosius, bishop of Philadelphia in Lydia,
Phoebus, bishop of Polychalandus in Lydia,
Magnus, bishop of Themisi in Phrygia,
Evagrius, bishop of Mitylene of the islands,
(6) Cyrion, bishop of Doliche,
Augustus, bishop of Euphrates,
Polydeuces, bishop . . . of the second province of Libya,
Pancras, bishop of Pelusium,
(7) Philicadus, bishop of Augustus in the province of Phrygia,
Serapion, bishop of Antipyrgus in Libya,
Eusebius, bishop of Sebaste in Palestine,
Heliodorus, bishop of Sozusa in Pentapolis,
Ptolemais, bishop of Thmuis in Augustamnica,
(8) Abgar, bishop of Cyrus in Euphrasia,
Exeresius, bishop of Gerasa,
Arabio, bishop of Adrai,
Charisius, bishop of Azotus,
Elisha, bishop of Diocletianopolis,
Germanus, bishop of Petra,
Baruch, bishop of Arabia; forty-three bishops in all.[113]
So far the document issued by the above-mentioned Semi-Arians
and Arians.

---

[113] The list contains 43 names; George of Alexandria is mentioned twice.

27,1   You men of sense who have gone through this and the
other creeds, be aware that the effort of both parties is a fraud
and nothing orthodox, with even a bit of the godly confession of
faith. (2) For the Lord says, "What ye have heard in the ear, that
proclaim ye upon the housetops."[114] And as the holy apostle says,
"Speak every man truth with his neighbor;"[115] but the prophet speaks
out to expose their mischief, "He speaketh peace with his neighbor,
but in his heart hath he war."[116] (3) In the same way, when these
followers of Acacius wanted to cast off the restraint of the true
confession after their separation from Basil and his adherents, they
issued a spurious, easily refutable, and entirely misleading creed,
so that, if they wanted to fool people, they could make a proper
confession in the words we have given—(4) but if they chose to
reveal the banefulness of their heresy they would have this declaration available, which is midway between the two positions and
possible as a confession of each of their creations.

27,5   But since, in this Acacian faction which was separated from
the other two—I have said that the Arian party was divided into
three groups. Eudoxius, Germanus, George of Alexandria and
Euzoeus of Antioch made one division, (6) and similarly Eleusius,
Eustathius, George of Laodicea, Silvanus of Tarsus, Macedonius of
Constantinople and many others made another. (7) But again
Acacius, as I said, Melitius, Eutychius and certain others formed
another group of their own. And the whole thing was pure trickery. (8) What each of them believed, the other believed. But they
were divided into schisms among themselves, either from mutual
hatred, since Cyril of Jerusalem was furious with Eutychius and
Eutychius with Cyril, but Cyril was in with Basil of Galate, Anianus
the newly consecrated bishop of Antioch, and George of Laodicea—
(9) but why wear myself out distinguishing between the factions
and describing them? I shall go on to the counter-arguments, and
the refutation of the guile of each of them. First, though, I must
speak of what happened later, for this contributed to the goodness
of some, and the wickedness of others.

28,1   For when Melitius was consecrated at Antioch by Acacius—
and for Acacius this has been the beginning of his retreat, if only
slightly, from his heretical views. By his support of Melitius' elec-
tion he shows that, of all things, he is in the orthodox camp. As
I was saying, when Melitius was consecrated by Acacius' own friends

---

[114] Matt. 10:27
[115] Eph. 4:25
[116] Ps. 27:3

they thought he shared their opinion. But as many report of him, he turned out not to. (2) For at present, since Melitius has been hounded and expelled from his see, those who favor him and his party are gradually and progressively becoming orthodox for the sake of God, due to the protracted length of the banishment. (3) For there were more [orthodox] laity than there were laity † of the < other* > party.[117] They profess their faith in the Son admirably through their episcopal elections, and do not reject the homoousion. Indeed they are prepared to confess and not deny it, they say, if there can just be a last council. (4) In fact the most honorable Melitius himself, who was consecrated at Antioch by the Arians around Melitius, gave a sort of first installment of this in church, in his first sermon at Antioch, and in orthodox terms, or so say the majority. I offer his sermon here, as follows:

A Copy of Melitius' Sermon[118]

29,1   The most wise Ecclesiastes says, "The end of any speaking is better than its beginning."[119] How much better and safer is it to cease from a struggle over words than to begin one, especially as the same Ecclesiastes says, "This wisdom of the poor is set at naught, and his words are not heard."[120] (2) < But > since "The body is not one member, but many,"[121] "All the members care one for another that there be no schism in the body,"[122] and "The head cannot say to the feet, I have no need of you,"[123] but "God hath tempered the body together, giving the more abundant honor to the part which lacks,"[124] it goes without saying that one cannot avoid being troubled by the troubling of the whole body.

29,3   But how should one begin to speak to you? Plainly, it is fitting that whoever embarks on speech or action should make peace its beginning and end, and that those who begin with it should also close with it. "For this shall turn to your salvation," says the apostle, "through your prayer and the supply of the Spirit"[125] which Jesus gives to those who believe in him. (4) And whether one speaks words of edification, "consolation, comfort of love, or fellowship of the Spirit,"[126] he comes in the peace of God—not,

---

[117] Holl: τῶν τῆς < ἄλλης > συνόδου; MSS: τοῦ τῆς συνόδου
[118] This sermon appears to be referred to at Theod. H. E. 2.31.8, where, however, Melitius speaks at a sort of public debate before the emperor.
[119] Eccles. 7:8
[120] Eccles. 9:16
[121] 1 Cor. 12:14
[122] 1 Cor. 12:25
[123] 1 Cor. 12:21
[124] 1 Cor. 12:24
[125] Phil. 1:19
[126] Cf. Phil. 2:1.

indeed, for all without discrimination, but peace "for those who love the Law,"[127] *as the prophet says. Not the written Law, the "image and shadow of things to come,"*[128] *but the spiritual law which wisely reveals the outcome of the things that were foretold. (5) "For peace," says the scripture, "is multiplied to them that love thee, and they have none occasion of stumbling."*[129]

Plainly, for those who hate peace, the occasion of stumbling remains, and it behooves those who long to be free from them to hold the love of the Lord before them as a shield. "For he himself is our peace, who hath made both one, and hath broken down the middle wall of partition, the enmity of the flesh, the Law of commandments contained in ordinances."[130] *(6) Nor is it possible to keep the commandment of the Lord without a prior love of God—for "If ye love me," says Christ, "keep my commandments."*[131] *Nor can the eyes or heart be enlightened unless the commandment enlightens them, for the scripture says, "The commandment of the Lord is clear, and giveth light unto the eyes."*[132] *Nor can one speak any truth unless he has Christ within him as the Speaker, in the words of him who says, "since ye seek a proof of Christ speaking in me"*[133]—*or rather, not simply "speaking in me," but, "having mercy in me." (7) "Let thy mercy and thy salvation come upon me," says the scripture, "and I shall make answer unto them that rebuke me,"*[134] *though this cannot be unless one "seek his statutes."*[135] *For those who are not so disposed, < or > apparently so, there is shame in his rebukes, and they cannot say, "Take from me shame and rebuke."*[136] *Instead the word of truth is taken out of his mouth, so that there is nothing more for him who prays < than >, "Take not the word of thy truth out of my mouth."*[137]

30,1   And when is this? When < one > does not continually observe the Law—when one does not journey on open ground. For one's "heart must be broadened"[138] *if one is to have room for the Christ who "walks within him,"*[139] *whose glory, not men but the heavens declare, for "The heavens declare the glory of God"*[140]—*or rather, the Father himself declares*

---

[127] Cf. Ps. 118:165.
[128] Cf. Heb. 8:15; 10:1.
[129] Ps. 118:165
[130] Eph. 2:14–15
[131] John 14:15
[132] Ps. 18:9
[133] 2 Cor. 13:3
[134] Ps. 118:41–42
[135] Ps. 118:56; 94; 145; 155
[136] Cf. Ps. 118:22.
[137] Ps. 118:43
[138] Cf. Ps. 118:32 (2 Cor. 6:11).
[139] Cf. Lev. 26:12 (2 Cor. 6:16).
[140] Ps. 18:2

by saying, "This is my Son, the beloved, in whom I am well pleased."[141]
(2) But one cannot confess this [Son] "if he haughtily speaketh iniquity"[142]
to his neighbor, if he joins the band of the antichrists and † adopts[143] *their*
name, abandoning the band and name of the Christians, of whom it is
said, "Touch not mine anointed ones."[144] *(3) For "Who is a liar," the*
scripture asks, "save he that denieth that Jesus is the Christ? This," it says,
"is the antichrist. For whosoever denieth the Son, the same hath not the
Father: but he that acknowledgeth the Son acknowledgeth the Father also.
That which ye have heard from the beginning," it says, "let this abide in
you. And if that abideth in you which ye have heard from the beginning,
ye also shall abide in the Son and in the Father."[145]

30,4   *But we shall "abide" when we confess before God and his elect*
angels—indeed, confess before kings, and not be ashamed, for the scripture
says, "I have spoken of thy testimonies before kings and was not ashamed."[146]
[We shall abide] when we confess that the Son of God is God of God,
One of One, Only-begotten of Ingenerate, the elect Offspring of his Begetter
and a Son worthy of him who has no beginning; the ineffable Interpreter
of the Ineffable, the Word, and the Wisdom and Power of Him who transcends
wisdom and power, beyond anything that the tongue can utter, beyond any
thought the mind can initiate. (5) He is the perfect and abiding Offspring
of Him who is perfect, and abides the same—not an overflow of the Father
or a bit or piece of the Father, but come forth without passion and entire,
from him who has lost none of what he had. (6) And because < the >
Son is, and is called, the "Word," he is by no means to be conceived of
as the Father's voice or verbal expression. For he subsists in himself and
acts, and by him and in him are all things. Similarly, although he is
Wisdom as well, he is not to be conceived of as the Father's thought, or
as a movement and activity of his reason, but as an Offspring who is
like the Father and bears the exact impress of the Father. (7) For the Father,
God, has sealed him; and he neither inheres in another nor subsists by
himself, but < is > an Offspring at work, who has made this universe and
preserves it. This is sufficient to free us from the error of the Greeks, the
willful worship of the Jews, and the heresy of the sectarians.

31,1   *But since some pervert the sense of the scriptural expressions,*
interpret them otherwise than is fitting, and understand neither the mean-
ing of the words nor the nature of the facts, they dare to deny the Son's
divinity because they stumble at the mention of creation in Proverbs, "The

---

[141] Matt. 3:17
[142] Ps. 72:8
[143] Holl: τάξειεν; R: καλέσειεν; MSS: ὁμολογήσειεν
[144] Ps. 104:15
[145] 1 John 2:22–24
[146] Ps. 118:46

Lord created me the beginning of his ways, for his works. "[147] *(They should follow the Spirit who gives life, and not the letter which kills, for "The Spirit giveth life.")*[148] *(2) Let me also, then, venture on a short discussion of this, not because it has < not > been fully discussed by those who have spoken before me—to say this, one would be mad!—and not because you are in need of a teacher, for "Ye yourselves are taught of God,"*[149] *but so that I may be "manifest in your consciences."*[150] *For I am one of those who desire to "impart unto you some spiritual gift."*[151]

31,3   *Believe me, neither elsewhere in the scripture nor here do the words of scripture contradict each other, even though, to those of unsound faith or weak wits, they may seem to be in conflict. Believe me also, it is not possible to find in this world an example adequate in itself to explain clearly the nature of the Only-begotten. (4) And for this reason the scripture employs many ideas and terms with reference to the Only-begotten, to help us grasp things that are above us with the aid of things familiar to us; to imagine things we do not know by means of things we do; and to advance, gently and by easy stages, from the seen to the unseen.*

31,5   *Believers in Christ, then, should < know > that the Son is like the Father, since he who is "through all," and by whom all things in heaven and earth were made, is the "image" of him who is "above all."*[152] *But [they should know] that he is an image, not as an inanimate object is the image of a living thing, or as a process is the image of an art, or a finished product the image of a process, but < as > an offspring is the image of its parent. (6) And [they should know] that the generation of the Only-begotten before the ages may not lawfully be portrayed < along the lines of > bodily human generation. And as < the Son is the* > Father's < wisdom* > in the pattern of the wisdom which embraces human thoughts, and though he is certainly not without a real existence of his own, the scripture made use of both terms, that of creation and that of generation, "He created me" and "He begot me." This was not to give the appearance of saying contraries about the same things and at the same time, but to show the real and enduring existence of the Only-begotten through "created," and his special and individual character through "begot." (7) For he says, "I proceeded forth from the Father and am come."*[153] *The very word, "wisdom," however, is enough to exclude any idea of passion.*

32,1   *But whither are we bound with our failure to remember him who*

---

[147] Prov. 8:22
[148] 2 Cor. 3:6
[149] 1 Thes. 4:9
[150] 2 Cor. 5:11
[151] Rom. 1:11
[152] Col. 1:15; Eph. 4:6; Rom. 9:5
[153] John 8:42

said, "O the depth of the riches both of the wisdom and knowledge of God! How unsearchable are his judgments, and his ways past finding out!"[154] (2) We have the Spirit of truth for our teacher, whom the Lord gave us after his assumption into the heavens, that we might "know the things that are freely given to us of God."[155] In him "we likewise speak, not in words which man's wisdom teacheth, but which the Spirit teacheth, comparing spiritual things with spiritual."[156] In him we serve and worship, for his sake we are despised, in him the prophets prophesied, in him by whom we are brought to the Son, the righteous have been guided.

But why do we meddle with nature? Am I speaking as with carnal persons, not spiritual? (3) "We cannot speak unto you as unto spiritual but as unto carnal,"[157] was said of others. It is to be feared that, from our contention over the incomprehensible and dispute about the unsearchable, we may fall into the depths of impiety. "And I said, I will get wisdom, and it was farther from me than that which was before, and its depth was unsearchable; who shall find it out?"[158] Let us be mindful of him who said, (4) "We know in part, and we prophesy in part. But when that which is perfect is come, then that which is in part shall be done away."[159] "If any man think that he knoweth, he knoweth nothing yet as he ought to know."[160] It is therefore to be feared that, if we attempt to speak of what we cannot, we may no longer be permitted to speak of what we can. We must speak because of faith, not believe because of what is spoken, for scripture says, "I believed, and therefore did I speak."[161]

32,5   Thus when we inquire, and try to contend, about the generation of God although we cannot describe our own, how can we avoid the risk that he who has given us not only "the tongue of instruction," but also the "knowledge of when to say a word,"[162] may condemn us to silence for our rashness of speech. (6) Such was the case with the blessed Zacharias. As he disbelieved the angel who had announced the child's conception, tested the grace and power of God by human reasonings, and despaired of his ability to father a child in his old age by an aged wife, what did he say? (7) "How shall I know that this will be? For I am old, and my wife well stricken in years."[163] And thus, since he was told, "Thou shalt

---

[154] Rom. 11:33
[155] 1 Cor. 2:12
[156] 1 Cor. 2:13
[157] Cf. 1 Cor. 3:1
[158] Eccles. 7:23–24
[159] 1 Cor. 13:9–10
[160] 1 Cor. 8:2
[161] Ps. 115:1 (2 Cor. 4:13)
[162] Isa. 50:4
[163] Luke 1:18

be dumb and not able to speak,"[164] *he could not speak when he left the temple.*

33,1   *We therefore cease to wrangle over the questions in dispute and the matters that are beyond us, and hold fast what we have received. Who dare be puffed up over knowledge, when even he who was vouchsafed "revelations," who was caught up "to the third heaven" and "heard unspeakable words," was recalled to his senses by his "thorn in the flesh," so as not to be "puffed up above measure?"*[165] (2) *The very prophet who said, "I believed, and therefore have I spoken," also said, "I was afflicted"— and not simply "afflicted," but "sore afflicted."*[166] *The nearer one's apparent approach to knowledge, the more should he reckon with his humanity. Hear the prophet say of him, "I said in my astonishment, All men are liars."*[167]

33,3   *Since we have the Teacher of the truth, let us make no further use of the teachings of men. Let us realize < our limitation, believe* >, and waste no more effort on "modes," or anything else. As we cannot say how the Son was generated or describe the mode of the Father's generation, we < must > consider "All things were made by him, and without him was not anything made"*[168] *as sufficient for teaching.*

33,4   *The Lord grant that with a spirit like Abraham's, who said, "Now I have begun to speak with the Lord, though I am dust and ashes"*[169]*— and not "exalted as the cedars of Lebanon,"*[170] *since equable, peaceable wisdom is not attained "by words which man's wisdom teacheth, but which faith teacheth"*[171]*—we inquire (5) only into what we must do to please our God and Father, and along with him, and together with him, < the Son > in the Holy Spirit, < to whom > be glory, might, honor and power, now, and forever, and to the ages of ages. Amen.*

The end of Melitius' sermon

34,1   To those < who had been eager > to bring Melitius from Pontus, it seemed that this < had > not < been said > to please or placate most of the Arians, but to annoy them. They then egged the emperor on, plotted against Melitius for not having confessed that the Son is a creature in the fullest sense of the word, and expelled him from his see. (2) He was driven into exile overnight,[172]

---

[164] Luke 1:20
[165] Cf. 2 Cor. 12:1 2; 4.
[166] Cf. Ps. 115:1.
[167] Ps. 115:2
[168] John 1:3
[169] Gen. 18:27
[170] Cf. Ps. 36:35.
[171] 1 Cor. 2:13
[172] Melitius was bishop of Antioch for less than a month, cf. Chrys. Panegyric on St. Melitius 1, MSG 50,516.

and is in exile to this day. Even now he resides in his own homeland, a man esteemed and beloved, especially because of the things
I am now told that he has accomplished, and which are the cause
of the confession his subjects in Antioch now make. They no longer
make even a passing mention of the word, "creature," but confess
that the Father, the Son and the Holy Spirit are co-essential—three
entities, one essence, one Godhead. (3) This is the true faith which
we have received from the ancients, the faith of the prophets,
Gospels and apostles, which our fathers and bishops confessed
when they met at the Council of Nicaea in the presence of the
great and most blessed emperor, Constantine. And may the most
honored Melitius himself make the same confession as his subjects
at Antioch and < those > who make it in certain other places! (4)[173]
For there are also some, apparently in communion with him and
his supporters, who blaspheme the Holy Spirit; and although they
speak correctly of the Son, they regard the Spirit as a creature and
altogether different from the Father. Later I shall give full information about them, as accurately as I can, in the refutation of the
heresy they hold.

35,1   As I said, I hold Melitius in honor for the good things
I have heard of him. And indeed his life is holy in the other
respects, he is well conducted, and is beloved in every way by the
laity for his way of life which all admire. (2) Some, however—I
do not know whether they are inspired by enmity, or jealousy, or
a desire to magnify themselves—[some] have said something about
him to the effect that the rebellion against him was not over his
orthodoxy, but because of canonical matters and the quarrel between
him and his priests, and because he received certain persons whom
he had previously expelled and condemned.[174] (3) But I have paid
no attention to this because, as I indicated above, of the rectifi-
cations and the confessions of the faith which, at long last, are
being made daily among his companions.

For I must tell the truth in this regard, as far as my weakness
in everything allows. (4) Suppose that he overlooked < something >
in the rush of the words of his exposition—I cannot say. Or suppose
that, in all innocence, a word escaped him—God knows. In one
way, two or three remarks in this exposition are questionable—
his treating at all, even nominally, of the Son of God in his divine
nature as a "creature," and his saying, "above wisdom," and perhaps something else.

---

[173] This paragraph is numbered 5 in Holl.
[174] Philost. 5;5: Jer. Chron. ed. Helm pp. 241–242

36,1 But I shall say a little about their allegations and get finished with this discussion. Tell us, people, why would it disturb you to say that the homoeousion is the homoousion? Confess your faith plainly, to let us know that you belong to us, and are not strangers. Brass can be of an essence *like* gold, tin of an essence *like* silver, lead of an essence *like* iron—but the story you have concocted and turned out will not fool us. (2) For if you want to fool people, you < make > the false excuses that we must not say, "homoousion," or we will make the Son identical with the Father, or the Spirit identical with the Son and the Father. Here too the argument you have invented fails. (3) We say, not, "identically essential,"[175] but, "co-essential," to confess, not that < the Son > is any different from the Father, but that he is God actually begotten of God—not originating from some other source or from nothing, but come forth < from > the Father. He was begotten at no time, without beginning, and inexpressibly, is forever with the Father and never ceases to be, but is begotten, and not his Father's kinsman or progenitor.

36,4 For "homo" means that there are two entities, < but > not different in nature. Thus the true union [of the two essences] revealed by the Holy Spirit, through the expression in the mouths of those who use the expression. And you see that you will have no excuse, and cannot speak against orthodoxy and frighten your followers who accept your false argument, [by claiming] that whoever says, "homoousion," has professed faith in an identity. (5) No way! [That there are] two will be shown by "*homo*ousion;" that the Offspring is not different from the Father will also be indicated by "homoousion."

36,6 But because of the word, "essence," you will be convicted of fabricating the homoeousion; and because of your altered confession of faith you will be condemned for not meaning what you say, but falsifying the teaching of what you mean. For if you mean that the Son is not of the Father at all, but is *like* him instead, you are a long way from the truth. (7) If one chooses to decorate a relief with any materials, no matter which, he cannot make it the same as the relief; indeed, the work is one of fabrication. But something begotten of something else retains the likeness of genus and the sameness of species which characterize true sonship. (8) Now if you say that the Son is not begotten of the Father himself but must be outside of him, and call him "of like essence" to do him a favor, you have given him nothing, but have been deprived

---

[175] ἀμαούσιον

of his favor. (9) "He that honoreth not the Son as the Father honoreth him," says the holy apostle, "the wrath of God abideth on him."[176] And again, he who said, "I proceeded forth from the Father and am come,"[177] [said] "I am in the Father and the Father in me"[178] in the same breath as, "Philip, he that hath seen me hath seen the Father."[179]

37,1 Since I have often discussed these things, I believe that will be enough of the same refutations here. The same ones I applied earlier to the root that put forth their heresy are capable of demolishing these Semi-Arians here—[them], and the ones who split off from them, (2) Acacius' friends and the others who issued a creed at Seleucia in Isauria which is contrary to the true one. Because I wanted bring it to light, I have also inserted the whole of the creed they issued at the end, after the creed of Basil of Ancyra and George of Laodicea which was written as representing them all. (3) But lest it appear that when I put this in the second place I did it from forgetfulness—because it did its fearful damage secretly and accepted a gag as though to < restrain its own teachings > with a bridle in the time of hypocrisy—I shall also say a little about it and its authors, the allies of Acacius, Euzoeus, Eutychius and the rest. (4) And the document before us has plainly altered the confession of the truth. But lest it be said that I have slandered these people, let me point out what was discovered and what, as time went by, became evident in this group of theirs.

37,5 One of them is Euzoeus of Caesarea, who is their disciple and Acacius' successor. [That was] after the consecration of Philumen, who was consecrated by Cyril of Jerusalem; and the consecration of the elderly Cyril who was consecrated by Eutychius and his friends; and the consecration of Gelasius who, once more, was consecrated by Cyril of Jerusalem. He was the son of Cyril's sister. After the consecration of these three and their suspension because of the quarrel between them, Euzoeus was consecrated in his turn. (6) Gemellinus was also one of them, and Philip of Scythopolis, and Athanasius of Scythopolis. These not only teach Arianism publicly and not in secret, as though they had never heard of anything better; they do battle for their heresy, what is more, and persecute those who teach the truth. They are no longer willing merely to refute orthodox believers verbally, but subject them to feuds, violence and murder. For they have done harm, not in one city and country

---

[176] John 5:23; 3:36
[177] John 8:42
[178] John 14:10
[179] John 14:9

but in many. (38,1) < And* > this Lucius, who has done so much
to those who confess the Son of God at Alexandria, is < one of
them* >.

Who, if he has God's good sense, can fail to see < the dreadful
things* > their fraternity < is doing* > every day? They preach in
public that the Son of God is a creature, and that the Holy Spirit
is a creature as well, and entirely different from the essence of
God. (2) < There is no need for me even to speak of all that* >
Eudoxius and his friends < are doing* > since George met his
shameful end at Alexandria and Eudoxius received the headship,
and the perquisites of high office. < He > was one of the group
around Hypatius and Eunomius, and to flatter them pretended
to be convinced; < but >, though he kept it a secret, he never
ceased to believe in the doctrines of the Anomoeans. (3) And he
himself promoted Demophilus, Hypatius and Eunomius, men whom
they had once exiled for this criminal exposition [of the creed].
They were disciples of Aetius, who was once exiled to the Taurus.
He was made a deacon by George of Alexandria, and the root of
the Anomoeans grew up from him. (4) As there is one thorny stem
and the same root, but it < bears* > schisms of different kinds as
though on each thorn, so it is with their malice. It has disgorged
this filth into the world < by putting forth* >, differently at different times, the misinterpretations of this heretical sect, which keep
getting worse. I shall say this again later about these Anomoeans.

38,5 But I think that for now, this much will do. Since we have
scotched and maimed this sect like a horrid serpent let us † stomp
on it,[180] leave it dead after trampling it, and turn away to hurry
on to the rest, likewise calling on God to help us keep our promise.

Against Pneumatomachi.[1] 54, but 74 of the series.

1,1 A sort of monstrous, half-formed people with two natures, as
the mythographers < described > the Centaurs, Pans and Sirens,
have been born to these Semi-Arians and orthodox believers, and
have risen up against us. (2) Some are Arian—though, if you please,
they declare that the Son is not a creature in the full sense of the
word, but a Son begotten outside of time. But they say with a hint

---

[180] Holl: συντρίψωμεν; MSS: ἀνετρέψαμεν

[1] This Sect is Epiphanius' comment on a controversy in which he was personally involved. Its main literary source, and the bulk of the Sect, is an excerpt
from Epiphanius' own work, the Ancoratus.

of time that he < has been in existence > † from of old[2] until now,
but that He "by whom all things were made"[3] was before all time,
and have thus by no means abandoned the formula originally spat
out by Arius, which said that "There was a time when was not;"
and they blaspheme the Holy Spirit < by saying that the Spirit is
a creature >. (3) Others hold the truly orthodox view of the Son,
that he was forever with the Father and has never ceased to exist,
but † has been begotten[4] without beginning and not in time. But
all of these blaspheme the Holy Spirit, and do not count him in
the Godhead with the Father and the Son.

1,4 I often have discussed this extensively, and have given
authoritative proof, at considerable length, in every Sect, that he
is to be called, "Lord," with the Father and the Son. For the "Spirit
of the Lord filleth the whole world"[5]—the "Spirit of truth,"[6] the
Spirit of God. He is called the Spirit of the Lord, who "proceeds
from the Father and receives of the Son,"[7] "giveth gifts severally
as he will,"[8] "searcheth the deep things of God,"[9] and is with the
Father and the Son, baptizing, sealing, and perfecting him whom
he has sealed. (5) But to keep from assuming a burden here, I
shall offer, for the reader's instruction and the enjoyment of those
who have been vouchsafed the Holy Spirit, the things I have already
said in opposition to the Spirit's blasphemers in my long work on
the faith, which I wrote [in the form of a letter] to Pamphylia.
It is as follows:

Excerpt from the Ancoratus[10]

2,1 *"The grace of our Lord Jesus Christ hath appeared, teaching us that,
denying ungodliness and worldly lusts, we should live soberly, godly and
righteously in this present world, looking for the blessed hope, and the
glorious appearing of the great God and our Savior Jesus Christ; who gave
himself for us, that he might redeem us from all iniquity, and purify unto
himself a peculiar people, zealous of good works."*[11] (2) He *"blotted out
the handwriting of ordinances, which was against us, and took it out of*

---

[2] Holl: ἀπ᾽ αἰῶνος; MSS: ἀπ᾽ οὐρανοῦ
[3] John 1:3
[4] Holl: ἐστὶ γεγεννημένος; MSS: αὐτὸ γεγεννημένον
[5] Wisd. Sol. 1:7
[6] John 16:13
[7] Cf. John 15:26; 16:14.
[8] Cf. 1 Cor. 12:11.
[9] 1 Cor. 2:10
[10] Anc. 65,1–73,9
[11] Tit. 2:11–14

the way, nailing it to his cross; and having spoiled principalities and powers he made a show of them openly, triumphing over them in it."[12] "He hath broken the gates of brass and burst the bars of iron in sunder."[13] He made the light of life visible again, stretching forth his hand, showing the way, baring the foundations of heaven and demanding a dwelling place in Paradise once more. He therefore also caused "the righteousness of the Law"[14] "to dwell in us,"[15] (3) and has given us the Spirit, so that we may know him and the truth about him. That is, he has become the beginning and end of our life, our "law of righteousness,"[16] "law of faith,"[17] and "law of the Spirit,"[18] free from the "law of the flesh of sin."[19]

2,4   Therefore "I delight in the law of God after the inward man."[20] But our inward man is Christ, provided that he dwells in us. (5) For it is he who, by dying, became our way to life "that they which live should not henceforth live unto themselves, but unto" the Cause of life, "who died for them, and rose again."[21] "Mindful of the oath which," as David said, "he sware many generations before"[22] "God was in Christ, reconciling the world unto himself, not imputing their transgressions unto them."[23]

2,6   "For it pleased the Father than in him should all fullness dwell, and by him to reconcile all things unto himself, having made peace through the blood of the cross."[24] (7) He came, then, "for the dispensation of the fullness of the times," as he promised to Abraham and the other saints, "to gather in one all things in him, things which are in heaven and things which are on earth."[25] (8) There was estrangement and enmity "during the [time of the] forbearance of God,"[26] but he "reconciled them in the body of his flesh, making both one through him. For he came to be our peace,"[27] and "as he who broke down the middle wall of partition, who abolished enmity in his flesh, the law of commandments contained in ordinances, for to make the twain one new man in himself."[28] And he commanded that the gentiles be "of the same body, and fellow partakers and fellow heirs

---

[12] Col. 2:14–15
[13] Cf. Isa. 45:2.
[14] Cf. Rom. 8:4.
[15] Cf. John 1:14.
[16] Rom. 9:31
[17] Rom. 3:27
[18] Rom. 8:2
[19] Rom. 7:25
[20] Rom. 7:22
[21] 2 Cor. 5:15
[22] Cf. Heb. 5:9; Ps. 104:8–9.
[23] 2 Cor. 5:19
[24] Col. 1:19–20
[25] Eph. 1:10
[26] Rom. 3:26
[27] Eph. 2:14
[28] Eph. 2:14–15

of the promise"[29] by saying, "Come unto me, all ye that labor and are heavy laden, and I will give you rest."[30] (9) And so "while I was weak, through the flesh,"[31] a Savior was sent to me "in the likeness of sinful flesh,"[32] and performed this gracious work, to "redeem"[33] me from slavery, corruption, death. And he became my "righteousness, sanctification and redemption."[34] (10) Righteousness, by destroying sin through faith in him; sanctification, by setting us free through water and Spirit, and by his word; redemption, by giving his blood, giving himself for me as a true lamb, an expiation for the world's cleansing, for the reconciliation of all in heaven and on earth, and so fulfilling, at the appointed time, the "mystery hidden before the ages and generations."[35] (11) And he "shall change our vile body, that it may be fashioned like unto his glorious body, according to the working whereby he is able even to subdue all things unto himself,"[36] for "In him dwelleth all the fullness of the Godhead bodily."[37]

3,1   Christ, the vessel of wisdom and of the Godhead, therefore as mediator "reconciles all things to God in him,"[38] "not imputing their trespasses,"[39] but fulfilling the hidden mysteries by faith in his covenant, which was foretold by the Law and the prophets. He is declared to be the Son of God, but called the Son of David, for he is both God and man, the "mediator between God and men,"[40] the true "house of God," the "holy priesthood."[41] He is the giver of the Holy Spirit, who in turn regenerates and renews all things for God; for "The Word was made flesh and dwelt among us, and we beheld his glory, even the glory of the Only-begotten of the Father."[42]

3,2   When the rain is absorbed by trees and plants it engenders bodies, each in the likeness of its fruit. The oil grows rich in the olive by receiving its essence from it, the sweet wine darkens in the vine, the fig sweetens on the fig tree, and [the rain] will generate new growth according to its kind in every seed. (3) So, I believe, God's Word was made flesh in Mary and became man in the seed of Abraham, in accordance with the promise, "We have found the Messiah of whom Moses did write."[43] As Moses said, "Let

---

[29] Eph. 3:6
[30] Matt. 12:28
[31] Rom. 8:3
[32] Rom. 8:3
[33] Cf. Gal. 4:5.
[34] 1 Cor. 1:30
[35] Col. 1:26
[36] Phil. 3:21
[37] Col. 2:9
[38] 2 Cor. 5:18
[39] 2 Cor. 5:19
[40] 1 Tim. 2:5
[41] 1 Pet. 2:5
[42] John 1:14
[43] John 1:41; 45

my word descend as the rain,"⁴⁴ (4) and David, "Let him come down as
dew on a fleece and, like drops watering the earth,"⁴⁵ the wool will then
increase the progeny of the fleece when it receives the dew. But when the
earth receives the rain, since it receives it by the Lord's command it will
increase the fruit for which husbandmen hope, yielding its essence gladly,
but in eagerness to receive more from him. (5) So, when the Virgin Mary
asked, "How shall I know that this will be to me?"⁴⁶ she was told, "The
Spirit of the Lord is upon thee, and the power of the highest shall overshadow thee. Therefore also that which shall be born of thee shall be holy,
and called, Son of the Most High.'"⁴⁷

3,6   Christ speaks in the angel, and by his fashioning of himself the
Lord refashions himself by "taking the form of a servant."⁴⁸ And Mary
absorbs the Word for conception as the earth absorbs the rain; but by taking
mortal nature God's Word makes himself a holy fruit. (7) He was [born]
of her who absorbed him, like earth and fleece—the fruit of the true hope,
awaited by the saints as Elizabeth said, "Blessed art thou among women,
and blessed is the fruit of thy womb."⁴⁹ This [fruit] the Word received from
humankind, and suffered although he was impassible. (8) He is the "living
bread which came down from heaven"⁵⁰ and gives life. He is the fruit of
the true olive, the oil of anointing and compounding, which, as a type,
Moses described.⁵¹ He is the "true vine"⁵² which only the Father tends, who
has produced a joyous vintage for us. (9) He is the "living water, after
taking which < the > man that thirsteth shall not thirst again, but it is
in his belly springing up into everlasting life."⁵³

The new husbandmen have taken of this water and given it to the world,
while the old husbandmen have withered and perished from unbelief. (10)
By his own blood he hallows the gentiles, but by his own Spirit he leads
the called to the heavens. "As many as live by the Spirit of God, they live
to God."⁵⁴ Those who are not so led are still reckoned as dead, and these
are called "natural" or "carnal."⁵⁵ (11) Christ commands us, then, to
abandon the works of the flesh which are the strongholds of sin, to put
to death the members of death by his grace, and to receive the Holy Spirit
which we did not have—the Spirit who gives me life, though I am long

---

⁴⁴ Deut. 32:2
⁴⁵ Ps. 71:6
⁴⁶ Luke 1:34
⁴⁷ Luke 1:35
⁴⁸ Phil. 2:7
⁴⁹ Luke 1:40
⁵⁰ John 6:51
⁵¹ Cf. Exod. 30:22–24.
⁵² John 15:1
⁵³ John 4:10; 13; 14
⁵⁴ Rom. 8:14
⁵⁵ 1 Cor. 2:14; 3:1; 3

dead and, unless I receive him, shall have died. For without his Spirit,
all are dead. (12) *"If, therefore, his Spirit be in us, he that raised him*
from the dead shall quicken our mortal bodies by his Spirit that dwelleth
in us."[56] *In my opinion, however, both dwell in the righteous—Christ, and*
his Spirit.

4,1 *If it is believed that Christ, as "God of God," is of the Father,*
and his Spirit is of Christ or of both—as Christ says, "who proceedeth from
the Father,"[57] *and, "He shall receive of me"*[58]*—and if it is believed that*
Christ is of the Holy Spirit—the angel's words are, "That which is conceived
in her is of the Holy Spirit"[59]*—[then] I know the Mystery that redeems*
me by faith, by hearing alone, by love for him who has come to me. (2)
For God knows himself, Christ proclaims himself, the Holy Spirit reveals
himself to the worthy.

A Trinity is proclaimed in the holy scriptures and is believed in with
all seriousness, without contention, by the hearing of the creeds. From this
faith comes salvation by grace—"righteousness is by faith without the works
of the Law."[60] *(3) < For > the scripture says that "the Spirit of Christ"*
is given to those who are saved "by the hearing of faith."[61] *(4) And in*
my opinion, as I am taught by the scriptures, the catholic faith is declared
by the voices of its heralds to be as follows:

Three Holies, three of equal holiness; three Actuals, three of equal actuality;
three Informed, three with the same form; three at work, three at one work;
three Subsistents, three of the same subsistence, in co-existence. This is called
a holy Trinity, one concord though they are three, one Godhead of the same
essence, the same divinity, the same subsistence, like [generated] of like,
resulting in the equality of the grace of the Father, of the Son, and of the
Holy Spirit.

To teach the how of this is left to them. (5) *"No man knoweth the Father*
save the Son; neither knoweth any man the Son, save the Father, and he
to whom the Son will reveal him."[62] *But he reveals him through the Holy*
Spirit. (6) *Thus, whether these Persons, who are three, are of him, from*
him, or with him is properly understood by each Person, just as they reveal
themselves as light, fire, wind, and I believe with other visionary likenesses,
as the seer is worthy. (7) *Thus the God who said "Let there be light" at*
the beginning, "and there was" visible "light,"[63] *is the same God who has*

---

56 Rom. 8:11
57 John 15:26
58 John 16:14
59 Matt. 1:20
60 Rom. 3:28
61 Gal. 3:2
62 Matt. 11:27
63 Gen. 1:3

given us the light to see "the true light, which lighteneth every man that cometh into the world"[64]—*"Send forth thy light and thy truth,"*[65] *says David—and the same Lord who said, "In the latter days I will pour out my Spirit upon all flesh, and their sons shall prophesy, and their daughters, and their young men shall see visions."*[66] *He has therefore shown us three Objects of sacred worship, of a triple subsistence.*

5,1 *"I say,"* therefore, *"that Christ was a minister of the circumcision for the truth of God, to confirm the promises."*[67] *But I understand from the sacred scriptures that the Holy Spirit is his fellow minister, for the following reasons. Christ is sent from the Father; the Holy Spirit is sent. Christ speaks in the saints; the Holy Spirit speaks. Christ heals; the Holy Spirit heals. Christ hallows; the Holy Spirit hallows. Christ baptizes in his name; the Holy Spirit baptizes.*

5,2 *The scriptures say, "Thou shalt send forth thy Spirit, and thou shalt renew the face of the earth,"*[68] *which is like saying, "Thou shalt send forth thy Word and melt them."*[69] (3) *"As they ministered to the Lord and fasted," says the scripture, "the Holy Spirit said, Separate me Barnabas and Saul for the work whereunto I have called them."*[70] *This is like saying, "The Lord said, Go into the city, and there it shall be told thee what thou must do."*[71] (4) *"So they, being sent forth by the Holy Spirit, departed unto Seleucia,"*[72] *is as much as to say, "Behold, I send you forth as sheep in the midst of wolves."*[73] (5) *"It seemed good to the Holy Spirit to lay upon you no greater burden than these necessary things,"*[74] *is as much as to say, "I say, yet not I, but the Lord, Let the wife not depart from her husband."*[75]

5,6 *"Now when they had gone throughout Phrygia and the region of Galatia, and were forbidden of the Holy Spirit to preach the word in Asia, after they were come to Mysia they assayed to go into Bithynia: but the Spirit suffered them not,"*[76] *is equivalent to Christ's saying, "Go, baptize all nations,"*[77] < or >, *"Carry neither scrip, nor staff, nor shoes."*[78] (7) *"Who*

---

[64] John 1:9
[65] Ps. 42:3
[66] Joel 2:28
[67] Rom. 15:8
[68] Ps. 103:30
[69] Ps. 147:7
[70] Acts 13:2
[71] Acts 9:6
[72] Acts 13:4
[73] Matt. 10:16
[74] Acts 15:28
[75] 1 Cor. 7:10
[76] Acts 16:6–7
[77] Matt. 28:19
[78] Matt. 10:10; Luke 10:4

said to Paul through the Spirit that he should not go up to Jerusalem"[79]—
or Agabus' prophecy, *"Thus saith the Holy Spirit, The man that owneth
this girdle"*[80]—*is equivalent to Paul's saying, "since ye seek a proof of
Christ speaking in me,"*[81] *or, "Remember the words of the Lord, that he
said, It is better to give than to receive."*[82]

5,8   *[Paul's], "And now, behold, I go bound in the Spirit"*[83] *is the
equivalent of his, "Paul, a prisoner of Jesus Christ."*[84] *(9) "Save that the
Holy Spirit witnesseth to me in every city,"*[85] *is equivalent to saying, "The
Lord testifieth to my soul that I lie not."*[86] *(10) [To say], "with power
according to the Spirit of holiness,"*[87] *is similar to saying, "Holy is he who
rests in the saints."*[88] *(11) [To say], "And circumcision is that of the heart,
in the Spirit,"*[89] *is similar to saying, "And ye are circumcised with the
circumcision made without hands, in the putting off the body of the sins
by the circumcision of Christ."*[90]

5,12   *[To say], "If so be that the Spirit of God dwelleth in you,"*[91] *is
similar to saying, "As ye have received Christ, walk ye in him."*[92] *And [to
say], "The Spirit of the Lord spake by me, and his word is in my mouth,"*[93]
(13) and "having the firstfruits of the Spirit,"[94] *is similar to saying, "Christ
is the firstfruits."*[95] *(14) [To say], "But the Spirit himself maketh intercession for us,"*[96] *is similar to saying, "who is on the right hand of God,
who also maketh intercession for us."*[97] *(15) [To say], "that the offering
up of the gentiles may be acceptable, being sanctified by the Holy Spirit,"*[98]
*is similar to saying, "Now the Lord sanctify you, that ye may be sincere
and without offense at the day of Christ."*[99] *(16) [To say], "But God hath
revealed them unto us by his Spirit,"*[100] *is similar to saying, "When it*

---

[79] Acts 21:4
[80] Acts 21:11
[81] 2 Cor. 13:3
[82] Acts 20:35
[83] Acts 20:22
[84] Philem. 1; Eph. 3:1
[85] Acts 20:23
[86] Cf. Gal. 1:20.
[87] Rom. 1:4
[88] Isa. 57:15
[89] Rom. 2:29
[90] Col. 2:11
[91] Cf. 1 Cor. 3:16.
[92] Col. 2:6
[93] 2 Kms. 23:2
[94] Rom. 8:23
[95] 1 Cor. 15:23
[96] Rom. 8:34
[97] Rom. 8:24
[98] Rom. 15:16
[99] Phil. 1:10
[100] 1 Cor. 2:10

pleased God, who separated me from my mother's womb and called me by his grace, to reveal his Son in me."[101] (17) *[To say], "Now we have received, not the spirit of the world, but the Spirit which is of God,"*[102] *is similar to saying, "Prove your own selves whether Christ be in you."*[103] (18) *[To say], "Ye are the temple of God, and the Spirit of God dwelleth in you,"*[104] *is similar to saying, "I will dwell in them and walk in them; and I will be their God, and they shall be my people."*[105]

6,1 *Paul says, moreover, that justification and grace come from both [the Son and the Holy Spirit]. [To say], "justified in the name of our Lord Jesus Christ and by the Spirit of our God"*[106] *is similar to saying, "Being justified by faith we have peace with God through our Lord Jesus Christ,"*[107] (2) *and "No man can say that Jesus is Lord but by the Holy Spirit;"*[108] *and no one can receive the Spirit except from the Lord. [To say], "There are diversities of gifts, but the same Spirit; there are differences of administrations, but the same Lord; and there are diversities of operations, but it is the same God which worketh all in all,"*[109] *"from glory to glory, even as by the Spirit of the Lord,"*[110] (3) *and "Grieve not the Holy Spirit, in whom ye are sealed unto the day of redemption,"*[111] *is similar to saying, "Do we provoke the Lord to jealousy? Are we stronger than he?"*[112]

6,4 *[To say], "The Spirit speaketh expressly,"*[113] *is like saying, "Thus saith the Lord, the almighty."*[114] (5) *To say, "The Spirit standeth within you,"*[115] *< is like saying >, "If any man open to me, I and the Father will come in and make our abode with him."*[116]

6,6 *Isaiah said, "And the Spirit of the Lord is upon him,"*[117] *but Christ said, "The Spirit of the Lord is upon me because he hath anointed me,"*[118] *"Jesus of Nazareth, whom God anointed with the Holy Spirit,"*[119] *or, "The Lord hath sent me, and his Spirit."*[120] (7) *And the voice of the seraphim,*

---

[101] Gal. 1:15
[102] 1 Cor. 2:12
[103] 2 Cor. 13:5
[104] 1 Cor. 2:16
[105] 2 Cor. 6:16
[106] 1 Cor. 6:11
[107] Rom. 5:1
[108] 1 Cor. 12:3
[109] 1 Cor. 12:4–6
[110] 2 Cor. 3:18
[111] Eph. 4:30
[112] 1 Cor. 10:22
[113] 1 Tim. 4:1
[114] Hag. 2:1
[115] Hag. 2:5
[116] Cf. Rev. 3:20; John 14:23.
[117] Isa. 11:2
[118] Luke 4:18
[119] Acts 10:38
[120] Isa. 48:16

which cries, "Holy, Holy, Holy is the Lord of Sabaoth," is an obvious example.[121]

6,8 *If you hear the words, "Being by the right hand of God exalted, having received of the Father the promise of the Spirit;"*[122] *or "Wait for the promise of the Father, which ye have heard,"*[123] *or "The Spirit driveth him into the wilderness;"*[124] *or the words of Christ himself, "Take no thought what ye shall say, for it is the Spirit of my Father that speaketh in you,"*[125] *or "If I cast out devils by the Spirit of God,"*[126] *or "He that shall blaspheme against the Holy Spirit hath never forgiveness,"*[127] *and so on—or "Father, into thy hands I shall commend my Spirit,"*[128] *or "The child grew and waxed strong in the Spirit,"*[129] *or "Jesus, being full of the Holy Spirit, returned from Jordan,"*[130] *or "Jesus returned in the power of the Spirit,"*[131] *or "That which is born of the Spirit is spirit;"*[132] *[any of this] is like saying, "That which was made, in him was life,"*[133] *or "And I will pray the Father, and he shall give you another Comforter, the Spirit of truth."*[134] *"Why hath Satan filled thine heart to lie to the Holy Spirit?"*[135] *as Peter said to Ananias, and further on, "Thou hast not lied unto men, but unto God."*[136] *In other words the Holy Spirit, to whom they lied by keeping part of the price of their land, is God of God, and is God, or "God was manifest in the flesh, justified in the Spirit"*[137]*—(9) I cannot give a better argument than this.*

The Son is God: the scripture says, "Of whom, as concerning the flesh, Christ came, who is over all God;"[138] *"Believe on the Lord Jesus, and thou shalt be saved,"*[139] *"He spake unto them the word of the Lord," and "When he had brought them into his house he set meat before them, and rejoiced, believing in God with all his house"*[140]*—or, "In the beginning was the Word, and the Word was with God, and the Word was God,"*[141] *or "The*

---

121 Isa. 6:3
122 Acts 2:33
123 Acts 1:4
124 Mark 1:12
125 Matt. 13:11
126 Matt. 12:28
127 Mark 3:29
128 Luke 23:46
129 Luke 1:80
130 Luke 4:1
131 Luke 4:14
132 John 3:6
133 John 1:3–4
134 John 14:16–17
135 Acts 5:3
136 Acts 5:4
137 1 Tim. 3:16
138 Rom. 9:5
139 Acts 16:31
140 Acts 16:32; 34
141 John 1:1

grace of our God and Savior hath appeared unto all men, teaching us,"[142] or "that they may adorn the doctrine of God our Savior in all things,"[143] or "looking for that blessed hope, and the glorious appearing of the great God and our Savior Jesus Christ."[144]

(6,10) But the service of the Spirit, and the service of the Word, is the same. [To say], "Take heed unto yourselves, and to all the flock, over the which the Holy Spirit hath made you overseers, to feed the church of God,"[145] is similar to saying, "I thank Christ Jesus our Lord, who hath enabled me, for that he counted me faithful, putting me into the ministry."[146]

7,1   As we have shown, the Son and the Holy Spirit work in cooperation with the Father: "By the Word of the Lord were the heavens established, and all the host of them by the Spirit of his mouth."[147] The Holy Spirit is an object of worship: "They that worship God must worship him in Spirit and in truth."[148] (2) But if the Spirit cooperates in the making of these things, a creature cannot make a creature; and the Godhead does not become a creature and is not known as God in some limited or circumscribed sense. For the Godhead is boundless, infinite and incomprehensible, and surpasses all that God has made. (3) Nor can a creature be an object of worship: "They worshiped the creature rather than the creator, and were made fools."[149] How can it not be foolish to make a god of a creature and break the first commandment, which says, "Hear, O Israel, the Lord thy God is one Lord,"[150] "There shall no strange god be in thee."[151]

7,4   However, there are various names in the sacred scriptures for the Father, the Son and the Holy Spirit. The Father's names are, "Father Almighty," "Father of all," "Father of Christ." The Son's are, "Word," "Christ," "true Light;" but the Holy Spirit's are, "Paraclete," "Spirit of truth," "Spirit of God," "Spirit of Christ." (5) Further, our God and Father is regarded as light—indeed, as brighter than light, power and wisdom. But if our God and Father is light, the Son is light of light and thus "dwelleth in light which no man can approach unto."[152] (6) But God is all power, and thus < the Son > is "Lord of powers."[153] God is all wisdom, and the Son is thus

---

142 Cf. Tit. 2:11–12.
143 Tit. 2:10
144 Tit. 2:13
145 Acts 20:28
146 1 Tim. 1:12
147 Ps. 32:6
148 John 4:24
149 Rom. 1:25; cf. v. 22.
150 Deut. 6:4
151 Ps. 80:10
152 1 Tim. 6:16
153 Ps. 58:6

wisdom of wisdom, "in whom are hid all the treasures of wisdom."[154] *God is all life, and the Son is thus life of life, for "I am the truth and the life."*[155]

7,7   *But the Holy Spirit is of both, as spirit of spirit. For "God is spirit,"*[156] *but † God's Spirit*[157] *is the giver of spiritual gifts, utterly true, enlightener, Paraclete, conveyor of the Father's counsels. (8) For as the Son is "angel of a great counsel,"*[158] *so is the Holy Spirit. Scripture says, "Now we have received the Spirit of God, that we might know the things that are freely given to us of God. Which things also we speak, not with the persuasion of words of wisdom, but in demonstration of the Spirit of God, comparing spiritual things with spiritual."*[159]

8,1   *But someone will say, "Then are we talking about two Sons? Why 'Only'-begotten?" "Nay, but who art thou that reckonest contrary to God?"*[160] *If God calls the One who is of him, the Son, and the One who is of Both, the Holy Spirit—things understood by the saints alone, by faith—things which are light, which give light, which have the power to enlighten, and create a harmony of light with the Father himself! (2) [If this is so], Sir, hear with faith that the Father is the Father of a true Son and is all light, and that < the > Son is the < Son > of a true Father and is light of light, [and] not merely in name, as artifacts or created things are. And the Holy Spirit is the Spirit of truth, a third light, from the Father and the Son.*

8,3   *But all the other ["sons" and "spirits"] are such by adoption or in name, and are not [sons or spirits] like these, in actuality, power, light or meaning, as one might say, "I have begotten sons and raised them up,"*[161] *"I have said, Ye are gods and ye are all children of the Most High,"*[162] *"Who hath begotten drops of dew,"*[163] *"of whom [is] the whole family in heaven and earth,"*[164] *or "I that establish thunder and create spirit."*[165] *(4) For the true Father has not begun to be a father [at some particular time], like the other fathers or patriarchs; nor does he ever cease to be a father. For if he begins to be a father he was at one time the son of another father, before being the Father of an Only-begotten himself. But fathers are presumed to be children in the likeness of their fathers, and*

---

154 Col. 2:3
155 John 14:6
156 John 4:24
157 Holl: πνεῦμα δὲ θεοῦ; MSS: θεότης
158 Isa. 9:5
159 1 Cor. 2:12–13 and 12:4
160 Cf. Rom. 9:20.
161 Isa. 1:2
162 Ps. 81:6
163 Job 38:28
164 Eph. 3:15
165 Am. 4:13

arriving at the true father of this ancient history is an endless process.

8,5 *Nor is the true Son new at being a son, like the others, who are children by adoption. For if he is new at being a son, there was a time when the Father was not the Father of an Only-begotten.*

8,6 *And the Spirit of truth is not created or made, like the other spirits, or called "the angel of the great counsel"*[166] *in the same sense as the other "angels." (7) Some things have a beginning and an end, but others have rule, (i.e.,* ἀρχή *playing on "beginning") and might of an inconceivable kind. Some create all things for endless ages, in cooperation with the Father; others are created by these, as they will. Some worship the creators; others are fit for worship by all creatures. Some heal created things; others receive healing from the former. (8) Some are judged in accordance with their deserts; others have the power of righteous judgment. And some things are < in > time; others are not in time. Some illumine all; others are illumined by them. Some summon babes on high; others are summoned by Him who is Mature. Some grant favors to all; others receive favors. And in a word, some hymn the Holiness in the heavens of heavens and the other invisible realms; others are hymned, and bestow their gifts on the worthy.*

9,1 *But the scripture speaks of a great many spirits. [It says], "who maketh his angels spirits, and his ministers a flame of fire,"*[167] *and "Praise the Lord, all ye spirits."*[168] *(2) The gift of "discernment of spirits"*[169] *is given to the worthy. Some spirits are heavenly and "rejoice in the truth;"*[170] *some are of the earth and apt at deceit and error. Some are subterrestrial, children of the abyss and darkness. For the Gospel says, "They besought him that he would not send them away to go out into the abyss,"*[171] *and he accordingly gave the spirits this command. And he cast out spirits with a word and "suffered them not to speak."*[172]

9,3 *We are told of "a spirit of judgment and a spirit of burning."*[173] *We are also told of a spirit of the world—"We have not received the spirit of the world,"*[174] *says scripture—and a spirit of man: "What man knoweth the things of a man save the spirit of man which is in him?"*[175] *[We are told of] "a spirit that passeth away and cometh not again,"*[176] *"for the spirit hath passed through him and he shall not be,"*[177] *and "Thou shalt*

---

[166] Isa. 9:5
[167] Ps. 103:4
[168] Cf. Ps. 150:6.
[169] 1 Cor. 12:10.
[170] Cf. 1 Cor. 13:6
[171] Luke 8:31; cf. Mark 5:10.
[172] Luke 4:41
[173] Isa. 4:4
[174] 1 Cor. 2:12
[175] 1 Cor. 2:11
[176] Ps. 77:39
[177] Ps. 102:16

take away their spirits and they shall perish. "[178]

9,4   And "*Spirits of prophets are subject to prophets,* "[179] *and* "*Behold, a lying spirit stood before the Lord, and he said unto him, Wherewith shalt thou deceive Ahab? And he said, I will be a lying spirit in the mouth of the prophets.* "[180]

9,5   *We are told of a* "*spirit of compunction,* "[181] *a* "*spirit of fear,* "[182] *a* "*spirit of divination,* "[183] *a* "*spirit of fornication,* "[184] *a* "*spirit of tempest,* "[185] *a* "*talkative spirit,* "[186] *a* "*spirit of infirmity,* "[187] *an* "*unclean spirit,* "[188] *a* "*deaf and dumb spirit,* "[189] *a* "*spirit with an impediment in its speech,* "[190] *a* "*spirit exceeding fierce, which is called Legion,* "[191] *and the* "*spiritual forces of wickedness.* "[192] *There is no end to what the wise have said about spirits.*

9,6   *But just as most* "*sons* " *are sons by adoption or in name but not actual sons, since they have beginnings and ends and < were conceived > in sin, so most spirits are spirits by adoption or in name—even though they are sinful. Only the Holy Spirit, however, is called the* "*Spirit of truth,* " "*Spirit of God,* " "*Spirit of Christ* " *and* "*Spirit of grace* " *by the Father and the Son. (7) For he graciously gives good to each in various ways—"to one a spirit of wisdom, to another a spirit of knowledge, to another a spirit of might, to another a spirit of healings, to another a spirit of prophecy, to another a spirit of discernment, to another a spirit of tongues, to another a spirit of interpretations,* "[193] *and as the scripture says,* "*One and the selfsame Spirit* " *[grants] the rest of the gracious gifts,* "*dividing to every man severally as he will.* "[194] (8) *For as David says,* "*Thy good Spirit, O God, will guide me,* "[195] *or* "*The Spirit doth breathe where he will*"—*with words like these he has shown us the Holy Spirit's reality—"and thou hearest his voice, but canst not tell whence he cometh or whither he goeth.* "[196]

---

[178] Ps. 103:24
[179] 1 Cor. 14:32
[180] 3 Kms. 22:21–22
[181] Isa. 29:10 (Rom. 11:8)
[182] 2 Tim. 1:7
[183] Acts 16:16
[184] Hos. 4:12
[185] Ps. 10:6
[186] Job 8:2
[187] Luke 13:11
[188] Mark 1:23 et al
[189] Mark 9:25
[190] Cf. Mark 7:32.
[191] Matt. 8:28; Mark 5:9; Luke 8:30
[192] Eph. 6:12
[193] Cf. 1 Cor.12:8–10.
[194] 1 Cor. 12:11
[195] Ps 142:10
[196] John 3:8

And the words, "except ye be born of water and the Spirit"[197] *are similar to Paul's, "In Christ Jesus I begot you."*[198]

9,9 *Of the Holy Spirit, the Lord said, "When the Comforter is come, whom I will send unto you from the Father, even the Spirit of truth which proceedeth from the Father, he shall testify of me,"*[199] *and "I have yet many things to say unto you, but ye cannot bear them now. When he, the Spirit of truth, is come, he shall guide you into all truth: for he shall not speak of himself, but whatsoever he shall hear, that shall he speak, and he will show you things to come. He shall glorify me, for he shall receive of mine and shall show it unto you."*[200]

10,1 *Now if the Spirit proceeds from the Father and, as the Lord says, is to receive "of mine," (2) I will venture to say that, just as "No man knoweth the Father save the Son, nor the Son save the Father,"*[201] *so no one knows the Spirit except the Son from whom he receives and the Father from whom he proceeds. And no one knows the Son and the Father except the Holy Spirit who truly glorifies them, who teaches all things, who testifies of the Son, is from the Father, is of the Son, is the only guide to truth, the expounder of holy laws, instructor in the spiritual law, preceptor of the prophets, teacher of the apostles, enlightener with the Gospel's doctrines, elector of the saints, true light of true light.*

10,3 *The Son is a real Son, a true Son, a legitimate Son, the unique Son of a unique Father. With him also is the Spirit— < not a Son >, but termed, "Spirit." (4) This is the God who is glorified in the church: Father forever, Son forever, Holy Spirit forever; Sublime < of > Sublime, and the Most High; spiritual, of glory unbounded; the One to whom all that is created and made—in a word, the universe with its measurements and each thing that is contained—is inferior.*

10,5 *The Godhead is chiefly declared to be a unity in the Law of Moses, but is vehemently proclaimed a binity in the prophets, and is revealed as a Trinity in the Gospels, for over the times and generations it accords more closely with the knowledge and faith of the righteous. And this knowledge is immortality, and adoption is by faith in it. (6) But as though it were erecting the temple's outer wall in the Law of Moses, it gives the ordinances of the flesh first of all. It expounds the ordinances of the soul second, as though it were putting the sacred objects in place in the remaining prophets. But third it gives the ordinances of the spirit, as though, in the Gospels, arranging the mercy seat and Holy of Holies for its dwelling,*

---

[197] John 3:5
[198] 1 Cor. 4:15
[199] John 15:26
[200] John 16:12–14
[201] Matt. 11:27

but as its holy tabernacle a holy people, < which > has none but the righteous
for its companions.*

10,7 *In this people there dwells one infinite Godhead, one imperishable
Godhead, one incomprehensible Godhead, unfathomable, inexpressible,
invisible. It alone knows itself; it reveals itself to whom it will. It raises
up its witnesses, calls, predestines and glorifies them, lifts them up from
hades, hallows them. (8) For its own glory and faith it makes these three
one: things in heaven, on earth, and under the earth; spirit, soul and
flesh; faith, hope and charity; past, present and future; the ages, the eternal
ages, and the ages of ages; Sabbaths of Sabbaths; the circumcision of the
flesh, the circumcision of the heart, and "the circumcision of Christ by the
putting off of the body of the sins."*[202] *(9) In a word, it purifies all things
for itself, things visible and invisible, thrones, dominions, principalities
authorities, powers. But in all is the same holy voice crying, "Holy, Holy,
Holy," from glory to glory, < to glorify > the Father in the Son, and the
Son in the Father with the Holy Spirit, to whom be glory and might unto
the ages of ages. Amen. And he who so believes will say "So be it! So be it!"*

11,1 And these are the things which I have already written,
with my extremely limited ability, in explanation of the faith in
the Father, the Son and the Holy Spirit, and have cited in the
preceding paragraphs. But as a testimony to my own salvation I
shall continue with the godly citation of texts, and the godly
discussion, based on right reason, of the Godhead.

11,2 [It is plain] that the Only-begotten has been shown by
many testimonies in the previous discussion to act in concert with
the Father, and to do the same things in all respects and grant
the same graces, since he is "of the Father," and is not different
from the Father's power and Godhead, but is co-essential with the
Father. And not only the Son—the Holy Spirit has been shown
to act in concert with the Son and the Father, to do the same
things, and to give and grant the same graces as he will, since he
too is truly "of God," and not different from the Father and the
Son, but co-essential with the Father and the Son. This is plain
to everyone, and has been and will be entirely proven by such a
large number of texts.

11,3 However, because of the Holy Spirit's opponents and
enemies I shall present the godly conclusions from right reason,
and the arguments from texts in the same sacred scripture, that
concern only the Holy Spirit, and present them in addition to the
other texts, in accordance with the true godly doctrine of the Holy
Spirit. (4) For as is the truth, the Holy Spirit too is unique, is

---

[202] Col. 2:11

worshiped by all, is beloved by all things created and made, and is not to be equated with anything—no angel, no spirit—but is one of a kind. (5) For there are indeed many spirits, but since the Holy Spirit is eternally of the Father, and is not engendered by other beings, which were made from nothing, this Spirit is high above all spirits. As there is one God, and one only-begotten Son of God, so there is < one > Holy Spirit of God, but *of* God and *in* God.

11,6   But the only-begotten Son is incomprehensible, and the Spirit is incomprehensible; however, he is of God, and is not different from the Father and the Son. He is not amalgamated with the Father and the Son; there is an eternal Trinity of the same essence, not an essence other than the Godhead and not a Godhead other than the essence, but the same Godhead. And of the same Godhead are the Son and the Holy Spirit. (7) And the Spirit is a holy spirit, but the Son is a son. The Spirit proceeds from the Father and receives of the Son, "searcheth the deep things of God,"[203] "sheweth"[204] the things of the Son to the world, and hallows the saints through the Trinity. He is third in the enumeration [of the Trinity]—the Trinity is the Father, the Son and the Holy Spirit, for scripture says, "Go baptize in the name of the Father, and of the Son, and of the Holy Spirit."[205] He is the confirmation of the grace (i.e., of baptism), different from its naming, and not other than its gift.[206] There is one God, one faith, one Lord, one gift, one church, one baptism.

12,1   For, as I have often said, the Trinity is forever a Trinity, and never receives an addition. It is sweet to confess this faith, and one never tires of saying it; for the prophet says, "Sweet are thy words unto my throat."[207] (2) And if the words are sweet, how much sweeter is the holy name, "Trinity," the fount of all sweetness? This, then, is the enumeration of the Trinity: "Father, Son and Holy Spirit." (3) The Trinity is not an amalgam and cannot be separated from its oneness, and yet the Father is perfect in the subsistence of perfection, the Son is perfect, the Holy Spirit is perfect—Father, Son and Holy Spirit. (4) Conversely, the Holy Spirit is enumerated among the spiritual gifts: "For there are diversities

---

[203] 1 Cor. 2:10
[204] Cf. John 16:15.
[205] Matt. 28:19
[206] The foregoing expressions concern the rite of baptism, in which the candidate is baptized "in the name of the Father, and of the Son, and of the Holy Spirit." This naming of the Trinity is its "enumeration," and the Holy Spirit's name comes last as "confirmation" or "seal."
[207] Ps. 118:103

of gifts, but the same Spirit, and there are differences of administrations, but the same Lord, and there are diversities of operations, but it is the same God that worketh all in all."[208]

12,5   And since such is the case, let us make sure not to be
deprived of the truth, but let us confess the truth instead—not
to plead for God, but to have a godly view of him, lest we perish.
To say or think that there is any created thing in the Trinity, or
anything added to it, is unacceptable; the Trinity was always the
Father, the Son and the Holy Spirit.

12,6   The Son is neither the Father's kinsman nor amalgamated
with him, and the Spirit is neither amalgamated with nor the kinsman
of the Father and the Son. (7) The Son is begotten of the Father
and the Spirit proceeds from the Father, though in some ineffable
way the Trinity exists in an identity of its glory and is incomprehensibly a Son, and likewise a Holy Spirit, with a Father, and never
ceases from the eternity of its threeness. (8) The Father, then, is
forever ingenerate, uncreated and incomprehensible. The Holy
Spirit is eternally—not generate, not created, not a kinsman, not
an ancestor, not an offspring, but a Holy Spirit of the same essence
as the Father and the Son, "For God is spirit."[209]

13,1   In every scripture there are testimonies to our salvation,
in all its sureness. I shall cite as few as I can of the many [there
are], in order, even at this stage, not to leave the exposition without
a witness to the Holy Spirit. (2) For example, to declare the divinity
of his Holy Spirit for the salvation of the faithful, the Father says
of the Son's human nature, "I shall put my Spirit upon him, and
he shall proclaim judgment to the gentiles."[210] (3) Next, by his own
testimony, the Only-begotten adds, "The Spirit of the Lord is upon
me, because he hath anointed me"[211]—a plain acknowledgment,
by Christ's testimony, that his human nature is certified and proclaimed to the faithful by the Holy Spirit, for the Spirit is not
different from God.

13,4   But again, the Lord says of the Spirit, "It is the Spirit of
my Father that speaketh in you."[212] And again, since the Spirit is
not different from the Father's divinity, "He breathed in the faces
of the disciples and said, Receive ye the Holy Spirit."[213] And again,
to show his equality and co-essentiality, and his Father's, with the

---

[208] 1 Cor. 12:4–6
[209] John 4:24
[210] Isa. 42:1
[211] Luke 4:18
[212] Matt. 10:20
[213] John 20:22

Holy Spirit, he said, "If ye love me, keep my commandments. And I shall pray the Father, and he will give you another advocate"[214]— since the Lord himself is an advocate, and the Holy Spirit likewise is his fellow advocate.

13,5 And to show that the Spirit is not a servant, but is of the same Godhead [as the Son], the apostles gave intimation of his authority by saying, "And the Holy Spirit said, Separate me Barnabas and Saul for the work whereunto I have called them,"[215] and so on. (6) But Paul says plainly of him, "The Lord is the Spirit, and where the Spirit of the Lord is, there is liberty,"[216] and, "Ye are the temple of God, and the Spirit of the Lord dwelleth in you."[217] (7) Now if we are called God's temple because of the Holy Spirit's indwelling, who would dare to reject the Spirit and separate him from the essence of God—when the apostle plainly says that we become God's temples because of the Holy Spirit who dwells in the worthy? And how can the Spirit who "searcheth the deep things of God"[218] be different from God?

And don't tell me, (8) "He *searches*, but he doesn't *know* yet," as some dare to blaspheme him to their own destruction. [If this were so] they should say < the > same of the Father, for even of him scripture says, "He *searcheth* the treasuries of the belly."[219] (9) And if you intend to take an impious view [of the Spirit] because knowledge does not follow searching in the Spirit's case, you must speak impiously of the Father too, and be compelled to express the same wrong notion. No "knowing" is added to "The Father searcheth the treasuries of the belly"—there would be no need to say it—since God's foreknowledge is made plainly evident, < and > is fully expressed by the word, "search." So please < understand > the one knowledge and foreknowledge in the Spirit, the Son and the Father, since the Holy Trinity is plainly perfect and identical.

14,1 An untold amount could be said about this, and it would be possible to cite a mass of texts from sacred scripture, and drag them out at length and burden the readers. (2) For by speaking at length in every Sect I, despite my weakness, have sufficiently refuted them all by the power of God, and have shown that all sects are strangers to the truth, and that each of them blasphemes and denies the truth, whether in a minor or in a major matter.

---

[214] John 14:15–16
[215] Acts 13:2
[216] 2 Cor. 3:17
[217] 1 Cor. 3:16
[218] 1 Cor. 2:10
[219] Prov. 20:17

So with these people < who > blaspheme the Lord and the Holy Spirit to no purpose and, as the Lord has said, have no "remission" of sins "here or in the world to come"[220] because of their blasphemy of the Holy Spirit—and who have been trodden underfoot by the truth itself, (3) like a dreadful horned asp with its single horn, since the blasphemous mind is capable of destroying the entire body. And they have been struck by the preaching of the cross and the true confession of the Only-begotten—for, as I said, for a blasphemer of the Holy Spirit "There shall be no forgiveness either in this world or in the world to come"—and have been trodden on and crushed; for they cannot prevail against the truth.

14,4　All the sects are truly "gates of hell," but "They will not prevail against the rock,"[221] that is, the truth. For even though some of them choose to say, "We too profess the creed that was issued at Nicaea; show me from it that the Holy Spirit is counted as divine," they will find themselves confounded even by this. (5) The dispute then was not about the Holy Spirit. The councils make sure of the matter that arises at a particular time. Since Arius was directing the insult at the Son, accuracy of language, with additional discussion, was required with regard to him. (6) But observe from the creed itself that there is no way in which the blasphemers of the Spirit, the Pneumatomachi who are strangers to his gift and sanctification, can make their point here either. (7) The creed at once confesses, and does not deny, "We believe in one God, the Father Almighty." But "We believe" is not left at that. The faith is in God "and in one Lord Jesus Christ." < And > this is not left at that. The faith is in God "and in the Holy Spirit." (8) And all this is not left at that. The three "We believes" make it evident that the faith is in one glory, one unity and one co-essentiality—three Perfects but one Godhead, one essence, one glory, one dominion. And here too their argument has failed.

14,9　And how long am I to go on? I believe that what I have said against them will suffice for those who love the truth. I shall therefore pass this sect by too, beseeching God to aid me as usual in the refutation of them all, so that, by his power, I may keep my promise and give him thanks in every way.

---

[220] Matt. 12:32
[221] Matt. 16:18

Against Aerius.[1] *55, but 75 of the series*

1,1 Again, a person named Aerius, whose brains are cracked and whose pride is inflated, has likewise become a great misfortune for the world. For from first to last, malice has been the cause of every sect that has arisen—[malice], or a spirit of vainglory or pride, or a lustful appetite, or envy of one's neighbors, or temper, or rashness. (2) In a word, blindness is of the devil, though the devil has no power to deceive anyone who does not want him to. Everyone is responsible for his own sinning, as the scripture says, "that they which are approved may be made manifest."[2]

1,3 Aerius is still alive and with us, and is a thoroughgoing Arian. Because he has inquired further into Arian speculations he holds beliefs that are no different, but are like Arius' and more so. And he has his tongue sharpened and his mouth battle-ready in his turn, to attract a deluded band, and a throng of people whose ears keep itching and whose minds are receptive. (4) For he too has invented a monstrous fictitious doctrine with nothing to it—a source of some amusement to the sensible, but all the same he has deceived and perverted many with it.

1,5 Aerius was the fellow student of Eustathius the son of Sebastius, of Sebaste, in the country called Pontus, or Lesser Armenia. For Eustathius and Aerius were ascetics together. (6) When Eustathius attained the episcopate, however, Aerius wanted this instead, but could not get it. This is the kind of thing that arouses jealousy. Still, Eustathius appeared to be standing by Aerius. (7) He made him a presbyter immediately afterwards, and entrusted him with the hospice, which in Pontus is called an alms-house. For they make arrangements of this kind out of hospitality, and the leaders of the churches there lodge the crippled and infirm, and supply < their needs* > as best they can.

2,1 But since Aerius' anger had not left him, there were more words between them every day, the jealousy between them increased, and evil reports and slanders of Eustathius were circulated by Aerius. But the bishop Eustathius sent for Aerius and cajoled him, admonished, threatened, rebuked, pleaded with him, and got nowhere. For what had been begun was going on, to very ill effect.

2,2 Aerius finally left the hospice and withdrew from the world, on the pretext < that Eustathius was embezzling the church's funds.

---

[1] Epiphanius' information about his contemporary, Aerius, may well have come from oral sources, or been common report. However, the succession of quotations at 3,4–7, sometimes introduced by such formulas as "Next he says," or "after this," suggest that Epiphanius had a literary source as well.
[2] 1 Cor. 11:19

From that time on* > he scrutinized < Eustathius' life* >, like a
man out to get something on an enemy or take a shot at a foe.
(3) And in the end he slandered Eustathius to everyone, and said,
"He is no longer the sort of man < you think he is* >, but has
turned to the acquisition of wealth, and all sorts of property." (4)
All this was calumny on Aerius' part. Eustathius was in fact in
charge of the church's affairs, and he could not do otherwise. And
yet the things Aerius had said sounded convincing.

2,5   Since I have introduced Eustathius while speaking against
Aerius, one might suppose that I also regard Eustathius as commendable. No few admire his life and conduct, and if his faith
were only orthodox too! (6) For he too believed in Arianism from
first to last, and not even the hardships of the persecutions set him
straight—he was persecuted with Basil, Eleusius and others.[3] (7)
But apparently he also went on an embassy with other bishops to
the blessed Liberius of Rome, and signed the creed of the Council
of Nicaea, and its confession of orthodoxy. (8) Later, however, as
though he had regained his memory and awakened from dreams,
he never ceased to look to his original principles, the Arian heresy.
But this is about Aerius—we must get back to him.

3,1   For the reasons we have given, Aerius originally preened
himself on renunciation of the world; but when he left the hospice
he took a large body of men and women with him. (2) With his
< fellowship > he was driven from the churches, and from cultivated
lands and villages, and the other towns. He often lived out in the
snow with his numerous band of followers, and lodged in the open
air and caves, and took refuge in the woods. (3) But his teaching
was more insane than is humanly possible, and he says, "What is
a bishop compared with a presbyter? The one is no different from
the other. There is one order," he said, "and one honor and one
rank. A bishop lays on hands," he said, "but so does a presbyter.
The bishop administers baptism, and the presbyter does too. The
bishop performs the eucharistic liturgy, the presbyter likewise. A
bishop occupies the throne, and the presbyter also occupies one."

With this he misled many, < who > regarded him as their leader.
(4) Next he says, "What is the Passover you celebrate? You are
giving your allegiance to Jewish fables again. We have no business
celebrating the Passover," he says; "Christ was sacrificed for our
Passover."[4]

3,5   Then, after this: "Why do you mention the names of the

---

[3] Eustathius was deprived of his see at the Synod of Constantinople in 360.
[4] 1 Cor. 5:7

dead after their deaths (i.e., in the liturgy)? < If > the living prays or has given alms, how will this benefit the dead? If the prayer of the people here has benefited the people there, no one should practice piety or perform good works! He should get some friends any way he wants, either by bribery or by asking friends on his death bed, and they should pray that he may not suffer in the next life, or be held to account for his heinous sins.

3,6 "And there can be no set time for fasting," he says. "These are Jewish customs, and 'under a yoke of bondage.'[5] 'The Law is not made for the righteous, but for murderers of fathers and murderers of mothers'[6] and the rest. If I choose to fast at all, I shall fast of my own accord, on the day of my choice, because of my liberty." (7) And they therefore make a point of fasting on Sunday instead [of the usual days], and eating on Wednesdays and Fridays. They often fast on Wednesday also, but by their own choice, they say, not by ordinance.

3,8 And during the days of Passover, while we sleep on the ground, purify ourselves, endure hardships, eat dry bread, pray, watch and fast, performing all the saving < mortifications* > of the holy Passovers, they buy meat and wine early in the morning, stuff their veins, < and > burst out laughing in mockery of those who keep this holy service of the week of the Passover.

3,9 Indeed, even though they have had the custom of renunciation they have not practiced it. < There is > a great deal of eating of meat and drinking of wine—unless there are a scant few of them who choose < to do > this by their own preference. But most of them indulge lavishly in meat dishes and wine-drinking, as I have often remarked. These are the teachings which Aerius has spat up into the world.

4,1 And once more, he shows the world his intent, his unbelief, and his teachings, perverse in their mischievous cunning. (2) But I shall go on to the arguments against him, make a few points, and then pass him by. < From > his saying that a bishop and a presbyter are the same, it is plain to people with sense that he is simply foolish. How can this be? The one is an order that generates fathers. For the episcopate produces fathers for the church. But the presbyterate, which cannot produce fathers, produces children through the laver of regeneration, but surely not fathers or teachers. (3) And since he is not ordained for the purpose of ordaining, how could a presbyter consecrate a bishop, or say that he is equal

---

5 1 Tim. 6,1
6 1 Tim. 1:9

to a bishop? Aerius' quarrel and his jealousy have deceived him.

4,4   For his own and his hearers' deception he alleges that the apostle writes to "presbyters and deacons"[7] and not to bishops, and tells the bishop, "Neglect not the gift that is in thee, which thou didst receive at the hands of the presbytery;"[8] and again, elsewheare he writes "to bishops and deacons"[9] so that, as Aerius says, bishops and presbyters are the same thing. (5) And as he does not know the true order of events, and has not read the most searching investigations, he does not realize that the holy apostle wrote about the problems which arose when the Gospel was new. He wrote to *bishops* and deacons where bishops had already been consecrated, for the apostles could not establish everything at once. (6) There was a need for presbyters and deacons, for the business of the church can be done by these two. But where there was no one worthy of the episcopate, the place remained without a bishop. Where there was a need for one, however, and there were persons worthy of the episcopate, bishops were consecrated.

4,7   But where the congregation was not large they had no presbyters for ordination, and were content simply with the local bishop. However, there can be no bishop without a deacon. And the holy apostle saw to it that the bishop had deacons to assist him; in this way the church got its business done. (8) This is what local churches were like at that time. All did not get each thing at the start, but what was needed was arranged for as time went on.

5,1   For according to the Old Testament, Moses was sent straight to Egypt by God with nothing but a staff. < But > on his entry into Egypt he was also given his brother Aaron to help him. (2) Then, after his brother believed him, the council of elders, and the leaders of the people at that time, were gathered for him. And after this, when his work was established and his following was gathered, he passed through the sea.

5,3   And they were not yet living by the Law, until < the > Lord called him into the mount. But he gave him the tablets, and told him how to make a tabernacle, and appoint officials, captains of tens, fifties, hundreds and thousands. (4) And do you see how things were expanded? "See," says God, "that thou make all things according to the pattern that was shown thee in Sinai."[10]

5,5   And you see how a seven-branched lampstand was added

---

[7] I.e., all communications apparently addressed to bishops are addressed to presbyters.
[8] 1 Tim. 4:14
[9] Phil. 1:1
[10] Exod. 25:40

to the legislation, and long robes, priestly vestments, bells and woolen cloaks, brooches and turbans, miters and jewelry made from various stones; ladles, censers, lavers, altars, bowls, "masmaroth," which are strainers, "midikoth," which means ladles, "machonoth," which are bases—and everything the Law speaks of, cherubim and the rest, the ark of the covenant, carrying poles and rings; the tabernacle, and hides and skins dyed scarlet; curtain rings and the rest; doorkeepers, wooden trumpets and curved trumpets, trumpets made of gold, silver, bronze < and > horn—and everything else the Law said, different kinds of sacrifices, teachings. (6) Because this was not in force from the beginning, were the things not given < permanent status > after they had been ordained? (7) Thus the things the apostle wrote applied until the church expanded, achieved its full growth, and < filled > the world with the knowledge < which > was most rightly revealed by the Father, the Son and the Holy Spirit. And Aerius' argument has failed.

5,8   And < by giving indication >, through the holy apostle, of who a bishop is and who a presbyter is, the word of God teaches that they cannot be the same. Paul says to Timothy, who is a bishop, "Rebuke not a presbyter, but entreat him as a father."[11] (9) What was the point of a bishop's not rebuking a presbyter, if he did not have the authority over the presbyter? Once more, it says, "Receive not hastily an accusation against a presbyter, save by two or three witnesses."[12] (10) And he never told any presbyter, "Receive not an accusation against a bishop," or wrote to any presbyter not to rebuke a bishop. And you see that the fall of anyone the devil shakes loose is no light one.

6,1   But let us see and investigate his other teachings. And let us speak first of the Passover, as scripture says, "Christ is sacrificed for our Passover."[13] Let's see whether the man who said that, didn't keep the Passover himself. Scripture says, "He hasted to keep the Feast of Pentecost at Jerusalem."[14] But what Pentecost was Paul keeping if he hadn't kept the Passover? (2) And who, anywhere in the world, does not agree that Wednesdays and Fridays are designated as fasts in the church? If, indeed, I need to speak of the Ordinance of the Apostles, they plainly decreed there that Wednesdays and Fridays be fasts at all times except Pentecost,[15]

---

[11] 1 Tim. 5:1
[12] 1 Tim. 5:19
[13] 1 Cor. 5:7
[14] Acts 20:16
[15] This is not in the Didascalia, but Const. Ap. 5.20.14 directs that festival be kept on Pentecost and the week following.

and directed that nothing at all be eaten on the six days of the Passover except bread, salt and water;[16] and which day to keep, and that we break our fast on the night before the Lord's Day. (3) But who has better knowledge of these things? The deluded man who has just arrived and is still alive today, or those who were witnesses before us, who have had the tradition in the church before us and received it in this form from their fathers—and their fathers in their turn, who learned it from those before them, just as the church possesses the true faith and the traditions to this day because she has received them from her fathers? And again, so much for his idea of the Passover!

6,4   But then, if the same apostles did not speak of this very subject of Wednesdays and Fridays in the Ordinance, I could prove it in all sorts of other ways. But they wrote about this in specific terms, the church has received it, and there was a world-wide agreement before Aerius and his Aerians. (5) Perhaps Aerius was very aptly named for this reason; he has received an unclean spirit of the air, the airish "spirit of wickedness"[17] which, in him, laid siege to the church.

7,1   And then, as to naming the dead, what could be more helpful? What could be more opportune or wonderful than that the living believe that the departed are alive and have not ceased to be, but are with the Lord and live with him—(2) and that the most sacred doctrine should declare that there is hope for those who pray for their brethren as though they were off on a journey?

7,3   And even though the prayer we offer for them cannot root out all their faults—[how could it], since we often slip in this world, inadvertently and deliberately—it is still useful as an indication of something more perfect. (4) For we commemorate both righteous and sinners. Though we pray for sinners, for God's mercy,[18] and *for*[19] the righteous, the fathers, the patriarchs, prophets, apostles, evangelists, martyrs and confessors, for bishops and anchorites and the whole band [of saints],[20] (5) we worship our Lord Jesus Christ to distinguish him from the whole of humanity by our honor of him, remembering that the Lord is not on a level with any man—even though each man has < performed > a million righteous deeds and more.

---

[16] Didascalia 21 (Achelis–Flemming p. 111)
[17] Eph. 6:12
[18] For example, in the Liturgy of St. James, Brightman, *Liturgies* p. 57
[19] I.e., rather than praying *to* them
[20] See Const. Apost. 8.12.43, and the Liturgies of St. Chryostom and St. Basil, Brightman, *Liturgies* pp. 230–232.

7,6 For how could this be? The one is God; the other, man. The one is in heaven and the other, because of his earthly remains, is on earth—except for those who have risen and entered the bridal chamber as the holy Gospel says, "And many bodies of the saints arose and went in with him into the holy city."[21]

7,7 But which holy city does he mean? [Both], for the words apply to both, the city here and the city on high. For they plainly entered the earthly Jerusalem with him first. But before the Savior's ascent into heaven, no one had ascended until the time at which they ascended with him, "For no man hath ascended into heaven but he that came down from heaven, the Son of Man."[22] Since I am on the subject, I have given the two proof-texts for this. But if anyone asks, "Did they go *into* Jerusalem?" he should learn that on that day, "When the doors were shut, Jesus came to where the disciples were gathered, and saith unto them, Peace be unto you."[23]

8,1 But I shall take up the thread of this topic one more. The church is bound to keep this custom because she has received a tradition from the fathers. (2) But who can violate a mother's precept or a father's law? As the words of Solomon < tell us >, "Hear, my son, the words of thy father, and reject not the precepts of thy mother,"[24] showing that the Father—God, that is—and the Only-begotten and the Holy Spirit taught both in writing and in unwritten form. But our mother the church had precepts which she kept inviolate, and which cannot be broken. (3) Now since these precepts have been ordained in the church, and are suitable, and all of them marvelous, this fraud is confounded in his turn.

8,4 But let us pass him by too, as though we had squashed a dung or blister-beetle, or the bug we call a buprestis, < and >, on the foundation of the church and with God's power, go on once more to the rest, calling on God for aid.

Against Anomoeans.[1] *56, but 76 of the series*

1,1 Again, there are some who are called Anomoeans. These are of recent origin. Their founder was a deacon named Aetius, who was advanced because of his foolishness by George of Alexandria.[2]

---

[21] Matt. 27:52–53
[22] John 3:13
[23] John 20:19
[24] Prov. 1:8

[1] The chief source of this Sect is the Syntagmation of Aetius the Anomoean, *On the Ingenerate God and the Generate,* which is reproduced in full at 11–12. 54,23–31 seem to reflect personal debate between Epiphanius and Anomoeans.
[2] Cf. Theodore bar Khouni in Pognon pp. 196–198. However, according to

George was the bishop of the Arians and Melitians at once, and as I have already indicated was paraded through the city on a camel during the reign of Julian.[3] (2) And first he was surrounded by the Greeks and badly mistreated, and was paraded, as I said, and beaten with cudgels, but was then dragged through almost the whole town, and this is how he died. After his death he was burned, reduced to ashes together with the bones of many domestic and wild animals, and then scattered to the four winds by the pagans, and this was the last of him.[4]

1,3   Should one say of a man who died like that, "Well, he became a martyr by undergoing these sufferings at the hands of the pagans?" Indeed, if his ordeal had been for the truth's sake, and the pagans had done this to him from envy and because of his confession of Christ, he would truly have ranked as a martyr, and no minor one. (4) The confession of Christ, however, was not the reason for his death. It was the great violence he had inflicted on the city and people during his so-called episcopate, if you please, sometimes by robbing people of their patrimony, < sometimes by levying unjust taxes* >.

1,5   And not to inform on the man—for he did a number of things to the Alexandrians. For example, he expropriated the entire nitre tax; and he thought of a way of controlling the papyrus and reed marshes and the salt marshes, and getting them for himself. (6) He overlooked no shameful way of making money by many methods, even small things. For instance, he thought of limiting the number of biers[5] for the bodies of the dying, and without his appointed officials no dead man's body, especially not strangers' bodies, could be carried out for burial. This was not for hospitality's sake, but, as I said, to support himself. (7) For if anyone buried a body on his own, he ran a risk. In this way George made a profit on every corpse that was buried. And I pass over the other things the man got for himself through luxuries < and in other dreadful ways* >, and by cruelty.

1,8   Thus because of all this the Alexandrians who cherished anger against him, the pagans most of all, inflicted this end on him. But my reason for saying how the Alexandrians destroyed him like this as soon as they heard of Constantius' death, is simply because of Aetius, whom George made a deacon.

Philost. 3.17 and Soc. 2.35.5, Aetius was ordained deacon in Antioch by Leontius.

[3] Hist. Aceph. 85; Soc. 3.2.10

[4] Soz. 5.7.3; Philost. 7.2

[5] Amidon: "instituting a certain number of litter bearers for the bodies of the deceased"

2,1   They say that even by worldly standards Aetius was unedu-
cated until his manhood.[6] (2) But he stooped to attending the
lectures of an Aristotelian philosopher and sophist at Alexandria[7]
and learning their dialectic, if you please, for no other purpose
than to give a figurative representation of the divine Word. < But >
he devoted full time to the project, getting up at dawn and keeping
at it till evening, I mean at discussing and defining God via a sort
of geometry and in figures of speech, and at teaching and perfecting his doctrine. (3) As an Arian of the deepest dye and a
holder of Arius' insane doctrine, he became the more destructive
by devoting his time to these things, and sharpening his tongue
each day against the Son of God and the Holy Spirit.

2,4   He was accused by certain persons, however, and denounced
to Constantius, and was banished to the Taurus.[8] Here he ampli-
fied and disclosed all of his wicked doctrine by teaching it openly;
< for > after hardening himself by further shamelessness, he dis-
gorged his heresy in full. (5) For he dared to say that the Son
is *un*like the Father, and not the same as the Father in Godhead.

And not that we rely on the likeness. Beyond the likeness, we
know that the Son is the same as the Father, and the Father's
equal, in Godhead, and not different at all. (6) Many things can
be likened to God, but they are not the same as he, < or > his
equals, in Godhead. For example, man is in God's image and
likeness, but is not the same as God in the sense of equality. (7)
And the kingdom of heaven is *like* a grain of mustard seed—though
< a grain > is not identical with the kingdom and has no part of
it—and like leaven, and ten virgins, and a householder in point
of likeness, but not identical.

2,8   But as the Son is like the Father—and more than "like"
him, because he is the same as the Father and his equal—my
concern is not merely to prove his likeness, but < his > sameness
and equality as God of God, Son of the Father, and not different
from < his > essence, but begotten of him. And the same with the
Holy Spirit. (9) But this fine heretic Aetius didn't even think he
should regard the Son as worthy of likeness to the Father. Now
I agree that I myself do not really enter upon the demonstration
of the faith and the honoring of the Trinity if I rely solely on the
likeness. (10) Silver is like tin too, gold is like bronze and lead

---

[6] Greg. Nys. C. Eunom. 1.36–38; Philost. 3:15–17
[7] Soc. 2.35.6; Soz. 3.15.8
[8] At the Council of Sirmium in 359 Aetius was banished to Pepuza in Phrygia,
Philost. 4.8. He had already been in the region of the Taurus after his banishment from Antioch, Philost. 2.15.

like iron, and precious stones are imitated by glass; and likeness
does not show nature, but resemblance.

3,1   But here, since I have also inquired the meaning (δύναμις)
of the scripture which confesses the Son to be the "image of the
invisible God"[9] from the divine Gift who told the Pharisees, "Ye
understand neither the scriptures nor the power (δύναμις) of God,"[10]
I understand that this relationship has a dual sense. But I explain
it as though I take enough for the expounding of the word from
the illustration of a man. (2) We speak of a man's image, and
< there is one image that is like him and > one that is not like
him. One image is made like him with paint, but the other is made
by the identity of his essence with his begetter's. As compared with
his father the newborn son represents his kind, but in the end
he is found to be his likeness < by his > sameness and co-essentiality
with him, and his resemblance to him. (3) And we believe in the
only–begotten Son of God who is the same as the Father's Godhead and rank, and his equal because of the true image, and
because of the likeness which admits of no variation but is indistinguishable, as becomes a son who is truly and co-essentially begotten
of a father. And so with the Holy Spirit, because of his procession
from the Father—even though he is not begotten, because the Son
is an *only*–begotten.

3,4   But from his wish to offer further resistance to the confession of the truth, Aetius tries not even to confess the Son's
likeness to the Father. (5) For other Arians, who took their cue
from Lucian and Origen and were companions of a sophist named
Asterius[11] who lapsed in the persecution under Maximian, < did
not disclose the whole of their wrong view of the Son* >. (6) For
some < said* > that he is a < creature* >, and it has been explained
in my earlier Sects that each of them declared the Son of God
a creature, and taught that the Holy Spirit is the creature of a
creature, while some said that even though they declared him a
creature, the Son of God is like the Father. (7) But this man
exposed the whole of their deception, and of his own impiety, by
< displaying > with full clarity the harshness and arrogance of their
doctrine of the Lord. And in fact, strictly speaking the argument
of this Aetius, who is also called the "Different," can very justly be
marshalled against those who introduce the notion of the Son's
creaturehood in some covert form.

3,8   For whatever is created is unlike its creator, even though

---

[9] Col. 1:15
[10] Matt. 22:27
[11] Cf. Ath. Syn. 18.

it be made like him by grace. And however one tries to decorate this with various sorts of paint, the creator is unlike the creature—unless the representation of him is a copy and likeness which is in imitation only of his appearance. (9) And as his argument would have prevailed against those Arians who regard the Son of God and the Holy Spirit as creatures, so even later, after his excommunication by those same Arians—I mean Eudoxius,[12] Menophilus and the others—he confounded them before the emperor and said, (10) "As they believe, I believe—as they all do! But what is honest in me, they hide, and what I say openly < and > acknowledge, all these say the same, but conceal themselves." And the emperor at that time was not opposed to the Arian fabrication, but considered it orthodox, if you please! But since he declined to confess the Son of God a creature, the emperor was annoyed and, as I have already said, sent < Aetius > into exile.

4,1   That was the origin of the sect, and from the one proposition the man was inspired to a great production of evils, and dealt fearful wounds to his own soul, and his converts'. (2) For he was so deluded—he and his disciples—as to say, "I understand God perfectly in this way, and understand and know him so well that I don't know myself any better than I know God!"

4,3   But I have heard as many things about him, the fearful way in which the devil contrived, through him, to destroy the souls of the people he had caught. (4) Indeed, they take no account of holiness of life, fasts, God's commandments, or any of God's other ordinances for men's salvation,[15] but only say glibly that they < have > it all through one text. (5) It is as though someone had lightened ship and completely jettisoned the whole cargo, but had kept just one article of the ship's freight, a jar or some other thing, to get himself across the whole sea and ensure his safety with one implement. But if he was wrong, and did not get what he expected from the implement he kept, he would drown, and lose the whole business and his life as well. (6) Similarly, both Aetius and his Anomoeans are wrong to cite the Lord's words in the Gospel, and repeat the expression without properly grasping the meaning. (7) For when someone falls in with them and reminds them of the commandments, they claim that, as the text is worded, there is

---

[12] Philost. 8.4; 9.3
[13] Philost. App. 7.31
[14] Soz. 4.23.4
[15] NHL Gr. Pow. 40,3–6, "Cease from the evil lusts and desires and (the teachings of) the Anomoeans, evil heresies that have no basis," is sometimes interpreted as a reference to Anomoean laxity.

nothing else that God requires of us but simply to know him. This is what Christ meant, they say, by saying, "Grant them, Father, to have life in themselves. And this is life, that they may know thee, the only true God, and Jesus Christ whom thou hast sent."[16]

4,8   Indeed, some people have told me what they distinctly heard him say when certain persons were charged with having been caught in a sexual offense, and were found guilty by them. He was not annoyed at this and even made an idle jest and said that something like this is not important; it is a physical need and the way of meeting it. (9) "When we itch by our ear," he said—I myself am embarrassed to repeat what < the > filthy man told them—"we take a feather or straw," he said, "and scratch our ear, and get rid of the itching by our ear. This is another natural thing," he said, "and if someone does it he doesn't commit a sin."

5,1   Aetius made as many such remarks, and all his teachings are lax and wicked, so that what he is may be seen from his works themselves. But the Lord's words have made this abundantly clear to us, (2) as he said, "Beware of false prophets, which come to you in sheep's clothing, but inwardly they are ravening wolves. Ye shall know them by their fruits. Do men gather grapes of thorns, or figs of thistles?"[17] Thus the utter impudence of his stupidity is exposed in the second phrase and the first. (3) [We are shown] how he opened his mouth in impudence against his Master and was not ashamed to blaspheme his Lord, and the wise will test him by the fruits of his licentiousness and laxity, and not harvest his fruit. There is no cutting of a cluster from thorns, or holiness might emerge even from false doctrine.

5,4   But this is what I have heard of the events of his life. However, there are many words which, as I said, he dared to say in consequence of the madness of his rebellion against the Lord, and I shall give a few examples, and make the replies to them myself which the Lord gives me in refutation. (5) Here are the nonsense of "Different's" faith, and the "likenesses" of the words he quotes from scripture. They do not mean what he thinks, but he takes them that way although they mean something else.

6,1   He says at the very outset, "The Ingenerate cannot be like the Generate. Indeed, they differ in name; the one is 'ingenerate,' the other, 'generate'" (2) But this is perfectly silly and has simply driven the man insane. If, to avoid losing the true view of Christ, we are to require an engenderer of the Ingenerate, there will no

---

[16] Cf. John 17:2–3.
[17] Matt. 7:15–16

longer be one Father, or < one > father of a Father; we will need
an infinite number of fathers' fathers. And there will [no longer]
be one God, who is forever, has nothing before him, and endures
and abides forever, of whom the only-begotten true Son is begotten and is, and of whom is his Holy Spirit. The gods we need will
be many, and the whole will turn out to be imposture, not truth.

6,3   But we must know that, as the fact is, there is one God,
the Father of our Lord Jesus Christ, of whom is the Holy Spirit
who "proceeds from the Father and receives of the Son."[18] (4) And
this is the one Godhead—one God, one Lord, Father, Son and
Holy Spirit. The Son is not identical with the Father and neither
is the Holy Spirit, but the Father is a Father, the Son, a Son, and
the Holy Spirit, a Holy Spirit. [They are] three Perfects, one Godhead,
one God, one Lord, as I have ascribed this praise to God many
times, in every Sect.

6,5   Now since God is one, and no one can suppose that there
is another God besides the one, the Father is wondrously both
ingenerate and uncreated; and God's only-begotten Son, < who >
is begotten of him, is not unlike him in any way. He is the same
as and perfectly equal to the Father in rank, even though he is
generate and the Father ingenerate. (6) For if the Father has begotten
any Son of himself, it is impossible that [the Son] not be the
Father's equal, and not be like him. Whatever begets, begets its
like—and not only its like, but the same in its equality. (7) A man
begets a man, and God begets God. The man begets through
sexual intercourse, but God has begotten an Only-begotten alone,
in an ineffable manner. [He has not done this] by overflow,
contraction or expansion; the Father, who is spirit, has begotten
the Son of himself without beginning and not in time, altogether
his like and equal. As the holy Gospel says, "The Jews sought to
kill him, because he had not only broken the Sabbath, but said
that he was the Son of God, making himself *equal* with God."[19]

6,8   How can the Son not be like the Father and entirely his
equal when he has life in himself, and says, "As the Father raiseth
the dead, even so the Son raiseth the dead,"[20] and, "He that hath
seen me hath seen the Father?"[21] (9) He cannot be different when
he identifies the Father through himself and says, "He that knoweth

---

[18] John 15:26; 16:14
[19] John 5:18
[20] John 5:21
[21] John 5:21

me, knoweth the Father,"[22] and, "He that hath seen me hath seen
the Father," meaning that he is not different from the Father. And
the Father means † the Son < when he says >,"[23] Let us make man
in our image and after our likeness."[24] (10) If the Son were not
like the Father, how could man be made in [*their*] image and
likeness? The Father did not say, "Let us make man in *my* image"
or in" *your* image," but, "in *our* image." (11) By saying, "our," he
indicated the equality with the Father that characterizes the Son—
and not only his likeness, but his sameness in all ways, without any
difference.

7,1   But as I have already said, how can he not be the Father's
equal and like the Father, when he says, "I am in the Father and
the Father in me?"[25] (2) For not only does he say this himself in
the Gospel. Isaiah, prophesying in the Holy Spirit, knew that the
Son is in the Father and is not other than, or different from the
Father, (3) as the verse which implies this says in Hebrew: "phthoou
saareim, ouiabo goi sadik, somer emmouneim, iesro samoch, thesaar
salom salom, shi bak batoou betou baadonai ada oth, chi baia
adonai sor olemeim."[26] (4) In Aquila's version it says, "Open the
gates, let the righteous nation enter that keepeth faith, the creation firmly established, the keeping of peace, for in him have they
trusted. Trust ye in the Lord forever, for in the Lord is the Lord
who established the ages." (5) In the Septuagint's it says, "Open
the gates, let < a righteous nation > enter that preserveth truth,
and layeth claim to truth and keepeth peace. For in thee have they
trusted forever, O Lord, God the great, the eternal." (6) The reader
should note that in the Septuagint "God" stands in the place of
"the Lord," and "the great" in place of "in the Lord."

7,7   And how much is there to say about this? I am afraid of
prolonging my treatment of these words to a burdensome length.
Everything in the sacred scripture is clear, to those who will approach
God's word with pious reason, and not harbor the devil's work
within them and turn their steps to the pits of death—as this
unfortunate man and his converts have attacked the truth more
vigorously than any who have become blasphemers of God and
his faith before them.

7,8   < I have shown > that the Son cannot be unlike the Father,
but have said that I do not rely on this either. The Son is not only

---

[22] This is not in the NT; Epiphanius' memory is at fault.
[23] Lietzmann: τὸν υἱὸν σημαίνει < λέγων >; Holl: πρὸς τὸν υἱὸν < λέγων >
[24] Gen. 1:26
[25] John 14:20
[26] This is a Greek transliteration of the Masoretic Text of Isa. 26:2.

"like," but equal, the same in Godhead, the same in eternity and power. And yet we do not say, "tautoousion," or the expression that some use might be compared with Sabellius. (9) We say that he is the same in Godhead, essence and power, and in all ways the equal of the Father and his Holy Spirit. And we say "homoousion" as the holy faith teaches, so that the perfections are clearly indicated by "homo;" for the Son is the perfect Son of a perfect father, but the Holy Spirit is likewise perfect.

8,1   These people will be detected by a first, a second, and a third piece of evidence. If it is admitted that a < Son > has been begotten by him at all, it will be admitted that the Son must be like his Begetter. (2) It is plain that Aetius calls him by the name, "Offspring," but holds and believes him < to be > a creature, though he is called a "Son" by grace—as the surveyor of the realms of the heavens, divider of the indivisible, and measurer of our salvation in Christ, has seen fit to call him. (3) But, like Aetius', the argument of all these people who covertly introduce the doctrine of the creaturehood of Christ falls flat. (4) For I shall say to him with perfect justice, "Tell me, Mister, what can you say of the Son of God? Do you call him a creature, or an offspring? If you say he is a creature, stop hiding your outrage with plausible-sounding language by terming him the Father's Offspring! (5) Nothing that is created, is 'begotten;' and if it is begotten, it is not created. Never mind even saying 'begotten!' You have no business pronouncing the words of the truth even with one expression. Tell us your whole scheme so that we may learn who you are and escape your plot, you fisher for souls, you schemer against those who trust you! (6) Come on, do you worship the Son of God, or don't you?"

"Yes," says Aetius, "I worship him."

"Do you worship him as God, or not?"

"Yes," he says, "I worship him as God."

"Then what kind of a God can be creature, as you say he is, and still be worshiped?"

8,7   For suppose that God, who is fit to be worshiped, made the one creature and consented that he be worshiped, but their creator did not want any of the others worshiped and instead censured the worshipers of a creature through a Law that taught them, "Thou shalt not make to thyself any likeness, and thou shalt not worship it, neither in heaven, nor in earth, nor in the waters."[27] (8) And the apostle says, "They worshiped the creature more than

---

[27] Exod. 20:4

the creator, and were made fools."[28] Why did God forbid the worship of all creatures, < but consent that this one be worshiped? > Is there "respect of persons with God,"[29] then? Never! (9) By the fact that this One is worshiped, God has shown, in every way, that the One who is worshiped is different from the creature and that the creature which is worshiped is different from the Lord, who is fit for worship—the Son of God, begotten of the Father. For because he is begotten of him, he is like him and is his Son. He is therefore fit for the worship of all: "Through him God made all things, and without him was not anything made."[30] (10) For by him, and by the Holy Spirit who "proceeds from the Father and receives of the Son,"[31] God made and established all things. "By the Word of the Lord were the heavens established, and all the host of them by the Spirit of his mouth."[32]

8,11   When the Only-begotten, as I mentioned above, said, "that they may know thee, the only true God, and Jesus Christ whom thou hast sent,"[33] he distinguished himself from creation, as the apostle says, "one God, of whom are all things, and we through him; and one Lord, Jesus Christ, by whom are all things, and we by him."[34] (12) And you see how he showed that there is one God, the Father, but one Lord, the Son begotten of him. And he didn't say, "one God, and one Lord together with all God's creatures," but, "one Lord, through whom are all things." But if there is one Lord through whom are all things, he is not one of them all, but the maker of all, the creator of all created things.

9,1   But since he through whom are all things is the Son, begotten of the Father and the Father's offspring, then, as befits the creator of all things, he is unlike them all. (2) Since God the Father, of whom are all things, is called "one," and the "Lord Jesus by whom are all things" is called "one," the text just mentioned has clearly shown that the Son is of the Father, since it is tied together by the "one" and the "one," and by "of whom" and "by whom." But by saying, "by whom are all things," it has declared wonderfully well that the Son cannot be one of the rest, showing that there is a Father, and there is a Son—the only-begotten Lord—of the One who is the Father.

---

[28] Rom. 1:25
[29] Rom. 2:11
[30] Cf. John 1:3.
[31] John 15:26; 16:14
[32] Ps. 32:6
[33] John 17:3
[34] 1 Cor. 8:6

9,3   But the apostle was saying these things by the Holy Spirit's inspiration; he therefore did not need to give any proof of the Spirit. This was not because the Spirit is not glorified with the Father and the Son, or so that Paul could mark him off from all the things created through the Son. (4) It was enough that the Spirit was included with the Father and the Son in the Son's sure confession, "Go baptize in the name of the Father, and of the Son, and of the Holy Spirit."[35] So when the apostle spoke—or rather, when the Holy Spirit spoke in him—he said nothing about himself. The knowledge of him was clear, and undisputed by the Jews; but it was treasured up [rather than published], so that the Holy Spirit would not be the one to commend himself. (5) But the apostle was inspired by the Holy Spirit and spoke of the Father and the Son, to show that the Holy Trinity is eternal, and never ceases to be.

But don't be surprised if you hear, "one *God*, of whom are all things, and one *Lord*, by whom are all things."[36] (6) By calling the Son, "Lord," the apostle by no means denied his Lordship and Godhead. And by saying, "one God, of whom are all things," he did not deny God's Godhead and Lordship. "Lord" goes together with "God" and "God" with "Lord," and this will make no difference to the tidings which God has truly proclaimed to us through the apostles, for our salvation.

9,7   But this Different and his followers have turned from the way of the truth, and by a clumsy construction of God's oracles turned < to falsehood >. In the end, through distracting their minds with debate and verbal arguments, they have turned their backs on the truth and been deprived of the heavenly realms. (8) For— if they are willing to pay attention to "the light of the Gospel"[37]— every word will convict them. Though the Only–begotten surely came in the flesh, he nowhere says, "The Father who created me hath sent me." Nor did the Father ever say, in the Gospel or the Old Testament, "I have created the Son for you." [We read], "The Father hath sent me,"[38] "I came forth from the Father and am come,"[39] and, "He who is in the bosom of the Father,"[40] and, "The Word was with God, and the Word was God."[41] (9) And there is

---

[35] Matt. 28:19
[36] 1 Cor. 8:6
[37] 2 Cor. 4:4
[38] John 10:36
[39] John 8:42
[40] John 1:18
[41] John 1:1

much that we can learn about our salvation, and not be carried
away with this devil's tricky teaching.

9,10   For, consumed with envy at man's glory, the devil is out
to destroy mankind, and has thought of various ways to do it. The
first was through ignorance, the second through idolatry, another
time it was through vice—but now, at length, it is through the
error and imposture of the sects, to turn man away from the heavens
by every possible method.

10,1   How much my poor mind will find to say to you, Different! It is quite true that you are "Different;" you have made your
way of life and your thinking different from those who have the
understanding of God and hold the faith of the truth. (2) You
have not become different from other people by your progress in
goodness; you have become different from the sons of God's church
by abandoning the way of the truth. By taking the relation of the
Son of God to his Father for your excuse and calling him "different
from" the Father, you have become "different from" [the rest of
us] and been awarded this title, since you are no longer like those
who are to be saved in God.

10,3   But now then, not to waste my time in investigating him,
let me refute him from the things he described himself in a
controversial communication to certain persons. (4) For it seems
that he gave some indication of his mistakes in argument in his
treatise itself—which contains not one word of faith which is wholly
innocent and pure faith, and ordered in the Holy and meek Spirit.
(5) First, I set down in full the work which has come into my
possession which is apparently his, so as to go on from that to the
rest of the refutation of his treatise. The work is as follows:

The Treatise of Aetius the Anomoean

11,1   *During the time of my persecution by the Temporists,*[42] *some of them,*
among many other things, appropriated a brief treatise I had composed with
particular effort of the subject of the Ingenerate God and the Generate,
corrupted it with insertions and omissions and issued it, after altering the
sequence of the argument. It fell into my hands afterwards because one
of the virtuous brought it to me, (2) *and I have been obliged, like a father,*
to correct the treatise again and send it to you, all you male and female
champions of piety, to show you that the brief discourse accords with the

---

[42] "Temporist" is a pejorative term for catholic. Epiphanius takes it to mean
that the catholic position on the Trinity is accused of having an origin recent
in time. Athanasius, Dial. II Trin. 11, takes it to mean that catholics are accused
of teaching that the Son was begotten in time.

sense of the holy scriptures. With its help you will be able, with brief counter-arguments, to put a stop to the impudence of everyone—the Temporists most of all—who tries to contradict you about the Ingenerate God and the Generate.

11,3 *For the ready comprehension and the clarity of my arguments I have separated objection from objection and solution from solution in the form of short paragraphs, and have begun with the Ingenerate God,*

12,1 *Whether it is possible for the Ingenerate God to make a generate thing ingenerate:*

2.[43] *If the Ingenerate God transcends every cause, he therefore must also transcend origination. But if he [indeed] transcends every cause he plainly transcends origination also. For he neither received his existence from another nature nor provided himself with existence.*

3. *But if, not from the inadequacy of his nature but because of his transcendence of every cause, he did not provide himself with existence, how can anyone concede that there is no difference of essence between the nature that provides existence and the nature that is provided with existence, when such a nature [as the first] does not admit of origination?*

4. *If God remains forever ingenerate and his Offspring forever an Offspring, the heresy of the homoousion and the homoeousion will be brought to an end. But the essential incomparability [of the two] remains, since either nature remains endlessly in the rank proper to its nature.*

5. *If God is ingenerate in essence, the Generate was not produced by a separation of essence, but God gave it being by virtue of his authority.[44] For no pious reason can allow that the same essence can be both generate and ingenerate.*

6. *If the Ingenerate was generated, what is there to prevent the Generate from having become ingenerate? For on the contrary, every nature tends < away from > that which is not natural to it toward that which is.*

7. *If God is not wholly ingenerate, there is nothing to prevent his having generated as an essence. But since God is wholly ingenerate, there was no separation of his essence for the purpose of generation, but he brought an Offspring into existence by his authority.*

8. *If the Ingenerate God is wholly generative, the Offspring was not generated as an essence, since God's essence is wholly generative and not generated. But if God's essence has been transformed and is called an Offspring, God's essence is not unalterable, since the transformation brought about the formation of the Son. But if God's essence is both unalterable and above generation, talk of "sonship" will admittedly be a mere verbal ascription.*

---

[43] Epiphanius' paragraph numbers in this chapter will serve as the numbers of the paragraphs of Holl's chapter 12.

[44] Wickham: ἐξουσίᾳ ὑπέστησεν αὐτό; Holl and MSS: ἐξ οὐσίας ὑποστησάσης

9.   *If the Offspring was in the Ingenerate God in germ, he was "brought to maturity," as one might say, after his generation by receiving accretions from without. Therefore the Son is not "mature" because of the causes of his generation, but because of the accretions he received. For things which receive accretions genetically, in the sense of being constituted by them, are characteristically termed "mature" in some distinctive way.*

10.   *If the Offspring was full grown in the Ingenerate, it is an Offspring by virtue of properties which were in the Ingenerate,[45] and not by virtue of those with which the Ingenerate generated it. [But this cannot be], for there can be no generacy in ingenerate essence. The < same > thing can< not > both be and not be. An offspring is not ingenerate, and if it were ingenerate it would not be an offspring, for to say that God is not homogeneous is to offer him sheer insult and blasphemy.*

11.   *If Almighty God, whose nature is ingenerate, knows that his nature is not generate, but the Son, whose nature is generate, knows that he is what he is, how can the homoousion not be a lie? For the one knows himself to be ingenerate, but the other, generate.*

12.   *If ingeneracy does not represent the reality of God but the incomparable name is of human invention, God owes the inventors thanks for their invention of the concept of ingeneracy, since in his essence he does not have the superiority the name implies.*

13.   *If ingeneracy is only something external observers observe to be God's, the observers are better than the One observed, for they have given him a name which is better than his nature.*

14.   *If ingeneracy is not susceptible of generation, this is what we maintain. But if it is susceptible of generation, the sufferings of generation must be superior to the real nature of God.*

15.   *If the Offspring is unchangeable by nature because of its Begetter, then the Ingenerate is an unchangeable essence, not because of its will, but because of its essential rank.*

16.   *If "ingeneracy" is indicative of essence, it may properly be contrasted with the essence of the Offspring. But if "ingeneracy" means nothing, all the more must "Offspring" mean nothing.*

But how < could > nothing be contrasted with nothing? If the expression, "ingenerate," is contrasted with the expression, "generate," but silence succeeds the expression, the hope of Christians may well begin and end [there], since it rests in a particular expression, and not in natures which are such as the meaning of their names imply.

17.   *If the term, "ingenerate," as against the term, "offspring," contributes nothing toward superiority of essence, the Son, who is [therefore] surpassed*

---

[45] Wickham: ἐξ ὧν ἦν ἐν ⟨ τῷ ⟩ ἀγεννήτῳ γέννημά ἐστί; Holl, Amidon, MSS: ἐν γεννητῷ γέννημα ἐστι

only verbally,[46] will know that those who have termed him, "Son," are his betters, and not He who is termed his "God" and "Father."

18.   *If the ingenerate essence is superior, and innately superior, it is ingenerate essence per se.[47] For it is not superior to generation deliberately, because it so wills, but because this is its nature. Since ingenerate nature per se is God, it allows no reasoning to think of[48] generation in connection with it.[49]*

19.   *If "ingenerate," when applied to God, connotes privation but "ingenerate" must be nothing, what reasoning can take away nothing from a non-existent thing? But if it means something that is, who can separate God from being, that is, separate him from himself?*

20.   *If the "privations" of states are the removals of them, "ingenerate" as applied to God is either the privation of a state, or a state of privation. But if "ingenerate" is the privation of a state, how can something God does not have be counted as one of his attributes? If "ingenerate" is a state, however, a generate essence must be assumed to precede it, so that it may acquire the [new] state and be called, "ingenerate." If, however, the generate essence partook of an ingenerate essence [to begin with], it has been deprived of its generation[50] by undergoing the loss of a state.*

Generacy must then be an essence but ingeneracy a state. But if "off-spring" implies a coming to be, it is plain that the word means a state, whether the Offspring is made out of some essence, or whether it is what it is called, an "Offspring."

21.   *If "ingeneracy" is a state and "generacy" is a state, the essences are prior to the states; but even though the states are secondary to the essences, they are more important.*

Now if ingeneracy is the cause of generacy and means that there is an offspring which implies the cause of its own being, "offspring" denotes an essence, not a state. < On the other hand >, since ingeneracy implies nothing besides itself, how can ingeneracy be not an essence, but a state?

22.   *If every essence is ingenerate like Almighty God's, how can one say that one essence is subject to vicissitudes while another is not? But if the one essence remains above quantity and quality and, in a word, all sorts of change because of its classification as ingenerate, while the other is subject to vicissitudes < and yet > is admitted to have something*

---

[46] Reading with Holl, Amidon, MSS: ὑπερεχόμενος; Wickham, without explanation: ὑπερχόμενος

[47] Wickham, Codex Jenensis: αὐτὸ οὐσία; Holl and MSS: αὐτοουσία

[48] Holl, tentatively, Wickham: παρά; MSS: κατά

[49] The translation of this clause is problematic. Wickham: "It thrusts aside all burden of inquiry and reasoning from generate beings;" so, approximately, Amidon.

[50] Wickham: γενέσεως; Holl, Amidon, MSS: ἀγεννησίας

unchangeable in its essence, we ought to attribute the characteristics of these essences to chance, or, as is at any rate[51] logical, call the active essence ingenerate, but the essence which is changed, generate.[52]

23.   *If the ingenerate nature is the cause of the nature that has come to be, and yet "ingenerate" is nothing, how can nothing be the cause of a thing that has come to be?*

24.   *If "ingenerate" is a privation but a privation is the loss of a state, and if a "loss" is completely destroyed or changed to something else, how can the essence of God be named for a changing or vanishing state by the title, "ingenerate?"*

25.   *If "ingenerate" denotes privation, which is not an attribute of God, why do we say that God is ingenerate but not generate?*

26.   *If, as applied to God, "ingenerate" is a mere name, but the mere expression elevates the being of God over against all generate things, then the human expression is worth more than the being of the Almighty, since it has embellished God the Almighty with incomparable superiority.*

27.   *If there is a cause to correspond with everything generate but the ingenerate nature has no cause, "ingenerate" does not denote a cause but means an entity.*

28.   *If whatever is made, is made by something, but ingenerate being is made neither by itself nor by something else, "ingenerate" must denote essence.*

29.   *If the ingenerate being is implicitly indicated to be the cause of the Offspring's existence and, in contrast with every [other] cause, is invariable, it is incomparable essence in itself[53] and its matchlessness is not implied for any reason external to itself but because, being ingenerate, it is incomparable and matchless in itself.*

30.   *If the Almighty surpasses every nature, he surpasses it because of his ingeneracy, and this is the reason for the permanence of generate things. But if "ingenerate" does not denote an essence, how will the nature of generate things be preserved?*

31.   *If no invisible thing preexists itself in germ, but each remains in the nature allotted to it, how can the Ingenerate God, who transcends any category, sometimes see his own essence in the Offspring as secondary but sometimes see it in ingeneracy as prior, on the principle of "first and second."*

32.   *If God retains an ingenerate nature, there can be no question of his knowing himself as [both] originated and unoriginated. If, on the other hand, we grant that his essence continues to be ingenerate and generate,*

---

[51] Wickham: ἢ τό γε οὖν; Holl and MSS: ἢ τὸ γοῦν

[52] Wickham: τῷ αὐτομάτῳ ἐπιτρέψαι ὀφείλομεν τὰ κατὰ τὰς προειρημένας; Holl and MSS: τῷ αὐτομάτῳ ἐπιτρέψαι τὸν φιλοῦντα κατὰ τὰ προειρημένα

[53] Wickham: αὐτὸ οὐσία; Holl and MSS: αὐτοουσία

he does not know his own essence, since his head is in a whirl from origination and non-origination. But if the Generate too partakes of ingeneracy and yet remains without cessation in his generate nature, he knows himself in the nature in which he continues to remain, but plainly does not know his participation in ingeneracy; for he cannot possibly be aware of himself as both of ingenerate and of generate essence.

If, however, the Generate is contemptible because of his proneness to change, then unchangeable essence is a natural rank, since the essence of the Ingenerate admittedly transcends every cause.

33.   *If the Ingenerate transcends all cause, but there are many ingenerates they will [all] be exactly alike in nature. For without being endowed with some quality common [to all], while yet having some quality of its own— [a condition not possible in ingenerate being]—one ingenerate nature would not make, while another was made.*

34.   *If every essence is ingenerate, one will not differ from another in self-determination. How, then, can we say that one [such] being is changed and another causes change, when we will not allow God to bring them into being from an essence that has no [prior] existence?*

35.   *If every essence is ingenerate, every one is exactly alike. But the doing and suffering of an essence that is exactly like [all the others] must be attributed to chance. However, if there are many ingenerates which are exactly alike, there can be no enumeration of their ways of differing from one another. For there could be no enumerations of their differences, either in general or in some respect, since every difference which implies classification is already excluded from an ingenerate nature.*

36.   *If "ingenerate" and "God" are exact parallels and mean the same thing, the Ingenerate begot an Ingenerate. But if "ingenerate" means one thing while "God" means something else, there is nothing strange in God's begetting God, since one of the two receives being from ingenerate essence. But if, † as is the case,[54] that which is before God is nothing, "ingenerate" and "God" do mean the same, for "Offspring" does not admit of ingeneracy. Thus the Offspring does not allow himself to be mentioned in the same breath with his God and Father.*

12,37   *May the true God, † who is ingenerate in himself[55] and for this reason is alone addressed as "the only true God" by his messenger, Jesus Christ, who truly came into being before the ages and is truly a generate entity, preserve you, men and women, from impiety, safe and sound in Christ Jesus our Savior, through whom be all glory to our God and Father, now and forever, and to the ages of ages. Amen.*

---

[54] Wickham: ὥσπερ οὖν ἐστί; Holl and MSS: ὥσπερ οὐκ ἔστι

[55] Wickham: αὐτὸ ἀγέννητος; Dummer: αὐτοαγέννητος, which is synonymous; Holl and MSS: αὐτογέννητος. This last cannot be what Aetius wrote, but is surely what Epiphanius read, cf. 54,2.

The end of Aetius' treatise

13,1   And this is the beginning of my refutation of his corruptible passages, part of which have come into my possession. (For they say that, in all, he composed 300 other paragraphs like these, filled with impiety.) (2) But I publish the treatise here for scholarship's sake, if you like, as though a snake's body were decaying and rotting, and a good man had gathered up the bones of the carcass of the snake whose treachery might do harm to somebody. Aetius boasts of having put this treachery into writing for certain persons, and his treatise begins as follows. (3) But < by > God's inspiration let me prepare a preventative antidote because of it, for those who would like to be cured of his poison, by culling out the medicines of the words of the sacred scripture, from the beginning [of the treatise] until its end. I shall place my refutations next to each passage in these paragraphs of syllogistic reasoning, as follows:

14,1   *During my persecution by the Temporists some of them, among many other things, appropriated a brief treatise I had composed with particular effort on the subject of the Ingenerate God and the Generate, corrupted it with insertions and omissions, and issued it after altering the sequence of the argument. It fell into my hands afterwards because one of the virtuous brought it to me,* (2) *and I have been obliged, like a father, to correct the treatise again and send it to you, all you male and female champions of piety, to show you that the brief discourse accords with the mind of the holy scriptures. With its help you will be able, with brief counter-arguments, to put a stop to the impudence of everyone—the Temporists most of all— who attempts to contradict you about the Ingenerate God and the Generate.*

14,3   *For the ready comprehension and the clarity of my arguments I have separated objection from objection and solution from solution in the form of short paragraphs, and have begun with the Ingenerate God.*

15,1   Whether you think they are lengthy, or indeed, brief, I shall give the refutation of the exact words of your pompous dialectic and uselessly laborious syllogisms, without either omitting or repeating the endless number of the passages. (2) And in the first place, you wrote to the "male and female champions" of your connection [in the words I have given] above, and said that certain "Temporists" had appropriated the portion of your treatise that was then in your hands, < and had corrupted > it. But < going by > the expression † we catch you using,[56] < one > would sooner convict you and your disciples—not to say, your dupes—of bearing this name.

---

[56] Holl: < διὰ > τῆς ἐφευρεθείσης παρά σοι λέξεως; MSS: ἐρωτήθεις παρά σοι λέξεως.

15,3   For God's holy faith, which was there from the beginning
and yet never grows old, is always in existence. Its foundation has
been established and it has its Master, who is not in time. Hence
it is not temporal; it is forever, shares the citizenship of the angels,
and adorns the saints in every generation. (4) No, you're the
temporist! You have been fed on imposture and become stuck up,
and you mix your fodder indiscriminately with the flock's thorny
pasturage. For none of the ancients held your views, Aetius—you
who write against the "temporal," but are "temporal" yourself, and
of no ancient origin. (5) But at the very beginning of your introduction, when you said you had written the little book, you startled
the world in the terribly brilliant introduction to your work by
saying, "Ingenerate and Generate God"[57]—excuse my making fun
of your use of the terms of such a lengthy coinage of new names.

16,1   For what Christian, in possession of God's saving message,
could be inspired by the imposture of your fiction to come and
hear from you about a "generate God," to make a fool of himself
by learning to "worship the creature more than the creator, who
is blessed forever. Amen?"[58] (2) We have no created God, no manu-
factured God, but One who is uncreated and unoriginate, begotten of the Father without beginning and not in time. (3) For even
though you play games with "generate" and choose to make "generate" a synonym for ["begotten]," I shall not accept your expression even if you mean no less by it than "begotten of the Father."
"Men do not gather grapes of thorns, or figs of thistles,"[59] and a
correct statement is not to be expected from a man who is in error.
The Lord silenced the demons too, when they confessed that he
was Christ.

But you claim that your dinky little book is in accordance with
the sense of the sacred scriptures. (4) Tell me, which sacred scripture
ever taught the worship of a created God? As to God's being
"ingenerate," we can all see that. (5) But even this is not in the
sacred scripture in so many words; we fitly think and say this with
piety on the basis of correct and godly reasoning and our understanding of God itself.

16,6   But you say that you arranged your propositions as a short,
simple statement in the form of short paragraphs, so that the male
and female champions, as you call them—(dupes, actually)—will
know how to answer everyone. (7) Therefore, though I am no-
body, stupid, and not important but worth far less than many in

---

[57] So Epiphanius appears to understand Aetius' title. See below at 16,1–2.
[58] Rom. 1:25
[59] Matt. 7:16

God's holy church, I < shall take up > those remarks which you
think are weighty and clever, and which you have worked up as
a reply to important people—or rather, as your shout against the
truth—and, as I said, give the refutation of this incoherent, completely worthless nonsense of yours.

17,1   And this will do as my modest response to your prologue.
But [next] I shall insert your propositions, one after another, and
beside each statement and proposition put the answers to and
refutations of your syllogistic arguments, so that God's real servants
and champions who read this can learn the whole of your absurdity, laugh at it, and say, "The haughtiness of thine heart"[60] has
made this for you. (2) "For thou didst say in thine heart, I shall
ascend to heaven, and above the stars of heaven will I set my
throne. I shall sit on a lofty mountain; upon the lofty mountains
of the north will I ascend above the clouds and be like unto the
Most High. But now shalt thou descend to hades, to the foundations of the earth," and so on.[61]

18,1   And this is the beginning of Aetius' propositions:

1. *Whether it is possible for the Ingenerate God to make a generate thing
ingenerate:*
    Refutation. It is impious to begin with to think of impossibility
in connection with God, except for < the impossibility > of anything unsuitable to his Godhead—and this not because he cannot
do it, but because evil is unsuitable to the God for whom nothing
is impossible. It is impossible for his mighty divine goodness, and
for him in his goodness, to do evil.

18,2   *And otherwise,* if God regards the < making > of the ingenerate
generate as a good work, but lacks the power to bring something
that was going on well to a good conclusion, this must be a defeat
for the God who wants to do the better thing, but cannot. (3) But
if the ingenerate is good, but the generate was well made in its
own order, then, since the order of the generate is a good order
which stems from a good God, and which God regards as good,
God would not make a thing ingenerate which had been well
generated. He is satisfied with its being good in its own way.

18,4   Therefore, since the order of a good thing is not unchanged because it cannot be changed, but because it is good that
it be as it is, the ingenerate God is good. And the things he makes
are good in their own order, without taking the name of "ingenerate."

---

[60] Obad. 3
[61] Isa. 14:13–15

For God did not make created "gods," so that one could be equated with the other and remove the opposition between "greater" and "lesser" by the title, ["god"]. (5) If the one is an ingenerate God and the other a generate God, since their natures have nothing in common the generate God cannot by his nature share < in > the rank of the name [of God], except by a kindly intended misuse of the word—and then only if the well endowed God grants this to the lesser God by participation.

18,6   But the lesser God would never call himself by the greater God's name, but knows that he is entirely ineligible to have the rank and title by nature. Someone ought to tell you, "The Word *was* God,"[62] Aetius—not, "The Word *became* God." If indeed the Word "became" anything, how will he get < the > title of nobility by nature, or how will he be made equal to God's rank? Or how can the phrase, "was God," be got rid of? The time implied by "was" does not allow for the slightest distinction [between Gods].

18,7   But let me inform you that the God who has no beginning, the ingenerate God, begot, of himself, a God like himself— and not only like him, but in every way equal to him. (8) And he did not create him. Otherwise, since the creature had been unlike [his creator], he would have made the name "God" inapplicable because of the extent of the difference [between the two]. For the begetter cannot beget an offspring which is unlike him and not his equal, and the begotten cannot be unlike his begetter. (9) Here, then, < pious reason* > will comprehend the fact of [the Son's] sameness [as the Father] from the Gospel's text, "All that the Father hath are mine."[63] In other words: "The Father is God; I am God. The Father is life; I am life." And everything else that fits the Father < fits > the Son and the Holy Spirit in one Godhead, with no distinction between the persons of the Trinity. (10) For we are plainly assured of the perfect knowledge that the subsistent Word < has been begotten > of the Father without beginning and not in time, and that the subsistent Holy Spirit < proceeds from > the Father and < receives of > the Son.

19,1   2. *If the Ingenerate God transcends every cause, he therefore must also transcend origination. But if he [indeed] transcends every cause he plainly transcends origination also. For he has neither received his existence from another nature nor provided himself with existence.*

19,2   *Refutation.* If the ingenerate God transcends every cause, and yet the One whom he generated was generated unworthily

---

[62] John 1:1
[63] John 17:10

of him and not his equal, yet still retains the Father's transcendent name, the Offspring disgraces his Begetter by having the dignity of a name different from creatures but not doing honor to his maker as creatures do. (3) For other things win glory for their creator without being their maker's equals or having his name, but by being made as servants to their maker's glory, so that the superiority, even to them, of Him < who is > superior to the things that have been made glorious, may be observed, by proportion, from the glorious creatures. (4) If, however, the one who is not yet given their name but who has his rank by co-essentiality with the higher Being because of being generated together with him, is [still of] a different kind than the higher Being < because of > the difference [between them], he will even reduce the higher Being's rank because the offspring's participation in the union is different as compared with the Superior. (5) The Offspring is therefore not understood by faith to be the like offspring of a like parent and equal offspring of an equal parent, on the analogy of a physical offspring. He is God of God, light of light, and the subsistent Word of the Father. The unchanging glory of the Superior is thus preserved, in that the Superior < is > not his own cause, but generates from himself the equal of his pure and incomprehensible essence—co-essentially generates the real and subsistent divine Offspring. This is not a lifeless image, but replicates the Father's kind—as, to assign equality with the Begetter to the Offspring, the sacred scripture says, "image of the invisible God."[64]

19,6   And lest it be supposed that there is a difference between image and identity, the Father himself, to provide for the restoration of our life, said, "*Let us make* man in our image and after our likeness"[65] before this last text (i.e., Col 1:15). He did not distinguish himself from the Son, but used a dual and equivocal expression, "*Let us make* man," to mean two, himself and the Son— or, indeed, I would also say the Holy Spirit. (7) And < by using the words, "in image and in likeness" > of the image's exactitude, and saying besides with two words that [the Son] is not < unlike > [the Father], he said that there is one image. But with "our" he declared that it is the image of two persons, and that the man who is being made, is not being made in the image of the one but in the likeness of the two, and is being made an exact image. This makes it entirely clear that the superiority of the Father, the Son

---

[64] Col. 1:15
[65] Gen. 1:26

and the Holy Spirit remains identical and unvarying.

19,8 For neither the Father, the Son nor the Holy Spirit has taken anything from another nature, or given another nature participation in his nature and rank. Nor did the Only-begotten and the Holy Spirit originate from the Father by an alteration of his nature, by the division of it or by an emanation from it. He has declared to us, plainly and consistently, that, as the ingenerate and uncreated nature was always superior, so a superior Offspring and Holy Spirit were always of him.

20,1 3. *But if, not from the inadequacy of his nature but because of his transcendence of every cause, he did not provide himself with existence, how can anyone concede that there is no difference of essence between the nature that provides existence and the nature that is provided with existence, when such a nature [as the first] does not admit of origination?*

20,2 *Refutation.* You should look up, Aetius, realize your pitiable condition, and put a stop to the worse than impiety of your rash notion, < or > no one will suppose that I have not been overawed by such temerity and caught your madness, but that I am giving godly counsel to you and myself. (3) For by supposing that, in the essentials and the things becoming to God, God is unlike and not the equal of the Son he has begotten, and by < seeing fit* > < to preach > with extreme imposture that † < the* > Son < is "of" him >[66] by some holy act of creation, you are preaching, if anything, that God is like the Son in the most unsuitable ways, which do not become his Godhead.

20,4 In the first place, to think of God with such profoundly stupid irreverence is the fruit of impiety, or rather, of a diseased mind. (5) By saying that < he > is [either] his own cause, or else that he < provided > himself with existence, you, in your search and quest for the origin of God, have entangled yourself in two wicked opinions: that is, either he always provided himself with existence or he exists by chance. And when I contemplate your wicked piece of reasoning I am frightened and shake with fear. (6) Stop it! Let's stop it! It is enough for us and our piety to understand and believe that the everlasting God was always God!

Indeed, you said, as though you had bestowed a great honor on God, that God neither provides himself with existence nor < is his own cause >, though here too there is no sense in what you say and think. On your premises, then, if the preservation of the faith depends upon words and arguments, < the divine nature would

---

[66] Holl: < ἡγούμενος >... ἐξ αὐτοῦ τὸν υἱον; MSS: ἐξελθεῖν θεόν

appear* > to be in a category similar to that of inferior beings and wretched bodies. (7) No creature, from bugs to man, from men to angels, is its own cause or has provided itself with existence. (8) No created thing has provided its own being; each has received the inception of its existence from the only Being who [truly] is. So since you have been foiled and beaten by the arguments you thought you could use, stop your unnatural effort to measure yourself against One higher than you! For you will be thwarted in every way since, even though he derives his rank from the Father < by > begetting—or by generation if you will—the Only-begotten is equal to and like the Father. (9) He will be no different from his equality with the Father because of this, just as he will be no different from his likeness because created things cannot provide themselves with being—in the same way that He who is their superior and in all ways perfect did not have his origin from anything before him. (10) For he did not begin to be, either. He was always and is always, even though he remains as he is and does not provide himself with being. We have no need of synonymous expressions, but of the consideration < which* > genuinely < makes for* > piety.

20,11 *And otherwise*, since you have said, "And if, not from the inadequacy of his nature but because of his transcendence of every cause, he did not provide himself with existence," learn for your own part that the Son's name cannot come from inadequacy, because he has the special fitness for it of co-essentiality with his Begetter. (12) For as transcendence of every cause is most becoming to the Father, so the same one Godhead is becoming to the only < Son > of the only Father, with the Holy Spirit—a Godhead which, not because of its inadequacy, but because of its transcendence of each and every thing < that has been made > from nothing, cannot admit of a cause. For there is one Godhead, which is enumerated by one name, "Trinity," and is proclaimed by candidates for baptism in their one profession of the names of "Father, Son and Holy Spirit," in the words that truthfully express the equivalence of the naming of a "Father," a "Son," and a "Holy Spirit."

20,13 But again, you said, "how can one concede that there is no difference of essence between the nature that provides existence and the nature that exists, when such a nature [as the first] does not admit of origination?" And you neither understand, nor have understood, how you have deprived yourself of knowledge of God's truth, because you are not taught the truth by the Holy Spirit, but are trying to penetrate the heavens by the wisdom of this world, which has been made foolish. (14) You will accordingly hear that [this wisdom] has been brought to naught for you: "The Lord knoweth the thoughts of the wise that they are vain."[67]

20,15   For He who begot the subsistent Word begot him equal to himself and not different from his Godhead because of the difference between him and the Offspring, but < in all ways like himself.* > For it would be entirely inappropriate for us to suppose that the Begetter himself has begotten the Offspring unworthily of himself, unequal to him, and inferior to the Begetter. (16) Scripture has said that all things were made through the Son, the subsistent Word, so as not to count him as a creature, but as the Father's like and equal in < everything >, as befits the name, "Father"—forever < like > Him Who Is, not strange to him but his true Son, a Son begotten of him with the same essence.

21,1   4. *If God remains forever ingenerate and his Offspring forever an Offspring, the heresy of the homoousion and the homoeousion will be brought to an end. But the essential incomparability [of the two] remains, since either nature remains endlessly in the rank proper to the nature.*

21,2   *Refutation.* If God remains ceaselessly in his ingenerate nature, as you have said, but the nature of God is eternal and in ceaseless possession of its rank, not because of something else but because it is God in his very essence and eternity in its very essence, then, if you call the Offspring "endless," he must surely be co-essential with God. For you have turned round and granted the Son the title on convincing natural grounds. (3) For you will grant, and will be forced to admit, that "endless" means entirely boundless and unlimited. Very well, how can he not be co-essential [with the Father]?

Since you have seen fit to mock the truth and tried to insult it with an heretical name, < you will be > defeated by the very words you have used. (4) For you will either admit that the essence you have blasphemously termed different [from the Father's] < has > an end—or, once you have declared him "endless," you will be obliged to teach the entire unalterability of his rank and the indistinguishability of the rank of the endless [Son from that of the endless Father]. The truth will not allow that the Son has an end for, because the scripture says, "Of his kingdom there shall be no end,"[68] he rules forever with the Father and the Holy Spirit.

Whatever has a beginning will also have an end, at the pleasure of Him who provided the thing that had a beginning with being. This is admissible in all cases, but inadmissible in the case of the Son. (5) For he is forever of the God Who Is and with the God

---

[67] 1 Cor. 3:20
[68] Luke 1:32

Who Is, and never ceases to be. Therefore he was, is and will be co-essential with the Father, the only Son of an only Father, and in no way different in essence—but is, as the ranks of the names imply, of a Godhead which remains identical [with the Father's], which has no amalgamation or beginning, which does not provide itself with being, and which admits of no unlikeness in itself. It is forever and never ceases to be, and is becoming to itself, for it is forever and ceaselessly in the rank of the Father of a Son, and of the Son of a Father, and of a Holy Spirit with a Father and a Son. For the Trinity cannot be compared within itself, since it admits of no distinction in rank.

22,1   5. *If God is ingenerate in essence, the Generate was not produced by a separation of essence, but God gave it being by virtue of his authority. For no pious reason can allow that the same essence is both generate and ingenerate.*

22,2   *Refutation.* You have come forward many times with your "ingenerate and generate," Mister, and brayed out God's name, and yet buried your notion of him underneath all sorts of lawlessness. For that name is an object of longing to one who is in doubt about it, and the resolution of his doubts is a consolation to the doubter, < but > if his doubts are not resolved, < he is ashamed* > even to say it. (3) And since you have no God you are < not > proud to say this name if only to mouth it, for you have never received it in the fear of him, in faith and hope, and in love for him. (4) Otherwise it would have been enough for you to say this once, and not go beyond the allowable limit for repetition. The Savior's pronouncement about you is plain, "By their fruits ye shall know them;"[69] for you are dressed in a sheep's fleece, but inside it you are a predator, like a wolf.

22,5   For if you were born of the Holy Spirit and a disciple of the apostles and prophets, you ought to go < looking > all the way from the Genesis of the World to the Times of Esther in the twenty-seven books of the Old Testament, which are counted as twenty-two—and in the four holy Gospels, the holy apostle's fourteen Epistles, the Acts of the Apostles before their time together with their Acts during it, the General Epistles of James, Peter, John and Jude, the Revelation of John, and the Wisdoms, I mean Solomon's and Sirach's—and, in a word, in all the sacred scriptures, and realize that you have come to us with a name, "ingenerate," which scripture never mentions. It is not inappropriate for God but an orthodox term for him, but it is nowhere to be found in the sacred

---

[69] Matt. 7:16

scripture, since no one < but > a madman would ever conceive of God as being generate.

22,6 But neither did they need to say that only the Father is the "ingenerate God" because his Son is generate, to avoid giving the impression that ingeneracy applies not only to the Father, but also to the Son and the Holy Spirit. Right-mindedness and the Holy Spirit teach all the sons of the truth of themselves not to be unclear about this, but to have the knowledge of God which is requisite, and which in itself belongs to < right > reasoning with regard to piety. (7) But if Anomoeans < say that* > < "ingenerate" is the proper name for God* >, since he is ingenerate—and I too agree— < I shall reply that this term is not inappropriate* >, but that they have no scriptural support for the use of the word. Piety knows of itself, by < correct > reasoning, that this < expression* > is accurate. For why will there be a difference[70] of essence < between the Ingenerate > and the Generate, if the latter really has the name because of his begetting, in some natural and ineffable sense—in a sense appropriate to God, and to the Son begotten of him without beginning and not in time, in reality and not in some accommodated sense of the word? (8) I therefore deny that his essence is created, or that it is different [from the Father's] because of being a created thing, but [maintain] that it is really begotten, and not different from its Begetter.

It thus remains not created and not made, but begotten of the very essence of God, and unaffected by time. For his true Begetter was not affected by time, so as to give being to an essence affected by time. For as is the Offspring, so is the Begetter; as is the Begetter, so is the Begotten.

23,1 6. *If the Ingenerate was generated, what is there to prevent the Generate from having become ingenerate? For on the contrary, every nature tends < away from > that which is not natural to it toward that which is.*

23,2 *Refutation.* If the Ingenerate made < the Generate >, and did not beget him, [then], since the name [of either one] is restricted to the one identity and neither is comparable with the other because of the real opposition of their meaning, the meaning of their relationship is the difference between the one and the other. For neither has anything in common with the other except only the authority of the superior nature, < which is > the cause of all it has created.

---

[70] διάστασις, as in 22,1. The word as Aetius employed it is best rendered, in context, "separation." Epiphanius appears to have understood it as "difference."

23,3   But since there is another term between "maker" and
"made," and between "creator" and "creature"—a term close to
"ingenerate" but a long way from "created"—you cannot confuse
all this, Aetius, and deliberately do away with the Son's share in
the perfect name, which reflects the true relation of the Son to
the eternal, uncreated Father. (4) < For > an ingenerate, uncreated
being can never become a creature, and change back from
creaturehood and return to its ingeneracy once more, even though
you construct a million Aristotelian syllogisms for us, abandoning
the simple, pure heavenly teaching of the Holy Spirit.

24,1   7. *If God is not wholly ingenerate, there is nothing to prevent
his having generated as an essence. But since God is wholly ingenerate,
there was no separation of his essence for the purpose of generation, but
he brought an Offspring into existence by his authority.*

24,2   *Refutation.* God is both wholly ingenerate and wholly
uncreated, and so is the Son he has begotten, and so is his Holy
Spirit < whom > you belittle, you carnal and natural Aetius who
are spiritually discerned! (For the Holy Spirit has his distinctive
character [from God] in a way peculiar to himself, and is not like
the many things which have been created of him, through him,
and because of him.)

24,3   And so [the Son] will have nothing in common with
creation, and no creature can share his rank. For all things are
transitory and pass away; and he leaves every logical argument
behind him, < defeated* > by the word of instruction from the
sacred scripture, "No man knoweth the Son save the Father, neither
knoweth any man the Father save the Son, and he to whom the
Son will reveal him."[71] (4) But the Son reveals him through the
Holy Spirit—not to those who argue about him, but to those who
truly and fully believe in him. For even though you come with a
million silly arguments, you pitiable object as I regard you, you
can neither "find out his judgments" nor "search out his ways,"[72]
as the scripture says.

25,1   8. *If the Ingenerate God is wholly generative, the Offspring was
not generated as an essence, since God's essence is wholly generative and
not generated. But if God's essence has been transformed and called an
Offspring God's essence is not unalterable, since the transformation brought
about the formation of the Son. But if God's essence is both unalterable
and above generation, talk of "sonship" will admittedly be a mere verbal
ascription.*

---

[71] Matt. 11:27
[72] Cf. Rom. 11:33.

25,2   *Refutation.* Not only you, Aetius, but every "heretic" should "be avoided after one admonition,"[73] as the holy and wise commandment directs. For you stand "self-condemned,"[74] inviting your own destruction and not compelled to this by anyone else. (3) Who can pity one who is "evil to himself and good to no one?"[75] But for my part, lest you think † in your self- < conceit >[76] that the evils you have propagated in the world are important objections [to the truth], I myself shall go patiently on grubbing up your thorny roots with "the two-edged sword, the word of Christ,"[77] by the sound, full and true confession of faith before God.

25,4   For glory to the merciful < God > who has found what sort you are—you who occupy the place of Judas, who was counted as one of the disciples but cut off from them, not by Christ's intent but because he had learned the denial of the Lord from Satan. (5) And what need is there to say anything more to you, since you are entirely different from Christians—from prophets, apostles, evangelists, martyrs and all the saints who are prepared to convict you at the day of judgment? For they endured the rack until death, they were scourged, torn, consigned to the beasts, fire, and death by the sword, rather than deny that he is God's Son and truly begotten of him.

25,6   For the Father is the Begetter of a sole Only-begotten, and of no one else after the One. And he is the Pourer forth of a Holy Spirit and of no other spirit. But he is the creator and the maker of all that he has made and continues to make. (7) Therefore, since many Sons are no longer begotten and many Spirits do not proceed from him, and since the same Godhead remains forever and is glorified in a Trinity and is never augmented, diminished, or supposed not to exist, the rank is not limited to a mere name in the Godhead's case. (8) [If it were], he would have many brothers like himself after him—as in the text, "I have begotten sons and exalted them,"[78] and, "who hath begotten the drops of dew,"[79] and, "of whom the whole family in heaven and earth is named,"[80] and,

---

[73] Cf. Tit. 3:10
[74] Tit. 3:11f
[75] Cf. Ecclus. 14:5.
[76] Holl: ἐν σεαυτῷ < πεφυσιωμένος >, and omit MSS ἔχων. Otherwise, read ἐν σεαυτῷ ἔνδον, also with the omission of ἔχων.
[77] Cf. Heb. 4:12.
[78] Isa. 1:2
[79] Job 38:28
[80] Eph. 3:15

"Have we not all one Father?"[81] and, "my son Jacob,"[82] and, "my firstborn Israel."[83] (9) These are all "sons" by analogy, by a mere verbal locution, because they have progressed from non-existence to existence, and are not sons essentially in the true sense of the word, but are merely [sons] < in name > and by grace. Therefore they have been created by the One who is not called Son by grace or merely in name, but < is > truly the Son. [They are] created by the One, through the One, with him who proceeds from the One and receives of the Other.

26,1   9. *If the Offspring was in the Ingenerate God in germ, he was "brought to maturity," as one might say, after his generation by receiving accretions from without. Therefore the Son is not "mature" because of the causes of his generation, but because of the accretions he received. For things which receive accretions genetically in the sense of being constituted by them are characteristically termed "mature" in some distinctive way.*

26,2   *Refutation.* If it had not been agreed that the Begetter is incorporeal, your entire performance might be worth staging. You scare no one else by staging it, however, but confuse your own mind [and deprive it] of the true confession of faith. (3) God, who is perfect in himself, begot of himself a perfect Son; he did not, contrary to nature, beget someone else. For the Son is not unsuited to his Begetter, and has no need to acquire anything from without. For, after the essence of God, there is nothing greater than God, which could share with God if he needed acquisition to come to maturity. (4) For He who is forever the incorporeal God has begotten the Incorporeal, by generation, to be with him forever; the Perfect has forever begotten the Perfect—God, who is spirit, begetting the subsistent Word, who is also spirit.

26,5   But what you say is silliness, Aetius, you treader on < the heights >, who get your ideas of God from syllogisms and out of your own logic-chopping head. For to the God who made all things from nothing and can do everything perfect at once, who needs no further benefaction and who governs these things by his decree, you are assigning the name of an essence that is subject to growth, < and > a Word in need of extra divinity, and are not even putting < him > on a level with his creatures. (6) For he made them perfectly at the beginning, and decreed by a wise ordinance that the further things that would spring from them would have no need to acquire anything. Those are the things in which successive

---

81 Mal. 2:10
82 Isa. 44:2; Jer. 26:28
83 Exod. 4:22

generations have been born and will be born—heaven, for example, the earth, water, air, the sun, the moon, the stars, and creatures which have been born from the waters—up to man himself. (7) God did not make heaven imperfect, or the earth in any way imperfect. He made the earth perfect and heaven perfect, though it was "invisible and chaos"[84] because of the order he was to impose on it. But he made water and the original light at the same time, making all things through the true Light, the uncreated and life-giving. (8) But then he made the things that have grown from the earth, and the firmament before that—not half-finished, but he made all things in their perfection. For < he says >, "Let the earth put forth herbiage of pasture, sowing seed in its likeness upon the earth, and fruit-bearing trees whose seed is in them in their likeness upon the earth."[85]

26,9 And you see that the things God had made full grown needed no additional endowment at the moment of their creation; they were "adult," as it were, and perfect at once, by God's decree. (10) But the things which were bestowed on man to be his subjects and were with him in germ for him to rule, were not entrusted to him full grown. For man always knew the Benefactor who bestows being on all, but who is over all, and who provides each created thing's benefactions for the sustenance of those who are of service to him.

26,11 God gave man the earth with the potential for growth, laying it out before him like a floor, as it were, and entrusting it to him as a womb, so that man could borrow the seeds produced by the plants which God had made perfect, and which were sown in the earth with spontaneous wisdom as a tree can do, [and the seeds] of other produce—borrow them from the mature plants in bits as small as a pebble (12) and sow this produce, and await what would be given for their increase < by > the perfect God. The crops man sowed would thus be increased from without, and man would not be unaware of the Provider of the bounty, think himself the creator, and be deprived of the truth.

26,13 For even though Noah planted a vineyard, scripture does not call him planter; he "was made an husbandman."[86] There is a difference between God who bestows the original gifts on things that are to be, and man to whom God's husbandry is entrusted. The one is meant to tend the gifts needed for growth to maturity,

---

[84] Gen. 1:2
[85] Gen. 1:11
[86] Gen. 9;20

but the other to provide the maturity, by his gift of his creatures
and of things that grow to maturity. (14) And so with beasts and
birds; so with domestic animals, reptiles and sea creatures. In the
beginning they were all made full grown by the God who commanded it, but by the will of his wisdom they now need a gift [from
him in order to grow]. This is intended for the benefit of man
who rules on earth, so that < he > will recognize the God above
all, the Provider of the seed-bearing plants and the gift of their
growth, as God and Lord.

26,15   For this reason God has left the heavenly bodies, which
are not sown by human hands and which neither beget nor are
begotten, in a full grown state. For they—the sun, moon and stars,
for example—did not spur the human mind on to treachery and
the pride of vainglory. (16) Not even the moon alters its appearance because it is born, wanes or waxes, but to mark and usher
in the seasons, which God has regulated by the luminaries. (17)
If God made corporeal things full grown at the outset when he
chose, although they cause other things to decay, and they themselves decay, why should he beget the One he has begotten of
himself—One [begotten] of one, the true God who is forever with
the true God by generation—in need of any benefaction?

26,18   All right, Aetius, stop bringing me your worthless Aristotelian syllogisms! I have had enough of them and am not to be
cheated of our Lord's true teaching, which says, "I came forth from
the Father and am come."[87] The saying is not meant loosely, but
gives indication of the essence of God's perfection and dignity.

27,1   10. *If the Offspring was full grown in the Ingenerate, it is an
Offspring by virtue of properties which were in the Ingenerate, and not
by virtue of those by which the Ingenerate generated it. [But this cannot
be], for there can be no generacy in ingenerate essence; the same thing
can< not > both be and not be. An offspring is not ingenerate, and if it
were ingenerate it would not be an offspring, for to say that God is not
homogeneous is to offer him sheer blasphemy and insult.*

27,2   *Refutation.* In his desire to understand God through logical terminology of human devising Aetius introduces opposition,
and † < falsely >[88] tries, with words, to mutilate the sure hope of
the plain faith. He contrasts unlike with unlike, and sets expression
against expression to force them to mean the impossible, the
unlikeness < of the Son > to the Father.

27,3   For he himself will be out-argued by the very arguments

---

[87] John 8:42
[88] Holl: ψευδῶς; MSS: καὶ ὡς

he has taught the world. He says, "If the Offspring were full grown in the Ingenerate, it must be an Offspring by virtue of the properties within the Ingenerate, and not by virtue of those with which the Ingenerate generated it. [But this cannot be], for there can be no generacy in an ingenerate essence. The < same > thing can< not > both be and not be. An offspring is not ingenerate, and if it were ingenerate it could not be an offspring, for to say that God is not homogeneous is to offer him insult and blasphemy." This means that the ground gained by the words is exposed to attack on all sides, for the Son *cannot be* unlike the Father, or unequal to his perfect Godhead.

27,4   For if he will insist on saying this, but turns < the > words he uses against each other and keeps saying that "ingenerate" and "generate" are opposites, he should learn from this < to contrast > the created and the uncreated. For the one cannot share the rank of the other, which is fit< ness > for any sort of worship. (5) If a thing that is unlike [God] is fit for any worship, since it is the equal of something [else that is] unlike [God] there will no longer be any sense in distinguishing the one thing from all of them. The unlike < being > cannot be compared, in the position of its rank, with the One, even though this one thing out of all the unlike things has greater glory; the unlikeness of < all > of them to the One has nothing in common with the One. (6) And the end result will be that the sun, the moon, the stars, the earth, and further things inferior to these, will be objects of worship—but no longer the One, with the One Spirit, that is, one Trinity, one Godhead, one Worship.

27,7   And so, if we must draw this inference for this reason, it will truly be the correct one. For the one Word is not like all the words, nor is the one Son the same as everything that is called a son by analogy; for he is not one of them all, but the one through whom they all were made. (8) The thing which Aetius himself at the outset termed impossible, and an insult to God and sheer blasphemy—because, as he said, there is < no > non-homogeneity in God—is not part of the difference [between the Son and the Father], but part of [the Son's] equality with the Father. And since the Godhead is not divided but is eternal perfection there are three Perfects, one Godhead. (9) But, if anything, the doctrine of unlikeness was confirmed for us as a proof of the true faith, so that we will neither hold with, nor believe those who, by a rash preconception, † have been unworthily < carried away >[89] with the

---

[89] Holl: Ἑλλήνων δόξαις ἀπαχθεῖσιν; MSS: Ἑλλήνων πταίειν

opinion of the pagans, who everyone knows worship the whole creation—which is unlike the Father who is worshiped in the Son, and the Son who is worshiped in the Father with the Holy Spirit, to whom be glory forever. Amen.

28,1   11. *If Almighty God, whose nature is ingenerate, knows that his nature is not generate, but the Son, whose nature is generate, knows that he is what he is, how can the homoousion not be a lie? For the one knows himself to be ingenerate, but the other, to be generate.*

28,2   *Refutation.* As a discriminator and surveyor who deals with the nature of God, Aetius, a human being who wants to know things that are beyond human nature, has said and declared that he knows—as a conclusion, not from scripture but from the arguments of mortals' notions—that "Almighty God, who is of an ingenerate nature, knows that he is not of a generate nature." (3) But never yet, from the very beginning of his treatise, does he say even by implication that the Only-begotten is a Son, as the original Arians did. (4) From the impudent remarks he keeps making, sons of the truth, observe at every point that he would like the Son to be entirely different from the Father, and to have no part at all in the divine nature. For there is no point < in his saying > that < God > knows he is ingenerate, and that he knows that he is not of a generate nature, and it is said < merely > < so as not > to call the Son a Son, even in name.

28,5   But his argument will be demolished. The Father is ingenerate and, because his nature is appropriate to him, has generated the Only–begotten eternally, < and is a Father* > by his generation of the Only–begotten as his one and only [Son], and his issuance of the Spirit. [The Holy Spirit is] an only Spirit who < co-exists >, in addition to the Only-begotten, with the only Begetter; and who co-exists with the Son who is begotten without beginning. The Father is spirit and begets spirit; he is not a body which can be divided physically, and which decays, grows, and can be cut. (6) Therefore, in the cases of all other things that beget and are begotten, they may have need of † each other for many reasons,[90] but here the rank of the One who is with the One, is not like all the others.

28,7   Therefore the Begotten himself, who has been uniquely begotten of him who has awesomely begotten him—just as he has been generated by the Ingenerate—is fit for his Begetter. He < therefore > begets no further sons himself—I mean, not of his essence—so that, because < the Son > begets no one else of his

---

[90] Holl: ἀλλ< ήλων >; MSS: ἀλλ'

essence and the Father is not begotten, the full glory of their rank may be preserved in both ways, in the single unity of the rank of Godhead: a perfect Father, a perfect Son, and a perfect Holy Spirit. (8) And thus the sacred scripture knows that the homoousion is no lie, and neither is the pious reason that has devoutly learned to glorify and worship the Father, the Son and the Holy Spirit by receiving the grace [for this] from God.

29,1   12. *If ingeneracy does not represent the reality of God but the incomparable name is of human invention, God owes the inventors thanks for their invention of the concept of ingeneracy, since in his essence he does not have the superiority the name implies.*

29,2   *Refutation.* I too, as I say to address Aetius, < confess the doctrine of > ingeneracy, and do not deny it even though it is not in sacred scripture; it is an orthodox idea. But in saying "ingenerate" I acknowledge that the Father is indeed ingenerate but do not deny that the Son is generate, though I do say that he is not created. Nor, if I declare that the Son is generate, can I deny that he has his being from God the Father. For the Father begot him by an act of generation, and did not create him.

29,3   For as you purposely pervert yourself—it can't be any-thing else—by thinking all crosswise about the "Generate and Ingenerate," you yourself must hear the words, "The thoughts of man are inclined to evil continually from his youth,"[91] of human arguments and contradictory syllogisms, and worthless human thought. (4) < But > I shall say for my part that, far sooner, it is inappropriate for the uncreated God to create creatures, and for the unmade God to make them. For if, as Aetius says, it is not proper that the ingenerate God beget, then it is inadmissible that the uncreated God create, and that the God who has not been made, make the things which are to be. (5) But since created things, and the greater part of their existing visible substance, are there to see, but do not befit the uncreated God < in the sense of > being his creatures, it will be desirable, in the end, that there be one uncreated God, and another who is created and, corre-spondingly, able to create. Otherwise the Incomparable will be cited for the change of created things, and, instead of what Aetius thinks of as suitable, will be regarded as unsuitable. (6) However, since the created God with the < power > to create is not self-generating but was created, another God will be required to be his creator, and another will therefore be invented. And there will be much idle talk about abysmal error, for our intellects will no

---

[91] Gen. 8:21

longer be sound, but will be instances of the saying, "The servants of God were made fools, and from knowledge, every man was made foolish."[92]

29,7 For no one "liveth to himself, and no man dieth to himself."[93] Nor will one learn to know anything but God, who has revealed his true faith to us < and said >, "This is my beloved Son, hear ye him"[94]—and his Begotten, who has revealed his Father to us and said, "I came forth from the Father, and am come."[95] (8) And God did not get his incomparability from a human name, nor will the rank of the true, subsistent divine Word, begotten of the Father without beginning < and > co-essentially, be impaired because of God's incomparability. For neither of them is indebted to human inventions for the names. (9) The Godhead receives no new rank, and no addition. The Godhead itself, of its fullness, provides for all—a fullness ever the same and never lessened, but ever bearing in its own essence the rank of its name, power and essence.

30,1 13. *If ingeneracy is only something external observers observe to be God's, the observers are better than the One observed, for they have given him a name which is better than his nature.*

30,2 *Refutation.* True it is that no one is better than God—say I to Aetius, the inventor of all this. How can anyone be better than God, when all things have received their being from God? (3) But since God is the cause of his creatures, rational and non-rational, visible and invisible, he himself is better than all, even if his rational creatures are of a mind right as to orthodoxy, so as to give partial, [not full], honor to That which is better than they. (If everything put together, and innumerably more, which has been thought to apply to God's praise, could compass the fullness of his glory, the Better < Being > would always be beyond the conception of its inferiors—even if they reach out with all their might, and beyond their might, towards the ascription of praise to their Better. For he is "better," not [merely] in word, but in power, name and word.)

30,4 But the praise of the Better by the inferiors will not distinguish between Incomparable and Incomparable. It knows the superiority through ingeneracy that is inherent in the Father, and the superiority that has been begotten of him. (5) Therefore the right mind God has granted men confesses < the > homoousion.

---

[92] Cf. Jer. 28:17.
[93] Rom. 14:7
[94] Matt. 17:5
[95] John 8:42

[It confesses this] to avoid inventing the unlikeness of the Son to the Father, and so dividing the superior, pure Perfection of Him through whom it knows [the Son] to have been truly begotten in an incomparable manner by his Begetter who, because of his superiority, is beyond any conception.

31,1   14. *If ingeneracy is not susceptible of generation, this is what we maintain. But if it is susceptible of generation, the sufferings of generation must be superior to the real nature of God.*

31,2   *Refutation.* To speak of any sufferings in God at all is the height of impiety. The Godhead is entirely immune to suffering, and very far above anything that occurs in our conflicting notions, < and > Aetius' argument will be completely defeated. For whatever takes place in us accompanied by suffering, exists in God without suffering. (3) For in us, willing is partly suffering—I do not mean the will to be godly, but the will to do something beyond our nature, because we cannot do what our will would like—say a man's will to fly, soar in the air, view the veins of the abyss, know the depths of the earth, and things of this sort.

But whatever in me involves suffering, is in existence without suffering in God. (4) For this reason God can do all he wills; for his nature does not conflict with his will, while our nature conflicts with as many desires as we have to reach out towards the impossible.

31,5   And because I have said that God does what he will, let no one say that he does the unsuitable. Not at all! God wills those things that he does, proportionately to his rank, with his will not in conflict with his capability, or his capability contrary to his will. But < God does not do the unsuitable* >, not because he cannot, but because he will not.

31,6   *And otherwise.* But come to think of it, after this freedom from suffering that exists in God, and < the nature > in us and in other creatures that is subject to suffering, we must admit that there is, in fact, still another "suffering;" after the second kind, a third kind can be distinguished. (7) We beget and are begotten with suffering, since our nature, and that of the other creatures which are begotten and beget, can be divided and drained, can expand and contract, can be burdened and lightened, and all the other things which are subject to suffering for such reasons.

But none of these were in God in his begetting of the Son. (8) If there were one such thing in God—in accordance with < the > doctrine which serves < them > as an excuse for repudiating the "Offspring"—I must reply to them, as the representative of the other side, that there is a second suffering, suffering in creating, and that we suffer in begetting and being begotten. (9) God, however, whom you conceive of as a creator and not a begetter and whom, as an argument against us, you accuse of suffering in begetting, in order to deny the legitimacy of the Son but consign suffering in creation to oblivion—(but this is not a form of suffering in God, heaven forbid! < God is entirely impassible* >. (10) We neither attribute suffering to God by the confession that he is the creator of all, nor, again, do we conceive of < another kind of > suffering in connection with him by confessing that he has begotten the true Son, truly without beginning and not in time.)

31,11   We therefore know that his nature is incomprehensible and not subject to suffering. Hence we confess him both as impassible begetter and as impassible creator. For he begot the Only-begotten without suffering, sent the Holy Spirit forth from himself without being divided, and created what has been and is being created without causing affliction or undergoing suffering. And he does what he will, in keeping with his Godhead, without reflecting first in order to determine by consideration whether the thing to be done ought to be done. Nor does he will to do a thing, and because of suffering lack the power to gratify will with performance. (12) He possesses at once will, deed, the begetting of the Only-begotten, and the creation of all things, for the divine nature and rank is far beyond the conception of Aetius' logic, and the logic of all mankind. God is superior to all invention, and gives way to no suffering but is far beyond all sufferings and any conception.

32,1   15. *If the Offspring is unchangeable by nature because of its Begetter, then the Ingenerate is an unchangeable essence, not because of his will, but because of its essential rank.*

32,2   *Refutation.* How long has this man been coming to me with the same thing to say, and never going beyond its content? From beginning to end he has described exactly the same things, and nothing else, about the same things. He has revealed no mysteries to me, (3) and has not taught me God as he professes to, nor taught me the faith through which the apostles worked when they raised the dead by the sound confession of the truth, cleansed lepers, and < performed > all the other acts of good concord, by which they gave examples of the real working [of miracles]. Instead he expounds useless, boastful syllogisms which do not go beyond their repetition, but are just that and nothing else. Please, then, none of you readers blame me if I attack the same points myself, since I am obliged to reply to his repetition.

32,4   For the Offspring is unchangeable as it befits Godhead to be, and the Begetter is unchangeable as, correspondingly, it

befits his unchangeable nature to be. The Begetter continues forever
to have the Son he has begotten, and allows his creatures no expectation of knowing the Father without the Son, and of ever
knowing the Begotten, and knowing his perfect Spirit who
proceeds from the Father and receives of the Son, without the
Father. (5) And this befits the rank of God's essence, which
needs no additional rank but is eternally of his own identical
rank.

33,1   16. *If "ingeneracy" is indicative of essence, it may properly be
contrasted with the essence of the Offspring. But if "ingeneracy" means
nothing, all the more must "Offspring" mean nothing.*

*But how < could > nothing be contrasted with nothing? If the expression,
"ingenerate," is contrasted with the expression, "generate" but silence succeeds
the expression, the hope of Christians may well begin and end [there] since
it rests in a particular expression, not in natures which are such as the
meaning of their names implies.*

33,2   *Refutation.* After learning to stupefy the minds of the simple,
why do these people love to anticipate the points against themselves! Aetius, whose hope is merely in an expression and not in
truth, has impudently come forward to pin it on me, although it
does not embarrass him to confess that the Son of God and God
the Father < differ > in a mere word. And yet I, of all people,
confess that the Father is real, the Son is real, and the Holy Spirit
is real; for nothing else can be compared with the Trinity.

33,3   And therefore the homoousion is truly the stay of my
confession, and not as an expression that can be canceled by use
and disuse, like Aetius' opinion of the Father, the Son and the
Holy Spirit. (4) There is actually a true Father, and actually a true
Son and Holy Spirit, however many worthless syllogisms Aetius
sows broadcast. As the sacred scripture says of such people, "I will
destroy the wisdom of the wise,"[96] and, "The Lord knoweth the
thoughts of man, that they are vain,"[97] and so on.

34,1   17. *If the term, "ingenerate," as against the term, "offspring,"
contributes nothing toward superiority of essence, the Son, who is [therefore]
surpassed only verbally, will know that those who have termed him "Son"
are his betters, not He who is termed his "God and Father."*

34,2   *Refutation.* No matter how much play-acting Aetius does
for me, no pious reason can allow that those who have received
being from Him Who Is are better < than the Son >. For he himself
agrees that they have been made through him. (3) For those who

---

[96] 1 Cor. 1:19
[97] Ps. 93:11

have been vouchsafed his kindness, < and > are privileged to be
called Christians because they truly know him and have been taught,
not by flesh and blood but by the Father, and who are therefore
rightly called blessed—like him (i.e., Peter) who recognized the
Son of God, with the addition of "living"[98] [to "God"]— have not
learned to call him "Offspring," as a verbal expression, but as a
"true Son begotten of a true Father." Nor are they spiritually discerned, < as > He who is spirit and only-begotten < discerns > the
soulish Aetius as incapable of receiving the things of the Spirit.

34,4   < For* > even though he says, "I go unto my Father and
your Father, unto my God and your God,"[99] < the Son remains
above the beings which have been created through him* >. (5)
Neither of these names can be equated with names of other sorts;
the truth abides forever, and each rank which can profitably be
discerned in the Son of God truly serves to clarify matters. (6) For
"my Father and your Father" cannot apply to them in the fleshly
sense; how can God, who did not assume flesh, be the Father of
flesh? And "my God and your God" cannot apply to the Son's
divine nature and the disciples' adoption as sons. (7) With < the
words >, "my God and your God," he who tells the truth in all
things for our < salvation > was mysteriously assuring the disciples
of his human nature. When he said, "my God and your God," he
< meant God's natural > relationship to him by the "my"—and at
the same time his relationship to us "which, in my kindness," < he
says >, "I allowed you to make your own by my coming," as the
scripture says, "He gave them power to become sons of God."[100]

34,8   Thus he himself took the form of a servant when he came
among them, and partook of something recent in recent days (i.e.,
Christ's human nature), though what was ancient (i.e., Christ's
divine nature) remained as it was and did not change in order
to be mixed [with anything new]. The sons of men were changed
to incorruption by participation in God, but not united with him
in co-essentiality; and he who took the form of a servant indicated
his recency by the word, "took," but did not undergo a change,
as is shown by "being in the form of God."[101] (9) Since these things
are so, and are wisely confessed, with full knowledge, by those
whom God has taught, neither "my God and your God" nor "my
Father and your Father" will express any difference from the right-
ful common possession of the pure divine essence, < or > from the

---

[98] Cf. Matt. 16:17.
[99] John 20:31
[100] John 1:12
[101] Phil. 2:6–7

transcendence of the Father's union with the Son, and the Son's, and the Holy Spirit's, with the Father.

35,1   18. *If the ingenerate essence is superior, and innately superior, it is ingenerate essence per se. For it is not superior to generation deliberately because it so wills, but because this is its nature. Since ingenerate nature per se is God, it allows no reasoning to think of generation in connection with it, and resists all examination and reasoning on the part of generate beings.*

35,2   *Refutation.* Aetius has involved me with the same bothers and, as I said, got me to repeat myself even frequently, because of his repetition, from beginning to end, of the same remarks about the same things. (3) The faith which saves every faithful person has never consisted of the speculation of human reasoning; human ideas are fallible, and cannot attain to the boundlessness of the essence of God. (4) Indeed, the whole of our salvation, the life-giving mystery of Christ, is "to the Jews a stumbling block, to Greeks foolishness. But to us who are called, both Jews and Greeks, Christ is the power of God and the wisdom of God. For the foolishness of God is wiser than men, and the weakness of God is stronger than men."[102]

35,5   Well then, wouldn't one class Aetius with the Jews because of the stumbling block of his syllogisms, but < regard > him as Greek because, in his own would-be wisdom, he considers God's truth foolishness? (6) For though the creator and artificer of all < is > one and is greater than all creation and handiwork, this does not mean that, because he is greater than his creatures, he does not make and create his creatures; he is not envious of his own goodness. For he is possessed of absolute goodness in his own right, and this is greater than all. He is not the victim of emotions, and it was not from envy or jealousy that he made what is out of what is not.

35,7   For he did not intend the things which he made, but which are inferior to his incomparable Godhead, to his own disadvantage, < making* > his creatures < to his own harm* >. He made them for his glory to manifest his own generous Godhead, for he is absolute goodness and self-existence[103] and imparts being to all the beings he has created from non-being because he wills them—each creature in proportion—to share the gift of each thing. (8) To the luminaries he has granted light, to the sky the beauties

---

[102] 1 Cor. 1:23–25
[103] This, and the other nouns beginning with αὐτό, suggest that Epiphanius read αὐτοουσία at 35,1.

of orderly arrangement, and portions of excellence to the earth and the rest, in accordance with his will. And on the angels themselves, and on other holy hosts, he has bestowed the gift of immortality; and on man he has bestowed the dignity of his image, and the gracious gift of life, knowledge and rationality. (9) And it was not after some hesitation that this came to him, by consent, as one might say, or after a change of mind or on reflection, but of his absolute goodness. For his nature, in his absolute goodness, is to have, to make, and to complete all things in a way that is becoming to himself.

35,10 Thus, as God procured nothing unbecoming his goodness < in > this, but glory and the knowledge of an awesome bounty, so there is no additional glory for his Godhead when he becomes known and perceived by his creatures. (11) The Godhead is never in need of an addition of glory. < It is > absolute glory, absolute excellence, absolute wonder and absolute praise, because the Father begot a Son though he himself was not begotten, < and the Son was begotten > to be with the Father as an eternal Wellspring of an everlasting Wellspring—stemming from him as Wellspring of Wellspring, God of God and light of light, with no beginning, not in time, but truly having a Father, while at the same time the Father truly has a Son not unbecoming to his Father, and without prejudice to the Father's incomparability. (12) For he is not a physical contraction but a subsistent Word, a Son of a Father, spirit of spirit and God of God. He excludes every speculation of logic, but is for the salvation of the faithful and of all that are made, through him and by him, by the Father, and who believe and know, and do not regard the power of God as foolishness—and do not regard the wisdom of God as foolishness, since it transcends all examination and all reasoning, particularly mortal men's, as Aetius himself has unwillingly admitted.

36,1 19. *If "ingenerate," when applied to God, connotes privation but "ingenerate" must be nothing, what reasoning can take away nothing from a non-existent thing? But if it means something that is, who can separate God from being, that is, separate him from himself?*

36,2 *Refutation.* Aetius tells me the things the pagan controversialists say about "privation" as though he were discussing it with reference to the knowledge of God and < for > a beneficial purpose. But to begin with, he does not know the cases in which "privation" is understood by the pagans. (3) Dialectic does not agree that "privation" can be spoken of with regard to everything, but only with regard to those things which are endowed with something by nature. For, [Aetius to the] contrary, one speaks of "privation" < in the cases of > things which admit of the cessation the things they have by nature; one does not say it of things which do not.

36,4   Thus one cannot say "blind" of a stone. A person who is sighted by nature and then loses his sight, is called blind. But surely if a bird, a man, or < any > beast whose nature is to see— when it is deprived of sight, it is called "blind" in the sense of a privation. (5) Similarly we cannot say "even-tempered" of < a stone >, or "harmless" or "ungrudging;" this is not a stone's nature. But of a man, or a beast with an irritable nature, one would speak of privation when it is not angry—but never in the case of things which cannot be angry.

36,6   I must apply this to God too, as though I were directing the argument at Aetius and cross-examining him. "Tell me, Aetius, do you know that God cannot be compared with all the things that are not of the same essence as his? Or would you even dare to count him as one of them all? (7) And if you would count him < with > all the things that are not of his essence, but which he has made from nothing through the Son who is begotten of his essence—[with all things, that is], with the sole exception of him (i.e., the Son) and the Holy Spirit, who is of the essence of the incomparable Father and his only-begotten Son—[if that is what you think of him], your confession of faith must be absurd in the extreme. (8) How can He by whom all things have been made from nothing, still be one of all things? This is impossible, and not even you would say it.

"But since he cannot possibly be like, or the same as, the beings which were made by him from nothing, he cannot possibly suffer like the beings which are unlike him—for whose emergence from non-being he is responsible, and all of whose qualities result from the privation of their opposites. (9) For some of them are sighted, not of themselves—(they do not have being of themselves, but by the generous grace of its Giver)—and suffering may < be caused > in these by the privation of things which they had by the gift of the Giver. He, meanwhile, is impassible and has his being from no one, and cannot be deprived, < like > the creatures which are made from nothing.

36,10   "Thus, if neither the Son, the Father nor the Holy Spirit is the same as they, but the Son is different from them and is not called by the same name, but has a special, incomparable name because < he is > absolute good and the Son of Absolute Good— [if all this is so], what can he have to do with privation < when* > there are < no* > opposites in < his nature* >?" (11) There is no need for Aetius' argument to tell me about privation, for it is not by the privation which is characteristic of creatures that the ingenerate God and his generate Son have their superior rank, but because of its natural and special appropriateness in itself to their being and Godhead.

So with God's freedom from anger. This is not because he is < not > angry, but because he is absolute freedom from anger. And the reason he is "ingenerate" is his absolute < in >generacy, even if the Son is generated from the Ingenerate. For talk of privation in the sense intended by the person suggesting [it] has no relevance to Him who is not comparable to the other beings. (12) For neither can the others be equated with the Generate, nor does the Ingenerate impart co-essentiality [with himself] to creatures. This is not because impossibility is an attribute of the Mighty [God], but because, due to the nature unique to the one God, and to his only-begotten Son with the Holy Spirit, impossibilities do not apply to the Mighty [God].

37,1   20. *If the "privations" of states are the removals of them, "ingenerate" as applied to God is either the privation of a state, or a state of privation. But if "ingenerate" is the privation of a state, how can something God does not have be counted as one of his attributes? If "ingenerate" is a state, however, a generate essence must be assumed to precede it, so that it may acquire [a new] state and be called "ingenerate." If, however, the generate essence partook of an ingenerate essence [to begin with], it has been deprived of its generation by sustaining the loss of a state.*

Generacy must then be an essence but ingeneracy a state. But if "offspring" implies a coming to be it is plain that the word means a state, whether the Offspring is made out of some essence or whether it is what it is called, an "Offspring."

37,2   *Refutation.* By already fighting fiercely, on the subject of privation, on the side of those who are strange to the faith, Aetius too has armed himself against the faith with the same weapons as they. But he says nothing that is based on the faith, and has not remembered what was said to those who say foolish things of their own invention and do not hold the Head of the faith—as the word says in refutation of them, "I said in my astonishment, All men are liars,"[104] after scripture had already said, "I am deeply humbled."[105]

37,3   Now, however, he again spends his time on the same things, and cites the rubbish of the terms, "privation" and "state," and the

---

[104] Ps. 115:2
[105] Ps. 115:1

reasonings of shaky human speculation. And though he is spiritually discerned he takes no trouble to check the special onslaught of the < idea stemming* > from human villainy that makes him < undertake > to say what he pleases about God. (4) Moreover, he once more obliges me to dwell on the same things myself although I have discussed the topic of privation at length, and to spend my time in refutations of him. (5) But we must not leave a hard-mouthed horse unbridled, whether it is galloping toward a ditch or has already been checked in its career. Nor may we give way to a man who is saying the same things against the faith, and not reply to him. So I shall speak again < to the question of > (6) "If the privations of states are the removals of them," and, "If it is the removal of a state, how can something God does not have be counted as one of his attributes?"

37,7   Even if < you pretend > to think of God in one way or another, Aetius, and guess at "states" in God, you will be deprived of your mind. No matter how many ideas about God enter your head to be stored away there—except just to believe him, marvel at him, and glorify him with all your heart!—you will be exposed as unable to out-argue God, his Son or his Holy Spirit, so that God will convict you, and you will be made a liar, as the scripture says. (8) There are states, wants and shaky ideas in us, since that is our nature and essence. But we can also speak of the nature and essence of God; and because we hear of God's nature and ours, and God's essence and ours, this does not mean that we are to compare the incomparable God with our nature. (9) And so with all that you say about God, Aetius. The Godhead is *per se* transcendent, incomparable, perfect in itself, with no need of anything; for it is absolute perception and absolute will.

37,10   Thus God has not been deprived of his < own > essence by incomparably begetting an incomparable only-begotten Son, nor < has he deprived the Offspring > of his rank, whom he has begotten of him as the only Offspring of an only Father—nor deprived the Holy Spirit of his rank. For the Offspring has no equality of nature, rank, or anything else with other beings. (11) God has not deprived himself of his incomparable Godhead in state or essence. Nor, as I said, has his Offspring been deprived of his Father's rank and his equality with the Father, (12) since it, like his Holy Spirit, cannot be compared with anything at all.

This makes a perfect Trinity; the Father is perfect, the Son is perfect, the Holy Spirit is perfect. It is not an amalgam, and does not differ from itself or have any subordination. (13) Otherwise what had been distinguished would remove the incomparability of

the Offspring, and what had been altered would cause a deprivation of [its] being, for it would either be called [an Offspring]
in appearance and not in truth, or else it would be named by a
mere word in passing, and not really exist. At any rate, this is the
way your idea is meant, Aetius, for it tries to exclude him from
the definition of faith, (14) "He that cometh unto God must believe
that he is, and that he is a rewarder of them that seek him."[106]
And this applies not only to the Father. "For he that hath not the
Son hath not the Father;"[107] and if one speaks of the Son, he cannot
do so "without the Holy Spirit."[108]

37,15   For the Father is truly "true God,"[109] as the Son, who
knows the Father, testifies. And the Son, who is known and witnessed to by the Father, is "true light."[110] And the Spirit, who is
not different [from God] but proceeds from the Father and receives
of the Son, is the "Spirit of truth."[111] (16) But these truths put an
end to all the syllogistic story-telling of your words, Aetius, and I
cannot be told to become a disciple of your master Aristotle, and
abandon < the teaching > of the fishermen who, though
"< un >learned and ignorant men,"[112] were enlightened in the Spirit
of God, and by God's power were heralds of the truth that was
vouchsafed them. For the kingdom of heaven is not in syllogistic
speech and boastful talk, but in power and truth. (17) Indeed I
have heard enough, from the beginning, of your argument about
the privation of states and accidents, and that generate essence
does and doesn't assume ingeneracy, and that it sustains the loss
of a state with a state, and the involvement of generate essence
with a state which is, however, ingenerate; and the passing mention
of an "offspring," though this means "only in the state [of being
an offspring]" and, because it has been remodeled from some
essence or other, indicate< s > a state, even though, as you have
said, it is called an offspring. (18) For your sick fancy says < the >
same things on the same subjects, and never utters the last of its
repetitions.

38,1   21. *If "ingeneracy" is a state and "generacy" is a state, the essences
are prior to the states; but even though the states are secondary to the
essences, they are more important.*

---

[106] Heb. 11:6
[107] John 2:23 (5:12)
[108] 1 Cor. 12:3
[109] John 17:3
[110] 1 John 2:8
[111] John 16:13
[112] Acts 4:13

Now if ingeneracy is the cause of generacy and means that there is an offspring which implies the cause of its own being, "offspring" denotes an essence, not a state. < On the other hand >, since ingeneracy implies nothing besides itself, how can ingeneracy be not an essence, but a state?

38,2 *Refutation.* As you see, friends of the truth, Aetius once more attempts an argument that distinguishes states in God, and states after God. And he puts some of them first, and others second. (3) But it is not right to assume firsts of God, or speak of seconds. God has all things at once and needs no additions. This is why pious reason does not allow the Offspring to be conceived of as born at some time. (4) < Nothing newer* > co-exists with God the Father, the Son and the Holy Spirit—that is, with the Trinity that *Is.* And so the God Who Is, is called the Father Who Is, and the Son Who Is is with Him Who Is, begotten without beginning and not in time. As the scripture says, "With thee *is* the will of life," and, "in thy light shall we see light;"[113] and "he who *is* in the bosom of the Father;"[114] and "In the beginning *was* the Word, and the Word was God."[115] And it says likewise of the Holy Spirit, "My Spirit *is* in the midst of you."[116] (5) And you see that there is nothing new in the Trinity. Therefore there is neither essence before state, nor state before essence.

38,6 And even if you make us say "state" of God, Aetius, we do not mean the precarious states, subject to change, which are in all the things that have non-essential states; and we do not mean anything in God that is more important [than He], or of later origin [than He]. We mean everything that, for his glory, is suitable to his rank. The one Godhead has one glory and one honor, "that they may honor the Son as they honor the Father,"[117] (7) and not blaspheme the Holy Spirit—because of the threat that does not forgive their sin either here or in the world to come. Nothing different [from this] can fitly be understood, worshiped or glorified in connection with the Trinity. We speak of, and truly glorify a Father in the Father, a Son in the Son, and a < Holy Spirit > in the Holy Spirit, just as the true faith fitly < requires > that we accord worshipful reverence to the one Trinity, and know its rank. (8) And the Ingenerate does not need the Generate to contribute to its essence, making the Generate the cause of its essence < because > it denotes < essence >. And the essence of the Begotten

---

[113] Ps. 35:10
[114] John 1:18
[115] John 1:1
[116] Hag. 2:15
[117] John 5:23

neither is, nor is called, a state of the Unbegotten.

38,9   For the Trinity is in need of nothing and receives no increment. Though the Trinity was always itself and no creature, this does not mean that it was by random chance, or for the honor of an additional title or an increase in dignity, that the Father thought of creating heaven, earth and all things visible and invisible through the Son, and stablishing the whole host of those very creatures of his by his Spirit—to gain the additional tribute of being called Creator and Artificer from the creation of the creatures and the making of creation, < and > of being perceived as Father besides, by the Son through whom and by whom the creatures had been made, and by the Holy Spirit in whom what was stablished had been stablished. (10) For God did not make his handiwork because he was changed from state to state and altered in his nature and essence, < or > as though by reflection and a changeable < mind >. He had eternal creativity and perfection in himself and needs no increment of glory. (11) And as no creature may conceive of an additional state in God and suppose that this is required by God's dignity, essence and glory, so Aetius, who wants to out-argue God about "ingenerate," "generate," and his argument about God's state and essence, will be stopped short. For it is agreed that all created things genuinely exist, and have not been contrived as an addition of glory to a God who needs none—just as we may not say that the Only-begotten and his Holy Spirit are the same as God's creatures, for this is not acceptable.

38,12   But since Aetius, with his chatter about high things and his impudent reaching towards the heavens, has come to me with syllogisms but draws his analogies from the creatures below, it will be found that he himself < has accomplished* > nothing < worthwhile* > with his logical arguments. For the wisdom of men passes away, and men's syllogisms are buried [with them]; "His spirit shall come forth and turn him to his dust."[118] (13) For all human argumentations are transitory and humankind will pass away, together with the artful reasoning of Aetius < and persons like himself* > about the faith. But as the scripture says, the faith, hope and the love † which he has despised[119] abide.

39,1   22. *If every essence is ingenerate like Almighty God's, how can one say that one essence is subject to vicissitudes while another is not? But if the one essence remains above quantity and quality and, in a word,*

---

[118] Ps. 103:2
[119] Holl and MSS: ὑπ᾽ αὐτοῦ συλλογιστικὴ πίστις; We conjecture ὑπ᾽ αὐτοῦ καταπεφρονημένη

all sorts of change because of its classification as ingenerate, while the other is subject to vicissitudes < and yet > is admitted to have something unchangeable in its essence, we ought to attribute the characteristics of these essences to chance, or, as is at any rate logical, call the active essence ingenerate but the essence which is changed, generate.

39,2 *Refutation.* I deny that every being is unbegotten,[120] or that every being is begotten of God. The God who has begotten the Son who has been begotten of him, and who has sent his Holy Spirit forth from himself, did not beget all beings. He begot One, who is therefore *only*-begotten; and he sent one Spirit forth from himself, who is therefore a *Holy* Spirit. But he created all beings through the One, and stablished them in the One, and some of them beget and are begotten after their creation, while some have been created, but neither beget nor are begotten.

39,3 But the uncreated being of the Trinity is far different from the beings that have been created, and not begotten, by the Trinity. (4) And so the Trinity is impassible and changeless, but all things after the Trinity < are > liable to suffering—unless the Impassible should grant impassibility by virtue of immortality, granting this as a generous gift to whom it will. They, however, do not have impassibility by virtue of an impassible nature, but by the generosity of the good and impassible God.

39,5 For not even the Only-begotten procures suffering in the flesh for his Godhead—although, by a true confession that stems from the true faith, it is believed that he suffered in the flesh although he was the impassible divine Word. But in his impassibility he remained the same, with no change or alteration of nature. (6) Therefore, since he was wisdom and impassible God, and knew that by suffering he would save those who are subject to the pain of death, he did not send "a messenger or an angel,"[120] or < anyone > further like the prophets before him, but came himself as Lord, assumed passibility and truly suffered, though his divine nature remained impassible.

39,7 For the incarnation did not weaken the power of his Godhead. We find him in his Godhead doing the works of God, and not prevented by flesh. He rebukes the wind, storm and sea, calls Lazarus by his sovereign authority, and does innumerable other things and more. (8) But he also allowed the flesh such things as were suitable—allowed the devil to tempt him, for example, men to strike him, the authorities to arrest him—so that

---

[120] So the context shows that Epiphanius understands ἀγένητος here.
[120] Cf. Isa. 63:9.

the Impassible would suffer in his passible nature, but remain impassible in his proper Godhead. (9) For he is not different from the impassible God, but does all things willingly in accordance with his awesome mystery—just as the Father contains all things, who is God with the Only-begotten himself and his Holy Spirit, one forever perfect Trinity and one impassible Godhead. He is one God and one sovereignty, for the same God contains all.

39,10 And his containing of all things does not make him passible, although the things he contains are subject to suffering. For God is within all and without all, not mingled with any. (11) And though God is everywhere, is without all things and contains all things, and all things are moved within him, they will not bring suffering on the impassible God—just as, < though > he has begotten the Only-begotten, or < because > the Only-begotten has been begotten, or though God's Holy Spirit has been sent forth, this will not bring suffering on the Holy Trinity. (12) For neither is the Holy Spirit passible, even though he descended to the Jordan in the form of a dove. Nor is the Only-begotten passible, even though he was baptized and touched by John; nor the Father, even though he cried from heaven in a voice audible to men, "This is my beloved Son; hear ye him."[121] (13) The Son, then, is immutable. And the Father is unbegotten, while the Son is begotten < but > impassible. And the Holy Spirit, who came forth, is also < impassible >. But all other things are creatures. The Holy Trinity, < however >, retains its quantity and uncreated name, with no change in the Supreme Being and no liability to suffering on the part of the Begotten; For neither does the Begetter suffer.

For the Offspring is not corporeal, but spirit [begotten] of spirit and Son of Father. (14) And the Spirit is likewise "of him," Spirit of the Father, Spirit of Christ, not created, not begotten, not their kinsman, not their ancestor, not their scion. For the incomparable being of the Father, the Son and the Holy Spirit surpasses all conception and all understanding, to speak not only of men, but of angels. (15) Neither the Only-begotten, nor his Father, nor his Holy Spirit underwent any change because the Only-begotten suffered in the flesh despite his impassibility, his Holy Spirit < descended > in the form of a dove, and the Father impassibly uttered a cry from heaven in the hearing of men. (16) Just so the angels when they were created, and the heavens, the earth and all things, underwent no change and suffering at the hands of their maker. The whole

---

[121] Matt. 3:17; 17:5

is an awesome mystery as the scripture says, "O the depth of the riches and wisdom and knowledge of God!"[122]

40,1   23. *If the ingenerate nature is the cause of the nature that has come to be but "ingenerate" is nothing, how can nothing be the cause of a thing that has come to be?*

40,2   *Refutation.* The ingenerate nature has a < causal > relationship in a different sense—not in the sense in which it is causally related to all things—to its only-begotten Offspring and the Holy Spirit who proceeds from it. But it is not causally related to them in the way in which that which exists is causally related to that which does not. For the Begotten is not begotten of nothing, and neither the Begetter nor the Holy Spirit who proceeds from him are non-existents—on the contrary, the Existent is the cause of the rest. (3) Therefore the holy Trinity co-exists in its own eternal glory, with a being proportionate to each name for its rank. For the things which have been made from nothing, have been made by the Trinity, and not by anything external to it.

This is why the Father by himself is not the cause of created things; the Father, the Son and the Holy Spirit made all things. (4) If the Son were different [from the Father], as though he < had been made > from nothing by a cause, he would have come forth along with everything else, and would himself have been the same < as they >. And God would have not been the cause by generation of the Son who had been brought forth, but would have been his cause by creation. And it could not be admissible that the one be called an offspring and the others creatures, but all should be called offspring along with him, or he should be called a creature like all the rest. And nothing would be exceptional (5) since, in that they were created from nothing, the One would be equivalent to all. I should say that not just angels would be equal to their maker and only-begotten creator, but men and cattle, and everything else that is infinitely inferior to his nature and rank.

40,6   < However >, He Who Is < forever > co-exists with Him Who Is Truly Begotten of him, though not in time—not [made] from nothing, but begotten of him. (7) And his Holy Spirit is in being, does not differ from his essence, and is not provided to God as though for his assistance, which is what Aetius says.

41,1   24. *If "ingenerate" is a privation but a privation is the loss of a state, and if a "loss" is completely destroyed or changed to something else, how can the essence of God be named after a changing or vanishing state by the title of "ingenerate?"*

---

[122] Rom. 11:33

41,2   *Refutation.* If the opinion of God which is to be derived from your syllogisms has been provided for God's glory only in your time—as your words above suggest—I too shall direct the same sort of remarks to you with God's permission, and address you myself. For since none of the ancient apostles or prophets in the Old and New Testaments held this opinion, you are asserting your superiority to God himself, and your unshakeability. (3) According to what you say, the Godhead acquired this subtlety of yours for its creed only in your time—this speaking about the privation of the ingenerate and generate, and giving God a name through the title of the divine essence.

41,4   No possibility of God's being deprived of things which are not his attributes has been found because God is the creator of all things after his Only-begotten and Holy Spirit. Nor has he come round to the acknowledgement of [new] attributes, so that his later creations add something better to God, and his purity can be conceived of both through its ability to be deprived of that in favor of this, and [also] through its changelessness. (5) The Godhead, however, is forever the same, and though it is wholly glory, and wholly incomprehensible by all its creatures, it is glorified by all, in accordance with the capacity of those who exert themselves in its praise. By the angels it is glorified in the tongue of angels, which the apostle declares to be preferable to men's. < But by men > it is glorified in the tongue of men, which is of a lower degree; < by the other creatures*, > in accordance with their still more inferior ability. (6) And God's glory has by no means been lessened or changed because God < is glorified > in each creature proportionately to < its ability >. It is unchangeable in itself, while all creation, in addition to its endless exertion of itself in praise, suffers deprivation; but the Supreme Being forever surpasses all understanding, and is neither changed, altered nor improved by the things everyone says are permitted it. For the same Godhead is superior, incomparable and glorified.

42,1   25. *If "ingenerate" denotes privation, which is not an attribute of God, why do we say that God is ingenerate but not generate?*

42,2   *Refutation.* God is indeed ingenerate, though this was nowhere said by any prophet, apostle or evangelist. To say this of God would be nothing surprising; pious reason would assume it from the natural law itself. (3) But because you coined the expression, Aetius, to say it to us, you think you are introducing another marvel. But you have confused and mixed your contrivance of the generate's equality of rank with the ingenerate with the godly law of nature, and with the rule of faith which God has granted to add an improvement, so that the One you worship as "different" (i.e., God the Son) may turn out to be the equal to the One you preach differently (i.e., God the Father).

42,4 If you worship the Father only in name, you have given him the honor deceitfully. And if you worship the Son while recognizing that he is unlike the Father, you have introduced confusion into the worship by honoring unlike equally with unlike. (5) If, however, you deny the Son worship from the prejudice of your unbelief, you will be reproved by all for failing to recognize Him who is rightly worshiped by all, and who is equal [to the Father]. "For all the angels of God shall worship him,"[123] and Mary and all his disciples worshiped him when he had risen gloriously in the flesh. (6) For they knew that he does not have the title of "born" or "created" < but > is begotten of the Father; and they worship him as the real God [begotten of] the real God, and worship the Holy Spirit, who is of him.

42,7 For they know that he differs in essence from creatures; he is not born or created, but begotten of the Father. And so, Aetius, after laboring over everything, spending a great deal of time, and introducing strange terms, < in the end you too* > will worship him.[124] (8) "For we must all stand before the judgment seat,"[125] and "every tongue will confess that Jesus Christ is Lord"— Jesus Christ, who is not different from God but "to the glory of God the Father,"[126] as scripture says and as we believe.

43,1 26. *If, as applied to God, "ingenerate" is a mere name, but the mere expression elevates the being of God over against all generate things, then the human expression is worth more than the being of the Almighty, since it is has embellished God the Almighty with incomparable superiority.*

43,2 *Refutation.* "Ingeneracy" is not a mere name when applied to God, and does not have any relationship of essence with created things. Thus "created things" is not a mere name either. But since another name in between "ingenerate" and "created" is needed, and this name is "Son"— < generate > and yet not created—which name shall we make the exception (i.e., exceptional in being a "mere" name, though the other two names represent reality)?

43,3 And if we grant that, [as Aetius says], created things are related [to the Son], then, since neither of the things we are

---

[123] Heb. 1: 6 (Ps. 96:7)
[124] Holl: . . . < τέλος καὶ σὺ > προσκυνήσεις αὐτῳ; Drexl, with MSS: . . . , καὶ λόγους ξενοὺς παρεισενέγκας προσκυνήσεις αὐτῷ
[125] 2 Cor. 5:10
[126] Phil. 2:11

mentioning (i.e., "creatures" and "Son") is spoken of with a mere name, (4) mere naming is not allowable in the case of the Generate and Son, just as mere naming is not allowable in the case of the Ingenerate and Creator, and in the case of created things. Aetius' senseless quibble will therefore show confusion in his reasoning, since, because created < nature > exists in reality and not < by > the mere naming of it, created beings cannot be equated with the name of "Son." For the Son himself does not permit the naming of "Son" to be the naming of a mere name.

43,5   But since the non-existent is not real, and the Son is not called "only-begotten" as a mere name, he is united with the Father's glory and is not to be mixed in with the category of creatures. (6) For the Godhead has no need of elevation, as though it did not exist. Nor does it need exaltation, even though, by some ignorant people, it is not exalted. And the being of the Godhead is not constituted by anyone's verbal locution. (7) No expression, of men or other creatures, can boast of winning glory as though for a God who needs it, or of embellishing God almighty, the God whom we worship, the God who is the master, creator and artificer of the expression. (8) For it does not suppose that it surpasses him in glory and is the beautifier of its own creator. Otherwise it would regard itself as worshipful, and certainly not worship Him who is to be worshiped. And your treatise, Aetius, starts a useless argument against all this to no purpose.

44,1   27. *If there is a cause to correspond with everything generate but the ingenerate nature has no cause, "ingenerate" does not denote a cause but means an entity.*

44,2   *Refutation.* Everything generate indeed has a cause, and I do not admit this as though I have learned it from you. The faith of the truth foresees, confesses at the outset, and teaches that God has no cause at all, and that he is uncompounded and entirely unequaled.

44,3   I myself, therefore, do not worship anything that is inferior to the essence of God himself, since it is proper to accord divine honor only to the Absolute—to the ingenerate Father, the Son [begotten] of him, and the Holy Spirit [who proceeds] from the Father and through the Only-begotten, since nothing in the Trinity is created and falls within the province of causation. (4) For nothing in the Trinity is made from nothing, like other things, which fall within the province of causation and have causes.

And so, since the Trinity is without such a cause, it has inerrantly taught that it alone can be worshiped; for it alone is without a cause. (5) But all other things must be categorized as caused. For they are things which have been made and created, while the Father is uncreated, and he has a Son who is begotten of him but not created, and a Holy Spirit who proceeds from him and yet is not his handiwork.

44,6   Since this is the case the Son, who is worshiped, has not inherited[127] the suffering of his cause even though, in the Father, he has a Begetter. And neither has the Holy Spirit. And other things, the creatures, cannot be the cause of any inheritance without suffering [themselves], since they are created by the Father, the Son and the Holy Spirit. (7) But the Only-begotten—and his Holy Spirit—can plainly be the cause of inheritance without suffering [themselves], for the Son is not a creature but an offspring and, since he has been begotten, will not inherit the causation of suffering. Neither will the Holy Spirit, since he proceeds from the Father. (8) For neither can the Father be classed as one who suffers in causing things because he has begotten [the Son], has sent the Holy Spirit forth from himself, and has created all the rest after the Son and the Spirit—though surely, all other things suffer in creating and begetting. (9) Therefore the Father, the Son and the Holy Spirit are uncaused; but the Trinity is the cause of all things, for it creates and fashions them jointly, meanwhile knowing that nothing within it is created or fashioned.

45,1   28. *If whatever is made, is made by something, but ingenerate being is made neither by itself nor by something else, "ingenerate" must denote essence.*

45,2   *Refutation.* To appear to be the inventor of a dialectical argument Aetius has come at me with this too, as though he were telling me something new and unheard of. There is simply no need for him to prove this particular thing. It is not in dispute, < its* > perennial < obviousness is not in contradiction* > to the truth, and it is confessed in the catholic church. (3) For "< If > whatever is made, is made by something else, but ingenerate being is made neither by itself nor by something else, 'ingenerate' must denote an essence." (4) What is more cogent than this? For Aetius has turned round and selected the term, "essence," which < is > regularly < rejected > by the Anomoeans themselves and the Arians, since he is plainly compelled by the truth to acknowledge it.

45,5   Ingeneracy, then, is an essence, and has generated the Only-begotten without defilement and without suffering, not in

---

[127] πάθος κεκλήρωται αἰτίου. This is either a misunderstanding of Aetius' vocabulary by Epiphanius, or association of ideas on his part. The reference is to Paragraph 27 of Aetius, which begins, εἰ παντὶ γεννητῷ αἰτία συγκεκλήρωται.

time and without beginning, not from non-existence but from itself. It has also sent the Holy Spirit forth, from itself and not from non-being. Therefore the holy Trinity is plainly declared co-essential by the orthodox teaching in the catholic church. But no created thing can be so termed, since neither by nature nor in divine majesty is it like the Only-begotten and the Holy Spirit. (6) Such things are created from nothing and cannot be worshiped, but the Trinity is eternal—the Father a perfect Father, the Son a perfect Son begotten of the Father, and the Spirit a perfect Spirit, proceeding from the Father and receiving of the Son. (7) And everything in the sacred scripture and the holy faith is crystal clear to us, and nothing is tortuous, contradictory or knotty.

46,1   29. *If the ingenerate being is implicitly indicated to be the cause of the offspring's existence and, in contrast with every [other] cause, is invariable, it is incomparable essence in itself [and] its matchlessness is not implied for any reason external to itself but because, being ingenerate, it is incomparable and matchless in itself.*

46,2   *Refutation.* Aetius attacks the same points many times, as I myself have said many times, and merely burdens me and nothing more. In the present instance I have had to add to my burden and repeat the same points to the same people, since Aetius has seen fit to do this. (3) For if the ingenerate being that begot is implied by the being of < the > offspring, the Begetter will not differ in rank from the Begotten < because of > begetting him. For he begot him of himself as an essence—spirit of spirit, and not body of body. Therefore the Begetter is implied to be incomparably well suited to the Begotten, and the Begotten to the Begetter. (4) For the Godhead needs no increment, or it would be called Father at one time but not at another. And neither can the Son be found < released* > from the heavenly bond (i.e., of the Trinity) by not being a Son at one time, but being a Son now. Thus God the Father, the Son and the Holy Spirit is of the same essence and not of different essences.[128] (5) For God is neither a kinsman nor a late arrival, but < a co-essential* Trinity >, with the name, "Father," ineffably well suited to the Son who is co-essential with him; and his Holy Spirit, who proceeds from the Father through the Son and < receives > what is the Son's, suitable to the Father and the Son.

46,6   Incomparability with all the creatures which are inferior to the Trinity and which have been created by the Trinity itself, is therefore characteristic of the Father, the Son and the Holy

---

[128] So we render αὐτοουσία and ἑτεροουσία.

Spirit. But the Trinity is not incomparable with itself, for it is uncreated, ingenerate and matchless. (7) Hence nothing can be equated with the Father, and nothing which has been made from non-existence and not begotten [by him] can be worshiped together with him. For he never said, "Sit thou on my right hand,"[129] to a creature. Nor, surely, did the Unbegotten say of any creature, "He that hath seen me, hath seen the Father,"[130] "I am in the Father and the Father in me,"[131] and, "No man knoweth the Father save the Son, and the Son save the Father, and he to whom the Son will reveal him."[132] (8) But he reveals him through the Holy Spirit, who knows, teaches and proclaims what is the Son's in the world "and searcheth all things, even the deep things of God."[133]

46,9   This is why Christ said, "He that honoreth not the Son as he honoreth the Father, the wrath of God abideth on him."[134] And he didn't say, "He that honoreth not angels as he honoreth the Father,"—or, in turn, "He that honoreth the Son as well (as the Father)"—but, "He that honoreth not the Son *as* he honoreth the Father." And to show that the incomparability and matchlessness of the Trinity is in the Father, the Son and the Holy Spirit, he likewise said, "It shall not be forgiven him that blasphemeth the Spirit, neither here nor in the world to come."[135]

47,1   30. *If the Almighty surpasses every nature he surpasses it because of his ingeneracy, which is the very reason for the permanence of generate things. But if "ingenerate" does not denote an essence, how will the nature of the generate things be preserved?*

47,2   *Refutation.* It is fitting to state and confess, and so hold fast to the doctrine that the Almighty, from whom the only-begotten divine Word and his Holy Spirit have inexpressibly come forth to us, surpasses all nature. (3) And therefore we surely do not acknowledge a creature as God, or we would be made fools of. But we glorify the Trinity which surpasses every nature, the Son with the Father, and the Holy Spirit, because of its ingeneracy and uncreatedness. (4) For since the Only-begotten and the Holy Spirit are not of another nature but are God of God and light of light, the Only-begotten too will be called, "Almighty," together with the Almighty Father, as the sacred scripture plainly says. (5) For the

---

129 Ps. 109:1
130 John 14:9
131 John 14:10
132 Matt. 11:27
133 Cf. 1 Cor. 2:10.
134 John 5:23; 3:36
135 Matt. 12:32

Only-begotten's rank is not different from the Father's, as the holy apostle expressly testifies in the Holy Spirit when he says of the children of Israel, "whose is the service and the covenants, and whose are the fathers, of whom is Christ according to the flesh, he that is God above all, blessed forever. Amen."[136]

47,6 Therefore the Only-begotten is also fit for worship and is God, the Holy Spirit is the divine Spirit, and there is no other God after the holy Trinity. (7) Instead the Father is almighty and so is his only-begotten Child, Jesus Christ, who is fit for the Father's rank and is called the Father of the world to come.[137] And he is also fit for his Holy Spirit, and the Trinity is forever manifest and known in its uncreatedness. (8) Because of this Trinity there is causation in all created things, and this is indicative of the perfect and incomparable essence—Father in Son, Son in Father with the Holy Spirit—which has eternal permanence in itself. For created things owe their preservation to this Trinity.

48,1 31. *If no invisible thing preexists itself in germ, but each remains in the nature allotted to it, how can the Ingenerate God, who transcends any category, sometimes see his own essence in the Offspring as secondary but sometimes see it in ingeneracy as prior, on the principle of "first and second?"*

48,2 *Refutation.* Aetius should give me warning of his questions in advance and put them clearly—especially this expression < he introduces >, (i.e., "in germ") which is reprehensible and in no way akin to his illustrations, since neither of the beings he has named (ἀοράτων and ἀγένητος θεός) can be equated with the other. For he has come to me with the names of many invisible beings.[138] (3) There are the spiritual invisible beasts, I mean the Seraphim and Cherubim, as well as angels, which are "spirits,"[139] and certain others of which it is true that nothing about them is "in germ." (4) For no one would say that invisible things are bodies, for they neither beget nor are begotten. Plainly, they were created in accordance with the will of the everlasting Godhead. Each creature has been assigned whatever virtue He Who Is has allotted it in the excellence of his generous lovingkindness, and each has received its allotted portion and abides by it. (5) And God is independent of all cause, contains all things, and does not have his Son—or his Holy Spirit— with hesitation, or regretfully after a lapse of time.

---

136 Rom. 9:4–5
137 Isa. 9:5 Aℵ*LC
138 A sarcastic reference to the "invisible being" which "preexists itself in germ"
139 Cf. Ps. 103:4; Heb. 1:7; 14.

He has a Son in a way that befits the eternal possession of a Son begotten—and only-begotten—with the Father always within him; and he also has the Holy Spirit who is of the Father and receives of the Son, and has him everlastingly.

48,6 For the abundance of the everlasting Godhead does not depend on a lack of glory or the addition of glory. But while no creature is everlasting, when did the Trinity see itself with its abundance lessened, and see this at one time, but at another time see itself with an increase of essence, as though it needed it—and at still another time see itself with a further increase of glory or abundance after the creation of its creatures? (7) And in sum, < the nonsense* > of those who choose to bring forward and advance the speculations of human reasoning against the truth and make them public, will do no harm. The rank of God, the Father, the Son and the Holy Spirit, surpasses all the understanding of angels and greater beings, let alone man's.

For human reasonings of are of no value, and men's thoughts are mortal because they skewer themselves on syllogisms and disputations. (8) Thus others have been condemned by their own arguments, and < have drawn inferences > from some quibbling speculation, some, about the origin of evil, others about the devil's origin or why he was made, others about God's purpose in creating man such that he would sin, others about God's reason for accusing man later after making him like that. (9) [All this] to learn, after ringing the changes on all their arguments, that they are mortal, and to ascribe majesty and knowledge to the < God who is glorified* > in the Father, the Son and the Holy Spirit, that is, to the one Trinity—(10) after asking and receiving the knowledge of the true faith from him—and not to try to overstep their bounds. Instead they will learn to desist from blind reasoning, and not talk cleverly with their wagging tongues and foolish arguments, but be circumspect at the wise command of the holy and divine scripture which says "not to think more highly than they ought to think, but to think soberly."[140]

49,1 32. *If God retains an ingenerate nature, there can be no question of his knowing himself as [both] originated and unoriginated. If, on the other hand, we grant that his essence continues to be ingenerate and generate, he does not know his own essence, since his head is in a whirl from origination and non-origination. But if the Generate too partakes of ingeneracy and yet remains without cessation in his generate nature, he knows himself in the nature in which he continues to remain, but plainly does not know*

---

[140] Rom. 12:3

his participation in ingeneracy; for he cannot possibly be aware of himself
as both of ingenerate and generate essence.

49,2   *Refutation.* There is no doubt that God retains an ingenerate
nature since he has created and made all things from nothing—
the Father < who > begot from himself a Son who is co-essential
with him and fit for his eternity, and [produced] the Holy Spirit
who came forth from him with the suitability for co-essentiality with
him. (3) And although the Trinity created all things, visible and
invisible, from nothing, this does not mean that that which corresponds with God's rank, the eternity of Him Who Is, is denied
by the recent origin of the name of the creatures. (4) But the
supreme essence on high is denied to the creatures, since it is not
co-essential with them, but called them out of non-being into being.

Thus the Son, who has not been begotten of non-being but of
Him Who Is, may properly be contemplated together [with God],
for [God's] essence neither stretched nor shrank [in begetting
him]. The Father, who is spirit, truly begot his Son as spirit, and
produced the Holy Spirit from himself—and is neither unknowing
of himself, nor aware of a shrinkage, a broadening or a division
of his essence. (5) It makes no sense that God should know all
these [latter] things < of himself >, just as it is unaccountable that
< the Son and the Spirit* > —that is, the Holy Spirit < that searches
the depths of God* > —should not know the Godhead.

And the Ingenerate does not fail to share co-essentiality with his
Offspring, nor the Generate to be eternal with the Father. (6) For
the Father knows the Son and the Son knows the Father, since
the Trinity remains endlessly uncreated and the Only-begotten is
endless, for he is begotten of Him Who forever Is, and in his own
perfect nature, himself truly Is. (7) He therefore knows himself.
And neither is the Son ignorant of the ingenerate essence of the
Father, nor the Ingenerate of the essence of the Son, for the only-
begotten divine Word is worthy of credence when he says, "No man
knoweth the Father save the Son, and the Son save the Father."[141]

49,8   Therefore never mind the pronouncement of this great
Aetius, "He cannot possibly have knowledge of himself both as of
ingenerate and as of generate essence." (9) The Only-begotten has
already delivered his verdict in the form that follows, by saying that
he and no one else knows the Father—(though at the same time
he allows for the inclusion of the Holy Spirit, as he says elsewhere,
"The Spirit of the Father shall teach you."[142] But if the Spirit is

---

[141] Matt. 11:27
[142] Luke 12:12; Matt. 10:20

the Spirit of the Father, he is not ignorant of the Father either.) (10) But by saying, "No man knoweth the Father save the Son,"[143] < the Son showed in the same breath* > that he always knows the Father—showing his own matchlessness, and the Father's and the Holy Spirit's matchlessness, in comparison with all other beings, which are not eternal but have been made.

49,11 But if he has already < said > that he always knows the Father, it is no use for Aetius to come tiptoeing in with his worthless teachings. For it is clear to everyone that he plainly thinks in human terms, and is condemned as fleshly and soulish by Him who knows himself, the Father and his Holy Spirit. (12) The Godhead, then, is exempt from all causation—not only the Father, but the Son and the Holy Spirit as well, since all are agreed that the Godhead of the Father, the Son and the Holy Spirit transcends every cause.

50,1 33. *If the Ingenerate transcends all cause but there are many ingenerates, they will [all] be exactly alike in nature. For without being endowed with some quality common [to all] while yet having some quality of its own—[a condition not possible in ingenerate being]—one ingenerate nature would not make, while another was made.*

50,2 *Refutation.* Of course the Unbegotten transcends all cause, since the Ingenerate is one and is an object of worship, but the object of worship is different from the worshipers. (3) But the Trinity is an object of worship because it is a unity and a Trinity enumerated in one name, Father, Son and Holy Spirit. And it includes nothing different from itself, but the Father has fittingly begotten, and not created, a Son. (4) For the Offspring is forever of the Begetter—as is the Holy Spirit who has come forth from him—since the Offspring is the < Son > of Him Who Is. The Trinity, then, exists in one uncreated unity, while all that has been created from nothing is caused by the Trinity itself. (5) The one Trinity is therefore one God, Father, Son and Holy Spirit, containing nothing different from itself: uncreated, unbegotten, unfashioned, a Trinity which is not made but makes, which includes the name of no creature but creates, which is one and not many. (6) And although they are many, all things are caused by it but are not enumerated with it.

Thus no share of the incomparable essence is allotted to any other nature. (7) There is therefore no created nature in the essence of God; God's essence is creative of all that cannot participate by co-essentiality in the incomparable—in the one essence of the Father, the Son and the Holy Spirit. To one who has received the knowledge

---

[143] Matt. 11:27

of the truth it is plain that the divine nature reveals this to him, < since > it alone is worshiped and not created things, just as it alone, and not created things, baptizes in its own name.

51,1   34. *If every essence is ingenerate, one will not differ from another in self-determination. How, then, can we say that one [such] being is changed and another causes change, when we will not allow God to bring them into being from an essence that has no existence?*

51,2   *Refutation.* Every opponent of the truth has gathered an amazing number of trivial sayings and expected to fall upon people, get them upset, remove them from the way of life, and ruin them. Aetius expects to overawe the simple here although he is not really saying anything with this proposition. For he says what he says unnecessarily, and has employed the term, < "ingenerate" >, at this time, from his usual habit of trotting it out for no good reason.

51,3   The ingeneracy of every essence is not acknowledged even by the wise themselves, or every essence would be regarded as God. (4) But since not all essences are treated as God, but one rather than all—the one Godhead in Trinity—how can this fine fellow still suppose that an awe of him will overcome the sons of the truth? (5) One essence will differ from another because the Trinity creates them; but all things are created by the Trinity and it alone is self-determined, while all that it has made is determined by it. The latter sort of essence in changeable but the Trinity's essence is changeless, though it is constantly changing the things that are changed by it, and is able to bring their essences and subsistences out of nothing. (6) For it is fitting that God should transform as he wills the ordering of < the > things he has made, and has brought into being out of non-being and nothing.

52,1   35. *If every essence is ingenerate, every essence is exactly alike. But the doing and suffering of an essence that is exactly like [all the others] must be attributed to chance. However, if there are many ingenerates which are exactly alike, there can be no enumeration of their ways of differing from one another. For there could be no enumerations of their differences, either in general or in some respect, since every difference which implies classification is already excluded from ingenerate nature.*

52,2   *Refutation.* Not every essence is ingenerate. It is foolish to think < this >, and whether Aetius intends it as a declaration or as a query, both the argument and its statement belong to pagan ignorance. But plainly, Aetius intends it as a query. (3) Then let him ask the pagans this, and let them agree with him that this follows from their argument; for they give the title, "matter," to something that is contemporaneous with God. And if Aetius agrees, let him get caught with them! The truth is that there is one Maker, which consists of one essence of a perfect Trinity, < which is >, and yet is not enumerated as an identity. But all other things are born and created, and not ingenerate.

52,4   But the Godhead is uncreated, with the Father begetting, the Son begotten, and the Holy Spirit sent forth from the Father himself and receiving of the Son, while all [other] things are created. Indistinguishability in power is properly confined to the Trinity. And all Godhead is ascribed to the Father because of the rightness and certainty of belief in one God, and the refutability of belief in many. But the rightness of the Son is fittingly reckoned in proportion to that of the Father and the Holy Spirit.

52,5   This being so, the device of the query will fail of its treacherous purpose from the start. There are not many indistinguishables; there is one Trinity in unity, and one Godhead in Trinity. (6) But all other things are separate, and their doing and suffering is not by chance. Nor can the holy Trinity suffer in doing a thing; the whole—I mean the Father, the Son and the Holy Spirit—is impassible and worshipful. (7) For God made all things through a Son, but he did not make the Son—(the Son is not one of all the creatures, for he assists the Father and is worshiped together with him)—nor did he make the Holly Spirit. (The Holy Spirit is not one of the totality of God's creatures; he strengthens the power of all, and he is worshiped.) (8) But all things are subject to the providence of the One, and each one endures, acts, suffers and < does* > everything else < in accordance with the will of the One* >.

Thus the one Trinity is indistinguishable from itself but the other things, < which > it has made, are different from it. (9) It alone is eternal, uncreated and unbegotten—though the Son is begotten independently of time and without beginning, but ever existent and never ceasing to be. (10) Thus for safety's sake the word of God has taught that the Father is the head—and yet not the beginning—of the Son,[144] because of their co-essentiality. The Holy Spirit also, who has been sent forth from the Father, is with the Father forever and has had no beginning in time.

53,1   36. *If "ingenerate" and "God" are exact parallels and mean the same thing, the Ingenerate generated an Ingenerate. But if "ingenerate" means one thing while "God" means something else, there is nothing strange in God's begetting God, since one of the two receives being from ingenerate essence. But if, † as is the case, that which is before God is nothing, "ingenerate*

---

[144] Cf. 1 Cor. 11:3.

*and "God" do mean the same, for "Offspring" does not admit of ingeneracy.
Thus the Offspring does not permit himself to be mentioned in the same
breath with his God and Father.*

53,2   *Refutation.* How does Aetius want me to grasp the meaning
of the questions which are raised by his arguments? And if he says
through arguments and syllogisms, my speculation will fail just like
his. (3) For no one can ever out-argue God, nor, as the scripture
says, "shall the thing formed say to him that formed it, Why hast
thou made me thus?"[145] But by pious reasoning and the right confirmation of it one must return, by means of the holy scripture,
to the teaching of the Holy Spirit.

53,4   Now since an unalterable pronouncement teaches us that
those who worship a creature have been made fools, how can it
not be < foolish > to take a creature for God and worship and
honor it, when faith by its nature denies worship to the creature
and the creature to worship. (5) Indeed, there will be no advantage in Christianity if it is in no way different from those who give
divine honor to the creature. Such faith will be idolatry rather than
piety.

53,6   For they too worship the sun, the moon and the heavenly
bodies, heaven and earth, and the other created things. And the
superiority of [certain] created things arouses no awe, and even
if one creature is outweighed by the other the special character
[of one creature] will not set it apart from the honor that is common
to them all because of their common name (i.e., "creature"). There
is One who has made both [of the creatures being compared],
and has allotted each, not a difference of name but a difference
of essence.

53,7   For in the case of all created things the creature's name
is "servitor," not "free." And if the servitor in any part [of creation]
is worshiped, the worship [of it] will be no different from [the
worship of] any other part, even if it is inferior. For it is the same
as the most exalted part, by its kinship with the creature which
has been made to be, after non-being, by Him Who Is.

53,8   "Ingenerate" is therefore a fit name for God, and "God"
for the ingenerate. Thus we do not call the Offspring a product
or artifact, but an offspring begotten essentially and without spot
of the Father, co-essential with the Father and fit to be worshiped
with him. And neither do we call the Holy Spirit, who is of him,
different; he too is fit to be worshiped. (9) But the word, "God,"
is not uttered in the same breath with any other being, a creature,

---

[145] Rom. 9:20

since the creature has been made different from ingeneracy because it has been allotted being after non-being. The Trinity, however, is eternal, and "God" and "Ingenerate" are not different things.

53,10 But your admission, Aetius, that the Son has been begotten of the Father, is deceptive and not sincere. Whatever is begotten is not created, and whatever is created is not begotten. But if a begotten thing is created, it is created in a different way, as, for example, men beget men but do not create them, since they themselves have been created by God on high. Thus the things they beget have been begotten by them, but all things have been created by God.

53,11 Now since God is uncreated but has begotten—not created—a Son, he begets nothing different from his own essence. How can his Offspring be created, then, when the Father is uncreated? If he calls the Offspring a creature, it cannot be called an Offspring.

And there is a great deal to say against such an absurd speculation. (12) But it does not become even God to be without a Son at one time, and be called "Father" later, after [begetting] a Son. Nor is it becoming to the Son that there be a time before him; if there is, the time will be greater than his greatness. (13) But the perpetual possession of unfailingness and eternity, in the identity of their qualities, is becoming to the Father. And nothing was before God, this is plain. It can be shown, then, that "God" and "Ingenerate" are the same, as Aetius has said; and in somehow implicating these with each other Aetius accuses himself rather than proving his point. (14) For if "God" is used together with God, as it is, "ingenerate" is also an acceptable term for the "Begotten Son;" ingeneracy is implicit in God. (15) The divine Word is mentioned in the same breath with the Father because of his Godhead, uncreatedness, and joint honor with the Father, even though this is of no help to Aetius; for all creatures worship the Son, and "every tongue confesses that Jesus Christ is Lord to the glory of God the Father,"[146] to whom be glory, the Father in the Son with the Spirit, unto the ages of ages. Amen.

54,1 *Aetius' closing valediction*

37. *May the true God, †who is ingenerate in himself*[147] *and for this reason is alone addressed as "the only true God" by his messenger, Jesus*

---

[146] Cf. Phil. 2:11.

[147] Wickham: αὐτὸ ἀγέννητος; Dummer: αὐτοαγένητος, which is synonymous; Holl and MSS: αὐτογένητος. This last cannot be what Aetius wrote, but is surely what Epiphanius read, cf. 54,3.

Christ, who truly came into being before the ages and is truly a generate entity, preserve you, men and women, safe and sound, from impiety in Christ Jesus our Savior, through whom be all glory to our God and Father, both now and forever, and to the ages of ages. Amen.

54,2 *Refutation.* Even at the close of Aetius' letter to his gang whom he addressed as "male and female champions," he did not desist from this sort of verbal wickedness. In his valediction too he gave proof of the strangeness of his doctrine. (3) For he says, "The true self-begotten God preserve you safe and sound," and without realizing that with one word he has destroyed all the implications of his inquiry. He spoke of the "Ingenerate God" in the propositions above, but by introducing a "self-begotten God" to us here he has made no allowance for < God's uncausedness* > and the fact that he did not make himself. For every < evil > notion forgets itself, the better to be detected.

54,4 Next he says, "he who for this reason is alone addressed as 'the only true God.'" But going by what Aetius says and thinks, he is either keeping the Son from being "God," and misrepresenting the name < because he wants > to be called a Christian, or else he believes that the Son is God but not a true one. And [in that case] he will have one true God, and one who is not true. (5) And because Aetius finds one Person below another in a descending order and assigns the Holy Spirit a still lower and inferior rank—or again, will hold that the Spirit is a lesser "God" or not count him as one of the Trinity—the pathetic object will be an entire stranger to Christians. May he be denounced in the end as a complete pagan and Sadducee, a stranger—as he is—to the Holy Spirit, and comparable to the pagans in his lot. (6) For he claims that there is one greater and one lesser God, one true God and one not true. The pagans confess that one God is supreme but call the others lesser. But the sacred scripture plainly confounds him. It says that the Father is "the true God",[147] and likewise says "God" of the Son[148]—and it says, "God is light,"[149] of the Father, and "He was the true light"[150] of the Son. And of the Holy Spirit it says, "the Spirit of truth."[151] Thus the Trinity is truly proclaimed to us in "wisdom and the depth of its riches."[152]

---

[147] John 17:3
[148] Cf. John 1:1.
[149] 1 John 1:5
[150] John 1:9
[151] John 16:13
[152] Cf. Rom. 11:33.

54,7   Next after this he even says, "by his messenger, Jesus Christ."
He was not ashamed to regard the Only-begotten as unworthy of
the name of God, but employed the mere verbal title, just as, in
the above propositions, he accorded the Son the honor of the
divine name only verbally.

54,8   However, he says, "who truly came into being and is of
a nature truly generate," but says, " He will keep you from impiety."
Any loose woman attributes her behavior to others from the start.
Not seeing how great his impiety has been, he believes himself
pious, as madmen suppose themselves sane but the others crazy.

54,9   But here < in writing >, "in Christ Jesus," he did not dare
to acknowledge him as "our Lord," but deceptively called him "our
Savior." (10) And he says, "through whom be all glory to < our
God and > Father, now and forever and unto the ages of ages.
Amen." Even *all* glory" is meant to strip the Son of honor and
glory. May none of the pious, who have received the gift of the
true faith from the Holy Spirit, ever acquiesce in this!

54,11   But now that I have discussed all these things that Aetius
has said in thirty-six syllogistic propositions with a certain skill in
debate and the inferential guesswork of human trickery, (12) I
urge you to read † them[154] attentively, and you will know his earth-
bound nonsense at once, Christian people, servants of Christ and
sons of the truth. (13) Aetius did not dare to mention the word
of God even in one paragraph, or any text of the Old or the New
Testament—not from the Law, the Prophets, the Gospels or the
Apostles. He did not dare quote a line of the patriarchs', of the
Savior himself; never one of the Father's, not one oracle of the
Holy Spirit delivered through apostles or prophets. He thus stands
fully self-exposed, to the friends of the truth, as an entire stranger
to God and his faith.

54,14   I believe that I have opposed his propositions, as best
I can even in untrained speech, but that I have confronted him
with proof from the sacred scriptures, and from pious reason itself.
(15) And since I have discussed the faith clearly enough in my
refutations of him I feel that this will do, so as not to create any
further difficulty in reading by making additions.

54,16   But once more, < I shall mention and indicate* > a few
of the ideas < he introduced* > in his vanity, after his foreign creed
and his hatred of Christ and his Holy Spirit, and take up, and
briefly state and discuss, all the < foolishness* > his mouth, and

---

[154] Holl: < αὐτ > οἷς; MSS: οἷς. Holl's alternative suggestion is νῦν τέλος τίθεμεν
τοῦ λόγου.

his disciples' mouths, dared to utter in his arrogant pride and inordinate blasphemy.

54,17 For with their idea of knowing God not by faith but by actual knowledge, he and his disciples were the most deluded of all. I mentioned somewhere above that they say they do not simply know God with the knowledge of faith, but as one might know anything which is visible and tangible. As one might pick up a rock or club, or a tool made of some other material, so this good chap says, "I know God as well as I know myself, and do not know myself as well as I know God."

54,18 But in the end, talking and hearing nonsense is a deception to many, but a joke to the wise. For what person who has contracted insanity and gone mad can fail to drive others mad, particularly his followers and subjects? (19) Suppose someone demanded of him and his pupils, "Don't tell me that you know the incomparable, incomprehensible God, whose form cannot be perceived, but who is known to his servants by faith! Describe the foundations of the earth to me, the storehouses of the abyss, the veins of the sea, the location of hades, the dimensions of the air, the form and thickness of the heavens! Tell me what the top of the heavens is, the bottom of the underworld, what is to the right, what is to the left of creation! Tell me how you yourself were made, and the number and dimensions of the innumerable things on earth!" (20) Then after hearing this, as some of their dupes have told me, his disciples resort to quibbling excuses and finally say deceitfully, "All these things are physical, and we cannot know them. But we know clearly what sort of God made them, how he is, what he is like, and who he is."

54,21 But who can hear this without at once laughing at them? It is sheer foolishness to say that one knows, and has accurately described, the incomparable, ineffable Artificer. And if only Aetius would say that he knows and has described him by faith, and he and they would not venture to say that they know him by a sort of direct knowledge! But the things the incomparable God himself has made, and which, because of their innumerable < kinds* >, can < only* > be wondered at by those who see them, he says that he and his followers do not know. (22) And most of all, the sacred scriptures everywhere plainly declare that God is invisible, incomprehensible and beyond our understanding, but that it is known only by faith "that he is, and that he is the rewarder of them that love him."[155]

---

[155] Heb. 11:6

54,23   But when anyone with an orthodox view of God's glory, faith, love and incomprehensibility tells them, "We know that God is incomprehensible, we know that God is invisible, ineffable, but we know that, in his invisibility and incomprehensibility, he actually is," this exponent of the new dialectic dares < to reply* > with light mockery, as though to tell a story, (24) "What are you and your faith like? Like a deaf, dumb and blind virgin who's been violated. Everyone who knows her can see that she has, but if they ask who her seducer is, she can't hear to know they're asking. And she hasn't seen her seducer because she's blind, and can't say who he is because she's dumb."

54,25   Now the reverse is true of him and his story, for as the scripture says, "His travail shall return on his own head, and he shall fall into the pit which he hath made,"[156] and the like. (26) Aetius himself is like a man who was born blind but can speak— indeed, speaks at length—and can hear, and knows the names of white and black, hyacinth, light green, red and the various other colors, and light and dark, and has been told their names. But he surely has no knowledge of their appearance and cannot possibly describe it, because he was born blind to begin with, and does not know the variation and appearance of the qualities of the colors. (27) The reality which answers to the distinction between each of their names is experienced by visual perceptions, but never by verbal explanation to one who does not know their appearance to start with, or by handling and touch. (28) So when people who are blind from birth talk about them and know enough to contrast black with white, and green with hyacinth, purple, scarlet and the other colors, but we ask them the quality of their appearance and the color of each quality, they cannot say, and cannot learn it from us. They can only convince each other by talking, but they deceive their hearers as though they know all about the distinction, even though they are describing < the indescribable* > in words and are ignorant because of their inability to comprehend it.

54,29   Even so Aetius himself, who jokes about the seduction of the deaf, dumb and blind virgin, has come to me to talk about God. In fact, going by his blasphemy, it is he who has been spoiled, and his ignorance is like blindness from birth, (30) because he talks about God but by describing < the indescribable > in words and ends even by making his disciples shameless.

For there is nothing that they do not dare. When they are under cross-examination by someone and are hard pressed, they blaspheme

---

[156] Ps. 7:17; 16

the names of prophets and apostles and leave at once, turning away with the words, "The apostle said this as a man," but sometimes, "Why quote the Old Testament to me?" (31) But this is no surprise in view of the Savior's words, "If they have called the master of the house Beelzebul, how much more them of his household."[157] If they deny the Lord himself and his true glory, how much more his prophets and apostles?

54,32   But his disciples have been inspired to still further madness, as has their successor, a person miscalled Eunomius (i.e., "law-abiding"), who is still alive to be a great evil, < and introduces* > another piece of impudence. For he rebaptizes persons already baptized—not only people who come to him from the orthodox and the sects, but even from the Arians. (33) He, however, rebaptizes them in the name of God the Uncreated, and in the name of the Created Son, and in the name of the Sanctifying Spirit created by the Created Son. (34) And to make it clear that it is no longer faith which their whole workshop of jugglery, theater and farce proclaims, but practically clowns' work, some maintain that he baptizes his candidates for rebaptism upside down, with their feet on top and their heads below. (35) And while they are in this position he obliges them to swear an oath that they will not abandon the sect he has cooked up. (36) But they say that when this same Aetius had been recalled from exile after Constantius' death by Julian on his accession to the throne, and when he was still a deacon in his sect, he was raised to the episcopate by a bishop of his sect.

54,37   This is < the > information I have < about > Aetius and his disciples, to whom some have given the name of Anomoean because he has come to an opinion still more frightful than the heresy of Arius. (38) With God's help I have gone through his doctrines in detail as best I can, as though I had stamped on the serpent called the many-footed millipede, or wood-louse, with the foot of the truth, and crushed it with the true confession of the Only-begotten. Giving our accustomed thanks to God, beloved, and summoning his power to the aid of our weakness, let us go on to the remaining sects (39) to the best of my ability and understanding, and call, as I said, on our Master himself, to come to my aid in the exposure of the sects and the refutation of them, so that, by his power, I may be able to keep the promise which, despite my unimportance and mediocrity, I have made.

---

[157] Matt. 10:25

ANACEPHALAEOSIS VII

Here too are the contents of the second Section of this same Volume Three. By the division of the Sections which we have been using, it is a seventh Section. It is Section Seven and the end of the whole work, and contains four Sects:

1. < 77 >. Dimoerites, also called Apolinarians, who do not confess that Christ's humanity is complete. Some of them at one time dared to say that Christ's body is co-essential with his Godhead, some denied that he ever took a soul, but some, in reliance on the text, "The Word was made flesh,"[1] denied that Christ received his fleshliness from created flesh, that is, from Mary. They merely said contentiously that the Word was made flesh; but after that, I do not know why, they say that he has not received a mind.

2. < 78 >. Antidicomarians, who say that the holy, ever-virgin Mary had relations with Joseph after bearing the Savior.

3. < 79 >. Collyridians, who offer a loaf in the name of this same Mary on a certain set day of the year. I have given them a name to correspond with their practice, and called them Collyridians.

4. < 80 >. A group < called > Massalians, which means, "people who pray." Of the sects current among pagans, the following, called Euphemites, Martyrians and Satanists, are associated with them.

This is the summary of the seventh Section, and the end of the three Volumes. There are eighty Sects in all. At the very end of the third Volume, and after Section Seven, is the Faith of the Catholic Church, the Defense of Truth, the Proclamation of the Gospel of Christ, and the Character of the Catholic and Apostolic Church which has been in existence from all ages, but which was fully manifest, in time, by Christ's incarnation.

Against Dimoerites, called < Apolinarians >[1] by some, who do not confess that Christ's humanity is complete. 57, but 77 of the series.

1,1   Though it is painful to me in the anticipation, another doctrine different from the faith sprang up directly after these. I cannot

---

[1] John 1:14

[1] The chief literary source of this Sect is Athanasius' Epistle to Epictetus the bishop of Corinth, which is quoted in full at 3–13. Also quoted is the apologia of Paulinus of Antioch, a document composed by Athanasius (21, 1–8). The Apolinarian controversy was one in which Epiphanius was personally involved.

tell why, but it was to make sure that the devil would not leave
< the church untroubled* >, for he is constantly disturbing the
human race and, as it were, warring on it, by putting his bitter
poisons into its choice foods. And as though he were dumping
its bitterness into honey, < he is introducing the heresy* > even
through people who are admired for their exemplary lives and
always renowned for their orthodoxy. (2) For this is the work of
the devil, who envied our father Adam at the beginning and is
the enemy of all men—as certain wise men have said, envy is always
the opponent of great successes (εὐπραγίαι).[2] (3) And so, not to
leave me and God's holy church untroubled but constantly in an
uproar and under siege, the devil planted certain occasions for
this [trouble] even through persons of importance.

1,4　For certain persons—people, indeed, who were originally
ours, who held high position, and who have always been esteemed
by myself and all orthodox believers, have seen fit to remove the
mind from Christ's human nature and say that our Lord Christ
took flesh and a soul at his coming, but not a mind—in other
words, that he did not take full humanity. (5) I cannot say how
they have contributed to the world with this, or who of their
predecessors they learned it from—or what benefit they have derived
from it or conferred on me, on their hearers, and on God's holy
church, by causing us nothing but disturbance and division among
ourselves, and grief, and the loss of our mutual affection and love.
(6) For they have abandoned the following and the righteousness
of the sacred scriptures, and the simple profession—the faith of
the prophets, Gospels and apostles—and introduced a sophistical,
fictitious doctrine, and a series of many dreadful teachings with
it, so that they are examples of the scripture, "They shall turn away
from sound doctrine and give heed unto fables and empty words."[3]

2,1　It was the elderly and venerable Apolinaris of Laodicea,
whom I, the blessed Pope Athanasius, and all the orthodox had
always loved, who originally thought of this doctrine and put it
forward. (2) When some of his disciples told me about it I did
not at first believe that a man like himself had introduced this
doctrine to the world, and I waited patiently, with hopeful expectation, till I could learn the facts of the matter. (3) For I thought
that his pupils who were coming to me from him had not understood the profound < utterances > of so well educated and wise

---

[2] Cf. Pindar, Pythian Odes 7.14–15: "I feel some rejoicing at a new success
(εὐπραγία); but I am grieved that envy is the requital for good works."
[3] 2 Tim. 4:3; 1 Tim. 1:4

a man and teacher, and had not learned this from him but had made it up on their own. (4) For even among the ones who were visiting me, a great deal was in dispute. Some of them dared to say that Christ had brought his body down from on high. But the heresy stayed in people's heads and drove them to shocking lengths, for others denied the doctrine that Christ had received a soul. (5) But some even dared to say that Christ's body was co-essential with his Godhead, and threw the east into great turmoil; it became necessary to call a council on their account and condemn persons of this kind.

2,6 Minutes were taken, moreover, and copies of them sent to the blessed Pope Athanasius. Because of the minutes the blessed Pope was obliged to write an Epistle himself against people who say such things, in which he harshly reproved the most venerable bishop Epictetus for even deigning to make a reply about this to the trouble-makers. (7) In the same letter the blessed Pope wrote plainly about the faith, and denounced those who were saying those things and making trouble. I feel obliged to present a copy of this letter here, in its entirety. It is as follows:

Athanasius the bishop of Alexandria to Epictetus the bishop of Corinth:

3,1 *I had believed that every worthless doctrine of all sectarians, however many there are, had been brought to an end by the council that convened at Nicaea. For the faith confessed by the fathers there, in conformity with the holy scriptures, is sufficient for the overthrow of all impiety and for the commendation of the godly faith in Christ. (2) And therefore, when various councils were held just lately in Gaul,[4] Spain and the metropolis of Rome,[5] all the participants, as though moved by one spirit, unanimously condemned those who still secretly held the opinions of Arius, I mean Auxentius of Milan and Ursacius, Valens and Gaius of Pannonia. (3) But because such persons contrive so-called councils of their own, [the participants in the orthodox councils] have written everywhere that none but the council of Nicaea alone is to be termed a council of the catholic church—the monument of victory over every sect, especially the Arian, on whose account the council was chiefly called at that time.*

3,4 *After so much [of this sort], how can anyone still undertake to doubt or dispute? If they are Arians, it would be no surprise that they complain of writings against themselves, just as, when they hear, "The idols of the heathen are silver and gold, the work of men's hands,"[6] pagans*

---

[4] The Synod of Paris, ca. 360 A.D. Cf. Hilarius Fr. 11.1–4.
[5] For the Council of Rome, see Soz. 6.23.7–15; Theod. H. E. 2.22.3–12.
[6] Ps. 113:12

consider the teaching concerning † the Holy Spirit[7] foolishness. (5) *But if it is persons who appear to be orthodox and to love the fathers' pronouncements who wish to revise them by disputation, they do nothing else than to "give their neighbor a foul outpouring to drink,"[8] as scripture says, and to dispute about words, to no purpose, but for the overthrow of the simple.*

4,1 *I write in this way after reading the minutes your Reverence has taken. They ought not even to have been put in writing, so as to leave not even a memory of these matters to posterity. For who has ever heard of such things? Who has taught or learned them?* (2) *"For from Zion shall go forth the word of the Lord, and the Law of God from Jerusalem;"[9] but where have these things come from?* (3) *What hell spewed forth the doctrine that "< the > body taken from Mary is co-essential with the Word's divine nature,"[10] or, "The Word was transformed into flesh, bones, hair and the rest of the body,[11] and changed from his own nature?"[12]* (4) *Who has ever heard Christians say that "The Son was clothed with a body by attribution, not nature?" Who has been so impious as both to say and to believe that "His divine nature, which was itself co-essential with the Father, has been curtailed, and from perfect become imperfect; and that which was nailed to the tree was not the body, but the very creative essence of wisdom?"[13]* (5) *And who can hear, "The Lord produced his passible body by transformation, not from Mary but from his own essence," and suppose that a Christian is saying this?*

4,6 *And who conceived of this wicked impiety, so as even to think of saying, "Whoever says that the Lord's body is from Mary no longer believes in a Trinity in the Godhead, but in a quaternity >?"[14] In other words, persons who hold such views are saying that the flesh which the Savior*

---

[7] Holl: ἁγίου πνεύματος; MSS: θείου σταυροῦ

[8] Hab. 2:15

[9] Isa. 2:3

[10] Apolinaris specifically says that Christ's flesh was not from heaven, cf. 1 Ep. Dion. 13 (Lietzmann p. 259); Fr. 164 (Lietzmann p. 259); Fr. 163 (Lietzmann p. 255). Timotheus the Apolinarian, however, calls "The Lord's flesh . . . co-essential with God," Fr. 181 (Lietzmann p. 279); cf. Apolinaris himself at De Unione 8 (Lietzmann p. 188).

[11] This might be a hostilely worded statement of Apolinaris' doctrine that Christ is μία φύσις, cf. Apol. 1 Ep. Dion. 2 (Lietzmann p. 257).

[12] Apolinaris appears to say the opposite at Epist. Dion. 10, "The one thing partakes of the other which differs from it in name (i.e., the Godhead and manhood of Christ, which are both the same Christ), not by the incorporeal's changing into the corporeal, or the corporeal's changing into the incorporeal . . ."

[13] Cf. Frag. 186 (Lietzmann p. 319), where Felix of Rome says, "We curse those who ascribe the sufferings to the Godhead, and those who call Christ a crucified man and do not confess that he was crucified in his whole divine hypostasis."

[14] Cf. Apol. Quod Unus Sit Deus 3.4 (Lietzmann pp. 295–297).

*assumed from Mary is of the essence of the Trinity. (7) And again, from
what source have certain persons spewn forth an equal impiety, so as to
say, "Christ's body is not younger than the Godhead of the Lord but is
forever begotten in co-eternity with him, since it arose from wisdom?"*[15] *(8)
But why have persons called Christians even presumed to doubt that the
Lord who came forth from Mary is the Son of God in essence and nature,
but that, humanly speaking, he is of the seed of David and St. Mary's
flesh? (9) Who, then, have become so audacious as to say, "The Christ
who suffered and was crucified in the flesh is not Lord, Savior, God and
Son of the Father?" (10) Or how can people wish to be called Christians
who say, "The Word has come to a holy man as to one of the prophets,
and has not become man himself by taking his body from Mary.*[16] *Christ
is one thing; the Son of God, the Son of the Father before Mary and before
all ages, is another?" Or how < can > people be Christians when they say,
"The Son is one person, and the Word of God is another?"*

5,1   *These things were said in various ways in your minutes, but their
intent is one and the same, and looks to impiety. Because of them, persons
who plume themselves on the confession of the fathers at Nicaea have been
differing and disputing with one another. (2) I am astonished that your
Reverence has put up with it, and has not stopped them from saying these
things and expounded the orthodox creed to them, so that they may either
hear it and be still, or dispute it and be recognized as sectarians. (3) For
the statements I have quoted are not to be said or heard among Christians,
but are in every way foreign to the teaching of the apostles. (4) For my
part, I have had their statements inserted baldly in my letter, as I have
said, so that one who merely hears them may observe the shame and impiety
in them. (5) And even though one ought to accuse them at greater length
and expose the shame of those who harbor these thoughts, it would be better
still to end my letter here and write no more. (6) It is not right to investigate
further and expend more effort on things whose wrongness has been so
plainly revealed, or the contentious may think that they are matters open
to doubt. In reply to such statements it is enough to say simply that they
are not of the catholic church, and that the fathers did not believe them.
(7) But lest the inventors of evils take shameless occasion from my complete*

---

[15] A theologian hostile to Apolinaris might draw this conclusion from such
passages as De Unione 1, (Lietzmann pp. 185–186), "There was a descent from
heaven, not merely a birth from a woman. For scripture says not only, 'Made
of a woman, made under the Law,' but likewise, 'No man hath ascended to
heaven save he that came from heaven, the Son of Man.'" Cf. De Unione 9
(Lietzmann pp. 188–189).

[16] Apolinaris consistently denies this doctrine: ἡ κατὰ μέρος πίστις 6 (Lietzmann
p. 169); Frs. 14; 15 (Lietzmann pp. 208;209); Fr. 51 (Lietzmann p.216); Ep.
Dioc. 2 (Lietzmann p. 256).

silence, it will be well to mention a few passages from the sacred scriptures. For perhaps if they are embarrassed even in this way, they will desist from these filthy notions.

6,1 *What has possessed you people to say, "The homoousion is the co-essentiality of Word's body with the Word's divine nature?"[17] For it is best to begin with this proposition in order that, from the demonstration of its unsoundness, all the rest may be shown to be the same.*

6,2 *It is not to be found in the scriptures, for they say that God has become incarnate in a human body. Furthermore, the fathers who met at Nicaea said, not that the body, but the Son himself is co-essential with the Father. And they confessed that the Son is of the Father's essence, but that— again, in accordance with the scriptures—his body is of Mary. (3) Therefore, either reject the Council of Nicaea < and > introduce these opinions as sectarians; or, if you desire to be the children of the fathers, do not believe otherwise than they have written.*

6,4 *Indeed, your absurdity can be seen from the following consideration as well. If the Word is co-essential with the body whose substance is of the earth, but the Word is co-essential with the Father in accordance with the fathers' confession, then the Father himself is co-essential with the body whose origin is of the earth. (5) And why do you still blame the Arians for calling the Son a creature, when you yourselves say that the Father is co-essential with created things, and—passing over to another impiety— that "The Word has been transformed into flesh, bones, hair, sinews and the whole body, and changed from his own nature?" (6) The time has come for you to say openly that he is made of earth; for the substance of the bones, and of the whole body, is made of earth.*

6,7 *What is this madness, of such severity that you even contradict yourselves? For by saying that the Word is co-essential with his body you distinguish the one from the other, but you imagine a change of the Word himself by his transformation into flesh. (8) And who will put up with you further if you so much as say these things? You have leaned farther towards impiety than any sect. If the Word is co-essential with his body mention of Mary is superfluous, and there is no need of her. If, as you say, the Word is co-essential with his body, the body is capable of existing eternally even before Mary, just as is the Word himself. (9) Indeed, what need is there for the Word's advent, to assume something co-essential with himself or be altered from his own nature and become a body? For the Godhead does not lay hold of itself, to assume something co-essential with*

---

[17] This might be a pardonable misunderstanding of Apolinaris' doctrine as it is stated, for example, at De Unione 8 (Lietzmann p. 188), "Thus he is both co-essential with God in his invisible spiritual nature, although the flesh is included in the term, since it is united with the Son's co-essentiality with God..."

it. (10) *Nor did the Word, who atones for the sins of others, sin and so turn into a body, offer himself as a sacrifice for himself, and atone for himself.*

7,1 *But none of this is so, perish the thought! "He took part of the seed of Abraham," as the apostle said, "wherefore in all things it behooved him to be made like unto his brethren"*[18] *and take a body like ours.* (2) *Thus Mary is indeed the foundation [of his body], so that he took it from her and offered it, as his own, for us. And Isaiah indicated Mary by prophecy when he said, "Behold, the Virgin shall conceive and bear."*[19] *And Gabriel was sent to her—not simply "to a virgin," but "to a virgin espoused to a man"*[20]—*to show Mary's true humanity through her suitor.* (3) *And scripture mentions her "bringing forth,"*[21] *and says, "She wrapped him in swaddling clothes,"*[122] *and, "Blessed were the paps which he hath sucked."*[23] *And a sacrifice was offered, as though for a son who had "opened the womb."*[24] *But these are all tokens of a virgin's giving birth.*

7,4 *And Gabriel surely did not simply tell her, "that which is conceived 'in' thee,"*[25] *or it might be supposed that a body had been introduced into her from without. He said, "that which is born 'of' thee,"*[26] *so that it might be believed that the child, when born, was actually born 'of her.' Nature shows this plainly besides, for the body of a virgin who has not given birth cannot have milk, and a body cannot be nourished with milk or wrapped in swaddling clothes without first being actually born.*

7,5 *This is the body that was "circumcised the eighth day."*[27] *Simon "took" this "up in his arms."*[28] *This became "a child and grew,"*[29] *reached the age of twelve, and attained his thirtieth year.* (6) *For "the very essence of the Word" was not "changed and curtailed," as some have supposed, for it is changeless and unalterable as the Savior himself says, "See that it is I, and I am not changed."*[30] *And Paul writes, "Jesus Christ is the same yesterday, today and forever."*[31] (7) *But the impassible and incorporeal Word of God was in the body that was circumcised, was carried*

---

[18] Heb. 2:16–17
[19] Isa. 7:14
[20] Luke 1:27
[21] Luke 1:31
[22] Luke 2:7
[23] Luke 11:27
[24] Luke 2:23
[25] Cf. Matt. 1:20.
[26] Luke 1:35
[27] Cf. Luke 2:21
[28] Luke 2:28
[29] Luke 2:40
[30] Cf. Luke 24:39 (Mal. 3:6).
[31] Heb. 13:8

*in its mother's arms, ate, grew weary, was nailed to the tree and suffered.
(8) This body was laid in the tomb when Christ himself "went to preach
to the spirits that were in prison,"*[32] *as Peter said.*

8,1   *This above all reveals the folly of those who say that the Word
was changed to bones and flesh. If this were so there would be no need
of a tomb. The body itself would have gone of itself to preach to the spirits
in hades. (2) As it is, Christ himself went to preach, but "Joseph wrapped"
the body "in a linen shroud, and laid it to rest"*[33] *on Golgotha. And it
has been shown to all that the body was not the Word, but the Word's
body.*

8,3   *And Thomas handled this body once it was risen from the dead,
and saw in it "the prints of the nails"*[34]—*the sight of which nails the Lord
had endured as they were hammered into his own body, and did not prevent
although he could have. Instead he, the Incorporeal, claimed the characteristics of the body for his own. (4) Of course he said, "Why smitest thou
me?"*[35] *as though he himself had been hurt, when he was struck by the
servant. And though by nature he was intangible, he still said, "I gave
my back to the scourges, and hid not my face from spitting."*[36] *(5) For
what the Word's human nature suffered, the Word united with the human
nature imputed to himself, so that we might participate in the Word's divine
nature.*

8,6   *And it was a paradox that the one who suffered was the same
as the one who did not suffer. He suffered in that his own body suffered,
and he was in the very body that suffered; but since the Word, who is
God by nature, is impassible, he did not suffer. (7) And the Incorporeal
himself was in the passible body, while the body had within it the impassible
Word, nullifying the weaknesses of the body itself. (8) But he did this,
and became what he was, in order to assume our characteristics, nullify
them by offering them in sacrifice, and finally, by enduing us with his
own characteristics, enable the apostle to say, "This corruptible must put
on incorruption, and this mortal must put on immortality."*[37]

9,1   *But this was not done by attribution as some have surmised in
their turn, perish the thought! Since the Savior truly became true man,
he truly became the salvation of man as a whole. (2) If the Word were
< in > the body by attribution, as they say, and something which is said
to be by attribution is imaginary, both men's salvation and their resurrection must be called [only] apparent, as the most impious Mani teaches.*

---

[32] 1 Pet. 3:19
[33] Mark 15:46
[34] John 20:25
[35] John 18:23
[36] Isa. 50:6
[37] 1 Cor. 15:53

9,3   *But our salvation has by no means been imaginary, or a salvation of the body alone. The salvation of man as a whole, soul and body, has truly been accomplished in Christ.* (4) *Therefore the Savior's true body, which he received from Mary as the sacred scriptures say, is really human. But it was a true body because it was the same as ours. For since all of us were Adam's descendants, Mary is our sister.*

9,5   *And no one can doubt this if he recalls what Luke wrote. For after the resurrection from the dead, when some thought that they were not beholding the Lord in the body he had taken from Mary but were seeing a spirit in its place, he said, "See my hands and feet, and the prints of the nails, that it is I myself. Handle me and see, for a spirit hath not flesh and bones as ye see me have. And when he had thus spoken, he showed them his hands and his feet."*[38] (6) *From this, again, those bones can be refuted. He did not say, "as ye see me 'be' flesh and bones," but 'have' flesh and bones," so that there can be no question of the Word himself being changed into these things. It must be believed that he himself was 'in' these things, both before his death and after his resurrection.*

10,1   *But since these things can be proved in this way, there is no need to deal with the rest and enter into a discussion of them.* (2) *For as the body in which the Word was is not co-essential with the divine nature but truly born of Mary; and as the Word himself was not changed into bones and flesh, but became incarnate in the flesh*—(3) *for this is the sense of the words in John, "The Word became flesh,"*[39] *as can be learned from a similar passage. For Paul writes, "Christ became a curse for us."*[40] *And as Christ did not himself become a curse, but [it is said] that he became a curse because he assumed the curse for us, so he became flesh, not by turning into flesh, but by assuming flesh for us and becoming man.*

10,4   *For—once more—to say, "The Word was made flesh," is the equivalent of saying that he became man, as we read in the Book of Joel, "I will pour out my Spirit upon all flesh."*[41] *< For > the promise did not < extend > to animals but is for men, for whom, indeed, the Lord became man.* (5) *And since this is the meaning of the text, those who have supposed that "The flesh that came from Mary was before Mary, and the Word had a human soul before her and had always been in it before his advent," must surely with good reason condemn themselves.* (6) *Those too who have said, "His flesh is not subject to death, but is of an immortal nature," will cease to say so. For if Christ did not die, how could Paul "deliver" to the Corinthians "that which I also received, that Christ died for our*

---

[38] Luke 24:39
[39] John 1:14
[40] Gal. 3:13
[41] Joel 3:1

sins according to the scriptures?[42] *How could Christ rise at all, if he did not first die?*

10,7 *But those who even suppose that there can be "a quaternity instead of the Trinity" if the body is said to be from Mary, must blush beet red. (8) "For," < they say >, "if we say that the body is co-essential with the Word, the Trinity remains a Trinity, since the Word imports nothing foreign into it. But if we say that the body born of Mary is a human body, then, since the body by its nature is other than [the Word], and since the Word is in it, there will necessarily be a quaternity instead of a Trinity because of the addition of the body." (11,1) But they do not realize how they fall foul of themselves by saying this. For if they say that the body is not from Mary but is co-essential with the Word, it will be shown nonetheless that they, on their notion, are speaking of a quaternity—the very misrepresentation that they made to avoid giving the impression that they believed it. (2) For as the Son who, in their view, is not the Father himself despite his co-essentiality with the Father, but is called a Son co-essential with the Father, so the body, which in their view is co-essential with the Word, is not the Word himself, but different from the Word. (3) But since it is different, on their own showing their Trinity will be a quaternity. For the true, and truly perfect and undivided Trinity receives no addition, but the Trinity of their invention does. And since they invent a God other than the true one, how can they still be Christians?*

11,4 *For once more, their foolishness can be seen in another of their sophisms. They are very wrong if they think that a quaternity is being spoken of instead of a Trinity because the Savior's body is, and is said in the scriptures to be, of Mary and human, since this makes an addition to the Trinity because of the body. For they are equating the creature with the creator, and supposing that the Godhead can receive an addition. (5) And they have not understood that the Word did not become flesh to add to the Godhead, but to enable the flesh to rise—nor that the Word did not come forth from Mary for his own betterment, but for the redemption of the human race.*

11,6 *How can they think that the body, which was redeemed and given life by the Word, makes an addition of Godhead to the life-giving Word? Rather, a great addition was made to < the > human body itself by the Word's fellowship and union with it. (7) Instead of a mortal body it became immortal; instead of an ensouled body it became spiritual. Though a body of earth, it passed through the heavenly gates. The Trinity is a Trinity even though the Word took a body from Mary. It allows of no addition or subtraction but is forever perfect, and is known as one Godhead in*

---

[42] 1 Cor. 15:3

Trinity; thus it is preached in the church that there is one God, the Father of the Word.

12,1 *Because of this, finally, those who once said, "The one who came forth from Mary is not the Christ himself, and Lord and God," will hold their tongues. (2) If he was not God in the body, why was he called "Immanuel, which, being interpreted, is, God is with us,"*[43] *as soon as he came forth from Mary? And if the Word was not in flesh, why did Paul write to the Romans, "of whom, according to the flesh, Christ came, who is God over all, blessed for evermore. Amen?"*[44] *(3) Let those who formerly denied that the Crucified is God admit their error and be convinced by all the sacred scriptures—most of all by Thomas who cried out, "My Lord and my God!"*[45] *after seeing the nail prints in his hands.*

12,4 *For though the Son was God and the Lord of glory, he was in the ingloriously nailed, dishonored body. The body suffered when it was pinned to the wood and blood and water flowed from its side, but all the while, as the temple of the Word, it was filled with the Word's Godhead. (5) Thus it was that the sun withdrew its rays and darkened the earth on seeing its maker lifted up in his tortured body. But though of a mortal nature, the body itself rose in transcendence of its nature. It ceased from the corruptibility of its nature, became the garment of the Word, and by donning the more than human Word, became incorruptible.*

12,6 *But there is no reason for me to discuss the imaginary thing some people say, "As a word came to each of the prophets, so the Word came to one particular man who was born of Mary." Their stupidity obviously carries its own condemnation. If this is the way he came, why is he born of a virgin, and not as the child of a man and a woman himself? Each of the saints was born like that. (7) Or, if this is how the Word came, why is every man's death not said to have been for us, but only the death of this man? If the Word arrived with each of the prophets, why is it said only of the son of Mary that he came "once, in the end of the ages?"*[46] *(8) Or, if he came in the same way that he came in the saints before him, why have all the others died and not yet risen, while the son of Mary alone arose the third day? (9) Or, if the Word came just like the others, why is only the son of Mary called Immanuel, because his body has been filled with Godhead and born of her? For Immanuel means "God is with us." (10) Or, if this is the way he came, since each of the saints eats, tires and dies, why is it not said that each one < was > eating, tiring and dying, but said only of the Son of Mary? For the things this body suffered are*

---

[43] Matt. 1:23
[44] Rom. 9:5
[45] John 20:28
[46] Heb. 9:26

mentioned because it was he himself who suffered them. And though of all the others it is said merely that they were born and begotten, only of Mary's offspring is it said, "And the Word was made flesh."[47]

13,1 *This will show that the Word came to all the others to help them prophesy, but that the Word himself took flesh from Mary and came forth as a man—God's Word in nature and essence, "but of the seed of David according to the flesh,"*[48]*—and was made man of Mary's flesh, as Paul said. (2) The Father identified him in the Jordan and on the mount by saying, "This is my beloved Son, in whom I am well pleased."*[49] *(3) The Arians have denied him but we know and worship him, not distinguishing the Son from the Word, but knowing that the Word himself is the Son, by whom all things were made, and we set free.*

13,4 *Thus I am surprised that there has been any contention among you over matters so < plain >. But God be thanked, my sorrow at reading your minutes is matched by my joy at their conclusion. (5) For [the participants] departed in harmony, and peaceably agreed on the confession of the orthodox faith. It is this that has led me to write these few lines after much prior consideration, for I am concerned that my silence not give pain rather than joy to those who, by their agreement, have given me cause to rejoice. (6) I therefore ask that, primarily your Reverence, and secondly your hearers, receive this with a good conscience, and, if < in any respect > it falls short of true religion, that you correct this and send me word. But if it has been unfitly and imperfectly written, as by one untrained in speaking, I ask the pardon of all for my feebleness of speech. Farewell!*

14,1 Since I have inserted this letter and not merely set out to write against the Apolinarians because of things I have heard from them or from others, it has been made plain to everyone that I have accused no one falsely. (2) But next I shall take up the case against them, so that there can be no suspicion on anyone's part that I am slandering my brethren—though I pray for them even now, that they may correct the things that appear to disturb me, so that they may not lose me, or I, them. (3) For I have often made this plea, and have begged, and still continue to beg that they remove the contention and follow the sacred ordinance of the apostles, the evangelists and the fathers, and the confession of the faith which is simple, firm, unshakeable, and in every way entirely right.

14,4 Others have told me in private that the Lord did not take this flesh of ours, or any flesh like it, when he came, but took

---

[47] John 1:14
[48] Rom. 1:3
[49] Matt. 3:17; 17:5

another flesh, different from ours. And if they would only speak to his glory and praise! (5) I too say that his body is holy and undefiled: "He did no sin, neither was guile found in his mouth."[50] And this is plain to everyone who speaks and thinks of Christ in a godly way. (6) And even though I speak of his actual body just as he took our actual body, < I still mean that* > his body < remained* > undefiled. In us who have offended, however, < our bodies have become different from the Lord's* >. [This is] not because our bodies are different, and alien to his in their inferiority and degradation; < our bodies have become different from the Lord's* > because of our sins and transgressions. (7) For the Lord did not take one sort of body while we have another sort; the very body which [in him] is preserved and kept undefiled, < in us has been sullied* >.

15,1 Others, even now motivated by contention, are led on by strange opinions and do not "hold fast to the head of the faith" as the fathers teach, "from whom the whole body, supplied and knit together by its joints and bands, increaseth with the increase of God,"[51] as the apostle says. (2) With their ears ringing, perhaps as with strange doctrines, they, very like Valentinus, Marcion and Mani, imagine things in pretended honor of Christ rather than telling the truth.

15,3 Whenever I tell them that Christ had a body like ours, they turn at once to their own contentious fabrications (4) and say that he had nails, flesh, hair and so on, but not the kind we have; he had different nails, different flesh, and all the rest not like what we have but different from ours. < They imagine their* > futile words because they would like to do Christ some sort of quibbling favor in their own turn, if you please, like Valentinus and the other sects I have mentioned. (5) For they say, "If we confess that Christ's < body > < has* > all [the features of a body] in their entirety,[52] † < we must also allow it all the natural functions." But "Meddle not with more than thy works."* >[53] This scripture refers to people of their kind, who are "busybodies and work not."[54] (6) To strike terror in the hearts of the simple, they say straight off, "[If Christ's body was like ours], he had the normal physical needs—evacuation, or going to the bathroom, or the other

---

[50] 1 Pet. 2:22
[51] Cf. Col. 2:19.
[52] Here Holl adds two lines of Greek. The MSS read simply περιέργως which is unsatisfactory.
[53] Sir. 3:23
[54] 2 Thes. 3:11

things." They think all this is wise, but it is horrid and silly, as the prophet said, "Who hath required this at your hands?"[55] (7) Of which of the saints did scripture mention such things, although the prophets were men and not gods, and the evangelists and others were unquestionably made of soul and flesh like ourselves? Where did scripture not witness instead to the more seemly things in the saints, let alone the Lord Christ?

16,1   Those who are frightening the sheep, startling the doves and stampeding Christ's lambs and flock, had better tell me where Moses went to the bathroom during the forty days! (2) Where did Elijah attend to his needs at the brook Kidron, when he ate bread in the morning and meat in the evening, brought by the ravens at God's command? (3) It would be foolish of the scripture to speak of these things, just as it was foolish of these people to inquire into them. What is the good of such things? What use are they—except to foster unbelief, since prejudice finds its opportunities in silly statement and worthless rebuttal.

16,4   What's more, better tell me why God kept the children of Israel's hair from getting long for forty years, and their shoes from wearing out, and their clothes from getting worn or torn, when that was his will. (5) Had they come from heaven too? Were they gods? Indeed, they were not in God's good graces, but had provoked God in many ways. Didn't they have the same frailties as we? God did this to show that in him all things are possible, and that he allows them to happen and not happen.

16,6   But for our sakes, lest anyone should attribute anything supernatural to them because of the miracles God did for them— that is, that their hair did not grow, and their clothes did not wear out and the rest, and because "Man ate the bread of angels"[56]— (7) the sacred scripture reassured us by saying, "Let each man take an iron peg in his girdle, that, when thou easest thyself in a place, thou shalt dig and cover thine own stool; for ye are people sanctified, and the Lord dwelleth in the midst of your camp."[57] (8) As to this, the native Hebrews tell the story that this was the standard for a while, until God willed to show this wonder in them, that even though they were eating both meat and land-rails,[58] they found they had no need of it.

17,1   And whether, < as seems more likely* >, the Hebrews have

---

[55] Isa. 1:12
[56] Ps. 77:25
[57] Deut. 23:13–14
[58] ὀρτυγομήτρα. a bird that migrates with quail

this tradition in their ancestors' honor, whether as a gratuitous addition or as a fact—though they surely know themselves that their clients were mortal and not gods, and were made of flesh, blood and soul—(2) who can put up with the Apolinarians' insufferable remarks about Christ, the divine Word who came from heaven, and his in all respects glorious and true human nature? In it he fulfilled the saying, "in all points tempted as a man, yet without sin."[59] (3) For even though Christ truly had our flesh, it was possible for him not to do the things that we regard as undignified, and to do such things as were seemly, and of a fitness in proportion to his Godhead. For it was by his doing that the hair of the children of Israel did not grow, their clothes did not get dirty, and these things < which >, according to tradition, happened to them. (4) But there is no doubt that Christ indeed had man-made clothing: "They parted his raiment, and upon his vesture did they cast lots."[60] (5) But if his garment was made by men it was plainly made of wool and linen, and woolen and linen things are inanimate and lifeless. (6) And yet when Christ willed to display the power of his Godhead "He was transfigured and showed his countenance as the sun, and his garments white as wool."[61] (7) "For to the Mighty One all things are possible,"[62] and in an instant he can change lifeless and inanimate things, contrary to expectation, to glory and splendor, like Moses' rod, like the shoes of the children of Israel. (8) For we all agree that the holy apostles were men, with mortal bodies like ours. But because of the glory of God that indwelt them they were immortal, and Peter's shadow healed all the sick who were brought to him, and napkins and kerchieves from Paul's clothing worked miracles.

18,1 And why do these people take the trouble to make shameful guesses about God, on subjects there has never been a need to discuss—for any prophet, evangelist, apostle or author? (2) However many of such things they say, even if they make a million more bad guesses, they won't overturn the faith of our fathers which declares Christ truly < man >.

18,3 For Christ was truly born in the flesh of Mary the evervirgin, by the agency of the Holy Spirit. He was called Immanuel, or "God is with us," < and > can have no second birth. (4) As a child he fled to Egypt with Joseph and Mary, since [enemies] were

---

[59] Cf. Heb. 4:15.
[60] John 19:24
[61] Matt. 17:2
[62] Cf. Mark 10:27.

seeking the child's life—which is as much as to say that he could be killed in the flesh. Still, he was worshiped by the magi as true God, begotten in the flesh < in reality >, not appearance. (5) And due to Joseph's fear because of Archelaus, he did not enter Jerusalem on his return from Egypt—showing that the child could be arrested, and could[63] suffer too soon what he was to suffer in the flesh.

18,6   < He came willingly to baptism* >, but was hindered by John, for the Master was recognized by the servant as God truly incarnate. But in this case, so as to "fulfill all righteousness"[64] in the flesh and "leave us an example"[65] of salvation in his true and perfect humanity, he did not accept his servant's honor.

18,7   Moreover, he grew truly weary from his journey—and he was not simply weary but sat down as well, because he had truly become man. < And yet > he cried, "Come unto me, all ye that labor and are heavy laden, and I will give you rest,"[66] to show that his Godhead is sufficient to give rest to all the world's multitudes who come to him. (8) Further, he was tempted by the devil, and remained forty days without food or drink, to show the self-sufficiency of his Godhead. (9) For he did not go hungry as you and I master ourselves like philosophers, and subject himself to discipline and restraint; because of his true Godhead, he went hungry without lacking anything. (10) And the scripture says, "He was afterwards an hungered,"[67] to show the true incarnation of his Godhead, which allowed the manhood the satisfaction of its lawful and true needs, so that the truth of the sequence [of these events][68] would not hide the true manhood. (11) For he was hungry at the fig tree too, and he made real clay. But as God he commanded the fig tree and was obeyed. And on the ship he rebuked the wind, and it dropped. (12) And with the spittle and clay he fashioned the missing member and bestowed it on the blind man, as upon Adam, by the command of his Godhead and the spittle of his humanity— and once again, by the clay. For all things were in him in their fullness; suffering in his flesh, impassibility in his Godhead, until he arose from the dead, never again to suffer, to "die no more"[69] at all.

---

[63] Drexl and MSS: δυναμένου... ἐν σαρκὶ παθεῖν; Holl: δυναμένου < ἀναγκασθῆναι > ἐν σαρκὶ παθεῖν

[64] Matt. 3:15

[65] Cf. 1 Pet. 2:21.

[66] Matt. 11:28

[67] Matt. 4:2

[68] I.e., he fasts for forty days without needing food, and only then becomes hungry.

18,13 But if there are any who suppose that, because he did not get it from a man's seed, he received a different body, this in no way makes it unlike our bodies. Since we agree that it was born of Mary, it was like ours. Mary was not different from our bodies—for Adam was not from a man's seed either, but was formed from earth! (14) And his body was by no means different from ours because of his being of the earth and not of a man's seed. For we are his descendants and our bodies are not different from his, even though we are of a man's seed and born of a woman's womb.

18,15 But by quibbling about this often and having it in their heads, some have lost touch with the question before us. In turn, some of those who come to see me have wasted a million other words and more on the accusation of a man who is widely esteemed. And in fact, I think they have caused more disturbance than necessary, whether < unintentionally* > from ignorance or stupidity, or whether they deliberately come forward and speak out. But with the readers' agreement, let this be enough about the non-essentials; < I have not written* > from motives of envy, or dislike of the man. (16) For I pray that he has not been parted from the church of Christ and the sweetness of the whole brotherhood, but that he has given up instigating the contention over this matter and returned, as scripture says, "Return, return, O Shunamite; return, and we will look on thee."[70] In any case, I shall once more take up the thread of the subject.

19,1 He will not say that Christ's human nature is complete. Furthermore, he hinders some people's salvation by frightening them and telling them we must not say that Christ has "taken up" (ἀνειληφέναι) perfect manhood, because, if you please, of the scripture, "The Lord taketh up (ἀναλαμβάνων) the meek."[71] (2) But no one can show that there is anything out of the ordinary, or different from our frequent use of synonymous expressions, in saying that he Lord "took up" (ἀναλαβεῖν) flesh, or "took" (λαβεῖν) perfect manhood. (3) Scripture says, "The Lord taketh up the meek," "He took me up from the flocks of sheep,"[72] "He was taken up,"[73] and, "The two men said, Ye men of Galilee, why stand ye?

---

[69] Rom. 6:9
[70] Song of Songs 7:1
[71] Ps. 146:6
[72] Cf. Ps. 77:70.
[73] Acts 1:2

This [Jesus], who hath been taken up from you."[74] (4) And there is no difference at all in the meaning of taking up, whether one says "Christ took up," or, "took," or, "formed (ἀναπλάσσειν) his own humanity." Nor can those who choose to attack the simple and < say that > we must < not > talk like this, frighten us with this word.

And no one need think that I am speaking slanderously, or jokingly, about this matter. (5) I have often thought of writing on this subject, but < held off > so that no one would think I was attacking him from enmity. Humanly speaking, he has done me no harm, and taken nothing of mine. (6) But though I considered not writing this, I am compelled to by the truth itself, so as to omit no < one > whose opinions are contrary to the faith, as pious readers will understand later that I am not speaking from worldly jealousy. (7) Indeed, the man would be of the utmost service to me— < he is the best* > in the world, both in < education* > and in love— if, in harmony with God's holy church, he would agree with us all in every way and not import any strange doctrine.

19,8   Whether he or his disciples use the expression in passing, in a different sense [but] in this form and appearance, I cannot say. (9) But I have often considered, and been perturbed that they justify contention and a battle to the death for the sake of this expression. (10) And this tells me that they probably use the expression in some rather strange sense.

20,1   For when you ask any of them they all tell you something different, but some say that the Lord has not taken perfect manhood or become perfect man. (2) But since many found this repugnant they finally turned to deception, as I learned directly from them in so many words. (3) For I visited Antioch and had a meeting with their leaders, one of whom was the bishop Vitalius, a man of the most godly life, character and conduct. (4) And I advised and urged them to assent to the faith of the holy church, and give up the contentious doctrine.

20,5   But Vitalius said, "But what quarrel is there between us?" For he was at odds with a respectable and eminent man, the bishop Paulinus, and Paulinus was at odds with Vitalius, whom I had summoned. (6) I hoped to reconcile the two; both appeared to be preaching the orthodox faith, and yet each of them disagreed [with the other] for some reason—(7) for Vitalius had accused Paulinus of Sabellianism. And thus, when I arrived < at Antioch* > I had refrained from full communion with Paulinus, until he

---

[74] Acts 1:11

convinced me by submitting a document < in > which, on a previous occasion, he had stated his agreement with the blessed
Athanasius to clear himself. (8) For he brought a signed copy of
this and gave it to me. It contains a clear statement about the Trinity
and the mind of Christ's human nature, composed by our blessed
father Athanasius himself. I append this statement; it is as follows:

A copy of the document written by Bishop Paulinus[75]

21,1   *I, Paulinus, bishop, believe as I have received from the fathers that
there is a perfect existent and subsistent Father and a perfect subsistent Son,
and that the perfect Holy Spirit is subsistent. (2) I therefore receive the
above account of the three entities and the one subsistence or essence, and
receive those who so believe; for it is godly to believe and confess the Trinity
in one Godhead. (3) And of the incarnation for us of the Word of the
Father, I believe as it has formerly been written that, as John says, "The
Word was made flesh."[76] (4) For I do not believe as the most impious
persons do, who say that he has undergone a change; but I believe that
he has become man for us, and was conceived of the holy Virgin and the
Holy Spirit.*

1,5   *Nor did the Savior have a lifeless body without sensation or intelligence. (6) For as the Lord has become man for us, it would be impossible
that his body be without intelligence. (7) I therefore condemn those who
set aside the creed of Nicaea, and do not confess that the Son is of the
Father's essence, or co-essential with the Father. (8) I also condemn those
who say that the Holy Spirit is a creature made by the Son. (9) I further
condemn the heresies of Sabellius and Photinus, and every heresy, for I
am content with the creed of Nicaea and with all that is written above.*

The End

22,1   But I said besides to my brother Vitalius and those who were
with him, "And what do you have to say? If there is anything wrong
between you, put it right!"

"Let them tell you < themselves >," said Vitalius. (2) But Paulinus
and his companions said that Vitalius and his denied that Christ
has become perfect man.

Vitalius answered at once, "Yes, we confess that Christ has taken
perfect manhood." And this was wonderful for the audience to
hear, and a great pleasure. (3) < But > since I know the spirit of

---

[75] This document is also appended to the Epistle of the Council of Alexandria, 362 A.D., as given in Athanasius, Tomus ad Alexandros 11.
[76] John 1:14

those who gain their brothers' agreement through pretenses, I kept asking for his exact meaning, and said, "Do you confess that Christ has truly taken flesh?"

"Yes," he agreed.

22,4   "Of the holy virgin Mary and by the Holy Spirit, without the seed of a man?" He agreed to this too.

22,5   "Did the divine Word, the Son of God, actually take flesh from the Virgin at his coming?" He emphatically agreed.

By this time I had become glad, for I had heard from some of those youngsters who came to me on Cyprus that he did not believe that Christ's flesh was from Mary at all. (6) But when this most godly man himself had confessed that our Lord Jesus Christ took flesh from Mary, I asked him, in turn, if he also took a soul . To this too he agreed with the same vehemence, and said, "One must not say otherwise, but must tell the truth in everything. (7) For whoever writes to men about the truth must disclose his whole mind, have the fear of God before his eyes, and include no false-hood in the message of the scripture."

23,1   Vitalius, then, agreed that Christ had also taken a human soul; for it was he who had said, "Yes, Christ was perfect man." But next, after my questions about the soul and the flesh, I asked, "Did Christ take a mind when he came?"

Vitalius at once denied this and said, "No."

23,2   Then I said to him, "Then why do you say that he has been made perfect man?" And he revealed his own notion of the meaning of this: "We are calling him perfect man if we make him the Godhead instead of the mind, and the flesh and the soul, so that he is perfect man composed of flesh, and soul, and Godhead instead of mind."

23,3   So now his contentiousness was out in the open and I discussed it at length, and proved from scripture that we must confess that the divine Word took everything in its perfection, that he provided < the human nature > in its fullness at his incarnation and < possesses > it in its fullness; and that he united it [with his Godhead] after his resurrection and possesses it, and none other, in glory, in its entirety and spiritual, united in his Godhead with himself; and that the whole fullness makes one Godhead, and he sits at the Father's right hand in heaven, on the glorious throne of its eternal sovereignty and rule. But in the end I got up without having convinced either side, because of their obvious conten-tiousness.

23,4   But this is how I realized that they were not talking about the mind, but that their doctrine of the mind is different [from

ours]. For at times they would not admit that Christ had taken
a soul. (5) But when I made the rejoinder, "Well, what is the
'mind?' then? Do you think it's a real thing inside a man? Is man
therefore a conglomerate?" some of them opined that the "mind"
is the "spirit" which the sacred scripture regularly says is in man.
(6) But when I showed them that the mind is not the spirit, since
the apostle plainly says, "I will sing with the mind, I will sing with
the spirit,"[77] there was a long discussion, but I could not convince
the contending parties.

24,1   Then in turn, I asked some of them, "What do you mean?
Are you saying that the mind is an actual thing?" And some of
them said it is not a thing, because I had convinced them with,
"I will sing with the mind, I will sing with the spirit," that we must
not believe that the mind is the thing called "the spirit of a man."
(2) And since they had no reply to this, I then said, "All right,
if the mind isn't a real thing but is a movement of our whole selves,
but you, in turn, say that Christ is the mind, do you therefore
imagine that Christ isn't a real thing, and that he has brought his
incarnation about only nominally, and in appearance?"

24,3   And I felt deeply † grieved[78] then, and the even tenor of
my life was made painful, because dissensions had been sown for
no good reason among these people who are brethren and praiseworthy, so that that enemy of man, the devil, may keep causing
differences among us. (4) But, brethren, considerable mutual damage
arises from this cause. It would be simplest if no discussion of this
had been stirred up in the first place. What good has this innovation done the world? How has it benefited the church—or rather,
hasn't it harmed it by causing hatred and strife? But because this
doctrine has been put forward, it has become frightening. (5) It
is not for the betterment of our salvation; it is a denial of our
salvation, not only on this point for one who does not confess it,
but in a very small point too.[79] One must not stray from the way
of the truth even in an unimportant matter.

24,6   Let me speak against this too, then, since I choose not
to stray from my own salvation or abandon the rule of God's holy
church and confession. (7) None of the ancients ever said this—
no prophet, apostle, evangelist, no interpreter down to our own
day, when this doctrine of such sophistry issued from the very

---

[77] 1 Cor. 14:15
[78] Holl: λύπη < καὶ ὀδυνηρ > ά. MSS: λυπηρά
[79] I.e., not only is the Apolinarian doctrine of Christ heretical, but they have
an unscriptural definition of "mind."

learned man I have spoken of. (8) For he has been equipped with no mean education. He began with elementary schooling and Greek learning, and was trained in the whole of dialectic and rhetoric. Moreover, his life is otherwise of the holiest, < and he > remained beloved † by the orthodox[80] and ranked with the foremost, until this business. (9) He suffered banishment too, because he < would > not associate with the Arians. And why should I say all this? I am very sorry, and my life is a grief to me because, as I have often said, the devil is always afflicting us.

25,1 Now then, to omit none of the truth, as I have said, I shall begin on this doctrine. What good has it done us to expel the mind from Christ's human nature? (2) If your argument was advanced to be a help—if I can say that—to our Lord Jesus Christ, the divine Word and the Son of God, and we are to deny that he took a mind so as not to conceive of any defect in his Godhead, the Manichaeans, the Marcionites and other sects deserve more credit than we. They will not ascribe flesh to him, so as not to make his Godhead defective.

25,3 But the meaning of the truth does not conform to human wishes, but to the wisdom that governs it, and the incomprehensibility that directs it. (4) Since we profess our faith in this form and do not agree with Mani—(though he thinks his denial that Christ took flesh redounds to his praise, Mani will do Christ no favor. Instead, by confessing Christ's incarnation [only] in appearance, he will be deprived of the truth.) Since this is what we believe, the vulgar chatter will be a favor of no use to our brothers even now. (5) Both they and we agree < that* >, unless they are willing to change their minds, < the Manichaeans will depart from our confession of faith entirely.* > And when pressed, certain Apolinarians have often been caught in the denial that Christ took true flesh, as I said, because some of them have dared to say that his flesh is co-essential with his Godhead. (6) But they should be cast out as < un >repentant, and exposed for such wickedness before those of them whose view of Christ's flesh is correct. Surely the most godly Apolinaris himself will not deny this.

26,1 Now if the Word took true flesh when he came, and truly took it from Mary, not by a man's seed but through the Holy Spirit; and if he was truly conceived and, since he was God and the fashioner of the first man and all things, fashioned his own < flesh >; then the Word was not diminished at his coming, but remained in his

---

[80] Holl: < ὃς > καὶ πρὸς τῶν ὀρθοδόξων ἀεὶ ἐν ἀγάπῃ ἐν πρώτῳ ἀριθμῷ < τε > ταττόμενος; MSS: καὶ τῶν πρὸς ὀρθοδόξων ἀεὶ ἐν ἀγάπῃ ἐν πρωτῷ ἀριθμῷ ταττόμενος

own unchanging nature. (2) For since he is co-essential with God the Father and not different from the Father and the Holy Spirit, he underwent no change when he took flesh. If we agree, therefore, that he has plainly taken flesh and come to maturity, then he is not without a soul. (3) For except for things which do not move, everything that matures is composed of soul and body, as the scripture says, "Jesus increased in wisdom and maturity," where "maturity"[81] implies flesh; but maturity, as I said, is attained by a soul and a body.

26,4   But after saying, "He increased in maturity," it next says, "and wisdom." And how could he who is the Father's wisdom increase in wisdom, if his body was without a human mind? And if he was without mind, how could he increase in wisdom in soul and body? And you see how forced people's notion is when they reject the mind.

"But," Apolinaris would say, "I deny that he took a human mind. [If we say that he did], we will make him covetous and ill-tempered; for the mind in us is covetous." And there certainly is a great deal of human contention; as the scripture has said, "God made man simple, but they have made for themselves many counsels."[82] (5) Now if, by the confession that he has taken a human mind, we attribute any of our defectiveness to him, all the more, by confessing that he has taken flesh, we will grant on the same principle that he has become defective in this respect, in flesh. But perish that thought! (6) Now as the Word was < not > defective in the flesh when he came even though he had true flesh, so he has not conceived of anything unbecoming his Godhead in his mind. The Lord, when he came, did whatever is right for flesh, and for a soul and a human mind, so as not to disturb the course of his true human life. (7) For hunger, thirst, weariness, sleep, journeying, grief, weeping and anger were right. But these right things duly taking place in him showed < the truth* > of his true human nature.

27,1   For scripture never says that he had a wrong desire. But he had a good desire when he said, "With desire I have desired to eat this Passover with you."[83] Desire, however, does not stem from his Godhead, or from the flesh alone or the irrational soul, but from the perfect manhood of body, < soul and > mind, and everything in man. (2) For the Word acquired these things when he came—body, soul, mind and all that is in man, except for sin,

---

[81] Luke 2:52
[82] Cf. Eccles. 7:29.
[83] Luke 22:15

except for defect, as the scripture says, "in all points tempted as a man except for sin."[84] But if he was tempted in *all* points, the Word acquired *all* things when he came. (3) If he had acquired everything, however, then in himself he was free from defect and kept them all undefiled—being perfect God born of flesh, and, as the Perfecter of the whole human nature, perfectly fulfilling all things. He was not divided by the unseemly behavior of the flesh, or distracted by the evil purpose of the mind within us.

27,4   For our mind was not made to sin with, but to examine all sides of the matters we compare mentally, and to perform righteousness and its opposite. "The mind discriminates words; the throat tastes foods,"[85] and, "Eye understands and mind sees."[86] Thus the mind is the sight, taste and discrimination within us and is granted us by God, but assents to nothing unless the man wants it to. (5) But the flesh is continually denounced in every scripture for the lust that arises in it. However, the text of course does not denounce flesh itself; the word denounced the deeds that spring from the flesh, as the apostle said because of the by-products of the flesh, "I know that in me, that is, in my flesh, dwelleth no good thing."[87]

27,6   But in rejection of the sects' idea that the flesh has nothing to hope for from the resurrection of the dead, Paul says, "This corruptible must put on incorruption, and this mortal must put on immortality."[88] Thus there can be no question of his rejecting the hope of the resurrection of the flesh because he rejects the works of the flesh, which scripture regularly calls, "flesh." (7) For he plainly denounced the deeds that are wickedly done in the flesh, but showed that, in a person who sanctifies his flesh, the flesh itself is a holy temple, as the scripture says, "Pure worship of God and our Father is this, to visit the fatherless and widows in their affliction, and to keep himself unspotted from the world,"[89] and elsewhere, "Blessed are they that keep pure the flesh."[90]

27,8   But though the scripture has often spoken against "flesh" and taught us that it is the source of lusts and pleasures, it says nothing against the mind. Instead it says, "I will sing with the mind, I will sing with the spirit,"[91] and, "if, in turn, I sing with the spirit,

---

[84] Cf. Heb. 4:15.
[85] Job 12:11
[86] Cf. Prov. 20:12.
[87] Rom. 7:18
[88] 1 Cor. 15:53
[89] Cf. Jas. 1:27.
[90] Acts of Paul and Thecla 5

but my mind is unfruitful."[92] (9) And you see that there is fruit in him in his mind. And even if there is no fruit, Paul never counted the mind as sinful, but made the fruit known by means of the mind.

28,1 But what harm did this do to the power of our Lord's Godhead? What weakened his power? The holy woman's belly? The Virgin's womb? His parents' journeys? Simeon's embrace? Anna's welcome? Being carried by Mary? The harlot's touch? A woman's hair touching his feet? Her tears? Being laid in a tomb? The shroud did not envelop that inviolate Lord and his supreme power by enwrapping his body.

28,2 Indeed, when he was still in the womb John leaped for joy at his Master's visit to him through the holy Virgin's pregnancy. But when he had been born and lay in a manger, it was no mystery to a choir of angels. Bands of angels were sent to serve as escorts at the coming of the everlasting king; hymns of victory were offered, peace was proclaimed to the shepherds.

28,3 But what caused any weakening of his power? While he was still a babe in arms a sign, the star, appeared in the east, magi arrived, worship was offered and gifts given. Scribes were questioned by the king, and in reply they confessed their faith in Christ. (4) And all the other things in the series, what harm did they do his Godhead? How did the possession of the flesh veil it, as is the case with us? He rebuked the waves, winds and sea, and the power of his Godhead was not prevented by the flesh from doing what it is the nature of the Godhead to do. (5) What is more, though the flesh is a burden and load, he was not encumbered by a load. As the changeless God, and in the flesh but not changed by the flesh, he walked on the water < as though on dry land >; and he was in the flesh and not altered from flesh. With a < loud > voice he called, "Lazarus, come forth!"[93] unhindered by the flesh, and with no enslavement of his Godhead in the flesh to his perfect manhood.

29,1 And I have a great deal to say < about this >. He rose from the dead, what is more, forced the gates of hades, took the captives, brought them upward; and after rising the third day in his holy flesh itself, and in his holy soul, mind and entire human nature, he became perfect man united with Godhead, for he had joined his manhood to his Godhead, and death "hath no more

---

[91] 1 Cor. 14:15
[92] Cf. 1 Cor. 14:14.
[93] John 11:43

dominion over him."[94] (2) But once united with his Godhead he made his coarseness fine and "entered where doors were barred."[95] And after his entrance he exhibited his "flesh and bones,"[96] suggesting the readiness of his power to save, and affording us a glimpse of our hope, for the Word has perfected all things by his coming. And he sat in glory at the Father's right hand after being taken up in his body itself, not burdened by the bulk [of his body and yet] not without a body; he had raised his body spiritual. (3) If our body is "sown in corruption, raised in incorruption, sown a natural body, raised a spiritual body,"[97] how much more the body of God's only-begotten Son? And thus the scripture, "Thou shalt not deliver thine holy one to see corruption, neither shalt thou leave my soul in hell,"[98] has been fulfilled.

29,4   But I have said all this about his perfect human nature so that no one will suppose that, because he took perfect flesh, he therefore did the unsuitable deeds of the flesh. No orthodox believer thinks or says this of him. But if no one thinks that he did the unsuitable deeds of the flesh, no one should suppose that he did the unsuitable deeds of the mind! (5) And it is plain that, when he came, the Word became man perfectly.

And if we say, "[became man] perfectly," we do not have two Christs, or two kings and sons of God, but the same God and the same Man—not as though he had come to dwell in a man, but the same God himself wholly made man. And not a man who advanced to Godhead but God come from heaven, who modeled his own manhood on himself in keeping with his mighty Godhead, as scripture says, "The Word became flesh."[99]

29,6   But as to "The Word became flesh," to avoid giving the impression that he was man first, and Christ came to a man, the holy Gospel put "Word" first, and then confessed the flesh with, "The Word was made flesh." (7) For it did not say, "The flesh was made Word." This shows that the Word came from heaven first, formed his own flesh from the holy Virgin's womb, and perfectly fashioned his entire human nature in his image. (8) For even though scripture says, "The Word was made flesh," this is not because the Word was turned into flesh and the Word became flesh in this way, or because the Godhead was transformed into flesh;

---

[94] Rom. 6:9
[95] Cf. John 20:19; 26.
[96] Luke 24:39
[97] 1 Cor. 15:42; 44
[98] Cf. Ps. 15:10.
[99] John 1:14

at his coming the divine Word took his own humanity as an accompaniment to his Godhead.

30,1   And scripture says that "Jesus increased in maturity and wisdom."[100] As I have said already, how could he "increase" [in wisdom] without a human mind? And God's holy prophet Isaiah also witnesses to this text by saying, "Behold, my beloved servant in whom I am well pleased shall understand."[101] (2) And do you see that "shall understand" refers to a perfect human nature? Without a mind, no one can "understand;" and the text does not apply to Godhead. For that which is understanding itself cannot be in need of understanding, and that which is Wisdom itself cannot be in need of wisdom; "He shall understand" is to be taken of the human mind.

30,3   And tell me, why was he hungry? If he was just flesh, how could he pay any attention to hunger? And if he was made only of body and soul, and his soul did not have the rationality of the mind which is the thought of the human nature—I don't mean wicked thought, but thought directed towards lawful need which is appropriate to his Godhead—then how could he be hungry or have a conception of hunger? (4) Tell me, how could he be grieved, if his soul was without a mind and reason? If a soul is irrational or if there is flesh without soul, it is not subject to grief or sorrow. (5) And I can think of many < replies* > which I should make to him. < For we must* > realize that quibbles are not to the point and that, if anything, they alarm those who want to think too far, and not measure themselves by the measure the most holy apostle recommended to us, "not to think more highly than we ought to think."[102]

31,1   They also confront us with certain words of scripture, "We have the mind of Christ,"[103] and say, "Do you see that the mind of Christ is different from our minds?" How simple people are! Each one leans in the direction he wants to go, and where he appears to be clever, turns out to be inept. (2) For though I am "inept in speech—but not in knowledge,"[104] as the scripture says—

---

[100] Luke 2:52
[101] Cf. Isa. 42:1.
[102] Rom. 12:3
[103] 1 Cor. 2:16. At Leontius Adversus Fraudes Apollinistarum 141 (Lietzmann Fr. 155, p. 249) Timotheus is represented as quoting Apolinaris: "Christ is a living God-animated body and divine spirit in flesh, a heavenly mind of which we are all partakers as it is said, "We have the mind of Christ." With this, however, cf. 34,3–4.
[104] 2 Cor. 11:6

and though I am very limited, and I admire these people even when they attack the mind because of words, I am baffled by their notion because they interpret this text as proof of what is simply such sterile contentiousness on their part. For the thing (i.e., 2 Cor. 11:16) has no meaning with any bearing on this position.

31,3   For Paul says, "We have the mind of Christ." But we need to ask what "Christ" means to them, or what the "mind of Christ" is. And here they show that they understand Christ as one thing, and his divine nature as something else. (4) For if they suppose that Christ [himself] replaces the [human] mind, and yet call only Christ's human nature "Christ," they are trying to lead me into one more dispute. And plainly, it is < not > [only] after the incarnation that he is described as the divine Word and Son of God. (5) < But > though the texts that call him Christ came earlier, even before the incarnation, it is in the incarnation that they are fulfilled. For his Godhead does not lack the name of Christ, and his incarnation and human nature cannot be mentioned without such a name, as the scripture says, "Say not in thine heart, who shall ascend into heaven, that is, to bring Christ down. Or who shall descend into the deep, that is, to bring Christ up from the dead."[105] (6) And the apostle, in turn, says, "that they may know thee, the only true God, and Jesus Christ whom thou hast sent."[106] Now "Thou hast sent" means "[sent] from on high;" and yet it cannot be separated from the words of Peter, "Jesus of Nazareth, a man approved among you by signs and wonders, whom God hath anointed with the Holy Spirit,"[107] and texts of this sort.

32,1   And next, in their desire to confront me with ideas that are in every way contentious, my very beloved brethren also preach, not without daring, that his divine nature has suffered, because of the text which says, "If they had known, they would not have crucified the Lord of glory."[108] (2) But some of Apolinaris' disciples, who, I suppose, do not understand this, want to invent something else by putting this forward with the rest. I would be surprised if Apolinaris himself says anything of the kind.

For it is no surprise if the sacred scripture says that the Lord of glory has been crucified. (3) We confess that his human nature

---

[105] Rom. 10:6–7
[106] John 17:3
[107] Acts 2:22
[108] 1 Cor. 2:8. At Antirrheticus 24, p. 179 (Apolinaris Fragment 48, Lietzmann p. 215) Gregory of Nyssa quotes Apolinaris as saying that Christ is called "Lord of glory" because he is an "incarnate mind . . . who did not become flesh in the Virgin but passed through her in transit and was before the ages."

too is the Lord of glory. The humanity is not separate from the Godhead, if we understand each of them properly and see the whole in combination as one person and one perfection. (4) For we preach and believe that Christ can suffer [but] not that he (i.e., the human nature) suffered for himself, or that the Sufferer and the Lord are different persons, or that the Godhead suffered. Our Lord Jesus Christ suffered while his Godhead remained unaltered and impassible and yet, though it remained impassible, suffered in the flesh. (5) For if Christ died for us—and truly died—his divine nature did not die. He died in the flesh—as the scripture says, "He was put to death in the flesh but quickened by the Spirit,"[109] and again, "Christ hath suffered for us in the flesh."[110]

32,6   It is remarkable that we confess that he truly suffered and yet is truly impassible. For because of its changelessness, impassibility and co-essentiality with the Father, his divine nature did not suffer; his flesh suffered, and yet the divine nature was not separate from the human nature in its suffering. (7) For the divine and the human nature were together when Christ suffered in his flesh on the cross yet remained impassible in his divine nature, so that we are no longer justified only in his flesh but also in his Godhead, and our salvation is effected in both ways, in the divine nature and in the flesh.

32,8   For Christ was no mere man for us, but a subsistent divine Word < become > incarnate, and God truly made man for us. Thus our hope is not in man but in the Godhead; and our God is not a God who suffers, but an impassible God. Still, he has not wrought our salvation without suffering, but by dying for us and offering himself to the Father as a sacrifice for our souls, "cleansing us with his blood,"[111] "tearing up the handwriting against us and nailing it to the cross,"[112] as the scripture everywhere teaches us.

33,1   And if the need arises, I shall have a great deal to say in proof of this. Elsewhere, in explaining this view of our sure salvation, I have said that if a garment is stained by a flow of blood, the blood has not stained the body of the wearer, but the stain on the garment is not considered the garment's, but the wearer's. (2) In the same way the passion did the divine nature no harm but was suffered in the human nature, and yet not only as the human nature's; otherwise the scripture, "Cursed be everyone whose hope

---

[109] 1 Pet. 3:18
[110] 1 Pet. 4:1
[111] Heb. 9:22
[112] Col. 2:14

is in man,"[113] might be applicable to the work of salvation. It was
also counted as the Godhead's though the Godhead does not suffer,
so that the salvation of the passion might be credited to God's holy
church in the Godhead.

33,3   And again, no pedant need wish to debate anything but
the point of the comparison. Not every parable in the scripture
is to be applied wholesale. For example, "Judah is a lion's whelp"[114]
is said because the animal is the strongest and kingliest, not because
it is irrational and a predator. (4) So with the garment. It is not
put on and taken off; "He put on majesty" once, as the scripture
says, but the second time "He put it on, and was girded with
strength,"[115] in fulfillment of the most holy apostle's words, "Christ
dieth no more, death hath no more dominion over him."[116]

33,5   But in spite of this my brethren would like to cite "We
have the mind of Christ"[117] to prove their point to me. However,
going by what they say in explanation of the subject, they lead me
to suspect that they may have understood "mind" [in the text] as
something different from "Christ." (6) Yet if they do not think that
the Godhead is separate from the humanity but that there is [only]
one person, what further thing will this so-called "mind of Christ"
be? Is the divine Word all by itself in the human nature, and
without a human mind, as they say? Does [the divine] Christ have
a "mind" other than the nature of his Godhead? Or is every difficult word used loosely, as proof of what goes on within us?

34,1   In fact every godly person lives, not in accordance with
the mind of man, but in accordance with the "mind of Christ."
This means the mind that is filled with understanding by Christ,
thinks righteously like Christ, lives in Christ by the confession [of
him], is preserved in well-doing for Christ's sake. For this is the
"mind of Christ," which is capable of being in us without confining
Christ in an enclosure. (2) The Father, the Son and < the > Holy
Spirit are everywhere, and Christ is in us spiritually if we become
worthy of him, since no space encloses him, his Father and his
Holy Spirit. By the power of his Godhead he is in all things, and
yet, because of his incommunicable and incomparable essence, he
is intermingled with nothing.

34,3   But when the apostle said, "We have the mind of Christ,"[118]

---

[113] Jer. 17:5
[114] Gen. 49:9
[115] Ps. 92:1
[116] Rom. 6:9
[117] 1 Cor. 2:16
[118] 1 Cor. 2:16

what should we think he means? Did Paul have his own human
< mind >? Or did he become filled with Christ's mind and lose
his own, but have the mind of Christ instead of his own? Hardly!
Each of his hearers would agree that he had his own mind but
that he was filled with Christ's, who had equipped him with piety,
knowledge, and God's heavenly way of life.

34,4 If, therefore, he was filled with Christ's mind while having
his own, this means that, if we have to say it, Christ himself, the
Word, was "mind"—for some have seen fit to call God "mind." (5)
I, though, do not regard our mind as an entity— nor does any
son of the church—but as a form of activity which God has bestowed
upon us, and which is in us. But I do call Christ an entity, as all
the faithful confess that he is; and I confess that he is God and
truly the Lord, begotten of the Father, Perfect of Perfect, Light
of Light, and God of God. (6) But still, going by the same text,
He who is mind in himself—as the holy apostle's teaching about
him is "We have the mind of Christ"—had his own mind. And they
to whom Paul testified had their own minds, and in turn were
filled with the Mind, Christ, since his grace is capable of coming
to fruition in them in this way.

35,1 Hence, on the exact analogy, it will make no difference
if we assume this of Christ as well. For surely, even though Christ,
who is mind in himself, shared the human mind as he shared flesh
and blood and had the human soul, he was not the prisoner of
the [human] mind. (2) For if the apostle who had the human
mind as his own by nature, and the mind [of Christ] by participation in the gift, benefit and grace, no longer lived in accordance
with his own mind but was directed, by a guidance transcending
nature, by the mind of Christ, how much more the divine Word!
He possessed all perfection in himself and was absolute perfection,
absolute God, absolute power, absolute light, and the Completer,
or rather, Perfecter, both of the mind and of the whole body, and
wrought our salvation in all things by his advent in the flesh.

35,3 We must reject this text, then, as having no significance
for this subject, and put aside the denial that all things, apart from
sin, are complete in Christ. For the Word truly did all things at
his coming, and brought the scriptural prophecies of himself to
fulfillment—as the scripture says, "Behold, the Virgin shall conceive,"[119] and so on. He was conceived truly and not in appearance,
was truly engendered in a womb. He truly lived in the flesh with

---

[119] Isa. 7:14

flesh, true soul and true mind, and all true human characteristics except for sin. (4) He was truly born of a virgin womb—and truly of a holy virgin, not by the seed of men—with true flesh and soul and, as I said, a true mind. He was truly with his parents on their journey, truly lay in a manger in swaddling clothes, was borne in Mary's arms, went down to Egypt and was brought back from Egypt and to Nazareth, (5) went to the Jordan and was baptized by John and tempted by the devil. He truly chose disciples and preached the kingdom of heaven, just as everything about him is true—his betrayal by Judas and arrest by Jews, being brought to Pontius Pilate and condemned to death by him, his crucifixion and saying, "I thirst, give me to drink."[120] He truly accepted vinegar with gall, tasted it, and accepted nothing else to drink. He was truly nailed to the cross and cried, "Eli, Eli, lema sabachthani."[121] He truly bowed his head and expired. His body was truly removed and taken away, truly wrapped in a shroud by Joseph and laid in a tomb, truly secured with a stone.

35,6   He descended to hades in his Godhead with his soul, bravely and mightily freed the prisoners, truly ascended the third day, the divine Word with his holy soul, with the captives he had rescued; truly raised with body, soul and all his human nature. He spent the forty days with his disciples, truly blessed them on the Mount of Olives, and truly ascended into heaven while his disciples watched him truly taken up to the clouds.

He took his seat and truly sits at the Father's right hand in his body itself and his Godhead, in his perfect human nature itself, (7) in which he has united the whole in one, and as a single spiritual perfection—seated in glory as God, who will truly come to judge the quick and the dead. And nothing has been altered; all perfect things have been perfectly done in him, in their perfection.

36,1   I believe that this will do for these questions, and judge that now is the time to drop the subject. But again, I must also give some indication of the nonsense I have been told < by > those who say such things. I cannot believe that this is what they say, but I still shall not leave out what I have been told. (2) For some have even dared to report that certain of them, in their turn, say that Mary had relations with her husband Joseph after Jesus' birth. But I would be surprised if even they say this. (3) There are people who do, and I have counted them as other schismatics, and by request have written a letter to certain persons in Arabia against

---

[120] Cf. John 19:28.
[121] Matt. 17:46

the people who say this. (4) But I have said a great deal about this in treating of them in that letter. With God's help I shall add it next, in a chapter of its own.

36,5   Others have reported the venerable man as saying that we will live for a thousand years in the first resurrection, doing the same things we do now—observing the Law and the other ordinances, for example, engaging in all the activities of daily life, and taking part in marriage, circumcision and the rest. I simply can't believe this of him, but some have reported him as having said this, and insisted on it.

36,6   And it is plain that this millennium has been described in John's Revelation, and that the book has been believed by the majority, and the orthodox. But when the majority and orthodox read the book they know about the spiritual meanings, and take its spiritual statements as true < in the spiritual sense >, and believe that they must be given a profound explanation. For this is not the only profound utterance in Revelation; there are many others besides.

37,1   But for brevity's sake I merely mention the matter for now, to show that the godly that, whenever one wants to overstep the bounds of God's holy church and the apostles' faith and teaching < which determine Christians'* > hope, his mind will finally be turned, by the brief, quick mention of the one subject in his momentary, chance thought in passing, (2) to many pieces of nonsense and shaky speculations—unsuitable and strange disputes, and, as the apostle has said, "endless genealogies."[123] (3) Anyone with sense can see that this is a very simple matter requiring no explanation; this sort of wisdom and subject for argument needs no investigation. (4) If we are raised to be circumcised again, why haven't we been circumcised before? In this regard, then, the ancients managed < to do > something more important than we, since they realized what perfection is, and were perfected in advance with what will be perfection then.

37,5   What becomes of the words of the apostle, "If ye be circumcised, Christ shall profit you nothing,"[124] and, "All ye that are justified by the Law are fallen from grace?"[125] What about the Lord's words, "For in the resurrection they neither marry nor are given in marriage, but are equal unto the angels?"[126] (6) On the other

---

[123] 1 Tim. 1:4
[124] Gal. 5:2
[125] Gal. 5:4
[126] Luke 20:35–36

hand, "Ye shall sit at the table < of the kingdom > of my Father eating and drinking,"[127] and, "when I drink it new with you in the kingdom of heaven,"[128] with the additional word, "new," and the phrase, "at the table of the kingdom," mean something different. (7) I myself agree with this, since I have learned from the sacred scriptures that there is a partaking of immortal food and drink. Of these it is said, "Eye hath not seen and ear hath not heard, neither have entered into the heart of man, what things God hath prepared for them that love him."[129]

38,1 Apolinaris though, says that we partake of the material pleasures first, in the millennium, without labor and grief, but that after the millennium we partake of the things of which "eye hath not seen and ear hath not heard" was said.[130] (2) But this is contrary to the whole view of scripture. For if "The Law made no one perfect,"[131] but we are commanded to observe the Law after our resurrection, [this is a contradiction].[132] And if the "holy Law"[133] which was given by the Lord through Moses "was our conductor to Christ"[134] because of its inferiority to the things which are perfected,[135] (3) but < is abolished > because Christ, the Perfect and the Lord, has come and received the holy bride and church from the conductor of its tutees, that is, of the faithful—and if we have recognized[136] "Jesus," the greater and the "Finisher," through the conductor's Law—how can their argument prove to be anything but a sign of shallow thinking and silliness, when they say such things as that (4) a conductor is needed again after the perfection of Christ, so that we may return to the "beginning" "of the rudiments"[137] and the teaching, and of "the laying on of hands,"[138] as the scripture says. But the apostle tells us plainly, as though < he meant > the Old Testament and the Law, that "That which decayeth and waxeth old is ready to vanish away."[139]

---

[127] Luke 22:30
[128] Mark 14:25
[129] 1 Cor. 2:9
[130] This teaching is attributed to Apolinaris at Basil Ep. 265,2; Greg. Naz. Ep. 102; Carmen Hist. I De Suo Ipso 30;179; Jer. Com. In Isa. XVIII, Prefatio.
[131] Heb. 7:19
[132] This insertion, and the one below, are devices used to divide an otherwise unmanageably long sentence. Holl tentatively suggests < πῶς σταθήσεται τοῦτο > at this point.
[133] Rom. 7:12
[134] Gal. 3:24
[135] Cf. Heb. 9:11.
[136] Heb. 12:2
[137] Heb. 5:12
[138] Heb. 6:2
[139] Heb. 8:13

3,5   *For it is in this way that foolishness, and the seed of the devil's words, is wont to cause such disturbance and confusion, and with blasphemous thoughts to incite the minds of created human beings to war < on > their Master with clumsy conjectures and denials of God.*

3,6   *But while avoiding this, some in their turn have dared to proceed to other evils by the denial of their Master who alone redeemed them, the only-begotten Child Jesus Christ, the Son of the living God, the truly existent Son—begotten of the Father without beginning and not in time, forever of the Father and with the Father, begotten incomprehensibly and without defilement, co-essential with the Father and not different from the Father.*

(7)   *Some, again, have gone mad and bark at their own Master like rabid dogs—as the Jews did at the first, and have been called "dumb dogs"[8] for not knowing him. With evident fitness they were awarded this name by the prophet, < because of > their shameless rage at the Lord and his coming. (8) For they say that mad dogs are called "dumb" because they are left toothless by their mind on its departure.*

4,1   *For dogs are like this when they have gone mad. Though they once knew their master, his children, his household, all the householder's other kin, when the madness takes them these persons' faces seem different to them, and they attack even their owner's kinsfolk, in whose honor they once wagged their tails, and to whose ways they once submitted. (2) When those who were awaiting the coming of Christ beheld their Master's arrival—though they were prepared to receive the bridegroom, boasted of having seen the prophets, professed to obey their sacred oracles, and covenanted with Moses, "Be thou [for us] to the Lord,"[9] and, "All that the Lord saith unto thee we will hear and do"[10]—[nonetheless] when they saw their Master's arrival they did not know the appearance and marks of the truth which the prophets before him had portrayed, depicted, proclaimed and pointed to before his incarnation, and at once said to him, first, "Who is this that speaketh blasphemies?"[11] (3) But on another occasion they shamelessly ventured to say that he had a demon, and did not blush to call him a Samaritan as well. (4) Finally, as I have said, they set on him like mad dogs, nailed his hands < and struck him in the face* >, as a dog in its madness always fastens < on the person before it* > and attacks his hands, and is not ashamed to scratch the faces of its owners.*

4,5   *They gave their own Lord up to crucifixion; and of the prophets, the household of that same Master, they sawed one in half, stoned another, and slew another with the sword. (6) But their successors, the new Jews*

---

[8] Isa. 56:40
[9] Cf. Exod. 18:19.
[10] Deut. 5:27
[11] Luke 5:21

after them, are now behaving in the same way. The Jews by birth denied him; but in their utter madness and incompetence those who are now denying the truth of the Son's relation to the Father maintain without intermission that he is a creature and product of creation, and is different from the Father.

5,1 *Others in turn have abandoned those blasphemous doctrines, and have still, as it were, seen the sight surpassing the nature of heaven itself, visited the heavenly realms, and pried into them. They make their arrogant announcement and confident affirmation as though they had come from the heaven, and banish the Holy Spirit from the Godhead.* (2) *They have not denied the Father, or the Son's relation to him, but they go by another route to ensure the complete fulfillment of the prophecy, "Faith hath failed from their lips."*[12] (3) *For what can this mean but that now—as though they had the authority—instead of being commanded by God they wish to command God about the Holy Spirit, who is not different from the Father and the Son, who is of the same Godhead, and who cannot possibly be alien to the Godhead? For they shamelessly say that the Spirit is alien to God, a servant, a creature, of recent origin, and something made, but contrive to get hold of anything else that is shameful for an opinion of him.*

5,4 *Thus, because of its incurable wound of unbelief, the world of our day has inclined more < and more to evil* >. And that the wickedness which is destroying humanity through perversity, ignorance and unbelief may leave no stone unturned, an idle, foolish notion has diverted the attention of those who have, as it were, escaped the blasphemy of the holy Trinity, to other things, leaving no one's sin unobserved.*

5,5 *For I hear that someone has a new notion about the holy, ever-virgin Mary, and dares to cast a blasphemous suspicion on her, so that our generation will be exactly like a dangerous serpent and poisonous snake. [Such a snake] lurks in a dark den and strikes everyone with its bites, one near the face, another near the heel, another near the hand,* (6) *so that no one can avoid the bite of unbelief. Though one suppose he has escaped it in one way he does not avoid the poison in another, while one whose faith is sound in one respect is exposed to some other form of harm.*

6,1 *Why this ill will? Why so much impudence? Isn't Mary's very name (i.e., "Virgin") a testimony, you trouble-maker? Doesn't it convince you? Who, and in which generation, has ever dared to say St. Mary's name and not add "Virgin" at once when asked? The marks of excellence show from the titles of honor themselves.* (2) *For the righteous received the honors of their titles appropriately for them and as it became them. "Friend of God"*[13] *was added to the name, "Abraham," and will not be detached from*

---

[12] Jer. 7:28
[13] Jas. 2:23

it. The title, "Israel," was added to "Jacob" and will not be changed. The title, "Boanerges," or "sons of thunder," was given to the apostles and will not be discarded. And St. Mary was given the title, "Virgin," and it will not be altered, for the holy woman remained undefiled. "Doth not nature itself teach you?"[14] *Oh, this new madness, these new troubles!*

6,3   *There are many other things which the fathers did not venture to say in times gone by. Now, however, one blasphemes Christ's incarnation by talking heresy about the Godhead itself, while another considers the entire matter of the incarnation defective, another is troubled about the resurrection of the dead, and someone else < by another > point. (4) And in a word, woe to our troubled generation with its salvation in peril, swamped on every side by the wicked second sowings of the devil's sick fancies and heretical reasonings! (5) How dare they < so degrade* > the undefiled Virgin who was privileged to become the Son's habitation, and was chosen for this from all the myriads of Israel, so that something deemed worthy to be a vessel and dwelling place is to become a mere sign of child-bearing?*

7,1   *For I have heard from someone that certain persons are venturing to say that she had marital relations after the Savior's birth. And I am not surprised. The ignorance of persons who do not know the sacred scriptures well and have not consulted histories, always turns them to one thing after another, and distracts anyone who wants to track down something about the truth out of his own head. (2) To begin with, when it fell to the Virgin's lot to be entrusted to Joseph*[15] *she was not entrusted to him for marriage, since he was a widower. (3) He was called her husband because of the Law, but it plainly follows from the Jewish tradition that the Virgin was not entrusted to him for matrimony. (4) It was for the preservation of her virginity in witness to the things to come—[a witness] that Christ's incarnation was nothing spurious but was truly attested, as without a man's seed < but > truly brought about by the Holy Spirit.*

7,5   *For how could such an old man,*[16] *who had lost his first wife so many years before, take a virgin for a wife? Joseph was the brother of Cleopas but the son of Jacob surnamed Panther; both of these brothers were the sons of the man surnamed Panther. (6) Joseph took his first wife from the tribe of Judah and she bore him six children in all, four boys and two girls, as the Gospels according to Mark and John have made clear.*[17] *(7) His firstborn son was James, whose surname was Oblias, or "wall,"*[18] *and who was also surnamed "The Just" and was a nazirite, or "holy man." (8)*

---

[14] 1 Cor. 14:14
[15] Cf. Protevangelium of James 9.1.
[16] Cf. Protevangelium of James 9.2.
[17] Cf. Mark 6:3; John 19:25.
[18] Cf. Hegesippus in Eus. H. E. 3.23.7.

He was the first to receive the episcopal throne,[19] *the first to whom the Lord entrusted his throne on earth.* (9) *He was also called the Lord's brother, as the apostle agrees by saying somewhere, "But other of the apostles saw I none, save James the Lord's brother,"*[20] *and so on. But he is called the Lord's brother not by nature but by grace, because of being brought up with him.* (10) *For because she had been betrothed to Joseph Mary appeared to be the wife of a husband, but she had no sexual relations with him. For this reason the degree of the kinship of Joseph's sons to the Savior was called, or rather, regarded as, that of brotherhood.*

7,11	*Similarly Joseph himself is held by dispensation to be in the position of a father, though he had had no part in the fleshly generation of the Savior. Thus Luke the evangelist says of the Savior himself that he was "the son of Joseph, as was supposed;"*[21] *and Mary too said to him the Gospel according to Luke, "Behold, thy father and I have sought thee sorrowing."*[22] (12) *Who, then, can call Joseph the Lord's father when he had no responsibility for his generation, especially when the incarnation took place without a man's seed? But by the dispensation of providence this is how matters fell out.*

8,1	*Joseph begot James when he was somewhere around forty years old. After him he had a son named Joses—then Simeon after him, then Judah, and two daughters, one named Mary and one, Salome; and his wife died.* (2) *And many years later, as a widower of over eighty, he took Mary. So we are told in the Gospel, for it says, "Mary, his espoused wife;"*[23] *it didn't say, "married wife." And again, in another passage it says, "And he knew her not."*[24] (3) *One can only wonder at all † < the allegations* >*[25] *of those who look for wicked allegations, who < strive* > to discover the causes which need no discovery and to investigate the uninvestigable, but who turn from the essentials to foolish questions, so that the plague of every kind of unbelief and blasphemy must surely be ascribed to us for the dishonoring of the saints.*

8,4	*In the first place, the course of nature entirely confutes them. An old man of over eighty did not take a virgin as a sexual partner to begin with; she was committed to his protection. Secondly, he himself was surely "just;"*[26] *and when he had heard that that which was in her was "of the*

---

[19] Cf. Clem. Hom. Epist. Clem. Ad Jac. 1.
[20] Gal. 1:19
[21] Luke 3:23
[22] Luke 2:48
[23] Matt. 1:18
[24] Matt. 1:25
[25] Holl: οἷς < προφασίζονται > οἱ προφάσεις θηρώμενοι πονηρὰς καὶ < σπουδάζοντες >; MSS: οἷς οἱ προφάσεις θηρῶνται αἱ πονηραί
[26] Cf. Matt. 1:19.

Holy Spirit,"[27] *he would not dare to keep wanting her after such a providence, < and > use the vessel which had been privileged to contain him whom heaven and earth could not contain because of his transcendent glory.* (5) *If even today < many of the faithful > strive to remain virgin, pure and continent in his name, wasn't Joseph more faithful? And Mary herself, "who," as scripture says, "pondered all things in her heart?"*[28] *After a dispensation of that sort, of such greatness and importance, < how could it not be wrong* > for an elderly man to have relations once more, with a pure and honored virgin, a vessel which had contained the Uncontainable and had received such a mystery of a heavenly sign and man's salvation?*

9,1 *Where can I not find proof that the Virgin remained pure? For a starter, let them show me that Mary bore children after the Savior's birth! Let these designers and reciters of deceit and mischief make the names up and give them! But they can't show them because she was still a virgin and, perish the thought, had no sexual relations!* (2) *If she had ever born children even though she was always with the Savior himself, her children too would be said to be with < him >.*

But the text, "Lo, thy mother and thy brethren stand without, seeking thee,"[29] *misleads them.* (3) *Besides, they do not know the wording of the earlier passage, "His brethren believed < not > on him."*[30] *As I myself grow older and am surprised at the triviality of the things in the sacred scriptures—I can tell you, as I become fully acquainted with them I thank God for taking the precaution to prove the truth of every text in the sacred scripture by the seemingly trivial words.* (4) *I always heard that James was called the Lord's brother, and I said in wonderment, "What's the use of this?" But now I understand why the sacred scripture said this beforehand. When we hear, "Lo, thy mother and thy brethren stand without, seeking thee,"* (5) *let us by all means learn that it is speaking of James and the other sons of Joseph, and not of sons of Mary whom she never had.*

For it was plain that, in comparison with the [years of] the Lord's incarnation, James was the elder. (6) *The scripture calls them brothers to confound [our opponents], and names James, Joses, Simeon, Judah, Salome and Mary, so that they will learn whose son James is and by which mother, and understand who is the elder.*

Jesus was crucified in the thirty-third year of his incarnation, but it was the twentieth year of Herod the son of Archelaus. (10,1) *For the Savior was born in Bethlehem of Judaea in the thirty-third year of the first Herod, the son of Antipater, which was the forty-second of the emperor Augustus.*

---

[27] Matt. 1:20
[28] Luke 2:19
[29] Matt. 12:47
[30] John 7:5

(2) *And at the age of two he was taken to Egypt by Joseph because of what the magi had told Herod, since Herod was seeking < to destroy > the child. But he went down to Egypt and spent another two years there.*

10,3 *King Herod died in the thirty-seventh year of his reign, but his son Archelaus reigned for nine years after him.* (4) *And the work [of salvation] was finished, and Jesus was crucified in the eighteenth year of Tiberius Caesar; it was the twentieth year of Agrippa called "The Great," or Herod the Younger, the son of Archelaus.* (5) *But nowhere have we heard that Joseph fathered [more] sons. Indeed, he did not live many years after his return from Egypt, for it was the Savior's fourth year, while Joseph was over eighty-four when he arrived from Egypt.* (6) *And Joseph survived for another eight years; and in Jesus' twelfth year, as it says in the Gospel according to Luke, he was sought for on their journey to Jerusalem, when he could not be found on the road.*

10,7 *But Joseph died during these years, and Jesus was no longer brought up by Joseph, but in Joseph's home. This is why the Gospel can no longer say that his father and mother and brethren came, but says, "Lo, thy mother and thy brethren stand without, seeking thee."*[31] (8) *Nor did it say that his father and brothers had spoken to him, when they said to him in Galilee, "No one that doeth these things would be in secret; if thou doest these things, show thyself."*[32] *It said that his brothers had spoken to him; Joseph was no longer alive in the flesh.* (9) *But then at his perfecting itself, when the Savior was on the cross, the Lord turned, as the Gospel according to John tells us, "and saw the disciple whom he loved, and said to him of Mary, "Behold thy mother." And to her he said, "Behold thy son."*[33] (10) *If Mary had children and her husband was alive, why did he entrust Mary to John and John to Mary? Why not rather entrust her to Peter? Why not to Andrew, Matthew and Bartholomew? But it is plain that he entrusted her to John because of virginity.*

10,11 *For < he says >, "Behold thy mother," even though physically she was not John's mother; [he says this] to show that < as > the originator of virginity she was his mother, since the life began with her.* (12) *And lest it be supposed that the work [of salvation] was appearance and not reality he said this to John to teach him to honor his own mother, even though, physically speaking, John was not his kin; for the Lord was truly born of her in the flesh.* (13) *For if she had not truly been the mother who bore him, he would not have taken care to entrust the Ever-virgin to John—his mother because of the incarnation, but in his honor undefiled and the wondrous vessel. But the Gospel says, "And from that day he took*

---

[31] Matt. 12:47
[32] Cf. John 7:4.
[33] John 19:26–27

her unto his own home."[34] *But if she had a husband, a home, children, she would return to her own home and not to someone else's.*

11,1   *But this must not be twisted to the harm of any who suppose that, by a clumsy conjecture, they can find an excuse here to invent their so-called "adoptive wives" and "beloved friends." The things done there were done by dispensation, and the case is different from all the other godly stringent rules that ought to be observed. Indeed, when this had been done and John had taken her to himself, she did not yet live with him.* (2) *If any think < I > am mistaken, moreover, let them search through the scriptures and neither find Mary's death, nor whether or not she died, nor whether or not she was buried—even though John surely traveled throughout Asia. And yet, nowhere does he say that he took the holy Virgin with him. Scripture simply kept silence because of the overwhelming wonder, not to throw men's minds into consternation.*

11,3   *For I dare not say—though I have my suspicions, I keep silent. Perhaps, just as her death is not to be found, so I may have found some traces of the holy and blessed Virgin.* (4) *In one passage Simeon says of her, "And a sword shall pierce through thine own soul also, that the thoughts of many hearts may be revealed."*[35] *And elsewhere the Revelation of John says, "And the dragon hastened after the woman who had born the man child, and she was given the wings of an eagle and was taken to the wilderness, that the dragon might not seize her."*[36] *Perhaps this can be applied to her; I cannot decide for certain, and am not saying that she remained immortal. But neither am I affirming that she died.*

11,5   *For scripture went beyond man's understanding and left it in suspense with regard to the precious and choice vessel, so that no one would suspect carnal behavior of her. Whether she died, I don't know; and [even] if she was buried, she never had carnal relations, perish the thought!* (6) *Who will choose, from self-inflicted insanity, to cast a blasphemous suspicion [on her], raise his voice, give free rein to his tongue, flap his mouth with evil intent, invent insults instead of hymns and glory, hurl abuse at the holy Virgin, and deny honor to the precious Vessel?*

12,1   *But if we need to take the matter up from another point of view, let's examine the findings of the naturalists. They say that a lioness never gives birth but once, for the following reason. A lion is very fierce, grim of visage, of extremely violent strength, and, as it were, the king of beasts.* (2) *A lioness conceives by one mate, but the implanted seed remains in the womb for a full twenty-six months. Thus the cub comes to maturity inside its mother because of the time, and already has all its teeth before*

---

[34] John 19:27
[35] Luke 2:35
[36] Cf. Rev. 12:13–14.

it is born, and its claws fully developed, and, as they call them, its "incisors, eye-teeth and molars," and all the beast's remaining features. (3) *Thus while it is in the belly it rakes it with its claws in the course of its upward and forward movements and its other twists, and scrapes the wombs and ovaries that are carrying it. And so, when the mother has come to birth, that very day her belly becomes incapable of labor.* (4) *For the naturalists say that the ovaries and wombs are expelled with the cub, so that the lioness no longer feels desire unless, perhaps, she is forced. And even if it should happen that she is forced to mate, she can never conceive again because she has no wombs or ovaries.*

12,5   *Now even this series of events has given me a notion, beneficial rather than harmful, on the subject in question.* (6) *If Jacob says, "Judah is a lion's whelp,"*[37] *as a symbol of Christ, somewhere in John's Revelation it says, "Behold, the lion of the tribe of Judah, and the seed of David, hath prevailed"*[38]—*(when the Lord is compared to a lion it is not because of his nature, but symbolically, and because of the kingliness of the beast, < the > boldest, strongest, and in all other respects the handsomest of the animals.) [If the Lord is a lion], then, I should call the mother who bore him a lioness;* (7) *how can any lion be born if the mother is not to be called a lioness? But a lioness does not conceive a second time. Therefore Mary never conceives again; the holy Virgin cannot have had marital relations.*

13,1   *But let us look to other considerations too, to < make the truth evident in every way* >; since it was always with him, the truth < was* > a follower of Jesus. "Jesus was called to a marriage," and "his mother < was > there."*[39] *And < nowhere > are his brothers mentioned, and nowhere Joseph. < For he says >, "Woman, what have I to do with thee? Mine hour is not yet come."*[40] *He didn't say, "People, what have I to do with you?"*

13,2   *Mary Magdalene stood by the cross, and Mary the wife of Cleopas, and Mary the mother of Rufus, and the other Mary, and Salome, and other women. And it didn't say, "Joseph was there"—or "James the Lord's brother," < who > died in virginity < at the age > of ninety-six.* (3) *No iron implement had touched his head, he had never visited a bath house, had never eaten meat.*[41] *He did not own a change of clothing and wore only a threadbare linen garment, as it says in the Gospel, "The young man fled, and left the cloth wherewith he was clad."*[42]

13,4   *John, James and James, these three, lived in virginity—the two*

---

[37] Gen. 49:9
[38] Rev. 5:5
[39] John 2:1–2
[40] John 2:4
[41] Cf. Hegesippus in Eus. H. E. 2.23.5–7.
[42] Mark 14:52

*sons of Zebedee and James, who was the son of Joseph and the Lord's brother
because he had lived with him, had been brought up with him, and had
the status of a brother because of Joseph's only relationship to Mary, her
betrothal to him. (5) Only this James was allowed to enter the Holy of
Holies once a year,*[43] *since he was a nazirite and a member of the priesthood.*

Thus Mary was related to Elizabeth in two ways[44] *and James was
distinguished by priesthood, since only the two tribes intermarried, the kingly
with the priestly and the priestly with the kingly. Thus long ago the head
of the tribe of Judah, Naason, took < the > ancient Elizabeth, Aaron's daughter, to wife during the exodus. (6) Hence many sects are unaware of < the >
Savior's earthly genealogy, and because of their puzzlement disbelieve, and
suppose that they can contradict the truth by saying, "How could Mary,
of the tribe of David and Judah, be related to Elizabeth, of the tribe of
Levi?"*

14,1 *James also wore the priestly diadem. And once he raised his hands
to heaven and prayed during a drought, and heaven immediately gave
rain. He never put on a woolen garment.*[45] *From their continual kneeling
before the Lord with extreme piety, his knees grew as hard as camels'. (2)
He was no longer addressed by name; his name was "The Just." He never
washed in the bath house, did not eat meat, as I have already said, and
did not put on a sandal. And a great deal could be said about James
and his virtuous life.*

14,3 *You see, then, that Joseph's home was most remarkable in every
way. For if Joseph's sons knew the state of virginity and the practice of
the nazirites, how much more did the elderly and honorable Joseph know
how to preserve the Virgin in purity, and pay honor to the vessel in which
humankind's salvation had once dwelt? "Doth not nature itself teach you?"*[46]
(4) *The man was aged, very far advanced in years, and a man of standing,
faithful character and pious demeanor. For the Gospel says, "From fear
of God the man sought to put her away privily."*[47]

14,5 *This James, the Lord's brother and Joseph's son, died in Jerusalem, after living for about twenty-four years after the assumption of the
Savior.*[48] *For at the age of ninety-six he was struck on the head with a
fuller's rod, was thrown from the pinnacle of the temple* (6) *and fell without
injury, but knelt in prayer for those who had thrown him down and said,
"Forgive them, for they know not what they do."*[49] *Meanwhile Simeon, his*

---

[43] The basis of this is probably the notice at Eus. H. E. 2.23.6.
[44] Cf. Jul. Af. Epistula Ad Aristidem, Reichardt, p. 54.
[45] Cf. Hegesippus in Eus. H. E. 2.23.6.
[46] 1 Cor. 11:14
[47] Cf. Matt. 1:19.
[48] Hegesippus in Eus. H. E. 2.23.16–18
[49] Luke 23:34

cousin but the son of Cleopas, stood at a distance and said, "Stop! Why are you stoning the Just? And look, he's praying for you the best he can!" And this was the martyrdom of James.

15,1   *Now if Joseph's son lived for so many years, how could his father dare to abuse and insult a holy body in which God had dwelt, after he had seen awesome sights, angels standing guard at the birth of the Son, singing hymns from heaven and saying, "Glory to God in the highest, and on earth peace, good will toward men?"*[50] *And the shepherds had come to the cavern where Christ was born (2) and told these things, so many signs and wonders, in the hearing of the aged Joseph, who was far advanced in years. (3) The incarnate Christ's human nature was provided for us from Mary's body—the body from which the holy and undefiled flesh was formed for us, in the Savior's Godhead. As the angel Gabriel < says > in the relevant passage, "The Spirit of the Lord shall come upon thee, and the power of the highest shall overshadow thee; therefore also that holy thing which shall be born of thee shall be called the Son of God."*[51]

15,4   *Now how could Joseph dare to have relations with the Virgin Mary whose holiness was so great? But even if she had sexual relations— and perish that thought!—what good would it do us to inquire into this? Which is the better choice, to leave the matter to God, or to insist on what is bad? Plainly, scripture has not told us that we may not have eternal life, but will go to judgment, unless we believe that Mary had relations again. (5) It has, however, told us < to seek > what is good and righteous, what is holy, "that we may give grace unto the hearers also."*[52] *But people have abandoned the essentials, things that relate to faith in the truth, that are to the glory of God, and provide themselves with harmful things wherever they can find them. How disgusting it is even to think of < them >, especially as scripture says nothing of the sort.*

16,1   *For if the scripture said it, I would expound the proof-text truth< fully*> and think nothing of it. Is marriage unholy, after all? Is the marriage bed profane? Isn't "the bed undefiled?"*[53] *Is marriage debased? But prophets and high priests refrain from it because their service is for a higher purpose. (2) After he became a prophet Moses had no more relations with his wife, she bore no more children, and he fathered no more. For he had adopted a way of life which afforded more leisure for his Master. How could he remain on Mount Sinai "for forty nights and forty days"*[54] *and still attend to his marriage? Or how could he ready for ministry to God in the wilderness for forty years, and find the leisure for priesthood?*

---

[50] Luke 2:13–15
[51] Luke 1:35
[52] Eph. 4:29
[53] Heb. 13:4
[54] Exod. 24:18

If he was married, how could be continually expound the mysteries and converse with God? (3) For if the holy apostle speaks expressly of us, and says, "< Let them be continent* > 'for a time, that they may be free for prayer,'"[55] *how much more will the saying be true of prophets?*

But Mary too was a prophetess. (4) Scripture says, "He went in unto the prophetess, and she conceived and bare a son. And the Lord said unto me, Call his name, Spoil Speedily, Plunder Fiercely."[56] *(5) The meaning here, however, is Gabriel's visit to Mary, when he went forth to bring her the tidings that she would bear God's Son, the Savior, for the world, not by the seed of a man but through the Holy Spirit.*

16,6 *Moreover, Philip the evangelist had "four daughters that did prophesy,"*[57] *but they prophesied because of the virginity that was vouchsafed them. (7) Thecla too met St. Paul and dissolved her marriage, although her betrothed was most handsome, the leading man in the town, extremely rich, of excellent family, and very prominent. And yet the saint despised earthly things to gain the heavenly.*[58] *(8) Now if these persons [did] these things, how much more Mary, to whom the whole wondrous providence has come? But where can I find ideas to benefit them? How can I dispel the darkness of those who have spawned these dreadful doctrines, as the scripture says, "He hath conceived pain and brought forth iniquity?"*[59] *For these people do indeed conceive the pain of sick fancies, and bring forth the iniquity of blasphemies.*

17,1 *But no one should have those suspicions and say, in his attempt to implant them within himself in a different way, "Why does the Gospel say, 'Mary was found with child of the Holy Ghost before they came together?'*[60] *They were expected to come together, and this is why it said, 'before they came together.' (2) Furthermore, the same Gospel says once more, in another passage, 'She brought forth her son, the firstborn,' and, 'He knew her not until she had brought forth her son, the firstborn.'"*[61]

17,3 *And yet those who profess to distinguish between the senses of the scriptures (i.e., literal, allegorical etc.) and try to meddle with the loftiest and the deepest matters, do not know that the sense of this is as follows. (4) For if Mary had given birth again, scripture should have given the other brothers' names too. But never fear, if the Only-begotten < is called "firstborn" >, it is because he is the "firstborn of all creation."*[62] *The Gospel*

---

55 1 Cor. 7:5
56 Isa. 8:3
57 Acts 21:9
58 Acts of Paul and Thecla 7.10
59 Ps. 7:15
60 Matt. 1:18
61 Matt. 1:25
62 Col 1:15

did not say, "She brought forth her firstborn," but, "He knew her not until she had brought forth her son"—and it didn't say, "'her' firstborn," but, "'the' firstborn." (5) By "her son," scripture meant that he had been born of her in the flesh. But it didn't add another "her" to the term, "firstborn," but said simply, "firstborn."

For he is the One the apostle calls, "firstborn of all creation"—not one with creation but begotten before creation. (6) The apostle didn't say, "first-created," but, "firstborn;" and the passage is divided for its better and sounder interpretation by saying "firstborn" first, and then mentioning creation as inferior. For "firstborn" is understood of the Son, but "creation" < was made > through the Son. (7) Thus "She brought forth her son, the firstborn;"—but not "her firstborn," as though she was to bear another.

"And he knew her not." For how could he know that a woman would receive so much grace? Or how could he know that < the > Virgin would be so highly glorified? (8) He knew that she was a woman by her appearance, and her womanliness by her sex, and knew that her mother was Ann and her father, Joachim, that she was related to Elizabeth, that she was of the house and lineage of David. But he did not know that anyone on earth, especially a woman, would be honored with such glory. (9) He did not know her, then, until he had seen the wonder; he did not know how wondrous she was until he had seen "that which was born of her."[63] But when she gave birth he also knew the honor God had done her, for it was she who had been told, "Hail, thou that art highly favored, the Lord is with thee."[64]

18,1   *It is Mary who is meant by the description of Eve, for she was symbolically given the title, "mother of the living." For Eve was called "mother of the living"[65] in that passage," and this after being told, "Earth thou art, and unto earth shalt thou return,"[66] following her transgression. And after this transgression, it was a surprise that she received this great title. (2) Physically speaking, every human being in the world is born of that Eve; but here life itself has truly been born into the world of Mary, so that Mary brings forth the Living One and becomes the mother of the Living. (3) Mary, then, was called the "mother of the living" in a riddle.*

For "Who has given the woman the wisdom < of weaving > and skill in embroidery?"[67] was said of the two women. The first wise woman, Eve, < was > the weaver of earthly garments for Adam whose nakedness she had caused; for this task was assigned to her. (4) Since the nakedness was her fault, she had been given the task of clothing the physical body to hide

---

[63] Luke 1:35
[64] Luke 1:28
[65] Gen. 3:20
[66] Gen. 3:19
[67] Job 38:36

*its physical nakedness. But God's assignment to Mary was that she bear
a lamb and sheep for us, and that, by his virtue, we receive a garment
of immortality wisely made—as though from his fleece—from the glory of
the lamb and sheep.*

18,5   *But there is another marvel to ponder in connection with these
women, Eve and Mary. Eve has become the occasion of human deaths,
for "Death entered into the world"*[68] *through her. But Mary, through whom
Life was born for us, is the occasion of life. (6) And this is why the Son
of God came into the world; and "Where sin hath abounded, grace did
much more abound."*[69] *And in the place from which death came, life got
the start of it, so that there might be Life in place of death. He who, in
his turn, had become our life through a woman, shut out the death that
came from a woman.*

18,7   *And since Eve in Paradise fell into the sin of disobedience while
still a virgin, the obedience of grace came in its turn through the Virgin,
when she was told of the descent from heaven of Christ's incarnation, and
life immortal. (8) For in Paradise God tells the serpent, "And I shall put
enmity between thee and her, and between thy seed and her seed."*[70] *But
there is no example of a woman's seed < with an enmity toward the physical
seed of a snake* >, unless, as the riddle suggests, the "enmity" is taken
to mean Eve's enmity towards the progeny of the snake itself, and of the
devil who dwelt in the snake, and his envy.*

19,1   *And in fact, the whole cannot have its complete fulfillment in
Eve. But it will truly be fulfilled in the holy Seed, the elect Seed, the unique
Seed, the Seed which originated from Mary alone, and not from union
with a man. For he came to "destroy" the "power of the dragon and crooked
serpent which flees"*[71] *saying that it has overcome the whole world. (2) And
so the Only-begotten came from a woman for the destruction of the serpent—
that is, of heresy, corruption and deceit, imposture and iniquity. (3) It
is he who truly "opens a mother's womb."*[72] *All the firstborn who have ever
been born—to put it delicately—could not manage this; none but the Only-
begotten, who "opened a virgin's womb." That has been accomplished in
him alone, and in no one else.*

19,4   *But this*[73] *can also be seen from the subject itself. The expression,
["mother of the living"], is to be understood of Mary, and I shall take
the one that says, "For this cause shall a man leave his father and his
mother and shall cleave unto his wife, and the two shall become one flesh,"*[74]

---

[68] Cf. Rom. 5:12.
[69] Rom. 5:20
[70] Gen. 3:15
[71] Isa. 27:1
[72] Cf. Luke 2:23 (Exod. 13:12).
[73] That not all the statements in Gen. 2–3 are to be taken of Eve.
[74] Gen. 2:24

(5) *as a reference to the church. The holy apostle also says, "This is a great mystery, but I say it concerns Christ and the church."*[75] (6) *And see the precision of the scriptures! It says, "formed,"*[76] *of Adam, but of Eve it no longer says that she was "formed," but that she was "built." For it says, "He took one of his sides and built it into a wife for him,"*[77] *to show that the Lord formed his body from Mary, but the church has been built from his side itself—when his side was pierced, and the mysteries of blood and water became atonements for us.*

20,1 *But in any case Joseph knew Mary, not with any knowledge of physical intimacy, not with the knowledge of intercourse—he knew her, and honored her whom God had honored. For he did not know how glorious she was until he saw the Lord who was born of a woman.* (2) *And "Before they came together she was found with child"*[78] *is said to keep the argument of those who think that the God-ordained mystery came from sexual commerce from prevailing. For it meant, "before this thing that was expected took place—but the thing did not take place."* (3) *For even if it was expected that the Virgin would have relations with Joseph, an impossibility because of his age, the holy scripture shows us in advance, and confirms our notion, < to > convince < us > that, although the thing is possible despite the sacred childbirth, no man < may > ever again approach the Virgin for sexual relations—convincing us in the same way in which the angel convinced Joseph that his suspicion was unfounded.* (4) *For there is a similarity between "before they came together," which means that this was expected but did not happen, and, "Being a righteous man he sought not to make her a public example but to put her away privily,"*[79] *which means that he would become evil if he made her a public example, but he did not. In the same way the angel teaches him, "Fear not to take unto thee Mary thy wife"*[80] *though she had not yet become his wife, "even if you suspect her of a fall;" but she is not what you think," and so on.* (5) *For he says directly after that, "for that which was conceived in her,"*[81] *as though it already † was,*[82] *but then, "she shall bear a son,"*[83] *as of a future event; and it was.* (6) *And the prediction*[84] *< has come down to us* > *because its truth has been demonstrated, just as "before they came together" < has*

---

[75] Eph. 5:32
[76] Gen. 2:7
[77] Gen. 2:21–22
[78] Matt. 1:18
[79] Cf. Matt. 1:25.
[80] Matt. 1:20
[81] Matt. 1:20
[82] Eltester: γεγενημένον; Holl and MSS: γεγεννηημένου
[83] Matt. 1:21
[84] I.e., "She shall bear a son."

come down to us* > † because we are satisfied[85] *that no such thing has occurred. "Until she brought forth her son, the firstborn," is to be interpreted along the same lines,*[86] *because of the marvel of the knowledge of the Virgin, with her honor in the sight of God.*

21,1   *But no one should suppose that because it says, "before they came together," they came together later on. No one can prove this or show it; scripture provided this added confirmation to show that the Savior's conception was undefiled. "[Joseph] knew her not" is said to her glory; (2) "firstborn" is said because he is the Firstborn, before there are any creatures, and the "firstborn among many brethren"*[87] *as the apostle said—not brethren by < birth > from Mary as though she bore other sons, but the brethren who were vouchsafed adoption as sons through him when, to remove any suspicion of docetism, he truly became her son in the flesh. (3) What is more, he was the firstborn and son of the Virgin herself—not, as I said, because she had other sons. For this is similar to his first birth before the incarnation. He who is truly the Father's heavenly Firstborn before all creation, is not called Firstborn because there were others begotten of the Father after him. Because he is Only-begotten, he has no second brother. (4) Thus he was always Mary's firstborn during his sojourn on earth, but since he had no second brother born of her, he was Mary's only child.*

Those who have invented things that will hurt and not help them must stop. Don't do it! Please don't! (5) He who honors the Lord, also honors his holy < vessel >; he who dishonors the holy < vessel >, dishonors his own Master as well. Leave Mary the holy vessel, the holy Virgin, alone! These harmful < contrivances > are of no use to us; we must think more reverently, or we will become proud, or contentious, or garrulous. (6) For as the scripture says, We shall "give account for every idle word."[88] *Let us look after ourselves, then, and mind our own business. Let us not attribute our behavior to the saints, not look at the saints' lives in terms of our own.*

22,1   *For some who are who are constrained and inclined to sensuality and nourish a pernicious expectation [of it], would doubtless like to smear the saints as well, to provide a plausible excuse for their wicked, weak-willed expectation. To them the apostle says, "I would that all men were as myself."*[89] *But why does he say, "myself," except because of his purity?*

22,2   *"But because of fornication, let each have his own wife!"*[90] *But the pronoun has been left out; Paul said this for a reproof, and to convert them. He could have said, "because of 'your' fornication." He left "your"*

---

[85] Holl: ἀρκουμένοις; MSS: ἀρκούμενοι
[86] Cf. 17,4–7.
[87] Rom. 8:29
[88] Matt. 12:36
[89] 1 Cor. 7:7
[90] 1 Cor. 7:2

out, however, not to appear to have said this as abuse of anyone. (3) But the words were spoken in condemnation of certain persons who were unwilling to free themselves for God, as our fathers of old used to do after living in accordance with the Law and knowing their own vessels fittingly for procreation. I have found a scripture somewhere that says, "Rebecca conceived of one."[91] *(4) By saying, "of one," he described it politely but showed that her conception was a righteous one. He is telling us that, once he had children, Jacob had no further relations with his wife.*

22,5 *But it is a simple and easy matter for our minds to be diverted to evils instead of the essentials. Our human reason is shaky, and not quick to direct its zeal into the Lord's straight path. It veers sometimes to the right and sometimes to the left, and finds it hard to obey Solomon's injunction, "Turn not to the right hand, nor to the left."*[92] *(6) Since our wickedness is taking another turn with regard to the same thoughts, and urges our good sense to go off on other paths, let us make sure that excessive praise of the Virgin does not become another occasion of delusion for anyone.*

23,1 *For in blasphemy of the Son, some, as I have already indicated, have done their best to make him literally different from the Father's Godhead. Others again, whose views are different, have said that the Father is the same, the Son is the same, and the Holy Spirit is the same, as though, if you please, they had been encouraged to honor the Son too highly.*

23,2 *Similarly, some have dared to speak insolently of this holy and blessed Ever-virgin, as though she had had sexual relations after that greatest and unsullied providence of the Lord, his incarnation. And of all wickedness, this is the most impious. (3) But even as I say < that I am astonished > to learn how some have dared to give themselves to [the] sin with the utmost readiness, I am once more astonished to hear the other. For < I have heard > in turn that others, who are out of their minds on the subject of this holy Ever-virgin, have done their best and are doing their best, in the grip both of madness and of folly, to substitute her for God. (4) For they say that certain Thracian women there in Arabia have introduced this nonsense, and that they bake a loaf in the name of the Ever-virgin, gather together, and < both > attempt an excess and undertake a forbidden, blasphemous act in the holy Virgin's name, and offer sacrifice in her name with woman officiants.*

This is entirely impious, unlawful, and different from the Holy Spirit's message, and is thus pure devil's work, and the doctrine of an unclean spirit. (5) The words, "Some shall depart from sound doctrine, giving heed to fables and doctrines of devils,"[93] *apply to these people as well. For as*

---

[91] Rom. 9:10
[92] Prov. 4:27
[93] 1 Tim. 4:1

the scriptures say, they will be "worshiping the dead"[94] *as the dead were given divine honors in Israel. And the timely glory of the saints, which redounds to God in their lifetimes, has become an error for others, who do not see the truth.*

23,6   *For in Shechem, that is, the present day Neapolis, the inhabitants offer sacrifices in the name of Core, because of Jephthah's daughter, if you please, who was once offered to God as a sacrifice. And for those who have been taken in by it, this has become the misfortune of idolatry and the worship of vain things.* (7) *And because Pharaoh's daughter honored God's servant Moses, and took him up and reared him, the Egyptians honored her to excess in place of God because of the fame of the child in those days, and by an evil tradition have handed this down as a creed to the foolish. And they worship Thermutis the daughter of Amenophis*[95] *who was Pharaoh until that time, because, as I said, she reared Moses.*

23,8   *And there have been many such things to mislead the deluded, though the saints are not responsible for anyone's stumbling; the human mind finds no rest, but is perverted to evils.* (9) *The holy virgin may have died and been buried—her falling asleep was with honor, her death in purity, her crown in virginity. Or she may have been put to death—as the scripture says, "And a sword shall pierce through her soul"*[96]*—her fame is among the martyrs and her holy body, by which light rose on the world, [rests] amid blessings. Or she may have remained alive, for God is not incapable of doing whatever he wills. No one knows her end.*

But we must not honor the saints to excess; we must honor their Master. (10) *It is time for the error of those who have gone astray to cease. Mary is not God and does not have her body from heaven but by human conception, though, like Isaac, she was provided by promise.* (11) *And no one should make offerings in her name, for he is destroying his own soul. But neither, in turn, should he be insolent and offer insult to the holy Virgin. Heaven forbid, she had no sexual relations after or before the Savior's conception.*

24,1   *I have thought these few points through and put them in writing for those who are willing to learn the truth of the scripture, and not talk wildly and sharpen their blasphemous tongues to no purpose.* (2) *But if any prefer to object, and receive not what is beneficial but the opposite, I too will have to say, despite my insignificance, "Let him that heareth, hear, and him that disobeyeth, disobey;"*[97] *'let no man trouble' the apostles any more, or 'me.'"*[98] (3) *What I knew to be reverent and of use to the church I have said of the holy Virgin, in defense of her who is in every*

---

[94] Cf. Didache 6.3.
[95] Josephus C. Ap. 1.26.230–232; Ant. 2.5.224–226; Theoph. Ad Autol. 3.20
[96] Cf. Luke 2:35.
[97] Ezek. 3:27
[98] Gal. 6:17

way favored, as Gabriel said, "Hail, thou that art highly favored, the Lord is with thee!"[99] *But if the Lord is with her, how can she be a partner in another union? How can she have intercourse with flesh, when she is preserved by the Lord? (4) The saints are in honor, their repose is in glory, their departure in perfection, their portion in blessedness, among the holy women alone. Their choir is with the angels, their dwelling in heaven, their manner of life in the sacred scriptures. Their fame is in incomparable and perpetual honor. Their rewards are in Christ Jesus our Lord, through whom and with whom be glory to the Father with the Holy Spirit forever. Amen.*

24,5   *All the brethren send you their greetings. And do you yourselves greet all the faithful, orthodox brethren among you, who detest pride and hate the fellowship of the Arians and the foolishness of the Sabellians, but honor the Trinity in its co-essentiality, Father, Son and Holy Spirit, three entities, one essence, one Godhead, and in a word, one glory—and are not in error about our Savior's saving incarnation and advent in the flesh, (6) but believe completely in the incarnation of Christ as perfect God and at the same time perfect man except for sin; who took his body itself from Mary, and took a soul and mind, and everything human except for sin— not a Christ who is two, but one Lord, one God, one king, one high priest, God and man, man and God, not two but one, united not as a mixture or as an unreal thing, but as a great dispensation of grace. Farewell!*

24,7   Since I am satisfied that the copy of my letter is correct, and am of the opinion that this much will do for a reply to them, I have also passed this sect by in God, as I would a snake peeping out of its hole. I have fully refuted it with God's wise doctrine and his power—a power that breathes a sweet odor, like storax, on the world in the virtue < of the faithful >, holy children of the virginity which began with Mary, through the light which has dawned on the world through her. I have showed what the evil poison of this serpent's reptilian wickedness is. Let us go on to the rest once more, to finish the entire work in God.

Against Collyridians,[1] *who make offerings to Mary. 59, but 79 of the series*

1,1   < Another > sect has come to public notice after this, and I have already mentioned a few things about it in the Sect preceding, in the letter about Mary which I wrote to Arabia. (2) This one, again, was also brought to Arabia from Thrace and upper Scythia, and word of it has reached me; it too is ridiculous, and

---

[99] Luke 1:28

[1] The sources of this Sect are oral; see 1,2.

in the opinion of the wise wholly absurd. (3) < So > let's begin
the discussion and description of it; as others like it were, it too
will be adjudged silly rather than wise.

1,4   For as those who, from an insolent attitude towards Mary,
have seen fit to suspect these things were sowing damaging suspicions in people's minds long ago, so these persons who lean in
the other direction are guilty of doing the worst sort of harm; they
too will exemplify the maxim of certain pagan philosophers,
"Extremes are equal." (5) For the harm done by both of these sects
is equal, since one belittles the holy Virgin while the other, in its
turn, glorifies her to excess.

1,6   And who but women are the teachers of this? Women are
unstable, prone to error, and mean-spirited. (7) As in our earlier
chapter on Quintilla, Maximilla and Priscilla, so here the devil has
seen fit to disgorge ridiculous teachings from the mouths of women.
For certain women decorate a barber's chair or a square seat,
spread a cloth on it, set out bread and offer it in Mary's name
on a certain day of the year, and all partake of the bread; I discussed
parts of this right in my letter to Arabia. Now, however, I shall
speak plainly of it and, with prayer to God, give the best refutations
of it that I can, so as to grub out the roots of this idolatrous sect
and with God's help, be able to cure certain people of this madness.

2,1   Now then, servants of God, let us adopt a manly frame of
mind and dispel the madness of these women. The speculation
is entirely feminine, and the malady of the deluded Eve all over
again. Or rather, it is still the malady of the snake, the seducing
beast, and the false promise of the one who spoke in it. This
promise made no < sound > suggestion and did not make its undertaking good, but only caused death by calling the untrue true, and
encouraging disobedience by the sight of the tree, and aversion
to the truth itself by attraction to many things.

2,2   But we shall have reason to suppose that the minds of these
women which have been ensnared by the pride of that snake, are
like the ideas the deceiver sowed by saying, "Ye shall be as gods."[2]
Once again he is bringing death on that sex, as I have often said.

2,3   For to begin with, to whom is it not immediately obvious,
< if he will > investigate the whole scope of the past, that their
teaching and behavior are devilish, and their undertaking a de-
viation? Never at any time has a woman been a priest—(4) Eve
herself, though she had fallen into transgression, still did not dare
to undertake anything so impious. Not one of her daughters did,

---

[2] Gen. 3:5

though Abel sacrificed to God at once, and, even though they were
not accepted, Cain offered sacrifices before the Lord. Enoch pleased
God and was translated. Noah made thank offerings to the Lord,
as a token of gratitude, with the extra animals in the ark, in
thanksgiving to the One who had preserved him. (5) The righteous Abraham offered God sacrifice, and Melchizedek the priest
of God Most High. Isaac was pleasing to God, and Jacob made
the best offering he could on the stone, by pouring oil from his
flask.

And the children of Jacob. We find that Levi was the next to
receive the priesthood, but that those who received the priestly
order came from his stock—I mean Moses the prophet and expositor,
Aaron and his sons Eleazar and Phinehas, and his grandson Ithamar.
(6) And why name the throngs of those who sacrificed to God
in the Old Testament? We find Ahitub sacrificing, and the sons
of Korah, and the Gershonites and the Merarites, to whom the
levitical order was entrusted. And the house of Eli, and his kins-
men after him in the household of Abimelech and Abiathar, Helkiah
and Buzi, down to the high priest Joshua, and Ezra the priest, and
the rest. And nowhere was a woman a priest.

3,1   But I shall go on to the New Testament. If it were ordained
by God that women should be priests or have any canonical function
in the church, Mary herself, if anyone, should have functioned as
a priest in the New Testament. She was counted worthy to bear
the king of all in her own womb, the heavenly God, the Son of
God. Her womb became a temple, and by God's kindness and an
awesome mystery was prepared to be the dwelling place of the
Lord's human nature. But it was not God's pleasure [that she be
a priest]. (2) She was not even entrusted with the administration
of baptism—for Christ could have been baptized by her rather
than by John. But John the son of Zacharias dwelt in the wilderness
entrusted with baptism for the remission of sins, while his father
served God as a priest and saw a vision at the time of the offering
of incense.

3,3   Peter and Andrew, James and John, Philip and Bartholomew,
Thomas, Thaddaeus, James the son of Alphaeus, Judas the son of
James and Simon the Zealot, and Matthias who was chosen to
make up the number of the Twelve—all these were chosen to be
apostles and "offer the Gospel"[3] < throughout > the world, together
with Paul, Barnabas and the rest. And with James, the Lord's brother

---

[3] Rom. 15:16

and the bishop of Jerusalem, [they were chosen] to preside over mysteries.

3,4 Successors to the episcopate and presbyterate in the household of God were appointed by this bishop and these apostles, and nowhere was a woman appointed. (5) Scripture says, "Philip the evangelist had four daughters which did prophesy,"[4] but they were certainly not priests. And "Anna the daughter of Phanuel was a prophetess,"[5] but not entrusted with the priesthood. For the words, "Your sons shall prophesy, and your daughters shall dream dreams, and your young men shall see visions,"[5] required fulfillment.

3,6 < It is plain > too that there is an order of deaconesses in the church. But this is not allowed for the practice of priesthood or any liturgical function, but for the sake of female modesty, at either the time of baptism or of the examination of some condition or trouble, and when a woman's body may be bared, so that she will be seen not by the male priests but by the assisting female who is appointed by the priest for the occasion, to take care of the woman who is in need of it when her body is uncovered. For the ordinance of discipline and good order in the church has been protected with understanding and care, in proportion to our rule. For the same reason the word of God does not allow a woman "to speak"[6] in church either, or "bear rule over a man."[7] And there is a great deal that can be said about this.

4,1 But it must be observed that the ordinance of the church required no more than deaconesses. It mentioned widows too, and called those of them who were still older, "elder," but nowhere did it prescribe "eldresses" or "priestesses." Indeed, not even the deacons in the hierarchy of the church have been commissioned to celebrate any mystery, but only to administer mysteries already celebrated. (2) But once more, where has this new story come from? The women's pride and female madness? What has nourished the wickedness that—through the female, once more!—[8] pours the feminine habit of speculation into our minds < and >, by encouraging its characteristic luxury, tries to compel the wretched human race to overstep its proper bounds?

4,3 But let us adopt the firm resolve of the champion Job,

---

[4] Acts 21:9
[5] Luke 2:36
[5] Joel 3:1; Acts 2:17
[6] 1 Cor. 14:34
[7] 1 Tim. 2:12
[8] πάλιν θήλεος. Eltester suggests that this is corrupt.

prepare ourselves with the righteous answer on our lips, and ourselves say, "Thou hast spoken as one of the foolish women."⁹ (4)
For how can such a thing not appear insane to every wise man
whose < mind is sound* > in God? How can the practice not seem
idolatrous, and the undertaking the devil's? But the devil has always
slipped into the human mind in the guise of someone righteous,
and made human images with a great variety of arts, to deify mortal human nature in human eyes. (5) And yet the men who are
worshiped have died, and their images, which have never lived,
are introduced for worship—and since they've never lived they
can't be called dead either! And with adulterous intent < they have
rebelled > against the one and only God, like a common whore
who has been excited to the wickedness of many relations and
rejected the temperate course of lawful marriage to one husband.

4,6   Yes, of course Mary's body was holy, but she was not God.
Yes, the Virgin was indeed a virgin and honored as such, but she
was not given us to worship; she worships Him who, though born
of her flesh, has come from heaven, from the bosom of his Father.
(7) And the Gospel therefore protects us by telling us so on the
occasion when the Lord himself said, "Woman, what is between
me and thee? Mine hour is not yet come."¹⁰ < For > to make sure
that no one would suppose, because of the words, "What is between me and thee?" that the holy Virgin is anything more [than
a woman], he called her "Woman" as if by prophecy, because of
the schisms and sects that were to appear on earth. Otherwise
some might stumble into the nonsense of the sect from excessive
awe of the saint.

5,1   For what it has to say is complete nonsense, and an old
wives' tale, as it were. Which scripture has spoken of it? Which
prophet permitted the worship of a man, let alone a woman? (2)
The vessel is choice but a woman, and by nature no different [from
others]. Like the bodies of the saints, however, she has been held
in honor for her character and understanding. And if I should
say anything more in her praise, she is like Elijah, who was virgin
from his mother's womb, always remained so, and was taken up,
but has not seen death. She is like John who leaned on the Lord's
breast, "the disciple whom Jesus loved."¹¹ She is like St. Thecla; and
Mary is still more honored than she, because of the providence
vouchsafed her. (3) But Elijah is not to be worshiped, even though

---

⁹ Job 2:10
¹⁰ John 2:4
¹¹ John 13:23

he is alive. And John is not to be worshiped, even though by his own prayer—or rather, by receiving the grace from God—he made an awesome thing of his falling asleep.[12] But neither is Thecla worshiped, nor any of the saints.

For the age-old error of forgetting the living God and worshiping his creatures will not get the better of me. (4) "They served and worshiped the creature more than the creator," and "were made fools."[13] If it is not his will that angels be worshiped, how much more the woman born of Ann, who was given to Ann by Joachim[14] and granted to her father and mother by promise, after prayer and all diligence? She was surely not born other than normally, but of a man's seed and a woman's womb like everyone else. (5) For even though the story and traditions of Mary say that her father Joachim was told in the wilderness, "Your wife has conceived,"[15] it was not because this had come about without conjugal intercourse or a man's seed. The angel who was sent to him predicted the coming event, so that there would be no doubt. The thing had truly happened, had already been decreed by God, and had been promised to the righteous.

6,1   And everywhere we see the scriptures saying < the same >. Isaiah predicted the things that would be realized in the Son of God and said, "Behold, the virgin shall be with child and shall bear a son and shall call his name Immanuel."[16] (2) And as the woman who bore him was a virgin, and the name of < the > child the woman had conceived meant, "God is with us," the prophet saw them in a vision and was compelled by the Holy Spirit to describe them, so that he would not doubt the meaning of the truth. He said, "And he went in unto the prophetess." He was describing Gabriel's entrance in the Gospel, who was sent by God to announce the entrance into the world of God's only-begotten Son, and his birth of Mary. And Isaiah said, "And she conceived and bare a son. (3) And the Lord said unto me, Call his name Spoil Speedily, Ravage Fiercely. For before the child shall know how to cry Father, or Mother, he shall take the power of Damascus and the spoil of Samaria,"[17] and so on.

And all of these things were still unfulfilled. But this would be

---

[12] Cf. Act. John 108–115.
[13] Rom. 1:25; 22
[14] Cf. Protevangelium of James 4.1–3.
[15] Cf. Protevangelium of James 4.2.
[16] Isa. 7:14
[17] Isa. 8:3–4

realized in the Son of God, and fulfilled about 1600 years later.
(Sic!) (4) And the prophet saw what would < happen > after so
many generations as though it had already happened.

Was it a lie, then? Never! God's providence was announced with
confidence as though it had already taken place, so that the truth
would not be disbelieved, and the arrival of such an astounding,
awesome event would not come to seem uncertain in the prophet's
estimation.

6,5 Or don't you see the very next declaration, as the holy
Isaiah himself says, "He was led as a sheep to the slaughter, and
as a lamb before its shearer is dumb, so opens he not his mouth.
But who can tell his generation? For his life is taken from the
earth, and I shall give the evil for his grave,"[18] and so on. And see
how he describes the earlier events as though they came later, and
explains the later ones as though they had already taken place,
by saying, "He *was* led as a sheep to the slaughter." (6) For this
is said to be a past event; he didn't say, "*is* led," and the subject
of Isaiah's pronouncement had yet to be led. But this was said to
the prophet as though it had already happened. God's revelation
was unalterable.

But when he went on he no longer spoke as of past events, so
as not to cause an error in his own turn, but said, "His life *is* taken
from the earth." He is giving the truth in the two ways, because
"was led" was already done, and "is taken" was done later. Thus
from its pastness you will know the truth and the sureness of God's
promise, and from its futurity you will imagine the time of the
mysteries' revelation.

7,1 And so in Mary's case. The angel foretold what her father
would receive from God on his return home—the favor her father
and mother had asked in prayer, "Lo, thy wife hath conceived in
her womb,"[19] as a certain fulfillment, by a promise, of the faithful
man's purpose. But for some this became an occasion of error.
No one in the world can be born in any but the normal human
way. Only < the Son* > was fit < for this* >; nature allowed it to
him alone. (2) As Maker and Master of the thing [to be made]
he formed himself from a virgin as though from earth—God come
from heaven, the Word who had assumed flesh from a holy Virgin.

But certainly not from a virgin who is worshiped, or to make
her God, or to have us make offerings in her name, or, again,
to make women priestesses after so many generations. (3) It was

---

[18] Isa. 53:7; 8; 9
[19] Protevangelium of James Codex B 4.2

not God's pleasure that this be done with Salome, or with Mary herself. He did not permit her to administer baptism or bless disciples, or tell her to rule on earth, but only to be a sacred shrine and be deemed worthy of his kingdom. (4) He did not order the woman called the mother of Rufus to † advance < to* > this rank,[20] or the women who followed Christ from Galilee, or Martha the sister of Lazarus and [her sister] Mary, or any of the holy women who were privileged to be saved by his advent < and > who assisted him with their own possessions—or the woman of Canaan, or the woman who was healed of the issue of blood, or any woman on earth.

7,5   Again, where has this coiled serpent come from? How are its crooked counsels renewed? Mary should be honored, but the Father, the Son and the Holy Spirit should be worshiped; no one should worship Mary. There is no commandment to < offer > the Eucharist even to a man, < as though > to God, let alone to a woman; not even angels are allowed such glory. (6) The bad writing on the hearts of the deluded should be erased, the sliver removed from their eyes. The creature must return to its Master; Eve, with Adam, must take care to honor only God, and not be influenced by the voice of the serpent but abide by God's commandment, "Thou shalt not eat of the tree."[21] (7) And yet the tree was not error; the disobedience of error came by the tree. Let no one eat of the error which has arisen on St. Mary's account. Even though "The tree is lovely"[22] it is not for food; and even though Mary is all fair, and is holy and held in honor, she is not to be worshiped.

8,1   But again, these women are "renewing the potion for Fortune and preparing the table for the demon[23] and not for God," as the scripture says. And they drink impious drinks as the word of God says, "And the women grind flour, and their sons gather wood to make cakes for the host of heaven."[24] (2) Such women should be silenced by Jeremiah, and not frighten the world. They must not say, "We honor the queen of heaven."[25] Taphnes knows how they must be punished; the places in Magdula know how to receive their bodies for the moth. Do not obey a woman, Israel; rise above a woman's evil counsel. "A woman snares men's precious souls."[26] "Her feet bring those who use her with death to hades."[27] (3)

---

[20] Holl: < εἰς > τοῦτο προάγειν; MSS: τοῦτο ποιεῖν
[21] Gen. 2:17
[22] Gen. 2:9
[23] Isa. 65:11
[24] Jer. 7:18
[25] Jer. 51:18
[26] Prov. 6:26
[27] Prov. 5:5

"Heed not a worthless woman. Honey drops from the lips of an harlot, who anointeth thy throat for a time; but afterwards shalt thou find her more bitter than gall, and sharper than a two-edged sword."[28]

Do not obey this worthless woman. Every sect is a worthless woman, but this sect more so, which is composed of women and belongs to him who was the deceiver of the first woman. (4) Our mother Eve should be honored because formed by God, but not be obeyed, or she may convince her children to eat of the tree and transgress the commandment. She herself must repent of her folly, must turn in shame clad with fig leaves. And Adam should look to himself, and no longer obey her. (5) Error's persuasion, and the contrary counsels of a woman, are the cause of her spouse's death—and not only his, but her children's. By her transgression Eve has overthrown creation, for she was incited by the voice and promise of the snake, strayed from God's injunction, and went on to another notion.

9,1   And so, since "death < had entered into > the world"[29] through a woman, the Master and Savior of all, whose desire was to heal the hurt, rebuild the ruins, and repair what was defective, came down and was himself born of a virgin woman to bar death out, complete what was missing, and perfect what was lacking. But evil returns to us, to perpetuate the defect in the world. Thanks to their God-given prudence, however, neither young men nor old obey the woman. (2) The Egyptian woman could not persuade or pervert the chaste Joseph, though she engineered her dire scheme against the boy with great ingenuity. But a man who had received prudence from the Holy Spirit was not persuaded, and so as not to demean his noble birth did not lose his chastity; he left his garments behind and did not ruin his body. To avoid the snare, he fled the place. He was punished for a while, but he reigns forever. He was thrown into prison, but better to remain under guard and "in the corner of a courtyard"[30] than with "a contentious and brawling woman."[31] (3) And how much is there to say? Whether these worthless women offer Mary the loaf as though in worship of her, or whether they mean to offer this rotten fruit on her behalf, it is altogether silly and heretical, and demon-inspired insolence and imposture.

---

[28] Prov. 5:3–4
[29] Rom. 5:12
[30] Prov. 21:9
[31] Prov. 21:19

9,4   But what I have said will do me, so as not to prolong the work. Mary is to be held in honor, but the Lord is to be worshiped! For the righteous deceive no one. "God cannot be tempted with evil, neither tempteth he any man"[32] to deceive him, and neither do his servants. "But every man is tempted of his own lust, and enticed and caught. Then lust conceiveth sin, and sin, when it is perfected, bringeth forth death."[33]

9,5   I believe I have said enough about all this, beloved. Now that we have squashed this blister-beetle too, as it were, with the speech of the truth—it looks golden, has something like wings, and flies, but it is poisonous and contains deadly venom—let us go on to the one sect still remaining. Once more let us call on God's support, so that we may find our way to the realm of the truth, and complete the refutation of our opponents.

Against Massalians,[1] with whom Martyrians, who are pagan, and the Euphemites and Satanians, are associated. 60, but 80 of the series

1,1   Shamelessness never gets enough, and foolishness is never satisfied. With mouth agape it has opened its mind to everything, to ruin the seed of Adam and Noah by bringing their chastity to an end in various ways, and going on to implant all kinds of whorishness in its victims. (2) For another sect has actually arisen after these, a foolish, entirely stupid one, wholly ridiculous, inconsistent in its doctrine, and composed of deluded men and women. They are called Massalians, which means "people who pray."[2]

1,3   For there were others a while ago in their own turn—from about the time of Constantius—who were called Euphemites and Massalians, and I suppose this [present] group has acquired its fervor in imitation of that one. (4) But those were pagan, and neither adherents of Judaism, Christians, nor Samaritans. They were simply pagans, if you please, and believed in the gods though they worshiped none < of them >, pretended to give divine honor to one only, and called him the Almighty.[3] They furnished certain

---

[32] James 1:13
[33] James 1:14–15

[1] 8,1 suggests that Epiphanius' sources of information about this group were oral. Other ancient accounts of the Christian Massalians are found at Ephrem Syrus Haer. 22; Theodoret H.E. 4.11; Haer. Fab. 4.11.
[2] מצלינא, from Aramaic צלי, "pray"
[3] Gregory of Nazianzus appears to describe this group under the name of Hypsistarii, Or. 8.5.

houses for their use, or flat places like fora, and called them prayer houses.

1,5 There were also places of prayer outside the cities in ancient times, among both the Jews and the Samaritans. I have found this in the Acts of the Apostles where Lydia the seller of purple met St. Paul. The sacred scripture describes it as follows: "It seemed to be a place of prayer;"[4] and the apostles came up and taught the women who had assembled on that occasion. (6) There is also a place of prayer at Shechem, the town now called Neapolis, about two miles out of town on the plain. It has been set up theater fashion outdoors in the open air, by the Samaritans who mimic all the customs of the Jews.

2,1 But the earlier, pagan Massalians—the predecessors of the present ones whose background is nominally Christian, if you please— would sometimes set up small sites like these themselves, like the ones called synagogues and oratories, in certain places; but in others they actually built something like a church. They would gather in the evening and at dawn with much lighting of lamps and torches (2) and offer God lengthy hymns by their sages and certain blessings, if you please, in the fond belief that they can appease God, as it were, < with > hymns and blessings.

But blind ignorance contrives all this, with the fancy of conceit, for those who have gone astray. (3) One such structure was struck by lightning a while ago, I cannot say where, but I may have heard of it in Phoenicia. Moreover, some zealous provincial governors have put many of these persons to death for debasing the truth and counterfeiting the customs of the church without being either Christians or Jews. I believe the general Lupician was one who punished these pagan Euphemites, but a second error arose because of this. (4) Some of them took the bodies of those who were put to death at that time for this pagan lawlessness, buried them in certain places, pronounced the same blessings there in turn, and called themselves Martyrians, because of those who had been martyred for the idols, if you please!

3,1 But others in their own turn thought of something still more crafty and said, as though consulting their own intelligence in their simplicity, "Satan is great and the strongest, and does people a great deal of harm. Why not take refuge in him, worship him instead [of God], and give him honor and blessing, so that < he will be appeased* > by our flattering service and do us no harm, but spare us because we have become his servants?" And so, again,

---

[4] Acts 16:13

they have called themselves Satanians.

3,2 I grouped their sect together with the ones I mentioned first and intend to speak of now, because, in their departure from the truth, they do the same things in the open air, and spend their time in prayer and hymns. (3) But all this was harmless because of its absurdity and could distract no one's mind from the truth, for those people were not said to be Christian but were altogether pagan. Today, however, these people who are now called Massalians < have adopted* > their customs. But they have no beginning or end, no top or bottom, they are unstable in every way, without principles, and victims of delusion. They are entirely without the foundation of a name, a law, a position, or legislation.

3,4 Saying that they have come to faith in Christ, if you please, they see fit < to gather* > [in mixed companies] of men and women, as though they had renounced the world and abandoned their homes. But in the summertime they sleep in the public squares, all together in a mixed crowd, men with women and women with men, because, as they say, they own no possession on earth. They show no restraint and hold their hands out to beg, as though they had no means of livelihood and no property.

3,5 But the things they say go beyond foolishness. Whichever of them you ask, he calls himself anything you want him to. If you say, "prophet," they will say, "I am a prophet," if you name Christ, he will say, "I am Christ," if you mention patriarch, he will shamelessly call himself that; if angel, he will say he is one. And in a word, how foolish people are![5]

3,6 They have no notion of fasting.[6] If they get hungry at their time of prayer, if you please, whether it is at the second hour or the third hour or nighttime, they do anything without restraint, and eat and drink. (7) As to vice or sexual misconduct, I have no way of knowing. But they can have no lack of this either, especially with their custom of sleeping all together in the same place, men and women. There are also Massalians, of Mesopotamian extraction, in Antioch.

4,1 But they got this harmful doctrine from the extreme simplicity of certain of the brethren. For some who are brothers of mine, and orthodox, do not know the moderation of Christian conduct, which tells us to renounce the world, abandon our possessions and property, sell what we have and give to the poor—

---

[5] Lietzmann comments, "Dies wird wohl eine karrikierte Äusserungsweise des bei Theodoret bezeugten Enthusiasmus = Einwirkung des heiligen Geistes sein."
[6] Cf. Theod. H. E. 4.11.7.

but really to take up the cross and follow, and not < be > idle and without occupation and eat at the wrong times, and not < be like > drones (2) but "work with one's own hands,"[7] like the holy apostle Paul who renounced the world. Though he was the herald of the truth "his hands sufficed not only for himself, but also for them that were with him."[8] Not that they were idle; they joined him in his work. He boasts of this somewhere and teaches us in the plainest of terms, "He that worketh not, neither let him eat."[9] (3) Some of these brethren < refrain from all mundane labor* > —as though they had learned this from the Persian immigrant, Mani, if I may say so. They have no business to be that way. The word of God tells us to mark such people, who will not work.

4,4   For the saying of the Savior, "Labor not for the meat that perisheth, but for that meat which endureth unto everlasting life,"[10] has given some a wrong notion. They believe that "the meat that perishes" is the honest labor < by > which we possess its product righteously. This applied to Abraham's work, because of the calf; to the widow's, because of Elijah; to Job's work because of his sons and cattle; and [it applies] to all these servants of God who labor righteously with their own hands "to suffice also for them that need"[11]—just as they perform this righteous labor in every monastery, in Egypt and every country. (5) As the bee, with the wax she has produced < in > her hands but a drop of honey in her mouth, hymns the Lord of all with her own voice of song, in proportion to her understanding—as Solomon testifies, "By honoring wisdom she was advanced"[12]—(6) so the servants of God who are truly founded on the solid rock of the truth and build their house securely, perform their light tasks, each in his own trade, with their own hands. And they recite nearly all of the sacred scripture and keep their frequent vigils without tiring or grudging, one in prayer, another in psalmody. They continually hold the assemblies that have been set by lawful custom, (7) and spend all their days in the offering of blameless prayers to God, with deep humility and woeful lamentation, < at > the hours which come without intermission at their fixed intervals. [And], as I said, besides their spiritual work they spend their days in manual labor, so that they will not become needy and fall into human hypocrisies, no longer able to

---

[7] Cf. 1 Cor. 4:12; 1 Thes. 4:11.
[8] Cf. Acts 20:34.
[9] 2 Thes. 3:10
[10] John 6:27
[11] Cf. Eph. 4:28.
[12] Prov. 6:8c

speak the truth to the impious (8) or be untouched by the defilement of those who are rich from unrighteousness and take advantage of the poor—and no longer able to do without maintenance by such people because they cannot support themselves by honest toil, but are forced by need to share the table of the idle rich.

5,1 And thus the word of God urges us, "Desire not the meats of the rich, for these are near a life of falsehood."[13] And again, in another passage, "Such things must thou prepare. But if thou art more greedy, desire not his meats."[14] (2) For the [three] children in Babylon gained glory from these, because they rejected the king's table and chose to satisfy their hunger with seeds instead of his table and food. They renounced wealth and glory as Moses "chose rather to suffer affliction with the people of God than to enjoy"[15] the treasures in Egypt.

But he attained to prophecy by working with his own hands. (3) For this aristocrat and son of the king's daughter was made a shepherd so that he would not eat the bread of idleness. And so our father Jacob teaches us this when he says to Laban, "Give me work, so that I may labor < and enjoy > mine own bread."[16] And Jacob himself was told by his own father-in-law to tend sheep in his turn, for the righteous must not eat the bread of idleness.

5,4 The apostles were told to earn their living by preaching the word, so that they would not spend their time in journeys from city to city and place to place to preach. For "The laborer is worthy of his hire,"[17] and, "Sufficient for him that laboreth is his sustenance."[18] (5) And because of their frequent business with the laity, their administration of the church, and their constant liturgical worship, the word of God also says to pastors, "Who feedeth a flock, and eateth not of its milk? Or who planteth a vineyard, and partaketh not of its fruit?"[19] It says besides, "The husbandman must be first partaker of the fruits,"[20] (6) so as not to leave the presbyter or bishop in want of his daily bread; it urges the laity to contribute from their just wages to the support of the priests, through firstfruits, offerings and the rest. And though the persons God has appointed to guide the laity have a right to these things,

---

[13] Prov. 23:3
[14] Prov. 23:2–3
[15] Heb. 11:25
[16] Cf. Gen. 29:15–16.
[17] Matt. 10:10
[18] Cf. 1 Tim. 6:8.
[19] 1 Cor. 9:7
[20] 2 Tim. 2:6

since they profess to please God wholly they do not use them to excess.

6,1   Indeed, besides their preaching of the word, some of God's priests imitate their holy father in Christ after God, I mean the holy apostle Paul, and most, though not all, work with their hands as far as possible and < ply > any trade which is in keeping with their rank and constant care for the church. (2) Thus, along with the word and its preaching, they will have a clear conscience because they produce with their own hands, maintain themselves and, with an excellent disposition towards God and their neighbors, willingly share the alms they have on hand, I mean < from > firstfruits, offerings and their own earnings, with the brethren and the needy.

6,3   True, they are under no compulsion [to do this], or condemned [for not doing it]; but even though they are engaged [both] in righteous labor and in the work of the church, and have a right to maintenance, they do this from an abundance of good will. (4) For their God-inspired souls also desire this, grounded, [as they are], in the fear of God, and taught by the Holy Spirit of the heavenly riches, which are righteously gained amid praise, a good report and excellence, and are won by sacred doctrines, the study of the holy scripture and the oracles of God, psalmody and solemn assemblies, holy fasts, purity and discipline, and voluntary manual work for righteousness' sake.

6,5   Besides, these same esteemed brethren of ours in the monasteries, or, as we say, the cloisters of Mesopotamia, have been detected in another form [of error], that of deliberately < having > their hair long like a woman's and wearing sackcloth openly. (6) The children of < Christ's > holy virgin, our mother the church, should be grave and retiring persons and secretly serve the God who, as the scripture says, knows our secrets and rewards us openly. They should < walk > decorously because of outsiders, and not desire reward and credit from those who see them. Visible sackcloth is out of place in the catholic church, as is < un >cut hair, because of the apostle's injunction, "A man ought not to have long hair, inasmuch as he is the image of God."[21]

7,1   But what is worse, and the opposite error, some cut off their beards, the mark of manhood, while often letting the hair of their heads grow long. And as to the beard, the sacred instruction and teaching in the Ordinances of the Apostles says not to "spoil," that is, not to cut the beard,[22] and not to wear gaudy or-

[21] 1 Cor. 11:7
[22] Didasc. 2 (Achelis-Flemming p. 5)

naments, and not to adopt a token of pride. (2) Long hair was proper only for nazirites, because of the type. The ancients were guided by the type of Him who was to come, and had long hair on their heads for prayer until the Answer to the world's prayer arrived. But Christ, God's only-begotten Son, was obviously a Head; and he who always was, was made known to the world—(and yet was not known to all mankind, but only to the few believers in him)—so that since we know the Head, we will not "dishonor the head."[23] (3) For the apostle is not speaking of his own head; the point of his joke, "Doth not nature itself teach you that, if a man hath long hair, it is shame to him?"[24] applies to Christ rather than to Paul's head. For the adornment is not [being worn] for God's sake, even though it is supposed to be; the style is a contentious one, since the type of the Law is gone and the truth has come.

7,4 But Paul says, "If any seem to be contentious, we have no such custom, neither the churches of God."[25] He rejected persons who had such customs and practices because, by the apostles's ordinance and in the eyes of God's church, they are contentious. (5) But I have been obliged to say this because of these Massalians, since they have contracted the sickness of mind from the same source (i.e., contention), have truly come to grief from perversity of mind, and have been made a sect with the horrid custom of idleness and the other evils.

8,1 This is what I have heard about these people in their turn. They have become a joke in the eyes of the world and have spat up their vulgar thought and words, though they are incoherent and irremediable, and have abandoned God's building. So I shall mention a few points about these things and, as usual, work them up for their refutation. (2) First of all, by the ancient usage of married persons right reason does not allow women to associate with men. [It allows] a man < to be > with his wife in private, as Adam was with Eve, as Sarah was with Abraham, as Rebecca was united with Isaac. (3) For even though some of the patriarchs had two and three wives, the wives were not in one house. This sort of thing is the intercourse of pigs and cattle. (4) If anything, these people astonish me because they profess not to have commerce with wives, while on the contrary they are having their joke and making a show of their utter shame. (5) For even if they had spouses, they should have them individually, not promiscuously.

---

[23] 1 Cor. 11:4–5
[24] 1 Cor. 11:14
[25] 1 Cor. 11:16

And even if they are married, they should not be caught making a public spectacle, by their own free choice, of God's institution, the union of man and wife with decency, dignity and understanding. (6) Even though some of them are continent and have abstained from women, and have [kept] their rule despite their extravagant, foolish behavior, this would not be by the example of the apostles, or at the command of the prophets who preceded the apostles.

9,1   Moses took up the hymnody in the wilderness when he came out of the sea, and sang to God, "Let us sing to the Lord, for he is held in glorious honor; horse and rider hath he thrown into the sea."[26] And the men responded together, but no women, to show their decorousness and teach the dignity of the decorum of God's Law. (2) And next it says, "And Miriam took the timbrel and led the women, and said, Let us sing to the Lord, for he is held in glorious honor."[27] And women responded together to her who was like them, was of the same sex, and was in some sort their leader—contrary to the ignorant, vulgar notion of those who practice heresies in mixed crowds.

9,3   But the prophet says of the resurrection, "And they shall mourn by tribes, the tribe of Nathan by itself and their women by themselves, the tribe of Judah by itself and their women by themselves,"[28] and so on. (4) The apostles enjoined this on the church, and the Lord enjoined it in the Gospel by illustrating it from one woman and telling his mother (sic!), "Touch me not, for I am not yet ascended to my Father."[29] (5) So Gehazi approached the Shunamite to thrust her away, to keep her from violating the commandment and flaunting the ordinance of the prophets. But by the Holy Spirit's inspiration the prophet saw the woman's sadness, transgressed the ordinance to console her, received her that one time for the woman's consolation, and overlooked her touching his feet contrary to custom < because of > her distress and grief of heart. And why should I say a lot about these people who mimic dogs and imitate swine?

9,6   But as to their calling themselves Christ, what sensible person can fail to see that the doctrine is crazy? Or < their > saying, "I am a prophet!" What kind of prophecy is to be seen among them, or which marvelous work of Christ do they perform? If someone is Christ himself, in which Lord has he hoped and believed? Why the errant nonsense? Why the idiotic doctrines? But the things I

---

[26] Exod. 15:1
[27] Exod. 15:20–21
[28] Zech. 12:12
[29] John 20:17

have said about it will also be sufficient for this sect.

10,1   And this is the place to seal my whole work on these sects and bring it to a close. God has appeared and come to my aid, as I can confess with all my soul and mind, < and > thank the Lord himself that I have been privileged to finish the undertaking I assumed in the Lord himself—I mean that I have composed a description and refutation of < eighty > sects, and at the same time, as far as my human frailty permitted, revealed what goes on in each. (2) For this is the end of my full account of the origins and causes of the eighty sects I have been told of, and whose number and names I know, and the formularies, proof-texts and positions of some of them. I am struck with wonder at the words of the sacred scripture, "There are threescore queens and fourscore concubines, and maidens without number; one is my dove, my perfect one,"[30] to see how—(3) after speaking of the eighty concubines to begin with and naming Barbarism, Scythianism, Judaism, Samaritanism [and the rest], which are not lawful wives and have no dowry from the king and no guarantee that their children can inherit—all I shall have left is the demonstration of the truth, the one and only dove herself, whom the bridegroom praises.[31] (4) (For there really are seventy-five concubines, and these five mothers of theirs—Hellenism, the mother of the pagans; Judaism, the mother of the Jews; the Samaritan sect, the mother of the Samaritans, and Christianity,[32] (5) from which the separated sects have been broken off like branches and are called by Christ's name but are not his. Some are very far removed from him, while others have disinherited and estranged themselves over some very small matter—[themselves] and their children, who are not children of lawful wives but of wives who have strayed, and are merely called by the name of Christ.)

11,1   And in what follows, now that I have the leisure and have made fervent supplication to God, I shall make the case for the truth, brief in its statement but sure in its teaching. Though the truth is not last; it is first, and I have already mentioned it some time ago, before the sects, in the Advent of Christ.[33] (2) < I sing its praises* > now, however, because it is the first, and ever since his incarnation has been united to Christ as his holy bride. (3)

---

[30] Song of Songs 6:8–9
[31] This last clause is Holl's paragraph #6. It follows a very long parenthesis in the text, and the sense is best conveyed by rendering it here.
[32] Without Barbarism and Scythianism, which Epiphanius omits here, there are 79 sects; with them, if Christianity is also to be counted, there are 81.
[33] *De Incarnatione*, the unnumbered tractate between Sects 20 and 21

It was created with Adam, proclaimed among the patriarchs before Abraham, believed with Abraham, revealed by Moses, and prophesied in Isaiah. But it was made manifest in Christ and exists with Christ, and is the object of our praise after< wards >.

11,4 For to receive the crown afterwards and continue happy with the crown, the contestant must first engage in the contest, and the toil and other struggles of the contest. Not that the crown comes last; it is there before the bout but is awarded afterwards, for the joy and gladness of him who has worked for it. (5) But now that I have said these things about the Massalians, let us go on to the words I have spoken of, < because we want > to show how there are eighty concubines but sixty queens, (6) [and] how one is at once virgin and holy bride, and dove and ewe lamb, but [also] God's holy city, "the pillar and ground of the truth"[34] and "the firm rock, over which the gates of hell shall not prevail."[35] (7) For, calling and having called upon God in all things, I have succeeded in keeping my promised undertaking, I mean the complete heresiology, and in this undertaking reached even the Massalians. Treading on it too with the shoe of the Gospel, like a many-footed, ugly, misshapen and foul-smelling chameleon, let us give thanks to God in all things and < glorify > the Father in the Son, the Son in the Father, with the Holy Spirit, forever and ever. Amen.

A Concise, Accurate Account of the Faith of the Catholic and Apostolic Church (De Fide)

1,1 We have discussed the various, multiform, and much divided teachings of the crooked counsels of our opponents, have distinguished them by species and genus, and, by God's power, have exposed them as stale and worthless. We have sailed across the shoreless sea of the blasphemies of each sect, with great difficulty crossed the ocean of their shameful, repulsive mysteries, (2) given the solutions to their < hosts > of problems, and passed their wickedness by. And we have approached the calm lands of the truth, after negotiating every rough place, enduring every squall, foaming, and tossing of billows, (3) and, as it were, seeing the swell of the sea, and its whirlpools, its shallows none too small, and its places full of dangerous beasts, and experiencing them through words.

And now, sighting the haven of peace, we make supplication to the Lord once more in prayer as we hasten to land in it. (4)

---

[34] 1 Tim. 3:15
[35] Matt. 16:18

Now, as we recover from all our fear, distress and illness, as we inhale the mainland breezes with the utmost relief, as we < have come to > safety and[1] won our way to the calm harbor, we rejoice already in our spirits. (5) If the truth must be told, we have borne many hardships in [all of] this, and no light ill treatment, and have marched and sailed, as it were, across land and sea—the earth's rugged mountains and desert wastes, and the perils of the deep which we have mentioned. (6) Let us hasten to the city the moment we spy it—the holy Jerusalem and Christ's virgin and bride, the firm foundation and rock, our holy mother < but > Christ's bride. At this most auspicious moment let us ourselves say, "Come, let us go up to the mountain of the Lord, and the house of the God of Jacob. And he shall teach us his way,"[2] and so on.

2,1   Now then, children of Christ and sons of God's holy church, who have read through this compilation of the eighty sects or a part of them, who have joined me in plowing through such a mass of their wicked doctrines and marching across such a vast desert, fearful and dryly set down! (2) As though we were in Mara and thirsty from the fearful, trackless waste, let us call upon the Lord of all, for we have always been in need of him and in every part of these Sects, in our continual encounters with their obscurities. (3) Let us cry out ourselves, "Like as the hart desireth the waterbrooks, so longeth my soul after thee, O God," and again, "When shall I come to appear before the presence of God?"[3] (4) Therefore let us ourselves be quick to call upon him—not as he called the bride, for he is her Bridegroom, Lord, Master, King, God and Champion. (5) But let us call upon him as his servants and ourselves say, in unison with him, "Hither from Lebanon, O bride, for thou art all fair and there is no spot in thee."[4]

2,6   [She is] the great Builder's garden, the city of the holy king, the bride of the unspotted Christ, the pure virgin betrothed in faith to one husband alone—she who is illustrious and "breaketh forth as the dawn, fair as the moon, choice as the sun, terrible as serried ranks;"[5] she who is called blessed by the "queens," and hymned by the "concubines."[6] She is praised by the daughters and "cometh from the wilderness,"[7] "made white and leaning upon her

---

[1] Dummer: καλοῦ τε; Holl: [καὶ] τοῦ τε
[2] Isa. 2:3
[3] Ps. 41:2–3
[4] Song of Songs 4:8; 7
[5] Song of Songs 6:10
[6] Song of Songs 6:8
[7] Song of Songs 3:6

sister's son."[8] She exudes myrrh and "cometh from the wilderness, exuding, like pillars of smoke, myrrh, and frankincense from the powders of the perfumer"[9] who has given his own sweet savor— (7) he whom she foresaw and said, "Ointment poured out is thy name; therefore the maidens have loved thee."[10]

She "standeth at the king's right hand clad in fringed garments, cunningly adorned with garments interwoven with gold."[11] There is no darkness in her though once she was "blackened."[12] (8) But now she is "fair"[13] and "made white."[14] Thus, on entering you, we shall recover from the hateful pains of the deeds of the sects that once shot through us, shall have respite from the tossing of their billows, and be truly refreshed in you, our holy mother the church, in the sacred doctrine that is in you, and God's sole true faith.

2,9 But I shall begin describing the wonders of this holy city of God. For glorious things have been spoken of her, as the prophet said, "Glorious things have been spoken of thee, O city of God."[15] They are beyond the reach of all but inaccessible to unbelievers, but are obtainable in part, with the promise of fullness, by the faithful and true, [and] will be provided by their Master in the kingdom of heaven, where, with her own heavenly bridegroom, his holy virgin and heiress has herself obtained her portion and inheritance.

3,1 In the first place, the God who is over all is God to us who have been born of this holy church. This is the first proof of the truth, and "the ground of the faith"[16] of this only, virgin, holy and harmless "dove" (2) whom the Lord revealed in the Spirit to Solomon in the Song of Songs and said, "There are threescore queens, and fourscore concubines, and maidens without number, but one is *my* dove, *my* perfect one"[17]—adding the two "my's." (3) For she is *his* "dove" and *his* "perfect one," since the others are said to be and are not, while she herself is named twice. He did not say, "They are *my* eighty concubines," of the others. He awarded the queens their honorable connection with him through the glorious

---

[8] Song of Songs 8:5
[9] Song of Songs 3:6
[10] Song of Songs 1:3
[11] Ps. 44: 10; 14
[12] Song of Songs 1:6
[13] Song of Songs 1:5
[14] Song of Songs 1:5
[15] Ps. 86:3
[16] Cf. 1 Tim. 3:15.
[17] Song of Songs 6:8–9

name; but he declared that the concubines have no connection with him at all.

3,4   When I note their numbers I am obliged to investigate the passage by the anagogical method of spiritual interpretation, so as not to pass them by. I am not speaking of trivialities, but truly comparing words with their true spiritual senses, by means of the true scriptures. (5) For < it is plain > that the number of each thing in scripture is unalterable, and that nothing which is assigned a number can be without value or be reduced to number in the scripture for no good reason. Now "queens" are the ones[18] named earlier on in a genealogy. (6) For vast throngs accompany a king, but the king is still their head. So just as one man will be identified by his head although there are many members in a body, the entire throng of the king's subjects will be reckoned as one through the one king.

4,1   Now a generation in Christ is called a "queen," not because the whole generation ruled, but because the one generation which knew the Lord is elevated < to > the royal rank and status by the name of its husband.[19] For example, Adam and his whole generation are to be counted as this, a "queen"—both his rule, and the ruling family which reigned with him—because of his knowledge of God, his privilege of being the first man created, and because he was given the first penance, as the sequel shows. (2) Then after him came Seth and all humankind with him, and Enosh, Cainan, Mahalaleel, Jared, Enoch, Methuselah, Lamech and Noah; these holy men have been listed individually by number, one generation after another, and the number of them is given in Matthew. (3) For in Matthew there are sixty-two generations and lineages, listed under the names of their finest men, who had the knowledge of God or shared the royal glory and dignity because of some other excellence. The roll of the number < of them > goes on until the incarnation of Christ.

4,4   For ten generations passed between Adam and Noah and another ten between Noah and Abraham. But there were fourteen generations from Abraham until David, fourteen generations from David until the captivity, and fourteen generations from the captivity until Christ, so that there are sixty-two generations from Adam to Christ, and they are rounded off to sixty. (5) For although there were seventy-two palm trees in the wilderness, scripture called them seventy. And although the seventy men were called to the mount,

---

[18] Literally, "souls;" ψυχαί, feminine
[19] γενεά, "generation," is feminine, making the word-play possible.

with Eldad and Medad they are seventy-two. And there were seventy-two translators under Ptolemy, but to round this off we always speak of the Septuagint version.

4,6   Here too, I believe, it says sixty queens with the omission of the first and the last, because of the < suitability of the* > middle sixty for types and an anagogical treatment of the entire subject. For since < the length of time between Adam and Christ is counted* > by six tens,[20] but the time of the creation was correspondingly over in < six days* >, < the number six seems a suitable one* > for the linking of < a throng > of holy souls from every generation, who have reigned in God by faith. (7) Thus there are six stone water jars at Cana of Galilee, which were emptied and filled again. By holding two[21] or three[22] firkins apiece they < symbolize* > the amounts of the Old and New Testaments, and the whole of the Trinity. They were changed from water into unmixed wine, and filled for the good cheer of a wedding and the sons of men. (8) And so the pagan writings speak of a hexagon, which is multiplied to twenty-one by three and seven.[23] The significance of this hexagon is the same as the whole visible vault (of the universe), since its rectangular base has a fourfold < "side" >, as it were, and the covering over the vaulting on top makes six.

5,1   But not to go on too long, I rest content, once more, with what I have said about the sixty queens, [or] generations counted up until Christ's incarnation. But for the rest, the number of the generations after Christ and until now is known only to the Lord. (2) No one has reported or arranged the numbers by generation any further, because the number of this sort of thing has been sealed and closed by the number of the queens, which is counted up to the incarnation itself. (3) For the rest, the later authors, or rhetoricians, annalists or historians no longer count generations but successions and times of the emperors, according to the number of the years of each emperor's reign.

From all this the wise will understand that, even without this inquiry, all time is divided into the sixty-two generations up until Christ—(4) for after Christ the world's time periods are no longer

---

[20] I.e., groups of ten or more generations, counted by their "heads," the persons who begin them. Epiphanius arrives at the figure, six, by counting Adam as one, and Christ as six. See 4,4.

[21] I.e., the Old and New Testaments

[22] The Persons of the Holy Trinity

[23] I,e, seven groups of three hexagons with their flat sides juxtaposed to form a kind of vaulted solid and thus represent the "vault of the universe(?)" Or might this be a very garbled reminiscence of Plato Timaeus 55B, where a twenty-sided geometrical solid is constructed from 210 equilateral triangles?

counted by lineages in this way, since < the number > [of them] is summed up in one unified whole which, by God's good pleasure, indicates an unshakeable stay. This [unit] will make it < evident > that the end of the age is separate from time, and will be over at the transition to the age to come.[24]

5,5   This is why he says, "*One* is my dove, my perfect one."[25] All things are completed in her, whether < they are > times and seasons, years and intervals of generations, and whether the age counts its dates by emperors, consuls, Olympiads or governorships. (6) But there are eighty concubines, who were to be found among the queens even before the earthly reign, that is, the reign of the faith and this bride and virgin herself, who is unspotted and a "dove," the "only daughter of her mother, even of her that bore her."[26]

6,1   For the church is engendered by one faith and born with the help of the Holy Spirit, and is the only daughter of the only mother, and the one daughter of her that bore her. And all the women who came after and before her have been called concubines. They have not been entire strangers to the covenant and inheritance, but have no stated dowry and are not receptacles of the Holy Spirit, but have only an illicit union with the Word. (2) For the Hebrew language gave a good explanation of the concubine by calling her "pilegeshtha." "Peleg" means "half," and "ishtha" is a wife, which is as much as to say that she is "half a wife."[27] (3) Insofar as she has come to the Lord, he called all to the light of liberty by saying, "While ye have the light with you, walk in the light."[28] And the holy apostle says, "Ye are children of the day and children of the light."[29] And again < it is said > in the sacred scripture, "He that doeth evil hateth the light neither cometh unto the light."[30] (4) And similarly even though concubines—who are not acknowledged or full wives, and are not married with a dowry by their husbands—have carnal relations with the husbands, they cannot have the honor, title, security, marriage portion, wedding gifts, dowered status and legitimacy of the free wife.

---

[24] The number which means "unshakeable support" is one. There is one "end of the age," i.e., the time between Christ's incarnation and the beginning of the "age to come." The oneness of the "end of the age" is shown by the fact that its chronology is not reckoned by successive generations, which were multiple.

[25] Song of Songs 6:9

[26] Song of Songs 6:9

[27] Epiphanius incorrectly adds the Aramaic emphatic ending to the Hebrew אישה.

[28] Cf. John 12:35.

[29] 1 Thes. 5:5

[30] John 3:20

And so, as I have said, the sects I have listed in succession are eighty concubines. (5) But no one need be surprised if each of them is given different names in every country. What is more, we must observe that each sect in turn has frequently divided into many parts on its own and taken different names. This is no surprise; it is the way things are. (6) But I find eighty-one in all—one [more than eighty] because of the one who is different from them all, but is the only one allotted to the bridegroom whom he has acknowledged by such a name as "One is my dove," and again, "my perfect one."[31] In other words all the concubines are low-born and of no particular harmlessness, purity and gentleness.

6,7   The concubines, then, include < the ones > that followed the so-called "Barbarism" and "Scythianism" in the beginning, down through the Massalians, a total of seventy-seven, and the source of the pagan sects, Hellenism, the source of < the > Jewish, Judaism, and the Samaritan sect, the source of the Samaritan. When < these > three are added to the seventy-seven the sum is eighty and the one is left, (8) namely, the holy catholic church, Christianity. By the will of the Father, the Son and the Holy Spirit Christianity was, in fact, named from the beginning, both with Adam and—before Adam and before all the ages—with Christ, and was believed with all who have pleased God in every generation. And it was plainly revealed in the world at Christ's coming. And I now sing its praises once more after all these sects, the ones < we called > concubines, following the order of the treatise.

7,1   For the Word himself counted the sects like this in the Song of Songs when he said, "Eighty queens and eighty concubines and maidens without number. But one," he says, "is my dove, my perfect one; the one daughter of her mother, elect for her that bore her."[32] (2) And he later shows how all will find her the most honored of them all, the mistress of them all, and his only choice, the one whose children are the king's heirs and legitimate children. For they are "children of the promise" and not "children of the bondmaid"[33] or the concubine, or of the others whose description is endless.

7,3   For even though Abraham had children by the concubine Keturah, Keturah's children were not joint heirs with Isaac. They received gifts, however, like gifts for a governor, to make sure that the type would be preserved for the anagogical interpretation of

---

[31] Song of Songs 6:9
[32] Song of Songs 6:7–8
[33] Gal 4:28; 31

the text, and that no one would despair of Christ's calling. (4) For the gifts Abraham gave Ishmael and Keturah's sons were a type of the good things to come, for the conversion of the gentiles to the faith and truth.

7,5 For Abraham gave Hagar, a bondmaid and cast out by Abraham—([she was] like the Jerusalem below who was in bondage with her children, of whom it is said, "I have cast out thy mother,"[34] and again, "I gave the bill of divorcement into her hands."[35]) Abraham gave this bondmaid, I mean Hagar, a skin full of water, the more of a type because of the hope of her conversion.[36] It showed the power of the "laver of regeneration,"[37] which has been given to unbelievers for a gift of life, and for the conversion of all the heathen to the knowledge of the truth.

7,6 But Abraham's gifts to Keturah's children were wealth— gold, silver, clothing, and whatever Abraham secretly hid in their wallets, the "frankincense, myrrh and gold"[38] of the companions of the kings of Sodom and Gomorrah, which < had been plundered by > Chedorlaomer's allies. They had taken prisoners from Sodom, Gomorrah and the other towns, had made off with their horses, captured most of the people, and seized the wealth of each king and most of the possessions of the others. (7) Abraham brought [all] this back "from the slaughter of the kings"[39] at that time. But he did not dare to return things already reserved for the Lord God and instead, as I find in the traditions of the Hebrews, gave them as gifts, along with his other gifts, to his sons by Keturah.

8,1 These children of Abraham by Keturah were cast out by Abraham, and settled in Magodia in Arabia. On Christ's arrival the same gifts < were offered > to Christ in Bethlehem < by > the descendants of Keturah's children, the magi, who offered gifts and presents to gain their share of the same hope, when they had seen the star and come to Bethlehem. (2) The prophet gives plain indication of these gifts by saying, "Before the child is able to cry Father or Mother, he shall take the power of Damascus and the spoil of Samaria before the king of the Assyrians."[40] For as I said, these were taken from Damascus in Abraham's time, and from Samaria, by the kings on their raid. (3) Now when did Christ

---

[34] Cf. Jer. 22:26.
[35] Jer. 3:8
[36] I.e., Hagar's, "return"
[37] Tit. 3:5
[38] Matt. 2:11
[39] Gen. 14:16–17
[40] Isa. 8:4

receive them "before he could cry Father or Mother," except when the magi came and "opened their wallets"—or "treasures," as some copies say—"and offered myrrh, frankincense and gold?"[41]

8,4   And do you see what the truth's expressions are, and the consequences of them? The sects too are concubines, and their children have received gifts. But the concubines have only received the name, and have only been called by Christ's name and received their few texts from the sacred scripture, so that, if they choose, they can understand the truth by these. (5) But if they prefer not to, but return to Herod—(for they are told not to return to Herod, but to go to their country by another way.) But if they do not do as they are told the gifts are no good to them, just as their coming would have done the magi no good if they had returned to Herod. For these same sects debase the teachings of God's oracles in a way that resembles Herod's.

9,1   These, then, are < the > eighty concubines, so numbered in scripture. And those queens are the individuals listed by generation, that is, men and their descendants. But the young girls without number consist of the further philosophies all over the world and the ways of life, one praiseworthy and one not, of each individual. (2) For who can count the variety of this world? How many other sects have not grown up among the Greeks after the four most famous ones which we have mentioned—and further, after those sects and the ones after them, how many individuals and ideas keep arising of themselves, with seeming "youth", in accordance with the opinion of each? (3) There are some called Pyrrhonians, for example, and many others. Since I have learned of many I shall give their names and their opinions in order below, but < this > is a fraction of the ones in the world. (4) And the ones which follow are Greek sects. As the first of them I should begin with the opinion and belief of Thales of Miletus.

9,5   For Thales of Miletus himself, who was one of the seven sages, declared that the primal origin of all things is water. For he says that everything originates from water and is resolved back into water.

9,6   Anaximander the son of Praxiades, also a Milesian, said that the infinite is the first principle of all things. For all things originate from this and all things are resolved into it.

9,7   Anaximenes the son of Eurystatus, also a Milesian, said that air is the first principle of all things, and that everything originates from this.

---

[41] Matt. 2:11

9,8   Anaxagoras the son of Hegesibulus, of Clazomene, said that identical particles are the first principles of all things.

9,9   Archelaus < the > naturalist, the son of Apollodorus—some say the son of Milton, but he was Athenian—says that all things have originated from earth. For this is the first principle of all things, or so he says.

9,10   Socrates the ethicist, the son of Sophroniscus † the statuary[42] and Phaenaretes the midwife, said that man must mind his own affairs but nothing more.

9,11   Pherecydes too said that earth came into being before all things.

9,12   Pythagoras of Samos, the son of Mnesarchus, said that God is the unit, and that nothing has come into being apart from this. But he said that the wise must not sacrifice animals to the gods, and must certainly not eat meat or beans, or drink wine. He said that everything from the moon down is passible, but that everything above the moon is impassible. And he said that the soul migrates into many animals. He also commanded his disciples to maintain silence for five years, and in the end pronounced himself a god.

9,13   Xenophanes the son of Orthomenus, from Colophon, said that all things are made of earth and water. All things are, or so he said, but nothing is true. Thus what is certain is not clear; all things, especially invisible things, are matters of opinion.

9,14   Parmenides the son of Pyres, an Elean, also said that the infinite is the first principle of all things.

9,15   Zeno of Elea, the controversialist. Like the other Zeno he said both that the earth is immoveable and that there is no void. He also says the following: That which must be moved is moved either in the place in which it is, or the place in which it is not. And it can neither be moved in the place in which it is, nor in the place in which it is not; therefore nothing is moved.

9,16   Melissus the son of Ithagenes, the Samian, said that everything is one, but that it is by not nature enduring; all things are potentially destructible.

9,17   Leucippus the Milesian—though some say that he was an Elean—was also a controversialist. He too said that everything is in the infinite, and that all events take place in imagination and appearance. There are no real events; they are apparent, like an oar in the water.

---

[42] Diels: ἑρμογλύφου; MSS: Ἐλμάγλου, an improbable name

9,18   Democritus of Abdera, the son of Damasippus, said that the world is infinite and is situated above a void. But he also said that there is one end of all, and that contentment is best, but that pains are the boundaries of evil. And what appears just is not just; the unjust is the opposite of nature. For he said that laws are an evil invention, and < that > the wise should not obey laws, but live freely.

9,19   Metrodorus of Chios said that no one understands anything. We have no precise understanding of the things we think we know; and we should pay no heed to our senses, for all things are appearance.

9,20   Protagoras of Abdera, the son of Menander, said that there are no gods, and that God does not exist at all.

9,21   Diogenes of Smyrna, or some say he was from Cyrene, held the same opinions as Protagoras.

9,22   Pyrrho of Elis collected all the doctrines of the other sages and wrote objections to them to demolish their opinions. He was not satisfied with any doctrine.

9,23   Empedocles of Agrigentum, the son of Meto, introduced fire, earth, water and air as the four primal elements, and said that originally there was enmity between the elements. For earlier they had been separated, he said, but now, as he says, they have been united in friendship. In his opinion, then, there are two first principles and powers, enmity and love, the one of which is unitive, the other, divisive.

9,24   Heraclitus of Ephesus, the son of Bleso, said that all things come from fire and are resolved back into fire.

9,25   Prodicus calls the four elements, and after them the sun and the moon, gods; for he said that the vital principle of all things comes from these.

9,26   Plato the Athenian said that there are God, matter and form, but that the world is generate and mortal while the soul is ingenerate, immortal and divine. But there are three parts of the soul, the rational, the spirited, and the appetitive. And he said that marriages and wives should be common to all, and that no one should have one spouse to himself, but that anyone who wishes may have relations with any women who are willing.

9,27   Aristippus of Cyrene. He was gluttonous and pleasure-loving, and said that the pleasure is the goal of the soul, and that whoever experiences pleasure is happy. But one who never experiences pleasure is thrice wretched, as he says, and unfortunate.

9,28   Theodorus, who is called the atheist, said that discussion of God is silly. For he believed that there is nothing divine, and therefore urged everyone to steal, forswear themselves, rob, and not die for their countries. For he said that the world is one country and that only the happy man is good, and that the unfortunate < must > be avoided even if he is wise. And a fool, if he is wealthy and an unbeliever, is preferable [to such a "wise" man].

9,29   Hegesias of Cyrene. This man said that there is no such thing as love or gratitude. They do not exist; one does a favor because he is in need [of a favor], or confers a benefit because he has suffered something worse [by not conferring it]. He also said the following: Life is profitable for a bad man, but death for a good one. Hence some have called him the advocate of death.

9,30   Antisthenes, who had a Thracian mother but was Athenian himself, was first a Socratic and then a Cynic. He said that we must not envy the good deeds of others or their shameful behavior to one another; and that the walls of a city are vulnerable to the traitor within, but the walls of the soul are unshakeable and unbreachable.

9,31   Diogenes the Cynic who was from Sinope in Pontus, agreed with Antisthenes in everything. He said that the good is † natural[43] to every wise man but that everything else is simply foolishness.

9,32   Crates of Thebes in Boeotia, also a Cynic, said that poverty is liberty.

9,33   Arcesilaus said that the truth is accessible to God alone, but not to man.

9,34   Carneades was of the same opinion as Arcesilaus.

9,35   Aristotle the son of Nicomachus is said by some to be a Macedonian from Stagyra, but a few say that he was Thracian. He said that there are two first principles, God and matter, and that things above the moon are subject to divine providence, but that what is below the moon is not ruled by providence but borne along at random by some unreasoned motion. But he says that there are two worlds, the world above and the world below, and that the world above is immortal while the world below is mortal. And he says that the soul is the entelechy of the body.

9,36   Theophrastus of Ephesus held the same opinions as Aristotle.

9,37   Strato of Lampsacus said that heat is the cause of all things. He said that the parts of the world are infinite, and that everything living is capable of having a mind.

9,38   Praxiphanes of Rhodes held the same opinions as Theophrastus.

9,39   Critolaus of Phasela held the same opinions as Aristotle.

---

[43] Zeller: οἰκεῖον; MSS: οἰστόν

9,40 Zeno of Citieum, the Stoic, said that we must not build temples for gods but keep the Godhead in our minds alone—or rather, regard the mind as God, for it is immortal. We should throw the dead to wild beasts or consign them to fire. We may indulge in pederasty without restraint. But he said that the divine permeates all things. The causes of things sometimes depend on us and sometimes do not depend on us—that is, some things are up to us while some are not.

He also said that < the soul persists for some time* > after its separation from the body, and called the soul a long-lived spirit but said that is certainly not fully immortal. For it is exhausted to the point of extinction by the length of its existence, or so he says.

9,41 Cleanthes says that pleasures are the good and noble, and he called only the soul man, and said that the gods are characters in mysteries, and holy calls. And he claimed that the sun is a torch and the world < is holy, and men are* > initiates, and the possessed are priests of the gods.

9,42 Persaeus taught the same doctrines as Zeno.

9,43 Chrysippus of Soli wrote infamous laws. For he said that sons must have relations with their mothers and daughters with their fathers. For the rest he agreed with Zeno of Citieum. But besides this, he said that we should eat human flesh. But he said that the goal of all is to live pleasantly.

9,44 Diogenes of Babylon said that all things consist of pleasure.

9,45 Panaetius of Rhodes said that the universe is immortal and unaging, ignored divination, and pooh poohed what is said about the gods. For he said that the discussion of God is chatter.

9,46 Posidonius of Apamaea said that man's highest good is wealth and health.

9,47 Athenodorus of Tarsus held the same opinions as Chrysippus, and taught the same doctrines as Zeno.

9,48 Epicurus the son of Neocles, who was reared in Athens, pursued a life of pleasure and, as I said of him at the outset, was not ashamed to have relations in public with licentious women.[44] He said in his turn that there are no gods, but that mere chance governs all things. And nothing in the world comes of our own will—not learning, lack of education, or anything else—but that all things happen to everyone unwilled. And it is no use to blame

[44] Epicurus is discussed at 1,1,8, but Epiphanius does not say this there. It is likely that he is here quoting a handbook, perhaps the same one in which he found the material for Sects 1,1,5–8.

anyone, as he says, or to praise anyone; people do not undergo these things voluntarily.

But he said that death is not to be feared. And as I have said already, he maintained both that everything consists of atoms, and that the universe is infinite.

10,1   And these are the Greek philosophers I have learned of. But there are as many others throughout the barbarian and Greek parts of the Roman realm and the other regions of the world. (2) There are seventy-two repulsive philosophies in the Indian nation, those of the gymnosophists, the Brahmans (these are the only praiseworthy ones), the Pseudo-brahmans, the corpse-eaters, the practitioners of obscenity, and those who are past feeling. Because of the great corruption in men, and their practice of evil and < obscenity* >, I consider it unnecessary and not worth my while to speak individually of the Indian sects and the disgusting things they do. (3) For again, it is said that there are six different sects in Media, and as many in Ethiopia—and among the Persians, or in Parthia, Elamitis, Caspia, Germany, and Sarmatia, or however many there are among the Dauni, or among the Zikchi, Amazons, Lazi, Iberians, Bosporenes, Geli, Chinese or the other nations, there are < any number > of different laws, philosophies and sects and a countless throng of varieties.

10,4   For instance, Chinese men stay at home and weave, and anoint themselves and do womanly things in readiness for their wives. And in reverse, the women cut their hair short, wear men's underclothing, and do all the field labor. But among the Geli, on the contrary, those who do evil are held by their laws to be praiseworthy.

10,5   And how many mysteries and rites do the Greeks have? For example, the women who go to the megara,[45] and those who celebrate the Thesmophoria, are different from each other. And there are as many others: the Eleusinian mysteries of Demeter and Persephone at Eleusis, and the shocking goings-on in the sanctuaries there—the unclothing of women, to put it politely, drums and cakes, the bull-roarer and the basket, the worked wool, the cymbal, and the potion prepared in the beaker.

And just as many others. The mysteries of Archemorus in Pythia (6) and others on the Isthmus, those of Athamas and Melicertes the child of Ino. And all the men who turn the phallus over, and the < women > who † celebrate[46] the obscene rites, and the men

---

[45] Pits into which pigs were thrown at the festival of the Thesmophoria
[46] Holl: ἑορτάζουσαι ... < γυναῖκες >; MSS: φαλλαρίζουσαι

who serve Rhea by castrating male children and living their lives
without male organs, certainly unable to be men any longer, but
without having become women. (7) And other Dionysians, those
who are initiated into the Curetes and their distribution of meat,
who are crowned with snakes and raise the cry of "Va, Va!" Either
they are still calling on that Eve who was deceived by the snake,
or else they are summoning the snake to their imposture in ancient
Hebrew. For by the plain interpretation "Eve" means the woman;
but in the ancient language native Hebrew speakers call the snake
"chavvah."

11,1   And "What shall I say? For the time will fail me if I tell"[47]
of the countless differences in people's various practices, as well
as in their virtue and their vice. (2) As many others in Egypt, who
are initiates of Cronus and make a show of putting iron collars
on their necks, having their hair loose on top, < wearing > filthy,
absurd clothing, and piercing their nostrils as though for nose
rings at each [festival] of Cronus in the town called Astus. (This
is a small town in Egypt, the chief village of the so-called nome
of Prosopitis.) This is how they follow the unclean rites of the
general assembly of deluded persons, and the mad instructions of
the drum beating ecstatics, if you please! But these people are
hopelessly lost.

11,3   But just as many of the others! For instance, the cult of
Harpocrates near Buticus, or the little town of Butus itself. They
are already elders in years, < but are children in behavior* >, and
are compelled by the daemon to enact the imaginary frenzies of
Horus at the sacred month. (4) But each citizen—even an elder
already far along in years, together with young women of the same
persuasion, and other ages from youth up—are priests of this Horus,
if you please, and of Harpocrates. Their heads are shaved and they
shamelessly carry his emblem—a slavish one, as well as accursed
and childish—and are willing participants in the games of the
daemon's initiates, make themselves ridiculous with their madness
and folly, and cast off all restraint. (5) First they smear their faces
with porridge, flour and other vulgarities, and then they dip their
faces in a boiling cauldron and deceitfully madden the crowds with
their faces, for a magical performance, if you please; and they wipe
the stuff off their faces with their hands, and give some to anyone
who asks, to eat for their health's sake and as a remedy for their ills.

12,1   But if I were to describe the woman ecstatics in Memphis
< and > Heliopolis who bewitch themselves with drums and flutes,

---

47 Heb. 11:32

and the dancing girls, and the performers at the triennial festival—
and the women at Bathys and in the temple of Menuthis who have
abandoned shame and womanliness—to what burdens for the
tongue, or what a long composition I could commit myself, by
adding the countless number [of these] to the number I have
already given! (2) For even if I were to take on the enormous task
I would leave our comprehension of these things incomplete, since
scripture says that there are "young women *without number*."[48] (3)
The rites at Sais and Pelusium, at Bubastis and Abydus, the temples
of Antinous and the mysteries there. The rites at Pharbetis, those
of Mendesius' goat, all the mysteries in Busiris, all the ones in
Sebennytus, all the ones in Diospolis, where they sometimes perform
rites for the ass in the name of Seth, or Typho, if you please, while
others < worship* > Tithambro, or Hecate, and others are initiates
of Senephthy, others of Thermuthi, others of Isis. (4) And how
many things of this sort can be said! < If one tries > to name them
specifically it will consume a great deal of time. The entire subject
will be summed up by the phrase, "young women without number."[49]

12,5   But again, < I omit* > the names of many other mysteries,
heresiarchs and fomenters of schism whose leaders are called
Magusaeans by the Persians but prophets by the Egyptians, and
who preside over their shrines and temples. And those Babylonian
magi who are called Gazarenes, sages and enchanters, and the
Indians' Evilei so-called, and Brahmans, < and > the Greeks' hiero-
phants and temple custodians, and a throng of Cynics, and the
leaders of countless other philosophers.

13,1   As I said, then, [there are] people in Persia called Magusaeans, who detest idols but worship † planets,[50] fire, the moon
and the sun. And in Greece, again, [there are] others called Abian
Musi, who drink mare's milk and live entirely in wild country. (2)
And however many of so many such things the human mind can
take in, which are called "great" and < regarded > as praiseworthy,
there are as many different "young women without number."[51]
some praiseworthy, some not. Some who make up their own practice and rule of asceticism and appear in public with long hair.
Others wear sackcloth openly, though other holy brethren sit in
sackcloth and ashes at home. Still others, from their "youth," add
to their burden with extra fasts and rules < for the sake of > a

---

[48] Song of Songs 6:8
[49] Song of Songs 6:87
[50] Holl: στοιχείοις; MSS: εἰδώλοις, which contradicts what has just been said
[51] Song of Songs 6:8

perfect conscience towards the bridegroom.

13,3 But others, as I said, do not act the part of "youths" rightly but arbitrarily from some preconception, in contradiction to the truth. Zacchaeus, who has recently died in the hill country around Jerusalem, would never pray with anyone. But for the same reason he freely undertook to handle and consecrate the sacred mysteries although he was a layman. And [there was] another—and he was once one of those who seemed to have led the finest kind of life, and he lived in the hermitages in a monastery in Egypt—(4) [he], and another man, near Sinai, who were made "young" by dreaming < that > they had received bishop's orders, and undertook to sit on thrones and perform episcopal functions.

13,5 Others, and not a few of them, have dared, from "youthfulness," to make themselves eunuchs, if you please, contrary to the commandments. (6) But others, whose origins are orthodox, seem to behave like "youths" and venture to gather their own congregations contrary to the canons. Moreover, they rebaptize the people who come to them from the Arians, if you please, without the judgment of an ecumenical council. (7) For because the Arian and the catholic laity are still intermingled, and many are orthodox but are joined with the Arianizers from hypocrisy, the matter, as I said, has not yet been settled by a judgment—not until there can be a separation of this blasphemous sect, and then its sentence will be determined.

13,8 Of the people who rebaptize this way by their own directive, I have heard that one is a presbyter in Lycia. And there are others as well, who each pray by themselves and never with anyone else; and others wear slave's collars contrary to the ordinance of the church. (9) And so, at the close of the entire work, I have said that those who are "young" in their own way, to suit their own tastes, are "without number"[52]—by no means for good, to practice the various forms of wisdom, judgment, courage, prudence and righteousness. Others of these act "young" more arbitrarily, and perversely < estrange > themselves from the truth, in numbers there is no way of counting.

14,1 But the one dove herself, the holy virgin, confesses that God is the Father, the Son and the Holy Spirit, a perfect Father, a perfect Son, and a perfect Holy Spirit. She confesses that the Trinity is co-essential and that the Trinity is not an amalgam, but that the Son is truly begotten of the Father, and that the Holy Spirit is not different from the Father and the Son, (2) but that

---

[52] Song of Songs 6:8

the Trinity is everlasting. It never needs an addition and contains no subordination, but is reduced to one unity, and one sovereignty of our God and Father.

And all things have been made by this Trinity of Father, Son and Holy Spirit. Once these things did not exist, and they are not contemporaneous with God and were not in being before him; they were brought from non-being into being by the Father, the Son and the Holy Spirit.

14,3 This Father, Son and Holy Spirit has always vouchsafed to appear in visions to his saints, as each was able to receive [the vision] in accordance with the gift which had been < given > him by the Godhead. This gift was granted to each of those who were deemed worthy, sometimes to see the Father as each was able, < sometimes > to hear his voice as well as he could. (4) When he said by the mouth of Isaiah, "My beloved servant shall understand,"[53] this is the voice of the Father. And when Daniel saw "the Ancient of Days,"[54] this is a vision of the Father. And again, when he says in the prophet, "I have multiplied visions and been portrayed by hands of the prophets,"[55] this is the voice of the Son. And when, in Ezekiel, "The Spirit of God took me" and "brought me out unto the plain,"[56] this refers to the Holy Spirit.

14,5 And there are many things of this kind that could be said. I have mentioned parts of a few of them in passing, and quoted the two texts to show what the church is like. But there are a million and more like them in the sacred scriptures of the Old and the New Testaments. (6) And [we find in the scriptures] that the Lord himself formed Adam's body and "breathed the breath of life into him" to make "a living soul" for him.[57] God himself, the Father, Son and Holy Spirit, the one Godhead, gave the Law to Moses. The prophets were sent by the same Godhead. He himself is our God, the God of Jews and Christians, and has called those Jews to justification who do not deny our Lord Jesus' advent, and saves all who live by his true faith and do not deny the truth of the proclamation of God's true Gospel doctrine. (7) For the Only-begotten has come! Come! And this is what our mother the church is like—the calm haven of peace, the good cheer redolent of the

---

[53] Isa. 52:13
[54] Dan. 7:9
[55] Hos. 12:11
[56] Ezek. 3:14; 22
[57] Cf. Gen. 2:7.

blossoming[58] of the vine, which bears the "cluster of blessing"[59] for us and daily grants us the drink that soothes all anguish, the blood of Christ, unmixed, true.

15,1 [And there are texts to show] that Christ was truly born of Mary the ever-virgin, by the Holy Spirit's agency, not by the seed of a man. No, he took his body from the holy Virgin herself, truly and not in appearance—truly flesh, truly body, with bones, sinews and everything of ours. He was no different from ourselves except for the glory of his holiness and Godhead, and the holiness and righteousness of his vessel. He had the fullness of everything without sin, and possessed a true human soul, a true human mind— not that I affirm the concreteness of the mind, as others do. (2) But he possessed them all unstained by sin, a "mouth" that did not lie, "lips that spoke no guile,"[60] a heart not inclined to rebellion, a mind not perverted to wrong, flesh that did not did not indulge in fleshly pleasure. He was perfect God from on high, but had not come to dwell *in* a man; he himself became wholly incarnate, without changing his nature but including his own manhood together with his Godhead.

15,3 He truly entered the Virgin's womb, was carried for the usual time, and was born without shame, unstained, undefiled, through the birth canals. He was nursed, was embraced by Simeon and Anna, was borne in Mary's arms. He learned to walk, went on journeys, became a boy and grew up in full possession of all human characteristics. His age was counted in years and his gestation in months, (4) for he was "made of a woman, made under the Law."[61]

He came to the Jordan and was baptized by John. This was not because he needed cleansing but, in keeping with his manhood under the Law, not to confuse what was right, and so that "all righteousness might be fulfilled,"[62] as he himself said—and to show that he had taken true flesh, true manhood. He went down into the water to give, not to receive; to provide generously, not from need; to enlighten the water, and empower it to become a type of those who would be perfected in it. Thus those who truly believe in him and hold the faith of the truth would learn that he had truly become man and truly been baptized, (5) and would there-

---

[58] Cf. Song of Songs 2:13.
[59] Cf. 1 Cor. 10:16.
[60] Cf. 1 Pet. 2:22.
[61] Gal. 4:4
[62] Matt. 3:15

fore come themselves with his assent, receive the power of his descent, and be illumined by his illumination. This is the fulfillment of the oracle in the prophet about a change of power,[63] about the giving of the power of salvation of the bread which is taken from Jerusalem, and the giving of the strength of the water. (16,1) But the power of the bread and the strength of the water are here made strong in Christ, so that not bread, but the power of bread will be our power. Indeed, the bread is food, but the power in it is for the generation of life. [And the water is strength], not merely so that the water will cleanse us, but so that we may have sanctifying < power > for the achievement of our salvation by the strength of the water, through faith, work, hope, the celebration of the mysteries, and the naming [of the Trinity].

16,2 He came up out of the Jordan and heard the Father's voice, < for the Father bore witness* > in the hearing of the disciples who were present, to show who it was for whom he was testifying. And as I have said in many Sects, the Holy Spirit descended in the form of a dove to prevent the Trinity's being thought an identity, since the Spirit is shown in his own person. The Spirit settled on him and "came upon him"[64] to make the Subject of his testimony manifest; to testify that his holy flesh is dear to the Father and the Holy Spirit and approved by them; to declare the Father's approval of the Son's incarnation; to make it evident that the Son is a true Son; and in fulfillment of the scripture, "And after these things he appeared on the earth and consorted with men."[65]

16,3 He came up out of the Jordan, was plainly and truly tempted by the devil in the wilderness, and grew hungry afterwards in keeping with and because of the reality of his human nature. (4) He chose disciples, preached truth and healed diseases; he slept, grew hungry, made journeys, performed miracles, raised the dead, gave sight to the blind, strengthened the lame and the palsied. He preached the Gospel, the truth, the kingdom of heaven, and the lovingkindness of himself, the Father and the Holy Spirit.

17,1 He truly underwent the passion for us in his flesh and perfect manhood. He truly suffered on the cross in company with his Godhead, though this was not changed to passibility but was impassible and unalterable. The two inferences can clearly be drawn:

---

[63] LXX Isa. 3:1, "Behold, the Master, the Lord of hosts, will take away from Judah and Jerusalem the strong man and the strong woman, the strength of bread and the strength of water."
[64] Matt. 3:16
[65] Bar. 3:38

Christ suffered for us in the flesh;"[66] but he remained impassible
in his Godhead. (2) It is not that the manhood is a separate thing
and the Godhead a separate thing; the Godhead accompanies the
manhood and yet, because of the purity and incomparability of
its essence, does not suffer. < Christ > suffered in the flesh, however, and was put to death in the flesh, though he lives forever
in his Godhead and raises the dead.

17,3   But his body was truly buried and remained lifeless, without breath and motion, for the three days—wrapped in the shroud,
laid in the tomb, shut in by the stone and the seal of those who
had imposed it. Yet the Godhead was not shut in, the Godhead
was not buried; (4) it descended to the underworld with the holy
soul, took the captive souls from there, broke the "sting of death,"[67]
"shattered" the bars and the unbreakable "bolts,"[68] and by its own
authority "loosed the pains of hades."[69]

It ascended with the soul, for "the soul had not been left in hell,
nor had the flesh seen corruption;"[70] (5) the Godhead had raised
it or the Lord himself, the divine Word and Son of God, had risen
with soul, body and entire vessel, with the vessel at last united with
spirit. His body itself was spirit though it had once been tangible,
had been subjected to scourging by the free consent of the Godhead,
had consented to temptation by Satan and had experienced hunger, sleep, weariness, grief and sorrow. (6) The holy body itself
was at last united with the Godhead, though the Godhead had
always been with the holy body which underwent such sufferings.
For Christ had risen and united his body with himself, as one spirit,
one unity, one glory, his own one Godhead.

17,7   For he truly appeared and was handled by Thomas, ate
and drank with the apostles and consorted with them for forty days
and forty nights. Indeed, he "entered where doors were barred,"[71]
and after entering displayed sinews and bones, the mark of the
nails and the mark of the lance. For it was indeed the body itself,
(8) since it had been joined to one unity and one Godhead, with
no further expectation of suffering, no further death, as the holy
apostle says, "Christ is risen, he dieth no more; death hath no more
dominion over him."[72] What had been passible remains forever

---

[66] 1 Pet. 4:1
[67] 1 Cor. 15:55–56
[68] Cf. Ps. 106:16.
[69] Acts 2:24
[70] Cf. Acts 2:27; Ps. 15:10.
[71] Cf. John 20:19; 26.
[72] Rom. 6:9

impassible, the divine nature with body, soul, and all its human nature. (9) He is very God and has ascended into the heavens and taken his seat at the Father's right hand in glory, not by discarding his body but by uniting it to spirit in the perfection of one Godhead, just as our own bodies, though "sown as natural bodies" for now, will be raised spiritual; though sown in corruption for now, will be raised in incorruption; though sown in mortality for now will be raised in immortality."[73]

17,10   Now if such is the case with our [own] bodies, how much more with that holy, inexpressible, incomparable, pure body united with God, the one body in its final uniqueness? The apostle also testifies to this and says, "Even if we knew Christ after the flesh, now know we him no more."[74] (11) It is not that he separated his flesh from his Godhead; < he displayed it* > as it was and united with his Godhead, no longer fleshly but spiritual, as the scripture says, "according to the Spirit of holiness after the resurrection from the dead of our Lord Jesus Christ."[75] At the same time [he displayed] this flesh divine, impassible and yet having suffered—and having been buried, having risen, having ascended in glory, coming to judge the quick and the dead as the scripture truly says, "Of his kingdom there shall be no end."[76]

18,1   For our mother, the holy church herself, believes as has been truly preached to her and enjoined upon her, that we shall all fall asleep and be raised with this body, with this soul, with our whole vessel, "that each may receive according to that he hath done."[77] (2) It is true that the resurrection of the dead, eternal judgment, the kingdom of heaven, and repose < are in store > for the righteous, and the inheritance of the faithful and an angelic choir is awaiting those who have kept the faith, purity, hope and the Lord's commandments. And it has been proclaimed, certified and believed that "These shall rise to life eternal,"[78] as we read in the Gospels.

18,3   For whatever the apostle and all the scriptures say is true, even though it is taken in a different sense by unbelievers and those who misunderstand it. (4) But this is our faith, this is our honor, this is our mother the church who saves through faith, who is strengthened through hope, and who by Christ's love is made

---

[73] Cf. 1 Cor. 15:44; 53.
[74] 2 Cor. 5:16
[75] Rom. 1:4
[76] Luke 1:33
[77] 2 Cor. 5:10
[78] John 5:29

perfect in the confession of faith, the mysteries, and the cleansing
power of baptism—(5) for < he says >, "Go, baptize in the name
of the Father, and of the Son, and of the Holy Spirit."[79] [Baptize,
that is], in the name of the divine Trinity, for the name admits
of no distinction; God is preached and proclaimed to us as one
in the Law, the Prophets, the Gospels and the Apostles, in the Old
and New Testaments, and is believed in as one—Father, Son and
Holy Spirit. (6) The Godhead is no identity but truly a perfect
Trinity. The Father is perfect, the Son is perfect, the Holy Spirit
is perfect, one Godhead, one God, to whom be glory, honor and
might, now and forever and to the ages of ages. Amen.

19,1   This is the faith, the process of our salvation. This is the
stay of the truth; this is Christ's virgin and harmless dove. This is
life, hope and the assurance of immortality. (2) But I beg all you
readers to pardon my mediocrity and the feebleness of my very
limited mind—torpid and ill as it is from a heavy dose of the sects'
poison, like the mind of a man vomiting and nauseated—for the
expressions I have been brought[80] to use in referring to certain
persons < with harshness* > or severity or calling them "offenders,"
"scum," "dupes" or "frauds." (3) Though I do not readily make
fun of anyone, I have had to dispose of them with expressions like
these to dispel certain persons' notions. Otherwise they might think
that, since I have publicly disclosed the things the sects say and
do, I have some measure of agreement with the heresy of each
of the sects.

19,4   I also composed a brief Proem[81] at the beginning of the
work to give advance assurance of this and ask for pardon, so that
no one would suppose that I turn to mockery because I am beaten,
and fault me for unpleasantness. In the Proem I also indicated
which sects I would cover, into how many Volumes I had divided
the whole work, and how many sects, and which ones, I had spoken
of in each Volume. Here again I remind us of these things, to
do the readers good at every point.

20,1   There are three Volumes, and seven Sections. In Volume
One there are forty-six Sects, enumerated by name and arranged
consecutively < throughout the > Volume from the first and the
second until the last. For Volume One contains forty-six Sects in
three Sections, Volume Two contains twenty-three Sects in two
Sections, but Volume Three, eleven in two. (2) I beg and plead

---

[79] Matt. 28:19
[80] Holl: ἠνέχθη< ν >; Drexl and MSS: ἠνέχθη.
[81] Pan. Proem I

with all of you who are sharing my labor and reading with patient effort, reap the benefit but put the sects' odious doctrines out of your minds. I have not made them public to do harm but to do good, and to make sure that no one falls under their spell.

20,3   As you go through the whole work, or even parts of it, pray for me and make request that God will give me a portion in the holy and only catholic and apostolic church and the true, life-giving and saving < faith >, and deliver me from every sect. (4) And if, in my humanity, I cannot reach the full measure of the incomprehensible and ineffable Godhead, but am still pressed to offer its defense < and > compelled to speak for God in human terms, and have been led by daring [to do so], you yourselves pardon me, for God does. (5) And once more, pray that the Lord may give me the portion in his holy faith which I have asked for, the only faith free of all inconsistency, and grant the pardon of my own sins, which are many, in Christ Jesus our Lord, through whom and with whom be glory to the Father with the Holy Spirit forever. Amen.

21,1   I have spoken briefly of the tenets of the faith of this only catholic church and harmless dove, her husband's only wife as the scripture says, "One is my dove."[82] I have likewise spoken of the countless "young women without number,"[83] the co-essentiality of the Father, the Son and the Holy Spirit, the fleshly and perfect advent of Christ, and other parts of the faith. (2) But as to her ordinances, I must once more partially describe, in a few words, as many ordinances as have actually been observed and are being observed in the church, some by commandment, others by voluntary acceptance. For God rejoices in the excellence of his church.

21,3   And to begin with, the basis and, as it were, the foundation in the church is the virginity which is practiced and observed by many, and held in honor. But for most monks and nuns, the single life is the concomitant of this virginity. (4) After virginity is continence, which sets out on the same course. Next comes widowhood with all soberness and a pure life. (5) Following these orders, lawful wedlock is held in high esteem, especially marriage to one partner only and with the observance of the commandments. (6) But if a person's wife or husband dies < and he [or she] wants > a spouse, it is allowable to marry a second wife or husband after the death of the first husband or wife.

21,7   But the crown, or, as it were, the mother and begetress

---

82   Song of Songs 6:9
83   Song of Songs 6:9

of all these, is the holy priesthood, which is drawn mostly from virgins, but if not from virgins, from single men. (8) If there are not enough single men to serve, it is composed of men who abstain from relations with their own wives, or widowers who have had only one wife. But beginning with the episcopal order and including presbyters, deacons and sub-deacons, it is not permissible to receive a twice-married person for priesthood in the church, even if he is continent < or > a widower. (9) Then, after this priesthood, comes the order of readers which is composed of all the orders—that is, of virgins, single men, the continent, widowers, and men who are still in lawful wedlock—if necessary, even of men who have married a second wife after the death of the first. For a reader is not a priest; he is like a scribe of the Law.

21,10   Deaconesses are also appointed—only to assist women for modesty's sake, if there is a need because of baptism or an inspection of their bodies. (11) Then, after these, come exorcists and translators < from > one language to another, either in readings or in sermons. But finally there are undertakers, who enshroud the bodies of those who fall asleep; and door-keepers, and the whole good order [of the laity].

22,1   On the apostles' authority services are set for the fourth day of the week, the eve of the Sabbath, and the Lord's Day.[84] But we fast till the ninth hour on the fourth day and the eve of the Sabbath, because the Lord was arrested at the beginning of the fourth day and crucified on the eve of the Sabbath. (2) And the apostles taught us to keep fasts on these days in fulfillment of the saying, "When the bridegroom is taken from them, that shall they fast on those days."[85] (3) Fasting is not enjoined upon us as a favor to Him who suffered for us, but so that we may confess that the Lord's passion to which he consented for us < has become > our salvation, and that our fasts may be acceptable to God for our sins. (4) And < this > fasting is observed throughout the year in this holy catholic church—I mean fasting till the ninth hour on the fourth day and the eve of the Sabbath—(5) with the sole exception of the full Pentecost of fifty days, during which neither kneeling nor fasting is enjoined, but services are held in the early morning hours as on the Lord's Day, in place of those at the ninth hour on the fourth day and the eve of the Sabbath. (6) But moreover, there is no fasting < or kneeling > during the fifty days of Pentecost, as I said, or on the Day of the Epiphany when the Lord was born

---

[84] Cf. Didascalia 21.
[85] Luke 5:35

in the flesh, even though it may be the fourth day or the eve of the Sabbath.

22,7 But the church's ascetics fast with a good will every day except the Lord's Day and Pentecost, and hold continual vigils. (8) This holy catholic church regards all the Lord's Days as days for enjoyment, however, and holds services at dawn, < but > does not fast; it is inappropriate to fast on a Lord's Day. (9) The church also observes the forty days before the seven days of the holy Passover with fasts every day, but never fasts on Lord's Days, or on the actual fortieth day [before Easter].

22,10 All of the laity eat dry fare every day—I mean by taking only bread, salt and water in the evening—during the six days of the Passover. (11) Moreover, the zealous do two, three and four times more than this, and some [fast] the entire week until cockcrow at the dawn of the Lord's Day, and keep vigil on all six days. Again, they hold services from the ninth hour until evening during these six days, and on the whole fortieth day [before the Passover]. (12) But in some places they hold vigils only from the dawn of the day after the fifth until the eve of the Sabbath, and the Lord's Day. (13) In some places the liturgy is performed at the ninth hour of the fifth day at the close of the vigil, but they are still on dry fare. (14) In other places there is no liturgy except at dawn on the Lord's Day when the vigil closes at about cockcrow on the Day of the Resurrection, and with a festal assembly on the principal day of the Passover, as has been prescribed. But the other mysteries, baptism and the private mysteries, are performed in accordance with the tradition of the Gospel and the apostles.

23,1 They make memorials for the dead by name, offering prayers and the liturgy. There are always hymns at dawn and prayers at dawn in this holy church, as well as psalms and prayers at lamplighting time.

23,2 Some of the church's monks live in the cities, but some reside in monasteries and retire far from the world. (3) Some, if you please, see fit to wear their hair long as a custom of their own devising, though the Gospel did not command this, and the apostles did not allow it. For the holy apostle Paul has forbidden this style.

23,4 But there are other, excellent disciplines which are observed in this catholic church, I mean abstinence from meat of all kinds—four-footed animals, birds, fish, eggs and cheese; and various other customs, since "Each shall receive his reward according to his labor."[86] (5) And some abstain from all of these, while

---

[86] 1 Cor. 3:8

some abstain only from four-footed animals, but eat birds and the rest. Others also abstain from birds, but eat eggs and fish. Others do not even eat eggs, while others eat only fish. Others abstain from fish too but eat only cheese, while others do not even eat cheese. And at the present time still others abstain from bread, and others from fruits and vegetables.

23,6   Many monks sleep on the ground, and others do not even wear shoes. Others wear sackcloth under their clothing—the ones who wear it properly, for virtue and repentance. It is inappropriate to appear publicly in sackcloth, as some do; and, as I said, it is also inappropriate to appear in public wearing collars, as some prefer to. But most monks abstain from bathing.

23,7   And some monks have renounced their means of livelihood, but devised light tasks for themselves which are not troublesome, so that they will not lead an idle life or eat at others' expense. (8) Most are exercised in psalms and constant prayers, and in readings, and recitations by heart, of the holy scriptures.

24,1   The custom of hospitality, kindness, and almsgiving to all has been prescribed for all members of this holy catholic and apostolic church. (2) The church has baptism in Christ in place of the obsolete circumcision, < and > rests in the Great Sabbath instead of on the lesser sabbath.

24,3   The church refrains from fellowship with any sect. It forbids fornication, adultery, licentiousness, idolatry, murder, all law-breaking, magic, sorcery, astrology, palmistry, the observation of omens, charms, and amulets, the things called phylacteries. (4) It forbids theatrical shows, hunting, horse < races >, musicians and all evil-speaking and slander, all quarreling and blasphemy, injustice, covetousness and usury. (5) It does not accept actors, but regards them as the lowest of the low. It accepts offerings from people who are not wrong-doers and law-breakers, but live righteously.

24,6   It continually enjoins prayers to God at the appointed night hours and after the close of the day, with all frequency, fervor, and bowing of the knee. (7) In some places they also hold services on the Sabbaths, but not everywhere. By the command of the Savior the best refrain entirely from swearing, abuse and cursing, and certainly from lying, as far as this is in their power. But most sell their goods and give to the poor.

25,1   Such is the character of this holy < mother of ours >, together with her faith as we have described it; and these are the ordinances that obtain in her. For this is the character of the church, and by the will of the Father, the Son and the Holy Spirit it is drawn from the Law, the Prophets, the Apostles and the Evangelists, like a good antidote compounded of many perfumes for the health of its users. (2) These are the features of this chaste bride of Christ; this is her dowry, the covenant of her inheritance, and the will of her bridegroom and heavenly < king >, our Lord Jesus Christ, by whom and with whom be glory, honor and might to the Father with the Holy Spirit, forever and ever. Amen.

25,3 All the brethren who are with me greet your Honors, especially Anatolius whose task, with much labor and the utmost good will, has been to transcribe and correct the work against these sects, I mean the eighty, in shorthand notes. (4) His most honored fellow deacon Hypatius also [greets you], who copied the transcription from notes to quires [of papyrus]. Please pray for them, my most honored and truly beloved brethren. (5) The peace of our Lord Jesus Christ and his grace, and his truth in accordance with his commandment, be with you all, my most scholarly beloved brethren! Amen.

SELECTED SUBJECT INDEX

NAG HAMMADI AND MANICHAEAN STUDIES

FORMERLY

NAG HAMMADI STUDIES

1. SCHOLER, D.M. *Nag Hammadi bibliography, 1948-1969.* 1971. ISBN 90 04 02603 7
2. MÉNARD, J.-E. *L'évangile de vérité.* Traduction française, introduction et commentaire par J.-É. MÉNARD. 1972.
   ISBN 90 04 03408 0
3. KRAUSE, M. (ed.). *Essays on the Nag Hammadi texts in honour of Alexander Böhlig.* 1972. ISBN 90 04 03535 4
4. BÖHLIG, A. & F. WISSE, (eds.). *Nag Hammadi Codices III, 2 and IV, 2. The Gospel of the Egyptians.* (The Holy Book of the Great Invisible Spirit). Edited with translation and commentary, in cooperation with P. LABIB. 1975.
   ISBN 90 04 04226 1
5. MÉNARD, J.-E. *L'Évangile selon Thomas.* Traduction française, introduction, et commentaire par J.-É. MÉNARD. 1975. ISBN 90 04 04210 5
6. KRAUSE, M. (ed.). *Essays on the Nag Hammadi texts in honour of Pahor Labib.* 1975.
   ISBN 90 04 04363 2
7. MÉNARD, J.-E. *Les textes de Nag Hammadi.* Colloque du centre d'Histoire des Religions, Strasbourg, 23-25 octobre 1974. 1975. ISBN 90 04 04359 4
8. KRAUSE, M. (ed.). *Gnosis and Gnosticism.* Papers read at the Seventh International Conference on Patristic Studies. Oxford, September 8th-13th, 1975. 1977. ISBN 90 04 05242 9
9. SCHMIDT, C. (ed.). *Pistis Sophia.* Translation and notes by V. MACDERMOT. 1978. ISBN 90 04 05635 1
10. FALLON, F.T. *The enthronement of Sabaoth.* Jewish elements in Gnostic creation myths. 1978. ISBN 90 04 05683 1
11. PARROTT, D.M. *Nag Hammadi Codices V, 2-5 and VI with Papyrus Berolinensis 8502, 1 and 4.* 1979. ISBN 90 04 05798 6
12. KOSCHORKE, K. *Die Polemik der Gnostiker gegen das kirchliche Christentum.* Unter besonderer Berücksichtigung der Nag Hammadi-Traktate 'Apokalypse des Petrus' (NHC VII, 3) und 'Testimonium Veritatis' (NHC IX, 3). 1978.
    ISBN 90 04 05709 9
13. SCHMIDT, C. (ed.). *The Books of Jeu and the untitled text in the Bruce Codex.* Translation and notes by V. MACDERMOT. 1978. ISBN 90 04 05754 4
14. McL. WILSON, R. (ed.). *Nag Hammadi and Gnosis.* Papers read at the First International Congress of Coptology (Cairo, December 1976). 1978.
    ISBN 90 04 05760 9
15. PEARSON, B.A. (ed.). *Nag Hammadi Codices IX and X.* 1981.
    ISBN 90 04 06377 3
16. BARNS, J.W.B., G.M. BROWNE, & J.C. SHELTON, (eds.). *Nag Hammadi Codices.* Greek and Coptic papyri from the cartonnage of the covers. 1981.
    ISBN 90 04 06277 7
17. KRAUSE, M. (ed.). *Gnosis and Gnosticism.* Papers read at the Eighth International Conference on Patristic Studies. Oxford, September 3rd-8th, 1979. 1981.
    ISBN 90 04 06399 4
18. HELDERMAN, J. *Die Anapausis im Evangelium Veritatis.* Eine vergleichende Untersuchung des valentinianisch-gnostischen Heilsgutes der Ruhe im Evangelium

Veritatis und in anderen Schriften der Nag-Hammadi Bibliothek. 1984.
ISBN 90 04 07260 8

19. FRICKEL, J. *Hellenistische Erlösung in christlicher Deutung.* Die gnostische Naassener-schrift. Quellen, kritische Studien, Strukturanalyse, Schichtenscheidung, Re-konstruktion der Anthropos-Lehrschrift. 1984. ISBN 90 04 07227 6

20-21. LAYTON, B. (ed.). *Nag Hammadi Codex II, 2-7, together with XIII, 2* Brit. Lib. Or. 4926(1) and P. Oxy. 1, 654, 655.* I. Gospel according to Thomas, Gospel according to Philip, Hypostasis of the Archons, Indexes. II. On the origin of the world, Expository treatise on the Soul, Book of Thomas the Contender. 1989. 2 volumes. ISBN 90 04 09019 3

22. ATTRIDGE, H.W. (ed.). *Nag Hammadi Codex I* (The Jung Codex). I. Introductions, texts, translations, indices. 1985. ISBN 90 04 07677 8

23. ATTRIDGE, H.W. (ed.). *Nag Hammadi Codex I* (The Jung Codex). II. Notes. 1985. ISBN 90 04 07678 6

24. STROUMSA, G.A.G. *Another seed. Studies in Gnostic mythology.* 1984. ISBN 90 04 07419 8

25. SCOPELLO, M. *L'exégèse de l'âme.* Nag Hammadi Codex II, 6. Introduction, tra-duction et commentaire. 1985. ISBN 90 04 07469 4

26. EMMEL, S. (ed.). *Nag Hammadi Codex III, 5.* The Dialogue of the Savior. 1984. ISBN 90 04 07558 5

27. PARROTT, D.M. (ed.) *Nag Hammadi Codices III, 3-4 and V, 1 with Papyrus Berolinensis 8502,3 and Oxyrhynchus Papyrus 1081.* Eugnostos and the Sophia of Jesus Christ. 1991. ISBN 90 04 08366 9

28. HEDRICK, C.W. (ed.). *Nag Hammadi Codices XI, XII, XIII.* 1990. ISBN 90 04 07825 8

29. WILLIAMS, M.A. *The immovable race.* A gnostic designation and the theme of sta-bility in Late Antiquity. 1985. ISBN 90 04 07597 6

30. PEARSON, B. (ed.). *Codex VII.* (in preparation)

31. SIEBER, J.H. (ed.). *Nag Hammadi Codex VIII.* 1991. ISBN 90 04 09477 6

32. SCHOLER, D.M. *Nag Hammadi Bibliography.* (in preparation)

33. WALDSTEIN, M. & F. WISSE, (eds.). *Apocryphon of John.* (in preparation)

34. LELYVELD, M. *Les logia de la vie dans l'Evangile selon Thomas.* A la recherche d'une tradition et d'une rédaction. 1988. ISBN 90 04 07610 7

35. WILLIAMS, F. (Tr.). *The Panarion of Epiphanius of Salamis.* Book I (Sects 1-46). 1987. ISBN 90 04 07926 2

36. WILLIAMS, F. (Tr.). *The Panarion of Epiphanius of Salamis.* Book II and III (Sects 47-80, De Fide). 1994. ISBN 90 04 09898 4